For selected older vintages, ref...

ITALY	1									
Barolo, Barbaresco	8◑									
Chianti Classico Ris.	7◑									
Brunello	8◑	8◑	8◑	8◑	8◑	9◑	8◑	9◑	8◑	8◑
Amarone	7◑	8◑	7◑	8◑	6●	8◑	5●	9◑	8●	3◑
SPAIN										
Ribera del Duero	7◑	8◑	9◑	7◑	6●	6●	9◑	8●	8●	5●
Rioja (red)	7◑	9◑	8◑	7◑	6●	6●	9●	9●	7●	6●
PORTUGAL										
South	7◑	6◑	7●	8◑	8●	7●	8●	8●	6●	5●
North	8◑	7◑	8●	8●	8●	5●	8●	8●	8●	7●
Port	9◑	7◑	7◑	8○	10●	7○	8○	8○	9●	5○
USA										
California Cabernet	8◑	8◑	9◑	8◑	9●	9●	8●	8●	7●	7●
California Chardonnay	9◑	9◑	9●	8●	9●	8●	7●	8●	9●	8●
Oregon Pinot Noir	7◑	6◑	8●	8●	6●	8●	7◑	8◑	8◑	8◑
Wash. State Cabernet	7◑	8◑	8◑	8●	8●	8●	8◑	7◑	8◑	7◑
AUSTRALIA										
Coonawarra Cabernet	6◑	9◑	9◑	9◑	8●	6●	9●	10●	8●	8●
Hunter Semillon	9◑	9◑	9◑	7◑	8◑	8●	9●	8●	8●	7●
Barossa Shiraz	6◑	9◑	8◑	9●	6●	8●	10●	8●	7●	10●
Marg. River Cabernet	9◑	10◑	9◑	9●	9●	6●	10◑	9●	8●	7●
NEW ZEALAND										
M'lborough Sauvignon	8●	10●	8●	5◑	9●	9●	7●	8◑	8◑	6◑
H'kes Bay Cab/Merlot	5◑	8◑	9◑	8◑	9●	8●	7●	8●	5●	9●
SOUTH AFRICA										
Stellenbosch Cabernet	8◑	9◑	10◑	8◑	9●	8●	7●	8●	9●	5◑
S'bosch Chardonnay	8◑	9◑	10◑	8◑	9●	8●	8●	9●	8●	7●

Numerals (1–10) represent an overall rating for each year.
◑ Not ready ● Just ready ● At peak ◐ Past best ○ Not generally declared

Oz CLARKE

POCKET
WINE
BOOK 2013

CONTENTS

Below: New vineyards at Aconcagua Costa, Chile.

A–Z OF WINES, PRODUCERS, GRAPES & WINE REGIONS   61–327

HOW TO USE THIS BOOK _____

The **World of Wine** section, starting on page 22, gives an overview of all the world's significant wine-producing countries. The most important countries are followed by a full list of the relevant entries in the A–Z section. Remember that regional A–Z entries guide you to further recommended producers in each region or appellation.

The A–Z section starts on page 61 and includes over 1600 entries on wines, producers, grapes and wine regions from all over the world. It is followed on page 328 by a **Glossary** of winemaking terms.

Detailed **Vintage Charts**, with information on which of the world's top wines are ready for drinking in 2013, can be found on the inside front and back covers; the front chart features vintages back to 2002; the back chart covers a selection of older vintages for premium wines.

Glass Symbols   These indicate the wines produced.

  Red wine   Rosé wine   White wine

The order of the glasses reflects the importance of the wines in terms of volume produced. For example:

  White followed by rosé wine

  Red followed by rosé, then white wine

Grape Symbols   These identify entries on grape varieties.

  Red grape   White grape

Star Symbols   These indicate wines and producers that are highly rated by the author.
★   A particularly good wine or producer in its category
★★   An excellent wine or producer in its category – one especially worth seeking out
★★★   An exceptional, world-class wine or producer

Best years   Recommended vintages are listed for many producer and appellation entries. Those listed in bold, e.g. **2010**, **05**, indicate wines that are ready for drinking now, although they may not necessarily be at their best; those appearing in brackets, e.g. (2011), (09), are preliminary assessments of wines that are not released at the time of going to press.

Cross References   Wine names, producers and regions that have their own entries elsewhere in the A–Z are indicated by SMALL CAPITALS. **Grape varieties** are not cross-referred in this way, but more than 70 varieties, from Airén to Zinfandel, are included.

Special Features   The A–Z section includes special 2-page features on the world's most important wine styles, regions and grape varieties. These features include recommended vintages and producers, as well as lists of related entries elsewhere in the A–Z.

Index   The Index contains over 4500 recommended producers. Some of the world's most famous brand names are also included.

Right: Marlborough, New Zealand.

4

INTRODUCTION _____

Don't do this to me, fellas. I've spent years promoting the libertarian approach to wine, the approach that says the tastiest will always triumph, the consumer will recognize the decent stuff and that's what they'll buy. Don't let the bureaucrats into your vineyards and your wineries. It's a simple formula. Just do the right thing, and we'll do the right thing – we'll buy your wine.

And then I hear that the New World champion of fresh original flavours, created from scratch and owing nothing to the European classics – Marlborough in New Zealand – wants to introduce an appellation system 'with strict controls over quality and yield', modelled on the French system. Why? How could such a standard bearer for the Brave New World admit that it needs to fall back on the French system of 'Appellation Contrôlée' – which over the decades has become one of the wine world's most notorious apologists for mediocrity protected by government decree.

But hang on, let me read that again. Marlborough wants an appellation system 'with strict controls over quality and yield.' Er…what's so wrong with that? Well, if the producers can't trust themselves to vigorously control yield and maximize quality, perhaps you do need a bunch of local enforcers to do the job. When an area's new and small, frankly, if someone isn't playing the game, a few of the beefier winegrowers can take them round the back of the bike shed and give them a good kicking. It usually works. But Marlborough

isn't new or small any more. Over 30 years it's built a reputation as the gold standard for Sauvignon Blanc around the world and has led New Zealand's charge to join the Premier League of world winemakers. Its production now dwarfs that of any other Kiwi region.

Late last year I took a helicopter ride up the Wairau Valley, Marlborough's heartland. We must have flown for half an hour up the valley – way, way past the limits old timers always told me were imposed on vineyard development by frost dangers and lack of heat to ripen the grapes. And it was nothing but vines. Vines whose substandard fruit would hit the market as Marlborough wine. And if you've wondered recently why so many Marlborough wines don't taste as good as they used to, are so often discounted and sport names you'd never heard of, well, what about because of uncontrolled expansion into unsuitable areas and no limit on how many tons of grapes each hectare can produce?

It goes back to the wine lover's oldest obsession. Do you want your wine to taste of where it comes from, do you want that badge of 'origin' to mean something? If so, sadly, human nature must often be reined in, and if a wine community becomes too big and too impersonal too fast, well, perhaps you do need laws. I was in Burgundy earlier this year. They've been defining, refining, re-defining the tiny minutiae of their vineyards for a thousand years to preserve nuances in both the quality and the personality of different wine sites. And Burgundy shows the good and bad side of an appellation system. There are still lots of poor producers in Burgundy, but the good ones create wines with such a precise sense of 'origin' that their subtly nuanced differences almost convert you into being a fan of appellation laws.

This takes us right back to the purpose of appellation systems, why they're created, what they ought to do. It's almost always to combat fraud, adulteration, dilution. But these have been occurring since for ever. Pliny complained about it in Roman times. Chianti in Italy and the Port producers in Portugal attempted rudimentary appellation systems in the 18th century at the same time as British writers were marvelling at local merchants who could 'squeeze Bordeaux out of a sloe and draw Champagne from an apple.' When the French really got serious about appellation in the 20th century, it was after generations of abuse of their most famous names.

Above: Elqui, Chile.
Right: Constantia, South Africa.

6

But appellations need bureaucrats and bureaucrats love to build empires, make laws, not streamline them. Sixty years ago about half of Bordeaux's vineyards – basically all the decent stuff – was part of the Bordeaux Appellation Contrôlée system. Now it's virtually 100%. Pretty well anything that isn't physically growing in a swamp can get in. So rather than protect the good name of Bordeaux, the result has been oceans of basic Bordeaux, unloved, unwanted, and unable to sell for a price that even covers the cost of production. The careless creation of appellations cheapens areas and their reputations rather than bolstering them.

If Marlborough does decide to go down the appellation route, it will need strong personalities to enforce controls on yield and the pursuit of visions of quality. A compromised appellation is worse than no appellation at all, and if it's only voluntary, and some of the worst offenders are big beasts locally, how do you force them to comply? Can you actually stop them using the name Marlborough? And with the vast increase in bulk wine shipping, can you stop a distant export market using the name 'Marlborough' at will?

Even so, I will be drinking **New Zealand** wine this year – more Chardonnay, Pinot Noir and Syrah than Sauvignon, because other parts of the world are now making Sauvignon at least as well. Some of the **Australian** stuff is pretty good, although it's Aussie Chardonnay that is making my mouth water at the moment, along with the newly restrained yet excitingly focused versions of Shiraz and Cabernet. **South Africa** thrills me more with whites than reds, and I'll pick Chardonnay, Semillon and Sauvignon

I'll drink the Americas enthusiastically south to north. **Chile** is proving it can make virtually any style it wants – fabulously crunchy Sauvignons, lush but refreshing Chardonnays, scented Pinot Noirs and Syrahs, blackcurranty Carmenères and Cabernets, and brooding Carignans from Maule. **Argentina**'s reds throb with ripeness and vitality and I'm finding more Malbecs and Cabernets from single estates with real personality to match their rip-roaring red blood, while scented Andean Torrontés gets better and

better. Is there a new wave building up in **Uruguay**? If so, I'll drink it. And I'll definitely drink **Brazilian** fizz and some of the lighter reds from the south.

I'm having a lot of fun with East Coast North American wine – Viognier from **Virginia**, Riesling from **New York**, Chardonnay from **Ontario**. And I'm getting more at ease with the power and grandeur of the West Coast. Or is it that they're quietly easing back on the throttle? Certainly **California** Pinot Noirs and Chardonnays get ever more drinkable and the mighty Cabernets seem to be shedding a little muscle and smiling a little more winsomely. So I'll be drinking them, along with blackberry-fruited Zinfandels, Petite Sirahs and a bunch of other non-mainstreamers from Lodi and Paso Robles.

Spain has some fantastic wines right now, led by refreshing white Albariño from Galicia in the north-west and dry sherry from Andalucía in the south-west. **Portugal**'s Douro and Alentejo regions are brim full of good, lightly oaked reds. In **Italy**, Sicily gets more exciting for reds and whites, while the whites from Campania are thrillingly different. Further east, there's a new dawn in **Lebanon**, and it's tasty and exotic. **Greece** is in a frightful economic mess, but there are some blindingly original wines to be had. Even **Cyprus** is waking up. So are the Adriatic nations of **Croatia** and **Slovenia**, and I'll be drinking their fragrant whites and light-boned reds.

As for **France**, I usually spend more time drinking the wines of the deep south rather than the classics, but 2009 and 2010 reds are so good that I'll be drinking more classics than normal this year, and not even the top stuff: 2009 petits châteaux in Bordeaux, and 2009 and 2010 Burgundies like Santenay, Savigny, Beaune and even Bourgogne Rouge. After that, a splosh of spicy southern Rhône red, a jug or two of appetizing **Austrian** Grüner Veltliner – and then I'll do my duty as a Brit by drinking as much **English** fizz as I can lay my hands on.

SOME OF MY FAVOURITES

The following are some of the wines I've enjoyed most this year. They're not definitive lists of 'best wines', but all the wines, regions and producers mentioned here are on an exciting roll in terms of quality. Some are easy to find; others are very rare or expensive – but if you get the chance to try them, grab it! You can find out more about them in the A–Z on pages 61 to 327: the cross-references in SMALL CAPITALS will guide you to the relevant entries.

WORLD-CLASS WINES THAT DON'T COST THE EARTH
- BOEKENHOUTSKLOOF Syrah, South Africa
- BROWN BROTHERS Heathcote Shiraz, Australia
- Dureuil-Janthial, RULLY, France
- FABRE MONTMAYOU Grand Vin, Argentina
- GEROVASSILIOU Malagousia, Greece
- GRAHAM's Crusted Port, Portugal
- GROSSET Springvale Watervale Riesling, Australia
- HIDALGO Manzanilla La Gitana, Spain
- Viña LEYDA, Las Brisas Pinot Noir, Chile
- MAN O'WAR Syrah, New Zealand
- MCWILLIAM's Mount Pleasant Lovedale Semillon, Australia
- PLANETA, Santa Cecilia, Sicily, Italy
- Ch. SOCIANDO-MALLET, France
- VALDESPINO Fino Inocente, Spain

BEST LOOKALIKES TO THE CLASSICS
Bordeaux-style red wines
- CATENA Alta Cabernet Sauvignon, Argentina
- CULLEN Diana Madeline, Australia
- OPUS ONE, California
Burgundy-style white wines
- CATENA Adrianna Vineyard Chardonnay, Argentina
- CULLEN, Kevin John Chardonnay, Australia
- LEEUWIN ESTATE Art Series Chardonnay, Australia
- Littorai, Charles Heintz Vineyard, SONOMA COAST, California
- TE MATA Elston Chardonnay, New Zealand
Champagne-style wines
- COATES & SEELY Rosé, England
- Jansz (Vintage), YALUMBA, Australia
- NYETIMBER Classic Cuvée, England
- ROEDERER ESTATE L'Ermitage, California

TOP-VALUE WINES
- ALENTEJO, Portugal
- CAMPANIA whites, Italy
- CORBIÈRES, France
- CÔTES DE GASCOGNE whites, France
- ENTRE-DEUX-MERS and GRAVES whites, France
- Old-vines Garnacha reds from CALATAYUD and CAMPO DE BORJA, Spain
- Hungarian whites
- Leyda whites and reds, SAN ANTONIO, Chile
- White RIOJA, Spain
- SICILY reds, Italy

REGIONS TO WATCH
- AWATERE VALLEY, New Zealand
- Brazil, for sparkling wine
- DÃO, Portugal
- ELQUI, Chile
- HEATHCOTE, Australia
- Lodi (CENTRAL VALLEY) and PASO ROBLES, California
- SICILY, Italy
- Sussex, England
- Tupungato, Uco Valley, MENDOZA, Argentina
- VIRGINIA, USA
- WALKER BAY, South Africa

PRODUCERS TO WATCH
- Alpamanta, MENDOZA, Argentina
- ASTROLABE, New Zealand
- Bressia, MENDOZA, Argentina
- CASA MARÍN, Chile
- COATES & SEELY, England
- Collector, CANBERRA, Australia
- DE MARTINO, Chile
- Elephant Hill, HAWKES BAY, New Zealand
- FALERNIA, Chile
- O FOURNIER, Chile
- Maycas del LIMARÍ, Chile
- S C PANNELL, Australia
- Dom. des Tourelles, Lebanon

AUSTRALIA
- BROKENWOOD Semillon and Graveyard Vineyard Shiraz
- Henschke HILL OF GRACE Shiraz
- Charles MELTON Nine Popes
- MOUNT HORROCKS Watervale Riesling
- PARKER COONAWARRA First Growth
- PRIMO ESTATE Moda Cabernet-Merlot
- ROCKFORD Basket Press Shiraz

- SKILLOGALEE Shiraz
- TYRRELL'S Vat 1 Semillon
- YALUMBA Bush Vine Grenache

RED BORDEAUX
- Ch. ANGÉLUS
- Ch. AUSONE
- Ch. CANON-LA-GAFFELIÈRE
- Ch. GRAND-PUY-LACOSTE
- Ch. Feytit-Clinet, POMEROL
- Les Forts de LATOUR
- Ch. LÉOVILLE-BARTON
- Ch. LÉOVILLE-POYFERRÉ
- Ch. LYNCH-BAGES
- Ch. la MISSION-HAUT-BRION
- Ch. PÉTRUS
- Ch. PICHON-LONGUEVILLE
- Ch. PICHON-LONGUEVILLE-LALANDE
- TERTRE-RÔTEBOEUF

BURGUNDY
- COCHE-DURY, Corton-Charlemagne (white)
- Confuron-Cotetidot, Charmes-CHAMBERTIN (red)
- DROUHIN, Musigny (red)
- B Dugat-Py, Charmes-CHAMBERTIN (red)
- J-M Fourrier, GEVREY-CHAMBERTIN Clos St-Jacques (red)
- J-N GAGNARD, Bâtard-Montrachet (white)
- Comte LIGER-BELAIR, Échezeaux (red)
- de MONTILLE, Puligny-Montrachet Le Cailleret (white)
- de Villaine, La Digoine BOURGOGNE-CÔTE CHALONNAISE (red)
- de VOGÜÉ, Bonnes-Mares (red)
- Dom. de la VOUGERAIE, Corton-Charlemagne (white)

CALIFORNIA
- Cline, Bridgehead ZINFANDEL, Contra Costa County
- CORISON Kronos Vineyard Cabernet-Sauvignon
- Lang & Reed Cabernet Franc, NAPA VALLEY
- Rubissow, MOUNT VEEDER
- Rudd Oakville Estate Red, NAPA VALLEY
- SHAFER Hillside Select Cabernet Sauvignon
- Sean Thackrey, SONOMA COAST
- SPOTTSWOODE
- TABLAS CREEK, Esprit
- VIADER

ITALIAN REDS
- ALLEGRINI Amarone and La Poja
- Andrea Oberto BAROLO
- Firriato Harmonium Nero d'Avola, SICILY
- GAJA Langhe Sperss
- Illuminati Zanna, MONTEPULCIANO d'Abruzzo
- ISOLE E OLENA Cepparello
- ORNELLAIA Masseto
- POLIZIANO Le Stanze
- SASSICAIA
- Terre Nere, ETNA, Sicily
- Vajra BAROLO
- VOERZIO, Barolo, Piedmont

RHÔNE VALLEY
- CLAPE Cornas
- Clos du Caillou CHÂTEAUNEUF-DU-PAPE
- Clos des Cazaux GIGONDAS and VACQUEYRAS
- Dom. du Colombier CROZES-HERMITAGE and HERMITAGE (red and white)
- CUILLERON Condrieu and St-Joseph
- JAMET Côte-Rôtie
- Dom. de la Mordorée CHÂTEAUNEUF-DU-PAPE
- PERRET Condrieu and St-Joseph
- Marc Sorrel HERMITAGE (red and white)
- F Villard CONDRIEU and CÔTE-RÔTIE

CABERNET SAUVIGNON
- BALNAVES, Australia
- CATENA Alta, Argentina
- DIAMOND CREEK, California
- HENSCHKE Cyril Henschke, Australia
- Ladera, HOWELL MOUNTAIN, California
- Long Meadow Ranch, NAPA VALLEY, California
- PENLEY ESTATE, Australia
- RIDGE Monte Bello, California
- TERRAZAS DE LOS ANDES Cheval des Andes, Argentina
- Miguel TORRES Manso de Velasco, Chile

CHARDONNAY
- CONCHA Y TORO Amelia, Chile
- Diamond Valley Vineyards, YARRA VALLEY, Australia
- Dog Point, MARLBOROUGH, New Zealand
- FELTON ROAD, New Zealand
- FLOWERS Andreen-Gale, California
- GIACONDA, Australia
- HdV, California
- NEUDORF, New Zealand

- RAMEY Hyde Vineyard, California
- RIDGE Monte Bello, California
- SHAW & SMITH M3, Australia
- TABALÍ Reserva Especial, Chile

MERLOT
- ANDREW WILL, Washington State
- Buccella, NAPA VALLEY, California
- CASABLANCA Nimbus Estate, Chile
- CONO SUR 20 Barrels, Chile
- CRAGGY RANGE, New Zealand
- Fermoy Estate, MARGARET RIVER, Australia
- LEONETTI CELLAR, Washington State
- Sacred Hill Broken Stone, HAWKES BAY, New Zealand
- VILLA MARIA Reserve, New Zealand
- WOODWARD CANYON, Washington State

PINOT NOIR
- ATA RANGI, New Zealand
- Bass Philip Reserve, GIPPSLAND, Australia
- ELK COVE Reserve, Oregon
- FELTON ROAD, New Zealand
- FLOWERS Camp Meeting Ridge, California
- Freycinet, TASMANIA, Australia
- Viña LEYDA, Lot 21, Chile
- SAINTSBURY Carneros, California
- Schubert, MARTINBOROUGH, New Zealand
- Talley, Rosemary's Vineyard, SAN LUIS OBISPO COUNTY, California
- WILLIAMS SELYEM Westside Road Neighbors, California

RIESLING
- Tim ADAMS, Australia
- CASA MARÍN, Chile
- Château Lafayette Reneau, FINGER LAKES, New York, USA
- DÖNNHOFF Oberhäuser Brücke, Germany
- Gritsch, 1000-Eimerberg, WACHAU, Austria
- GROSSET, Clare Valley, Australia
- JACOB'S CREEK, Steingarten, Australia
- PEGASUS BAY, New Zealand
- Horst SAUER Escherndorfer Lump, Germany
- ZIND-HUMBRECHT Brand, France

SAUVIGNON BLANC
- CASA MARÍN, Chile
- CASAS DEL BOSQUE, Chile
- Ch. DOISY-DAËNE Sec, France
- Neil ELLIS Groenekloof, South Africa

- LUIS FELIPE EDWARDS Leyda, Chile
- Ch. MALARTIC-LAGRAVIÈRE, France
- MAN O'WAR, New Zealand
- Ch. SMITH-HAUT-LAFITTE, France
- TE MATA Cape Crest, New Zealand
- VAVASOUR, New Zealand
- VILLA MARIA Reserve Clifford Bay, New Zealand

SYRAH/SHIRAZ
- CAYUSE Cailloux Vineyard, Washington State
- CLONAKILLA, Australia
- CRAGGY RANGE Gimblett Gravels, New Zealand
- FALERNIA Reserva, Chile
- Heathcote Winery Slaughterhouse, HEATHCOTE, Australia
- Jamsheed Silvan, YARRA VALLEY, Australia
- Krupp Brothers, Black Bart, NAPA VALLEY, California
- Peter LEHMANN Stonewell, Australia
- MATETIC VINEYARDS EQ, Chile
- TRINITY HILL Homage, New Zealand

FORTIFIED WINE
- Argüeso MANZANILLA Las Medallas
- Buller Fine Old Muscat, RUTHERGLEN
- CHAMBERS Rutherglen Muscat
- Cossart Gordon Vintage Bual, MADEIRA WINE COMPANY
- GONZALEZ BYASS En Rama Fino
- GONZALEZ BYASS Noé Pedro Ximénez
- GRAHAM'S Vintage Port
- HENRIQUES & HENRIQUES 15-year-old Madeira
- MAURY, Pla del Fount
- PENFOLDS Great Grandfather Grand Old Liqueur Tawny

SPARKLING WINE
- BILLECART-SALMON Cuvée N-F Billecart Champagne
- CAMEL VALLEY Pinot Noir Rosé Brut, England
- CLOUDY BAY Pelorus, New Zealand
- Geisse Brut Rosé, Brazil
- Alfred GRATIEN Vintage Champagne
- Charles HEIDSIECK Champagne
- Charles MELTON Sparkling Red, Australia
- Le Mesnil Blanc de Blancs CHAMPAGNE
- QUARTZ REEF Vintage, New Zealand
- SCHRAMSBERG Blanc de Blancs, California

11

MODERN WINE STYLES ─────────

Not so long ago, if I were to have outlined the basic wine styles, the list would have been strongly biased towards the classics – Bordeaux, Burgundy, Sancerre, Mosel Riesling, Champagne. But the classics have, over time, become expensive and unreliable – giving other regions the chance to offer us wines that may or may not owe anything to the originals. *These* are the flavours to which ambitious winemakers the world over now aspire.

WHITE WINES

Ripe, up-front, spicy Chardonnay is the main grape and fruit is the key: apricot, peach, melon, pineapple and tropical fruits, spiced up with the vanilla and butterscotch richness of some new oak to make a delicious, approachable, fruit cocktail of taste. Australia, South Africa and Chile are best at this style, but all have begun to tone down the richness. Oak-aged Chenin from South Africa, Semillon from Australia and Semillon-Sauvignon from South-West France can have similar characteristics.

Green and tangy New Zealand Sauvignon was the originator of this style – zingy lime zest, nettles and asparagus and passionfruit – and South Africa now has its own tangy, super-fresh examples. Chile's San Antonio and Casablanca regions produce something similar, and there are good, less expensive versions from southern France and Hungary. Bordeaux and the Loire are the original sources of dry Sauvignon wines, and an expanding band of modern producers are matching clean fruit with zippy green tang. Spain's Rueda is zesty. Riesling in Australia is usually lean and limy.

Bone-dry, neutral The most famous, and most appetizing, examples are from Chablis. Producers of unoaked Chardonnay in cool parts of Australia, New Zealand and the USA are doing a good, but fruitier, impression. Many Italian and Greek whites from indigenous varieties fit this bill. Southern French wines are often like this, as are many basic wines from Bordeaux, South-West France, Muscadet and Anjou. Modern young Spanish whites and dry Portuguese Vinho Verdes are good examples. I don't like seeing too much neutrality in New World wines, but cheap South African and California whites are 'superneutral'. More interesting are Verdelhos and Chenins from Australia.

White Burgundy By this I mean the nutty, oatmealy-ripe but dry, subtly oaked styles of villages like Meursault at their best. Few people do it well, even in Burgundy itself, and it's a difficult style to emulate. California makes the most effort. Washington, Oregon, New York State and British Columbia each have occasional successes, as do top Australian, South African and New Zealand Chardonnays.

Perfumy, dry or off-dry Gewurztraminer, Muscat and Pinot Gris from Alsace or, in southern Germany, Gewürztraminer, Scheurebe, Grauburgunder (Pinot Gris) and occasionally Riesling will give you this style. In New Zealand look for, Riesling, Pinot Gris and Gewürztraminer. Irsai Olivér from Hungary and Torrontés from Argentina are both heady and perfumed. Albariño in Spain is leaner but heady with citrus scent. Viognier is apricotty and scented in southern Europe, Australia, Chile and California. Croatian Malvasia and Greek Malagousia are bright and subtly scented.

Mouthfuls of luscious gold Good sweet wines are difficult to make. Sauternes is the most famous, but Monbazillac, the Loire, and sometimes Alsace, can also come up with rich, intensely sweet wines that can live for decades. Top sweeties from Germany and Austria are stunning. Hungarian Tokaji has a wonderful sweet-sour smoky flavour. Australia, California and New Zealand produce some exciting examples and South Africa, the USA and Croatia have a few excellent sweeties. Canadian Icewines are impressive.

RED WINES

Spicy, warm-hearted Australia is still out in front through the ebullient brashness of her Shiraz reds – ripe, almost sweet, sinfully easy to enjoy. France's southern Rhône Valley is also motoring, and the traditional appellations in the far south of France are looking good. In Italy, Piedmont is producing delicious beefy Barbera and juicy exotic Dolcetto, Puglia has chocolaty Negroamaro and Sicily has Nero d'Avola. Portugal's Tejo and Alentejo also deliver the goods, as does Malbec in Argentina. California Zinfandel made in its most powerful style is spicy and rich; Lebanese reds have the succulent scent of the kasbah.

Juicy, fruity Beaujolais can be the perfect example, but leafy, raspberryish Loire reds, and simple Grenache and Syrah are equally good bets. Modern Spanish reds from Valdepeñas, Bierzo and La Mancha, and old-vine Garnachas from Campo de Borja and Calatayud, do the trick, as do unoaked Douros from Portugal and young Valpolicella and Teroldego in Italy. Young Chilean Merlots are juicy, and Argentina has some good examples from Bonarda, Tempranillo, Sangiovese and Barbera.

Deep and blackcurrant Chile has climbed back to the top of the Cabernet tree, though good producers in cooler parts of Australia produce Cabernets of thrilling blackcurrant intensity. New Zealand Merlot and Cabernet Franc are dense and rich yet dry. California too frequently overripens its Cabernet and Merlot, though restrained examples can be terrific. Top Bordeaux is on a rich blackcurrant roll since 2000: it's expensive but exciting – as is top Tuscan Cabernet.

Tough, tannic long-haul boys Bordeaux leads this field, and the best wines are really good after 10 years or so – but, except in years like 2009, minor properties won't age in the same way. It's the same in Tuscany and Piedmont – only the top wines last well – especially Brunello di Montalcino, Vino Nobile di Montepulciano, some IGT, and DOCG wines from Chianti Classico, Barolo and Barbaresco. Portugal has some increasingly good Dão and Douro reds, and Spain's Toro and Ribera del Duero reds need aging.

Soft, strawberryish charmers Good Burgundy tops this group. Rioja in Spain can sometimes get there, as can Navarra and Valdepeñas. Pinot Noir in California, Oregon, Chile and New Zealand is frequently delicious, and South Africa and Australia increasingly get it right too. Germany can hit the spot with Spätburgunder (Pinot Noir). Over in Bordeaux, of all places, St-Émilion, Pomerol and Blaye can do the business.

Rosé There's been a surge in rosé's popularity, probably led by California's blush Zinfandel and Grenache. But far better, drier rosés are also becoming popular, with Spain, Italy and France leading the way for drier styles and Chile and New Zealand the best for fuller pinks.

SPARKLING AND FORTIFIED WINES

Fizz This can be white, pink or red, dry or sweet, and I sometimes think it doesn't matter what it tastes like as long as it's cold enough and there's enough of it. Champagne can be best, but frequently isn't – and there are lots of new-wave winemakers making good-value lookalikes. California, Tasmania, England and New Zealand all produce top-quality fizz. Spain can also excel, but mostly pumps out oceans of good basic stuff.

Fortified wines Spain is unassailable as the master of dry fortifieds with its fino sherries. Ports are the most intense and satisfying rich red wines – but Australia, California and South Africa have their own versions of both these styles. Madeira's fortifieds have rich, brown smoky flavours, and luscious Muscats are made all round the Mediterranean and in Rutherglen, Australia.

MATCHING FOOD AND WINE

Give me a rule, I'll break it – well, bend it anyway. So when I see the proliferation of publications laying down rules as to what wine to drink with what food, I get very uneasy and have to quell a burning desire to slosh back a Grand Cru Burgundy with my chilli con carne.

The pleasures of eating and drinking operate on so many levels that hard and fast rules make no sense. What about mood? If I'm in the mood for Champagne, Champagne it shall be, whatever I'm eating. What about company? An old friend, a lover, a bank manager – each of these companions would probably be best served by quite different wines. What about place? If I'm sitting gazing out across the shimmering Mediterranean, hand me anything, just as long as it's local – it'll be perfect.

Even so, there are some things that simply don't go well with wine: artichokes, asparagus, spinach, kippers and mackerel, chilli, salsas and vinegars, salted peanuts, chocolate, all flatten the flavours of wines. The general rule here is avoid tannic red wines and go for juicy young reds, or whites with plenty of fruit and fresh acidity. And for chocolate, liqueur Muscats, raisiny Banyuls or Italy's grapy, frothy Asti all work, but some people like powerful Italian reds such as Barolo or Amarone. Don't be afraid to experiment. Who would guess that salty Roquefort cheese and rich, sweet Sauternes would go together? But they do. So, with these factors in mind, the following pairings are not rules – just my recommendations.

FISH

Grilled or baked white fish White Burgundy or other fine Chardonnay, white Bordeaux, Viognier, Australian and New Zealand Riesling and Sauvignon, South African Chenin.

Grilled or baked oily or 'meaty' fish (e.g. salmon, tuna, swordfish) Alsace or Austrian Riesling, Grüner Veltliner, fruity New World Chardonnay or Semillon; reds such as Chinon or Bourgueil, Grenache/Garnacha, or New World Pinot Noir or Cabernet Franc.

Fried/battered fish Simple, fresh whites, e.g. Soave, Mâcon-Villages, Verdelho, Vinho Verde, Pinot Gris, white Bordeaux, or a Riesling Spätlese from the Pfalz.

Shellfish Chablis or unoaked Chardonnay, Sauvignon Blanc, Pinot Blanc; *clams and oysters* Albariño, Aligoté, Vinho Verde, Seyval Blanc; *crab* Riesling, Viognier; *lobster, scallops* fine Chardonnay, Champagne, Viognier; *mussels* Muscadet, Pinot Grigio.

Smoked fish Ice-cold basic fizz, manzanilla or fino sherry, Riesling, Sauvignon Blanc, Alsace Gewurztraminer or Pinot Gris.

MEAT

Beef and lamb are perfect with just about any red wine.

Beef/steak *Plain roasted or grilled* tannic reds, Bordeaux, New World Cabernet Sauvignon, Shiraz, Ribera del Duero, Chianti Classico.

Lamb *Plain roasted or grilled* red Burgundy, red Bordeaux, especially Pauillac or St-Julien, Rioja Reserva, New World Pinot Noir, Merlot or Malbec.

Pork *Plain roasted or grilled* full, spicy dry whites, e.g. Alsace Pinot Gris, lightly oaked Chardonnay; smooth reds, e.g. Rioja, Alentejo, Sicily; *ham, bacon, sausages, salami* young, fruity reds, e.g. Beaujolais, Lambrusco, Teroldego, unoaked Tempranillo or Garnacha, New World Malbec, Merlot, Zinfandel/Primitivo.

Veal *Plain roasted or grilled* full-bodied whites, e.g. Pinot Gris, Grüner Veltliner, white Rioja; soft reds, e.g. mature Rioja or Pinot Noir; *with cream-based sauce* full, ripe whites, e.g. Alsace or New Zealand Pinot Gris, Vouvray, oaked New World Chardonnay; *with rich red-wine sauce* (e.g. *osso buco*) young Italian reds, Zinfandel.

Venison *Plain roasted or grilled*
Barolo, St-Estèphe, Pomerol,
Côte de Nuits, Hermitage, big
Zinfandel, Alsace or German
Pinot Gris; *with red-wine sauce*
Piedmont and Portuguese reds,
Pomerol, St-Émilion, Priorat, New
World Syrah/Shiraz or Pinotage.

Chicken and turkey Most red
and white wines go with these
meats – much depends on the
sauce or accompaniments. Try
red or white Burgundy, red
Rioja Reserva, New World Pinot
Noir or Chardonnay.

Duck Pomerol, St-Émilion, Côte
de Nuits or Rhône reds, New World
Syrah/Shiraz (including sparkling)
or Merlot; also full, soft whites from
Austria and southern Germany.

Game birds *Plain roasted or grilled*
top reds from Burgundy, Rhône,
Tuscany, Piedmont, Ribera del
Duero, New World Cabernet or
Merlot; also full whites such as
oaked New World Semillon.

Casseroles and stews Generally
uncomplicated, full-flavoured
reds. The thicker the sauce, the
fuller the wine. If wine is used in
the preparation, match the colour.
For strong tomato flavours
see Pasta.

HIGHLY SPICED FOOD

Chinese Riesling, Sauvignon,
Pinot Gris, Gewürztraminer,
unoaked New World Chardonnay
or Semillon; fruity rosé; light Pinot
Noir.

Indian Aromatic whites,
e.g. Riesling, Sauvignon Blanc,
Gewürztraminer, Viognier;
non-tannic reds, e.g. Valpolicella,
Rioja, Grenache.

Mexican Fruity reds, e.g. Merlot,
Cabernet Franc, Grenache,
Syrah/Shiraz, Zinfandel.

Thai/South-East Asian Spicy
or tangy whites, e.g. Riesling,
Gewürztraminer, New World
Sauvignon Blanc, dry Alsace
Muscat. Coconut is tricky: New
World Chardonnay may work.

EGG DISHES

Champagne and traditional-method
fizz; light, fresh reds such as
Beaujolais or Chinon; full, dry
unoaked whites; New World rosé.

PASTA, PIZZA

With tomato sauce Barbera,
Valpolicella, Soave, Verdicchio,
New World Sauvignon Blanc; *with
meat-based sauce* north or central
Italian reds, French or New World
Syrah/Shiraz, Zinfandel; *with cream-
or cheese-based sauce* gently oaked
Chardonnay, Soave, Verdicchio,
Campania whites; Valpolicella or
Merlot; *with seafood/fish* dry, tangy
whites, e.g. Verdicchio, Vermentino,
Grüner Veltliner, Istrian Malvasia
from Croatia, *with pesto* New World
Sauvignon Blanc, Campania whites;
Dolcetto, Languedoc reds
*Basic pizza, with tomato, mozzarella
and oregano* juicy young reds, e.g.
Grenache/Garnacha, Valpolicella,
Austrian reds, Languedoc reds.

SALADS

Sharp-edged whites, e.g. New
World Sauvignon Blanc, Chenin
Blanc, dry Riesling, Vinho Verde.

CHEESES

Hard Full reds from Italy, France
or Spain, New World Merlot or
Zinfandel, dry oloroso sherry,
tawny port.

Soft LBV port, Zinfandel, Alsace
Pinot Gris, Gewürztraminer.

Blue Botrytized sweet whites such
as Sauternes, vintage port, old
oloroso sherry, Malmsey Madeira.

Goats' Sancerre, Pouilly-Fumé,
New World Sauvignon Blanc,
Chinon, Saumur-Champigny.

DESSERTS

Chocolate Asti, Australian Liqueur
Muscat, Banyuls, Canadian
Cabernet Franc Icewine.

Fruit based Sauternes, Eiswein,
fortified European Muscats.

Christmas pudding Asti,
Australian Liqueur Muscat.

MATCHING WINE AND FOOD

With very special bottles, when you have found an irresistible bargain or when you are casting around for culinary inspiration, it can be a good idea to let the wine dictate the choice of food.

Although I said earlier that rules in this area are made to be bent, if not broken, there are certain points to remember when matching wine and food. Before you make specific choices, think about some basic characteristics and see how thinking in terms of grape varieties and wine styles can point you in the right direction.

In many cases, the local food and wine combinations that have evolved over the years simply cannot be bettered (think of ripe Burgundy with *coq au vin* or *boeuf bourguignon*; Chianti Riserva with *bistecca alla Fiorentina*; Muscadet and Breton oysters). Yet the world of food and wine is moving so fast that it would be madness to be restricted by the old tenets. Californian cuisine, fusion food, and the infiltration of innumerable ethnic influences coupled with the re-invigoration of traditional wines, continuous experiment with new methods and blends and the opening up of completely new wine areas mean that the search for perfect food and wine partners is, and will remain, very much an on-going process.

Here are some of the characteristics you need to consider, plus a summary of the main grape varieties and their best food matches.

Body/weight As well as considering the taste of the wine you need to match the body or weight of the wine to the intensity of the food's flavour. A heavy alcoholic wine will not suit a delicate dish, and vice versa.

Acidity The acidity of a dish should balance the acidity of a wine. High-acid flavours, such as tomato, lemon or vinegar, should need matching acidity in their accompanying wines, but, almost by mistake, I've tried a few reds with salad dressing and the wine's fruit was enhanced, not wrecked. Was I lucky? More research needed, I think. Use acidity in wine to cut through the richness of a dish – but for this to work, make sure the wine is full in flavour.

Sweetness Sweet food makes dry wine taste unpleasantly lean and acidic. With desserts and puddings, find a wine that is at least as sweet as the food (sweeter than the food is fine). However, many savoury foods, such as carrots, onions and parsnips, taste slightly sweet and dishes in which they feature prominently will go best with ripe, fruity wines that have a touch of sweetness.

Salt Salty foods, such as blue cheese, and sweet wines match. Salty foods and tannin are definitely best avoided.

Age/maturity The bouquet of a wine is only acquired over time and should be savoured and appreciated: with age, many red wines acquire complex flavours and perfumes and simple food flavours are the best accompaniment.

Tannin Red meat, when cooked rare, can have the effect of softening tannic wine. Mature hard cheeses can make rough wine seem gentle. Avoid eggs and fish with tannic wines.

Oak Oak flavours in wine vary from the satisfyingly subtle to positively strident. This latter end of the scale can conflict with food, although it may be suitable for smoked fish (white wines only) or full-flavoured meat or game.

Wine in the food If you want to use wine in cooking it is best to use the same style of wine as the one you are going to drink with the meal (it can be an inferior version though).

RED GRAPES

Barbera Wines made to be drunk young have high acidity that can hold their own with sausages, salami, ham, and tomato sauces. Complex, older or oak-aged wines from the top growers need to be matched with rich food such as beef casseroles and game dishes.

Cabernet Franc Best drunk with plain rather than sauced meat dishes, or, slightly chilled, with grilled or baked salmon or trout.

Cabernet Sauvignon All over the world the Cabernet Sauvignon makes full-flavoured reliable red wine: the ideal food wine. Cabernet Sauvignon seems to have a particular affinity with lamb, but it partners all plain roast or grilled meats and game well and would be an excellent choice for many sauced meat dishes such as beef casserole, steak and kidney pie or rabbit stew and substantial dishes made with mushrooms.

Dolcetto Dolcetto produces fruity purple wines that go beautifully with hearty meat dishes such as calves' liver and onions or casseroled pork, beef or game.

Gamay The grape of red Beaujolais, Gamay makes wine you can drink whenever, wherever, however and with whatever you want – although it's particularly good lightly chilled on hot summer days. It goes well with pâtés, bacon and sausages because its acidity provides a satisfying foil to their richness. It would be a good choice for many vegetarian dishes.

Grenache/Garnacha Frequently blended with other grapes, Grenache nonetheless dominates, with its high alcoholic strength and rich, spicy flavours. These are wines readily matched with food: barbecues and casseroles for heavier wines; almost anything for lighter reds and rosés – vegetarian dishes, charcuterie, picnics, grills, and even meaty fish such as tuna and salmon.

Merlot Merlot makes soft, rounded, fruity wines that are some of the easiest red wines to enjoy without food, yet are also a good choice with many kinds of food. Spicier game dishes, herby terrines and pâtés, pheasant, pigeon, duck or goose all team well with Merlot; substantial casseroles made with wine are excellent with Pomerols and St-Émilions; and the soft fruitiness of the wines is perfect for pork, liver, turkey, and savoury foods with a hint of sweetness such as Iberico, Parma or honey-roast ham.

Nebbiolo Lean but fragrant, early-drinking styles of Nebbiolo wine are best with Italian salami, pâtés, *bresaola* and lighter meat dishes. Top Barolos and Barbarescos need substantial food: *bollito misto*, rich hare or beef casseroles and *brasato al Barolo* (a large piece of beef marinated then braised slowly in Barolo) are just the job in Piedmont, or anywhere else for that matter.

Pinot Noir The great grape of Burgundy has taken its food-friendly complexity all over the wine world. However, nothing can beat the marriage of great wine with sublime local food that is Burgundy's heritage, and it is Burgundian dishes that spring to mind as perfect partners for the Pinot Noir: *coq au vin*, *boeuf bourguignon*, rabbit with mustard, braised ham, chicken with tarragon, *entrecôtes* from prized Charolais cattle with a rich red-wine sauce … the list is endless.

Pinot Noir's subtle flavours make it a natural choice for complex meat dishes, but it is also excellent with plain grills and roasts. New World Pinots are often richer and fruitier – excellent with grills and roasts and a good match for salmon or tuna.

In spite of the prevalence of superb cheese in Burgundy, the best Pinot Noir red wines are wasted on cheese.

Sangiovese Only in Tuscany does Sangiovese claim to be one of the world's great grapes, though Australia and Argentina are starting to succeed. Sangiovese definitely 'needs' food and Chianti, Rosso di Montalcino, Vino Nobile di Montepulciano and the biggest of them all, Brunello, positively demand to be drunk with food. Drink them with grilled steak, roast meats and game, calves' liver, casseroles, hearty pasta sauces, *porcini* mushrooms and Pecorino cheese.

Syrah/Shiraz Modern Syrah/Shiraz can be rich and exotic or scented and savoury, but it always offers loads of flavour and is superb with full-flavoured food. France and Australia lead the pack, followed by South America, South Africa, California and Washington, and even New Zealand. The classic barbecue wine, also brilliant with roasts, game, hearty casseroles and charcuterie. It can be good with tangy cheeses such as Manchego or Cheshire.

Tempranillo Spain's best native red grape makes juicy wines for drinking young, and matures well in a rich (usually) oaky style. Good with game, cured hams and sausages, casseroles and meat grilled with herbs, particularly roast lamb. It can partner some Indian and Mexican dishes.

Zinfandel California's much-planted, most versatile grape is used for a bewildering variety of wine styles from bland, sweetish pinks to rich, succulent, fruity reds. And the good red Zinfandels themselves may vary greatly in style, from relatively soft and light to big and beefy, but they're always ripe and ready for spicy, smoky, unsubtle food: barbecued meat, haunches of lamb, venison or beef, game casseroles, sausages, Tex-Mex, the Beach Boys, The Eagles – anything rowdy – Zin copes with them all.

WHITE GRAPES

Albariño Light, crisp, aromatic in a grapefruity way, this goes well with crab and prawn dishes as well as Chinese-style chicken dishes.

Aligoté This Burgundian grape can, at its best, make very versatile food wine. It goes well with many fish and seafood dishes, smoked fish, salads and snails in garlic and butter.

Chardonnay More than almost any other grape, Chardonnay responds to different climatic conditions and to the winemaker's art. This, plus the relative ease with which it can be grown, accounts for the marked gradation of flavours and styles: from steely, cool-climate austerity to almost tropical lusciousness. The relatively sharp end of the spectrum is one of the best choices for simple fish dishes; most Chardonnays are superb with roast chicken or other white meat; the really full, rich, New World-style blockbusters need rich fish and seafood dishes. Oaky Chardonnays are, surprisingly, a good choice for smoked fish.

Chenin Blanc One of the most versatile of grapes, Chenin Blanc makes wines ranging from averagely quaffable dry whites to the great sweet whites of the Loire. The lighter wines can be good as aperitifs or with light fish dishes or salads while the medium-sweet versions usually retain enough of their acidity to counteract the richness of creamy chicken and meat dishes. The sweet wines are superb with foie gras or blue cheese, and with fruit puddings – especially those made with slightly tart fruit.

Gewürztraminer Spicy and perfumed, Gewürztraminer has the weight and flavour to go with such hard-to-match dishes as *choucroute* and smoked fish. It is also a good choice for Chinese or any lightly spiced Oriental food, with its use of lemongrass, coriander and ginger, and pungent soft cheeses, such as Munster from Alsace.

Grüner Veltliner In its lightest form, this makes a peppery, refreshing aperitif. Riper, more structured versions keep the pepper but add peach and apple fruit, and are particularly good with grilled or baked fish.

Marsanne These rich, fat wines are a bit short of acidity, so match them with simply prepared chicken, pork, fish or vegetables.

Muscadet The dry, light Muscadet grape (best wines are *sur lie*) is perfect with seafood.

Muscat Fragrant, grapy wines coming in a multitude of styles, from delicate to downright syrupy. The drier ones are more difficult to pair with food, but can be delightful with Oriental cuisines; the sweeties really come into their own with most desserts. Sweet Moscato d'Asti, delicious by itself, goes well with rich Christmas pudding or mince pies.

Pinot Blanc Clean, bright and appley, Pinot Blanc is very food-friendly. Classic fish and chicken dishes, modern vegetarian food, pasta and pizza all match up well.

Pinot Gris In Alsace, this makes rich, fat wines that need rich, fat food: *choucroute*, *confit de canard*, rich pork and fish dishes. Italian Pinot Grigio wines are light quaffers. New World Pinot Gris is often delightfully fragrant and ideal with grilled fish.

Riesling Good dry Rieslings are excellent with spicy cuisine. Sweet Rieslings are best enjoyed for their own lusciousness but are suitable partners to fruit-based desserts. In between, those with a fresh acid bite and some residual sweetness can counteract the richness of, say, goose or duck, and the fuller examples can be good with Oriental food and otherwise hard-to-match salads.

Sauvignon Blanc Tangy green flavours and high acidity are the hallmarks of this grape. Led by New Zealand, New World Sauvignons are some of the snappiest, tastiest whites around and make good, thirst-quenching aperitifs. Brilliant with seafood and Oriental cuisine, they also go well with tomato dishes, salads and goats' cheese.

Sémillon Dry Bordeaux Blancs are excellent with fish and shellfish; fuller, riper New World Semillons are equal to spicy food and rich sauces, often going even better with meat than with fish; sweet Sémillons can partner many puddings, especially rich, creamy ones. Sémillon also goes well with many cheeses, and Sauternes with Roquefort is a classic combination.

Viognier Fresh, young Viognier is at its best drunk as an aperitif. It can also go well with mildly spiced Indian dishes or chicken in a creamy sauce. The apricot aroma that typifies even inexpensive Viognier suggests another good pairing – pork or chicken dishes with apricot stuffing.

MAKING THE MOST OF WINE

Most wine is pretty hardy stuff and can put up with a fair amount of rough handling. Young red wines can knock about in the back of a car for a day or two and be lugged from garage to kitchen to dinner table without coming to too much harm. Serving young white wines when well chilled can cover up all kinds of ill-treatment – a couple of hours in the fridge should do the trick. Even so, there are some conditions that are better than others for storing your wines, especially if they are on the mature side. And there are certain ways of serving wines which will emphasize any flavours or perfumes they have.

STORING

Most wines are sold ready for drinking, and it will be hard to ruin them if you store them for a few months before you pull the cork. Don't stand them next to the central heating or the cooker, though, nor on a sunny windowsill, as too much warmth will flatten the flavour and give a 'baked' taste.

Light and extremes of temperature are also the things to worry about if you are storing wine long-term. Some wines, Chardonnay for instance, are particularly sensitive to exposure to light over several months, and the damage will be worse if the bottle is made of pale-coloured glass. The warmer the wine, the quicker it will age, and really high temperatures can spoil wine quite quickly. Beware in the winter of garages and outhouses, too: a very cold snap – say −4°C (25°F) or below – will freeze your wine, push out the corks and crack the bottles. An underground cellar is ideal, with a fairly constant temperature of 10°–13°C (50°–55°F). And bottles really do need to lie on their sides, so that the cork stays damp and swollen, and keeps out the air.

TEMPERATURE

The person who thought up the rule that red wine should be served at room temperature certainly didn't live in a modern, centrally heated flat. It's no great sin to serve a big, beefy red at the temperature of your central heating, but I prefer most reds just a touch cooler. Over-heated wine tastes flabby, and will lose some of its more volatile aromas. In general, the lighter the red, the cooler it can be. Really light, refreshing reds, such as Beaujolais, are nice lightly chilled. Ideally, I'd serve Burgundy and other Pinot Noir wines at larder temperature (about 15°C/59°F), Bordeaux and Rioja a bit warmer (17°C/62°F), Rhône wines and New World Cabernet at a comfortable room temperature, but never more than 20°C (68°F).

Chilling white wines makes them taste fresher, emphasizing their acidity. White wines with low acidity especially benefit from chilling, and it's vital for sparkling wines if you want to avoid exploding corks and a tableful of froth. Drastic chilling also subdues flavours, however – a useful ruse if you're serving basic wine, but a shame if the wine is very good. A good guide for whites is to give the cheapest and lightest a spell in the fridge, but serve bigger and better wines – Australian Chardonnays or top white Burgundies – perhaps half-way between fridge and central-heating temperature. If you're undecided, err on the cooler side, for whites or reds. To chill wine quickly, and to keep it cool, an ice bucket is much more efficient if filled with a mixture of ice and water, rather than ice alone.

OPENING THE BOTTLE

There's no corkscrew to beat the Screwpull, and the Spinhandle Screwpull is especially easy to use. Don't worry if bits of cork crumble into the wine – just fish them out of your glass. Tight corks that refuse to budge might be loosened if you run hot water over the bottle neck to expand the glass. If the cork is loose and falls in, push it right in and don't worry about it.

Opening sparkling wines is a serious business – point the cork away from people! Once you've started, never take your hand off the cork until it's safely out. Remove the foil, loosen the wire, hold the wire and cork firmly and twist the bottle. If the wine froths, hold the bottle at an angle of 45 degrees, and have a glass at hand.

AIRING AND DECANTING

Contact with air *does* change wine. Opening a bottle and pouring out half a glass will help mix oxygen with the wine and improve the flavour. Screw-capped wines are greatly improved by exposure to oxygen – the screw cap is such an efficient closure that the wine won't have experienced air before it's opened and typically its flavours will blossom after 5 or 10 minutes – i.e. by the second glass.

Decanting is good fun – and makes the wine look lovely. Some older wines with sediment need decanting to separate the liquid from the deposit: mature Bordeaux, Rhône, Burgundy and Vintage Port usually benefit. Ideally, if you are able to plan that far in advance, you need to stand the bottle upright for a day or two to let the sediment settle in the bottom. Draw the cork extremely gently. As you tip the bottle, shine a bright light through from underneath as you pour in a single steady movement. Stop pouring when you see the sediment approaching the bottle neck. Contrary to many wine buffs' practice, I would decant a mature wine only just before serving; elderly wines often fade rapidly once they meet with air, and an hour in the decanter could kill off what little fruit they had left.

A good-quality young white wine can benefit from decanting, and mature white Burgundy looks fabulous – all glistening gold – in a decanter.

GLASSES

If you want to taste wine at its best, to enjoy all its flavours and aromas, to admire its colours and texture, choose glasses designed for the purpose and show the wine a bit of respect. The ideal wine glass is a fairly large tulip shape, narrower at the top, to concentrate aromas, and is made of fine, clear glass, with a slender stem. When you pour the wine, fill the glass no more than halfway to allow space for aromas. For sparkling wines choose a tall, slender flute glass, as it helps the bubbles to last longer.

KEEPING LEFTOVERS

Leftover white wine keeps better than red, since the tannin and colouring matter in red wine is easily attacked by the air. Any wine, red or white, keeps better in the fridge than in a warm kitchen. And most wines, if well made in the first place, will be perfectly acceptable, if not pristine, after 2 or 3 days re-corked in the fridge. Young, screw-capped wines, especially whites, might even improve and can easily last a week and still be good to drink.

A variety of gadgets are sold for the purpose of keeping wine fresh. The ones that work by blanketing the wine with heavier-than-air inert gas are much better than those that create a vacuum in the air space in the bottle.

FRANCE

I've visited most of the wine-producing countries of the world, but the one I come back to again and again, with my enthusiasm undimmed by time, is France. The sheer range of its wine flavours, the number of wine styles produced, and indeed the quality differences, from very best to very nearly worst, continue to enthral me, and as each year's vintage nears, I find myself itching to leap into the car and head for the vineyards of Champagne, of Burgundy, of Bordeaux and the Loire. France is currently going through a difficult period – aware that the New World is making tremendous strides and is the master of innovation and technology, yet unwilling to admit to the quality and character of this new breed of wines. But the best French producers learn from the newcomers while proudly defining their Frenchness.

CLIMATE AND SOIL

France lies between the 40th and 50th parallels north, and the climate runs from the distinctly chilly and almost too cool to ripen grapes in the far north near the English Channel, right through to the swelteringly hot and almost too torrid to avoid grapes overripening in the far south on the Mediterranean shores. In the north, the most refined and delicate sparkling wine is made in Champagne. In the south, rich, luscious dessert Muscats and fortified wines dominate. In between is just about every sort of wine you could wish for.

The factors that influence a wine's flavour are the grape variety, the soil and climate, and the winemaker's techniques. Most of the great wine grapes, like the red Cabernet Sauvignon, Merlot, Pinot Noir and Syrah, and the white Chardonnay, Sauvignon Blanc, Sémillon and Viognier, find conditions in France where they can ripen slowly but reliably – and slow, even ripening always gives the best flavours to a wine. Since grapes have been grown for over 2000 years in France, the most suitable varieties for the different soils and mesoclimates have naturally evolved. And since winemaking was brought to France by the Romans, generation upon generation of winemakers have refined their techniques to produce the best possible results from their different grape types. The great wines of areas like Bordeaux and Burgundy are the results of centuries of experience and of trial and error, which winemakers from other countries of the world now use as role models in their attempts to create good wine.

WINE REGIONS

White grapes generally ripen more easily than red grapes and they dominate the northern regions. Even so, the chilly Champagne region barely manages to ripen its red or white grapes on its chalky soil. But the resultant acid wine is the ideal base for sparkling wine: with good winemaking and a few years' maturing, the young still wine can transform into a golden honeyed sparkling wine of incomparable finesse.

Alsace, on the German border, is warmer and drier than its northerly location might suggest (the vineyards sit in a rain shadow created by the Vosges mountains that rise above the Rhine Valley). It produces mainly dry white wines, from grapes such as Riesling, Pinot Gris and Gewurztraminer that are seldom encountered elsewhere in France. With its clear blue skies, Alsace can provide ripeness, and therefore the higher alcoholic strength of the warm south, but also the perfume and fragrance of the cool north.

South-east of Paris, heading into limestone country, Chablis marks the northernmost tip of the Burgundy region, and the Chardonnay grape here produces very dry wines, usually with a streak of green acidity and minerality, but nowadays with a fuller, softer texture to subdue any harshness.

It's a good 2 hours' drive further south to the heart of Burgundy – the Côte d'Or, which runs between Dijon and Chagny. World-famous villages such as Gevrey-Chambertin and Vosne-Romanée (where the red Pinot Noir dominates) and Meursault and Puligny-Montrachet (where Chardonnay reigns) produce the great Burgundies that have given the region renown over the centuries. Lesser Burgundies – but they're still good – are produced further south in the Côte Chalonnaise, while between Mâcon and Lyon are the Mâconnais white wine villages (Pouilly-Fuissé and St-Véran are particularly tasty) and the villages of Beaujolais, famous for bright, easy-going red wine from the Gamay grape. The 10 Beaujolais Crus or 'growths' are the most important communes and should produce wine with more character and structure.

East of Burgundy, Jura makes unusual whites, good sparkling and light reds; further south, Savoie and Bugey make crisp whites and light, spicy reds.

South of Lyon, in the Rhône Valley, red wines begin to dominate. The Syrah grape makes great fine wine at Côte Rôtie, Hermitage and Cornas in the north, while in the south the Grenache and a host of supporting grapes (most southern Rhône reds will add at least Syrah, Mourvèdre or Cinsaut to their blends) make full, satisfying reds, of which Châteauneuf-du-Pape is the richest, most famous and most expensive. The white Viognier makes lovely wine at Condrieu and Château-Grillet in the north.

The whole of the south of France has undergone considerable change over the last 25 years. Despite the financial woes of growers who over-extended themselves in the late 1990s, new ownership and a new generation are

Main vineyard areas

0   50   100 km
0   50 miles

producing exciting wines from previously unpromising lands. The traditional Provence, Languedoc and Roussillon vineyards make increasingly impressive reds from Grenache, Syrah, Mourvèdre and Carignan, as well as a growing number of surprisingly fragrant whites. And with the new Languedoc appellation (covering the whole of Languedoc and Roussillon), the possibilities and freedom to improve by blending will be extended. Some of the tastiest and most affordable wines are vins de pays/IGP, often examples of Cabernet Sauvignon, Chardonnay and other international grape varieties. Roussillon also makes fine sweet Muscats and Grenache-based fortifieds.

South-West France is emerging from its domination by Bordeaux; its often unique grape varieties yield gems that combine novelty with good value. Dry whites from Gascony, Bergerac and Gaillac are crisp and fresh, while sweeter styles such as Jurançon are increasingly successful, and Monbazillac and Saussignac make some of the finest of all French sweet wines. Madiran, Cahors, Fronton, Gaillac and Bergerac produce top-quality reds.

But Bordeaux is the king here. Cabernet Sauvignon and Merlot are the chief grapes, the Cabernet dominating the production of deep reds from the Médoc peninsula and its famous villages of Margaux, St-Julien, Pauillac and St-Estèphe on the left bank of the Gironde river. Round the city of Bordeaux are Pessac-Léognan and Graves, where Cabernet and Merlot blend to produce fragrant refined reds. On the right bank of the Gironde estuary, the Merlot is most important in the plump rich reds of St-Émilion and Pomerol. Sweet whites from Sémillon and Sauvignon Blanc are made in Sauternes, with increasingly good dry whites produced in the Entre-Deux-Mers, and especially in Graves and Pessac-Léognan.

The Loire Valley is France's northernmost Atlantic wine region but, since the river rises in the heart of France not far from the Rhône and extends over 1000km (600 miles), styles from no less than 77 appellations vary widely. Sancerre and Pouilly in the east produce tangy, *terroir*-influenced Sauvignon whites and some surprisingly good Pinot Noir reds and rosés. Along the river Cher, which joins the Loire at Tours, the best varieties are Sauvignon and Romorantin for whites, Gamay and Côt/Malbec for reds, while new Châteaumeillant AC is making promising Gamay and Pinot Noir blends. In central Touraine, Saumur and Anjou the focus is on Chenin Blanc in styles which range from bone dry to lusciously sweet, even sparkling, and for reds (and rosés), Cabernet Franc with a little Cabernet Sauvignon. Down at the mouth of the river, as it slips past Nantes into the Atlantic swell, the vineyards of Muscadet produce dry whites that take on the salty notes of the sea. At the vanguard of the natural wine movement – some 2415 hectares (6000 acres) are cultivated organically – the Loire Valley is teeming with producers working as naturally as possible both in the vineyard and winery, the best of whom make highly characterful wines – look out for ambitious vins de France.

CLASSIFICATIONS

Not for the first time, France is making an attempt to simplify its wine classification system, this time in partnership with general changes in the EU wine industry. The basic Vin de Table category has become **Vin de France** and can now show both grape variety and vintage on the label. The middle-ranking **Vin de Pays** category has been morphed into a pretty similar **IGP** (Indication Géographique Protégée) category. For instance, Vin de Pays d'Oc may now appear with Pays d'Oc IGP on the label. It'll taste exactly the same, but there'll be another gaggle of contented bureaucrats somewhere in Europe. The top quality classification is Appellation d'Origine Protégée, or **AOP**, which will gradually replace **AC** (Appellation d'Origine Contrôlée).

2011 VINTAGE REPORT

You'll need to cherry-pick Bordeaux 2011s. Climatically, it was an upside-down year. There were summer temperatures in April; drought-like conditions in May and June; a cool July and August with some much-needed rain; heat and humidity in late August–early September which led to the threat of rot; and to cap it all, hail in May and September which hit, respectively, the southern part of the Médoc and St-Estèphe. An early harvest and relatively clement weather for the rest of September helped save the day. The rest was down to the growers and the time they spent in the vineyards and sorting the grapes during the harvest. Some estates had a large crop, others small, so it's a perplexing year. But some good wines have been made. As in 2010, dry whites are fresh and aromatic. Sauternes producers are satisfied with the vintage. And the better reds look to have more structure than the 2007s and be similar to 2004 or 2008 in terms of quality. If prices drop drastically there could even be some bargains among the top estates.

South-West France, at last, had a year that brought smiles to nearly every grower's face. A precocious warm and dry spring brought a good budbreak and flowering. By contrast most of early summer was cold but still dry. Late summer and autumn were hot, with intermittent showers and storms to swell the grapes. The harvest took place on time and in perfect conditions. Late November rain may have spoiled some of the ultra-stickies.

In Burgundy the weather patterns were very similar to those in 2007 – an early and amazingly fine season guaranteed an August start to the harvest, but as the summer wore on the weather got worse, with storms in August, taking the edge off quality. Thankfully it did not rain during the picking. Decent whites, though erratic in the Mâconnais, and plenty of them. The thicker skins of the red grapes should produce more structured wines than in 2007, but probably without the sumptuous quality of 2009 or precision of 2010.

The exceptionally warm spring helped bring Beaujolais' vineyards to early maturity, and ripening continued evenly over the course of summer, with a rainy July providing refreshment for the vines. An early harvest resulted in wines with depth and concentration, positioned somewhere between the ripe 2009s and the more classic 2010s in character, with a bit more freshness than the former and more power than the latter.

Northern Rhône reds have attractive fruit, are easy to drink and risk being underestimated. In the best cases, they combine elegance with medium depth. Quality is uneven in the southern Rhône, with wines of dodgy balance and high alcohol here and there. Their fruit can be expressive, but they may need time to come together. It is a decent year for the fresh whites.

In Provence the weather was very mixed. January, February and March were wet, providing much-needed water for the development of the vines and a replenishing of the water table. April, May and June were, by contrast, unusually warm and dry. July saw temperatures around 2°C lower than usual – but still warm at around 23°C. Nights continued cool and rain slowed the ripening of the grapes but allowed for great freshness. Odd storms continued into early August but from mid-August to mid-September the weather was hot and dry and the grapes ripened successfully. The harvest was large and replenished stocks which have diminished after a number of smaller vintages.

A warm spring in Languedoc and Roussillon, which prompted predictions of an early harvest, but a cool early summer slowed down the ripening and everything came right with a fine sunny September. Yields much higher than 2010, and some beautifully balanced wines, both red and white.

After good vintages in 2009 and 2010, 2011 offered up a challenge to many producers in the Loire. The heat in spring brought on early ripening, with harvest starting up to 3 or 4 weeks early in some appellations. However, a cool and occasionally rainy summer resulted in uneven ripening. Growers of Muscadet and Sauvignon Blanc in Touraine struggled to curb fungal infections, and careful selection and clever winemaking was necessary in order to avoid 'off' flavours. Chenin fared better, with some great wines – particularly sweet styles – coming out of the vineyards surrounding Anjou. Red wines were also challenged by the damp summer, and *terroir* told, as growers with vineyards on well-drained slopes were able to wait for the late September sunshine in order to pick beautifully ripe grapes, while those working with the early-ripening sand and gravel vineyards on the flat were forced to harvest early in order to prevent rot from developing.

In Alsace, winter saw some very low temperatures, but spring was mild, sunny and dry. This led to early flowering in warm conditions with low disease pressure, followed by enough late summer heat to allow for full ripeness and a fairly early harvest. Rieslings are looking to be the best of the bunch, showing classic aromas and acidity. Botrytis was not terribly abundant, so sweet wines may be thinner on the ground.

In Champagne, after a very warm, dry spring and early flowering, a rich, mature crop was expected, but a cool summer slowed ripening. Most producers, however, are pleased with the quality and nearly all see it as significantly superior to 2010, with some making the comparison with the classic balance of the 1995 vintage.

French entries in the A–Z section (pages 62–327), by region.

ALSACE	PRODUCERS	Mann, Albert	Trimbach
ACs	Adam, Jean-Baptiste	Muré, René	Turckheim, Cave de
Alsace	Deiss, Marcel	Ostertag, Dom.	Weinbach
Crémant d'Alsace	Hugel	Schoffit, Dom.	Zind-Humbrecht

BORDEAUX	Médoc	Batailley	Falfas
ACs	Montagne-St-	Beau-Séjour Bécot	de Fargues
Barsac	Émilion	Belair	Ferrière
Blaye-Côtes de	Moulis	Beychevelle	de Fieuzal
Bordeaux	Pauillac	le Bon Pasteur	Figeac
Bordeaux	Pessac-Léognan	Bonnet	La Fleur de Boüard
Bordeaux Supérieur	Pomerol	Branaire-Ducru	la Fleur-Pétrus
Cadillac	Premières Côtes de	Brane-Cantenac	Gazin
Cadillac-Côtes de	Bordeaux	Calon-Ségur	Gilette
Bordeaux	Puisseguin-St-	Canon	Gloria
Canon-Fronsac	Émilion	Canon-la-Gaffelière	Grand-Puy-Ducasse
Castillon-Côtes de	St-Émilion	Cantemerle	Grand-Puy-Lacoste
Bordeaux	St-Émilion Grand	Chasse-Spleen	Gruaud-Larose
Cérons	Cru	Cheval Blanc	Guiraud
Côtes de Bourg	St-Estèphe	Dom. de Chevalier	Haut-Bages-Libéral
Entre-Deux-Mers	St-Georges-St-	Clarke	Haut-Bailly
Francs-Côtes de	Émilion	Climens	Haut-Batailley
Bordeaux	St-Julien	La Conseillante	Haut-Brion
Fronsac	Ste-Croix-du-Mont	Cos d'Estournel	Haut-Marbuzet
Graves	Sauternes	Coutet	d'Issan
Haut-Médoc		Doisy-Daëne	Kirwan
Lalande-de-Pomerol	**CHATEAUX**	Doisy-Védrines	Lafaurie-Peyraguey
Listrac-Médoc	Angélus	Ducru-Beaucaillou	Lafite-Rothschild
Loupiac	d'Angludet	Duhart-Milon	Lafleur
Lussac-St-Émilion	l'Arrosée	l'Église-Clinet	Lafon-Rochet
Margaux	Ausone	l'Évangile	Lagrange

CHAMPAGNE
Champagne AC
Champagne Rosé
Coteaux
  Champenois AC
Rosé des Riceys AC

PRODUCERS
Billecart-Salmon
Bollinger
Deutz
Duval-Leroy
Gratien, Alfred
Gosset
Heidsieck, Charles
Henriot
Jacquesson
Krug
Lanson
Laurent-Perrier
Moët & Chandon
Mumm, G H
Paillard, Bruno
Perrier, Joseph
Perrier-Jouët
Philipponnat
Piper-Heidsieck
Pol Roger
Pommery
Roederer, Louis
Ruinart
Taittinger
Veuve Clicquot

JURA AND SAVOIE
Arbois AC
Bugey AC
Château-Chalon
  AC
Côtes du Jura AC
Crémant du Jura AC
l'Étoile AC
Roussette de Savoie
  AC
Savoie

LOIRE VALLEY
ACs
Anjou Blanc
Anjou Rouge
Anjou-Villages
Bonnezeaux
Bourgueil
Cabernet d'Anjou
Cheverny
Chinon
Côte Roannaise
Coteaux de
  l'Aubance
Coteaux du
  Giennois
Coteaux du Layon
Crémant de Loire
Jasnières
Menetou-Salon
Montlouis-sur-Loire
Muscadet
Pouilly-Fumé
Pouilly-sur-Loire
Quarts de Chaume
Quincy
Reuilly
Rosé de Loire
St-Nicolas-de-
  Bourgueil
Sancerre
Saumur
Saumur-Champigny
Saumur Mousseux
Savennières
Touraine
Val de Loire, IGP
Vouvray

PRODUCERS
Baudry, Bernard
Blot, Jacky
Bourgeois, Dom.
  Henri
Chidaine, François
Clos Naudin, Dom.
  du
Coulée de Serrant,
  Vignobles de la
Dagueneau, Didier
Druet, Pierre-
  Jacques
Huet
Hureau, Ch. du
Luneau-Papin, Dom.
Mabileau, Frédéric
Mellot, Alphonse
Ogereau, Dom.
Pierre-Bise, Ch.
Ragotière, Ch. de la
Roches Neuves,
  Dom. des
Vacheron, Dom.
Villeneuve, Ch. de

RHÔNE VALLEY
ACs
Beaumes-de-Venise
Château-Grillet
Châteauneuf-du-
  Pape
Clairette de Die
Collines
  Rhodaniennes,
  IGP des
Condrieu
Cornas
Costières de Nîmes
Côte-Rôtie
Coteaux de
  l'Ardèche, Vin de
  Pays des
Côtes du Rhône
Côtes du Rhône-
  Villages
Côtes du Vivarais
Crémant de Die
Crozes-Hermitage
Gigondas
Grignan-les-
  Adhémar
Hermitage
Lirac
Lubéron
Muscat de
  Beaumes-de-
  Venise
Rasteau
St-Joseph
St-Péray
Tavel
Vacqueyras
Ventoux
Vinsobres

PRODUCERS
Allemand, Thiérry
Beaucastel,
  Ch. de
Chapoutier, M
Chave, Jean-Louis
Clape, A
Clos des Papes
Colombo, Jean-Luc
Coursodon, Pierre
Cuilleron, Yves
Delas Frères
Font de Michelle,
  Dom.
Graillot, Alain
Guigal
Jaboulet Aîné,
  Paul
Jamet
Oratoire St-Martin,
  Dom.
Perret, André
Rayas, Ch.
Réméjeanne,
  Dom. la
Rostaing, Réné
St Gayan, Dom.
Sang des Cailloux,
  Dom. le
Tain, Cave de
Vidal-Fleury
Vieux Télégraphe,
  Dom. du

SEE ALSO
Cairanne

ITALY

Is Italian wine too complicated for the rest of the world to understand? There are so many wines, so many grape varieties, so many producers. One could look at this in a positive light, as being part and parcel of that great diversity which we so often praise. Or one could see this plethora of names as the source of a confusion which puts us off, just as we are put off by corrupt politicians, criminal organizations, economic turbulence. So we retrench and limit ourselves to the few names that do mean something – Pinot Grigio, Prosecco, Chianti, Valpolicella, Barolo. Understandable. But this is to miss out on the wealth of different flavours and styles that Italian wine offers, were we adventurous enough to throw caution to the winds and take a punt on something about which we know little or nothing. It would be nice to say there's an easy way to understand Italian wine – but it would be wrong. There is no magic key, other than our own experience. And of course this book.

GRAPE VARIETIES AND WINE REGIONS

Nonetheless, there are ways of partially demystifying Italian wines. One is to think not in terms of the 20 political divisions or 'regions' into which Italy is divided, but rather in terms of 4 macro-zones: North-West, North-East, Central and South & Islands. The North-West is dominated by two major black grape varieties, Nebbiolo (the grape of Barolo) and Barbera, and is also home to some of Italy's best sparklers: dry Franciacortas and fragrant sweet Moscatos. The North-East has bubbles too, mainly in the form of Prosecco,

but apart from Valpolicella, with its increasingly famous Amarone, it is home to a host of grape varieties of French and Germanic origin. Central Italy is dominated by a few major black varieties like Sangiovese and Montepulciano plus a couple of whites – Verdicchio and Trebbiano. The South and the islands of Sicily and Sardinia are a treasure trove of local vines and wines too numerous to specify, but too exciting to dismiss.

CLASSIFICATIONS

Another way of categorizing Italian wines is by quality designation or 'denomination'. At the bottom of the pyramid is **Vino da Tavola** (table wine), i.e. wine subject to few regulations and theoretically of inferior quality, although for a while until the mid-1990s some of the best wines of Italy, like Sassicaia and Tignanello, had to take shelter in this category for lack of anywhere else to go. Vino da tavola is supposed not to display on the label any mention of vintage, provenance or grape variety, although that seems to be changing for select wines under new EU rules..

IGT (Indicazione Geografica Tipica), which began taking effect in the mid-1990s to identify wines from certain areas, is the next level of the pyramid. IGT's regulations are lax compared with those of higher denominations, and for this reason a lot of wines are to be found under this title, some of them of high quality. Today there are well over 120 IGTs, some of them of marvellous obscurity, others very important such as IGT Toscana and IGT Sicilia.

DOC (Denominazione di Origine Controllata) is the principal designation for wines from specific zones, and constitutes the lower level of the 'quality wine' section of the pyramid. Through most of the last third of the 20th century the DOC regulations in many cases were lumbered with a lot of unnecessary baggage from the past, but rules are being updated and made more sensible, allowing for recognition of communes, estates and single vineyards, and banning the use of grapes or musts from other zones. What is needed today is a more enlightened attitude towards alternative closures like the screw cap – at present, many DOCs and all DOCGs forbid any closure other than cork. Another problem today is a surfeit of DOCs. There are now almost 400, a good number of which are unnecessary or repetitive.

DOCG (Denominazione di Origine Controllata e Garantita), the top of the pyramid, was conceived as a 'super-league' for DOCs that promised high class – but didn't always provide it. Wines are made under stricter standards that have favoured improvements, but the best guarantee of quality remains the producer's name. Currently DOCGs number around 80.

What Italy's denominations need is a good pruning, which is what the EU would like to give them. The plan from Brussels was to reduce the total number of DOCGs, DOCs and IGTs to just 182 DOPs and IGPs: **DOP** (Denominazione di Origine Protetta) and **IGP** (Indicazione Geografica Protetta). These were indeed introduced from August 2009, but with an open-ended option to carry on using the old designations, which is what the Italians will doubtless continue to do until forced to do otherwise.

2011 VINTAGE REPORT

The 2011 vintage was notable mainly for a blistering August, with temperatures from north to south hovering between 35 and 40°C for the best part of 3 weeks. Photosynthesis was interrupted in many places, and growers who had resorted to leaf-thinning in early summer regretted it when the August sun's rays pounded down on the unprotected bunches. With low to non-existent rainfall the grapes were healthy enough, but there was more than a little raisining and a lot of concentration. Quantity, which seemed promising in July, finished up at 40.3 million hl, 14% down on 2010, making 2011 the smallest harvest in 60 years. Quality, while patchy, was better than might have been expected, and was generally reckoned distinctly superior to that of 2003, the previous super-hot year. This was variously explained by good levels of ground water from abundant spring rains and by advances in canopy management techniques.

Italian entries in the A–Z section (pages 62–327).

REGIONS
Abruzzo-Molise
Alto Adige
Basilicata
Calabria
Campania
Emilia-Romagna
Friuli-Venezia Giulia
Lazio
Liguria
Lombardy
Marche
Piedmont
Puglia
Romagna
Sardinia
Sicily
Trentino
Tuscany
Umbria
Valle d'Aosta
Veneto

DOCs/DOCGs
Aglianico del Vulture
Amarone della Valpolicella
Asti
Barbaresco
Barbera d'Alba
Barbera d'Asti
Bardolino
Barolo
Bianco di Custoza
Bolgheri
Breganze
Brunello di Montalcino
Carignano del Sulcis
Carmignano
Castel del Monte
Chianti
Chianti Classico
Chianti Rufina
Cirò
Colli Orientali del Friuli
Colli Piacentini
Collio
Conero/Rosso

Conero
Dogliani
Etna
Franciacorta
Frascati
Friuli Grave
Friuli Isonzo
Gattinara
Gavi
Langhe
Lugana
Marsala
Montecarlo
Montefalco
Morellino di Scansano
Moscato d'Asti
Moscato Passito di Pantelleria
Nebbiolo d'Alba
Oltrepò Pavese
Orvieto
Primitivo di Manduria
Prosecco
Recioto della Valpolicella
Recioto di Soave
Roero
Rosso di Montalcino
Rosso Piceno
Salice Salentino
Soave
Taurasi
Teroldego Rotaliano
Valpolicella
Valtellina Superiore
Verdicchio dei Castelli di Jesi, di Matelica
Vernaccia di San Gimignano
Vino Nobile di Montepulciano

PRODUCERS
Allegrini
Altare
Ama, Castello di
Anselmi

Antinori
Argiolas
Avignonesi
Banfi
Bellavista
Biondi-Santi
Boscarelli
Bussola, Tommaso
Ca' del Bosco
Case Basse
Clerico
Conterno, Aldo
Conterno, Giacomo
Contucci
Costanti
Dal Forno, Romano
De Bartoli, Marco
Falesco
Felluga, Livio
Felsina, Fattoria di
Ferrari
Folonari,Tenute Ambrogio & Giovanni
Fontanafredda
Fonterutoli, Castello di
Fontodi
Foradori
Frescobaldi
Gaja
Giacosa, Bruno
Gravner
Isole e Olena
Jermann
Lageder, Alois
Lungarotti
le Macchiole
Maculan
Mascarello, Bartolo
Mascarello, Giuseppe
Masi
Mastroberardino
Monsanto
Montevertine
Ornellaia, Tenuta dell'
Pieropan
Planeta
Il Poggione

Poliziano
Prunotto
Querciabella
Quintarelli
Racemi
Rampolla, Castello dei
Ratti, Renato
Ricasoli, Barone
Ruffino
Salaparuta, Duca di
San Leonardo
Sandrone, Luciano
Schioppetto
Selvapiana
Tasca d'Almerita
Terriccio, Castello del
Tiefenbrunner
Tua Rita
Viviani
Voerzio, Roberto
Volpaia, Castello di

SEE ALSO
Arneis
Barbera
Brachetto
Cannonau
Cortese
Dolcetto
Fiano
Friulano
Grechetto
Lagrein
Lambrusco
Malvasia
Maremma
Montepulciano
Nebbiolo
Nero d'Avola
Pecorino
Sangiovese
Sassicaia
Solaia
Tignanello
Trebbiano
Vermentino
Vin Santo

GERMANY

The dull semi-sweet wines with names like Liebfraumilch and Niersteiner Gutes Domtal that used to dominate the export market are rapidly vanishing off all but the most basic radar screens. Instead, we are seeing an expanding range of single-estate wines of fine quality, although the choice, except at specialist wine merchants, remains limited. Throughout Germany, both red and white wines are year by year, region by region, grower by grower, becoming fuller, better balanced and drier.

GRAPE VARIETIES

Riesling makes the best wines, at least in northerly regions such as the Mosel and Rheingau, in styles ranging from dry to intensely sweet. Other white wines come from Grauburgunder/Ruländer (Pinot Gris), Weissburgunder (Pinot Blanc), Gewürztraminer, Silvaner, Scheurebe and Rieslaner, although Müller-Thurgau produces much of the simpler wine. Plantings of red grape varieties now account for over 35% of the nation's vineyards. Good reds are being made in the south of the country from Spätburgunder (Pinot Noir) and Lemberger.

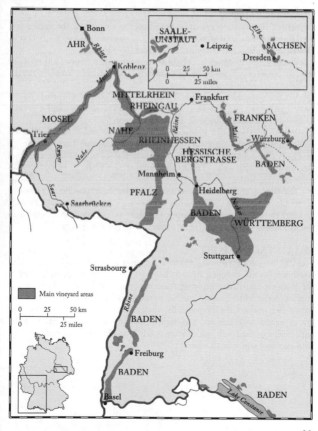

WINE REGIONS

Many of the most delectable Rieslings come from villages such as Bernkastel, Brauneberg, Ürzig and Wehlen on the Mosel, and Kiedrich, Johannisberg and Rüdesheim in the Rheingau. Characterful dry Mosel Rieslings are the speciality of villages such as Winningen near Koblenz. The Nahe makes superb Rieslings in Schlossböckelheim and Traisen, and Niederhausen has the region's best vineyards. Rheinhessen's top wines are the excellent racy Rieslings produced on steep riverside slopes in Nackenheim and Nierstein, but growers such as Keller and Wittmann have shown the real potential of some inland sites. Franken is the one place the Silvaner grape excels, often made in a powerful, dry, earthy style. The Pfalz is climatically similar to Alsace and has a similar potential for well-rounded, dry whites, plus rapidly improving reds. Baden also produces fully ripe but dry wine styles, which, were they better marketed, should enjoy wider international success. In Württemberg many red wines are thin and dull, but a few producers understand the need for weight and flavour. The other smaller wine regions make little wine and little is exported, although the Ahr has a growing reputation for Pinot Noir.

CLASSIFICATIONS

Germany's classification system is based on the ripeness of the grapes and therefore their potential alcohol level.

Deutscher Wein (German wine) is the most basic term.

Landwein (country wine) is a slightly more upmarket version, linked to 19 regional areas (only Franken being excluded). These must be Trocken (dry) or Halbtrocken (medium-dry).

QbA (Qualitätswein bestimmter Anbaugebiete) is 'quality' wine from one of 13 designated regions, but the grapes don't have to be very ripe, and sugar can be added to the juice to increase alcoholic content.

QmP (Qualitätswein mit Prädikat) or 'quality wine with distinction' is the top level; in 2007 the term was replaced by 'Prädikatswein'. There are 6 levels of QmP (in ascending order of ripeness): **Kabinett**, **Spätlese**, **Auslese**, **Beerenauslese**, **Eiswein**, **Trockenbeerenauslese** (**TBA**). The addition of sugar is forbidden.

The Rheingau has introduced an official classification – Erstes Gewächs (First Growth) – for its best sites. Other regions have evolved a widely adopted classification called Grosses Gewächs (GG), restricted – except in the Mosel – to dry and nobly sweet wines of the highest quality.

2011 VINTAGE REPORT

Frost in early May radically reduced the crop in southern Germany. Hot weather followed, bringing an early flowering. The summer provided one of the warmest and driest growing seasons of the last 50 years. Hail in late August in the Mosel caused further damage and crop reduction, but a hot September ripened the grapes fully, though there was little botrytis. The grapes were disease-free and had high sugars but lower acidity than in 2010, and, except in the south, yields were good. Overall, a ripe and healthy crop, with excellent wines in all styles.

German entries in the A–Z section (pages 62–327).

AUSTRIA

I can't think of a European nation where the wine culture has changed so dramatically in recent times as it has in Austria. Austria still makes great sweet wines, but a new order based on world-class medium- and full-bodied dry whites and increasingly fine reds has emerged.

WINE REGIONS AND GRAPE VARIETIES

The Danube runs through Niederösterreich, scene of much of Austria's viticulture. The Wachau produces great Riesling and excellent pepper-dry Grüner Veltliner. The Riesling is powerful and ripe, closer in style to Alsace than Germany. Next up the Danube are Kremstal and Kamptal, both increasingly reliable sources of lush dry whites plus a few good reds. The Weinviertel, in the north-east, produces large quantities of decent reds and Grüner Veltliner whites. Burgenland, south-east of Vienna, produces the best reds, mostly from local varieties Zweigelt, Blaufränkisch and St-Laurent. Also, around the shores of the Neusiedler See, especially near the towns of Rust and Illmitz, Burgenland produces some superb dessert wines. Further south, in Steiermark (Styria), Chardonnay and Sauvignon are increasingly oak-aged, though many drinkers still prefer the racy unoaked 'classic' wines from these varieties.

CLASSIFICATIONS

Wine categories are similar to those in Germany, but in practice the only ones frequently encountered are those defining the sweeter styles: **Auslese**, **Beerenauslese**, **Ausbruch** (a style only found around Rust in the Burgenland), **Trockenbeerenauslese** (**TBA**), **Eiswein** and **Strohwein**. The Wachau has its own ripeness scale for dry whites: Steinfeder wines are made for early drinking, Federspiel wines can last three years or so, and the most powerful wines are known as Smaragd. Over recent years Austria has developed a geographical appellation system with stylistic constraints, called DAC. As each DAC has different rules and restrictions – for example, there are three different Blaufränkisch DACs in the Mittelburgenland alone – the system is hard to understand and often ignored even by producers.

2011 VINTAGE REPORT

Despite some blips – frost in early May, some hail in June and drought in July – this was a good growing season with an even flowering, a hot June and more moderate July, with the ripening boosted by some rain in late August, and then an Indian summer that meant grapes could be harvested without rush. Wachau and Kamptal whites are excellent, while the Burgenland had hotter conditions and an earlier harvest of fine quality, especially for reds. In the Steiermark the harvest was early too, with top-quality whites. The crop was larger than in 2010. The sweet-wine harvest only began in mid-November as dry conditions kept noble rot at bay: good Beerenauslese but tiny amounts of TBA.

Austrian entries in the A–Z section (pages 62–327).

REGIONS	PRODUCERS		SEE ALSO
Burgenland	Bründlmayer	Pichler, Franz X	Blaufränkisch
Carnuntum	Feiler-Artinger	Pichler, Rudi	Grüner Veltliner
Kamptal	Hirtzberger, Franz	Polz	Schilcher
Kremstal	Knoll, Emmerich	Prager	
Steiermark	Kollwentz	Tement	
Thermenregion	Kracher, Alois	Umathum	
Wachau	Krutzler	Velich	
Wagram	Nigl	Wieninger	
Wien	Nikolaihof		

SPAIN

The technical makeover of Spain's long-dormant wine scene was largely complete by 2000. Since then, we have witnessed a progressive refinement of the wines, as increasing numbers of producers eschewed the over-oaking and ultra-powerful style that had been a hallmark of this country's revolution. Not coincidentally, forgotten regions and forgotten native grape varieties have now come to the fore.

WINE REGIONS

Galicia in the green, hilly north-west grows Spain's most aromatic whites. The heartland of the great Spanish reds, Rioja, Navarra and Ribera del Duero, is situated between the central plateau and the northern coast. Further west along the Duero, Rueda produces fresh whites and Toro good chunky reds. Cataluña is principally white wine country (much of it sparkling Cava), though there are some great reds in Priorat and increasingly in Terra Alta, Empordà-Costa Brava, Costers del Segre and Montsant. Aragón's reds are looking good too, with an impressive relaunch of Aragón's great (but long-neglected) native grape Garnacha. In the Madrid region, the sleepy Vinos de Madrid DO has sprung to life, with some remarkable reds from Garnacha and whites from Albillo. The central plateau of La Mancha makes mainly cheap reds and whites, though smaller private estates are improving spectacularly and neighbouring Manchuela is on the march with beefy reds. Valencia and neighbouring Murcia, known for simple, inexpensive wines, are now producing increasingly ambitious and rich reds, for example from Utiel-Requena and Jumilla. Andalucía's specialities are the fortified wines – sherry, Montilla and Málaga. There has been a notable rebirth of viticulture and winemaking in both the Balearics and the Canary Islands.

CLASSIFICATIONS

Vino de Mesa (table wine) is the lowest level. For a while, it was used for some non-DO 'super-Spanish'. Under new European regulations, producers may use simply Vino.

Vino de la Tierra or VT (country wine) followed by a geographical

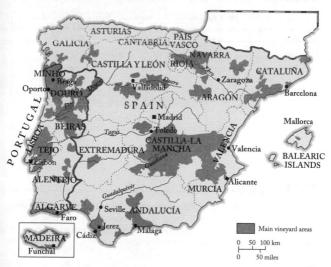

designation. These wines may be labelled Indicación Geográfica Protegida (IGP).

DO/DOP (Denominación de Origen/Protegida) is the main classification for wines from designated zones, which are subject to various regulations. In Castilla-La Mancha and Navarra, this category now encompasses single-estate DOs (Denominación de Origen **Vino de Pago**).

DOCa (Denominación de Origen Calificada) is a super-category. Only two regions (Rioja and Priorat) have been promoted.

2011 VINTAGE REPORT

An unusual and often challenging vintage, marked by a cool wet spring followed by a severe drought extending into 2012. A hot spell in late August and early September marked the vintage, leading to unusually early harvesting throughout the country as the grapes, even before full ripeness, shrivelled and became raisined on the vine. While Atlantic-influenced regions in the north-west enjoyed a copious, quality harvest, the Mediterranean regions were particularly hard hit by the heatwave, particularly in younger vineyards. In Rioja and Ribera del Duero the vintage was considered as uneven at best.

Spanish entries in the A–Z section (pages 62–327).

REGIONS			
Andalucía	Montilla-Moriles	CVNE	Raïmat
Aragón	Navarra	Enate	Remelluri
Balearic Islands	Penedès	Faustino	Rioja Alta, La
Canary Islands	Priorat	Fournier, O	Riojanas, Bodegas
Castilla-La Mancha	Rías Baixas	Freixenet	Rodríguez, Telmo
Castilla y León	Ribera del Duero	González Byass	Romeo, Benjamin
Cataluña	Rioja	Hidalgo	Sandeman
Galicia	Rueda	López de Heredia	Terroir al Límit
Valencia	Somontano	Lustau	Torres
	Toro	Marqués de	Valdespino
DO/DOCa	Utiel-Requena	Cáceres	Vall Llach
Bierzo	Valdepeñas	Marqués de Griñón	Vega Sicilia
Calatayud		Marqués de	Viñas del Vero
Campo de Borja	**PRODUCERS**	Murrieta	
Cariñena	Aalto	Marqués de Riscal	**SEE ALSO**
Cava	Allende	Martínez Bujanda	Airén
Costers del Segre	Artadi	Mas Doix	Albariño
Jerez y Manzanilla	Barbadillo	Mauro	Bobal
Jumilla	Campo Viejo	Muga	Graciano
Madrid, Vinos de	Chivite	Osborne	Grenache Noir
Málaga	Clos Erasmus	Palacios, Alvaro	Mencía
Mancha, La	Clos Mogador	Pérez, Raúl	Mourvèdre
Manchuela	Codorníu	Pesquera	Tempranillo
	Contino	Pingus, Dominio de	Xarel-lo

PORTUGAL

Investment and imagination have paid off in this attractive country, with climates that vary from the mild, damp Minho region in the north-west to the subtropical island of Madeira. Use of native grapes, occasionally blended with international varieties, means that Portugal is now a rich source of characterful wines of ever-increasing quality.

WINE REGIONS

The lush Vinho Verde country in the north-west gives very different wine from the winding valleys of the neighbouring Douro, with its drier, more continental climate. The Douro, home of port, is also the source of some of Portugal's best unfortified red wines. In Bairrada, Dão and Beira Interior, soil types are crucial in determining the character of the wines. Lisboa and Tejo (formerly known as Estremadura and Ribatejo) use native and international varieties in regions influenced either by the maritime climate or by the river Tagus. South of Lisbon, the Península de Setúbal and Alentejo produce some exciting table wines – and the Algarve is waking up. Madeira is unique: a volcanic island 850km (530 miles) out in the Atlantic Ocean.

CLASSIFICATIONS

Vinho is the lowest level, but commercially important as so much off-dry to medium-dry rosé is exported in this category.

Vinho Regional, or Indicação Geográfica Protegida (**IGP**), is the next level, with laws and permitted varieties much freer than for DOC. There are currently 14 IGPs.

DOC/DOP (Denominação de Origem Controlada/Protegida) is the most strictly regulated; there are now 31 DOC/DOPs.

2011 VINTAGE REPORT

Winter rains helped regions whose soils could retain and release water through the summer (mainly Douro and Bairrada). Spring was warm and occasionally wet, resulting in mildew and oidium, which reduced overall yields. Summer was cool and very dry until some refreshing rain towards the end of August and at the beginning of September. It was only in some high, late-ripening regions (Beira Interior and the higher parts of the Douro) that a very hot September and October caused some grapes to over-ripen. Generally, the cool, dry summer allowed the limited crop plenty of time to ripen slowly and well. So hopes are very high for reds from the Douro and Bairrada, and good for Dão, the Alentejo, Algarve, Tejo, Setúbal and Lisboa. Whites from cooler regions are very good, particularly in Vinho Verde, Bairrada, Dão, Beira Interior, Lisboa and Setúbal. A vintage port declaration seems likely.

Portuguese entries in the A–Z section (pages 62–327).

REGIONS	PRODUCERS	Henriques &	Taylor's
Alentejo	Aliança	Henriques	Vesúvio, Quinta do
Algarve	Bacalhôa Vinhos de	Madeira Wine	Warre's
Beira Atlântico	Portugal	Company	
Lisboa	Barbeito, Vinhos	Malhadinha Nova,	**SEE ALSO**
Península de Setúbal	Burmester	Herdade de	Albariño
Tejo	Churchill	Niepoort	Baga
Terras da Beira	Cockburn's	Noval, Quinta da	Graciano
	Cortes de Cima	Pato, Luís	Tempranillo
DOC	Côtto, Quinta do	Ramos, Joao	Touriga Nacional
Alenquer	Crasto, Quinta do	Portugal	
Bairrada	Croft	Ramos Pinto	
Bucelas	D F J Vinhos	Roques, Quinta dos	
Dão	Dow's	Rosa, Quinta de la	
Douro	Esporão	Sandeman	
Madeira	Ferreira	Santos Lima, Casa	
Port	Fonseca	São João, Caves	
Setúbal	Fonseca, José Maria da	Smith Woodhouse	
Vinho Verde	Graham's	Sogrape	

USA

The United States has more varied growing conditions for grapes than any other country in the world, which isn't so surprising when you consider that the 50 states of the Union cover an area that is larger than Western Europe; and although Alaska doesn't grow grapes in the icy far north, Washington State does in the north-west, as do Texas in the south and New York State in the north-east; even Hawaii, way out in the Pacific Ocean, manages to grow grapes and make wine. Every state, including Alaska (thanks to salmonberry and fireweed), now produces wine of some sort or another; it ranges from some pretty dire offerings, which would have been far better distilled into brandy, to some of the greatest and most original wines in the world today.

GRAPE VARIETIES AND WINE REGIONS

California is far and away the most important state for wine production. In its determination to match the best red Bordeaux and white Burgundy, California proved that it was possible to successfully re-interpret the classic European role models in an area thousands of miles away from their home. However, there is more to California than this. The Central Valley produces the majority of the simple beverage wines that still dominate the American market, but the northern end around Lodi and Clarksburg is proving that real quality is possible here. Napa and Sonoma Counties, north of San Francisco Bay, do produce great Cabernet and Chardonnay, but grapes like Zinfandel and Merlot also make their mark; the Carneros, Russian River Valley and

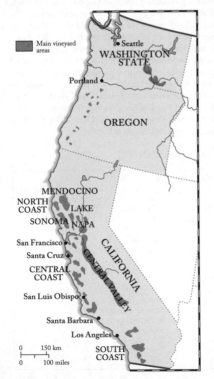

Sonoma Coast areas are highly successful for Pinot Noir, Chardonnay and sparkling wines. In the north, Mendocino and Lake Counties produce good grapes and Anderson Valley is superb for fizz and Pinot Noir. South of San Francisco, in the cool, foggy valleys between Santa Cruz and Santa Barbara, and the Santa Lucia Highlands in Monterey County, Chardonnay, Pinot Noir and Syrah are producing exciting cool-climate but ripe-flavoured wines.

Oregon, with a cooler and more capricious climate than most of California, perseveres with Pinot Noir, Chardonnay, Pinot Gris, Pinot Blanc and Riesling, with patchy success. Washington State, so chilly and misty on the coast, becomes virtual desert east of the Cascade

Mountains and it is here, in irrigated vineyards, that superb Cabernet Sauvignon, Merlot and Syrah can be made, with thrillingly focused fruit.

In New York, winemakers in the Finger Lakes continue to develop a regional style and national reputation for dry Riesling. Long Island impresses with classically styled Merlot, Cabernet Sauvignon and Cabernet Franc, as well as Chardonnay to pair with the local lobster. Improved vineyard practices have enabled growers to cope with the vagaries of the region's inconsistent weather, resulting in an overall increase in quality from year to year.

A growing consumer appreciation of wines from 'The Other 47' states (not California, Oregon or Washington) has helped fuel a 'locapour' movement. Virginia's wine industry nearly doubled in size over the last 5 years, and Maryland, Texas, Colorado, Arizona, Missouri and Michigan grew dramatically. Nearly anywhere you go in the USA today, 'local' wine is worth trying.

CLASSIFICATIONS

The AVA (American Viticultural Area) system does not guarantee a quality standard, but merely requires that at least 85% of grapes in a wine come from the specified AVA. There are over 190 AVAs, more than 100 of which are in California. AVAs come in all shapes and sizes, varying from the largest, Ohio River Valley, which spans an area of 67,340 sq km (26,000 sq miles) to the smallest, Cole Ranch, which covers a little less than a quarter of a square mile.

2011 VINTAGE REPORT

California vintners who hoped for a break after the tough 2010 harvest faced many of the same issues in 2011 – minus the heat spikes. From devastating frost damage in the Central Coast to delayed flowering and poor fruit-set in northern California vineyards, growers certainly had their hands full. Cooler-than-normal summer temperatures and overcast conditions slowed crop development by about 3 weeks, and rain in early October caused rot problems that led to yield losses across many varieties. Dry, warm weather eventually arrived to ripen the remaining grapes, and harvest wrapped up by early November. 2011 fruit shows lower-than-normal sugar levels, good tannin maturation and higher-than-normal acid levels. For those who prefer European-style wines, 2011 is your year.

In Oregon, 2011 was the coolest growing season on record. The season began exceptionally late, with record late flowering in mid-July. Summer was cooler than growers were hoping for, but the lack of rain during September, October and early November allowed grapes a long hang time. While potential grape sugar and resulting alcohol levels are lower than normal, the grapes achieved physiological maturity. Most Willamette Valley producers expressed a desire not to undergo another vintage like 2011. The Umpqua Valley enjoyed an easier season. Both red and white wines have plenty of acidity and lowish alcohol – delicious to drink young. Top-notch sparkling wines.

In Washington, a hard freeze on 23 November 2010 left quite a few vineyards in Yakima Valley and Walla Walla Valley without a 2011 crop. Budbreak was a month later than normal. A very cool spring and early summer pushed harvest back by a month. Cooler than usual weather in September left nervous growers worrying about ripeness levels, but warm days and nights in October, with little rain and no frost, allowed the fruit to reach full maturity. For the second year in a row, the vintage yielded wines with lower alcohol and higher acidity than the norm, vibrant colours and fine potential.

After a warm and promising summer, a series of hurricanes swept up the East Coast during harvest season; reds will be weak except for the best producers, but many whites were harvested before the deluge.

USA entries in the A–Z section (pages 62–327) by state.

CALIFORNIA

AVAs
Alexander Valley
Anderson Valley
Cameros
Central Coast
Dry Creek Valley
Howell Mountain
Mendocino Ridge
Mount Veeder
Napa Valley
Oakville
Paso Robles
Russian River Valley
Rutherford
Santa Cruz
  Mountains
Santa Maria Valley
Sta. Rita Hills
Sierra Foothills
Sonoma Coast
Sonoma Valley
Spring Mountain
Stags Leap District

PRODUCERS
Acacia
Alban
Alysian
Araujo
Arrowood
Au Bon Climat
Beckmen
Beringer
Bonny Doon
Bronco Wine Co.

Calera
Caymus
Chateau Montelena
Chateau St Jean
Chimney Rock
Clos du Bois
Clos du Val
Cobb
Coppola, Francis
  Ford
Corison
Dalla Valle
DeLoach
Dehlinger
Diamond Creek
Domaine Cameros
Domaine Chandon
Dominus
Dry Creek Vineyard
Duckhorn
Dunn Vineyards
Dutton Goldfield
Gary Farrell
Ferrari-Carano
Fetzer
Flora Springs
Flowers
Franciscan
Freestone
Gallo
Grgich Hills Estate
Gundlach Bundschu
Handley
Harlan Estate
Hartford Family
Hartwell

HdV
Heitz Cellar
Iron Horse
J Vineyards
Jordan
Kendall-Jackson
Kenwood
Kistler
Kunde Estate
Landmark
Laurel Glen
Lynmar
Marcassin
Mariah
Marimar Estate
Matanzas Creek
Merryvale
Michael, Peter
Miner Family V'yards
Mondavi, Robert
Morgan
Moshin
Mumm Napa
Murray, Andrew
Nalle
Navarro
Newton
Opus One
Phelps, Joseph
Pine Ridge
Qupé
Ramey
Rasmussen, Kent
Ravenswood
Ridge Vineyards
Rochioli

Roederer Estate
St Supéry
Saintsbury
Sanford
Scharffenberger
Schramsberg
Screaming Eagle
Sea Smoke
Seghesio
Shafer
Silver Oak Cellars
Silverado Vineyards
Sonoma-Cutrer
Spottswoode
Stag's Leap Wine
  Cellars
Steele
Stony Hill
Swan, Joseph
Tablas Creek
Talbott
Turley
Viader
Williams Selyem

SEE ALSO
Central Valley
Mendocino County
Monterey County
Napa Valley
San Luis Obispo
  County
Santa Barbara
  County
Sonoma County
Zinfandel

NEW YORK STATE
Finger Lakes AVA
Long Island

PRODUCERS
Anthony Road
Bedell Cellars
Channing Daughters

Fox Run
Frank, Dr Konstantin
Lamoreaux Landing
Lenz Winery

Wiemer, Hermann J
Wölffer Estate

OREGON
Willamette Valley
  AVA

PRODUCERS
Abacela
Adelsheim Vineyard
Argyle
Beaux Frères
Bergström

Domaine Drouhin
Domaine Serene
Elk Cove
Evening Land
Patricia Green
King Estate

Ponzi Vineyards
St Innocent
Soter Vineyards
WillaKenzie Estate
Wright, Ken

WASHINGTON STATE

AVAs
Columbia Valley
Walla Walla Valley
Yakima Valley

PRODUCERS
Abeja
Andrew Will
Betz
Cadence
Cayuse Vineyards
Chateau Ste Michelle
Columbia Crest

Corliss
DeLille Cellars
Dunham Cellars
Gramercy Cellars
Hedges
Januik
K Vintners
L'Ecole No 41

Leonetti Cellar
Long Shadows
Owen Roe
Pepper Bridge
Quilceda Creek
Spring Valley V'yard
Syncline
Woodward Canyon

SEE ALSO
Colorado
Maryland

Pennsylvania
Texas
Virginia

PRODUCERS
Barboursville
Chaddsford Winery

Horton Vineyards
Linden Vineyards
Llano Estacado

AUSTRALIA

Australia finds itself at a bit of a crossroads nowadays. Its reputation, which soared sky-high on a relatively small volume of wine produced, has begun to teeter as volumes have mushroomed. Its ability to overdeliver quality at a fair price, which fuelled the New World wine revolution, has been undermined by the need to soak up large amounts of excess production from poorly thought-out expansion of vineyards. And despite the fact that its winemakers, especially those of independent companies and estates, are creating some of Australia's best-ever wine, the country has increasingly been saddled with the downmarket reputation of 'critter' brands, based on whatever marsupial had not yet featured on a label, and deep-discounted junk. These are wines to avoid. Now is the time to rediscover Australia's genius, sometimes rough and ready, but frequently finely balanced and sublime, and unlike the wines of any other country in the world.

GRAPE VARIETIES

Varietal wines remain more prized than blends. Shiraz has long been a key varietal and is more fashionable than Cabernet Sauvignon, especially in its ever increasing cool-climate manifestations. Renewed respect for old-vine Grenache and Mourvèdre has seen these former workhorse varieties transformed into sought-after stars. Cool-climate Pinot Noir and, to a lesser degree, Merlot lead the pack of alternative red varieties and Australia's endless appetite for experiment has found prospective new stars in Petit Verdot, Tempranillo, Nebbiolo and Sangiovese. Among white grapes, the position of Chardonnay has been challenged by the upstart Sauvignon Blanc, despite the fact that modern Australian Chardonnay is some of the best in the world. Sales of Sauvignon (70% of which comes from New Zealand) have exceeded

Chardonnay in Australia and although one in four of the whites Australians drink is Chardonnay, its popularity has declined by about 7% per year: a serious problem when one realizes how much continues to be produced. At the top end of the market, tauter, finer, ultra-cool Chardonnay is fighting back and challenges as Australia's finest white variety. Semillon and Riesling follow, with the Italians Fiano and Vermentino and Rhône varieties Marsanne and Viognier (now fashionably included in blends with Shiraz) both impressing; Verdelho and, particularly, Pinot Gris are making a case for themselves as alternatives to Chardonnay. Sweet whites are produced from Semillon and Muscat – both the top-class Brown Muscat (a sub-variety of Muscat Blanc à Petits Grains) and the more workaday Muscat Gordo Blanco.

WINE REGIONS

South Australia dominates the wine scene – it grows the most grapes, makes the most wine and is home to most of the nation's biggest wine companies. There is more to it, however, than attractive, undemanding, gluggable wine. The Clare Valley produces outstanding cool-climate Riesling, as well as excellent Shiraz and Cabernet. The Barossa is home to some of the planet's oldest vines, particularly Shiraz and Grenache. Eden Valley is great for Riesling, Coonawarra for Cabernet.

Victoria was Australia's major producer for most of the 19th century until her vineyards were devastated by phylloxera. Victoria has now regained her position as provider of some of the country's most startling wine styles: stunning liqueur Muscats; thrilling dark reds from Central Victoria; impressive Chardonnays from Yarra Valley and Pinots from Mornington Peninsula; plus both varieties from trendy Beechworth and up-and-coming Geelong.

New South Wales (specifically the Hunter Valley) was home to the revolution that propelled Australia to the front of the world wine stage; a clutch of new regions in the Central Ranges are now grabbing headlines. The state is also a major bulk producer in Riverina.

Western Australia's viticultural heartland, Margaret River and the Great Southern, has a short history, stretching back little more than 40 years, but produces some of the country's finest wines. Margaret River has a thriving wine tourism industry thanks largely to the quality of its Chardonnay and Cabernet Sauvignon; the Great Southern excels with increasingly impressive Shiraz and Riesling; both regions make outstanding Semillon-Sauvignon Blanc blends. Pemberton is gaining a reputation for its whites and its Pinots.

Tasmania, with its cooler climate, is benefiting from more mature vines and better viticultural expertise, and attracting attention for top-quality Pinot Noirs and Champagne-method sparkling wines – and there is excellent potential for Riesling, Pinot Gris and Gewürztraminer.

CLASSIFICATIONS

In a country so keen on inter-regional blending for its commercial brands, formal appellation control, restricting certain grapes to certain regions, is virtually unknown; regulations are more of a guarantee of authenticity than a guide to quality. The Label Integrity Program (LIP) guarantees all claims made on labels and the Geographical Indications (GI) committee is busy clarifying zones, regions and sub-regions – albeit with plenty of lively, at times acrimonious, debate about where some regional borders should go.

2012 VINTAGE REPORT

After the difficulties of the previous harvest, the quality of the 2012 vintage in most parts of Australia has occasioned much joy among Australia's winemaking community, although yields are generally down – not a bad thing considering the current surplus of grapes caused by the weakness of export markets. In South Australia, the winemakers of McLaren Vale, the Barossa, Clare, Coonawarra and Langhorne Creek are all looking forward to making stunning wines. The Murray Darling and the Riverland had an exceptional harvest with executives at Jacob's Creek worrying about the excellent quality of the lowest ranked grapes. 'They may be too good' is a cry that's rarely heard. In Victoria, the Grampians has had its finest year in a decade, while Heathcote, the Yarra Valley and Mornington Peninsula are upbeat about quality. Queensland and Tasmania are abuzz with delight.

In New South Wales, monsoon weather brought rain and flooding and affected regions such as the Hunter Valley, Riverina, Mudgee, Orange and Cowra. Although the younger winemakers in the Hunter have been horrified by the rain and hideous weather, the older generation remain philosophical and believe that they may yet make some decent wines. Riverina's major player, Casella, suffered flooding of the winery but soldiered on, making their wines on other sites.

Western Australia, especially Margaret River, continued its long-running good fortune with good spring rains and ideal conditions at fruit set ensuring average yields. A hot summer with hotter than usual nights led to a harvest that was about three weeks earlier than usual, but of high quality.

Australian entries in the A–Z section (pages 62–327).

STATES	Riverland	Fox Creek	Penley Estate
New South Wales	Rutherglen	Giaconda	Petaluma
Queensland	Swan District	Glaetzer	Pierro
South Australia	Yarra Valley	Grosset	Plantagenet
Tasmania		Hanging Rock	Pondalowie
Victoria	**PRODUCERS**	Hardys	Primo Estate
Western Australia	Adams, Tim	Harewood	Rockford
	Balnaves	Henschke	St Hallett
WINE REGIONS	Bannockburn	Houghton	Sandalford
Adelaide Hills	Barry, Jim	Howard Park	Seppelt
Barossa	Bay of Fires	Jacob's Creek	Shaw, Philip
Beechworth	Best's	Katnook Estate	Shaw & Smith
Bendigo	Binder, Rolf	Knappstein	Skillogalee
Canberra District	Blass, Wolf	Kooyong	Stonier
Central Victoria	Boireann	Leeuwin Estate	Tahbilk
Clare Valley	Brand's	Lehmann, Peter	Tapanappa
Coonawarra	Brokenwood	Lindemans	Tarrawarra
Geelong	Brown Brothers	Lubiana, Stefano	Thomas
Gippsland	Burge, Grant	Majella	Torbreck
Grampians and	Cape Mentelle	McWilliam's	Tower Estate
Pyrenees	Capel Vale	Meerea Park	Tyrrell's
Great Southern	Carlei	Melton, Charles	Vasse Felix
Heathcote	Chambers	Merrill, Geoff	Voyager Estate
Hilltops	Chapel Hill	Mitchell	Weaver, Geoff
Hunter Valley	Cherubino, Larry	Morris	Wendouree
Limestone Coast	Clarendon Hills	Moss Wood	Westend
Margaret River	Clonakilla	Mount Horrocks	Wirra Wirra
McLaren Vale	Coldstream Hills	Mount Langi Ghiran	Wynns
Mornington	Cullen	Mount Mary	Yalumba
Peninsula	D'Arenberg	Oakridge	Yellowtail
Mudgee	De Bortoli	Pannell, S C	
Orange	Domaine Chandon	Paringa Estate	**SEE ALSO**
Padthaway	Duval, John	Parker Coonawarra	Grange
Pemberton	Farr, By	Estate	Hill of Grace
Riverina	Ferngrove	Penfolds	

45

NEW ZEALAND

New Zealand's wines, though diverse in style, are characterized by intense fruit flavours, zesty acidity and pungent aromas – the product of cool growing conditions and high-tech winemaking.

GRAPE VARIETIES

New Zealand is a small, cool-climate wine-producing country which has done a brilliant job of selling itself on rarity, exclusivity, high quality and high price. Its fame was based firmly on Sauvignon Blanc – deservedly so, because Sauvignon's explosion onto the world's consciousness during the 1980s and 1990s changed forever our views of how tangy and refreshing a white wine could be. Sauvignon Blanc is still the Kiwi flag-waver – too much so, since we are now seeing discounted cheap examples of Marlborough Sauvignon Blanc all around the world as sales fail to keep up with excessive planting. Hopefully the smaller 2012 vintage will ease things, but unless things quickly get back into balance, New Zealand's reputation for producing only high-quality, high-price wine is seriously at risk. That would be a tragedy, since the country also produces superb, full-bodied, oatmealy Chardonnay, succulent Pinot Gris, fragrant Riesling and Gewürztraminer and excellent fizz. For a long time thought of as too cool for high-quality reds, New Zealand is now creating sensational, scented Pinot Noir, dark, serious Bordeaux-style blends usually based on Merlot and Cabernet Sauvignon, and a small amount of exquisite Syrah. Wines of such quality are rare and should be high-priced.

WINE REGIONS

Nearly 1600km (1000 miles) separate New Zealand's northernmost wine region from the country's (and the world's) most southerly wine region, Central Otago. In terms of wine styles it is useful to divide the country into two parts. The warmer climate of Hawkes Bay and one or two pockets around Auckland produce the best Cabernet Sauvignon, Merlot and Cabernet Franc, as well as increasingly good Syrah. Waiheke Island and Hawkes Bay's Gimblett Gravels have some of the most exciting red wine vineyards. Martinborough and Wairarapa are noted for Pinot Noir. In the South Island, Nelson is good for Pinot Noir and aromatic whites, while Marlborough is the hub of the industry, famous for Sauvignon Blanc, but also excellent for fizz, Chardonnay, Riesling and Pinot Noir. Waipara is small but produces very characterful reds and whites, while Central Otago produces fabulous Pinot Noir, vibrant Riesling and an increasing amount of flavoursome Pinot Gris.

CLASSIFICATIONS

Labels guarantee geographic origin. The broadest designation is New Zealand, followed by North or South Island. Next come the 10 or so regions. Labels may also name specific localities and individual vineyards.

2012 VINTAGE REPORT

New Zealand's wine surplus seems to have well and truly ended with the cool, rain-affected 2012 vintage. Some winemakers are expecting a reduction on the previous year of around 30%. Grape and bulk wine prices have risen dramatically in response to the likely shortfall. Much of the drop can be traced to a cool, wet flowering and fruit-set period that reduced crops from the outset. With the exception of Central Otago, cool and sometimes wet weather continued during the early part of ripening until just after Easter, when warm, sunny weather rewarded anyone brave enough to have delayed harvesting their grapes.

The northern part of the North Island, including Auckland, Gisborne and Hawkes Bay, took the brunt of the wet conditions. South Island regions were less affected by rain, although a lack of sunshine until well into autumn caused concern. Marlborough Sauvignon Blanc appears to have survived well in quality, if not in quantity. As in every challenging vintage, well-managed vineyards carrying modest crop loads will make excellent wine, while less diligent growers will produce variable results. 2012 is a year of contrasts, with Central Otago Pinot Noir likely to be the most outstanding wine.

New Zealand entries in the A–Z section (pages 62–327).

REGIONS	PRODUCERS		
Auckland	Astrolabe	Fromm	Palliser Estate
Awatere Valley	Ata Rangi	Hunter's	Pask, C J
Canterbury	Babich	Jackson Estate	Pegasus Bay
Central Otago	Brancott	Kumeu River	Quartz Reef
Gisborne	Church Road	Man O' War	Saint Clair
Hawkes Bay	Cloudy Bay	Martinborough	Seresin
Kumeu/Huapai	Coopers Creek	Vineyard	Stonyridge
Marlborough	Craggy Range	Matua Valley	Te Mata
Martinborough/	Delegat	Millton	Trinity Hill
Wairarapa	Dry River	Morton Estate	Vavasour
Nelson	Felton Road	Neudorf	Villa Maria
Waiheke Island	Framingham	Ngatarawa	Wither Hills
		Nobilo	Yealands

SOUTH AFRICA

The challenges of 2010 continued through 2011, again due to the strength of the Rand. Nevertheless, there were several areas for optimism: exports to other African countries, Russia and China showed positive growth. The UK, however, remains South Africa's biggest export destination. The focus on sustainability is growing: 82% of wine certified under the South African classification system complies with the country's environmental sustainabilty criteria, but for producers, better prices are required to invest in sustainability. Despite global economic difficulties, the South African wine industry remains attractive for international investors; a major sale in 2011 was the historic Klein Constantia. For all the difficulties, enthusiasm and innovation abound, along with a great diversity of variety and style.

GRAPE VARIETIES AND WINE REGIONS

The Cape's winelands run roughly 400km (250 miles) north and east of Cape Town, although small pockets of new vineyards are taking the winelands way outside their traditional territory. Wine, albeit in tiny quantities, is now being produced from grapes grown in the mountains above the Eastern Cape town of Plettenberg Bay – better known for its holidaymakers than its vines – from vineyards in the Drakensberg region of KwaZulu-Natal, and most recently near the northern Cape town of Sutherland, home also to the South African astronomical observatory, where the vineyards, 1500m (5000ft) above sea level, are covered in snow in winter.

Plantings overall continue to decrease. White grapes currently make up 56% of vineyard area. Major white varieties are Chenin Blanc (paradoxically the most planted and uprooted of all varieties), Sauvignon Blanc, Colombard and Chardonnay, with Cabernet Sauvignon and Shiraz way ahead of the red pack, though there has been a recent increase in Pinotage plantings. Rhône

varieties still generate the most excitement: as well as Shiraz/Syrah, there's Grenache, Cinsaut and Mourvèdre for reds, and Viognier, Grenache Blanc and Roussanne for whites. Much interest is being shown in old vines, in part due to their age, but also for some of the rare varieties included, such as red Semillon. There are approximately 3500ha (8650 acres) of vines 34 years or older, the oldest dating back to 1900. Thanks to Johann Rupert, owner of L'Ormarins, winemaker Eben Sadie and viticulturist Rosa Kruger, among others, many of these old vineyards are now producing distinctive wines.

With the major grape varieties being planted over the entire Western Cape winelands, there is little typicity of origin, although some areas are historically associated with specific varieties or styles. Stellenbosch lays claim to some of the best red wines; maritime-influenced Constantia and Cape Point produce exhilarating Sauvignon Blanc, a variety also showing great promise in other coastal areas, from Upper Langkloof, a ward in the eastern part of Klein Karoo, to Durbanville and Darling on the west coast and even further north to Bamboes Bay near Vredendal in the Olifants River region, as well as upland Elgin between Stellenbosch and Walker Bay. Many of these areas are also producing distinctive blends of Semillon and Sauvignon Blanc. In cool Walker Bay, the focus is Pinot Noir. Chardonnay, long associated with inland Robertson, is now making its mark with Cap Classique sparkling wines as well as citrous, nutty still wines. This warmer area is also recognized for fortifieds, mainly Muscadel (Muscat). Further to the east, Calitzdorp makes some highly regarded port styles. Inland areas such as Swartland along the west coast have good affinity with Syrah and other Rhône varieties, with white blends from Chenin, Chardonnay and Viognier.

CLASSIFICATIONS

The Wine of Origin (WO) system divides wine-producing areas into regions, districts, wards and single vineyards. Varietal, vintaged wines must be made from at least 85% of the named grape and vintage.

2012 VINTAGE REPORT

Winter 2011 was dry with some very cold spells, allowing the vines complete dormancy. Spring was cool and quite wet, but a couple of heat spikes in January and early February hastened ripening. Thanks to cool nights, the fruit retained freshness and purity of flavour. Healthy, physiologically ripe fruit at lower-than-normal sugar levels should provide top-quality white and red wines, especially aromatic whites and Shiraz. Dryland (non-irrigated) vineyards fared less well.

South African entries in the A–Z section (pages 62–327).

WINE REGIONS			
Constantia WO	Boekenhoutskloof	Hartenberg Estate	Spice Route
Durbanville WO	Bouchard Finlayson	Jordan	Springfield Estate
Elgin WO	Buitenverwachting	Kanonkop	Steenberg
Franschhoek WO	Cape Chamonix	Klein Constantia	Thelema
Paarl WO	Cape Point	KWV	Veenwouden
Robertson WO	Cluver, Paul	L'Avenir	Vergelegen
Stellenbosch WO	De Trafford	Meerlust	Villiera
Swartland WO	Distell	Morgenhof	Warwick
Walker Bay WO	Ellis, Neil	Mulderbosch	
	Els, Ernie	Rust en Vrede	**SEE ALSO**
	Fairview	Rustenberg	Pinotage
PRODUCERS	Glen Carlou	Sadie Family	
Beck, Graham	Grangehurst	Saxenburg	
Beyerskloof	Hamilton Russell	Simonsig	

SOUTH AMERICA

ARGENTINA

Argentina has been a major wine producer since the 19th century, but its current success is very much a 21st-century phenomenon, with Malbec its cheerleader. Basic Malbec is attractive, juicy and damsony; at its best it is thrilling, perfumed, complex and long lived. The best hail from Mendoza, in particular the Upper Mendoza River region and the Uco Valley in the shadows of the Andes mountains. The cooler regions of Neuquén and Río Negro in Patagonia are noted for minerally, deep Malbecs, while the extreme altitude vineyards of Salta in the north produce the most dense yet scented expressions. Argentina has other treasures: Bonarda with its sweet-sour, juicy fruit; aromatic, perfumed white Torrontés. Add those to Cabernet Sauvignon, Tempranillo, Shiraz and over 100 other grape varieties and the possibilities are endless. Foreign investment and personnel made this possible, but now many of the most thrilling wines, those with the purest expressions of *terroir*, are coming from a new generation of hugely talented Argentine winemakers and viticulturalists.

CHILE

In a remarkably short space of time, Chile has not only taken on the leadership of South America's wine community, but it has gone head to head with giants California and Australia in terms of the personality of its different wine types, innovation both in its winemaking and in establishing new vineyard areas, and in the influence its wines are having on wine lovers' drinking habits worldwide. Looking at Chile, that long, thin pencil of a nation tacked on to the Pacific edge of South America, with most of its landmass seeming to comprise mighty mountain ranges, led by the majestic Andes, you might wonder where exactly there was room for any expansion of vineyards. But from the Andes great rivers flow to the sea, and with every

mountain range they cut through, they create valleys, broad or narrow, ripe for planting vines, from Copiapó, 665km (413 miles) north of the capital Santiago, way down to the Malleco Valley 650km (403 miles) to the south. It is in these numerous valleys, the sunshine tempered by the cold Pacific winds, that many of Chile's most exciting wines are being made, often from vineyards so young the vines have scarcely taken root. However, there is a traditional wine scene too, based south of Santiago in Maipo and spreading down the Central Valley through Rapel, Curicó and Maule, hemmed in by the Andes and the Coastal Ranges, that is also shaking off its cobwebby past and beginning to contribute numerous challenging, thought-provoking wines to Chile's heady mix.

Carmenère, with its dark, rich, savoury flavours, is called Chile's flagship grape variety, but Merlot and Cabernet Sauvignon from Maipo, Syrah from Elqui, Limarí, Leyda and Colchagua, Carignan from Maule, and Pinot Noir from Leyda and Casablanca all offer superbly individual flavours. Chile's Chardonnay, especially from Limarí, Leyda and the south, is world class. Sauvignon Blanc from the coastal valleys such as Leyda and Aconcagua can be stunning, and Riesling and Gewürztraminer from the south are delicate and delightful. There are other grape varieties, too, which will increasingly make their mark, but these are a good bunch to be getting on with.

2012 VINTAGE REPORT

In Argentina, frost, rain, hail and the Zonda wind ensured that the 2012 crop was about 10% smaller than average, with the area of San Juan being the worst affected. Small doesn't mean poor, however, and 2012 will be remembered for its high quality, highly concentrated wines.

An unusually hot summer and early autumn resulted in record temperatures in many of Chile's warmer wine valleys, and grape picking commenced 10–15 days earlier than normal. Even in the cooler coastal regions such as Casablanca and Leyda, above-average daytime temperatures meant that picking times had to be carefully planned. Only the high altitude vineyards in

South American entries in the A–Z section (pages 62–327).

51

the Elqui Valley were not affected by the high temperatures. The grapes were healthy and red wines should be good to very good in all regions. White wines, especially Sauvignon Blanc, will present more of a challenge for the winemakers, but acidity levels are being reported as satisfactory. Following two short harvests – 2010 on account of the earthquake, and 2011 because of spring frosts – production in 2012 should be back to normal levels.

BRAZIL
Brazil dominates the map of South America, and you'd have thought there'd be loads of places ideal for growing grapes. But look at its place on the globe: largely between the equator and the Tropic of Capricorn – that's the degree of latitude that runs bang through the hot heart of Australia, subtropical, tropical or desert. And given that Brazil also possesses the world's largest tracts of rainforest, you'd expect it to be pretty humid, if not downright sodden – and an awful lot of it is. Remarkably, there is a fascinating subtropical operation at Vale do São Francisco, only 9° south, which in blistering conditions produces two crops a year of pretty tasty wine – the Moscato is particularly juicy. Otherwise you have to head way south to find decent stuff. The traditional area – the Rio Grande do Sul centred on the mountain city of Bento Gonçalves – was settled by Italians in the 1840s. It's still pretty humid, but good wines are increasingly possible, and the need to pick early in wet conditions means that lowish-alcohol reds from grapes like Merlot, Cabernet Franc and Teroldego can be delightful, as can the Moscatos. Sparkling wine, dry or sweet, from Pinot Noir and Chardonnay, or Moscato, is always good, and sometimes outstanding. The most promising areas for dry reds and whites are the high Planalto Catarinense vineyards north of Bento Gonçalves and the dry and temperate vineyards of the Serra do Sudeste down near the Uruguayan border. Further inland along the border is the Campanha region: also promising, but less temperate, drier and hotter, giving ripeness but less perfume and character than the grapes of the Sudeste.

URUGUAY
Most of the vines are on very fertile clay soils in the rainy, coolish Canelones region around Montevideo. Those soils plus that climate is not a great recipe for ripening most grape varieties before they rot on the vine, which is why the thick-skinned, rot-resistant black Tannat grape is the leading variety. Modern wineries have managed to soften the tannic Tannat; they are also producing snappy Sauvignon Blanc and fresh Cabernet Franc and Merlot. Efforts to find more suitable vineyard areas initially focused on inland sites – a few in the middle or west of the country – and more successfully in the far north, right on the Brazilian border in the Cerro Chapeu region. However, the most exciting new plantings are on the Atlantic seaboard around Maldonado in the south-east. The area is barely developed and thinly populated, but could end up as Uruguay's finest wine region. Best producers: Bouza, Carrau, Castillo Viejo, Filgueira, Juanicó, Pisano, Stagnari, Toscanini, Viñedo de los Vientos.

OTHER COUNTRIES
Peru has seemingly good vineyard sites in the Ica Valley south of Lima. I first tasted wines from the Tacama vineyards donkey's years ago; they're a lot better now. Bolivia has few vineyards, but they're incredibly high. Venezuela's chief claim to fame is that some of her subtropical vines give three crops a year – which makes a vintage chart rather complicated!

OTHER WINE COUNTRIES

ALGERIA With many vines over 40 years old, there should be great potential here, but political uncertainty hinders progress. The western coastal province of Oran produces three-quarters of Algeria's wine, including the soft but muscular Coteaux de Tlemcen wines and dark, beefy reds of the Coteaux de Mascara.

BELGIUM Belgium's vineyards were established by the Romans, but it is only within the past 20 years that climate change has once again allowed vines to thrive, and the country now has a budding wine industry, admittedly on a very small scale. Pinot Noir and Chardonnay are grown for sparkling and still wines, most notably some Chablis-like Chardonnay.

BULGARIA After success in the 1980s and disarray in the 90s, some progress followed the introduction of new wine legislation in 2001, and investment in new vineyards is beginning to gather pace. New World influences are having some effect, although few wines shine. Cabernet Sauvignon and Merlot dominate, but local grapes – plummy Mavrud, meaty Gamza, deep Melnik, fruity white Dimiat and Misket – can be good. Established wineries such as Boyar Estates, Khan Krum and Suhindol are being joined by new operations every year, some financed locally, others with international backing. Stork Nest and Bessa Valley are two of the largest, and anyone doubting Bulgaria's potential should taste the eminently affordable and excellent Enira wines from Bessa Valley (owned by Stephan von Neipperg of Ch. CANON-LA-GAFFELIÈRE in St-Émilion in France).

CANADA The strict VQA (Vintners Quality Alliance) maintains high standards in British Columbia and Ontario, and there is continuing progress in the two most important regions – OKANAGAN VALLEY in British Columbia and the NIAGARA PENINSULA in Ontario. Also jutting into Lake Ontario is the up-and-coming PRINCE EDWARD COUNTY. Sweet Icewine, made primarily from Vidal and Riesling, but occasionally from Cabernet Franc and other varietals, is still Canada's trump card. But producers have realized they also make high-quality Chardonnay and have begun to market Canadian Chardonnay more aggressively. Pinot Gris, Riesling, Sauvignon Blanc and Gewurztraminer also do well; Merlot, Cabernet Franc, Cabernet Sauvignon, even Syrah in British Columbia and Pinot Noir in Ontario, are producing tasty red wines. Some credible sparklers are now being made, especially in Prince Edward County and Nova Scotia. Latest rumblings are of good fizz in Nova Scotia.

CHINA With its massive population, burgeoning middle class and taste for luxury, China is unquestionably an appealing prospective market for wine producers throughout the world. In 2005 China's tariffs on imported wines were reduced from 64% to 14%, opening the door for imported wines. Currently wine from grapes only accounts for about 1.5% of alcohol consumed in China and consumption per capita is 0.5 litres per person each year – but it is growing at a very exciting rate. Interest is overwhelmingly for red wine, considered an auspicious colour, with Bordeaux red wines being perceived as the 'best'. That Ch. LAFITE continues to hold onto its title as 'the best of the best' in the eyes of aspiring Chinese collectors remains a curious fascination to outsiders, with many hopeful wineries looking to make their flagships the next lucratively placed Lafite.

Production of wine in China has been stepped up to meet the increase in demand. Around 95% of wine consumed in the country is produced domestically from locally grown grapes that are often blended with a large proportion of cheap bulk wine imports and sold as 'Chinese Wine'. There is, however, a growing number of wineries that are seeking to make genuine China-reared wines. Cabernet Sauvignon is almost without exception the emphasis – something of a quixotic pursuit for wineries looking to make the Chinese equivalent of Lafite. The best results of recent vintages range from drinkable wines that are recognizably Cabernet to some very good efforts indeed, but for the most part the finest are nothing to strike fear in the hearts of Bordeaux First Growths just yet. That said, in 2009 Domaines Barons de Rothschild (DBR) Lafite famously partnered with CITIC, China's biggest state-owned investment company, to establish vineyards in China with the aim of producing wine for domestic consumption.

China currently has more than 500 wineries. Vineyards in China are mainly located in the Shanxi and Shandong provinces, south-west and south-east of Beijing respectively. Many larger operations, international companies and joint ventures, including DBR Lafite, have based themselves around the city of Penglai in the coastal province of Shandong. This area has a relatively mild climate compared to the frigid

winters in regions further north, but summer rains and ensuing rot can be troublesome. Moving inland, drier, temperate-to-warm continental parts of China, such as parts of Shanxi province and the Mount Helan region in Ningxia province, seem climatically compatible to producing quality red wine grapes. Slightly cooler than Bordeaux, Ningxia appears a logical choice for quality wine vineyards. Impressive results from Ningxia wines such as Silver Heights' 'The Summit' and Jia Bei Lan seem to confirm this. Also promising is the Xinjiang area, which is considerably further inland, to the extreme west of China. This is warmer and even drier, receiving just 150mm of rain annually, with a particularly dry late summer/autumn spell during the critical

period after the onset of ripening. It also has significant diurnal swings in temperature with hot summer days and very cool nights, which could slow the ripening process and extend hang-time.

Dynasty, Changyu, Great Wall and Huadong are the major producers in China in terms of volume, controlling around half of grape wine production. Top boutique wineries that are making real quality inroads include Grace Vineyards in Shanxi province and Silver Heights, Jia Bei Lan and Helan Mountain in Ningxia province.

Since its abolition of wine taxes in 2008, Hong Kong has become a wine hub for mainland China. Large-scale exhibitions such as the Hong Kong International Wine and Spirits Trade Fair (held in November each year) and Vinexpo Hong Kong (held bi-annually in June) have proved highly popular.

CROATIA Croatia has a strong viticultural heritage and an undercurrent of rising potential: bulk whites dominate but small private producers are emerging and big companies are improving. What the country needs now is more investment, more technology in the vineyard and winery, and winemakers with a vision of what is happening elsewhere in the wine world. Tourism is flourishing and this should help popularize the wines – so long as foreigners can pronounce them.

The most established red vineyards are on the Dalmatian coast, where international varieties are being planted alongside gutsy indigenous grapes: deep, tannic Plavac Mali – related to Zinfandel – has long produced the best known red wines, but there are several other indigenous varieties, and Croatian Merlot is surprisingly good. The most popular white grapes are Malvazija (Malvasia) from Istria up towards the Italian border – ideally zippy and fresh – and the fleshier Graševina (Welschriesling) in the centre of the country. On the Serbian border at Fruska Gora there is good Traminac (Traminer). GRGICH of California has a winery on the Pelješac peninsula. Frano Miloš (also on the Pelješac peninsula), Zlatan Otok on Hvar island, Krauthaker in Kutjevo, and Coronica, Kozlovic, Vina Laguna and Matoševic in Istria are other names to look for.

CYPRUS Slowly the Cypriot wine industry is becoming more focused on quality. Small wineries are leading the way, especially Vlassides for red wines and Kyperounda for whites, and also Hadjiantonas, Tsiakkas, Vasa and Zambartas. Xynisteri can produce lively whites if grown at altitude, but the best variety may be Shiraz, on its own or blended with the local Marathefdiko and Lefkada. Historic sweet COMMANDARIA is the world's oldest wine brand.

CZECH REPUBLIC The vineyards of Bohemia in the north-west and Moravia in the south-east are mainly planted with white varieties – Grüner Veltliner, Müller-Thurgau, Riesling, Pinot Blanc, Pinot Gris – with pockets of red such as St-Laurent and Lemberger (Blaufränkisch).

DENMARK Grapes shouldn't grow this far north. But as global warming pushes the threshold for viticulture ever northward and new grape varieties are developed to thrive here, the EU permitted commercial wine production in 2000. The industry is still tiny, with about 40 growers taking advantage of the long hours of sunshine to ripen their grapes. Neighbouring southern Sweden, with very similar conditions, is also getting in on the act, with both white and red wines.

ENGLAND The first commercial vineyard of the modern era in the UK was planted in 1952 and since then the tiny industry has come a long way. Today, the UK boasts around 1550ha (3830 acres) of vines with over 500 vineyards (many very small), 125 wineries and an average annual output of around 2.5 million bottles. Gone are many of the old German crosses and hybrid vine varieties, largely replaced by cool-climate international varieties. Producers have learnt which varieties are successful: Bacchus, Schönburger and Seyval Blanc for still whites; Rondo, Regent, Dornfelder and Pinot Noir for still reds; but above all, Chardonnay, Pinot Noir and Pinot Meunier for quality sparklers. In particular, sparkling wines have shown they can equal CHAMPAGNE in quality and the area planted to the classic Champagne varieties is now approaching 50% of the UK total; most of the new plantings are of the Champagne varieties. The quality is likely to be excellent, but I fear there'll be a glut of grapes in a few years time. Growers from Champagne are taking notice and several famous houses have been looking for sites; a producer from Avize, who planted a 4ha (10 acre) vineyard in 2004/5, has just released his first wine, Meonhill, to much acclaim. Labelling regulations for UK wines are changing. Bottles will soon be labelled with PDO (Protected Designation of Origin) for Quality Wines or PGI (Protected Geographical Indication) for Regional Wines. Wines that have not been tested will fall into a new category known as 'varietal wines', the rules for which have yet to be invented.

The most popular winemaking counties are: West Sussex (Bolney, NYETIMBER, RIDGEVIEW, Stopham), Kent (BALFOUR, Biddenden, CHAPEL DOWN, GUSBOURNE, Meopham Valley, Sandhurst), Surrey (DENBIES), Essex (New Hall), Hampshire (COATES & SEELY, Jenkyn Place, Meonhill, Wickham), East Sussex (BREAKY BOTTOM, Davenport, PLUMPTON COLLEGE), Devon (SHARPHAM, Yearlstone), Gloucestershire (THREE CHOIRS), Berkshire (STANLAKE PARK) and Cornwall (CAMEL VALLEY). A new vineyard has been planted on Sark (Channel Islands) by the multimillionaire Barclay brothers; varieties include Chardonnay, Pinot Gris, Pinot Noir, Albariño and Savagnin; the first crop was in 2011.

2009 was an amazing year (*the* best year that UK vineyards have ever had). As with much of Europe, 2010 was a year of two halves: excellent early conditions (although some UK vineyards did get frosted) with a good flowering and then a wet, indifferent summer leading to grapes with surprisingly high sugars, but also very high acidities. 2011 had a very warm dry spring and early summer, followed by one of the worst flowering periods anyone can remember, which resulted in very small crops in most vineyards. However, a very warm September and October saw the grapes achieve record sugar levels (but also high acids) which should result in some good wines, especially Pinot Noir-based reds and, in time, bottle-fermented sparklers.

GEORGIA Georgia faces many challenges – lack of regulation, counterfeiting, and a recent ban on exports to Russia, its biggest market – but its diverse climates (from subtropical to moderate continental) and soils could produce every style imaginable. The tourist industry is helping introduce Georgian wines to a wider audience. International and indigenous varieties abound; the peppery, powerful red Saperavi could be a world-beater. Most wine is still pretty rustic, but investment is beginning to have an effect, with GWS (Georgian Wines & Spirits Company, 75% owned by Pernod Ricard) leading the way, and dozens more wine producers keen to excel.

GREECE The reputation, distribution and sales of Greek wines, both red and white, continue to improve, particularly in the US, but the Greek financial crisis has badly affected their domestic market. The new generation of winemakers and grape growers, many of them trained in France, Australia or California, have a clear vision of the flavours they want to achieve and their wines are modern but marvellously original too. Polarization between cheap bulk and expensive boutique wines continues, but large companies such as Boutari, Kourtaki and Tsantali are upping the quality stakes and flavours improve every vintage. More vineyard and marketing work – many labels are still difficult to understand – is needed. Retsina – resinated white and rosé wine – is common throughout Greece: poor retsina is diabolical but the best are deliciously oily and piny. Successful blends of international and indigenous varieties, but also tremendous unblended examples of the red Agiorgitiko, Limnio and Xynomavro, and white Assyrtiko, Malagousia, Moschofilero and Roditis. Quality areas: Santorini for whites, Nemea and Naoussa for reds, SAMOS for

56

sweet Muscats, Patras for dessert red Mavrodaphne. Wineries to watch include: Aidarinis, Alpha, Argyros, Antonopoulos, Biblia Chora, Gaia, Gentilini, GEROVASSILIOU, Hatzimichalis, Kyr Yianni, Domaine Costa LAZARIDI, Mercouri, Papaïoannou, Strofilia and Tselepos.

HUNGARY Hungary makes remarkably good whites and reds and outstanding sweet TOKAJI wines. Stringent regulations and investment/advice from Australian and western European companies and consultants – for example at the BALATONBOGLÁR winery – have put Hungary back on the international wine map. It has had some success with Sauvignon Blanc and Pinot Gris (also known as Szürkebarát) and there is renewed interest in native varieties such as Furmint, Hárslevelü and Irsai Olivér for whites, Kékfrankos (Blaufränkisch) and Kadarka (the traditional grape used in BIKAVÉR) for reds, and top Hungarian winemakers – Akos Kamocsay (at HILLTOP), Vilmos Thummerer, Attila Gere and others – are now a solid force. But price and reputation remain low and many vineyards are being abandoned out of desperation.

INDIA In spite of a population of about 1.1 billion people, wine consumption in India is minuscule. The urban/tourist centres of Delhi, Mumbai (Bombay), Bangalore and Goa account for about 80% of the country's wine consumption. Around 25% of wine is imported, the remainder is produced domestically. There is a long tradition of growing table grapes in India, but wine grape production is very recent. The major area of wine grape production is in the state of Maharashtra, focused around the town of Nashik. The vineyards are located at around 600m (2000ft) above sea level and so are cooler than the surrounding areas and certainly cooler than nearby Mumbai. In 2001 there were only 6 wineries in India. Today there are 47, most of them based in Maharashtra.

India is now starting to produce some consistent, good-quality wines, thanks mainly to the groundbreaking work of major player Chateau Indage in Maharashtra and concerted efforts in recent years of two quality-focused producers, Sula Vineyards in the Nashik area and Grover Vineyards located in the Nandi Hills just outside of Bangalore in the state of Karnataka. Newcomer Fratelli at Akluj, south of Pune, is worth keeping an eye on.

ISRAEL Israel is making the best wines produced in this area for over 2000 years. The higher-altitude Upper Galilee, Golan Heights and Judean Hills are the best regions. Leading wineries include Barkan, Carmel, CASTEL, Clos de Gat, Dalton, Margalit, Yarden and YATIR. Many of the top wines are Bordeaux-style blends or made from Bordeaux varieties such as Cabernet Sauvignon. However, some enterprising wineries, including Avidan, Carmel, Chateau Golan, Sea Horse and Vitkin are specializing in Mediterranean and Rhône varieties. These are more suitable for the climate and will produce interesting results, with particularly characterful wines from old-vine Carignan and Petite Sirah. Binyamina's Reserve Carignan, Carmel's Single Vineyard Shiraz, Segal's Dishon Cabernet Sauvignon, YATIR's Bordeaux blend, Yarden's Cabernet Sauvignon and CASTEL's Chardonnay are particularly good.

Kosher wines are necessary for Jews observing the Jewish dietary laws. These are the oldest of all codified wine laws. Regular winemaking methods are used, but there has to be a religious Jewish workforce and materials have to be certified as kosher. Israel makes some of the finest kosher wines. YATIR, CASTEL and Yarden make top-quality wines, which happen also to be kosher. The finest kosher wines from outside Israel are Covenant and Herzog from

California and Celler de Capçanes from Spain. Even Ch. LÉOVILLE-POYFERRÉ, Ch. PONTET-CANET, Ch. VALANDRAUD and others have made kosher cuvées. Some kosher wines are suitable for vegans and vegetarians.

JAPAN It's not easy to grow wine grapes in Japan. The major viticulture regions, Nagano and Yamanashi, are located near the centre of the main island of Honshu, and producers face a number of climate challenges during the growing season. 90% of the grapes grown in Japan are table grapes; very few are of the European wine grape species *Vitis vinifera*. Some wineries do try to use table grapes or wine grape hybrids (which are easier to grow than *vinifera*), and wines made from Delaware, Kyoho, Ryugan and Muscat Bailey A are common, but can have that distinctive and generally unappealing 'foxy' or chemical/epoxy character that is found in species other than *vinifera*.

Some particularly interesting Japanese wine is made from Koshu, a pink-skinned, predominantly *vinifera* grape, believed to have come to Japan from Europe many centuries ago, via the Silk Road. Koshu usually produces a clean, dry, light-bodied wine with a delicate citrus character that pairs very well with sushi and sashimi. Good Koshu producers include Grace, Château Mercian, Katsunuma Winery (good sparkling Koshu), Marufuji Rubaiyat and Asagiri Wine Company. Also worth trying are red and white wines from Suntory in Yamanashi, Yamazaki Winery in Hokkaido, and some of the upper level Château Mercian wines – their Private Reserve Chardonnay is surprisingly good.

LEBANON Vineyards are spreading outside the Bekaa Valley to Batroun in the north, Mount Lebanon in the west and Jezzine in the south. Lebanon has some excellent red blends, usually featuring French grape varieties such as Cabernet Sauvignon, Cinsaut and Carignan. The prominent wineries remain CH. MUSAR, Ksara, Kefraya, Massaya, Clos St Thomas and Dom. des Tourelles, but they are being challenged by the new order of small boutique wineries dedicated to quality and individuality, such as Dom. de Baal, Ch. Belle-Vue, Karam and Ch. Khoury. There are also new wineries with strong financial backing like Ch. Marsyas (who also own Ch. Bargylus in Syria), Ch. Ka and the very impressive Ixsir Winery.

LUXEMBOURG With one of the world's highest levels of wine consumption per capita, very little wine is exported. Co-operatives dominate here and quality is about what you would expect. Plantings of Elbling and Rivaner (Müller-Thurgau) are in decline, and are being replaced with quality varietals such as Riesling, Pinot Noir, Chardonnay and Gewürztraminer. *Crémant* (sparkling) wines continue to increase in quality and popularity.

MALTA The first impression of Malta is of an arid rocky island squeezed full of people and with barely enough soil to grow basic food crops. And it *never* seems to rain. Well, it does rain, and its limestone rock is able to absorb and hold a significant amount of water in reserve. Even so, water is scarce, but the vine doesn't need much – often the morning and evening dews from the sea breezes is enough to keep it going. Most wines used to be made from imported Italian grapes, and they weren't bad. But, especially on the small island of Gozo, vineyards are being developed and attractive wines are now available from 100% Maltese grapes. They're good, but you can taste the sun.

MEXICO In the far north-west of Mexico, in Baja California, some good reds are made by L A CETTO as well as by smaller companies such as Monte

Xanic and Casa de Piedra. In the rest of the country, only high-altitude areas such as the Parras Valley and Zacatecas have the potential for quality wines. Casa Madero, in the Parras Valley, has some success with Cabernet Sauvignon. Other promising grape varieties include Nebbiolo, Petite Sirah, Tempranillo, Zinfandel and Barbera, with Viognier and Chardonnay also planted.

MOLDOVA Standards of winemaking and equipment leave much to be desired, but fruit quality is good, and international players, including PENFOLDS and winemakers Jacques Lurton, Hugh Ryman and Alain Thiénot, have worked with local wineries. However, chaotic social conditions have led to many attempts being abandoned.

MONTENEGRO This red-wine-dominated part of the former Yugoslavia shows some potential in the beefy Vranac grape with its bitter cherry flavours – but the worst wines are really poor.

MOROCCO Known for big, sweet fruited reds that once found a ready blending market in France. France is still the biggest export market, but the wines have improved dramatically since the 1990s and domestic consumption is increasing, especially among young urban professionals. Massive investment by Castel Frères kickstarted the renaissance, and quality is on the rise at Morocco's leading producer, Celliers de Meknès. Domaine el Baraka and Domaine Larroque are promising, and French producers Bernard Magrez (sometimes in harness with Gérard Depardieu) and Alain GRAILLOT (Tandem) are making some good wines here, especially from Syrah.

NETHERLANDS The vineyard area has expanded rapidly in the past decade: there are currently around 175ha (430 acres), in the hands of more than 150 commercial growers, most of whom sell all their wines locally. The best vineyards are in the southern part of the country, in the rolling hills of Limburg. Chardonnay is the most promising grape variety.

ROMANIA The huge vineyard area has declined somewhat in recent years as hybrid grape varieties are pulled up, to be replanted with *Vitis vinifera* grapes such as Pinot Noir, Cabernet Sauvignon, Merlot and the native Feteasca Negra for reds, Pinot Gris and Chardonnay for whites. International-backed ventures such as Cramele Recas, Halewood (Prahova Valley) and Carl Reh are a sign of the mini-revolution, but challenges remain. Recent forays into the export market showed marked improvements but no really memorable flavours yet. The appellation system is of limited value, although Dealul Mare, Murfatlar and Cotnari all have ancient reputations.

SLOVAKIA The eastern part of the old Czechoslovakia, with its cool-climate vineyards, is dominated by white varieties – Pinot Blanc, Riesling, Grüner Veltliner, Irsai Olivér – with the occasional fruity Frankovka (Blaufränkisch) red. Western investment is rapidly improving the quality.

SLOVENIA Many of the old Yugoslav Federation's best vineyards are here. Potential is considerable, and some interesting wines are emerging, with whites generally better than reds. A simplified appellation system and the increasing popularity of Slovenia as a holiday and second-home region should increase availability. On the Italian border, Brda and Vipava have go-ahead co-operatives, and Kraski Teran is a red wine of repute. The Movia range, from the Kristancic family, looks promising.

SWITZERLAND Fendant (Chasselas) is the main grape for spritzy but neutral whites from the VALAIS and VAUD. Like the fruity DÔLE reds, they are best drunk very young. German-speaking cantons produce whites from Müller-Thurgau (sometimes labelled Riesling-Sylvaner) and mostly light reds and rosés from Pinot Noir (Blauburgunder); top producers, such as Daniel GANTENBEIN, make more powerful versions. Italian-speaking TICINO concentrates on Merlots, which have been increasingly impressive since 2000. Serious wines, especially in Valais, use Syrah, Chardonnay, Marsanne and traditional varieties like Amigne and Petite Arvine. Indeed, the traditional varieties, of which there are many, are undergoing a revival. Pinot Noir from the Valais is greatly improved. See also NEUCHÂTEL.

THAILAND The very concept of growing wine grapes anywhere within Thailand's tropics calls for a viticultural suspension of disbelief, but Thailand, close to the equator, has no less than 8 major wineries, producing nearly a million bottles of wine a year.

The first still wines appeared in 1995 from Chateau de Loei in north-eastern Thailand, using Chenin Blanc and Syrah. Siam Winery, which had begun producing wine coolers in 1986, launched its Monsoon Valley label in 2003; the wines are now exported to Thai restaurants in more than 15 countries. Entry-level red and white blends are made mainly from hybrid grapes, but premium range wines made from grapes such as Colombard and Shiraz grown in the Hua Hin Hills vineyard show quality potential.

TUNISIA Ancient wine traditions have had an injection of new life from international investment, and results so far are encouraging. Tourism soaks up most of the production and little is exported. It remains to be seen what effect recent political upheaval will have.

TURKEY There is new fascination with Turkey as we are being introduced to exotic indigenous grape varieties. The tannic, muscular yet scented Bogazkere, softer, plummy Öküzgözü and juicy, fruity Kalecik Karasi are all varieties worth trying, as are the delicate whites like Emir and Narince.

There is a move toward greater quality, led by the three dynamic large wineries, Kavaklidere, Kayra and Doluca (including the Sarafin label). These are being joined by new wineries including Baküs Butik, Buyülübag, Corvus, Idol, Likya, Pamukkale, Prodom, Umurbey and Vinkara.

There is an incredible variety of terroirs in Turkey, from east to west and north to south. Turkey remains the world's sixth-largest grape producer, but only 2–4% of this ends up as wine. The winery revolution is happening. The next objective is for wineries to gain control of vineyard activity in order to direct quality.

UKRAINE The Crimea's vineyards are the most important, producing hearty reds, sparkling reds and whites, and tremendous sweet stickies from Muscatel and other varieties, especially under the Massandra label. The Odessa region is successful with its sparkling wines, the best-known facilities being the Inkerman winery, Novyi Svet and Zolotaya Balka. Kolonist has raised the stakes for high-quality reds on the Moldovan border, and Trubetskoy is waking things up on the Dnieper.

A–Z

OF WINES, PRODUCERS, GRAPES & WINE REGIONS

In the following pages there are over
1600 entries covering the world's top wines, as well as leading
producers, main wine regions and grape
varieties, followed on page 328 by a glossary of wine terms
and classifications.

*On page 4 you will find a full explanation of
how to use the A–Z.*
*On page 337 there is an index of all wine producers
in the book, to help you find the world's best wines.*

AALTO *Ribera del Duero DO, Castilla y León, Spain* Former VEGA SICILIA winemaker Mariano García and ex-RIBERA DEL DUERO appellation boss Javier
Zaccagnini created this winery in 1999. From the outset, they have
produced dense but elegant reds, Aalto★★ and old vines cuvée Aalto
PS★★. Best years: (2010) 09 08 07 **06 05 04 03 01 00 99**.

ABACELA *Umpqua Valley AVA, Oregon, USA* Earl and Hilda Jones planted the
first Tempranillo vines in the Pacific Northwest, in the Umpqua Valley,
southern OREGON, in 1995. Today they grow Tempranillo, Syrah, Merlot,
Dolcetto, Malbec, Grenache, Viognier and Albariño. The Tempranillo★
(Reserve★★) has been the most successful wine; the Albariño★★ is
surprisingly similar to those of GALICIA. Best years: (2010) 09 **08 07 06**.

ABEJA *Walla Walla Valley AVA, Washington State, USA* A state-of-the-art facility
located on a century-old farmstead in the foothills of the Blue Mountains.
Winemaker John Abbott produces crisp Viognier★★ in small quantities,
rich and concentrated Chardonnay★, spicy Syrah★, supple Merlot★ and
fine Cabernet Sauvignon★★, plus a tiny amount of Cabernet Sauvignon
Reserve★★. Best years: (Cabernet Sauvignon) (2010) 09 **08 07 06 05**.

ABRUZZO-MOLISE *Italy* Abruzzo, with its (viniculturally speaking)
satellite Molise, is part maritime, part mountainous. White Trebbiano
d'Abruzzo DOC, occasionally impressive, is usually dry and neutral; tastier
whites come from the Pecorino grape. The fruity, full-coloured
Montepulciano d'Abruzzo DOC, despite high production, can be a red of real
character, as can its rosé partner, Cerasuolo. Training techniques are being
revised to favour quality over quantity, and new DOCs and DOCGs are
being introduced. Good producers include Contesa★★, Illuminati★★,
Marramiero★★, Masciarelli★★, Nicodemi, Orlandi Contucci Ponno★,
Tollo★, Valentini★★★. See also MONTEPULCIANO.

ACACIA *Carneros AVA, California, USA* Chardonnay and Pinot Noir specialist.
Restrained but attractive CARNEROS Chardonnay★. Pinot Noirs include
Carneros★ and some very good single-vineyard examples (Lone Tree
Vineyard★★). Best years: (Pinot Noir) (2010) 09 **08 07 06 05 03 02 01 00**.

ACHAVAL FERRER *Mendoza, Argentina* Founded in 1998, and now one of
Argentina's most sought-after labels. 80-year-old vines in the La
Consulta area of Uco Valley produce Finca Altamira★★, a dark, rich
Malbec. Also very good single-vineyard Malbecs Bella Vista★★ and
Mirador★★, as well as regular Malbec★★ and a more approachable red
blend, Quimera★. Best years: 2009 08 **06 05**.

ACONCAGUA *Chile* A warm region and home to some of Chile's best
reds, from Cabernet Sauvignon, Syrah and Carmenère. Recent
vineyard developments in the Aconcagua Costa region, close to the sea,
are proving very exciting for Sauvignon Blanc and Syrah. Best
producers: ERRÁZURIZ★★, VON SIEBENTHAL★.

JEAN-BAPTISTE ADAM *Alsace AC, Alsace, France* Long-established family
vineyard in Ammerschwihr with a reputation for luscious, classically
perfumed Gewurztraminer★★ from the Kaefferkopf Grand Cru, as well
as concentrated Riesling★★, herbaceous Pinot Gris★ and an exciting
Pinot Noir★★ given 18 months in oak. Best years: (Kaefferkopf
Gewurztraminer) (2011) 10 **09 08 07 05 04 02 01 00**.

TIM ADAMS *Clare Valley, South Australia* Important maker of fine, traditional
wine whose need to buy in grapes may disappear since his bargain
purchase of 75ha (185 acres) of vines from Leasingham in 2009. He

has subsequently snapped up the Leasingham winery (closed by Constellation), which he will use for contract winemaking. Classic dry Riesling★★★, oaky Semillon★★ and rich, opulent Shiraz★★ (both often ★★★) and Cabernet-Malbec★★. Newcomers Tempranillo★★ and Pinot Gris★ are exciting. The Fergus★★ can be a glorious Grenache-based blend, and minty, peppery Aberfeldy Shiraz★★ (can be ★★★) is a remarkable, at times unnerving, mouthful of brilliance from 100-year-old vines. The botrytis Riesling★ can be super. Protégé★ label is used for some of his newly acquired vineyards' fruit. Best years: (Aberfeldy Shiraz) (2010) 09 08 06 05 **04 03 02 01 00 99 98 96 94**.

ADELAIDE HILLS *South Australia* Small, exciting region 30 minutes' drive from Adelaide. High altitude affords a cool, moist climate ideal for fine table wines and superb sparkling wine. Consistently good Sauvignon Blanc and Chardonnay, promising Pinot Noir, small amounts of classy Nebbiolo, and increasingly exciting, fleshy Shiraz from warmer southern vineyards. Best producers: Ashton Hills★, Barratt, Bird in Hand★, HENSCHKE★★, The Lane★, Longview▲, Nepenthe★, PETALUMA★, SHAW & SMITH★★, Geoff WEAVER★★.

ADELSHEIM VINEYARD *Willamette Valley AVA, Oregon, USA* Over the past 3 decades, Adelsheim has established a reputation for excellent, generally unfiltered, Pinot Noir – especially cherry-scented Elizabeth's Reserve★ and Bryan Creek Vineyard★ – and for rich Chardonnay Caitlin's Reserve★. Also a bright, minerally Pinot Gris★. Best years: (Elizabeth's Reserve) (2010) 09 **08 07 06 05**.

AGLIANICO DEL VULTURE DOC *Basilicata, Italy* Wine from the Aglianico grape grown on the steep slopes of extinct volcano Mt Vulture. Despite the zone's location almost on the same latitude as Naples, the harvest here is sometimes later than in BAROLO, 750km (470 miles) to the north west, because the Aglianico grape ripens very late at altitude. The best wines are structured, complex and long-lived. Best producers: Basilium★, Bisceglia★, D'Angelo★★, Elena Fucci★, Cantine del Notaio▲▲, Tenuta del Portale, Le Querce★, Consorzio Viticoltori Associati del Vulture (Carpe Diem★). Best years: (2011) (10) 09 08 07 06 **05 04 01**.

AHR *Germany* The Ahr Valley is a small, 558ha (1380-acre), mainly red wine region south of Bonn, best known for Spätburgunder (Pinot Noir). Adeneuer★, Deutzerhof★, MEYER-NÄKEL★★ and Stodden★★ are the best of a growing band of serious producers.

AIRÉN Spain's – and indeed the world's – most planted white grape can make fresh, modern, but generally neutral-flavoured wines, with some eye-opening exceptions, such as Ercavio's stunning old-vines white from Toledo. Airén is grown all over the centre and south of Spain, especially in La MANCHA, VALDEPEÑAS and ANDALUCIA (where it's called Lairén).

ALBAN *San Luis Obispo County, California, USA* Based in the cool Arroyo Grande district of Edna Valley, John Alban is a RHÔNE specialist. He offers 2 Viogniers★★ and a Roussanne★★ laden with honey notes. There are 3 Syrahs (Reva★★★, Lorraine★, Seymour's Vineyard★★), intense Grenache★★ and Pandora★★, a blend of about 60% Grenache, 40% Syrah. These have been some of America's purest expressions of Rhône varietals, so hopefully a move toward even greater ripeness is purely temporary. Best years: (Syrah) (2009) 08 **07 06 05 04 03 02 01 00**.

A | ALBARIÑO

ALBARIÑO Possibly Spain's most characterful white grape. It is a speciality of RIAS BAIXAS in Galicia in Spain's rainy north-west and, as Alvarinho, in Portugal's VINHO VERDE region. California is having a go. When well made, Albariño wines have fascinating flavours of apricot, peach, grapefruit and Muscat grapes, refreshingly high acidity, highish alcohol – and unrefreshingly high prices. The ever-present danger to quality is excessive yields.

ALENQUER DOC *Lisboa, Portugal* Maritime-influenced hills north of Lisbon, producing wines from (mostly) local grape varieties such as Castelão (Periquita) and Trincadeira, but also from Cabernet, Syrah and Chardonnay. Many wines are simply labelled LISBOA (formerly Estremadura). Best producers: Quinta de Chocapalha★, Quinta da Cortezia★, Quinta do Monte d'Oiro★★, Quinta da Romeira, Casa SANTOS LIMA★. Best years: (reds) 2007 05 04 03 01 00.

ALENTEJO *Portugal* A large chunk of southern Portugal south and east of Lisbon and, along with the DOURO, one of Portugal's fastest-improving red wine regions. Already some of Portugal's finest reds come from here. Vinho Regional wines are labelled Alentejano. Best producers: (reds) ALIANÇA (Quinta da Terrugem★★), BACALHÔA★ (Tinto da Ânfora Grande Escolha★★), Borba co-op★, Cartuxa★ (Pera-Manca★★), Quinta do Centro, CORTES DE CIMA★, Dona Maria★, ESPORÃO★, Fita Preta★, Paulo Laureano★, MALHADINHA NOVA★★, Monte da Penha, Mouchão★★, Quinta do Mouro★, Pato Frio, Quinta da Plansel (Plansel Selecta★), João Portugal RAMOS★, Herdade do Rocim, Herdade de São Miguel, SOGRAPE★, José de Sousa★, Terras d'Alter★. Best years: (reds) 2009 08 07 05 04 01 00.

ALEXANDER VALLEY AVA *Sonoma County, California, USA* AVA centred on the northern Russian River, which is fairly warm, with only patchy summer fog. Cabernet Sauvignon is highly successful here, with lovely, juicy fruit not marred by an excess of tannin. Chardonnay may also be good when not over-cropped. Merlot and old-vine Zinfandel can be outstanding from hillside vineyards. Best producers: Alexander Valley Vineyards★, CLOS DU BOIS★, De Lorimier★, Geyser Peak★, Hanna★, JORDAN★, Murphy-Goode★★, RIDGE (Geyserville★★), Sausal★, SEGHESIO★★, SILVER OAK★★, Simi★, Skipstone★, Trentadue★★. See also RUSSIAN RIVER VALLEY AVA, SONOMA COUNTY. Best years: (reds) 2009 08 07 06 04 03 02 01 99 97 95.

ALGARVE *Portugal* Holiday region with mostly red wines in 4 DOCs: Lagoa, Lagos, Portimão and Tavira. Look out for reds and rosés from Sir Cliff Richard's Vida Nova, Quinta do Barranco Longo and Morgado da Torre.

ALIANÇA *Beira Litoral, Portugal* Aliança makes crisp, fresh whites and soft, approachable red BAIRRADAS★. Also made, either from its own vineyards or bought-in grapes or wines, are reds from the DÃO (Quinta da Garrida★) and ALENTEJO (Quinta da Terrugem★★). Quinta dos Quatro Ventos★★ from the DOURO is the top red, a blend of Tinta Roriz, Touriga Franca and Touriga Nacional.

ALICANTE BOUSCHET French grape, found (illegally) in Provence. This workhorse variety was largely grubbed up 20–30 years ago as lacking finesse and quality, but a few producers (Ch. de Berne, Ch. de Rouët) are now 'discovering' some old vines and are producing robust vins de

France. In Spain it's known as Garnacha Tintorera. Portugal is making excellent use of it, proving that every grape variety can have its day. South America is using its dark, brooding qualities.

ALIGOTÉ French grape, found mainly in Burgundy, whose basic characteristic is a lemony tartness. It can make extremely refreshing white wine, especially from old vines, but is generally rather lean. The best, from a subtype called Aligoté Doré, combining buttermilk texture with lemon zestiness, comes from the village of Bouzeron in the CÔTE CHALONNAISE, where Aligoté has its own appellation. Occasionally found in Moldova and Bulgaria. Drink young. Best producers: (Burgundy) COCHE-DURY★, A Ente★, J-H Goisot★, les Temps Perdus, Ponsot★, TOLLOT-BEAUT, de Villaine★.

ALLEGRINI *Valpolicella DOC, Veneto, Italy* High-profile producer in VALPOLICELLA Classico, making single-vineyard IGTs La Grola★★ (Corvina with a bit of Syrah) and La Poja★★★ (100% Corvina) wines which show the great potential that exists for Veronese red as a table wine. Outstanding AMARONE★★★ and RECIOTO Giovanni Allegrini★★. Best years: (Amarone) (2011) (10) 09 08 07 **06 04 03 01 00**.

THIÉRRY ALLEMAND *Cornas AC, Rhône Valley, France* Thiérry Allemand has 5ha (12 acres) of high-quality granite hillside vines. He uses little sulphur and makes top-class wines with clear fruit and dashing depth. He produces 2 unfiltered expressions of CORNAS at its intense and powerful best: Chaillot★★ has bold fruit, lively tannins; the complex, sustained Reynard★★★ is from a parcel of very old Syrah. Best years: (Reynard) (2011) 10 09 08 07 **06 05 04 03 01 00** 99 98 96 95 94 91 90.

ALLENDE *Rioja DOCa, Rioja, Spain* One of the most admired new names in RIOJA, making a mix of single-vineyard (*pago*) and high-quality blends. Scented, uncompromisingly concentrated reds include Aurus★★★, Calvario★★ and fresh, vibrant Allende★★. Also a marvellous, scented white★★. Best years: (reds) (2010) 09 08 **07 06 05** 04 03 02 01 00 99.

ALMAVIVA★★★ *Maipo, Chile* State-of-the-art joint venture between CONCHA Y TORO and the Baron Philippe de Rothschild company (see MOUTON-ROTHSCHILD), located in MAIPO Valley's Tocornal vineyard at the foot of the Andes. A memorably powerful red from old Cabernet Sauvignon vines planted in alluvial, stony soils; it can be drunk at 5 years but should age for 10. Best years: (2010) 09 07 06 **05 03 01**.

ALOXE-CORTON AC *Côte de Beaune, Burgundy, France* An important village at the northern end of the CÔTE DE BEAUNE producing mostly red wines from Pinot Noir. Its reputation is based on the 2 Grands Crus, CORTON (mainly red) and CORTON-CHARLEMAGNE (white only). There's an argument raging that some of the Grand Cru red vineyards should be 1er Cru, and most of the 1er Crus downgraded to village level. I think that's too severe, but look out for village Boutières and Valozières as worthy of 1er Cru status. Almost all the white wine is classified as Grand Cru. Best producers: d'Ardhuy★, CHANDON DE BRIAILLES★, M Chapuis★, Marius Delarche★, Dubreuil-Fontaine★, Follin-Arbelet★, Camille Giroud★, Antonin Guyon★, JADOT★, Mallard, Rapet★, Senard★, TOLLOT-BEAUT★. Best years: (reds) (2011) 10 09 **08 07 06** 05 03 02 99.

A | DOM. JEAN-MICHEL ALQUIER

DOM. JEAN-MICHEL ALQUIER *Faugères AC, Languedoc, France* This estate shows how good FAUGÈRES can be. Barrel aging of all wines, and low yields for the special cuvées, Les Bastides★★ and La Maison Jaune★. Grand Blanc is a good white blend of Marsanne and Grenache Blanc. **Best years:** (Bastides) (2011) 10 **09 08 07 06 05 04**.

ALSACE AC *Alsace, France* Tucked away on France's border with Germany, Alsace produces some of the most individual white wines of all, rich in aroma and full of ripe, distinctive flavours. Alsace is almost as far north as CHAMPAGNE, but its climate is considerably warmer and drier. Wines from the 51 best vineyard sites can call themselves Alsace Grand Cru AC and account for 4% of production; quality regulations are more stringent and many individual crus have further tightened the rules. Riesling, Muscat, Gewurztraminer and Pinot Gris are generally considered the finest varieties in Alsace. Pinot Blanc can produce good wines too – although confusingly Pinot Blanc can legally be made from 100% Auxerrois (a variety whose parentage is Pinot Blanc and Gouais Blanc). Reds from Pinot Noir are improving fitfully. Alsace labels its wines by grape variety and, apart from the Edelzwicker blends and CREMANT D'ALSACE fizz, most Alsace wines are made from a single variety, although blends from certain Grand Cru sites, such as Altenberg de Bergheim and Kaefferkopf, are now recognized. Vendange Tardive means 'late-harvest'; the grapes (Riesling, Muscat, Pinot Gris or Gewurztraminer) are picked late and almost overripe, giving higher sugar levels and potentially more intense flavours. The resulting wines are usually rich and mouthfilling and often need 5 years or more to reach their full potential. Sélection de Grains Nobles (made from botrytized grapes of the same varieties) are among Alsace's finest, but are very expensive to produce (and to buy). **Best producers:** J-B ADAM★★, Lucien Albrecht★, Barmès-Buecher★, J Becker, Léon Beyer★, P Blanck★★, Bott-Geyl★★, A Boxler★, Ernest Burn★★, DEISS★★, Dirler-Cadé★★, Pierre Frick★, Rémy Gresser★, HUGEL★, Josmeyer★★, Kientzler★, Klur, Kreydenweiss★★, Seppi Landmann★, A MANN★★, Meyer-Fonné, Mittnacht Frères, MURE★★, OSTERTAG★★, Pfaffenheim co-op, Ribeauvillé co-op, Rieflé★, Rolly Gassmann★, Martin Schaetzel★★, Charles Schléret, Schlumberger★, SCHOFFIT★★, Louis Sipp, Bruno Sorg★, Marc Tempé, TRIMBACH★★, TURCKHEIM co-op★, WEINBACH★★, Paul Zinck★, ZIND-HUMBRECHT★★★. **Best years:** (2011) 10 **09 08 07 05 04 02 01 00**.

ALTARE *Barolo DOCG, Piedmont, Italy* Elio Altare of La Morra led the winemaking revolution in traditionalist Alba, drastically shortening maceration times for Nebbiolo and other grapes. Though a professed modernist, Elio's wines are intense, full and structured while young, but with clearly discernible fruit flavours, thanks to an almost fanatical diligence in the vineyard. Recently added Barolo Cerretta★ from Serralunga. Also outstanding BAROLO Arborina★★★ and Brunate★★★ and 3 barrique-aged wines under the LANGHE DOC: Arborina★★★ (Nebbiolo), Larigi★★★ (Barbera) and La Villa★★ (Nebbiolo-Barbera). **Best years:** (Barolo) (2011) (10) (09) 08 07 06 **04 01 00 99**.

ALTO ADIGE *Trentino-Alto Adige, Italy* A largely German-speaking province, originally called Südtirol. The DOC covers dozens of different types of wine. Reds range from light and perfumed when made from the ubiquitous (but diminishing in importance) Schiava grape, to fruity and more structured when made from Cabernet or Merlot, to dark and velvety if Lagrein is used. Oak aging, once inclined to excess, is being handled ever better. Whites

66

include Chardonnay, Gewürztraminer, Pinot Grigio, Riesling and Sauvignon, among others, and world appreciation is increasing for the steely, minerally and potentially long-lived Pinot Bianco wines (aka Weiss-burgunder). There is also some good sparkling wine. Production is dominated by well-run co-ops, although there are excellent individual producers. Best producers (private): Abbazia di Novacella★, Casòn Hirschprunn★, Peter Dipoli★★, Egger-Ramer★, Franz Gojer★, Franz Haas★★, Haderburg★★, Hofstätter★★, Kränzl★, LAGEDER★★, Laimburg★, Loacker★, Josephus Mayr★, Muri-Gries★★, Josef Niedermayr★, Ignaz Niedriest★, Plattner-Waldgries★, Peter Pliger/Kuenhof★★, Hans Rottensteiner★, Heinrich Rottensteiner★, TIEFENBRUNNER★★, Elena Walch★★, Baron Widmann★; (co-ops) Caldaro★, Colterenzio★★, Girlan-Cornaiano★, Gries★★, Nals-Margreid★★, Prima & Nuova/Erste & Neue★, San Michele Appiano★★, Santa Maddalena★, Terlano★★★, Termeno★★.

ALTOS LAS HORMIGAS *Mendoza, Argentina* When visionary Tuscan winemaker Alberto Antonini fell in love with Argentina and its Malbec, Altos Las Hormigas was born. A relentless pursuit of *terroir* expression through Malbec has spanned 15 years and some 216ha (530 acres) of vineyards. The MENDOZA Classic★ label is benchmark stuff. At the top end the Vista Flores Single Vineyard Malbec★★ is deeply perfumed and lush with blue fruit. Fine Bonarda under the Colonia Las Liebres★ label.

ALVARINHO See ALBARIÑO.

ALYSIAN *Russian River Valley, Sonoma County, California, USA* Joint venture between Gary FARRELL and investor William Hambrecht, started in 2007, has released a string of superb Pinot Noirs★★ that emulate the delicate, balanced style that Farrell pioneered at his own RUSSIAN RIVER outfit.

CASTELLO DI AMA *Chianti Classico DOCG, Tuscany, Italy* High-profile CHIANTI CLASSICO estate, with outstanding Chianti Classico★★, plus single-vineyard Riservas★★★ (Bellavista and La Casuccia). L'Apparita★★★ is one of Italy's best Merlots. Also good Chardonnay Al Poggio★. Best years: (Chianti Classico) (2011) (10) 09 00 **07 06 04 01 00 99 97 95**.

AMARONE DELLA VALPOLICELLA DOCG *Veneto, Italy* A brilliantly individual, bitter-rich style of VALPOLICELLA made from grapes shrivelled on mats for months after harvest. The wine, which can reach 16% of alcohol and more, differs from the sweet RECIOTO DELLA VALPOLICELLA in that it is fermented to near-dryness. Wines from the Classico zone are generally the best (exceptions from DAL FORNO, Corte Sant'Alda, Roccolo Grassi and Prà's Morandina). Best producers: Accordini★★, ALLEGRINI★★★, Bertani★★, Brigaldara★, Brunelli★, BUSSOLA★★★, Michele Castellani★★, Corte Sant'Alda★, Valentina Cubi★★, DAL FORNO★★★, Guerrieri-Rizzardi★★, MASI★★, Prà★, QUINTARELLI★★★, Le Ragose★★, Roccolo Grassi★, Le Salette★★, Serègo Alighieri★, Speri★★, Tedeschi★★, Tommasi★, Villa Monteleone★★, VIVIANI★★, Zenato★★. Best years: (2010) 09 08 **06 04 03 01 00**.

AMIGNE Ancient Swiss grape variety that is virtually limited to 40ha (100 acres) around Vétroz in the VALAIS. The wine has an earthy, nutty intensity and benefits from a few years' aging. Best producers: Bonvin, Cottagnoud★, A Fontannaz, Jean-René Germanier★, Kurt★, Vieux Moulin.

ANAKENA *Cachapoal, Rapel, Chile* A modern winery producing one of Chile's best Viogniers★★, Ona Pinot Noir★ and the unusual Ona white blend of Riesling, Viognier and Chardonnay★.

DOM. DE L'ANCIENNE CURE *Bergerac AOP and Monbazillac AOP, South-West France* Christian Roche is best known for his luscious MONBAZILLACS★★, but his dry whites and his reds are no less remarkable. Top cuvées L'Abbaye★ and L'Extase★★ for all three styles. Best years: (reds and dry whites) (2011) 10 09 **08 06 05**; (sweet whites) 2010 **09 06 05**.

ANDALUCÍA *Spain* Fortified wines, or wines naturally so strong in alcohol that they don't need fortifying, are the speciality of this southern stretch of Spain. Apart from sherry (JEREZ Y MANZANILLA), there are the lesser, sherry-like wines of Condado de Huelva DO and MONTILLA-MORILES, and the rich, sweet wines of MÁLAGA. These regions also make some modern but bland dry whites; the best are from Condado de Huelva. Red and unfortified white wines are also appearing from Málaga, Cádiz, Seville, Granada and Almería provinces.

ANDERSON VALLEY AVA *California, USA* Small appellation (243ha/600 acres) in western MENDOCINO COUNTY that produces brilliant wines. Most vineyards are within 15 miles of the Pacific Ocean, making this one of the coldest AVAs in California. Delicate Pinot Noirs and Chardonnays, and one of the few places in the state for first-rate Gewürztraminer and Riesling. Superb sparkling wines with healthy acidity and creamy yeast are highlights as well. Best producers: Brutocao★, Goldeneye★, Greenwood Ridge★, HANDLEY★, Lazy Creek★, Littorai★, NAVARRO★★★, ROEDERER ESTATE★★, SCHARFFENBERGER CELLARS★★.

ANDREW WILL WINERY *Washington State, USA* Winemaker Chris Camarda makes delicious blends of BORDEAUX varietals from a range of older WASHINGTON vineyards. At the top are the complex Champoux Vineyard★★★ and the opulent Ciel du Cheval★★★. Wine from the estate vineyard, Two Blondes Vineyard★, will improve as the vines age. Sorella★★, a blend of the best barrels each vintage, can be outstanding with age. Best years: (reds) (2010) 09 **08 07 06 05 04 03**.

CH. ANGÉLUS★★★ *St-Émilion Grand Cru AC, 1er Grand Cru Classé, Bordeaux, France* One of the best-known ST-ÉMILION Premiers Grands Crus Classés, with an energetic owner and talented winemaker. Rich, dark, spicy, modern St-Émilion with lots of lovely old-vine Cabernet Franc. On flying form. Best years: 2010 09 08 **07** 06 **05** 04 03 02 01 00 99 98 96 95 93.

MARQUIS D'ANGERVILLE *Volnay, Côte de Beaune, Burgundy, France* Succeeding generations of d'Angervilles have provided an exemplary range of elegant Premiers Crus from VOLNAY, the subtlest of the CÔTE DE BEAUNE's red wine appellations. Quality continues to improve, though oak sometimes needs to be kept in check – now with biodynamic approach. Clos des Ducs and Taillepieds are ★★★. All should be kept for at least 5 years. Best years: (top reds) (2011) 10 09 08 **07** 06 05 03 **02 99 98** 96 95 91 90.

CH. D'ANGLUDET★ *Margaux AC, Haut-Médoc, Bordeaux, France* This English-owned château makes a gentle, charming style that is always good value – getting better and better in the last decade. It ages well for at least 10 years. Best years: 2010 09 08 **06 05 04 03 02 00 98 96 95** 94.

ANJOU BLANC AC *Loire Valley, France* Wines range from bone dry to sweet, from excellent to dreadful; the best are dry. Up to 20% Chardonnay or Sauvignon can be added, but many leading producers – some preferring the IGP VAL DE LOIRE or Vin de France labels – use 100% Chenin from top sites once dedicated to sweet COTEAUX DU LAYON. Best producers: M Angeli/Sansonnière★, C Battais, P Baudouin, S Bernardeau★, D Chaffardon, des Chesnaies, B Courault, P Delesvaux★★, Fesles★, Dom. F L, La Grange aux

Belles, de Juchepie★, Richard Leroy★★, Montgilet, Mosse★, OGEREAU★, de Passavant★, PIERRE-BISE★, Pithon-Paillé★, Richou★, Roulerie★, Soucherie★. Best years: (top wines) 2011 **10 09 08 07 06 05 04.**

ANJOU ROUGE AC *Loire Valley, France* Anjou reds (from Cabernets Sauvignon and Franc or Pineau d'Aunis) are increasingly successful. Usually fruity, easy-drinking wine, with less tannin than ANJOU-VILLAGES. Wines made from Gamay are sold as Anjou Gamay. **Best producers:** Brizé★, B Courault, P Delesvaux★, La Grange aux Belles, OGEREAU★, PIERRE-BISE★ (Anjou Gamay), Pithon-Paillé★, Putille, Richou★, Rochelles★, Roulerie, Sablonnettes. **Best years:** (top wines) (2011) **10 09 08 06 05 04 03.**

ANJOU-VILLAGES AC *Loire Valley, France* Superior Anjou red from 46 villages, and made from Cabernet Franc and Cabernet Sauvignon. Anjou-Villages Brissac's schist-dominated soils produce particularly firmly structured wines, which reward aging. **Best producers:** Bablut/Daviau★★, P Baudouin, Brizé★, de Conquessac, Deux Arcs, Haute Perche, Montgilet★, de la Motte, OGEREAU★, PIERRE-BISE★★, Putille★, Richou★★, Rochelles★★, Sauveroy, la Varière/Beaujeau★. **Best years:** (2011) **10 09 08 06 05 04 03 02 01.**

ANSELMI *Veneto, Italy* Roberto Anselmi was one of the first after PIEROPAN to show that SOAVE can have real personality when carefully made. Using ultra-modern methods he has honed the fruit flavours of his San Vincenzo★★ and Capitel Foscarino★★, and introduced small-barrel-aging for single-vineyard Capitel Croce★★ and luscious, SAUTERNES-like I Capitelli★★ (sometimes ★★★), as well as the Cabernet Sauvignon Realdà. All sold under the regional IGT rather than Soave DOC. **Best years:** (I Capitelli) (2011) (10) 09 **08 05 04 03 01 00.**

ANTHONY ROAD *Finger Lakes AVA, New York State, USA* Located on the west edge of Seneca Lake, Anthony Road specializes in dry★, semi-dry★ and sweet Rieslings, as well as an ALSACE-styled Gewurztraminer. The winery is part of a group effort to define the region's style of dry Riesling.

ANTINORI *Tuscany, Italy* Florentine wine merchants since 1385, Antinori, under the leadership of Piero, were at the forefront of the so-called 'wine renaissance' from the 1970s. Still a major force for modernization in Tuscan winemaking circles, while building a national portfolio in places like Umbria (Castello della Sala with its famous white wine Cervaro★★), Piedmont (PRUNOTTO), Puglia (Tormaresca) and Franciacorta (Montenisa). Best Tuscan offerings include Marchese Antinori CHIANTI CLASSICO Riserva★★, VINO NOBILE La Braccesca★★, BRUNELLO DI MONTALCINO Pian delle Vigne★★ and BOLGHERI's Guado al Tasso★★. But the wines that helped to revolutionize Tuscan – indeed Italian – wines are the 'super-Tuscans' TIGNANELLO★★★ (Sangiovese-Cabernet) and SOLAIA★★★ (Cabernet-Sangiovese): barrique-aged and aimed at the top echelons of the wine world. **Best years:** (reds) (2011) (10) 09 08 **07 06 04 01 00 99.**

DOM. D'ANTUGNAC *Limoux AC, Languedoc, France* Jean-Luc Terrier and Christian Collovray, who own the MÂCON Domaine des Deux Roches, are producing impressive Pinot Noir and Chardonnay in the cool LIMOUX region. Côté Pierre Lys★ (Pinot Noir) exhibits finesse and complexity. Chardonnay Les Gravas★ is barrel-fermented and aged, balancing richness with apples and cream freshness.

ARAGÓN *Spain*   Aragón stretches south from the Pyrenees to Spain's central plateau. Winemaking has improved markedly, first of all in the cooler, hilly, northern SOMONTANO, and now also further south in CALATAYUD, CAMPO DE BORJA and CARIÑENA; these 3 DO areas have the potential to be a major budget-price force in a world mad for beefy but juicy reds.

ARAUJO *Napa Valley AVA, California, USA*   Boutique winery whose great coup was to buy the Eisele vineyard, traditionally a source of superb Cabernet. Araujo Cabernet Sauvignon★★★ is one of California's most sought-after reds, combining great fruit intensity with powerful but digestible tannins. Impressive Syrah★★ and attractively zesty Sauvignon Blanc★★.

ARBOIS AC *Jura, France*   The largest of the ACs in the Jura region, with sub-appellation Pupillin. The region's best reds, from Trousseau and Poulsard, are made here. Dry whites from Chardonnay and/or the local Savagnin, are varied in style: some sherry-like, the most concentrated being the sallow *vin jaune*; others fruity or more 'Burgundian' and mineral. Also rare, sweet *vin de paille*. See also CRÉMANT DU JURA. Best producers: L Aviet★, P Bornard, Dugois★, Gahier, Ligier, F Lornet★, l'Octavin★, Overnoy/Houillon★, la Pinte★, J Puffeney★★, Renardière, Rijckaert★, Rolet, A & M Tissot★★, J Tissot, Tournelle★. Best years: 2010 **09 08 07**.

ARDÈCHE, IGP See COTEAUX D'ARDÈCHE.

DOM. ANTOINE ARENA *Patrimonio AC, Corsica, France*   Family-owned bio-dynamic vineyard in Patrimonio, which specializes in white wines based on Vermentino, white Bianco Gentile (a local grape that had fallen into disuse) and stunning reds under the Carco, Morta Maio and Grotte di Sole★ labels. Best years: (Grotte di Sole) (2011) 10 **09 08 07** 06.

ARGIOLAS *Sardinia, Italy*   Sardinian star making DOC wines Cannonau (Costera★), Monica (Perdera) and Vermentino (Costamolino★) di Sardegna as well as red and white Iselis blends. Top wines are powerful, spicy reds Turriga★★ and Korem★, and golden sweet white Angialis★★.

ARGYLE *Willamette Valley AVA, Oregon, USA*   Founded in 1987 by Brian Croser and Rollin Soles. The cool WILLAMETTE VALLEY is ideal for late-ripened Pinot Noir and Chardonnay, used for Argyle sparkling wine★. Also barrel-fermented Chardonnay★ and Pinot Noir★ (Reserve★★, Nuthouse★★, Spirithouse★★). Best years: (Pinot Noir) (2010) 09 **08 07 06 05**.

ARNEIS   Italian grape grown in the ROERO hills in PIEDMONT. Arneis is DOCG in Roero, producing dry white wines which, at best, have an attractive appley, herbal perfume. Can be expensive, but cheaper versions rarely work. COOPERS CREEK and TRINITY HILL make good ones in New Zealand and Crittenden, First Drop and Sam Miranda in Australia. Best producers: Brovia★, Correggia★, Deltetto★, GIACOSA★, Malvirà★, Angelo Negro★, PRUNOTTO★, Vietti★, Gianni Voerzio★.

ARRAS See BAY OF FIRES.

DOM. ARRETXEA *Irouléguy AOP, South-West France*   Michel and Thérèse Riouspeyrous are considered the stars of IROULÉGUY. Whites are crisp, full and dry; unusually, the minerally rosé is made from Grenache. High-quality reds★, with top cuvée Haitza★★ rather like a refined MADIRAN in style, but still gutsy and macho. Best years: (2011) (10) 09 **07** 05.

CH. L'ARROSÉE★ *St-Émilion Grand Cru AC, Grand Cru Classé, Bordeaux, France*   This small property, just south-west of the historic town of ST-ÉMILION, makes really exciting wine: rich, chewy and wonderfully luscious, with a comparatively high proportion (40%) of Cabernet. On great form since new ownership in 2002. Drink after 5 years, but may be cellared for 10 or more. Best years: 2010 09 08 **07 06 05 04 03 02 00 98 95**.

ARROWOOD *Sonoma Valley AVA, California, USA* Richard Arrowood started his winery in 1986. It was acquired by Jackson Family Wines in 2006, and Arrowood left in 2010 to focus on his Amapola Creek brand. The wines have mostly been tip-top – including beautifully balanced Cabernet★★, superb Merlot★★, deeply fruity Syrah (Saralee's★★, Le Beau Mélange★), velvety Chardonnay★ (Alary Vineyards★★), fragrant Viognier★★. Best years: (Cabernet Sauvignon) 2008 **07 06 05 04 03 02 01 00 99 97 96 95 94**.

ARTADI *Rioja DOCa, País Vasco, Spain* This former co-op is now producing some of RIOJA's deepest, most ambitious reds, but they in no way overshadow the excellent, scented and fairly priced Viñas de Gain★★. Viña El Pisón★★★ and fascinating, richly ripe Pagos Viejos★★ are blockbusters. Best years: (2010) 09 08 **07 06 05 04 03 01 00 98 96 95**.

ASTI DOCG *Piedmont, Italy* The world's best-selling sweet sparkling wine, made from Moscato Bianco grapes, was long derided as light and cheap, though promotion to DOCG signalled an upturn in quality. Its light sweetness and refreshing sparkle make it ideal with fruit and a wide range of sweet dishes. Drink young. Best producers: Araldica, Bera★, Cinzano★, Contero, Giuseppe Contratto★, Cascina Fonda★, FONTANAFREDDA, Gancia★, Martini & Rossi★, Cascina Plan d'Or★.

ASTROLABE *Marlborough, South Island, New Zealand* High-flying winery launched in 2001. The Province range includes a powerful Sauvignon Blanc★★, taut dry Riesling★ and subtly oaked Chardonnay. The Valleys range showcases MARLBOROUGH sub-regions and includes two excellent Sauvignon Blancs, from AWATERE★★ and Kekerengu Coast★★. The Vineyards range is restricted to tiny parcels of experimental wines. Best years: (Sauvignon Blanc) 2011 10 09 07 06.

ATA RANGI *Martinborough, North Island, New Zealand* Small, high-quality winery. Stylish, concentrated reds include seductively perfumed cherry/plum Pinot Noir★★★ and an impressive Cabernet-Merlot-Syrah blend called Célèbre★★. Whites include big, rich Craighall Chardonnay★★, a more accessible Petrie★, delicately luscious Lismore Pinot Gris★★★ and a concentrated, mouthwatering Sauvignon Blanc★. A succulent Kahu Botrytis Riesling★★ is made when vintage conditions allow. Best years: (Pinot Noir) (2011) 10 **09 08 07 06 03 01 00**.

AU BON CLIMAT *Santa Maria Valley AVA, California, USA* Pace-setting winery in this cool region, run by talented, ebullient Jim Clendenen, whose early inspiration was BURGUNDY. The result is a range of lush Chardonnays★★ and intense Pinot Noirs★★ (Isabelle and Knox Alexander bottlings can be ★★★). He also makes BORDEAUX-style reds, Italian varietals (both red and white) and occasional exotic sweeties. Clendenen's wife, Morgan runs Cold Heaven Cellars specializing in cool-climate Viognier. Best years: (Pinot Noir) (2010) 09 **08 07 06 05 04 03 02**; (Chardonnay) (2010) **09 08 07 06 05 04 03**.

AUCKLAND *North Island, New Zealand* Vineyards in this region are concentrated in the districts of Henderson, KUMEU/HUAPAI, Matakana on the mainland and high-quality red producer WAIHEKE ISLAND, out in the gulf. Clevedon, south of Auckland, is a fledgling area that shows promise. Best years: (Cabernet Sauvignon) 2010 **09 08 07 06 05 04 02**.

CH. AUSONE★★★ *St-Émilion Grand Cru AC, 1er Grand Cru Classé, Bordeaux, France*
This beautiful property is situated on what are perhaps the best slopes in
ST-ÉMILION. Owner Alain Vauthier has taken it to new heights since 1996
and the wines now display stunning texture and depth and the promise of
memorable maturity. A high proportion (50%) of Cabernet Franc beefs
up the Merlot. Second wine: La Chapelle d'Ausone. Best years: 2010 09 08
07 06 05 **04 03 02 01 00 99 98 97 96 95 90 89**.

AUXEY-DURESSES AC *Côte de Beaune, Burgundy, France* Auxey-Duresses is
a backwater village up a valley behind MEURSAULT. The reds should be light
and fresh but can lack ripeness. At its best, and at 3–5 years, the white is
dry, soft, nutty and hinting at the creaminess of a good Meursault, but at
much lower prices. Of the Premiers Crus, Les Duresses is the most
consistent. Best producers: (reds) Comte Armand★★, J-P Diconne★, Maison
Leroy, M Prunier★, P Prunier★; (whites) M Ampeau★, d'Auvenay★★ (Dom.
LEROY), J-P Diconne★, J-P Fichet★, Gras, Olivier LEFLAIVE★, Maison Leroy★,
M Prunier★. Best years: (reds) (2011) 10 09 08 **07 06 05 03 02 99**; (whites)
(2011) 10 09 **08 07**.

AVIGNONESI *Vino Nobile di Montepulciano DOCG,*
Tuscany, Italy Ex-proprietors the Falvo
brothers brought a revolutionary viticultural
system to Tuscany with their high-density,
bush-trained system known as *settonce*.
Ownership has changed but VINO NOBILE is
still the top wine, especially the Riserva

Grandi Annate★★★. Fine Cortona DOC varietals from Chardonnay (Il
Marzocco★), Merlot (Desiderio★) and Sauvignon. The most sought-
after wine is Vin Santo★★★, with its partner (from Sangiovese) Occhio
di Pernice★★★. Best years: (Vino Nobile) (2011) (10) 09 08 **07 06 04 01**.

AWATERE VALLEY *Marlborough, South Island, New Zealand* MARLBOROUGH sub-
region that's cooler than the better-known Wairau Valley. In terms of
vineyard area Awatere is larger than HAWKES BAY. Awatere Sauvignon offers a
concentrated Marlborough style with nettle, tomato leaf and green
capsicum characters, while Chardonnay is taut and mineral. Pinot Noir can
be good but may lack ripeness in cool vintages. Best producers:
ASTROLABE★★, Blind River★★, Clifford Bay★, Clos Marguerite★, O:TU★,
Tohu★, VAVASOUR★, VILLA MARIA★★, YEALANDS★. Best years: (Sauvignon Blanc)
2011 10 09 07 06.

CH. D'AYDIE *Madiran AOP, South-West France* The old-established Laplace
family is spreading its wings. As well as a full-blown Tannat-based
MADIRAN★★, named after the château (now restored after a bad fire), there
is a softer Madiran called Odé d'Aydie★ and a softer one still called
Autour du Fruit. The Laplaces are also making excellent Madirans for
Patrick Ducournau (Chapelle Lenclos★★ and Domaine Mouréou★).
Also very fine PACHERENCS★ and a quaffable range of IGPs. Best years:
(reds) (2011) (10) 08 **06 05**; (sweet whites) (2011) **10 07 06 05**.

BABICH *Henderson, North Island, New Zealand* Family-run winery with prime
vineyard land in MARLBOROUGH and HAWKES BAY. Irongate Chardonnay★ is
an intense, steely wine that needs plenty of cellaring, while full-flavoured
reds under the Winemakers' Reserve label show even greater potential
for development. Flagship wine The Patriarch★★ is a red BORDEAUX
blend from Hawkes Bay. Marlborough whites include stylish Sauvignon
Blanc★, tangy Riesling and light, fruity Pinot Gris. Best years: (premium
Hawkes Bay reds) **2009 08 07 06 05 04**.

BACALHÔA VINHOS DE PORTUGAL *Península de Setúbal, Portugal*
Forward-looking operation, using Portuguese and foreign grapes with equal ease. Quinta da Bacalhôa★ is an oaky, meaty Cabernet-Merlot blend, Palácio da Bacalhôa★★ even better; Tinto da Ânfora★ a rich and figgy ALENTEJO red (Grande Escolha★★ version is powerful and cedary); and Cova da Ursa★ a toasty, rich Chardonnay. Portugal's finest sparkling wine, vintage-dated Espumante Loridos Chardonnay★, is a decent CHAMPAGNE lookalike. Só Syrah ('só' means 'only' in Portuguese) is characterful. Also excellent 20-year-old Moscatel de SETÚBAL★★.

BADEN *Germany* Very large, 15,900ha (39,290-acre) wine region stretching from FRANKEN to the Bodensee (Lake Constance). Its dry whites and reds show off the fuller, softer flavours Germany can produce in the warmer climate of its southerly regions. Many of the best non-Riesling German wines come from here, as well as many good barrel-fermented and barrel-aged wines. Germany's best co-operatives are located here, but the number of quality-oriented private estates is growing. See also KAISERSTUHL, ORTENAU.

BAGA Important red grape in BAIRRADA. Also planted in smaller quantities in DÃO and the TEJO. In the best years, it can give deep, complex, blackberryish wine, but aggressive tannin is a continuing problem.

BAIRRADA DOC *Beira Atlântico, Portugal* Bairrada, along with the DOURO, DÃO and ALENTEJO, can be the source of many of Portugal's best red wines. These can brim over with intense raspberry and blackberry fruit, though with austere tannins that take quite a few years to soften. Traditionally made from a minimum of 50% of the tannic Baga grape; rules changed in 2003 to admit a load of 'international' grapes into the Bairrada fold. The whites are coming on fast with modern vinification methods. With an Atlantic climate, vintages can be very variable. Best producers: (reds) ALIANÇA★, Quinta das Bágeiras★, Quinta de Baixo★, Campolargo★, Cantanhede co-op, Quinta do Encontro, Caves do Freixo, Caves Messias (Quinta do Valdoeiro Reserva★), Casa de Saima★★, Caves SÃO JOÃO★★, SOGRAPE, Sidónio de Sousa★★, (whites) Caves São João★★, Luís Pato (Reserva★). Best years: (reds) 2009 **08 05 04 03 01 00 97**.

BALATONBOGLÁR WINERY *Transdanubia, Hungary* Premium winery in the Lake Balaton region, which has benefited from heavy investment and the expertise of viticulturist Dr Richard Smart and wine consultant Kym Milne, but still needs to work to improve quality – particularly in the inexpensive but dumbed-down range sold under the Chapel Hill label.

BALEARIC ISLANDS *Spain* Medium-bodied reds and soft rosées were the mainstays of Mallorca's 2 DO areas, Binissalem and Plà i Llevant, until Anima Negra began making impressive, deep reds from the native Callet grape. Best producers: 4 Kilos Vinícola★★, Anima Negra★★, Hereus de Ribas, Miquel Gelabert★, Toni Gelabert★, Macià Batle, Miquel Oliver, Son Bordils★.

BALFOUR *Kent, England* Consistent quality from this Kent vineyard, Hush Heath Estate, which covers 11.5ha (28 acres). The award-winning Balfour Brut Rosé★★ is the UK's highest priced wine.

BALNAVES *Coonawarra, South Australia* Long-term residents of COONAWARRA, the grape-growing Balnaves family decided to become involved in making wine in the mid-1990s and are among the best producers in the region. Reserve Cabernet The Tally★★★ is complex, wonderfully structured and deeply flavoured; the regular Cabernet★ is well priced and an excellent example of Coonawarra style.

BANDOL AC *Provence, France* A lovely fishing port with vineyards high above the Mediterranean, producing some of the best reds and rosés in Provence. The Mourvèdre grape gives Bandol its character – dense colour, warm, smoky black fruit and a herby fragrance. The reds happily age for 10 years, sometimes more, but should be very good at 3–4. The rosés, delicious and spicy but often too pricey, should be drunk young. A small amount of neutral, overpriced white. Best producers: la Bastide Blanche★, la Bégude★, Bunan★, Frégate★, le Galantin★, J-P Gaussen★, Gros' Noré★, l'Hermitage★, Lafran-Veyrolles★, la Laidière★, Mas Redorne★, la Noblesse★, PIBARNON★★, Pradeaux★★, Ray-Jane★, Roche Redonne★, Ste-Anne★, Salettes★, SORIN★, la Suffrène, Tempier★, Terrebrune★, la Tour du Bon★, VANNIÈRES★★. Best years: (2011) 10 09 **08 07 06 05 03 01**.

BANFI *Brunello di Montalcino DOCG and Toscana IGT, Tuscany, Italy* American-owned huge estate in iconic Montalcino. Despite many awards and much work on Sangiovese clones, their BRUNELLOS (Poggio all'Oro★, Poggio alle Mura★) remain a bit stodgy, if potent, and are exceeded, quality-wise, by 'super-Tuscans' Summus★★ and Excelsus★★. Also have cellars in PIEDMONT for GAVI and fizz. Best years: (top reds) (2011) (10) (09) (08) 07 06 **05 04 01 00**.

BANNOCKBURN *Geelong, Victoria, Australia* The Hooper family has 27ha (67 acres) of mature vines, from which all the estate's wines are sourced. Michael Glover is proving to be an idiosyncratic and brilliant winemaker. Most notable are Sauvignon Blanc★★, Chardonnay★★, Pinot Noir★★ and Shiraz★, and four limited-release wines: my favourite, the complex and classy Alain GRAILLOT-influenced Range Shiraz★★; MEURSAULT-like SRH Chardonnay★★; powerful, gamy Serré Pinot Noir★★; and dense, tightly coiled yet elegant Stuart Pinot★★. Best years: (Shiraz) (2011) (10) (09) 08 06 05 **04 03 02 01 00 99 98 97 96 94 92 91**.

BANYULS AC *Roussillon, France* One of the best *vins doux naturels*, made mainly from Grenache, with a strong plum and raisin flavour. *Rimage* – early bottlings of vintage wine – and *rancio* tawny styles are the best. Best drunk after dinner, though often served as an apéritif in France. Best producers: Cellier des Templiers★, CHAPOUTIER, Clos de Paulilles★, la Coume du Roy★, l'Étoile★, MAS BLANC★★, Piétri-Géraud★★, la Rectorie★★, la Tour Vieille★, Vial Magnères★.

BARBADILLO *Jerez y Manzanilla DO, Andalucía, Spain* The largest sherry company in the coastal town of Sanlúcar de Barrameda makes a wide range of good to excellent wines, in particular salty, dry manzanilla styles (Solear★★, En Rama unfiltered★★★) and intense, nutty, but dry amontillados and olorosos (Amontillado Príncipe★★, Oloroso Cuco★★). Neutral dry white Castillo de San Diego is a bestseller in Spain.

BARBARESCO DOCG *Piedmont, Italy* This prestigious red wine, grown in the LANGHE hills south-east of Turin, is often twinned with its neighbour BAROLO to demonstrate the nobility of the Nebbiolo grape. Barbaresco can be a shade softer and less powerful, and is not required by law to age as long (2 years minimum compared with 3), but at the top level is often indistinguishable from Barolo. As in Barolo, traditionalists excel, led by Bruno GIACOSA. Even though the area is relatively compact (575ha/1420 acres), styles can differ significantly between vineyards and producers. Best vineyards: Asili, Bricco di

Neive, Crichet Pajè, Gallina, Marcorino, Martinenga, Messoirano, Moccagatta, Montestefano, Ovello, Pora, Rabajà, Rio Sordo, Santo Stefano, Serraboella, Sorì Paitin. Best producers: Barbaresco co-op★★, Ceretto★★, Cigliuti★★, Stefano Farina★★, Fontanabianca★★, GAJA★★★, GIACOSA★★★, Marchesi di Gresy★★, Lano★, Moccagatta★★, Fiorenzo Nada★★, Castello di Neive★★, Oddero★, Paitin★★, Pelissero★★, Pio Cesare★★, PRUNOTTO★★, Rizzi★, Albino Rocca★★, Bruno Rocca★★, Sottimano★★, La Spinetta★★, Castello di Verduno★★, Vietti★★. Best years: (2011) (10) 09 08 **07 06 04 01 00 99 98.**

VINHOS BARBEITO *Madeira DOC, Portugal* Most modern of the MADEIRA producers, making elegant, pale-coloured Madeiras. Pioneer of single-harvest wines and single-cask bottlings. Good 10 Years Old★ range, excellent 20 Years Old★★ and Colheita Single-Cask★★ bottlings.

BARBERA A native of north-west Italy, Barbera vies with Sangiovese as the most widely planted red grape in the country. When grown for high yields its natural acidity and low tannin show through, producing vibrant quaffers. Low yields from the top PIEDMONT estates create intensely rich and complex wines. Oaked versions can be stunning. Significant plantings in California, Argentina and Australia.

BARBERA D'ALBA DOC *Piedmont, Italy* Barbera plays second fiddle to Nebbiolo among Alba wines, yet some of the finest come from this appellation, often benefiting from barrique aging. The most modern examples are supple and generous and can be drunk almost at once. More intense, dark-fruited versions require at least 3 years' age, but might improve for as much as 8. Best producers: G Alessandria★★, ALTARE★, Azelia★★, Boglietti★★, Brovia★★, Burlotto★★, Ceretto★, Cascina Chicco★, Cigliuti★★, CLERICO★, Elvio Cogno★★, Aldo CONTERNO★★, Giacomo CONTERNO★★, Conterno-Fantino★, Corino★★, Correggia★★, Elio Grasso★, Giuseppe MASCARELLO★, Moccagatta★, M Molino★★, Monfalletto-Cordero di Montezemolo★★, Oberto★★, Parusso★★, Pelissero★, F Principiano★★, PRUNOTTO★★, RATTI★, Albino Rocca★★, Bruno Rocca★, SANDRONE★★, P Scavino★★, La Spinetta★★, Vajra★★, Mauro Veglio★★, Vietti★★, Gianni Voerzio★★, Roberto VOERZIO★★. Best years: (2011) 10 **09 08 07 06 04**.

BARBERA D'ASTI DOCG *Piedmont, Italy* In the province of Asti, Barbera is king and is capable of making outstanding wine. Unoaked versions are fruity and intense, while barrique-aged examples, especially those labelled 'Superiore', can rival the best Barbera d'Alba and even some of the better Nebbiolo-based reds. Best examples can be kept for 5–6 years, occasionally longer. Best producers: Araldica/Alasia★, La Barbatella★★, Pietro Barbero★★, Bava★, Bertelli★★, Braida★★, Cascina Castlèt★, Coppo★★, Hastae (Quorum★), Martinetti★★, Il Mongetto★★, Perrone★★, PRUNOTTO★★, La Spinetta★★, Vietti★★, Vinchio-Vaglio Serra co-op★. Best years: (2011) 10 **09 08 07 06 04.**

BARBOURSVILLE VINEYARDS *Virginia, USA* Founded by Italy's Zonin winemaking family in 1976, on property that features the ruins of a mansion designed by Thomas Jefferson for his friend, James Barbour. Under winemaker Luca Paschina since 1990, the wines have shown consistent improvement. There's an enticing range of French and Italian styles: minerally, scented Viognier★, good Cabernet Franc Reserve★ and Nebbiolo. Octagon★, a BORDEAUX blend based on Merlot, combines New World flair with Old World finesse.

BAROSSA
South Australia

 The Barossa Valley, an hour or so's drive north of Adelaide in South Australia, is the heart of the Australian wine industry and home to many of its giant producers – Jacob's Creek, Wolf Blass, Penfolds and Yalumba – alongside around 50 or so smaller wineries, producing or processing up to 60% of the nation's wine. However, this percentage is based mostly on grapes trucked in from other regions, because the Barossa's vineyards themselves grow less than 10% of Australia's grapes. Yet Barossa-grown grapes, once rejected as uneconomical for their low yields, are now increasingly prized for those same low yields.

Why? Well, it's highly likely that the world's oldest wine vines are in the Barossa. The valley was settled in the 1840s by Lutheran immigrants from Silesia, who brought with them vines from Europe: most importantly, as it turned out, cuttings of Syrah (or Shiraz) from France's Rhône Valley. And because the Barossa has never been affected by the phylloxera louse, which destroyed most of the world's vineyards in the late 19th century, today you can still see gnarled, twisted old vines sporting just a few tiny bunches of priceless fruit that were planted by refugees from Europe more than a century and a half ago, and are still tended by their descendants. A new wave of winemakers has taken up the cause of the Barossa vines with much zeal and no small amount of national pride, and they now produce from them some of the deepest, most fascinating wines, not just in Australia, but in the world.

GRAPE VARIETIES
Shiraz is prized above all other Barossa grapes, able to conjure head-swirling, palate-dousing flavours. The Barossa Valley is the main source of Shiraz grapes for Penfolds Grange, the wine that began the revolution in Australian red wine in the 1950s. Cabernet Sauvignon can be very good in the best years and similarly potent, as are the Rhône varieties of heady Grenache and deliciously earthy Mourvèdre; some of the most exciting examples are from the original vines planted in the 19th century. All these varieties are largely grown on the hot, dry valley floor, but just to the east lie the Barossa Ranges, and in these higher, cooler vineyards, especially in those of the neighbouring Eden Valley, some of Australia's best and most fashionable Rieslings are grown, prized for their steely attack and lime fragrance. But even here you can't get away from Shiraz, and some thrilling examples come from the hills, not least Henschke's Hill of Grace and Mount Edelstone, and Torbreck's The Gask.

CLASSIFICATIONS
The Barossa was among the first zones to be ratified within the Australian system of Geographical Indications and comprises the regions of Barossa Valley and Eden Valley. The Barossa lies within South Australia's collective 'super zone' of Adelaide.

See also GRANGE, SOUTH AUSTRALIA; and individual producers.

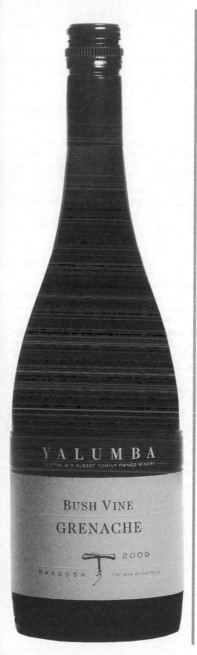

YALUMBA
AUSTRALIA'S OLDEST FAMILY OWNED WINERY

BUSH VINE

GRENACHE

2009

BAROSSA · FINE WINE OF AUSTRALIA

BEST YEARS

(Barossa Valley Shiraz) (2010) 09
**00 06 05 04 03 02 01 00 99 98
97 96 94 91 90 86**;
(Eden Valley Riesling) **2011 10 09
08 07 06 05 04 03 02 01 00 99
98 97 96 95**

BEST PRODUCERS

Shiraz-based reds
Barossa Valley Estate, Bethany,
Rolf BINDER, Grant BURGE, Burge
Family, Chateau Tanunda,
Dutschke, John DUVAL, Elderton
(Command), GLAETZER, Greenock
Creek (Block Shiraz, Seven
Acre), HENSCHKE, Hentley Farm,
Heritage, Hewitson, JACOB'S
CREEK (Centenary Hill), Jenke,
Trevor Jones, Kaesler, Kalleske,
Langmeil, Peter LEHMANN,
Maverick, Charles MELTON,
Murray Street, PENFOLDS (RWT,
GRANGE), Chris Ringland,
ROCKFORD, ST HALLETT, Tim Smith,
Spinifex, Teusner, Thorn Clarke,
TORBRECK, Torzi Matthews,
Turkey Flat, Two Hands, The
Willows, YALUMBA (Octavius).

Riesling
Bethany, Wolf BLASS (Gold Label),
Grant BURGE, Leo Buring (Leonay),
HENSCHKE, Hewitson, JACOB'S
CREEK (Steingarten),
Peter LEHMANN, McLean, Mesh,
Radford, ROCKFORD, Ross Estate,
ST HALLETT, Thorn Clarke, Torzi
Matthews, YALUMBA (Heggies,
Pewsey Vale).

**Cabernet Sauvignon-based
reds**
Rolf BINDER, Grant BURGE,
Greenock Creek, HENSCHKE, Peter
LEHMANN, ST HALLETT, The Willows.

**Other reds (Grenache,
Mourvèdre, Shiraz)**
Rolf BINDER, Grant BURGE, Burge
Family (Garnacha, Olive Hill),
Charles Cimicky, Elderton (Ode
to Lorraine), HENSCHKE, Jenke
(Mourvèdre), Kalleske, Langmeil,
Peter LEHMANN, Charles MELTON,
PENFOLDS (Bin 138), Teusner,
TORBRECK, Turkey Flat, Two Hands,
YALUMBA.

Semillon
Grant BURGE, HENSCHKE, Heritage,
Jenke, Peter LEHMANN, ROCKFORD,
Turkey Flat, The Willows.

BARDOLINO DOC *Veneto, Italy* Zone centred on Lake Garda, giving, traditionally, light, scented red and rosé (*chiaretto*) wines to be drunk young, from the same grape mix as neighbouring VALPOLICELLA, but some estates are now adding more character to their wines. Bardolino Superiore is DOCG. Best producers: ALLEGRINI★, Cavalchina★, Corte Gardoni★, Guerrieri-Rizzardi★, Le Fraghe, MASI, Le Vigne di San Pietro★, Zeni.

BAROLO DOCG *Piedmont, Italy* Arguably Italy's greatest wine, named after a village south-west of Alba, from the Nebbiolo grape grown in around 1800ha (4450 acres) of vineyards on the steep LANGHE hills, the best coming from near the top (*bricco*) of those hills. Having in the post-WWII period gone to excesses of austerity, Barolo in the 1990s almost threatened to go too far in the other direction, its subtle floral/wild fruit aromas being drowned all too often under expensive but intrusive oak smells of vanilla and toast. Thankfully, in the 21st century, producers are finding their way back to the 'tar and roses' of the grape while managing to keep Nebbiolo's fierce tannins and biting acidity under control. The villages of Barolo and La Morra are said to make the most perfumed wines, Monforte and Serralunga the most structured, Castiglione Falletto perhaps the best balanced. Barolo is frequently labelled by vineyard, though the producer's reputation often carries more weight. Best vineyards: Arione, Bricco delle Viole, Brunate, Bussia Soprana, Cannubi, Cerequio, Conca dell'Annunziata, Fiasco, Francia, Gavarini, Ginestra, Monfalletto, Monprivato, Rocche dell'Annunziata, Rocche di Castiglione, Santo Stefano di Perno, La Serra, Vigna Rionda, Villero. Best producers: G Alessandria★★, ALTARE★★, Azelia★★, Baudana★★, Boglietti★★, Brovia★★, Burlotto★★, Cappellano★★, Ceretto★, Chiarlo★, Ciabot Berton★, CLERICO★★★, Aldo CONTERNO★★, Giacomo CONTERNO★★★, Paulo Conterno★★, Conterno-Fantino★★, Corino★★, Luigi Einaudi★★, GIACOSA★★★, Elio Grasso★★, M Marengo★★, Bartolo MASCARELLO★★★, Giuseppe MASCARELLO★★★, Massolino★★, Monfalletto-Cordero di Montezemolo★★, Andrea Oberto★★, Oddero★★, Parusso★★, Pio Cesare★★, Pira★★, E Pira & Figli★★, F Principiano★, PRUNOTTO★★, Renato RATTI★, Revello★★, Giuseppe Rinaldi★★, Rocche dei Manzoni★★, SANDRONE★★★, P Scavino★★, M Sebaste★★, Vajra★★, Mauro Veglio★★, Castello di Verduno★★, Vietti★★, Vigna Rionda★★, Gianni Voerzio★★, Roberto VOERZIO★★★. Best years: (2011) (10) (09) 08 07 06 04 01 00 99 98 97 96 95.

BAROSSA VALLEY See pages 76–7.

JIM BARRY *Clare Valley, South Australia* Flagship white, The Florita★, heads a quartet of classy, perfumed Rieslings (Watervale★★, Lodge Hill★★). Inexpensive Lodge Hill Shiraz★ is impressive, but the winery is best known for its rich, fruity McRae Wood Shiraz★★ and heady, palate-busting Armagh Shiraz★★. Best years: (Armagh Shiraz) (2009) 06 05 **04** 02 01 **99** 98 96 95 92 89.

BARSAC AC *Bordeaux, France* Barsac, lying close to the river Garonne and with the little river Ciron running along its eastern boundary, is the largest of the 5 communes in the SAUTERNES AC, and also has its own AC, which is used by most, but by no means all, of the top properties. Less power and more finesse than Sauternes. Best producers: CLIMENS★★★, COUTET★★, DOISY-DAËNE★★, DOISY-VEDRINES★★, Myrat★, NAIRAC★★, Piada, Suau★. Best years: (2011) 10 09 **07** 05 03 02 01 99 98 97 96 95 90 89 88 86 83.

BASILICATA *Italy* Southern Italian region best known for one wine, the potentially excellent, complex red called AGLIANICO DEL VULTURE.

BASSERMANN-JORDAN *Deidesheim, Pfalz, Germany* Famous 50ha (124-acre) estate, making rich yet elegant dry Rieslings ★ ★ from Deidesheim and FORST. Best years: (2011) 10 09 08 **07 06 05 04 03 02 01 99**.

CH. BATAILLEY★ *Pauillac AC, 5ème Cru Classé, Haut-Médoc, Bordeaux, France* A byword for reliability and value for money among the PAUILLAC Classed Growth estates. Marked by a full, obvious blackcurrant fruit, not too much tannin and a luscious overlay of creamy vanilla. Lovely to drink at only 5 years old, the wine continues to age well for at least 15 years. Best years: 2010 09 08 06 **05 04 03 02 00 98 96 95 90 89**.

BÂTARD-MONTRACHET AC *Grand Cru, Côte de Beaune, Burgundy, France* This Grand Cru produces some of the world's greatest whites – full, rich and balanced, with a powerful mineral intensity of fruit and fresh acidity. There are 2 associated Grands Crus: Bienvenues-Bâtard-Montrachet and the minuscule Criots-Bâtard-Montrachet. All should be able to age for a decade. Best producers: Blain-Gagnard★★, CARILLON★★★, DROUHIN★★, FAIVELEY★★, Fontaine-Gagnard★★, J-N GAGNARD★★★, JADOT★★★, Louis LATOUR★★, Dom. LEFLAIVE★★★, Olivier LEFLAIVE★★, Marc MOREY★★★, Pierre MOREY★★★, RAMONET★★★, SAUZET★★★, VERGET★★. Best years: (2011) 10 09 08 07 06 **05 04 02 00 99**.

BERNARD BAUDRY *Chinon AC, Loire Valley, France* Supple, elegant CHINON. Aspect and soil type differentiate four site-specific cuvées: Les Granges (sand/gravel) and Les Grézeaux★ (gravel/clay) are for earlier drinking, while Le Clos Guillot★★ (limestone/clay/tuffeau) and La Croix Boissée★★ (clay/limestone) reward patience. Good dry white and rosé too. Best years: (top reds) (2011) 10 09 **08 06 05 04 03 02 01 00**.

LES BAUX-DE-PROVENCE AC *Provence, France* This AC has proved that organic and biodynamic farming can produce spectacular results in a warm dry climate. Good fruit and intelligent winemaking produce some of the more easily enjoyable reds in Provence. Best producers: Hauvette★, Lauzières, Mas de la Dame★, Mas de Gourgonnier★, Mas Ste-Berthe★, ROMANIN★★, Terres Blanches★. Best years: (2011) 10 09 **08 07 06 05 04 03 02**.

BAY OF FIRES *Tasmania, Australia* The Tasmanian arm of Accolade. There's a renewed focus on table wines under the Bay of Fires label, especially its complex, minerally Chardonnay★ and smooth, tightly structured, ageworthy Pinot Noir★★. Also a sublime Riesling, impressive Pinot Gris and an intense, steely Sauvignon Blanc. In the past decade Accolade's chief sparkling wine maker, Ed Carr, has concentrated on the region's ultra-cool climate. He's making brilliant fizz, now labelled House of Arras (Brut Elite★★, Grand Vintage★★ and EJ Carr Late Disgorged★★).

BÉARN AOP *South-West France* Best known for quaffable rosés, sometimes from growers in MADIRAN and JURANÇON (where pink wines do not qualify for AOP). Whites dull but some good reds, mostly from independent growers such as CAUHAPÉ, Guilhemas★, Lapeyre★, Nigri★.

CH. DE BEAUCASTEL *Châteauneuf-du-Pape AC, Rhône Valley, France* The Perrin family makes some of the richest, most profound reds in CHÂTEAUNEUF-DU-PAPE★★, with an unusually high percentage of Mourvèdre (Hommage à Jacques Perrin★★★ is 60% Mourvèdre), which can take at least a decade to show their best. The white Roussanne Vieilles Vignes★★★ is enticing, mysterious and long-lived. They also produce stylish red★★ and white★ CÔTES DU RHÔNE Coudoulet de Beaucastel and GIGONDAS Dom. des Tourelles★★. Under the Famille Perrin label there are fine, authentic southern reds, including organic Côtes du Rhône

Nature★, VENTOUX La Vieille Ferme★, RASTEAU★ and VINSOBRES★. Best years: (reds) (2011) 10 09 07 **06 05 04 03 01 00 99 98 97 96 95 94 90 89 88 85**; (whites) 2010 09 **08 07 06 05 04 03 01 00 99 98 97 96 95 94 90 89**.

BEAUJOLAIS AC *Beaujolais, Burgundy, France* Wine region in the beautiful hills that stretch down from Mâcon to Lyon, producing predominantly red wine from the Gamay grape. Beaujolais is best known for BEAUJOLAIS NOUVEAU, accounting for just over 30% of the production, which represents a substantial drop over the past decade. The better-quality reds, each having their own appellation, come from the north of the region and are BEAUJOLAIS-VILLAGES and the 10 single-Cru villages: from north to south these are ST-AMOUR, JULIENAS, MOULIN-A-VENT, CHENAS, FLEURIE, CHIROUBLES, MORGON, REGNIE, BROUILLY and CÔTE DE BROUILLY. There is a growing buzz about the area: standards have improved dramatically in recent years as a new wave of producers (a younger generation of locals, and winemakers from both Burgundy in the north and the Rhône in the south) have begun investing here. Growing consumer demand for food-friendly wines with lower alcohol levels has helped to spark renewed interest in the area. In good vintages simple Beaujolais is light, fresh, aromatic and delicious to drink, but in poorer vintages the wine can be drab and acidic. A little rosé is also made from Gamay, and a small quantity of Beaujolais Blanc is made from Chardonnay. Best producers: J-P Brun/Terres Dorées (l'Ancien★), Ch. de Cercy, A Chatoux★, Coquard, H Fessy, Y Métras★.

BEAUJOLAIS NOUVEAU *Beaujolais AC, Burgundy, France* Also known as Beaujolais Primeur, this is the first release of bouncy, fruity Beaujolais on the third Thursday of November after the harvest. Once a simple celebration of the new vintage, nouveau was badly over-hyped and, as a result, is nowhere near as popular as it once was. Quality is generally reasonable and the wine can be delicious until Christmas and the New Year, but thereafter is likely to throw a slight sediment and soon loses the vivacious fresh fruit that made it so appealing in its youth.

BEAUJOLAIS-VILLAGES AC *Beaujolais, Burgundy, France* Beaujolais-Villages can come from one of 38 villages in the north of the region. Top examples have more body, character and elegance than simple BEAUJOLAIS and represent all the pleasure of the Gamay grape at its best. Best villages: Lancié, Quincié and Perréon. Best producers: DUBOEUF, Dubost/Tracot, Ch. de Grandmont, J-C Lapalu, Ch. du Pavé★, JADOT (Combe aux Jacques), Gilles Roux/de la Plaigne★.

BEAUMES-DE-VENISE AC *Rhône Valley, France* Area rightly famous for its scented, honeyed fortified sweet wine, MUSCAT DE BEAUMES-DE-VENISE. The red wine from high vineyards is forceful, full of smoky dark fruit and crisp tannins, and can show well for 8–10 years. Best producers: (reds) Beaumalric, Bernardins, Cassan★, Durban★, Fenouillet, Ferme Saint-Martin, les Goubert, Ch. Redortier★, Saint-Amant (good whites).

BEAUNE AC *Côte de Beaune, Burgundy, France* Most of the wines are red, with delicious, soft red-fruits ripeness. There are no Grands Crus but some excellent Premiers Crus, especially Boucherottes, Bressandes, Clos des Mouches, Fèves, Grèves, Marconnets, Teurons, Vignes Franches. White-wine production is increasing – DROUHIN makes outstanding, creamy, nutty Clos des Mouches★★★. Other good whites from Chanson★★, LAFARGE★★ and Prieur★★. Best producers: (growers) BELLENE★, Croix★, Germain/Ch. de Chorey★, LAFARGE★★, de MONTILLE★, Albert Morot★, J Prieur★★, Rateau, TOLLOT-BEAUT★★; (merchants) BOUCHARD

PÈRE ET FILS★★, Champy★★, Chanson★★, DROUHIN★★, Camille Giroud★★, JADOT★★. Best years: (reds) (2011) 10 09 08 **07** 06 05 **03 02** 99; (whites) (2011) 10 09 08 **07 06 05**.

CH. BEAU-SÉJOUR BÉCOT★★ *St-Émilion Grand Cru AC, 1er Grand Cru Classé, Bordeaux, France* Demoted from Premier Grand Cru Classé in 1986 and promoted again in 1996, this estate is on top form. Brothers Gérard and Dominique Bécot produce firm, ripe, richly textured wines that need at least 8–10 years to develop. Best years: 2010 09 08 **07** 06 05 04 03 02 01 00 99 98 96 95 90 89.

BEAUX FRÈRES *Willamette Valley AVA, Oregon, USA* The goal here is to make ripe, unfiltered Pinot Noir★★ that expresses the essence of their 10ha (24-acre) vineyard atop Ribbon Ridge in the Chehalem Valley. A parcel known as The Upper Terrace★★★ yields exceptional fruit from Dijon clones. Best years: (2010) 09 08 **07** 06 05.

GRAHAM BECK WINES *Robertson WO, South Africa* Since the passing of Graham Beck in 2010 and sale of the Franschhoek cellar, fruit from the Stellenbosch is now vinified at Beck-owned STEENBERG. Top wines include new spicy aromatic Cabernet Sauvignon-Shiraz blend Ad Honorem★, The Joshua Shiraz-Viognier★★, DURBANVILLE-sourced Pheasants' Run Sauvignon Blanc★★, and single-vineyard Coffeestone Cabernet★. The very popular sparkling range, under Pieter 'Bubbles' Ferreira's leadership, continues to be made at the ROBERTSON cellar and is headed by Chardonnay-based Cuvée Clive★★ with 5 years on the lees; there's also rich NV Brut★ and creamy, barrel-fermented and ageworthy Blanc de Blancs★. Best Robertson table wines are single-vineyard The Ridge Syrah★ and succulent Lonehill Chardonnay★. Viognier is good too.

BECKMEN *Santa Ynez Valley AVA, California, USA* Estate-grown Rhône-style wines show beauty and structure at moderate alcohol levels. Grenache★ and Grenache-based Cuvée Le Bec★ are bright and juicy. The Purisma Mountain Syrahs★★ are richer in style, yet wonderfully balanced.

BEDELL CELLARS *Long Island, New York State, USA* Winemaker Kip Bedell helped establish LONG ISLAND's reputation with his Bordeaux-styled Merlot★ and red blends. The wines have continued to improve under new ownership, with Bedell still chief winemaker. Sister winery Corey Creek produces a noteworthy Gewürztraminer.

BEECHWORTH *Victoria, Australia* Beechworth was best known as Ned Kelly country before Rick Kinzbrunner of GIACONDA planted these slopes of sub-Alpine north-east Victoria. Now boutique wineries produce tiny volumes of Chardonnay, Pinot Noir and Shiraz at high prices. BROKENWOOD sources fruit from a major new vineyard here, called Indigo. Best producers: Amulet (Shiraz★★), BROKENWOOD, Castanga★ (Syrah★★), Cow Hill★, GIACONDA★★★, Savaterre (Chardonnay★★), Sorrenberg★.

BEIRA ATLÂNTICO *Portugal* The coastal part of what used to be the Beiras, includes BAIRRADA DOC. Beira Atlântico Vinho Regional wines use Portuguese red and white varieties along with international grapes such as Cabernet Sauvignon and Chardonnay. Best producers: ALIANCA, Quinta dos Cozinheiros, Quinta de Foz de Arouce★, Filipa Pato★, Luís PATO★★, Caves SÃO JOÃO (Quinta do Poço do Lobo). Best years: (2010) **09 08 05** 04 03 01 00.

CH. BELAIR-MONANGE★★ *St-Émilion Grand Cru AC, 1er Grand Cru Classé,*
Bordeaux, France Used to be simply Belair until renamed by new owner
négociant J-P MOUEIX in 2008. The soft, supremely stylish wines are
drinkable at 5–6 years, but also capable of long aging. Best years: 2010 09
08 06 05 04 03 02 01 00 99 98 95 90 89 88 86.

BELLAVISTA *Franciacorta DOCG, Lombardy, Italy* Specialist in FRANCIACORTA
sparkling wines, with a very good Cuvée Brut★★ and 4 distinctive Gran
Cuvées★★ (including an excellent rosé). Vittorio Moretti★★ is made in
exceptional years. Also produces lovely still wines, including white blend
Convento dell'Annunciata★★★, Chardonnay Uccellanda★★ and red
Casotte★ (Pinot Nero) and Solesine★★ (Cabernet-Merlot).

BELLENE *Beaune, Cote de Beaune, Burgundy, France* New name for Nicolas
Potel's own businesses. Domaine de Bellene has vineyards in BEAUNE★,
NUITS-ST-GEORGES, SAVIGNY, VOLNAY and VOSNE. Maison Roche de Bellene is
the merchant label. Best years: (Domaine) (2011) 10 09 08.

BELLET AC *Provence, France* Tiny AC in the hills behind Nice; the wine is
usually expensive, although domaines such as Toasc produce cheaper
IGP wines from young vines. Best producers: Ch. de Bellet★, Clos St
Vincent★, Ch. de Crémat, de la Source, Toasc. Best years: (2011) 10 09 08 07.

BENDIGO *Central Victoria, Australia* Warm, dry, former gold-mining region,
which is now home to about 40 small-scale, high-quality wineries. The
best wines are rich, ripe, distinctively minty Shiraz and Cabernet. Best
producers: Balgownie, Blackjack★, Bress, Chateau Leamon, Passing Clouds,
PONDALOWIE★, Turner's Crossing★, Water Wheel★. Best years: (Shiraz)
(2010) 08 06 05 04 03 02 01 00 99 98 97 95 94 93 91 90.

BERCHER *Burkheim, Baden, Germany* A top KAISERSTUHL estate. High points
are the powerful oak-aged Spätburgunder★★ (Pinot Noir) reds, Grau-
burgunder★★ (Pinot Gris) and Chardonnay★ dry whites, which marry
richness with perfect balance, and elegant, tangy Muskateller★. Best
years: (whites) (2011) 10 09 08 06 05; (reds) (2011) 10 09 08 07 06 05.

BERGERAC AOP *South-West France* With Bordeaux prices getting steeper
and steeper, Bergerac is seen as a good alternative for more modest
purses. The claret-like reds have a good, raw blackcurrant fruit and hint
of earth, and the wines under the superior Côtes de Bergerac AOP, often
oak-aged, can age well. The fresh dry whites are for early drinking. The
best sweet whites are produced under their own more specific
appellations: MONBAZILLAC, SAUSSIGNAC, MONTRAVEL and ROSETTE. Best
producers: (red and dry white) l'ANCIENNE CURE★, Bélingard★, Eyssards,
Fontenelles★, la Jaubertie★, Marnières★, les Miaudoux★, Monestier-la-Tour★,
TOUR DES GENDRES★★, VERDOTS★★. Best years: (reds) (2011) 10 09 06 05.

BERGSTRÖM *Willamette Valley AVA, Oregon, USA* The Bergström family uses
biodynamic farming to bring out the best character from the *terroir* of
their estate vineyards. The focus is on Pinot Noir, with Bergström
Vineyard★★ and de Lancellotti Vineyard★★ forming the greater part of
the production. Cumberland Reserve★★★ is a multi-vineyard blend that
can rival many fine Burgundies in its complexity. Also small amounts of
Chardonnay★ and Riesling★★. Best years: (reds) (2010) 09 08 07 06 05.

BERINGER *Napa Valley AVA, California, USA* Beringer, part of the Treasury
group, mass-produces some fairly average varietal labels, but also offers a
range of top-class Cabernet Sauvignons. Private Reserve Cabernet can be
★★★ and is one of NAPA VALLEY's most approachable; Chabot Vineyard★★
can be equally impressive. The Knight's Valley Cabernet Sauvignon★ is
made in a lighter style and is good value. Alluvium red★★ and white★

(meritage wines) are also from Knight's Valley. Private Reserve Chardonnay★★ is powerful, ripe and toasty. Bancroft Ranch Merlot★★ from HOWELL MOUNTAIN is also very good. Best years: (Cabernet Sauvignon) 2009 08 **07** 06 05 03 02 01 00 **99** 98 **97** 96 95 94 93.

BERNKASTEL *Mosel, Germany* Both a historic wine town in the Middle MOSEL and a large Bereich. Top wines, however, come only from vineyard sites around the town – the most famous of these is the overpriced Doctor vineyard. Wines from the excellent, if less glamorous, Graben and Lay sites are often as good. Best producers: Dr LOOSEN★★, MOLITOR★, Pauly-Bergweiler★, J J PRÜM★★, S A PRÜM★, SELBACH-OSTER★★, Studert-Prüm, Dr H Thanisch★, WEGELER★★. Best years: (2011) 10 09 08 **07** 06 05 04 02 01.

DOM. BERTHOUMIEU *Madiran AOP, South-West France* Didier Barré offers a worthy challenge to Alain Brumont of Ch. MONTUS, with his more accessible reds, especially Charles de Batz★★ (the real name of d'Artagnan, fictionalized in *The Three Musketeers*). His PACHERENCS★★ are just as good. Best years: (reds) (2011) 10 **08** 06 05; (Pacherenc) (2011) 10 **09** 07 06 05.

BEST'S *Grampians, Victoria, Australia* After 50 vintages, Viv Thomson has handed over the running of this historic winery (vineyards date back to 1868) to his son Ben and a well-qualified young winemaker, Justin Purser. The premium range is called Great Western, with superb fleshy Bin No. 0 Shiraz★★★, good Cabernet★ and a fresh, citrus Riesling★. The Thomson Family Shiraz★★ is an outstanding cool-climate Shiraz. Best years: (Thomson Family Shiraz) (2010) 08 06 05 **04** 01 99 98 97 95 94 93 91 90.

BETZ *Columbia Valley AVA, Washington State, USA* Since 1997, Bob Betz MW has crafted wines of uniquely stylish character. Two BORDEAUX-style red blends: Clos de Betz★ and ageworthy, powerful Cabernet Sauvignon-based Père de Famille★★. The Syrah La Côte Rousse★, named for its Red Mountain origin, is opulent; Syrah La Serenne★★ shows more polish and finesse. Best years: (2010) 09 **08** 07 06 05.

CH. BEYCHEVELLE★★ *St-Julien AC, 4ème Cru Classé, Haut-Médoc, Bordeaux, France* This beautiful château can make wine of Second Growth quality. It has a charming softness even when young, but takes at least a decade to mature into ST-JULIEN's famous cedarwood and blackcurrant flavour. Over the years, it's given me as much pleasure as any Bordeaux – I drank an awful lot of the 1961 at university with a monumentally indulgent tutor. Then it became inconsistent through the 1970s and 80s, but since 1996 has steadily regained its enticing, scented form. Second wine: Amiral de Beychevelle. Best years: 2010 09 08 **07** 06 05 04 03 02 00 99 98 96 95 89 86.

BEYERSKLOOF *Stellenbosch WO, South Africa* Variations on the Pinotage theme abound at Beyers Truter's property: the Pinot-like Diesel★★ (named for a beloved dog), from gravel soils, sets the standard. Blended with Cabernet and Merlot, Faith★ is showy but elegant, with Pinotage-led Synergy more succulent. Pinotage also contributes to good fizz (!) and traditional port style Lagare Cape Vintage. Striking Cabernet Sauvignon-based Field Blend★★ (previously named Beyerskloof). Best years: (Field Blend/Beyerskloof) 2007 05 04 03 01 00 99 98.

BIANCO DI CUSTOZA DOC *Veneto, Italy* Dry white wine from the shores of Lake Garda, made from a blend of grapes including SOAVE's Garganega and GAVI's Cortese. Drink young. Best producers: Cavalchina★, Gorgo★, Montresor★, Le Vigne di San Pietro★, Zeni★.

BIDDENDEN *Kent, England* Established in 1969, this is one of the oldest UK vineyards and produces good wines using little-known grapes such as Ortega★ and Huxelrebe. Also great apple juices and ciders.

BIENVENUES-BÂTARD-MONTRACHET AC See BÂTARD-MONTRACHET.

BIERZO DO *Castilla y León, Spain* Sandwiched between the rainy mountains of GALICIA and the arid plains of CASTILLA Y LEÓN. The arrival of Alvaro PALACIOS, of PRIORAT fame, and his nephew Ricardo Pérez Palacios with their inspired Corullón★★ red, shed an entirely new and exciting light on the potential of the Mencía grape, while native winemaker Raúl PÉREZ has made a name for himself on the national scene. Best producers: Bodega del Abad★, Casar de Burbia★, Castro Ventosa★, Estefanía★, Gancedo★, Losada, Luna Beberide★, Paixar★★, Descendientes de J Palacios★★, Peique★, Raúl PÉREZ★★, Pittacum★, Dominio de Tares★.

BIKAVÉR *Hungary* Formerly known by its anglicized name, Bull's Blood, Kékfrankos (Blaufränkisch) grapes sometimes replace robust Kadarka in the blend; some producers include Cabernet Sauvignon, Kékoporto or Merlot. New regulations should improve the quality of Bikavér in the 2 permitted regions, Eger and Szekszárd. Winemakers such as Vilmos Thummerer are working hard on this front.

BILLECART-SALMON *Champagne AC, Champagne, France* High-quality family-controlled CHAMPAGNE house that makes extremely elegant wines which become irresistible with age. Greatly increased volumes diluted the non-vintage Brut★, but quality is improving again and non-vintage Brut Rosé★★, Blanc de Blancs★★★, vintage Cuvée Nicolas François Billecart★★★ and Cuvée Elisabeth Salmon Rosé★★ are all excellent. Impressive bone-dry Extra Brut★★. Clos Saint-Hilaire★★★ is a single-vineyard vintage Blanc de Noirs. Best years: 2004 (02) **00 99 98 97 96 95 90 89 88 86 85 82**.

ROLF BINDER *Barossa, South Australia* Rolf and Christa Binder's family winery was known as Veritas until 2004. Top wines are the Hanisch Shiraz★★★ and Heysen Shiraz★★★. The Shiraz-Mataro Pressings★★ (known locally as Bull's Blood) and Heinrich Shiraz-Grenache-Mataro★★ blends are lovely big reds; Cabernet-Merlot★★ also impresses, as does Riesling★. Under the Christa Rolf label, Shiraz-Grenache★ is good and spicy with attractive, forward black fruit.

BINGEN *Rheinhessen, Germany* A small town and also a Bereich, the vineyards of which fall in both the NAHE and RHEINHESSEN. The best vineyard is the Scharlachberg, which produces some exciting wines, stinging with racy acidity and the whiff of minerals. Best producers: Kruger-Rumpf, Rheingraf. Best years: (2011) 10 09 08 **07** 06 05.

BÍO BÍO *Chile* One of Chile's most southerly vineyard regions. Cool and wet, but showing promise for Riesling, Pinot Noir and Gewürztraminer. Agustinos, Porta and Veranda are making good Pinot here with help from Burgundian winemakers. Best producers: Agustinos, CONCHA Y TORO, CONO SUR, Porta, Veranda.

BIONDI-SANTI *Brunello di Montalcino DOCG, Tuscany, Italy* Franco Biondi-Santi's Greppo estate has created both a legend and an international standing for BRUNELLO DI MONTALCINO. The Biondi-Santi style has remained deeply traditional, while that of other producers has moved on. The very expensive Riserva★★★, with formidable levels of tannin and acidity, deserves a minimum 10 years' further aging after release before serious judgement is passed on it. Franco's son, Jacopo, has created his own range of wines at Castello di Montepò, including Sassoalloro★★, a barrique-aged Sangiovese, and Sangiovese-Cabernet-Merlot blend Schidione★★. Best years: (Brunello Riserva) (2011) (10) (09) (08) 07 06 04 **01 99 97 95 90 88 85 75 64 55 45.**

BLAGNY AC *Côte de Beaune, Burgundy, France* The red wine from this tiny hamlet above MEURSAULT and PULIGNY-MONTRACHET can be fair value, if you like a rustic Burgundy. Actually much more Chardonnay than Pinot Noir is grown here, but this is sold as Puligny-Montrachet, Meursault Premier Cru or Meursault-Blagny. Best producers: Ampeau★, Lamy-Pillot★, Martelet de Cherisey★★, Matrot★. Best years: (2011) 10 09 **07 06 05 03 02 99.**

BLANQUETTE DE LIMOUX AC *Languedoc, France* Refreshing fizz from the Mauzac grape, which makes up a minimum 90% of the wine and gives it its striking 'green apple skin' flavour – the balance is made up of Chardonnay and Chenin Blanc. The traditional (CHAMPAGNE) method is used. Best producers: Collin, Fourn★, Guinot, Martinolles★, Rives-Blanques★, SIEUR D'ARQUES co-op. See also CREMANT DE LIMOUX AC and pages 294–5.

WOLF BLASS *Barossa Valley, South Australia* Wolf Blass, with its huge range, remains a cornerstone (with PENFOLDS) of Australia's largest wine company, Treasury Wine Estates. The wines do still faintly reflect the founder's dictum that they must be easy to enjoy, though I long for them to do better. The reds sometimes show clumsy oak, and rarely capture the traditional Blass mint and blackcurrant charm. Whites are on the oaky side, except for the Rieslings, which are good, though sweeter and less vibrant than they used to be, including Gold Label Riesling★. White Label Riesling★ and Chardonnay★, released at 5 years of age, have lifted the bar at the top end. Top of the range reds include red blend Black Label★★ and Platinum Label Shiraz★★, which can be quite impressive and do age well. The Eaglehawk range is reliable. Best years: (Black Label) (2011) 10 09 08 **06 03 02 01 99 98 97 96 95 91 90 88 86.**

BLAUBURGUNDER See PINOT NOIR.

BLAUER LEMBERGER See BLAUFRANKISCH.

BLAUFRÄNKISCH Good Blaufränkisch, when not blasted with new oak, has a taste similar to raspberries and white pepper or even beetroot. Hungarian in origin, it does well in Austria, where it is the principal red grape of BURGENLAND. The Hungarian vineyards (where it is called Kékfrankos) are mostly just across the border on the other side of the Neusiedlersee. Called Lemberger in Germany, where almost all of it is grown in WÜRTTEMBERG. Croatia calls it Frankovka or Borgogna and makes crunchy, juicy reds. Also successful in NEW YORK STATE and (as Lemberger) in WASHINGTON STATE (getting better with global warming!).

BLAYE-CÔTES DE BORDEAUX AC *Bordeaux, France* Much improved AC on the right bank of the Gironde. Formerly Premières Côtes de Blaye; part of Côtes de Bordeaux AC from 2008. The fresh, Merlot-based reds are ready at 2–3 years but will age for more. Top red wines can be labelled under the quality-driven Blaye AC. Good modern whites. Best producers: (reds) Bel-Air la Royère★, Confiance★, Gigault (Cuvée Viva★), Haut-Bertinerie★, Haut-Colombier★, Haut-Grelot, Haut-Sociando, les Jonqueyres★, Monconseil-Gazin★, Mondésir-Gazin★, Montfollet★, Roland la Garde★, Segonzac★, Tourtes★; (whites) Charron (Acacia★), Haut-Bertinerie★, Cave des Hauts de Gironde (Chapelle de Tutiac★), Tourtes (Prestige★). Best years: **2010 09 08 05 04 03.**

BORDEAUX RED WINES

Bordeaux, France

 This large area of South-West France, centred on the historic city of Bordeaux, produces a larger volume of fine red wine than any other French region. Wonderful Bordeaux-style wines are produced in California, Australia, South Africa and South America, but the home team's top performers still just about keep the upstarts at bay. Around 650 million bottles of red wine a year are produced here. The best wines, known as the Classed Growths, account for a tiny percentage of this figure, but some of their lustre rubs off on the lesser names, making this one of the most popular wine styles.

GRAPE VARIETIES

Bordeaux's reds are commonly divided into 'right' and 'left' bank wines. On the left bank of the Gironde estuary, the red wines are dominated by the Cabernet Sauvignon grape, with varying proportions of Cabernet Franc, Merlot and Petit Verdot. At best they are austere but perfumed with blackcurrant and cedarwood. The most important left bank areas are the Haut-Médoc (especially Margaux, St-Julien, Pauillac and St-Estèphe) and, south of the city of Bordeaux, Pessac-Léognan and Graves. On the right bank, Merlot is the predominant grape, which generally makes the resulting wines more supple and fleshy than those of the left bank. The key areas for Merlot-based wines are St-Émilion, Pomerol, Fronsac and Castillon-Côtes de Bordeaux.

CLASSIFICATIONS

At its most basic, the wine is simply labelled Bordeaux or Bordeaux Supérieur. Above this are the more specific ACs covering sub-areas (such as the Haut-Médoc) and individual communes (such as Pomerol, St-Émilion or Margaux). Single-estate Crus Bourgeois (although, after a legal challenge, this is no longer a classification but as of 2008 a certificate awarded on a yearly basis) are the next rung up on the quality ladder, followed by the Crus Classés (Classed Growths) of the Médoc, Graves and St-Émilion. The famous classification of 1855 ranked the top red wines of the Médoc (plus one from Graves) into 5 tiers, from First to Fifth Growths (Crus); there has been only one change, in 1973, promoting Château Mouton-Rothschild to First Growth status. Since the 1950s the Graves/Pessac-Léognan region has had its own classification for red and white wines. St-Émilion's classification (for red wines only) has been revised several times, the latest modification being in 2012; the possibility of re-grading can help to maintain quality, but not if you can't also get relegated. Curiously, Pomerol, home of Château Pétrus, arguably the most famous red wine in the world, has no official pecking order. Many top châteaux make 'second wines', which are cheaper versions of their Grands Vins.

See also BLAYE-CÔTES DE BORDEAUX, BORDEAUX, BORDEAUX SUPÉRIEUR, CADILLAC-CÔTES DE BORDEAUX, CANON-FRONSAC, CASTILLON-CÔTES DE BORDEAUX, CÔTES DE BOURG, FRANCS-CÔTES DE BORDEAUX, FRONSAC, GRAVES, HAUT-MEDOC, LALANDE-DE-POMEROL, LISTRAC-MEDOC, LUSSAC-ST-EMILION, MARGAUX, MEDOC, MONTAGNE-ST-EMILION, MOULIS, PAUILLAC, PESSAC-LEOGNAN, POMEROL, PUISSEGUIN-ST-EMILION, ST-EMILION, ST-ESTÈPHE, ST-GEORGES-ST-EMILION, ST-JULIEN; and individual châteaux.

BEST PRODUCERS

Graves, Pessac-Léognan
Carbonnieux, Dom. de
CHEVALIER, HAUT-BAILLY, HAUT-
BRION, la LOUVIERE, MALARTIC-
LAGRAVIERE, la MISSION-HAUT-
BRION, PAPE-CLEMENT, SMITH-
HAUT-LAFITTE.

Margaux BRANE-CANTENAC,
FERRIÈRE, ISSAN, MALESCOT ST
EXUPERY, MARGAUX, PALMER,
RAUZAN-SEGLA, SIRAN, du Tertre.

Pauillac GRAND-PUY-LACOSTE,
HAUT-BAGES-LIBERAL, LAFITE-
ROTHSCHILD, LATOUR, LYNCH-
BAGES, MOUTON-ROTHSCHILD,
PICHON-LONGUEVILLE, PICHON-
LONGUEVILLE-LALANDE, PONTET-
CANET.

Pomerol le BON PASTEUR,
Certan-de-May, Clinet, Clos
l'Eglise, la CONSEILLANTE, l'EGLISE
CLINET, l'EVANGILE, la FLEUR-
PETRUS, GAZIN, Hosanna, LAFLEUR,
LATOUR-A-POMEROL, PETIT-
VILLAGE, PETRUS, le PIN,
TROTANOY, VIEUX-CHATEAU-
CERTAN.

St-Émilion ANGELUS, AUSONE,
BEAU-SEJOUR BECOT, BELAIR-
MONANGE, CANON, CANON-LÀ-
GAFFELIERE, CHEVAL BLANC, Clos
Fourtet, la Dominique, FIGEAC,
Grand Mayne, Larcis-Ducasse,
MAGDELAINE, MONBOUSQUET, La
Mondotte, PAVIE, PAVIE-MACQUIN,
Rol Valentin, TERTRE-ROTEBOEUF,
TROPLONG MONDOT,
VALANDRAUD.

St-Estèphe CALON-SEGUR, COS
D'ESTOURNEL, HAUT-MARBUZET,
LAFON-ROCHET, MONTROSE,
Ormes de Pez, PEZ, Phélan
Ségur, Tronquoy-Lalande.

St-Julien BEYCHEVELLE,
BRANAIRE-DUCRU, DUCRU-
BEAUCAILLOU, GRUAUD-LAROSE,
LAGRANGE, LANGOA-BARTON,
LEOVILLE-BARTON, LEOVILLE-LAS-
CASES, LEOVILLE-POYFERRE,
ST-PIERRE, TALBOT.

BORDEAUX WHITE WINES

Bordeaux, France

 This is France's largest fine wine region, but, except for the sweet wines of Sauternes and Barsac, Bordeaux's international reputation is based almost entirely on its reds. From 52% of the vineyard area in 1970, white wines now represent only 11% of the present 117,500ha (290,350 acres) of vines. Given the size of the region, the diversity of Bordeaux's white wines should come as no surprise. There are dry, medium and sweet styles, ranging from dreary to some of the most sublime white wines of all. Bordeaux's temperate southern climate – moderated by the influence of the Atlantic and of two rivers, the Dordogne and the Garonne – is ideal for white wine production, particularly south of the city along the banks of the Garonne.

GRAPE VARIETIES

Sauvignon Blanc and Sémillon, the most important white grapes, are both varieties of considerable character and are usually blended together. They are backed up by smaller quantities of other grapes, the most notable of which is Muscadelle (unrelated to Muscat), which lends perfume to sweet wines and spiciness to dry.

DRY WINES

With the introduction of new technology and new ideas, many of them influenced by the New World, Bordeaux has become one of France's most exciting white wine areas. There are both oaked and unoaked styles. The unoaked are leafy, tangy and stony-dry. The barrel-fermented styles are delightfully rich yet dry, with custard-cream softness mellowing leafy acidity, and peach and nectarine fruit.

SWEET WINES

Bordeaux's most famous whites are its sweet wines made from grapes affected by noble rot, particularly those from Sauternes and Barsac. The noble rot concentrates the flavours, producing rich, honeyed wines replete with pineapple and peach flavours, and which develop a lanolin and beeswax depth and a barley sugar and honey richness with age. On the other side of the Garonne river, Cadillac, Loupiac and Ste-Croix-du-Mont also make sweet wines; these rarely attain the richness or complexity of a top Sauternes, but they are considerably less expensive.

CLASSIFICATIONS

The two largest dry white wine ACs in Bordeaux are Bordeaux Blanc and Entre-Deux-Mers. There are plenty of good dry wines in the Graves and Pessac-Léognan regions; the Pessac-Léognan AC, created in 1987, contains all the dry white Classed Growths. The great sweet wines of Sauternes and Barsac were classified as First or Second Growths in 1855.

See also BARSAC, BLAYE-CÔTES DE BORDEAUX, BORDEAUX, BORDEAUX SUPERIEUR, CADILLAC, CERONS, CÔTES DE BOURG, ENTRE-DEUX-MERS, FRANCS-CÔTES DE BORDEAUX, GRAVES, LOUPIAC, PESSAC-LEOGNAN, PREMIÈRES CÔTES DE BORDEAUX, STE-CROIX-DU-MONT, SAUTERNES; and individual châteaux.

BEST YEARS

(dry) (2011) **10 09 08 07 06 05 04 02 01 00**;
(sweet) (2011) 10 09 **07 05 03 02 01** 99 98 97 96 95 90 89 88 86

BEST PRODUCERS

Dry wines

Pessac-Léognan Brown, de CHEVALIER, Couhins-Lurton, FIEUZAL, La Garde, HAUT-BRION, Larrivet-Haut-Brion, LATOUR-MARTILLAC, LAVILLE-HAUT-BRION (since 2009 la MISSION-HAUT-BRION blanc), la LOUVIERE, MALARTIC-LAGRAVIERE, SMITH-HAUT-LAFITTE; *Graves* Archambeau, Brondelle, Chantegrive, Clos Floridène, Crabitey, Magneau, Rahoul, Respide, Respide-Médeville, St-Robert (Cuvée Poncet-Deville), Toumilon, Tourteau-Chollet, Vieux-Ch.-Gaubert, Villa Bel Air.

Entre-Deux-Mers BONNET, de Fontenille, Landereau, Marjosse, Nardique-la-Gravière, Ste-Marie, Toutigeac, Turcaud.

Bordeaux AC l'Abbaye de Ste-Ferme, Bauduc, DOISY-DAENE (Sec), LYNCH-BAGES, Ch. MARGAUX (Pavillon Blanc), MONBOUSQUET, REYNON, Roquefort, TALBOT, Thieuley, Tour de Mirambeau.

Blaye-Côtes de Bordeaux Charron (Acacia), Haut-Bertinerie, Cave des Hauts de Gironde co-op (Chapelle de Tutiac), Tourtes (Prestige).

Sweet wines

Sauternes and Barsac CLIMENS, Clos Haut-Peyraguey, COUTET, DOISY-DAENE, DOISY-VEDRINES, FARGUES, GILETTE, GUIRAUD, LAFAURIE-PEYRAGUEY, NAIRAC, Raymond-Lafon, RIEUSSEC, Sigalas-Rabaud, SUDUIRAUT, la TOUR BLANCHE, YQUEM.

Cadillac Fayau, Manos, Mémoires.

Cérons Ch. de Cérons, Grand Enclos du Ch. de Cérons.

Loupiac Clos Jean, Cros, Noble.

Ste-Croix-du-Mont Loubens, Pavillon, la Rame.

89

B JACKY BLOT

JACKY BLOT *Loire Valley, France*   When he created Domaine de la Taille aux Loups in MONTLOUIS-SUR-LOIRE and VOUVRAY in 1988, Blot's use of barrel fermentation and new oak caused controversy. However, rigorous selection of pristine, ripe grapes produces sparkling, dry and sweet whites with tremendous fruit purity. Top Montlouis-sur-Loire cuvées Rémus (*sec*)★★ and Romulus (*liquoreux*)★★ are groundbreaking – with staggeringly good 'Plus' versions in exceptional vintages. He has recently acquired two propitious vineyards in Montlouis: Clos de Mosny and Clos Michet. Also new is a fine Triple Zéro sparkling rosé (from Gamay), as well as the white version (from Chenin). Since 2002 Blot has made four powerful but ultra-refined reds at Domaine de la Butte★★ in BOURGUEIL AC from separate parcels of south-facing vineyards. Best years: (whites) (sec) (2011) 10 **08 07 06**; (moelleux) (2011) 09 **05 03 02 97 96 95 90**.

BOBAL Occupies the second largest area (some 90,000ha/222,400 acres) among red varieties in Spain, surpassed only by Tempranillo. Once doomed to bulk wine's netherworld, some producers in MANCHUELA and UTIEL-REQUENA (Cerrogallina, Finca Sandoval, Ponce, Mustiguillo) have rescued it and its fruity, vivacious, structured, somewhat rustic character.

BOEKENHOUTSKLOOF *Franschhoek WO, South Africa*   Perched high in the FRANSCHHOEK mountains, this small winery is named after the surrounding Cape beech trees. The flagship range includes punchy, savoury Syrah★★, deep, long-lived Cabernet Sauvignon★★, sophisticated Semillon★★ partly from 100-year-old vines, sumptuous Noble Late Harvest★★ from Semillon and burly, expressive Chocolate Block★★ (Syrah-led, with Grenache, Cabernet Sauvignon, Cinsaut and Viognier). Fruit-focused Porcupine Ridge★ and Rhône-style The Wolftrap white★ and red★ offer great value. Best years: (premium reds) **2009 08 07 06 05 04 03 02 01 00 99 98 97**.

BOIREANN *Queensland, Australia*   Peter and Therese Stark established Boireann in 1995 as a retirement project to specialize in red wines, with 400 Cabernet vines. It's now QUEENSLAND's most impressive boutique winery, with a 1.5ha (3.5-acre) vineyard planted to 10 red varieties plus Viognier for the flagship fragrant, plush Shiraz-Viognier★★. Other stunning reds include Merlot★★, Cabernet Sauvignon★ and, from 2008, the seductive Lurnea★ (a blend of Merlot, Cabernets Sauvignon and Franc and Petit Verdot).

BOISSET *Burgundy, France*   Jean-Claude Boisset bought his first vineyards in 1964 and began a *négociant* company whose extraordinary success has enabled him to swallow up many other long-established names such as Jaffelin, Ponelle, Ropiteau and Héritier Guyot in the CÔTE D'OR, Moreau in CHABLIS, Cellier des Samsons and Mommessin in BEAUJOLAIS and most recently Rodet in Côte Chalonnaise. Most of these companies are designed to produce commercially successful rather than fine wine, excepting Domaine de la VOUGERAIE and now the Boisset label itself. Also projects in California, Canada, Chile and Uruguay.

BOLGHERI DOC *Tuscany, Italy*   Zone named after an arty village in the Tuscan coastal commune of Castagneto Carducci. Until the 1980s simple white and rosé wines were made there – later, major reds based on Cabernet, Merlot and/or Syrah. There is a special sub-zone for SASSICAIA, the only DOC in Italy for a single property. Best producers: Argentiera, Ca' Marcanda★ (GAJA), Collemassari, Grattamacco★★, Guado al

Tasso★★ (ANTINORI), Le MACCHIOLE★★, ORNELLAIA★★, Poggio al Tesoro★, Michele Satta★★. Best years: (reds) (2011) (10) 09 **08 07 06 05 04 01 00**.

BOLLINGER *Champagne AC, Champagne, France* One of the great CHAMPAGNE houses, with good non-vintage (Special Cuvée★) and vintage wines (Grande Année★★★), made in a full, rich, rather old-fashioned style. (Bollinger is one of the few houses to ferment its base wine in barrels.) It also produces a range of rarer vintages, including Vintage RD★★★, and a Vieilles Vignes Françaises Blanc de Noirs★★ from ancient, ungrafted Pinot Noir vines. Delightfully soft, creamy non-vintage Brut Rosé. Bollinger bought Champagne Ayala, a neighbour in Aÿ, in 2005. Best years: (Grande Année) (2004) 02 **00 99 97 96 95 92 90 89 88 85 82 79**.

CH. LE BON PASTEUR★★ *Pomerol AC, Bordeaux, France* Owned by Michel Rolland, Bordeaux's most famous winemaker. The wines are expensive, but they are always deliciously soft and full of lush fruit. Best years: 2010 09 08 **06 05 04 03 02 01 00 99 98 96 95 90 89**.

BONNES-MARES AC *Grand Cru, Côte de Nuits, Burgundy, France* A large Grand Cru straddling the communes of CHAMBOLLE-MUSIGNY and MOREY-ST-DENIS, commendably consistent over the last few decades. Bonnes-Mares generally has a deep, ripe, smoky plum fruit, which starts rich and chewy and matures over 10-20 years. Best producers: d'Auvenay★★★ (Dom. LEROY), BOUCHARD PÈRE ET FILS★★, CLAIR★★, DROUHIN★★★, Drouhin-Laroze★★, DUJAC★★★, Robert Groffier★★★, JADOT★★★, ROUMIER★★★, de VOGÜE★★★, VOUGERAIE★★★. Best years: (2011) 10 09 08 **07** 06 05 **03 02 01** 99 98 96 95 93 90.

CH. BONNET *Entre-Deux-Mers AC, Bordeaux, France* This region's pioneering estate for quality and consistency. Large volumes of good, fruity, affordable ENTRE-DEUX-MERS★ and BORDEAUX AC rosé and red, particularly the barrel-aged Reserve★. Drink this at 3–4 years and the others young. Also a special cuvée, Divinus★. Owner André Lurton is also the proprietor of Ch. La LOUVIERE and other properties in PESSAC-LEOGNAN.

BONNEZEAUX AC *Loire Valley, France* One of France's great sweet wines, Bonnezeaux is a zone within the COTEAUX DU LAYON AC. Quality is variable, but top wines are world class. It can age well in good vintages. Best producers: M Angeli/Sansonnière★★, Fesles★★, Les Grandes Vignes★, Petit Val★★, la Petite Croix★, Petits Quarts★★, Terrebrune★★, la Varière★★. Best years: (2011) 10 09 **07 06 05 04 03 02 01 99 97 96 95 90 89**.

BONNY DOON *Santa Cruz Mountains AVA, California, USA* Randall Grahm has a particular love for Rhône and Italian varietals: Le Cigare Volant★★ is a blend of Grenache and Syrah and is Grahm's homage to CHÂTEAUNEUF-DU-PAPE. Cigare Blanc★ is lush yet dry. His biodynamic-certified Ca' del Solo wines are delightful, particularly the Albariño★.

BORDEAUX AC *Bordeaux, France* One of the most important ACs in France, covering reds, rosés and the dry, medium and sweet white wines of the entire Gironde region. Most of the best wines are allowed specific district or commune ACs (such as MARGAUX or SAUTERNES), but a vast amount of Bordeaux's wine – delicious, atrocious and everything in between – is sold as Bordeaux AC. At its best, straight red Bordeaux is marked by bone-dry leafy fruit and an attractive earthy edge, and as global warming kicks in, raw, tannic examples are becoming less common. Good examples usually benefit from a year or so of aging. Bordeaux Blanc has joined the modern world with an increasing number of refreshing, pleasant wines. These may be labelled as Bordeaux Sauvignon. Drink young. Bordeaux Clairet is a pale red wine, virtually rosé but with a little more substance. Best producers: (reds) Beauregard-Ducourt, BONNET★, Dourthe (Numéro 1), Ducla, d:vin★, Fontenille★, Gadras, Girolate, Sirius, Thieuley★, Tour de Mirambeau; (whites) l'Abbaye de Ste-Ferme★, Bauduc★, DOISY-DAËNE★, Dourthe (Numéro 1★), LYNCH-BAGES★, MARGAUX (Pavillon Blanc★★), MONBOUSQUET★, REYNON★, Roquefort★, TALBOT★, Thieuley★, Tour de Mirambeau★, Vieux Ch. Lamothe. See also pages 86–9.

BORDEAUX SUPÉRIEUR AC *Bordeaux, France* Covers the same area as the BORDEAUX AC but the wines must have an extra 0.5% of alcohol, a lower yield and a longer period of maturation. Many of the best petits châteaux are labelled Bordeaux Supérieur. Best producers (reds): Barreyre★, Beaulieu Comtes des Tastes★, de Bouillerot★, de Courteillac★, La France★, Grand Village★, Parenchère★, Penin★, Pey la Tour★, Pierrail★, le Pin Beausoleil★, Reignac★, Roques Mauriac★, Thieuley (Réserve Francis Courselle★), Tire-Pé★.

BORIE LA VITARÈLE *St-Chinian AC, Languedoc, France* The Izarn family produces several ST-CHINIANs, as well as vins de pays/IGPs, which express the different soils of their organic vineyard: Les Crès★, dominated by Syrah, is spicy and warm; Les Schistes, with more Grenache, is ripe and concentrated. Best years: (2011) 10 **09 08 07 06 05 04**.

BOSCARELLI *Vino Nobile di Montepulciano DOCG, Tuscany, Italy* Arguably Montepulciano's best producer, crafting rich and stylish reds with guidance from star enologist Maurizio Castelli. VINO NOBILE★★, Riserva del Nocio★★ and the barrique-aged Boscarelli★★ are all brilliant. Best years: (2011) (10) 09 08 **07 06 04 01 99**.

BOUCHARD FINLAYSON *Walker Bay WO, South Africa* Pinotphile Peter Finlayson produces classy Pinot Noir (Galpin Peak★ and occasional Tête de Cuvée★★). His love of Italian varieties is reflected in Hannibal★★, a multi-cultural mix led by Sangiovese with Pinot Noir, Nebbiolo, Barbera and Shiraz. Chardonnays (Kaaimansgaat/Crocodile's Lair★ – now fresher, more citrusy and less obviously oaky – and full, nutty home-grown Missionvale★) are plausibly Burgundian. Sauvignon Blanc★ is tangy and fresh. Best years: (Pinot Noir) **2010 09 08 07 06 05 04 03**.

BOUCHARD PÈRE & FILS *Beaune, Burgundy, France* Important merchant with superb holdings such as Chevalier-Montrachet★★, le MONTRACHET★★★, BEAUNE Grèves Vigne de l'Enfant Jésus★★, as well as a 1er Cru blend labelled Beaune du Château. Reds and whites equally good. Best years: (top reds) (2011) 10 09 08 **07 06** 05 02 **99**.

BOUCHES-DU-RHÔNE, IGP *Provence, France* Wines from 3 areas: the coast, a zone around Aix-en-Provence and the Camargue. Mainly full-bodied, spicy reds, with estates like TREVALLON (now IGP Alpilles) breaking with local tradition and using a high percentage of Cabernet Sauvignon. Unusual varieties include Caladoc (Grenache x Malbec) at la Michelle and Arinarnoa (Merlot x Petit Verdot) at Isle St-Pierre. Rosé can be good too. Best producers: Ch. Bas, Isle St-Pierre, Mas de Rey, la Michelle. Best years: (reds) (2011) 10 09 **08 07 06**.

DOM. HENRI BOURGEOIS *Sancerre AC, Loire Valley, France* A major presence with 67ha (166 acres) of domaine vineyards and a substantial *négociant* business extending into POUILLY-FUMÉ, MENETOU-SALON, QUINCY and COTEAUX DU GIENNOIS, plus Clos Henri label in New Zealand. Quality remains consistently high. Bourgeois owns 8 out of 10ha of La Côte des Monts Damnés' precipitously steep slopes after which the family have named a wonderfully mineral Sancerre★ – and also their stylish hotel-restaurant. Ageworthy old-vine Jadis★★, an impressively structured Sauvignon Gris, is from *terre blanche* soils, while d'Antan★★ is from silex soils.

Together with rare barrel-fermented Étienne Henri★★, they are among
the finest in Sancerre. Good red Sancerre too. Best years: (top wines) 2011
10 09 08 07 06 05 04.

BOURGOGNE AC *Burgundy, France* Bourgogne is the French name
anglicized as 'Burgundy'. This generic AC mops up all the Burgundian
wine with no AC of its own, resulting in massive differences in style and
quality. The best wines will usually come from a single grower's vineyards
just outside the main village ACs of the COTE D'OR; such wines may be the
only way we can afford the joys of fine Burgundy. If the wine is from a
grower, the flavours should follow a local style. However, if the address
on the label is that of a *négociant*, the wine could be from anywhere in
Burgundy. Pinot Noir is the main red grape, but Gamay from a
declassified BEAUJOLAIS Cru is, absurdly, allowed. Red Bourgogne is
usually light, fruity in an upfront strawberry and cherry way, and should
be drunk within 2–3 years. The rosé (Pinot Noir) can be pleasant, but
little is produced. Bourgogne Blanc is a usually bone-dry Chardonnay
wine and most should be drunk within 2 years. Bourgogne Passe-tout-
Grains is made from Gamay with a minimum 33% of Pinot Noir, while
the oxymoronically named Bourgogne Grand Ordinaire (now renamed
COTEAUX BOURGUIGNONS AC) is rarely more than a quaffing wine, drunk in
local bars. Best producers: (reds/growers) Arnoux-Lachaux★★,
G Barthod★★, S CATHIARD★, Dugat-Py★★, G Jourdan★, LAFARGE★, MÉO-
CAMUZET★★, Parent★, P RION★, ROUMIER★, C Tremblay★, VOUGERAIE★;
(reds/merchants) Roche de BELLENE, DROUHIN★, GIRARDIN, JADOT★, Maison
Leroy★★; (reds/co-ops) BUXY★, Caves des Hautes-Côtes★; (whites/growers)
Bachelet-Monnot★, M Bouzereau★, Boyer-Martenot★, J-M BROCARD★, COCHE-
DURY★★, P-Y COLIN-MOREY★, Dancer★, J-P Fichet★, P Javillier★, A Jobard★,
Matrot★, Ch. de Meursault★, Pierre Morey★, ROULOT★; (whites/merchants)
DROUHIN★, FAIVELEY, JADOT★, Olivier LEFLAIVE, Rodet★; (whites/co-ops) BUXY,
Caves des Hautes-Côtes. Best years: (reds) (2011) 10 **09** 05, (whites) (2011) **10
09**. See also pages 94–7.

BOURGOGNE ALIGOTÉ AC See ALIGOTÉ.

BOURGOGNE-CÔTE CHALONNAISE AC *Burgundy, France* AC for vine-
yards to the west of Chalon-sur-Saône around the villages of Bouzeron,
RULLY, MERCUREY, GIVRY and MONTAGNY. Best producers: X Besson, BUXY★,
Villaine (La Digoine★). Best years: (reds) (2011) 10 **09**; (whites) (2011) **10 09**.

BOURGOGNE-CÔTE D'OR AC *Burgundy, France* New AC for wines from
COTE DE BEAUNE and COTE D'OR grapes. These should be superior to simple
'BOURGOGNE'.

BOURGOGNE-HAUTES-CÔTES DE BEAUNE AC *Burgundy, France* The
hills behind the great CÔTE DE BEAUNE are a good source of affordable
Burgundy. The red wines are lean but drinkable, as is the slightly sharp
Chardonnay. Best producers: Caves des Hautes-Côtes★, J-Y Devevey★,
L Jacob★, J-L Joillot★, Mazilly★, Naudin-Ferrand★, C Nouveau★. Best years:
(reds) (2011) 10 **09** 05; (whites) (2011) **10 09**.

BOURGOGNE-HAUTES-CÔTES DE NUITS AC *Burgundy, France*
Attractive, lightweight wines from the hills behind the CÔTE DE NUITS.
The reds are best, with an attractive cherry and plum flavour. The whites
tend to be rather dry and flinty. Best producers: (reds) D Duband★,
FAIVELEY★, A-F GROS★, M GROS★, A Guyon★, Caves des Hautes-Côtes★, Jayer-
Gilles★★, T LIGER-BELAIR★, A Verdet★; (whites) Caves des Hautes-Côtes★,
Champy★, Jayer-Gilles★★, Thévenot-le-Brun★. Best years: (reds) (2011) 10 **09
08** 05; (whites) (2011) **10 09**.

BURGUNDY RED WINES

Burgundy, France

 Rich in history and gastronomic tradition, the region of Burgundy (Bourgogne in French) covers a vast tract of eastern France, running from Auxerre, south-east of Paris, down to the city of Mâcon. As with its white wines, Burgundy's red wines are extremely diverse. The explanation for this lies partly in the fickle nature of Pinot Noir, the area's principal red grape, and partly in the historical imbalance of supply and demand between growers – who grow the grapes and make and bottle much of the best wine – and merchants, whose efforts originally established the reputation of the wines internationally.

WINE STYLES

Pinot Noir shows many different flavour profiles according to climate, soil and winemaking. The reds from around Auxerre (Épineuil, Irancy) in the north will be light, chalky and strawberry-flavoured. Also light, and somewhat rustic, are the generic Bourgognes from outlying areas such as the Couchois and Châtillonais, while the Côte Chalonnaise offers solid reds from Givry and Mercurey.

The top reds come from the Côte d'Or, the heartland of Burgundy. Flavours sweep through strawberry, raspberry, damson and cherry – in young wines – to a wild, magnificent maturity of Oriental spices, chocolate, mushrooms and truffles. The greatest of all – the world-famous Grand Cru vineyards such as Chambertin, Musigny, Richebourg and Clos de Vougeot – are in the Côte de Nuits, the northern part of the Côte d'Or from Nuits-St-Georges up toward Dijon. Other fine reds, especially Volnay, Pommard and Corton, come from the Côte de Beaune. Some villages tend toward a fine and elegant style (Chambolle-Musigny, Volnay), others toward a firmer, more tannic structure (Gevrey-Chambertin, Pommard).

The Beaujolais should really be considered as a separate region, growing Gamay on granitic soils rather than Pinot Noir on limestone, though a small amount of Gamay has also crept north to be included in the lesser wines of Burgundy as well as all red Mâcon.

CLASSIFICATIONS

Most of Burgundy has 5 increasingly specific levels of classification: regional ACs (e.g. Bourgogne), specified ACs covering groups of villages (e.g. Côte de Nuits-Villages), village wines taking the village name (Pommard, Vosne-Romanée), Premiers Crus (better vineyard sites) and Grands Crus (the best individual vineyard sites). At village level, vineyard names in small letters are called *lieux-dits*.

See also ALOXE-CORTON, AUXEY-DURESSES, BEAUJOLAIS, BEAUNE, BLAGNY, BONNES-MARES, BOURGOGNE, BOURGOGNE-COTE CHALONNAISE, BOURGOGNE-HAUTES-COTES DE BEAUNE/NUITS, CHAMBERTIN, CHAMBOLLE-MUSIGNY, CHASSAGNE-MONTRACHET, CHOREY-LÈS-BEAUNE, CLOS DE LA ROCHE, CLOS ST-DENIS, CLOS DE VOUGEOT, CORTON, CÔTE DE BEAUNE, CÔTE DE NUITS, CÔTE D'OR, CRÉMANT DE BOURGOGNE, ÉCHÉZEAUX, FIXIN, GEVREY-CHAMBERTIN, GIVRY, IRANCY, LADOIX, MÂCON, MARANGES, MARSANNAY, MERCUREY, MONTHELIE, MOREY-ST-DENIS, MUSIGNY, NUITS-ST-GEORGES, PERNAND-VERGELESSES, POMMARD, RICHEBOURG, la ROMANÉE-CONTI, ROMANÉE-ST-VIVANT, RULLY, ST-AUBIN, ST-ROMAIN, SANTENAY, SAVIGNY-LÈS-BEAUNE, la TÂCHE, VOLNAY, VOSNE-ROMANÉE, VOUGEOT; and individual producers.

BEST YEARS

(2011) 10 09 08 **07 06** 05 03 **02 99 98 96 95 90**

BEST PRODUCERS

Côte de Nuits B Ambroise, Arlaud, l'Arlot, Arnoux-Lachaux, Denis Bachelet, G Barthod, A Burguet, Cacheux-Sirugue, S CATHIARD, Charlopin, J Chauvenet, R Chevillon, Chopin-Groffier, B CLAIR, CLOS DES LAMBRAYS, CLOS DE TART, J-J Confuron, P Damoy, Drouhin-Laroze, C Dugat, B Dugat-Py, DUJAC, Sylvie Esmonin, J-M Fourrier, Geantet-Pansiot, H Gouges, GRIVOT, R Groffier, GROS, Hudelot-Noëllat, Jayer-Gilles, F Lamarche, Lechenaut, Philippe Leclerc, Dom. LEROY, LIGER-BELAIR, H Lignier, MEO-CAMUZET, Denis MORTET, MUGNERET-GIBOURG, J-F MUGNIER, Perrot-Minot, Ponsot, J Prieur, RION, Dom. de la ROMANÉE-CONTI, Rossignol-Trapet, Rory, E Rouget, ROUMIER, ROUSSEAU, Sérafin, Taupenot-Merme, J & J-L Trapet, de VOGÜÉ, VOUGERAIE.

Côte de Beaune M Ampeau, d'ANGERVILLE, Comte Armand, Bize, H Boillot, J-M Boillot, CHANDON DE BRIAILLES, de Courcel, Germain/Ch. de Chorey, Michel LAFARGE, LAFON, de MONTILLE, J Prieur, N Rossignol, TOLLOT-BEAUT.

Côte Chalonnaise Dureuil Janthial, Joblot, M Juillot, Lorenzon, F Raquillet, de Suremain, de Villaine.

Merchants Roche de BELLENE, Bichot, BOISSET, BOUCHARD PÈRE & FILS, Champy, Chanson, DROUHIN, FAIVELEY, Alex Gambal, V GIRARDIN, Camille Giroud, JADOT, D Laurent, Benjamin Leroux, Maison Leroy, Remoissenet.

Co-ops Vignerons de BUXY, Caves des Hautes-Côtes.

BURGUNDY WHITE WINES

Burgundy, France

 White Burgundy has for generations been thought of as the world's leading dry white wine. The top wines have a remarkable succulent richness of honey and hazelnut, melted butter and sprinkled spice, yet are totally dry. Such wines are all from the Chardonnay grape and the finest are generally produced in the Côte de Beaune, the southern part of the Côte d'Or, in the communes of Aloxe-Corton, Meursault, Puligny-Montrachet, Chassagne-Montrachet and St-Aubin, where limestone soils and the aspect of the vineyard provide perfect conditions for the even ripening of grapes. However, Burgundy encompasses many more wine styles than this, even if no single one quite attains the peaks of quality of those 5 villages on the Côte de Beaune.

WINE STYLES

Chablis in the north traditionally produces very good steely wines, aggressive and lean when young, but nutty and rounded – though still very dry – after a few years. Modern Chablis is frequently a softer, milder wine, easy to drink young, and sometimes enriched (or denatured) by aging in new oak barrels.

There is no doubt that Meursault and the other Côte de Beaune villages can produce stupendous wine, but there have been problems of late with wines oxidizing prematurely for various reasons still insufficiently understood. Consequently, white Burgundy from these famous villages must be approached with caution, although growers now believe they have dealt with the problem. Lesser-known villages such as Pernand-Vergelesses and St-Aubin often provide good wine at lower prices. There can be interesting whites from some villages in the Côte de Nuits, such as Morey-St-Denis, Nuits-St-Georges and Vougeot, though amounts are tiny compared with the Côte de Beaune.

South of the Côte d'Or, the Côte Chalonnaise is becoming more interesting for quality white wine now that better equipment for temperature control is becoming more widespread and oak barrels are being used more often for aging. Rully and Montagny are the most important villages, though Givry and Mercurey can produce nice white too. The minor Aligoté grape makes some refreshing wine, especially in Bouzeron.

Further south, the Mâconnais is a large region, two-thirds planted with Chardonnay. There is some fair sparkling Crémant de Bourgogne, and some very good vineyard sites, in particular in St-Véran and in Pouilly-Fuissé. Increasingly stunning wines can now be found, though there's still a lot of dross.

See also ALOXE-CORTON, AUXEY-DURESSES, BÂTARD-MONTRACHET, BEAUJOLAIS, BEAUNE, BOURGOGNE, BOURGOGNE-CÔTE CHALONNAISE, BOURGOGNE-HAUTES-COTES DE BEAUNE/NUITS, CHABLIS, CHASSAGNE-MONTRACHET, CORTON, CORTON-CHARLEMAGNE, CÔTE DE BEAUNE, CÔTE DE NUITS, CÔTE D'OR, CRÉMANT DE BOURGOGNE, FIXIN, GIVRY, LADOIX, MÂCON, MÂCON-VILLAGES, MARANGES, MARSANNAY, MERCUREY, MEURSAULT, MONTAGNY, MONTHELIE, MONTRACHET, MOREY-ST-DENIS, MUSIGNY, NUITS-ST-GEORGES, PERNAND-VERGELESSES, POUILLY-FUISSÉ, POUILLY-VINZELLES, PULIGNY-MONTRACHET, RULLY, ST-AUBIN, ST-ROMAIN, ST-VERAN, SANTENAY, SAVIGNY-LÈS-BEAUNE, VIRÉ-CLESSÉ, VOUGEOT; and individual producers.

BEST YEARS

(2011) 10 **09 08 07 06 05 04**
02 00 99

BEST PRODUCERS

Chablis and Auxerrois
Barat, J-C Bessin, Billaud-
Simon, P Bouchard,
A & F Boudin, J-M BROCARD,
D Dampt, V DAUVISSAT, Droin,
Durup, N & G Fèvre, W Fèvre,
J-H Goisot, J-P Grossot,
LAROCHE, Long-Depaquit,
Malandes, Louis Michel,
Christian Moreau, Moreau-
Naudet, Picq, Pinson, RAVENEAU,
Vocoret.

Côte d'Or (Côte de
Beaune) M Ampeau,
d'Auvenay (LEROY), Blain-Gagnard,
H Boillot, J-M Boillot, Bonneau
du Martray, M Bouzereau,
Boyer-Martenot, CARILLON,
Coche Debord, COCHE DURY,
Marc COLIN, P-Y COLIN-MOREY,
Dancer, A Ente, J-P Fichet,
Fontaine Gagnard,
J-N GAGNARD, A Gras,
P Javillier, A Jobard, R Jobard,
LAFON, H Lamy, Dom. LEFLAIVE,
Matrot, MOREY, M Niellon,
P Pernot, J & J-M Pillot, J Prieur,
RAMONET, M Rollin, ROULOT,
SAUZET, VERGET, VOUGERAIE.

Côte Chalonnaise
S Aladame, Bureuil Janthial,
H & P Jacqueson.

Mâconnais D & M Barraud,
A Bonhomme, Bret Brothers,
Cordier, Corsin, Deux Roches,
J-A Ferret, Ch. Fuissé, Guffens-
Heynen/VERGET, Guillot-Broux,
LAFON, O Merlin, Ch. des
Rontets, J & N Saumaize,
Saumaize-Michelin, la
Soufrandière, J Thévenet.

Merchants BOUCHARD PÈRE &
FILS, Champy, Chanson,
DROUHIN, FAIVELEY, V GIRARDIN,
JADOT, Louis LATOUR, Olivier
LEFLAIVE, Maison Leroy,
Rijckaert, Rodet, VERGET.

Co-ops Vignerons de BUXY, la
CHABLISIENNE, Lugny, Viré.

BOURGUEIL AC *Loire Valley, France* Fine red from between Tours and Angers, made with Cabernet Franc, sometimes with a little Cabernet Sauvignon. A concerted quality drive, together with a good run of vintages, is shedding its reputation for rusticity; expect spicy wines with plump raspberry and plum fruit. Best producers: Y Amirault★★, Audebert★, la Butte★★/BLOT, T Boucard★, P Breton★★, la Chevalerie★★, Clos de l'Abbaye★, L et M Cognard-Taluau, DRUET★★, S Guion★, Lamé-Delisle-Boucard★, la Lande/Delaunay★, F MABILEAU★, Nau Frères★, Ouches★, Raguenières★. Best years: (2011) 10 **09 08 06 05 04 03 02 01**. See also ST-NICOLAS-DE-BOURGUEIL.

BRACHETTO An unusual Italian grape native to Piedmont, Brachetto makes every style from dry and still to rich, sweet passito and sweet, frothy light red wines with a Muscat-like perfume, as exemplified by Brachetto d'Acqui DOCG. Best producers: (dry) Contero, Correggia★, Scarpa★; (Brachetto d'Acqui) BANFI★, Braida★, G Marenco★.

CH. BRANAIRE-DUCRU★★ *St-Julien AC, 4ème Cru Classé, Haut-Médoc, Bordeaux, France* After a period of mediocrity, 1994 saw a return to full, soft, chocolaty form, with some added muscle in the new millennium. Best years: 2010 09 08 **07 06 05 04 03 02 01 00 99 98 96 95**.

BRANCOTT *Auckland, Gisborne, Hawkes Bay and Marlborough, New Zealand* Owned since 2005 by French giant Pernod Ricard, which produces an estimated 40% of New Zealand's wine, the new regime has replaced the well-known Montana brand with Brancott. Estate bottlings of whites are generally good (Sauvignon Blanc★) and they are now one of the world's biggest producers of Pinot Noir★, and with each vintage the quality improves and the price stays fair. The Stoneleigh label has top-selling Marlborough Sauvignon Blanc★, Riesling★ and tasty Rapaura Series★. Waipara wines use the Camshorn label. Austere yet full-bodied Deutz Prestige Cuvée Brut★★, elegant Deutz Blanc de Blancs★★ and refreshing sparkling Sauvignon Blanc. See also CHURCH ROAD.

BRAND'S *Coonawarra, South Australia* Owned by MCWILLIAM'S, with 100ha (250 acres) of new vineyards as well as some ancient COONAWARRA vines planted in 1893. Ripe Laira Cabernet★ is increasingly attractive; Patron's Reserve★★ (Cabernet with Shiraz and Merlot) is excellent. Shiraz★ and opulent Stentiford's Reserve★★ (from 100-year-old vines) show how good Coonawarra Shiraz can be. Merlot★★ is among Australia's best examples. Best years: (reds) (2010) 09 08 **06 05 04 03 02 01 00 99 98 97 96**.

CH. BRANE-CANTENAC★ *Margaux AC, 2ème Cru Classé, Haut-Médoc, Bordeaux, France* After a drab period, Brane-Cantenac returned to form during the late 1990s when Henri Lurton took over the family property. He is making some lovely wines, particularly the 2000, 2005 and 2009, although don't expect flavours to be mainstream – 2002 and 03 are tasty but wild. Best years: 2010 09 08 **07 06 05 04 03 02 01 00 99 98 96 95 89**.

BRAUNEBERG *Mosel, Germany* Small village with 2 famous vineyard sites, Juffer and (especially) Juffer Sonnenuhr, whose wines have a honeyed richness and creaminess rare in the Mosel. Best producers: Bastgen, Fritz HAAG★★★, Willi Haag★, von Kesselstatt, Paulinshof★, M F RICHTER★★, SCHLOSS LIESER★★. Best years: (2011) 10 09 08 **07 06 05 04 02 01**.

BREAKY BOTTOM *Sussex, England* Small vineyard in the South Downs. Peter Hall is a quirky, passionate grower, making delicious sparkling wines★★, mainly Seyval Blanc, but from the 2007 vintage using increasing percentages of Chardonnay and Pinot Noir.

BREGANZE DOC *Veneto, Italy* This hilly zone, north-east of Verona, is a major source of the world's favourite 'Italian' (except it's not) grape variety, Pinot Grigio. The native Vespaiolo can produce racy, very dry, if sometimes acidic whites, still and sparkling, plus an amazing sweet wine called Torcolato. Main grapes for red wines include Pinot Nero and Cabernet. Main producers are MACULAN and the Cantina Beato Bartolomeo da Breganze. Best years: (reds) (2011) (10) 09 **08 07 06 04**.

GEORG BREUER *Rüdesheim, Rheingau, Germany* Intense dry Riesling from RÜDESHEIM Berg Schlossberg★★★, Berg Rottland★ and RAUENTHAL Nonnenberg★★. Also a remarkable Sekt★. Best years: (Berg Schlossberg) (2011) 10 09 08 **07 06 05 04 03 02 01 00**.

JEAN-MARC BROCARD *Chablis, Burgundy, France* Dynamic winemaker who has built up this 80ha (200-acre) domaine almost from scratch. The Premiers Crus (including Montée de Tonnerre★★, Montmains★★) and slow-evolving Grands Crus (les Clos★★★) are tremendous, as is the Chablis Vieilles Vignes★★. Basic Chablis is a little erratic just now. Brocard also produces a range of BOURGOGNE Blancs★ from different soil types. Now adopting an increasingly organic – and in some cases biodynamic – approach to his vineyards. Best years: (2011) 10 **09 08 07**.

BROKENWOOD *Hunter Valley, New South Wales, Australia* High profile winery; celebrated its 40th anniversary in 2010. Delicious traditional unoaked HUNTER Semillon★★ (ILR Reserve ★★★). Very good Shiraz★★; best wine is classic Hunter Graveyard Vineyard Shiraz★★★. Cricket Pitch reds and whites are cheerful, fruity ready-drinkers. The Indigo vineyard at BEECHWORTH is making increasingly attractive Shiraz★, Chardonnay, Viognier and Pinot Noir. Also excellent Forest Edge Chardonnay★★ from ORANGE. Best years: (Graveyard Vineyard Shiraz) (2011) 09 07 05 **04 03 02 00 99 98 96 94 93 91 90 89 86**.

BRONCO WINE CO. *California, USA* Maker of the Charles Shaw range of wines – known as 'Two-Buck Chuck' because of their $2 price tag. There's now a $3.99 organic line called Green Fin. Makes you wonder how? The company is run by Fred Franzia, grand-nephew of the late Ernest GALLO. He is California's biggest vineyard owner with 16,000ha (40,000 acres), marketing 20 million cases of wine under more than a dozen brands.

BROUILLY AC *Beaujolais, Burgundy, France* Largest of the BEAUJOLAIS Crus; at its best, the wine is soft, fruity, rich and brightly coloured. Best producers: DUBOEUF (Ch. de Nervers), H Fessy★, J-C Lapalu★★, A Michaud★, Point du Jour (Les Bruyères★), Ch. Thivin★. Best years: (2011) 10.

BROWN BROTHERS *North-East Victoria, Australia* Highly successful and energetic family winery, producing a huge range of varietal wines, which have improved significantly in recent years – they have been an Australian leader in introducing new varietals. Their sparkling wines have long been regarded as among Australia's finest, and so the inspired 2010 purchase of Tasmania's sizeable Tamar Ridge is scarcely surprising. Top-of-the-range Patricia wines (Cabernet★★, sparkling Pinot-Chardonnay★★, Noble Riesling★★) are Brown's best yet. Premium grapes are from cool King Valley, mountain-top Whitlands and HEATHCOTE (potentially ★★★ Shiraz).

BRÜNDLMAYER *Kamptal, Niederösterreich, Austria* Willi Bründlmayer makes wine in a variety of Austrian and international styles, but his dry Riesling (Alte Reben★★★, Lyra★★) from the great Zöbinger Heiligenstein vineyard and superb, ageworthy Grüner Veltliner (Ried Lamm★★★) are superlative; high alcohol is matched by stunning fruit and mineral flavours. Also excellent Chardonnay★★ and good Sekt★. Best years: (Heiligenstein Riesling) (2011) 10 09 **08 07 06 05 04 02 00**.

BRUNELLO DI MONTALCINO DOCG *Tuscany, Italy* Iconic, full but elegant red 'created' by BIONDI-SANTI in the late 19th century. The number of producers soared in the late 20th century as the price of the wine (and land) took off, but the 'Brunellogate' scandal of the early 21st century (some big-name producers were accused of blending French grapes in with what is supposed to be a 100% Sangiovese wine) put a damper on sales, especially in the US, Brunello's main market. Released 4 years or more after vintage. Best producers: Agostina Pieri★★, Altesino★ (Montosoli★★), BIONDI-SANTI★, Gianni Brunelli★★, Camigliano★★, Caparzo★ (La Casa★★), Casanova di Neri★★★, Casanuova delle Cerbaie★★, CASE BASSE★★★, Castelgiocondo★ (FRESCOBALDI), Centolani★ (Pietranera★★), Cerbaiona★★, Ciacci Piccolomini d'Aragona★★, Donatella Cinelli Colombini★, Col d'Orcia★★, COSTANTI★★, Fuligni★★, La Gerla★★, Greppone Mazzi★, Maurizio Lambardi★★, Lisini★★, Mastrojanni★★ (Schiena d'Asino★★★), Siro Pacenti★★★, Pian delle Vigne★★ (ANTINORI), Pian dell'Orino★★, Piancornello★★, Pieve Santa Restituta★★ (GAJA), La Poderina★, Poggio Antico★★, Poggio San Polo★★, il POGGIONE★★, Le Potazzine★★, Salvioni★★, Livio Sassetti-Pertimali★★, Talenti★★, La Togata★★, Valdicava★★, Villa Le Prata★★. Best years: (2011) (10) (09) (08) 07 **06 04 01 00 99 97 95 90 88 85**.

BUCELAS DOC *Lisboa, Portugal* A tiny but historic DOC. The wines are whites based on the Arinto grape (noted for its high acidity). For attractive, modern examples try Quinta da Murta or Quinta da Romeira (Morgado de Santa Catherina★).

BUGEY AC *France* In the hills between the Jura (see ARBOIS, CÔTES DU JURA) and SAVOIE regions. Mainly Chardonnay and Altesse (also known as Roussette) for whites; Gamay, Mondeuse, Pinot Noir and Poulsard for rosés and light reds. A speciality is Bugey-Cerdon, a semi-sweet pink sparkling wine made from Gamay and Poulsard in the *méthode ancestrale*. Best producers: Angelot, Bartucci, Charlin, Lingot-Martin, Monin, Peillot★, Renardat-Fâche, Rondeau.

VON BUHL *Deidesheim, Pfalz, Germany* Large estate, since 2005 under the same ownership as BASSERMANN-JORDAN. Top Rieslings now invariably ★★. Best years: (Grosses Gewächs Rieslings) (2011) 10 09 **08 07 06 05 04 01**.

BUITENVERWACHTING *Constantia WO, South Africa* Beautiful old property, part of the Cape's original CONSTANTIA wine farm. Best known for penetrating and zesty Sauvignon Blanc★; Husseys Vlei Sauvignon Blanc★★ is bigger, more pungent, but slower to develop. Also fruit-laden Chardonnay★ and classically-styled reds, headed by Christine★★, one of the Cape's most accurate BORDEAUX lookalikes. Exciting new experiments include G, a dry Gewürztraminer smoothed in older oak. Best years: (Christine) **2008 07 06 05 04 03 02 01 00**.

BULL'S BLOOD See BIKAVÉR.

GRANT BURGE *Barossa Valley, South Australia* A leading BAROSSA producer with extensive vineyard holdings. A wide range, including chocolaty Filsell Shiraz★, rich Meshach Shiraz★★, Cameron Vale Cabernet★, Shadrach Cabernet★, RHÔNE-style Holy Trinity★ (Grenache-Shiraz-Mourvèdre) and fresh Thorn Riesling★. Excellent-value Barossa range and hugely popular Barossa bubbly. Recent vintages have shown a welcome reduction in oak with the reds. Best years: (Meshach) (2010) (09) (08) 06 **05 04 02 99 98 96 95 94**.

BURGENLAND *Austria* 4 regions: Neusiedlersee, with red wines from the Zweigelt grape and sweet wines from the Seewinkel area; Neusiedlersee-Hügelland, famous for sweet wines, and now also big reds and fruity dry whites; Mittelburgenland and Südburgenland, for robust Blaufränkisch reds. Best producers: Paul Achs★, FEILER-ARTINGER★★★, Gesellmann★★, Gernot Heinrich★★, Juris★, Kerschbaum★, KOLLWENTZ★★★, KRACHER★★★, KRUTZLER★★, Helmut Lang★★, A & H Nittnaus★★, Opitz★, Pöckl★★, Prieler★, Schröck★, Ernst Triebaumer★★, Tschida★, UMATHUM★★, VELICH★★.

BURGUNDY See BOURGOGNE AC and pages 94–7.

BÜRKLIN-WOLF *Wachenheim, Pfalz, Germany* One of Germany's largest privately owned estates, with 86ha (212 acres) of vineyards in some exceptional sites in WACHENHEIM, FORST and Deidesheim. Biodynamic since 2005. Since the mid-1990s it has been in the first rank of the PFALZ'S producers. The powerful, spicy dry Rieslings are ★★ to ★★★. Best years: (Grosses Gewächs Rieslings) (2011) 10 09 **08 07 06 05 04 01**.

BURMESTER *Port DOC, Douro, Portugal* Shipper established in 1730: now owned by the Galician firm Sogevinus, which also owns Cálem, Barros and Kopke. Burmester vintage PORT has improved. As well as refined 10- and 20-year old tawnies★, there are some outstanding old colheitas★★ which extend back over 100 years. Also decent Late Bottled Vintage and oak-aged DOURO red, Casa Burmester. Gilberts is a range of ports aimed at younger drinkers. Best years: (Vintage) **2007 03 00 97 95 94**.

CLEMENS BUSCH *Pünderich, Mosel, Germany* The little-known village of Pünderich lies north-east of the Middle MOSEL and is blessed with one exceptional site: Marienburg. Busch has long made the most of steep grey slate soils. Initially known for powerful dry Rieslings★★, he has added exquisite nobly sweet Rieslings▲▲▲ to the range. Biodynamic since the late 2000s. Best years: (2011) 10 09 08 07 **06 05**.

TOMMASO BUSSOLA *Valpolicella DOC and Amarone/Recioto DOCG, Veneto, Italy* Tommaso Bussola's AMARONE Vigneto Alto★★★ combines elegance with stunning power; Amarone Classico TB★★ is close behind, and even the basic Amarone★ is a challenge to the palate. The Ripasso VALPOLICELLA Classico Superiore TB★★ is one of the best of its genre, and the RECIOTO TB★★★ is excellent. Best years: (2011) (10) 09 08 **07 06 05 04 03 01 00**.

VIGNERONS DE BUXY *Côte Chalonnaise, Burgundy, France* One of Burgundy's top co-operatives. The light, oak-aged BOURGOGNE Pinot Noir★ and the red and white Clos de Chenôves★, as well as the nutty white MONTAGNY★, are all good, reasonably priced, and best with 2–3 years' age. Look out also for separate single vineyard and single domaine bottlings.

BUZET AOP *South-West France* Plummy BORDEAUX-style red wines from Merlot and Cabernets Sauvignon and Franc – affordable, too. Whites are rarely exciting and there's very little rosé. Buzet co-op is successful but uninspiring, despite new management. Dom. du Pech★ is a quirky and biodynamic independent. Best years: (reds) (2011) **10 09 06 05**.

CA' DEL BOSCO *Franciacorta DOCG, Lombardy, Italy* Model estate, headed by Maurizio Zanella, making some of Italy's finest and most expensive international-style wines. Outstanding sparklers include FRANCIACORTA Brut★★, Dosage Zero★, Satèn★★ and Cuvée Annamaria Clementi★★★. Still wines include excellent Chardonnay★★★, Pinéro★★ (Pinot Noir) and BORDEAUX blend Maurizio Zanella★★★. Also a varietal Carmenère, Carmenero★, and occasional Merlot★.

CABERNET SAUVIGNON

Wine made from Cabernet Sauvignon in places like Australia, California, Chile, Bulgaria, even in parts of southern France, has become so popular that many people may not realize where it all started – and how Cabernet became the great, omnipresent red wine grape of the world.

WINE STYLES

Bordeaux Cabernet It all began in Bordeaux. With the exception of a lively bunch of Merlot-based beauties in St-Émilion and Pomerol, the greatest red Bordeaux wines are based on Cabernet Sauvignon, with varying amounts of Merlot, Cabernet Franc and possibly Petit Verdot blended in. The blending is necessary because by itself Cabernet makes such a strong, powerful, aggressive and assertive wine. Dark and tannic when young, the great Bordeaux wines need 10–20 years for the aggression to fade, the fruit becoming as sweet and perfumed as fresh blackcurrants, with a fragrance of cedarwood, of cigar boxes, mingling magically among the fruit. It is this character that has made red Bordeaux famous for at least two centuries.

Cabernet worldwide When winemakers in other parts of the world sought role models to try to improve their wines, most of them automatically thought of Bordeaux and chose Cabernet Sauvignon. It was lucky that they did, because not only is this variety easy to grow in almost all conditions – cool or warm, dry or damp – but that unstoppable personality always powers through. The cheaper wines are generally made to accentuate the blackcurrant fruit and the slightly earthy tannins. They are drinkable young, but able to age surprisingly well. The more ambitious wines are aged in oak barrels to enhance the tannin, and also to add spice and richness capable of developing over a decade or more. Sometimes the Cabernet is blended – usually with Merlot, sometimes with Cabernet Franc, and occasionally with other grapes: Shiraz in Australia, Sangiovese in Italy, Tempranillo in Spain, Carmenère in Chile.

Europe Many vineyards in southern France now make good, affordable Cabernet Sauvignon. In the Loire, Anjou's warmest sites produce well-structured examples in top years. Spain produces some good varietal Cabernets and blends, as does Portugal. Italy's red wine quality revolution was sparked off by the success of Cabernet in Tuscany, and all the leading regions now grow it – to the detriment, some say, of authenticity. Eastern Europe grows lots of Cabernet, but of widely varying quality, while the Eastern Mediterranean and North Africa are beginning to produce tasty examples.

New World There is a general move toward darker, denser, more serious Cabernets, even in countries like Chile and Australia, whose Cabernet triumphs have until now been based on gorgeous blackcurrant fruit. I hope they don't ditch too much of the fruit, but I have to say that a lot of these new contenders are excellent. Argentina is also pitching in with some powerful stuff, and South African Cabernets are showing better balance and ageworthiness. California's reputation was created by its strong, weighty Cabernets. It should be possible to exhibit power with balance, since thudding tannins, excess alcohol and low acid fruit defeat Cabernet's purpose. Some Napa producers are well aware of this and are creating marvellous wines of a gaudy, ferocious beauty, increasingly aided by judicious blending with other varieties. Other, more self-indulgent, producers need to be reminded: less is more.

BEST PRODUCERS

France

Bordeaux CALON-SÉGUR, COS D'ESTOURNEL, GRAND-PUY-LACOSTE, LAFITE-ROTHSCHILD, LATOUR, LÉOVILLE-BARTON, LÉOVILLE-LAS-CASES, LÉOVILLE-POYFERRÉ, LYNCH-BAGES, Ch. MARGAUX, MONTROSE, MOUTON-ROTHSCHILD, PICHON-LONGUEVILLE, PICHON-LONGUEVILLE-LALANDE, PONTET-CANET, RAUZAN-SEGLA; *South-West* TOUR DES GENDRES, VERDOTS; *Provence* TREVALLON

Other European Cabernets

Italy CA' DEL BOSCO, GAJA, ISOLE E OLENA, LAGEDER, MACULAN, ORNELLAIA, Castello dei RAMPOLLA, SAN LEONARDO, SASSICAIA, SOLAIA, TASCA D'ALMERITA, TUA RITA. *Spain* Blecua, Enate, Jané Ventura, TORRES.

New World Cabernets

Australia BALNAVES, CAPE MENTELLE, CULLEN, Forest Hill, Fraser Gallop, HARDYS (Thomas Hardy), HENSCHKE, HOUGHTON (Jack Mann, Gladstones), HOWARD PARK, LEEUWIN, MAJELLA, MOSS WOOD, PARKER COONAWARRA ESTATE, PENFOLDS (Bin 707), PENLEY ESTATE, SANDALFORD, VASSE FELIX (Heytesbury), VOYAGER, The Willows, WIRRA WIRRA, Woodlands, WYNNS, Zema.

New Zealand BABICH, CRAGGY RANGE, Esk Valley, MAN O'WAR, MATUA VALLEY, STONYRIDGE, TE MATA, Vidal, VILLA MARIA.

USA (California) ARAUJO, BERINGER, Bryant Family, Cakebread, CAYMUS, CHIMNEY ROCK, CORISON, DALLA VALLE, DIAMOND CREEK, DOMINUS, DUNN, Grace Family, HARLAN, HARTWELL, Ladera, LAUREL GLEN, Long Meadow Ranch, Peter MICHAEL, MINER, NEWTON, Oakville Ranch, PHELPS, RIDGE, ST SUPÉRY, SCREAMING EAGLE, SHAFER, SILVER OAK, SPOTTSWOODE, STAG'S LEAP, Terra Valentine, Titus, VIADER; *(Washington)* ANDREW WILL, CADENCE, CORLISS, DELILLE CELLARS, DUNHAM, Fidelitas, JANUIK, LEONETTI, QUILCEDA CREEK, Three Rivers, WOODWARD CANYON.

Chile ALMAVIVA, Altaïr, Aristos, CARMEN, CONCHA Y TORO, ERRÁZURIZ, HARAS DE PIRQUE, SANTA RITA, Miguel TORRES.

Argentina CATENA ZAPATA, COBOS, MENDEL, TERRAZAS DE LOS ANDES.

South Africa BEYERSKLOOF, BOEKEN-HOUTSKLOOF, BUITENVERWACHTING, De Toren, DE TRAFFORD, Neil Ellis, GRANGEHURST, KANONKOP, Le Riche, MEERLUST, RUSTENBERG, SAXENBURG, THELEMA, VERGELEGEN.

CABARDÈS AC *Languedoc, France* Next door to MINERVOIS. Cabernet Sauvignon and Merlot are allowed, as well as French Mediterranean varieties such as Syrah and Grenache. At best, full-bodied, chewy, rustically attractive – and attractively priced. Best producers: Cabrol★, Cazaban★, Font Juvenal, Jouclary, Pennautier★, Salitis★. Best years: (2011) **10 09 08 07 06 05.**

CABERNET D'ANJOU AC *Loire Valley, France* Rosé made from both Cabernets: generally medium-dry or semi-sweet. Rosé d'un Jour is an alternative vin de France rosé, a riposte to commercial wines, made by several rebellious growers led by Mark Angeli; it is picked overripe and not chaptalized. Drink young. Best producers: M Angeli/Sansonnière, Bergerie, de Clayou, Hautes-Ouches, OGEREAU, des Petites Grouas, Terrebrune.

CABERNET FRANC Cabernet Franc comes into its own in cool zones or areas where the soil is damp and heavy. It can have a leafy freshness linked to raw but tasty blackcurrant-raspberry fruit; lighter wines drink well slightly chilled. In France it thrives in the LOIRE VALLEY, where single varietal wines are the norm. It is blended with Cabernet Sauvignon and Merlot in BORDEAUX, especially ST-ÉMILION (AUSONE, CHEVAL BLANC) and POMEROL (LAFLEUR, VIEUX-CHÂTEAU-CERTAN). Moderately successful where not overproduced in northern Italy, especially ALTO ADIGE and FRIULI – although some plantings here have turned out to be Carmenère – and increasingly preferred to Cabernet Sauvignon in Tuscany (LE MACCHIOLE's Paleo Rosso is an outstanding example of pure Cabernet Franc). It is the red of choice for many winemakers in Canada and the eastern US, performing especially well in the FINGER LAKES and VIRGINIA. Experiments with Cabernet Franc in WASHINGTON STATE and on CALIFORNIA's North Coast show promise, and it's at last gaining some respect in NAPA VALLEY. There are also some good South African, Argentine, Brazilian, Chilean, Australian and Israeli examples.

CABERNET SAUVIGNON See pages 102–3.

CADENCE *Red Mountain AVA, Washington State, USA* A range of vineyard-specific reds. Tapteil Vineyard★★★, a powerful Cabernet Sauvignon-dominated blend, is the flagship; Ciel du Cheval Vineyard★★★ is more forward and juicy. Bel Canto★★, a Cabernet Franc-Merlot-dominant blend, and Camerata★★, based on Cabernet Sauvignon, are both from the estate Cara Mia Vineyard. Best years: (2010) **09 08 07 06 05.**

CADILLAC AC *Bordeaux, France* Sweet wine from the southern half of CADILLAC-CÔTES DE BORDEAUX. Styles vary from fresh, semi-sweet to richly botrytized. The wines have greatly improved in recent years. Drink young. Best producers: Fayau (Réserve★), Ch. du Juge, Manos★, Mémoires★, REYNON★. Best years: **2010 09 07 05 03 02 01 99 98.**

CADILLAC-CÔTES DE BORDEAUX AC *Bordeaux, France* Formerly (pre-2008) Premières Côtes de Bordeaux. Hilly region overlooking GRAVES and SAUTERNES across the Garonne. For a long time the region was best known for its sweet wines, but the juicy reds have now forged ahead. Usually delicious at 2–3 years old, but should last for 5–6 years. Best producers: Bauduc★, Carignan★, Chelivette, Clos Ste-Anne, Le Doyenné, Grand-Mouëys★, Lamothe-de-Haux, Lezongars★, Mont-Pérat★, Plaisance★, Puy-Bardens★, REYNON★, Ste-Marie (Alios★), Suau★. Best years: **2010 09 08 05.**

CAHORS AOP *South-West France* One of the oldest French wine regions and springboard for the worldwide development of the Malbec grape. All Cahors must contain at least 70% Malbec. Traditionally the wines are dark, austere but elegant, and have an unforgettable rich plum and tobacco flavour when ripe and well made. The best need aging, although many growers are now making softer wines for early drinking. Best producers: Armandière, la Caminade★, du CÈDRE★★, Clos la Coutale★, CLOS DE GAMOT★★, CLOS D'UN JOUR★, CLOS TRIGUEDINA★★, COSSE-MAISONNEUVE★★, Gaudou★, Lamartine★, Latuc, Mas del Périé★, la Reyne★, les Rigalets★. Best years: (2011) (10) (09) **06 05 04 01 98**.

CAIRANNE *Rhône Valley, France* The top village in the CÔTES DU RHÔNE-VILLAGES appellation, home of full, lively, herb-scented reds and solid, food-friendly whites. Best producers: Alary★★, Ameillaud★, Armand, Berthet-Rayne, Brusset★, Camille Cayran, les Grands Bois, les Hautes Cances★, ORATOIRE ST-MARTIN★★, Présidente★, Rabasse-Charavin★, M Richaud★★. Best years: (reds) (2011) **10 09 07 06 05**.

CALABRIA *Italy* Italy's poorest and most backward region. CIRÒ, Donnici, Savuto and Scavigna DOC reds from the native Gaglioppo grape, and whites from Greco, are much improved thanks to greater winemaking expertise. In a very restricted field the two leading producers remain Librandi – with reds Duca San Felice★ (Gaglioppo) and Magno Megonio★★, from once endangered Magliocco, and white Efeso★★ from Mantonico and Oduardi, with their excellent Scavigna Vigna Garrone★.

CALATAYUD DO *Aragón, Spain* Over 5000ha (12,500 acres) of old Grenache vines on schistose slopes in the mountains between Madrid and Zaragoza: this is a recipe for vinous success that for too long went ignored as local co-ops made mostly bulk wines. Now, a number of more ambitious Spanish and foreign winemakers are making juicy, herb-scented reds which show some depth. Best producers: Albada★, Ateca★, Escocés Volante★, Bodegas y Viñedos del Jalón★, Langa, San Alejandro★, San Gregorio★.

CALERA *San Benito, California, USA* A pace-setter for California Pinot Noir with 6 estate wines: Reed★★, Selleck★★, Jensen★★, Mills★★, Ryan★ and de Villiers – complex, fascinating and capable of aging. Mt Harlan Chardonnay★★ is excitingly original too. CENTRAL COAST Chardonnay★ and Pinot Noir★ are good value. Small amounts of Viognier★★ are succulent with sensuous fruit. Best years: (Pinot Noir) 2010 09 **08 07 06 05 04 03 02 01**; (Chardonnay) 2010 **09 08 07 06 05 04 03 02**.

CALIFORNIA *USA* California's importance is not simply in being the fourth largest wine producer in the world (behind France, Italy and Spain). Most of the revolutions in technology and style that have transformed the expectations and achievements of winemakers in every country of the world – including France – were born in the ambitions of a band of Californian winemakers during the 1960s and 70s. They challenged the old order, with its regulated, self-serving elitism, and democratized the world of fine wine, to the benefit of every wine drinker. Other countries, notably Australia, have now taken the lead, but California is still important. A few figures: there are around 216,506ha (535,000 acres) of wine grape vineyards, producing more than 20 million hectolitres (500 million gallons) of wine annually – about 90% of all wine made in the US. A large proportion (more than 75%) comes from the hot, inland CENTRAL VALLEY. See also CENTRAL COAST, MENDOCINO COUNTY, MONTEREY COUNTY, NAPA VALLEY, SAN LUIS OBISPO COUNTY, SANTA BARBARA COUNTY, SIERRA FOOTHILLS, SONOMA COUNTY.

CH. CALON-SÉGUR★★ *St-Estèphe AC, 3ème Cru Classé, Haut-Médoc, Bordeaux, France* Long considered one of ST-ESTÈPHE's leading châteaux, but in the mid-1980s the wines were not as good as they should have been. Vintages from the mid-1990s have been more impressive, with suppler, riper fruit and greater finesse since 2008. Now on top form. One for aging. Second wine: Marquis de Calon. Best years: 2010 09 08 **07** 06 **05** 04 03 02 01 00 98 96 95 90 89 86.

CAMEL VALLEY *Cornwall, England* Top-quality producers of both still and sparkling wines, using classic CHAMPAGNE grapes as well as English varieties. Best wines are Pinot-based sparklers★★ and their Pinot Noir Rosé Brut★★ regularly wins top awards against international opposition. Bacchus★ and Atlantic Dry★ still whites are fragrant and delightful.

CAMPANIA *Italy* Three regions – PUGLIA, SICILY and Campania – lead the revolution in Italy's south. Campania has made excellent progress in the white department, with characterful varietals from Greco, Fiano, Falanghina and several other native grapes. On the red side, other producers besides the venerable MASTROBERARDINO have begun to realize the potential of Campania's soil, climate and grapes, especially with the red Aglianico. The leading red wines are Montevetrano★★★ (Cabernet-Merlot-Aglianico) and Galardi's Terra di Lavoro★★★ (Aglianico-Piedirosso), but also look for top Aglianicos from Antonio Caggiano★★, De Conciliis★, Feudi di San Gregorio★★, Luigi Maffini★, Michele Moio★, Salvatore Molettieri★, Orazio Rillo★, San Paolo and co-operatives Cantina del Taburno★ and La Guardiense★. DOC(G)s of note are Falerno del Massico, Fiano di Avellino, Greco di Tufo, Ischia, TAURASI and Vesuvio.

CAMPO DE BORJA DO *Aragón, Spain* Located to the south-east of RIOJA and NAVARRA, Campo de Borja boasts that its native clones of Grenache are the finest in all of Spain. Best producers: Alto Moncayo★★, Aragonesas★, Borsao★, Pagos del Moncayo.

CAMPO VIEJO *Rioja DOCa, Rioja, Spain* The largest producer of RIOJA is owned by Pernod Ricard. Tempranillo is a good modern young Rioja, packed with fresh, pastilley fruit; there's also an unoaked, 100% Viura white Rioja. Reserva and Gran Reserva★ are reliably good. The elegant Alcorta Reserva (100% Tempranillo) is now made separately.

CANARY ISLANDS *Spain* The Canaries have a treasure trove of pre-phylloxera vines, and a total of 9 DOs. The sweet Malvasia from Lanzarote DO and La Palma DO is worth a try, and there are a couple of remarkable fresh dry whites; otherwise stick with the young reds. Best producers: El Grifo, Monje, Viña Norte, Tacande★, Tanajara★, Teneguía, Viñátigo★.

CANBERRA DISTRICT *New South Wales, Australia* Cool, high altitude (800m/2600ft) may sound good, but excessive cold and frost can be problematic. Even so, with global warming kicking in, the smart money is on Canberra really shining in the next decade or so. Lark Hill and Helm make exciting Riesling; Lark Hill and Brindabella Hills have some smart Cabernet blends; Mount Majura has classy Tempranillo; Collector, Nick O'Leary and Capital are making impressive Shiraz, and CLONAKILLA Shiraz is sublime. Best producers: Brindabella Hills★, Capital, CLONAKILLA★★, Collector★★, Doonkuna★, Helm★, Lake George★, Lark Hill★, Madew★, Mount Majura, Nick O'Leary.

DOM. CANET-VALETTE *St-Chinian AC, Languedoc, France* Marc Valette is
uncompromising in his quest to make great wine: organic cultivation,
low yields and traditional *pigeage* (foot-stomping) are just some of his
methods. The wines offer an enticingly rich expression of ST-CHINIAN's
grape varieties and clay-limestone soils. Cuvées include Une et Mille
Nuits (1001 Nights)★ and the elegant, complex Syrah-Mourvèdre
Maghani★★. Best years: (Maghani) 2008 07 **06 05 04**.

CANNONAU See GRENACHE NOIR.

CH. CANON★★ *St-Émilion Grand Cru AC, 1er Grand Cru Classé, Bordeaux, France*
Canon can make some of the richest, most concentrated ST-ÉMILIONs, but
was in decline before being bought in 1996 by Chanel (also owns RAUZAN-
SEGLA). Following extensive work on the vineyard and cellars it's now back
on succulent form. In good vintages the wine is tannic and rich at first
but is well worth aging for at least 10–15 years. Second wine: Clos
Canon. Best years: 2010 09 08 **07 06 05 04 03 02 01 00** 98 89 88.

CANON-FRONSAC AC *Bordeaux, France* This AC is the heart of the
FRONSAC region. The wines are quite sturdy when young but can age for
10 years or more. Best producers: Barrabaque (Prestige★), Cassagne Haut-
Canon (La Trufière★), Canon-Pécresse, la Fleur Cailleau, Gaby★, Grand-
Renouil★, Haut-Bellet, Haut-Mazeris, Moulin Pey-Labrie★★, Pavillon, Vrai
Canon Bouché★. Best years: 2010 09 08 **06 05 03 01 00** 98.

CH. CANON-LA-GAFFELIÈRE★★ *St-Émilion*
Grand Cru AC, Grand Cru Classé, Bordeaux, France
Owner Stephan von Neipperg has put this
property up with the elite of ST-ÉMILION.
The wines are firm, rich and concentrated.
He also owns Clos de l'Oratoire★★, Ch.
d'Aiguilhe★★ in CASTILLON-CÔTES DE
BORDEAUX, and the remarkable micro-cuvée
La Mondotte★★. Best years: 2010 09 08 **07
06 05 04 03 02 01 00** 99 98 96.

CH. CANTEMERLE★ *Haut-Médoc AC, 5ème Cru Classé, Bordeaux, France* With
La LAGUNE, the most southerly of the Crus Classés. The wines are delicate
in style and delightful in ripe vintages. Second wine: Les Allées de
Cantemerle. Best years: 2010 09 08 **07 06 05 04 03 01 00** 98 96 95.

CANTERBURY *South Island, New Zealand* The long, cool ripening season of
the arid central coast of South Island favours white varieties, particularly
Chardonnay, Pinot Gris, Sauvignon Blanc and Riesling, as well as Pinot Noir.
The northerly Waipara district produces Canterbury's most exciting wines,
especially Riesling and Pinot Noir. Best producers: Bell Hill★★, Greystone★,
Mountford★, Muddy Water★, Omihi Road, PEGASUS BAY★★, Waipara West★. Best
years: (Pinot Noir) (2011) **09 08 07 06 03 02**; (Riesling) (2011) **09 08 07 06**.

CAPE CHAMONIX *Franschhoek WO, South Africa* FRANSCHHOEK property, best
known for seamlessly oaked, long-lived Chardonnays: citrus/creamy
standard★; Reserve★★ with lengthy maturation. Barrel-fermented
Sauvignon Blanc Reserve★ shows both richness and cool minerals. Pure-
fruited, silky Pinot Noir Reserve★★ gains in complexity with every
vintage. Best years: (Chardonnay) **2011 10 09 08 07 06 05 04 03 02 01**.

CAPE MENTELLE *Margaret River, Western Australia* Leading MARGARET RIVER
winery, owned by LVMH, with Rob Mann providing winemaking
expertise. Superb cedary, gamy Cabernet★★★, impressive Shiraz★★ and

Chardonnay★★, tangy Semillon-Sauvignon Blanc★★ and wonderfully chewy Zinfandel★★. Wallcliffe wines include taut Sauvignon Blanc-Semillon★★ and concentrated Shiraz★★. New Wilyabrup Cabernet blend is rich and lush. All wines benefit from cellaring: whites up to 5 years, reds 8–15. Best years: (Cabernet Sauvignon) (2011) 10 09 08 07 **05 04 01**.

CAPE POINT VINEYARDS *Cape Point WO, South Africa* Duncan Savage crafts brilliant whites from this pioneering property influenced by bracing Atlantic breezes. Sauvignon Blanc (standard★, Reserve★★) is astonishing, ocean-fresh and original. Semillon contributes with Sauvignon Blanc in the barrel-fermented Isliedh★★★, which effortlessly combines power with subtlety and good aging potential. Also elegant Chardonnay★. The Splattered Toad range offers drinkability and value – despite the name. Best years: (whites) **2011 10 09** 08 07 06 05 04 03 02.

CAPEL VALE *Geographe, Western Australia* The Pratten family's winery sources fruit from its own vineyards in Geographe, Mount Barker, PEMBERTON and MARGARET RIVER. Cheap and cheerful Debut range includes velvety Merlot★ and easy-drinking Pinot Noir. There's an impressive Regional Series, and three single-vineyard wines: intense yet fine Whispering Hill Riesling★★, elegant, powerful Whispering Hill Shiraz★★, and structured 'The Scholar' Cabernet★ from youngish vines in Margaret River. Best years: (Whispering Hill Riesling) 2011 10 **09 08 07 06 04 03 02 01 00 98 97.**

CARIGNAN The dominant red grape in the south of France is responsible for much boring, cheap, harsh wine. But when made gently or by carbonic maceration, the wine can have delicious spicy fruit. Old vines are capable of dense, tarry, rich, impressive reds, as shown by increasing successes in southern France, California, Lebanon, Israel and especially in Chile's Maule Valley, where dry-grown old-vine Carignan is making a serious comeback. In South Africa it is mainly used in Rhône-style blends. Although initially a Spanish grape (as Cariñena or Mazuelo), it is not that widespread there, but is useful for adding colour and acidity in RIOJA and CATALUÑA, and has gained unexpected respect in PRIORAT (some stunning cuvées from TERROIR AL LIMIT). In south-west Sardinia it is behind some excellent wines, including Santadi's CARIGNANO DEL SULCIS.

CARIGNANO DEL SULCIS DOC *Sardinia, Italy* Carignano is capable of producing wines of quite startling quality, as is demonstrated mainly by the excellent Santadi co-op, whose Rocca Rubia★, a barrique-aged Riserva with rich, fleshy and chocolaty fruit, is one of Italy's best-value reds. Baie Rosse★★ is a step up; even better is the more structured and concentrated Terre Brune★★. Best years: (2011) (10) 09 **08 07 06**.

LOUIS CARILLON & FILS *Puligny-Montrachet, Côte de Beaune, Burgundy, France* Excellent family-owned estate, split from 2010 vintage between sons Jacques and François. The emphasis is on traditional, finely balanced whites of great concentration, rather than new oak. Look out for PULIGNY-MONTRACHET Premiers Crus les Referts★★, Champs Canet★★ and les Perrières★★★, and the tiny production of Bienvenues-BÂTARD-MONTRACHET★★★. Best years: (whites) (2011) 10 **09 08 07 06 05 04 02.**

CARIÑENA DO *Aragón, Spain* The largest DO of ARAGÓN, baking under the mercilessly hot sun in inland eastern Spain, Cariñena has traditionally been a land of cheap, deep red, alcoholic wines from the Garnacha grape. (Confusingly the Carignan grape is called Cariñena in Spain, but is practically absent from the Cariñena region.) Since the late 1990s, however, temperature-controlled fermentation has been working wonders with the Garnacha, and Tempranillo and international grape varieties like Cabernet Sauvignon have been planted widely. **Best producers: Añadas★, Monfil, San Valero (Monte Ducay, Don Mendo), Solar de Urbezo★, Victoria★.**

CARLEI *Victoria, Australia* Outstanding biodynamic producer, with Chardonnay★★ and Pinot Noir★ from YARRA VALLEY and Shiraz★★ from HEATHCOTE. Sergio Carlei's signature blends are Tre Rossi★ (Shiraz-Barbera-Nebbiolo), Tre Amici (Sangiovese-Cabernet-Merlot) and Tre Bianchi (Sauvignon with small amounts of Semillon and Chardonnay). Green Vineyards range for good, modestly priced regional varietals, including Yarra Chardonnay and Pinot Noir, and Heathcote Shiraz.

CARMEN *Maipo, Chile* Some of the best reds in MAIPO, including Gold Reserve★★, a limited release made with Carmen's oldest Cabernet Sauvignon vines, balanced, complex Wine Maker's Reserve★★ and Reserva Merlot★★. Organic Nativa range (Cabernet Sauvignon★★) is now made separately. **Best years: (reds) 2009 07 05 03 01 99.**

CARMENÈRE An important but forgotten constituent of BORDEAUX blends in the 19th century, historically known as Grande Vidure. Widely planted in Chile, where it thrives on the warm climate and long growing season, it is sold under its own name or mixed with Merlot and Cabernet to greatly improve the blend. When ripe and made with care, it has rich blackberry, plum and spice flavours, with an unexpected but delicious bunch of savoury characters – grilled meat, soy sauce, celery, coffee bean thrown in. A true original. Also found in northern Italy – where it has been confused with Cabernet Franc – Argentina and China. Being replanted experimentally in Bordeaux.

CARMIGNANO DOCG *Tuscany, Italy* Red wine from the west of Florence, renowned since the 16th century and revived in the 1970s by Capezzana. The blend (Sangiovese, plus 10–20% Cabernet) gives one of Tuscany's more refined wines and can be quite long-lived. Although Carmignano is DOCG, DOC applies to a lighter red Barco Reale, rosé Vin Ruspo and fine VIN SANTO. **Best producers: Ambra★ (Vigne Alte★★), Artimino★, Capezzana★★, Piaggia★★, Pratesi★, Villa di Trefiano★. Best years: (2011) (10) 09 08 07 06 04 03 02 01.**

CARNEROS AVA *California, USA* Hugging the northern edge of San Francisco Bay, Carneros includes parts of NAPA and SONOMA Counties. Cool and windswept, with morning fog off the Bay, it is a top temperate area, suitable for Chardonnay and Pinot Noir as table wine and as a base for sparkling wine. Merlot and Syrah can also be exciting. **Best producers: ACACIA★, Ancien★, Artesa★, Buena Vista★, Carneros Creek★, DOMAINE CARNEROS★, Gloria Ferrer, HdV★★, RAMEY★★, RASMUSSEN★★, SAINTSBURY★★, Tor (Las Madres Syrah★★), Truchard★★. Best years: (Pinot Noir) 2009 08 07 06 05 04 03 02 01.**

CARNUNTUM *Niederösterreich, Austria* 950ha (2350-acre) region south of the Danube and east of Vienna, with sturdy Grüner Veltliner and a strong red wine tradition. **Best producers: Artner★, Glatzer★, Markowitsch★, Netzl★, Pitnauer★.**

CASA MARÍN *San Antonio, Chile* Impressive whites, led by single-vineyard Sauvignon Blancs: Laurel★★ is powerful, full of mineral and intense chilli and fruit flavours, while Cipreses★★★ shows the influence of the Pacific

Ocean in its haunting citrus and stony aromas. Casona Vineyard Gewürztraminer★, Miramar Riesling★ and Estero Sauvignon Gris★★ are delightful too – and there's juicy, cool-climate Pinot Noir★ as well as the outstanding Miramar Syrah★★★.

CASA SILVA *Colchagua, Chile* Well-run family dynasty heavily involved in the local *huaso* (horsemen) culture and protectors of COLCHAGUA style, especially with Carmenère. Much development in sub-regions such as Los Lingues, Lolol and, more recently, Paredones near the coast, where they are making the crisp and salty 'Cool Coast' Sauvignon Blanc★. Best wines are Los Lingues Gran Reserva Carmenère★ and red Quinta Generación★.

CASABLANCA *Chile* Coastal valley with a cool-climate personality. Whites dominate, with best results from Sauvignon Blanc, Chardonnay and Gewürztraminer. That said, the Pinot Noir is some of Chile's best, and some producers (Casas del Bosque, Kingston, Loma Larga) make top-quality cool-climate Syrah. **Best producers:** Viña CASABLANCA★, CASAS DEL BOSQUE★, CONCHA Y TORO★, CONO SUR★★, EMILIANA★, ERRÁZURIZ★, Kingston★, LOMA LARGA★, MONTES★, Quintay★, Veramonte.

VIÑA CASABLANCA *Casablanca, Chile* Cool CASABLANCA vineyards are the source of some top wines under the Nimbus label – quince-edged Chardonnay★, rose- and lychee-filled Gewürztraminer★ and tangy, intense Sauvignon Blanc★ – as well as flagship red blend Neblus★. Inky-black Cabernet Sauvignon★ (from MAIPO) and scented Merlot★★ (from COLCHAGUA).

CASAS DEL BOSQUE *Casablanca, Chile* This winery has a special focus on Sauvignon Blanc★ (Reserva★★) with Kiwi winemaker Grant Phelps. The reds are good too, especially the red blend Estate Selection★, Gran Reserva Syrah★ and Pinot Noir★. **Best years:** (whites) **2011** 10 09 08 07.

CASE BASSE *Brunello di Montalcino DOCG, Tuscany, Italy* Gianfranco Soldera unblushingly proclaims his BRUNELLO DI MONTALCINO★★★ and Brunello di Montalcino Riserva★★★ wines to be the best of their genre and, maddeningly, he's pretty much right. A fanatical biodynamist, Soldera believes perfect grapes are all you need to make great wine. He ages his wines for a minimum of 5 years in large old (and hence neutral) oak barrels; the result is a wine of brilliant colour and an amazing intensity and complexity of perfumes. **Best years:** (2011) (10) (09) (08) (07) 06 **04 01 99 98 97 95 93 90 88 85**.

CH. LA CASENOVE *Côtes du Roussillon AC, Roussillon, France* Former photojournalist Étienne Montès, with consultant enologist Jean-Luc COLOMBO, has developed an impressive range, including a perfumed white vin de pays made from Macabeu and Torbat, MUSCAT DE RIVESALTES★, RIVESALTES★ and 2 predominantly Syrah CÔTES DU ROUSSILLON reds: La Garrigue★★ and Commandant François Jaubert★★. Drink the latter with at least 5 years' bottle age. **Best years:** (François Jaubert) **2007 06 05 04**.

CASSIS AC *Provence, France* A picturesque fishing port near Marseille. The white wine, based on Ugni Blanc and Clairette, is overpriced but can be good if fresh. Light red wine, and the rosé can be pleasant. **Best producers:** Bagnol★, Ch. Barbanau, Caillol, Clos Ste-Magdelaine★, la Ferme Blanche★, Fontblanche, Ch. de Fontcreuse, Mas de Boudard. **Best years:** (whites) 2011 **10 09 08**.

DOM. DU CASTEL *Judean Hills, Israel* The Grand Vin★ is complex and refined, made from 5 BORDEAUX varieties. Delightfully well-balanced barrel-fermented 'C' Blanc de Castel★ (100% Chardonnay) from Jerusalem vineyards. **Best years:** (reds) 2009 08 **07 06 05 04**.

CASTEL DEL MONTE DOC *Puglia, Italy* An arid, hilly zone, and an ideal habitat for the Uva di Troia grape, producing long-lived red wine of occasionally astonishing character. There is also varietal Aglianico, some good rosé, and the whites produced from international varieties are improving. Best producers: Rivera★, Santa Lucia, Tormaresca★ (ANTINORI), Torrevento★. Best years: (2011) (10) 09 **08 07 06 04 01**.

CASTELL *Castell,   Franken,   Germany* Since medieval times the Castell family has owned the town of that name and its vineyards. The dry Silvaners and Rieslings are exemplary, especially from Casteller Schlossberg★★. Occasional Powerful TBA★★ too. Best years: (2011) 10 09 **08 07 06 05**.

CASTILLA-LA MANCHA *Spain* The DOs of the central plateau, La MANCHA and VALDEPEÑAS, make white wines from the Airén grape, and some good reds from the Cencibel (Tempranillo). Fast-improving reds and whites from Méntrida DO, MANCHUELA DO, Ribera del Júcar DO, Almansa DO and Uclés DO, as well as several single-estate (*pago*) appellations. The most ambitious single-estate wines made here are those from MARQUES DE GRIÑON's Dominio de Valdepusa★ estate near the Tagus river; the Dehesa del Carrizal and Pago de Vallegarcía★ estates, both in the Toledo mountains; Manuel Manzaneque's Cabernet-based reds★ and Chardonnay★ from Sierra de Alcaraz in Albacete province; and Uribes Madero's elegant Calzadilla reds★ in Cuenca province. Manzaneque and Calzadilla now have their own DOs, Finca Élez and Pago de Calzadilla, as do the Dominio de Valdepusa and Dehesa del Carrizal. Other top wines are Ercavio★ and La Plazuela★★ from Toledo, Adaras from Almansa, Arrayán★ and Jiménez-Landi★★ from Méntrida.

CASTILLA Y LEÓN *Spain* This is Spain's harsh, high plateau, with long cold winters and hot summers (but always cool nights). A few rivers, notably the Duero, temper this climate and afford fine conditions for viticulture. After many decades of winemaking ignorance, with a few exceptions like VEGA SICILIA, the situation has changed radically for the better in all of the region's DOs. In addition to RIBERA DEL DUERO, RUEDA, BIERZO, Cigales and TORO, there is now a bevy of new appellations which were approved in 2009, in coincidence with new EU regulations, covering quality viticultural areas formerly lumped together under the vino de la tierra umbrella: Arlanza, Arribes, Tierra de León, Tierra del Vino de Zamora, Valles de Benavente and Valtiendas. Dynamic winemakers such as Telmo RODRIGUEZ and Mariano García (AALTO and MAURO) have won huge critical acclaim for the region.

CASTILLON-CÔTES DE BORDEAUX AC *Bordeaux, France* Area east of ST-ÉMILION that has surged in quality recently: part of Côtes de Bordeaux AC from 2008. The best wines are full and firm, yet have the lushness of St-Émilion without the high prices, though they are no longer cheap. Best producers: Dom. de l'A★★, Aiguilhe★★, Belcier, Cap-de-Faugères★, la Clarière Laithwaite★, Clos l'Eglise★, Clos Les Lunelles★ (from 2001), Clos Puy Arnaud★★, Côte-Montpezat, Joanin Bécot★, Montlandrie★, Poupille★, Robin★, Veyry★, Vieux-Ch.-Champs-de-Mars★. Best years: 2010 **09 08 06 05 04 03 02 01 00**.

CATALUÑA *Spain* Standards vary among the region's DOs. PENEDÈS, between Barcelona and Tarragona, has the greatest number of technically equipped wineries in Spain, but doesn't make a commensurate number of superior wines. In the south, mountainous PRIORAT has become a new icon for its heady, raging reds, and the neighbouring DOs of Montsant and Terra Alta are following in its footsteps, albeit more affordably, with top wines from Acùstic, Joan d'Anguera★, Celler de Capçanes★, Europvin Falset★, Venus La Universal★ (Montsant), Bàrbara Forés and Celler Piñol★★ (Terra Alta). Inland COSTERS DEL SEGRE and Conca de Barberá, with top natural wine producer Escoda Sanahuja★, make potentially excellent reds and whites. Up the coast, Alella makes attractive whites and Empordá-Costa Brava, by the French border, is improving noticeably. Cataluña also makes most of Spain's CAVA sparkling wines. The Catalunya DO allows (generally) inexpensive blends from anywhere in the region.

CATENA ZAPATA *Mendoza, Argentina* Owner Nicolás Catena and his daughter Laura continue to keep Catena Zapata to the forefront of the Argentine wine industry. Mid-priced wines under the Alamos label are hugely successful. The winery also owns some of the best vineyards in the best *terroirs* of MENDOZA, where fruit for creamy Alta Chardonnay★, superripe Alta Malbec★ and blackcurranty Alta Cabernet Sauvignon★★ is grown. Nicolás Catena Zapata★★ (sometimes ★★★) is a masterpiece based on Cabernet, and recent releases of Malbec Argentino★★ are thrilling. Very impressive single-vineyard Malbecs Adrianna★★ and Nicasia★★, and Chardonnay White Bones★★ from the Adrianna vineyard. Best years: (top reds) 2010 09 08 **07 06 05.**

SYLVAIN CATHIARD *Vosne-Romanée, Côte de Nuits, Burgundy, France* Sylvain Cathiard achieved international recognition in the late 1990s and has made brilliant wines, even in difficult vintages, since then. The stars are VOSNE-ROMANÉE Aux Malconsorts★★★ and ROMANÉE-ST-VIVANT★★★, but his village Vosne-Romanée★★ and NUITS-ST-GEORGES Aux Murgers★★ are excellent too. Best years: (2011) 10 09 08 **07 06** 05 **03 02 00 99.**

DOM. CAUHAPÉ *Jurançon AOP, South-West France*
Henri Ramonteu is the largest as well as the best-known producer in JURANÇON, his complex dry whites equalling in quality his more traditional sweet wines. Chant des Vignes★ and Geyser★ are unoaked JURANÇONS SEC; Sève d'Automne★ is skilfully oaked. Top wines are dry La Canopée★★, sweet Noblesse du Temps★★ and fabulous barrel-fermented Quintessence★★★. Best years: (sweet) **2010 07 05 04 03.**

DOM. DE CAUSSE MARINES *Gaillac AOP, South-West France* Patrice Lescarret makes eccentric but much admired GAILLAC wines: famously his splendid but expensive sweet wines★★ using the rare Ondenc grape, and a sparkler called Préambulles. Best years: 2010 09 **07 05 03.**

CAVA DO *Spain* Cava, the Catalan name for CHAMPAGNE-method fizz, is made throughout Spain, but most comes from CATALUÑA. Grapes are the local trio of Parellada, Macabeo and Xarel-lo, although some good Cavas in Cataluña as well as VALENCIA include Chardonnay and Pinot Noir in their blends. The best-value, fruitiest Cavas are generally the youngest, with no more than the minimum 9 months' aging, although top producers such as Gramona and Recaredo are developing ambitious, long-lived, Xarel-lo-based wines. The top Cavas are seldom seen abroad, since their prices are too close to those of Champagne to attract international customers. Best producers: Can Feixes, Can Ràfols dels Caus★, Castell de Vilarnau, Castellblanch, CODORNÍU★, FREIXENET, Gramona★★, Jané Ventura, Juvé y Camps, Marqués de Monistrol, Parxet★, RAÏMAT, Raventós i Blanc, Recaredo★★, Rovellats, Signat★, Agustí Torelló★, Dominio de la Vega.

CAYMUS VINEYARDS *Napa Valley AVA, California, USA* Caymus Cabernet Sauvignon★ is ripe, intense and generally tannic; it can be outstanding as a Special Selection★★★. Conundrum★ (sometimes ★★) is an exotic, full-flavoured white blend. Also successful MONTEREY Chardonnay under the Mer Soleil★ label. Best years: (Special Selection) 2009 08 **07 06 05 04 03 02 01 00 99 98 97 95 94 91 90.**

CAYUSE VINEYARDS *Walla Walla Valley AVA, Washington State, USA* Winemaker Christophe Baron has created a cult label here. His superb Viognier★★★ is crisp, floral and spicy, yet he is best known for his Syrahs. Using French clones, he farms a vineyard reminiscent of some in CHATEAUNEUF-DU-PAPE for its large stones. Vineyard-designated Syrahs include Cailloux★★, with a distinctive mineral flavour and chocolate depth, and En Cerise★★, with more cherry and raspberry flavour but equal richness. The Bionic Frog★★ sports a cartoon label but is a serious Syrah, reminding me of a northern RHÔNE version. Camaspelo★ is a fascinating Cabernet-based red. Best years: (Syrah) (2010) 09 **08 07 06.**

DOM. CAZES *Rivesaltes, Roussillon, France* The Cazes family produce outstanding MUSCAT DE RIVESALTES★★, RIVESALTES Tuilé★★ and superb RIVESALTES Aimé Cazes★★, and also a range of table wines. Soft red, white and rosé Le Canon du Maréchal★ are good, as are the CÔTES DU ROUSSILLON-VILLAGES Syrah-Grenache-Mourvèdre blends Ego★, Alter★ and Le Credo★★. Also intriguing white Libre Expression★ from Macabeo. Now part of Jeanjean group, but still family run.

CH. DU CÈDRE *Cahors AOP, South-West France* The brothers Verhaeghe lead the generation of modern CAHORS winemakers. Their wines are dark and richly textured, with a generous coating of chocolaty oak. Their entry-level Ch. du Cèdre★★ (formerly Le Prestige) is the most approachable; Le Cèdre, which is 100% Malbec, aged in new barrels for 20 months, and GC★, which is fermented in oak as well, need considerable aging. Also a tasty white IGP wine. Best years: (2011) (10) **06 04 03 01.**

CENCIBEL See TEMPRANILLO.

CENTRAL COAST AVA *California, USA* Huge AVA covering virtually every vineyard between San Francisco and Los Angeles, with a number of sub-AVAs such as SANTA CRUZ MOUNTAINS, Santa Ynez Valley, SANTA MARIA VALLEY and Santa Lucia Highlands in MONTEREY COUNTY. See also SAN LUIS OBISPO COUNTY, SANTA BARBARA COUNTY.

CENTRAL OTAGO *South Island, New Zealand* The only wine region in New Zealand with a continental rather than maritime climate. Technically the ripening season is long and cool, suiting Pinot Noir, Gewürztraminer, Chardonnay and Pinot Gris, but there are usually periods of considerable heat during the summer to intensify flavour. Long autumns have produced some excellent Rieslings. There are nearly 100 wineries and an explosion of plantings, both in good areas like Bannockburn and Lowburn, and in marginal zones. Latest expansion is to the Waitaki Valley in northern Otago. Best producers: Akarua★, Carrick★, Chard Farm★, FELTON ROAD★★★,

Gibbston Valley★, Kawarau Estate★, Mt Difficulty★★, Mount Edward★★, Mount Maude, Nevis Bluff, Peregrine★★, Pisa Range★, QUARTZ REEF★★, Rippon★★, Tarras★, Two Paddocks★, Wild Earth★. Best years: (Pinot Noir) 2010 **09 08 07 06 05 03 02**.

CENTRAL VALLEY *California, USA*   This vast area grows 75% of California's wine grapes, used mostly for cheaper wine, along with brandies and grape concentrate. It is a hot area, where irrigated vineyards tend to produce excess tonnages of grapes. It is often said that it is virtually impossible to produce exciting wine in the Central Valley, but in fact the climatic conditions in the northern half are not unlike those in many parts of Spain and southern France and, viewed overall, quality has improved in recent years. Vineyards in the increasingly good Lodi AVA have expanded to around 40,470ha (100,000 acres), making Lodi the value for money quality leader for a variety of styles – mainstreamers like Merlot and Cabernet, but more excitingly old-vine Zinfandel, Carignan, Cinsaut and outsiders like Petite Sirah, Tannat, Teroldego, Vermentino and much else besides. If California wants an experimental hothouse, Lodi could fit the bill. Other sub-regions with claims to quality include the Sacramento Delta area, and especially Clarksburg. **Best producers:** (Lodi) Ironstone★, Jessie's Grove★, McManis★, Mettler Family★, Michael-David★, Old Ghost★, RAVENSWOOD (Lodi★), Woodbridge/MONDAVI.

CENTRAL VALLEY *Chile*   (Bottles in Europe may have Valle Central on the label.) The heart of Chile's wine industry, and an appellation encompassing the valleys of MAIPO, RAPEL, CURICÓ and MAULE; most major producers are located here. The key factor determining mesoclimate differences is the distance relative to the Coastal Ranges and the Andes Mountains: the closer you get to the mountains, the cooler you are.

CENTRAL VICTORIA *Victoria, Australia*   This zone comprises the regions of BENDIGO, HEATHCOTE, Goulburn Valley and the cooler Strathbogie Ranges and Upper Goulburn. Central Victoria, with its mostly warm conditions, produces powerful and individual wines. The few wineries on the banks of the Goulburn River feature fine Shiraz and Marsanne; reds from the high country are rich but scented and dry, with Heathcote excelling for texture and taste; whites are delicate and scented. **Best producers:** Heathcote Estate★★★, Heathcote Winery★★, Jasper Hill★★★, Mitchelton★, Paul Osicka★, PONDALOWIE★, TAHBILK★, Wild Duck Creek★.

CÉRONS AC *Bordeaux, France*   Sweet, soft, mildly honeyed wine from the GRAVES region of Bordeaux – not quite as sweet as SAUTERNES and not so well known, nor so highly priced. Most producers now make dry wine under the Graves AC. **Best producers:** Ch. de Cérons★, Chantegrive★, Grand Enclos du Château de Cérons★, Haura, Seuil. Best years: 2010 **09 07 05 03 02 01 99 98 97 96 95**.

LA CETTO *Baja California, Mexico*   One of Mexico's most successful wineries; it relies on mists and cooling Pacific breezes to temper the heat of the Valle de Guadalupe in the northern part of Baja California. Italian Camillo Magoni makes ripe, fleshy Petite Sirah★, oak-aged Cabernet Sauvignon, Zinfandel and Nebbiolo. Chardonnay and Chenin Blanc lead the whites. Also good fizz.

CHABLAIS *Vaud, Switzerland*   A sub-region of the VAUD, south-east of Lake Geneva along the right bank of the Rhône. Most of the vineyards lie on the alluvial plains, but 2 villages, Yvorne and Aigle, have much steeper slopes. Most of the thirst-quenchingly dry whites are made from

Chasselas. The reds are from Pinot Noir, as is a rosé speciality, Oeil de Perdrix. Best producers: Badoux, la Baudelière, Conne, Dillet, J & P Testuz★.

CHABLIS AC *Burgundy, France* Chablis, lying closer to CHAMPAGNE than to
the COTE D'OR, is Burgundy's northernmost outpost. When not destroyed by frost or hail, the Chardonnay grape makes a crisp, dry white wine with a steely mineral fruit, which can be delicious. Several producers have taken to barrel-aging for their better wines, resulting in some full, toasty, positively rich dry whites. Others are intentionally producing a soft, creamy, early-drinking style, which is nice but not really typical Chablis. Outlying vineyards come under the Petit Chablis AC and these wines are becoming very good but should be drunk young. The better straight Chablis AC should be drunk at 2–4 years, while a good vintage of a leading Chablis Premier Cru may take 5 years to show its full potential. About a quarter of Chablis is designated as Premier Cru, the best vineyards on the rolling limestone slopes being Fourchaume, Mont de Milieu, Montmains, Montée de Tonnerre and Vaillons. Best producers: Barat★, J-C Bessin (Fourchaume★★), Billaud-Simon★ (Mont de Milieu★★), Pascal Bouchard★, A & F Boudin★★, J-M BROCARD★, la CHABLISIENNE★, Collet★, D Dampt★, V DAUVISSAT★★, Droin★, DROUHIN★, Durup★ (Montée de Tonnerre★★), N & G Fèvre★, W Fèvre★★, J-P Grossot (Côte de Troesme★★), LAROCHE★★, Long-Depaquit, Malandes (Côte de Léchêt★★), Louis Michel★★, de Moor★, Christian Moreau★★, Moreau-Naudet★, Picq (Vaucoupin★), Pinson★, RAVENEAU★★, les Temps Perdus, Vocoret★★. Best years: (Chablis Premier Cru) (2011) 10 **09 08 07 05 02 00**.

CHABLIS GRAND CRU AC *Burgundy, France* The 7 Grands Crus
(Bougros, les Preuses, Vaudésir, Grenouilles, Valmur, les Clos and les Blanchots) facing south-west across the town of Chablis are the heart of the Chablis vineyards. Oak barrel aging takes the edge off taut flavours, adding a rich warmth to these fine wines. Droin and Fèvre are the most enthusiastic users of new oak, but use it less than they used to. Never drink young: 5–10 years are needed before you can see why you spent your money. Best producers: J-C Bessin★★, Billaud-Simon★★, Pascal Bouchard★, J-M BROCARD★★, la CHABLISIENNE★★, V DAUVISSAT★★★, Droin★★, W Fèvre★★★, LAROCHE★★, Long-Depaquit★★, Louis Michel★★, Christian Moreau★★★, Moreau-Naudet★★, Pinson★★, RAVENEAU★★, Servin★, Vocoret★★. Best years: (2011) 10 09 08 07 **06** 05 **02 00** 99 98 96 95 90.

LA CHABLISIENNE *Chablis, Burgundy, France* Substantial and reliable co-op
producing nearly a third of all CHABLIS. The best are the oaky Grands Crus – especially les Preuses★★ and Grenouilles (sold as Ch. Grenouilles★★) – but the basic unoaked Chablis★, the Vieilles Vignes★★ and the numerous Premiers Crus★ are good, as is the red BOURGOGNE Épineuil. Best years: (whites) (2011) 10 **09 08 07 06 05**.

CHADDSFORD WINERY *Pennsylvania, USA* This winery has gained a
following across the US since its founding in 1982. Winemaker Eric Miller uses primarily Cabernet Sauvignon and Merlot, both as varietals and for red blend Merican; he also uses Sangiovese in Due Rossi red blend and makes a juicy picnic red from Chambourcin. Chardonnays★ can be powerful and elegant.

CHAMBERS *Rutherglen, Victoria, Australia* Legendary family winery making
sheer nectar in the form of Muscat and Muscadelle (Tokay). The secret of success is their ability to draw on ancient stocks put down in wood by earlier generations. The Grand★★ and Rare★★★ blends are national treasures. Cabernet and Shiraz table wines are good.

CHAMPAGNE AC

Champagne, France

 The Champagne region produces the most celebrated sparkling wines in the world. It is the most northerly AC in France – a place where (even with the advent of global warming) grapes struggle to ripen fully, but provide the perfect base wine to make fizz. Champagne is divided into 5 distinct areas – the best are the Montagne de Reims, where the Pinot Noir grape performs brilliantly, and the Chardonnay-dominated Côte des Blancs, south of Épernay. In addition to Chardonnay and Pinot Noir, the other main grape permitted for the production of Champagne is Pinot Meunier.

The wines undergo a second fermentation in the bottle, producing carbon dioxide which dissolves in the wine under pressure. Through this method Champagne acquires its crisp, long-lasting bubbles and a distinctive yeasty, toasty dimension to its flavour, becoming one of the most delightfully exhilarating wines of all.

That's the theory anyway, and for 150 years or so the Champenois have persuaded us that their product is second to none. It can be, too, except when it is released too young or sweetened to cover up a sour unripeness. When that periodically happens you know that, once again, the powers of marketing have triumphed over the wisdom and skills of the winemaker. But Champagne expertise now turns out excellent fizz all around the globe – especially in California, Australia, New Zealand and England. With a recession weakening demand, there has never been a better time for Champagne producers to remind us their supreme marketing is matched by excellent quality.

The Champagne trade is dominated by large companies or houses, called négociants-manipulants, recognized by the letters NM on the label. The récoltants-manipulants (RM) are growers who make their own wine, and they are becoming increasingly important for drinkers seeking characterful Champagne.

STYLES OF CHAMPAGNE

Non-vintage Most Champagne is a blend of 2 or more vintages. Quality varies enormously, depending on who has made the wine and how long it has been aged. Brut is a dry, but rarely bone-dry, style. More completely dry styles – called things like Brut Zéro, Brut Sauvage or Extra Brut – are appearing and tasting good, primarily because climate change is providing riper grapes that don't need sugar to hide their rawness. Strangely, Extra Dry denotes a style less dry than Brut.

Vintage Denotes Champagne made with grapes from a single harvest. As a rule, it is made only in the best years, but far too many mediocre years were declared in the 1990s.

Blanc de Blancs A lighter, and at best highly elegant, style of Champagne made solely from the Chardonnay grape.

Blanc de Noirs White Champagne made entirely from black grapes, either Pinot Noir, Pinot Meunier, or a combination of the two.

Rosé Pink Champagne, made either from black grapes or (more usually) by mixing a little still red wine into white Champagne.

De luxe cuvée In theory, the finest Champagne and certainly always the most expensive, residing in the fanciest bottles.

See also CHAMPAGNE ROSE; and individual producers.

BEST YEARS
2007 04 **02 99 98 96 95 90 89 88 85 82**

BEST PRODUCERS

Houses BILLECART-SALMON, BOLLINGER, Cattier, Delamotte, DEUTZ, Drappier, DUVAL-LEROY, GOSSET, Alfred GRATIEN, Charles HEIDSIECK, HENRIOT, JACQUESSON, KRUG, LANSON, LAURENT-PERRIER, Bruno PAILLARD, Joseph PERRIER, PERRIER-JOUET, PHILIPPONNAT, PIPER-HEIDSIECK, POL ROGER, POMMERY, Louis ROEDERER, RUINART, Salon, TAITTINGER, Thienot, VEUVE CLICQUOT.

Growers Agrapart & Fils, Michel Arnould, Paul Bara, Barnaut, Beaufort, Bérèche & Fils, Franck Bonville, Francis Boulard, Roger Brun, Claude Cazals, Chartogne-Taillet, Dehours, Paul Déthune, Diebolt-Vallois, Egly-Ouriet, René Geoffroy, Gimonnet, Henri Giraud, H Goutorbe, André Jacquart, Benoît Lahaye, Larmandier, Larmandier-Bernier, Maillart, Margaine, Serge Mathieu, Moncuit, Franck Pascal, Jérôme Prévost, Alain Robert, Selosse, Tarlant, G Tribaut, Vilmart.

Co-ops Beaumont des Crayères, H Blin, Nicolas Feuillatte, Jacquart, Mailly, Le Mesnil, Union Champagne.

De luxe cuvées Belle Époque (PERRIER-JOUET), N-F Billecart (BILLECART-SALMON), Blanc de Millénaires (Charles HEIDSIECK), Celebris (GOSSET), Clos des Goisses (PHILIPPONNAT), Clos de Mesnil (KRUG), Comtes de Champagne (TAITTINGER), Cristal (Louis ROEDERER), Dom Pérignon (MOËT & CHANDON), Dom Ruinart (RUINART), Femme (DUVAL-LEROY) Grand Siècle (LAURENT-PERRIER), Grande Dame (VEUVE CLICQUOT), Josephine (Joseph PERRIER), Noble Cuvée (LANSON), RD (BOLLINGER), Sir Winston Churchill (POL ROGER), William Deutz (DEUTZ).

117

CHAMBERTIN AC *Grand Cru, Côte de Nuits, Burgundy, France* The village of GEVREY-CHAMBERTIN, the largest CÔTE DE NUITS commune, has no fewer than 9 Grands Crus (Chambertin, Chambertin-Clos-de-Bèze, Chapelle-Chambertin, Charmes-Chambertin, Griotte-Chambertin, Latricières-Chambertin, Mazis-Chambertin, Ruchottes-Chambertin and the rarely seen Mazoyères-Chambertin), which can produce some of Burgundy's greatest and most intense red wine. Its rough-hewn fruit, seeming to war with fragrant perfumes for its first few years, creates remarkable flavours as the wine ages. Chambertin and Chambertin-Clos-de-Bèze are neighbours on the slope above the village and the two greatest sites, but overproduction is a recurrent problem with some producers. Best producers: (Chambertin) LEROY★★★, MORTET★★★, J Prieur★★, Rossignol-Trapet★★★, ROUSSEAU★★★, Trapet★★★; (Clos de Bèze) BOUCHARD PÈRE & FILS★★, CLAIR★★★, Damoy★★★, FAIVELEY★★★, F Magnien★★, ROUSSEAU★★★; (other Grands Crus) Bachelet★★, Bernstein★★, Bize★★, Confuron-Cotetidot★★, DROUHIN★★, Dugat★★, Dugat-Py★★, FAIVELEY★★, J-M Fourrier★★, HOSPICES DE BEAUNE★, LEROY★★, T LIGER-BELAIR★★, Maume★★, MUGNERET-GIBOURG★★, Perrot-Minot★★, Rossignol-Trapet★★, Roty★★, ROUMIER★★, ROUSSEAU★★, Trapet★★, Tremblay★★; VOUGERAIE★★. Best years: (2011) 10 09 08 07 06 05 03 **02 01 00** 99 98 96 95 93 90.

CHAMBOLLE-MUSIGNY AC *Côte de Nuits, Burgundy, France* AC with the potential to produce the most fragrant, perfumed red Burgundy when in good hands – and, encouragingly, standards in the village are high. More young producers are now bottling their own wines. Best producers: Amiot-Servelle★, G Barthod★★, Digioia-Royer★, DROUHIN★★, DUJAC★★, Felletig★, R Groffier★★, Hudelot-Baillet★, Hudelot-Noëllat★, JADOT★★, Dom. LEROY★★, F Magnien★, J-F MUGNIER★★, RION★★, ROUMIER★★, Sigaut★, de VOGÜÉ★★. Best years: (2011) 10 09 **08** 07 05 **03** 02 01 00 99 98 96 95 93 90.

CHAMPAGNE See pages 116–17.

CHAMPAGNE ROSÉ *Champagne AC, France* Good pink CHAMPAGNE – usually a little weightier than white – has a delicious fragrance of cherries and raspberries. The top wines can age well, but most rosé Champagne should be drunk on release, with youth to the fore. Best producers: (vintage) BILLECART-SALMON★★, BOLLINGER★★, GOSSET★★, Charles HEIDSIECK★★, JACQUESSON★★, LAURENT-PERRIER (Grand Siècle Alexandra★★★), MOËT & CHANDON★★ (Dom Pérignon★★), PERRIER-JOUET (Belle Époque★), POL ROGER★★, POMMERY (Louise★★), Louis ROEDERER★★ (Cristal★★★), RUINART (Dom Ruinart★★), TAITTINGER (Comtes de Champagne★★), VEUVE CLICQUOT★★ (Grande Dame★★★); (non-vintage) Paul Bara★, E Barnaut★★, Beaumont des Crayères★, BILLECART-SALMON★★, Chanoine★, Drappier★, Egly-Ouriet★★, Henri Giraud★, Jacquart★, KRUG★★, LANSON★, LAURENT-PERRIER★, MOËT & CHANDON, RUINART★, TAITTINGER, Thienot★, Vilmart★. Best years: 2007 05 04 03 **02 00** 99 98 96 95 90 89 88 85 82. See also pages 116–17.

CHANDON DE BRIAILLES *Savigny-lès-Beaune, Côte de Beaune, Burgundy, France* François de Nicolay and his sister Claude produce old-fashioned, savoury reds, notably PERNAND-VERGELESSES★ (Premier Cru Île des Vergelesses★★) and CORTON★★, and tasty whites from Pernand-Vergelesses★ and Corton★★. Best years: (reds) (2011) 10 09 **07 06** 05 03 02 99.

CHANNING DAUGHTERS *Long Island, New York State, USA* Boutique winery in LONG ISLAND's Hamptons AVA that uses small lots from mature vineyards to produce exciting wines, including a racy Sauvignon Blanc★, Muscat-based Sylvanus★ and a juicy Blaufränkisch★. Newer plantings include unusual reds such as Teroldego, Lagrein and Refosco.

CHAPEL DOWN *Kent, England* Important UK winery, producing around 500,000 bottles a year. Most grapes are grown under contract, although 30ha (74 acres) of Chardonnay and Pinot Noir were planted in 2008 and are now producing. Good to very good wines, especially non-vintage Chapel Down Brut, sparkling English Rosé★★, vintage Pinot Reserve★, and Bacchus★ and Rosé still wines. Best years: (sparkling) **2007 06 05**.

CHAPEL HILL *McLaren Vale, South Australia* Chief winemaker Michael Fragos's efforts and some exceptional vintages have added a further dimension to the powerful, classy reds of Chapel Hill. The Cabernet Sauvignon★★ and Shiraz★★ are from mature MCLAREN VALE vines; The Vicar★★ is a top reserve Shiraz. Good Bush Vine Grenache★, Chardonnay★ and fascinating, bone-dry, honey-scented Verdelho★★, as well as bright, lively Savagnin★. The Il Vescovo range impresses, especially the Tempranillo and Sangiovese★. Best years: (Shiraz) (2010) 08 06 05 04 02 01 98 97 96 95 94 93 91.

CHAPELLE-CHAMBERTIN AC See CHAMBERTIN AC.

M CHAPOUTIER *Rhône Valley, France* The house of Chapoutier is a big mover in the world of biodynamic viticulture, and is producing serious, exciting wines. The red HERMITAGE la Sizeranne★ and special plot-specific Ermitages (les Greffieux★★, l'Ermite★★★, le Méal★★★, le Pavillon★★★), rich white Hermitage (de l'Orée★★, l'Ermite★★★ and Vin de Paille★★), CÔTE-RÔTIE La Mordorée★, CROZES-HERMITAGE les Varonniers★, ST-JOSEPH les Granits★★ (red and white) and CHÂTEAUNEUF-DU-PAPE Barbe Rac★ and Croix de Bois★ are all good, and have recently been more *terroir*-specific. Good white ST-PÉRAY Les Tanneurs★ and CONDRIEU Coteau de Chery★★. Large-volume, lively Crozes-Hermitage les Meysonniers and CÔTES DU RHÔNE Belleruche★ are good value. Also BANYULS, CÔTES DU ROUSSILLON-VILLAGES, ALSACE and Australian joint ventures. Best years: (la Sizeranne) (2011) 10 09 07 06 05 04 03 01 00 99 98 95 94 91 90 89 88.

CHARDONNAY See pages 120–21.

CHARMES-CHAMBERTIN AC See CHAMBERTIN AC.

CHASSAGNE-MONTRACHET AC *Côte de Beaune, Burgundy, France* Some of Burgundy's greatest white wine vineyards (part of le MONTRACHET and BÂTARD-MONTRACHET, all of Criots-Bâtard-Montrachet) are within the village boundary. The white Chassagne Premiers Crus are not as well known, but can offer nutty, toasty wines, especially if aged for 4–8 years; Blanchots Dessus, Caillerets, Romanée, Grandes Ruchottes and Morgeots are among the best. Ordinary white Chassagne-Montrachet is usually enjoyable; the red is a little earthy, peppery and plummy and can be an acquired taste. Best Premiers Crus for reds include Clos de la Boudriotte, Clos St-Jean and Clos de la Chapelle. Best producers: (whites) Blain-Gagnard★★, Coffinet-Duvernay★, B COLIN★, M COLIN★★, P COLIN★, P-Y COLIN-MOREY★★, J-N GAGNARD★★, V GIRARDIN★★, H Lamy★, B Moreau, M MOREY★★, T MOREY★★, V MOREY★★, M Niellon★★, J & J-M Pillot★★, P Pillot★, RAMONET★★; (reds) V GIRARDIN★★, B Moreau★, V MOREY★★, RAMONET★★. Best years: (whites) (2011) 09 08 07 06 05 02 00 99; (reds) (2011) 09 08 07 06 05 03 02 99.

CHASSELAS Chasselas is considered a table grape worldwide. Only in BADEN (where it is called Gutedel), Switzerland (as FENDANT) and SAVOIE is it thought to make decent light, dry wines with a slight prickle. A few Swiss examples, notably from CHABLAIS and Dézaley, rise above this.

CHARDONNAY

Chardonnay is at a real crossroads. From being lauded as the world's greatest white grape, it has suffered an astonishing fall from grace; so much so that I have conducted tastings where no one admitted to liking Chardonnay. Dear oh dear. It is still one of the world's star grapes, as numerous examples from Burgundy, Calfornia, Australia, South Africa, New Zealand and Chile demonstrate. But the world has suffered an avalanche of cheap sugary junk sadly bearing the name Chardonnay, which has massacred Chardonnay's reputation, especially among the next generation of wine enthusiasts. There is now a move toward more balanced, less oaky and even oak-free Chardonnay at all levels, from cheap to expensive, but too much commercial Chardonnay is still lifeless and flat. Luckily, excellent affordable Chardonnays are starting to appear in southern France and the New World, and at higher levels the wines are increasingly elegant and irresistible. But the consumer has yet to be convinced. Courage! Quality will out in the end.

WINE STYLES
Using oak The reason for Chardonnay's wonderful versatility lies in its susceptibility to the winemaker's aspirations and skills. The most important manipulation is the use of the oak barrel for fermenting and aging the wine. Chardonnay is the grape of the great white Burgundies and these are fermented and matured on their creamy lees in oak (not necessarily new oak); the effect is to give a marvellous round, nutty richness to a wine that is yet savoury and dry.

The New World winemakers sought to emulate the great Burgundies, planting Chardonnay and employing thousands of oak barrels (mostly new), and their success has caused winemakers everywhere else to see Chardonnay as the perfect variety – easy to grow, easy to turn into wine and easy to sell to an adoring public. But, as in all things, familiarity can breed contempt.

France Although a relatively neutral variety if left alone (this is what makes it so suitable as a base wine for top-quality Champagne-method sparkling wine), the grape can ripen in a surprising range of conditions, developing a subtle gradation of flavours going from the sharp apple-core greenness of Chardonnay grown in Champagne or the Loire Valley, through the exciting, bone-dry yet succulent flavours of white Burgundy, to a round, tropical flavour in Languedoc-Roussillon.

Other regions The most significant move currently is to reduce oak influence to the bare minimum or, indeed, none. Italy produces Chardonnay that can be bone dry and lean, or fat, spicy and lush. Spain does much the same. California and Australia virtually created their reputations on great, viscous, almost syrupy, tropical fruits and spice-flavoured Chardonnays, but both are re-focusing on top-quality full-bodied, oatmealy styles or unoaked versions. Some of the best New World Chardonnays, dry but ripe, fresh and subtly oaked, or fruit-led and unoaked, are coming from South Africa. New Zealand is producing beautifully balanced Chardonnays, their fragrant fruit only subtly oaked, while Chile and Argentina, in their different ways, have rapidly learned how to make fine Chardonnay, oaked and unoaked. Add Germany, Austria, Canada, New York State, Oregon, Greece, Portugal, Croatia, Slovenia, Moldova, Romania, England, Belgium, even China, and you'll see it can perform almost anywhere.

BEST PRODUCERS

France *Chablis* Billaud-Simon, DAUVISSAT, Droin, Fèvre, Louis Michel, C Moreau, RAVENEAU; *Côte d'Or* M Ampeau, H Boillot, J-M Boillot, Bonneau du Martray, BOUCHARD, CARILLON, COCHE-DURY, M COLIN, DROUHIN, A Ente, J-P Fichet, J-N GAGNARD, V GIRARDIN, JADOT, A Jobard, LAFON, H Lamy, Dom. LEFLAIVE, MOREY, M Niellon, RAMONET, ROULOT, SAUZET; *Mâconnais* D & M Barraud, Bret, Guffens-Heynen/VERGET, O Merlin, Saumaize-Michelin, J Thévenet.

Other European Chardonnays *Austria* BRÜNDLMAYER, KOLLWENTZ, TEMENT, VELICH, WIENINGER; *Germany* HUBER, Johner, REBHOLZ, WITTMANN; *Italy* BELLAVISTA, CA' DEL BOSCO, GAJA, ISOLE E OLENA, LAGEDER, Lis Neris, Castello della Sala (Cervaro), TIEFEN-BRUNNER (Linticlarus), Vie di Romans; *Spain* CHIVITE, ENATE, Muñoz, TORRES.

New World Chardonnays *Australia* BANNOCKBURN, Bindi (Quartz), Brookland Valley, CAPE MENTELLE, Chapman Grove (Atticus), COLDSTREAM HILLS (Reserve), CULLEN, Curly Flat, GIACONDA, GROSSET, HOWARD PARK, LEEUWIN, Marchand & Burch, Moorooduc, OAKRIDGE (864), PENFOLDS, PIERRO, Savaterre, SHAW & SMITH, TAPA-NAPPA, TARRAWARRA, TYRRELL'S, VASSE FELIX, VOYAGER, Woodlands, Yabby Lake.

New Zealand ATA RANGI, BABICH, Bell Hill, BRANCOTT, CHURCH ROAD, CLOUDY BAY, CRAGGY RANGE, DRY RIVER, Escarpment, FELTON ROAD, FROMM, KUMEU RIVER, MATUA VALLEY, MORTON ESTATE, NEUDORF, PALLISER, PEGASUS BAY, Peregrine, SAINT CLAIR, SERESIN, TE MATA, TRINITY HILL, VAVASOUR, Vidal.

USA ARROWOOD, AU BON CLIMAT, CALERA, CHATEAU ST JEAN, DOMAINE DROUHIN OREGON, DOMAINE SERENE, DUTTON GOLDFIELD, EVENING LAND, Gary FARRELL, FLOWERS, HdV, IRON HORSE, KISTLER, Littorai, MARCASSIN, MATANZAS CREEK, MERRYVALE, Peter MICHAEL, RAMEY, RIDGE, SAINTSBURY, SANFORD, SHAFER, STEELE, STONY HILL, TALBOTT.

Canada Le CLOS JORDANNE, Flat Rock, TAWSE.

South Africa ATARAXIA, BOUCHARD FINLAYSON, CAPE CHAMONIX, Neil ELLIS, HAMILTON RUSSELL, JORDAN, MULDERBOSCH, THELEMA, VERGELEGEN.

Chile, Argentina Aquitania (Sol de Sol), CATENA, Clos des Fous, COBOS, CONCHA Y TORO, DE MARTINO, ERRÁZURIZ, LEYDA, Maycas del Limarí, MONTES, TABALÍ.

121

CH. CHASSE-SPLEEN★ *Moulis AC, Haut-Médoc, Bordeaux, France* Chasse-Spleen is not a Classed Growth – but during the 1980s it built a tremendous reputation for ripe, concentrated and powerful wines under the late proprietor, Bernadette Villars. The château has been run by Villars' daughter Céline since 2000, and recent vintages are starting to show the form of the old days. Second wine: l'Ermitage de Chasse-Spleen. Best years: 2010 09 08 **07** 06 05 04 03 02 01 00 99 96.

CHÂTEAU-CHALON AC *Jura, France* The most prized – and pricey – *vin jaune*. But beware – the flavour will shock your taste buds like no other French wine. Made from the Savagnin grape and aged like sherry under a yeast *flor*, but in old barrels, it is not released until at least 6 years after the vintage and can be kept for decades. Best producers: Baud★, Berthet-Bondet★★, Bourdy★, Butin★★, J-C Crédoz★, J Macle★★, F Mossu★, A & M Tissot★. Best years: (2005) 04 **03** 02 00 99 98 97 96 95 93 92 90 89.

CHÂTEAU-GRILLET AC★★ *Rhône Valley, France* This rare and expensive RHÔNE white from a 3.4ha (8-acre) terraced amphitheatre vineyard, made from Viognier and aged in young oak, has magic wisps of orchard fruit and harvest bloom when young, but is best drunk after 5 years. More reserved than CONDRIEU, and recently much improved. Now owned by Ch. LATOUR. Best years: (2011) 10 09 **08** 07 06 05 04 03 01 00 98 95.

CHATEAU MONTELENA *Napa Valley AVA, California, USA* NAPA winery producing classic California Chardonnay★★ and an Estate Cabernet★★ that are impressive, if slow to develop. The Napa Valley Cabernet★ and Zinfandel are gentle and delightful. Best years: (Chardonnay) (2010) **09** 08 **07** 06 05 04 03 02 01; (Cabernet) 2008 07 06 05 03 02 01 00 99 98 91 90.

CHATEAU MUSAR *Ghazir, Lebanon* Founded in the 1930s. Owner Serge Hochar is now handing over to the next generation. The legendary Ch. Musar★ comes from an unlikely blend of Cabernet Sauvignon, old-vine Carignan and Cinsaut. A wine of real, if wildly exotic, character, with sweet dried fruits and incredible aging potential: the style oscillates between classic Bordeaux and spicy Rhône but doesn't really resemble either. An absolute original gem to some, but to others passé. White Ch. Musar★ is made from indigenous Obaideh (like Chardonnay) and Merwah (similar to Semillon). Hochar Père & Fils and the younger Musar Cuvée are less complex, more fruit-forward alternatives. Best years: (red) 2004 03 02 **00 99** 98 97 95 94 91 88.

CHATEAU ST JEAN *Sonoma Valley AVA, California, USA* Once known almost entirely for its range of Chardonnays (Belle Terre★★, Robert Young★★), St Jean has emerged as a producer of delicious reds, including a BORDEAUX-style blend called Cinq Cépages★★ and a Reserve Merlot★★. Now owned by Treasury Wine Estates. Best years: (Chardonnay) 2010 **09** 08 07 06 05 04 03 02 01 00; (Merlot) 2009 **08** 07 05 04.

CHATEAU STE MICHELLE *Washington State, USA* Pioneering winery with an enormous range of wines, including several attractive vineyard-designated Chardonnays★ (some ★★), Cabernet Sauvignons★ and Merlots★, especially Cold Creek Vineyard★★ and Indian Wells★★. Good Riesling, both dry and sweet, and increasingly interesting red Meritage★ and Syrah★. Partnership with Italy's ANTINORI and Germany's Ernst LOOSEN has produced dark, powerful Tuscan-style red Col Solare★★, attractive Riesling Eroica★ and a thrilling sweet version, Single Berry Select★★★, made in tiny quantities. Quality generally seems to be moving upward. Best years: (premium reds) (2010) 09 **08** 07 06.

CHÂTEAUNEUF-DU-PAPE AC *Rhône Valley, France* A large (3200ha/
7900-acre) vineyard area between Orange and Avignon. The sweetly
fruited, aromatic red wine is based on Grenache, plus Syrah and
Mourvèdre (10 other varieties are also allowed). Heady and powerful, it
should also be balanced and succulent. Always choose Châteauneuf from
a single estate, denoted by the papal coat of arms or mitre embossed on
the bottle neck. Top reds, particularly old-vine cuvées, will age for 10
years or more, but don't feel you have to pay extra for 'prestige' cuvées:
from a good estate, the normal release will be far cheaper, less dense
and often more easily enjoyable. Only 5% of Châteauneuf is white;
made mainly from Grenache Blanc, Bourboulenc, Clairette and
Roussanne, these wines can be surprisingly good. Many whites are best
young. Best producers: (reds) L Barrot★, BEAUCASTEL★★, Beaurenard★★, Bois
de Boursan★★, H Bonneau★★, Bosquet des Papes★★, les Cailloux★★,
Chante-Perdrix★, CHAPOUTIER★, la Charbonnière★★, Charvin★★, Clos du
Caillou★, Clos du Mont Olivet★★, CLOS DES PAPES★★★, Clos St-Jean★,
Cristia★, Cros de la Mûre★★, Font du Loup★, FONT DE MICHELLE★★, Fortia★,
la Gardine★★ Gigognan★ Giraud★ Grand Tinel★ Grand Veneur★, la
Janasse★★★, Marcoux★★, Mathieu★, Monpertuis★★, Mont-Redon★,
la Mordorée★★, la Nerthe★★, Pégaü★★, RAYAS★★★, Roquète★, Roger
Sabon★★, Sénéchaux★, St-Siffrein, Solitude★★, Tardieu-Laurent★,
P Usseglio★★, Vieille Julienne★★, Le Vieux Donjon★★, VIEUX TÉLÉGRAPHE★★★;
(whites) BEAUCASTEL★★★, CLOS DES PAPES★★, Clos St-Michel, FONT DE
MICHELLE★★, Grand Veneur★, Marcoux★★, Mont-Redon★, RAYAS★★,
Vaudieu, VIEUX TÉLÉGRAPHE★★. Best years: (reds) 2010 09 **08** 07 **06 05 04 03
01 00 99 98 96 95 90 89 88**.

CHAUME See COTEAUX DU LAYON AC.

JEAN-LOUIS CHAVE *Rhône Valley, France* Jean-Louis Chave's red
HERMITAGE★★★ is one of the world's great wines, a supreme Syrah,
surpassed only by the cellar-selected Cathelin★★★, produced
occasionally (2003, 2000, 1998, 95, 91, 90). His wonderful white
Hermitage★★★ (Marsanne with some Roussanne) sometimes outlasts
the reds, as it evolves toward its honeyed, nutty, complex peak. Also
excellent, improving red ST-JOSEPH★★ and occasional stunning sweet Vin
de Paille★★. Expensive, but worth the money. *Négociant* business makes
sound red and white Hermitage, and well-fruited CÔTES DU RHÔNE Mon
Coeur and St-Joseph Offerus. Best years: (reds) 2011 10 09 07 **06** 05 **04 03
01 00** 99 98 97 96 95 94 92 91 90 89 88 86 85 83 82 79 78; (whites) 2011
10 09 08 07 06 05 04 03 01 00 99 98 97 96 95 94 93 92 91 90 89 88 85 83.

CHÉNAS AC *Beaujolais, Burgundy, France* The smallest BEAUJOLAIS Cru, Chénas
styles range from light and elegant to austere and needing time to develop
Burgundian tones. Best producers: Ch. Bonnet (Vieilles Vignes★), DUBOEUF,
H Lapierre (Vieilles Vignes★), Piron-Lameloise (Quartz), B Santé★. Best years:
(2011) 10 **09**.

CHENIN BLANC One of the most underrated and versatile white wine
grapes in the world. In the LOIRE VALLEY, where it is also called Pineau de
la Loire, it is responsible for sweet, medium, dry and sparkling wines.
The great sweet wines of COTEAUX DU LAYON, QUARTS DE CHAUME,
BONNEZEAUX and VOUVRAY are some of the longest-lived of all wines. There
is an increasing emphasis on barrel-fermented and aged dry wines,
especially in ANJOU and now in TOURAINE, the best of which are a
revelation. In South Africa, Chenin Blanc remains both the most planted

and most uprooted variety; styles range from sparkling, through easy-drinking, dryish wines and modern barrel-fermented versions, to botrytized dessert wines. Chenin is also influential in quality white blends. New Zealand and Australia have produced good varietal examples, and it is also grown in California (DRY CREEK VINEYARD, Graziano), Argentina and Spain (Can Ràfols dels Caus, Escoda Sanahuja).

LARRY CHERUBINO *Western Australia* Larry Cherubino has an intimate knowledge of the vineyards of WESTERN AUSTRALIA that he gained as chief winemaker at HOUGHTON. Since 2003, he has been making small volumes of wine for his family company. As a winemaker, he appears to have a magic touch and his wines are regarded as among Australia's finest. Wines change from year to year, particularly in the good-value Ad Hoc range; The Yard label (Riesling★) is for single-vineyard wines; premium Cherubino range includes Margaret River Cabernet★, Frankland River Shiraz★★, Pemberton Sauvignon Blanc★ and Porongurup Riesling★★.

CH. CHEVAL BLANC★★★ *St-Émilion Grand Cru AC, 1er Grand Cru Classé, Bordeaux, France* Along with AUSONE, the leading ST-ÉMILION estate. Right on the border with POMEROL, it seems to share some of its sturdy richness, but with an extra spice and purity of fruit that is impressively, recognizably unique. An unusually high percentage (60%) of Cabernet Franc is often used in the blend. Gorgeous when young, yet with a remarkable ability to age for many decades. Best years: 2010 09 08 **07** 06 **05** 04 03 02 01 00 99 98 96 95 90 89 88 86 85.

DOM. DE CHEVALIER *Pessac-Léognan AC, Cru Classé de Graves, Bordeaux, France* Some of Bordeaux's finest wines. The red★★ starts out firm and reserved, but over 10–20 years gains heavenly cedar, tobacco and blackcurrant flavour. Recent vintages have greater purity of fruit. The brilliant

white★★★ is both fermented and aged in oak barrels; in the best vintages it will still be improving at 15–20 years, but 2006 and 2007 were so irresistible I'd be surprised if there's any left now, let alone in 15 years. Best years: (reds) 2010 09 08 **07** 06 **05** 04 03 02 01 00 99 98 96 90 89; (whites) 2010 **09** 08 07 06 05 04 02 01 00 99 98 96 90 89 88.

CHEVALIER-MONTRACHET AC See MONTRACHET AC.

CHEVERNY AC *Loire Valley, France* A little-known area south of Blois. The local speciality is the white Romorantin grape, which makes a bone-dry wine under the AC Cour-Cheverny, but the best whites are from Chardonnay. Also pleasant Sauvignon, Pinot Noir, Gamay and bracing CRÉMANT DE LOIRE. Drink young. Best producers: Cazin★, Cheverny co-op, Clos du Tue-Boeuf★, la Désoucherie, la Gaudronnière, Gendrier/Huards★, Maison, H Marionnet, de Montcy★, du Moulin, Luc Percher★, Salvard, F Saumon, Veilloux★.

CHIANTI DOCG *Tuscany, Italy* It may be the best-known name in Italian wine, but plain Chianti has slid so far down the price ladder in recent years that the best one could say of it is that it is cheap and cheerful – and therefore probably ought not to be categorized DOCG, supposedly reserved for Italy's finest. 'Chianti', when followed with a zonal name, such as Rufina, Colli Aretini, Colli Fiorentini or Colli Senesi, can be altogether superior, but don't bet on it. Chianti must be composed 75–100% of Sangiovese, the optional 25% being made up of Tuscan varieties like Canaiolo or Colorino, or (for more expensive but usually atypical examples) of varieties like Cabernet, Merlot and Syrah. Best producers: (Chianti Colli Fiorentini) Il Corno, Corzano e Paterno, Malenchini, Pasolini dall'Onda, Poppiano★, La Querce; (Chianti Colli Senesi) Casale-Falchini★, Castello di Farnetella★, Pietraserena. See also CHIANTI RUFINA.

CHIANTI CLASSICO DOCG *Tuscany, Italy* The historic CHIANTI zone, in the hills between Florence and Siena; in the 1930s it was thrown in with all the other yoiks (see above) and fobbed off with the epithet 'Classico'. It was only in 1996 that it acquired legal separation from anything else called Chianti, although regulations still allow substantial quantities of international grapes into the blend – with a minimum of 80% Sangiovese – something that many feel should not be allowed in Chianti Classico. The finest Riserva wines can improve for a decade or more. Many of the estates also offer regular bottlings of red wine, round and fruity, for drinking about 2–5 years after the harvest. Best producers (Riserva or top cru): Castello di AMA★★★, ANTINORI★ (Riserva★★), Badia a Coltibuono★, Il Borghetto★★, Brancaia★, Cacchiano★★, Capaccia★★, Carpineto★, Casaloste★★, Castellare★, Castell'in Villa★, Collelungo★, Colombaio di Cencio★, Casa Emma★★, FELSINA★★, Le Filigare★, FONTERUTOLI★★, FONTODI★★, ISOLE E OLENA★★★, Il Mandorlo★★, MONSANTO★★★, Monteraponi★★, Il Palazzino★★, Paneretta★★, Panzanello★★, Poggerino★★, Poggio al Sole (Casasilia★★★), Poggiopiano★★, Querceto★, QUERCIABELLA★★, Castello dei RAMPOLLA★★, RICASOLI (Castello di Brolio★), Riecine★★, Rignana★★, Rocca di Castagnoli★★, San Felice★★, San Giusto a Rentennano★★, San Polo in Rosso★, Casa Sola★★, Terrabianca★, Vecchie Terre di Montefili★★, Vignamaggio★, Villa Cafaggio★★, VOLPAIA★★. Best years: (2011) (10) 09 **08 07 06 04 01 99 97 95 90**.

CHIANTI RUFINA DOCG *Tuscany, Italy* CHIANTI sub-zone in the Apennine foothills east of Florence, where wines were noted for exceptional structure and longevity long before they joined the ranks of Chianti. Today the wines, particularly the long-lived Riserva Bucerchiale from SELVAPIANA and FRESCOBALDI's Montesodi, match the best of CHIANTI CLASSICO. Pomino DOC is a higher zone, almost entirely surrounded by Chianti Rufina; dominated by Frescobaldi, it makes greater use of French varieties such as Merlot, Cabernet and Chardonnay. Best producers: (Riserva) Basciano★, Tenuta di Bossi★, Colognole★, Frascole★, FRESCOBALDI★, Grati/Villa di Vetrice★, Grignano★, Lavacchio★, SELVAPIANA★★★, Castello del Trebbio★. Best years: (2011) (10) 09 **08 07 06 04 03 01**.

FRANÇOIS CHIDAINE *Montlouis-sur-Loire AC, Vouvray AC, Loire Valley, France* Along with Jacky BLOT, François Chidaine has inspired a new generation of MONTLOUIS-SUR-LOIRE vignerons with wines of wonderful purity, precision and length, with a dozen wines differentiated by soil type (clay, silex and limestone) and aspect sourced from Montlouis-sur-Loire and VOUVRAY including, since 2006, Prince Poniatowski's famous vineyard, Le Clos Baudoin. Dry wines account for 80% of Chidaine's range. Montlouis Les Lys★★, a *moëlleux* Sélection de Grains Nobles, is made only in exceptional vintages. Biodynamic since 1999. Best years: (sec/demi-sec) 2011 **09 08 07 06**; (moelleux) (2011) 09 **03 97**.

CHIMNEY ROCK *Stags Leap District AVA, California, USA* Powerful yet elegantly sculpted Cabernet Sauvignon★★ and a meritage blend called Elevage★★. There's also an ageworthy Elevage Blanc★ (a blend of Sauvignons Blanc and Gris) and a tangy Fumé Blanc★. Best years: (Elevage) 2008 07 **06 05 04 03 02 01 00 99 98 97**.

CHINON AC *Loire Valley, France* Fine red wine made mainly from Cabernet Franc with an occasional dash of Cabernet Sauvignon. Lovely light reds full of raspberry fruit and fresh summer earth to drink young (from gravelly soils), and heavyweights for keeping (from clay and limestone slopes); it is always worth buying a single-estate wine. Small amount of white (from Chenin Blanc). Best producers: P Alliet★★, B Baudry★★, Baudry-Dutour★, P Breton★, Coulaine★, Couly-Dutheil★, DRUET★, Grosbois, C Joguet★★, B & P Lambert★, la Noblaie★, de Pallus★★, Wilfrid Rousse, P Sourdais★. Best years: (2011) 10 09 **08 06 05 04 03 02 01**.

CHIROUBLES AC *Beaujolais, Burgundy, France* The highest in altitude of the BEAUJOLAIS Crus, producing a light, fragrant, delicious Gamay wine. Best producers: D Bouland★, Cheysson★, la Combe au Loup★, D Desvignes★, Trenel. Best years: **(2011)** 10.

CHIVITE *Navarra DO, Navarra, Spain* Longtime leader in exports from NAVARRA. The Gran Feudo★ red and rosé are very good easy drinkers; unoaked Chardonnay★ is excellent. The more upmarket reds have improved steadily in a restrained, claret-like style. The top range, Colección 125, includes a red Reserva★ (sometimes ★★), classy white Blanco★★ (barrel-fermented Chardonnay) and a characterful sweet Vendimia Tardía★★ (from Muscat Blanc à Petits Grains). Chivite's northerly estate, Pago de Arínzano★★, has its own Vino de Pago appellation since 2008.

CHOREY-LÈS-BEAUNE AC *Côte de Beaune, Burgundy, France* One of those tiny, forgotten villages that make good, if not great, Burgundy at prices most of us can afford, with some committed producers too. Can age for 5 years. Best producers: Arnoux★, DROUHIN★, Germain/Ch. de Chorey★, Maillard★, TOLLOT-BEAUT. Best years: (2011) 10 09 08 **07 05**.

CHURCH ROAD *Hawkes Bay, North Island, New Zealand* Premium-wine project owned by Pernod Ricard. The reds originally attempted to be Bordeaux lookalikes, but are now unashamedly Kiwi and all the better for it. Reserve Chardonnay★★ leapt in quality in recent years to become one of the country's best. Flagship wine Tom makes outstanding Cabernet-Merlot★★ and Chardonnay★★★ only in top vintages. Best years: (reds) 2010 **09 08 07 05 02**.

CHURCHILL *Port DOC, Douro, Portugal* Established in 1981, it was the first new PORT shipper for 50 years. The wines can be good, notably Vintage★, LBV★, Crusted★, single-quinta Gricha★ and a well-aged, nutty dry white port★, and are more consistent since Quinta da Gricha was bought in 1999. Churchill Estates★ is an unfortified DOURO red. Best years: (Vintage) **2007 03 00 97 94 91 85**; (Quinta da Gricha) (2009) **07 03 01 99**.

CINSAUT Also spelt Cinsault. Found mainly in France's southern RHÔNE VALLEY, PROVENCE and LANGUEDOC-ROUSSILLON. Ideal for rosé wine. In blends, Cinsaut's low alcohol calms high-degree Grenache and freshens the wine. Rare as a single varietal, but CLOS CENTEILLES and Clos du Serres make fine examples. Mainstay of the blend for Lebanon's CHATEAU MUSAR. Traditionally popular as a bulk blender in South Africa, enthusiasts of the Rhône style are bringing out serious quality. California has some fine old vines, and there is resurgence in Chile.

CIRÒ DOC *Calabria, Italy* Cirò Rosso, a Gaglioppo-based wine of ancient pedigree, has improved remarkably this century. Non-DOC Gaglioppo-based IGTs, like Librandi's Gravello★★ (an oak-aged blend with

Cabernet), can be exciting. The DOC also covers a dry white from Greco and a dry rosé. Best producers: Caparra & Siciliani★, Librandi★ (Riserva★★), San Francesco★. Best years: (reds) (2011) (10) 09 **08 07 06 05 04**.

BRUNO CLAIR *Marsannay, Côte de Nuits, Burgundy, France* Top producer from MARSANNAY with several single-vineyard cuvées there, and an impressive range from other top vineyards including CHAMBERTIN Clos de Bèze★★ and Gevrey-Chambertin Clos St-Jacques★★. Also good-value SAVIGNY La Dominode★★ and a delicious Marsannay rosé★. Best years: (top reds) (2011) 10 09 08 **07 06 05 03 02 01 99 98 96 90**.

CLAIRETTE DE DIE AC *Rhône Valley, France* Underrated sparkling wine made from a minimum of 75% Muscat: off-dry, with a creamy bubble and a honeyed, grapy, orchard-fresh fragrance. The *méthode Dioise* is used, which preserves the Muscat scent. A delightful light apéritif. Drink young. Best producers: Achard-Vincent★, Clairette de Die co-op, D Cornillon, Jacques Faure, J-C Raspail★. See also CRÉMANT DE DIE.

A CLAPE *Cornas AC, Rhône Valley, France* Leading 5ha (12-acre) estate in CORNAS. Dense, tannic wines that reward patient cellaring, full of rich, roasted fruit – though occasionally, as in 2004, scented and sublime – consistently excellent and often ★★★. Younger vine Renaissance★ is good lower-key Cornas. Also fine red CÔTES DU RHÔNE★ and authentic ST-PÉRAY★. Best years: (Cornas) 2011 10 09 08 07 **06 05 04 03 02 01 00 99 98 97 96 95 94 91 90 89 88 85 83 78**.

LA CLAPE *Grand Vin du Languedoc AC, Languedoc, France* The mountain of La Clape rises above the flat coastal fields south-east of Narbonne; its vineyards produce some excellent whites from Bourboulenc and Clairette, plus fine, herb-scented reds and rosés, mainly from Grenache, Syrah and Mourvèdre. Whites and reds can age. Best producers: d'Anglès, Camplazens★, Capitoul, l'HOSPITALET★, Mas du Soleilla★, Mire l'Étang, Moyau★, Négly, Pech-Céleyran★, Pech Redon★, Ricardelle★. Best years: (reds) (2011) 10 09 08 07 **06 05 04**.

CLARE VALLEY *South Australia* This historic upland region to the north of Adelaide has a deceptively moderate climate and is able to grow both hot-climate and cool-climate grapes successfully, including fine, aromatic Riesling, marvellously textured Semillon, scented Viognier, rich, robust Shiraz and Cabernet blends, and peppery but voluptuous Grenache. Best producers: (whites) Tim ADAMS★★★, Jim BARRY★★, Wolf BLASS (Gold Label★), Leo Buring (Leonay★★), Crabtree★, GROSSET★★★, Kilikanoon★★, KNAPPSTEIN★★, KT★★, Leasingham★, MITCHELL★, MOUNT HORROCKS★★, O'Leary Walker★★, PETALUMA★★, Pikes★, SKILLOGALEE★, Taylors/Wakefield★; (reds) Tim ADAMS★★, Jim BARRY★★, GROSSET★★, Kilikanoon★★, KNAPPSTEIN★, Leasingham★, MITCHELL★, MOUNT HORROCKS★, O'Leary Walker★, Pikes★, SKILLOGALEE★, Taylors/Wakefield, WENDOUREE★★. Best years: (Shiraz) 2010 09 08 **06 05 04 03 02 01 99 98 97 96 94 92 91 90**; (Riesling) **2010** 09 08 06 05 04 03 02 01 99 98 97 96 95.

CLARENDON HILLS *McLaren Vale, South Australia* Winery with a name for high-priced, highly extracted, unfined, unfiltered and unobtainable reds. Single-vineyard Astralis★★ is a hugely concentrated Syrah from old vines, aged in 100% French new oak. Other Syrah ★★ labels offer slightly better value, while Merlot★ and Cabernet Sauvignon★ aim to rub shoulders with great red BORDEAUX – although for the life of me I can't think which ones. Several cuvées of old vines Grenache★★ are marked by saturated black cherry fruit and high alcohol. Best years: (Astralis) (2010) 09 08 06 05 03 **02 01 00 98 96 95 94**.

CH. CLARKE★ *Listrac-Médoc AC, Bordeaux, France* This property had millions spent on it by the late Baron Edmond de Rothschild during the late 1970s, and from the 1998 vintage leading Bordeaux winemaker Michel Rolland has been consultant enologist. The wines can have an attractive blackcurrant fruit and now a lot more Merlot (70%) is giving them more ripeness and polish. There is also a small production of dry white wine, le Merle Blanc★. Best years: 2010 09 **08 07 06 05 04 03 01 00 99 98**.

DOMENICO CLERICO *Barolo DOCG, Piedmont, Italy* Domenico Clerico produces consistently superlative BAROLO (Ciabot Mentin Ginestra★★★, Aeroplan Servaj★★★, Per Cristina★★★) and excellent BARBERA D'ALBA★ (Trevigne★★), all wonderfully balanced. His range also includes LANGHE Arte★★, a barrique-aged blend of Nebbiolo and Barbera. Best years: (Barolo) (2011) (10) (09) 08 07 06 **04 01 00 99**.

CH. CLIMENS★★★ *Barsac AC, 1er Cru Classé, Bordeaux, France* The leading estate in BARSAC, with a deserved reputation for fabulous, sensuous wines: rich and succulent, yet streaked with lively lemon acidity. Easy to drink at 5 years, but a good vintage will be richer and more satisfying after 10–15 years. Second wine: les Cyprès (also delicious). Best years: 2010 09 **07 06 05 04 03 02 01 00 99 98 97 96 95 90 89**.

CLONAKILLA *Canberra, Australia* Tim Kirk has gained a reputation as one of the country's finest winemakers, initially on the strength of his flagship Shiraz-Viognier★★★, which is the benchmark for the style in Australia: elegant, lavender-scented, fleshily textured and complex, with the structure to age beautifully. His small family winery also produces increasingly impressive Riesling★, sublime Viognier★, a new  Sauvignon Blanc-Semillon as well as the more modestly priced O'Riada Shiraz★ (from local growers) and HILLTOPS Shiraz.

CLOS DE L'ANHEL *Corbières AC, Languedoc, France* Organic since 2003, Sophie Guiraudon and Philippe Mathias produce remarkable wines with a power unusual even for the CORBIÈRES. Top wine is smooth, rich Les Dimanches★★; also Les Terrassettes★, Les Autres and Le Lolo de l'Anhel. Best years: (Les Dimanches) (2011) 10 **09 08 07 06 05 04**.

CLOS DU BOIS *Alexander Valley AVA, Sonoma County, California, USA* I've always been partial to the house style here: gentle, fruit-dominated SONOMA Chardonnay, Merlot and Cabernet. Top vineyard selections can be exciting: Calcaire Chardonnay★★, rich, strong Briarcrest Cabernet Sauvignon★★ and Marlstone★★, a red BORDEAUX-style blend. Riesling is the latest project. Now owned by Constellation. Best years: (reds) 2010 09 08 07 06 05 04 03 02 01 00 99 97.

CLOS CENTEILLES *Minervois AC, Languedoc, France* Excellent MINERVOIS and Minervois La Livinière, as well as innovative vins de pays, reviving long lost grape varieties. Impressive Clos Centeilles★★ is the top wine; Capitelle de Centeilles★ and Carignanissime★ are 100% Cinsaut and 100% Carignan respectively; Campagne de Centeilles is also pre-dominantly Cinsaut. Best years: (reds) (2011) 10 **09 08 07 06 05 04 03 02**.

CLOS ERASMUS★★★ *Priorat DOCa, Cataluña, Spain* Profound and personal PRIORAT from Daphne Glorian's tiny estate. Convincing second wine, Laurel★. Best years: (2009) 08 07 05 **04 03 02 01 00 99 98 97 96 94**.

CLOS DE GAMOT *Cahors AOP, South-West France* The Jouffreau family, proud of their 400-year heritage, produce benchmark CAHORS★★. The wines are far from big blockbusters, but they need aging to develop ever-increasing subtlety and complexity. A cuvée from centenarian vines★★ is made in the best vintages. Clos St-Jean★★★, from a relatively new vineyard, is world-class. Best years: (2011) (10) 09 **06** 05 02 01 98.

LE CLOS JORDANNE *Niagara Peninsula VQA, Ontario, Canada* A joint venture between Canadian giant Vincor (part of Constellation) and Burgundy's BOISSET, making BURGUNDY-style Pinot Noir★ and Chardonnay★★. At the top end Le Grand Clos faintly echoes Burgundy's Grand Cru; the single-vineyard wines show *terroir* differences; Village Reserve wines are from the winery's vineyards in the village of Jordan. All organic.

CLOS D'UN JOUR *Cahors AOP, South-West France* In 10 years, Véronique and Stéphane Azémar have proved that their meteoric rise to celebrity is no flash in the pan. Le Clos d'un Jour★ is exceptional value for money; Un Jour★ is 100% Malbec and aged in oak. Unofficially organic. Best years: (2011) (10) 09 **06** 05.

CLOS DES LAMBRAYS AC *Grand Cru, Côte de Nuits, Burgundy, France* This 8.8ha (22-acre) Grand Cru vineyard in MOREY-ST-DENIS is almost entirely owned by the domaine of the same name, though Taupenot-Merme also has a few rows – not quite enough to make a barrel a year. Thierry Brouin, manager at the Dom. des Lambrays★★★, favours early picking and the use of stems to make a vibrant, spicy style of wine. Best years: (2011) 10 09 **07** 06 05 **03** 02 00.

CLOS MARIE *Pic St-Loup AC, Languedoc, France* Powerful, Syrah-dominated reds: Glorieuses★, Métairies du Clos★, Simon★ and L'Olivette★. Also white cuvée Manon. Best years: (2011) 10 **09 08 07** 06 05.

CLOS MOGADOR★★★ *Priorat DOCa, Cataluña, Spain* René Barbier Ferrer was one of the pioneers who relaunched the reputation of PRIORAT in the 1980s. The wine is a ripe, intense, brooding monster built to age. Best years: (2009) 08 07 06 05 **04 03** 01 00 99 98 97 96 95 94.

DOM. DU CLOS NAUDIN *Vouvray AC, Loire Valley, France* Philippe Foreau runs this first-rate 11.5ha (28-acre) VOUVRAY domaine. Depending on the vintage, he produces a range of styles: dry★★, medium-dry★★ and sweet★★ (rare Réserve★★★), as well as a sparkling Mousseux★★ that accounts for 40% of production. The wines are supremely ageworthy. As with HUET, in 2006, 2007 and 2008 the emphasis was on drier wines. Best years: (Moelleux Réserve) (2011) 09 **05** 03 97 96 95 90 89.

CLOS DES PAPES *Châteauneuf-du-Pape AC, Rhône Valley, France* The red CHÂTEAUNEUF-DU-PAPE★★★ has a high 20% of Mourvèdre, which gives structure, complexity and added longevity. More ample, fleshy and heady recently – a stylistic change – with enough very ripe Grenache to make the wine approachable in its youth and provide an initial blast of coated fruit. The marvellous, refined, long-lived white★★ takes on the nutty, complex character of aged Burgundy after 5 or 6 years. Best years: (red) 2011 10 09 08 07 06 05 04 03 01 00 99 98 97 96 95 94 90 89 88.

CLOS DE LA ROCHE AC *Grand Cru, Côte de Nuits, Burgundy, France* The biggest and often best of the 5 MOREY-ST-DENIS Grands Crus. The wine has a lovely, bright, red-fruits flavour when young, and should become richly chocolaty or gamy with age. Best producers: DROUHIN★★★, DUJAC★★★, HOSPICES DE BEAUNE★★, Dom. LEROY★★★, H Lignier★★, Perrot-Minot★★, Ponsot★★★, ROUSSEAU★★. Best years: (2011) 10 09 08 **07** 06 05 **03** 02 01 99 98 96 95 93 90.

CLOS ST-DENIS AC *Grand Cru, Côte de Nuits, Burgundy, France* This small (6.5ha/16-acre) Grand Cru, which gave its name to the village of MOREY-ST-DENIS, produces wines that are sometimes light, but should be wonderfully silky, with the texture that only great Burgundy can regularly achieve. Best after 10 years or more. Best producers: Arlaud★★, Charlopin★★, DUJAC★★★, JADOT★★, Ponsot★★★. Best years: (2011) 10 09 08 07 06 05 **03 02 01** 99 98 **96** 95 93 90.

CLOS DE TART AC *Grand Cru, Côte de Nuits, Burgundy, France* 7.5ha (18-acre) Grand Cru, a monopoly of the Mommessin family, run by Sylvain Pitiot. Intense, concentrated wines made by traditional methods with a modern result. Now exceptional quality★★★ – and price! Best years: (2011) 10 09 08 07 06 05 **03 02 01 00** 99 **96** 95 90.

CLOS TRIGUEDINA *Cahors AOP, South-West France* Jean-Luc Baldès makes some of the best-known and admired CAHORS★. Top cuvée Probus★★ manages to combine tradition and modernity. The New Black Wine revives a historical tradition for cooked and fortified wine perhaps best forgotten. Best years: (2011) (10) 09 **06** 05 02 01 98.

CLOS DU VAL *Napa Valley AVA, California, USA* Elegant Cabernet Sauvignon★ (STAGS LEAP DISTRICT★★), Chardonnay★, Merlot★, Pinot Noir★ and Zinfandel★. Reserve Cabernet★ can age well. Best years: (Reserve Cabernet) 2007 **06** 05 04 03 02 01 00 99 97 **96** 95 94 91 90.

CLOS DE VOUGEOT AC *Grand Cru, Côte de Nuits, Burgundy, France* Enclosed by Cistercian monks in the 14th century, and today a tourist attraction, this large (50ha/125-acre) vineyard is now divided among 80+ owners. As a result of this division, Clos de Vougeot is one of the less reliable Grands Crus; better wine tends to come from the upper and middle parts. When it is good it is wonderfully fleshy, turning deep and exotic after 10 years or more. Best producers: H. Boillot★, Chopin★★, J-J Confuron★★★, Eugénie★★★ (formerly Engel), FAIVELEY★, GRIVOT★★★, Anne GROS★★★, JADOT★★★, F Lamarche★★, Dom. LEROY★★★, T LIGER-BELAIR★★, MEO-CAMUZET★★★, Millot★★, Denis MORTET★★★, MUGNERET-GIBOURG★★★, Ch. de la Tour★★, VOUGERAIE★★. Best years: (2011) 10 09 08 **07** 06 05 **03 02 01 00** 99 98 **96** 95 93 90.

CLOT DE L'OUM *Côtes du Roussillon-Villages AC, Roussillon, France* Eric Monné makes powerful, dense wines from 18ha (45 acres), which he works organically. Wines include La Compagnie des Papillons★, Saint Bart Vieilles Vignes★ and Numéro Uno★★ (Syrah with a little Carignan).

CLOUDY BAY *Marlborough, South Island, New Zealand* New Zealand's most successful winery, Cloudy Bay achieved cult status with the first release of its zesty, herbaceous Sauvignon Blanc in 1985. After a dip in the early 2000s, the winery is getting back on form despite high production levels. Sauvignon Blanc★★ has regained a lot of its leafy zest. Sauvignon Blanc Te Koko★★ is very different: rich, creamy, oak-matured and bottle-aged. Cloudy Bay also makes Chardonnay★★, superb ALSACE-style Gewurztraminer★★ and Riesling★★ (late-harvest Riesling★★) and very good Pinot Noir★. Vintage Pelorus★★ is a high-quality old-style CHAMPAGNE-method fizz and non-vintage Pelorus★★ is excellent too. Best years: (Sauvignon Blanc) 2011 10 09 08 06 04.

PAUL CLUVER *Elgin WO, South Africa* Cool-loving varieties respond well in ELGIN: minerally, refined Sauvignon Blanc; compact, layered Chardonnay★★; subtle Gewurztraminer★★; vibrant, dryish Riesling★ and thrilling Noble Late Harvest★★ botrytis dessert version. Pinot Noir improves each vintage: standard Pinot Noir★ is silky and refreshing; the ethereal charm of single-vineyard Seven Flags★★ belies its complexity and ageworthiness. Best years: (whites) 2011 **10 09 08 07 06**.

COATES & SEELY *Hampshire, England* A new sparkling wine venture led by Christian Seely, the Brit who runs AXA Millésimes (Ch. PICHON-LONGUEVILLE, Ch. SUDUIRAUT, Quinta do NOVAL). Exciting wines, currently from bought-in grapes, include tasty Rosé★★ and Blanc de Blancs★★.

COBB WINES *Sonoma Coast AVA, California, USA* Small, prestigious Pinot Noir producer in one of the coolest areas of SONOMA COUNTY. Most wines are light in colour, but brilliantly scented and structured (Diane Cobb★★, Emmaline Ann★★). Best years: 2009 08 **07 06** 05.

COBOS *Mendoza, Argentina* Small Argentine-American operation. *Terroir* and the blockbuster come together spectacularly here. Top-of-the-range uNico★★★, an intense, dramatic Cabernet-based blend, showcases old-vine fruit from the Marchiori vineyard in the Perdriel district of MENDOZA. The Marchiori vineyard is also the source of Malbec★★, Cabernet★★ and rich, exotic Chardonnay★★ under the Bramare label. A varietal range named Felino★ offers dazzling purity of fruit and great quality for the price. Best years: (uNico): 2008 **06** 05.

J-F COCHE-DURY *Meursault, Côte de Beaune, Burgundy, France* Jean-François Coche-Dury, now joined by his son Raphaël, is a modest superstar, quietly turning out some of the finest wines on the CÔTE DE BEAUNE. His best wines are his CORTON-CHARLEMAGNE★★★ and MEURSAULT Perrières★★★, but even his BOURGOGNE Blanc★★ is excellent. His red wines, from VOLNAY★★ and MONTHELIE★, are delicious to drink even when young. Best years: (whites) (2011) 10 09 **08 07 06** 05 **04 02** 01 00 99 95.

COCKBURN'S *Port DOC, Douro, Portugal* Best known for Special Reserve ruby port. Also stylish Vintage★ and Quinta dos Canais★. Cockburn's is now owned by Symington Family Estates. Best years: (Vintage) 2007 03 00 97 94 91 70 63 60 55; (dos Canais) 2007 03 01 00 95 92.

CODORNÍU *Cava DO, Cataluña, Spain* The biggest CHAMPAGNE-method sparkling wine company in the world. Anna de Codorníu★ and Jaume Codorníu★ are especially good, but all the sparklers are better than the CAVA average. Drink young for freshness. Codorníu also owns RAÏMAT in COSTERS DEL SEGRE, Masía Bach in the PENEDES and Bodegas Bilbaínas in RIOJA, and has a stake in Scala Dei in PRIORAT.

COLCHAGUA *Rapel, Chile* RAPEL sub-region and home to several exciting estates, such as the Apalta hillside vineyard, where LAPOSTOLLE, MONTES, VENTISQUERO and others have plantings. Syrah and Carmenère do very well here. Chimbarongo and Los Lingues to the east are cooler due to the influence of the Andes. New vineyards toward the coast in Lolol and Marchíhüe are delivering exciting reds and whites, especially Syrah and Viognier. New coastal region Paredones is showing great promise for salty Sauvignon Blancs. Best producers: CASA SILVA★, CONO SUR★★, EMILIANA★★, Hacienda Araucano/Lurton★, Koyle, LAPOSTOLLE★★, Los Vascos, LUIS FELIPE EDWARDS★, MONTES★★, MontGras, Neyen★★, VENTISQUERO★ (Pangea★★), Viu Manent★.

COLDSTREAM HILLS *Yarra Valley, Victoria, Australia* Founded by Australian wine guru James Halliday; owned by Foster's (now Treasury) since 2005. Chardonnay★ (Reserve★★★) has subtlety and delicacy, but real depth as well. Pinot Noir★ (Reserve★★) is usually good: sappy and smoky with cherry fruit and clever use of all-French oak. Reserve Cabernet★ can be very good, though not always ripe; Merlot★★ ripens more successfully. Best years: (Reserve Chardonnay) 2011 **10 07 06 05** 03.

131

COLIN *Chassagne-Montrachet, Côte de Beaune, Burgundy, France* Extended family in ST-AUBIN and neighbouring CHASSAGNE-MONTRACHET, producing much fine white Burgundy. Michel Colin-Deleger's Chassagne domaine is now split between sons Bruno★ and Philippe★. Marc Colin★★ has handed over to three of his children, while his eldest, Pierre-Yves Colin-Morey★★, who has set up on his own, could be the one to watch.

COLLI ORIENTALI DEL FRIULI DOC *Friuli-Venezia Giulia, Italy* Many Italian denominations begin with 'Colli' (hills). This one covers 20 varietal types of wine, plus Bianco and Rosso blends – not including famous sweet wines Picolit and Ramandolo. But the most exciting wines are mostly reds – from the indigenous Refosco and Schioppettino, as well as varieties like Cabernet – and dry whites, from Friulano, Ribolla, Pinot Bianco, Pinot Grigio and Malvasia Istriana. Best producers: Ca' Ronesca★, Dario Coos★, Dorigo★, Le Due Terre★★, Livio FELLUGA★★, Walter Filiputti★, Adriano Gigante★, Livon★, Meroi★, Miani★★, Davide Moschioni★★, Rocca Bernarda★, Rodaro★, Ronchi di Cialla★, Ronchi di Manzano★★, Ronco del Gnemiz★★, Scubla★, Sirch★, Specogna★, Le Vigne di Zamò★★, Zof★. Best years: (whites) (2011) 10 **09 08 07 06 04**.

COLLI PIACENTINI DOC *Emilia-Romagna, Italy* Reds and whites from the hills of Piacenza. The best-known red, which may or may not be frothing, is Gutturnio, a Barbera-Bonarda blend. Other grape varieties include the Pinot family, Cabernet and oddballs Ortrugo and Trebbianino. With the exception of the more serious Gutturnios, most wines are best drunk young. Best producers: Luretta★, Lusenti, Castello di Luzzano/Fugazza★, Il Poggiarello★, La Stoppa★, Torre Fornello★, La Tosa (Cabernet Sauvignon★). Best years: (reds) (2011) 10 **09 08 07 06 04**.

COLLINES RHODANIENNES, IGP DES *Rhône Valley, France* Exciting granite/schist hillside region on the east bank between Vienne and Valence includes new vineyard of Seyssuel. Best wines are Syrah, and a few juicy Merlots and Gamays. Good Viogniers, with CONDRIEU-like finesse. Best producers: les Alexandrins, Barou (Viognier), P & C Bonnefond★, COLOMBO★, CUILLERON (Viognier★), P Gaillard★, J-M Gérin (Viognier), JAMET★★, P Jasmin, Monteillet, S Ogier★, A PERRET★, Pichat, G Vernay★, Vins de Vienne★ (Sotanum★★). Best years: (reds) **2010 09 07 06 05**.

COLLIO DOC *Friuli-Venezia Giulia, Italy* Some of Italy's best and most expensive dry white wines are from these hills on the Slovenian border. There are 19 types of wine, from local Friulano and Malvasia Istriana to international varieties. The best are ageworthy. Best producers: Borgo Conventi★, Borgo del Tiglio★★, La Castellada★, Damijan★, Livio FELLUGA★★, Marco Felluga★, Fiegl★, GRAVNER★★, JERMANN★★, Edi Keber★, Renato Keber★, Livon★, Primosic★, Princic★, Puiatti★, Roncùs★★, Russiz Superiore★, SCHIOPPETTO★, Matijaz Tercic★★, Venica & Venica★★, Villa Russiz★★, Villanova★, Zuani★★. Best years: (whites) (2011) 10 **09 08 07 06**.

COLLIOURE AC *Roussillon, France* Tiny fishing port in the Pyrenean foothills. Throat-warming red wine that is capable of aging for a decade but is marvellously rip-roaring when young. Best producers: (reds) Abbé Rous, Baillaury★, Clos de Paulilles★, MAS BLANC★★, la Rectorie★★, la Tour Vieille★, Vial Magnères★. Best years: (2011) 10 09 **08 07 06 05**.

COLOMBARD In France, Colombard traditionally has been distilled to make Armagnac and Cognac, but has now emerged as a table wine grape in its own right, notably as a mainstay of CÔTES DE GASCOGNE. At its best, it has a lovely, crisp acidity and fresh, aromatic fruit. The largest plantings of the grape are in California, where it generally produces rather less distinguished wines, although French winemaker Yannick Rousseau of NAPA VALLEY makes a superb dry version from old vines in RUSSIAN RIVER VALLEY. South Africa can produce attractive refreshing wines, though much is used in brandy production. Australia also has some bright-eyed examples (especially PRIMO ESTATE).

JEAN-LUC COLOMBO *Cornas AC, Rhône Valley, France* Colombo is an unashamed modernist. His wine CORNAS is more opulent and less tannic than most. Top cuvées are les Ruchets★★ and the lush old-vines la Louvée★★. Among his *négociant* wines, CONDRIEU Amour de Dieu★★, CHÂTEAUNEUF-DU-PAPE les Bartavelles★ and red and white HERMITAGE le Rouet★ stand out, although some offerings don't always seem fully ripe. Also fragrant ST-PÉRAY la Belle de Mai★ (sometimes ★★), plus good red and white CÔTES DU RHÔNE★ and COLLINES RHODANIENNES★. Best years: (Cornas) (2011) 10 09 **07** 06 05 04 03 01 00 **99 98**.

COLOMÉ *Salta, Argentina* Established in the early 19th century, Colomé is one of the oldest, most remote and beautiful wineries in South America. As well as a 5-star boutique hotel and art museum, Swiss billionaire owner Donald Hess has invested in a state-of-the-art winery and has been renovating and planting vineyards at extreme altitude. Altura Maxima, at 3100m (10,000ft) above sea level, is the world's highest commercial vineyard, and is biodynamic. The Estate Red★★ (Malbec with Cabernet Sauvignon and Tannat) is an aromatic, wild, herby wine. Reserve Malbec★★ is impressively plush, dense with blue fruit and alcohol. Torrontés★★ is thrillingly lush and scented. Bodegas Amalaya★ is a nearby Hess-owned but independent project, specializing in Malbec and Torrontés blends. Best years: (top reds) 2010 09 **08** 07 06 05.

COLORADO *USA* With their high altitudes, many regions in the Rocky Mountains seem perfect to grow wine grapes, but arid conditions, soil anomalies and cold winters make much of Colorado unsuitable. As a result, 90% of the fruit used by Colorado's 80 wineries comes from one of the two appellations: the warmer Grand Valley AVA and the slightly cooler (and higher in altitude) West Elks AVA. Most vineyards are at 1200–2100m (4000–7000ft). Riesling and Gewürztraminer do well here, with reds from Cabernets Franc and Sauvignon. Best producers: Balistreri, BookCliff Vineyards★, Boulder Creek★, Canyon Wind★★, Carlson, Colorado Cellars, Guy Drew, Alfred Eames Cellars★, Garfield Estates★, Infinite Monkey Theorem★, Jack Rabbit Hill★, Plum Creek★, Sutcliffe, Terror Creek★, Two Rivers★, Winery at Holy Cross Abbey★.

Grand Valley, Colorado

COLUMBIA CREST *Washington State, USA* An offshoot of CHATEAU STE MICHELLE, and now the largest winery in Washington State, producing top-calibre wines at everyday prices. Two Vines budget label is good. Grand Estates Shiraz★, Cabernet Sauvignon★ and Chardonnay★ are strong suits, as is the H3★ label for Horse Heaven Hills fruit; these are good young but will age for several years. Reserve Syrah★ can be heavily oaked but has impressive style. Best years: (reds) (2010) 09 **08 07** 06.

COLUMBIA VALLEY AVA *Washington State, USA* The largest of WASHINGTON's viticultural regions, covering a third of the state's landmass and encompassing both the YAKIMA VALLEY and WALLA WALLA VALLEY, as well as the newer AVAs of Red Mountain, Wahluke Slope, Rattlesnake Hills, Horse Heaven Hills, Snipes Mountain, Columbia Gorge and Lake Chelan. It produces 98% of the state's wine grapes: Merlot, Cabernet Sauvignon and Chardonnay are the most widely planted varieties. Best producers: ANDREW WILL★★, BETZ★, CADENCE★★, CHATEAU STE MICHELLE★, COLUMBIA CREST★, CORLISS★★, DELILLE CELLARS★★, DUNHAM★, Goose Ridge, GRAMERCY★, HEDGES★, JANUIK★, L'ECOLE NO 41★★, LONG SHADOWS★★, Matthews Cellars★★, OWEN ROE★, QUILCEDA CREEK★★★, SYNCLINE★, WOODWARD CANYON★★. Best years: (reds) (2010) 09 **08 07 06 05 04**.

COMMANDARIA *Cyprus* Liquid history from the time of the Crusades! Sun-dried Mavro and Xynisteri grapes produce an amber, treacly wine. Many are disappointing, but the rare Etko Centurion is very special. The main brands are Etko St Nicholas, Keo St John and Sodap St Barnabas.

CONCHA Y TORO *Maipo, Chile* Chile's biggest wine company, Concha y Toro has around 8500ha (21,000 acres) of vineyards and a talented group of winemakers led by Marcelo Papa. Casillero del Diablo is the 'international' label, best for oddballs like Pinot Grigio and Malbec, less good for Cabernet, Merlot and Carmenère. Stepping up, Trio★, Marqués de Casa Concha★ and Terrunyo★★ are good labels for reds and, especially, whites. Amelia★★ is the top Chardonnay, and small amounts of excellent reds come out under the Winemaker's Lot label (usually ★★). The classic Cabernet Sauvignon-based Don Melchor★★★ is impressively velvety and complex in recent releases. Recent Ucúquer cool-climate development at the mouth of Rapel River is exciting. The related Maycas del Limarí winery offers crisp Sauvignon Blanc★, tangy, mineral Chardonnay★★ and ripe, scented yet dense Syrah★★. Palo Alto winery in MAULE. Trivento★ is an important Argentinian project. Acquired FETZER of California in 2011. See also ALMAVIVA, CONO SUR.

CONDRIEU AC *Rhône Valley, France* The home of Viognier. Fragrant but expensive wine from mainly granite soils. Ranges from scented, full and opulent to sweet, late-harvested; the best have a mineral streak. Quality varies, so stick to top names. Classic aperitif. Best drunk young. Best producers: G Barge★, P Benetière★, P & C Bonnefond★★, CHAPOUTIER★, du Chêne★, L Chèze★, Clusel-Roch★, COLOMBO★★, CUILLERON★★★, DELAS★★, C Facchin★, Faury★★, P Gaillard★★, Y Gangloff★★, J-M Gérin, GUIGAL★★, F Merlin★★, Monteillet★★, Mouton★, R Niéro★★, A Paret★★, A PERRET★★, C Pichon★★, ROSTAING★★, St-Cosme★★, G Vernay★★★, F Villard★★★.

CONERO DOCG/ROSSO CONERO DOC *Marche, Italy* Denomination now split between the superior production, Conero DOCG, and Rosso Conero DOC. Conero (with lower yields) has a minimum of 85% Montepulciano and a maximum of 15% Sangiovese, while Rosso Conero's optional 15% may include international varieties. Best producers: Garofoli★★, Leopardi Dittajuti★, Mecella★, Monte Schiavo★★, Moroder★★, Le Terrazze★★, Umani Ronchi★★. Best years: (2011) (10) 09 **08 07 06 04**.

CONO SUR *Colchagua, Chile* Dynamic sister winery to CONCHA Y TORO, whose Pinot Noir put the grape on the Chilean map. Basic releases have lost a little character recently. The CASABLANCA-sourced 20 Barrels Pinot Noir★★ is rich and perfumed; top-of-the-range Ocio★★ is positively unctuous, yet refreshing. Minerally, crunchy 20 Barrels Sauvignon Blanc★★ is from one of Casablanca's coolest sites. Chardonnay★★,

Merlot★★ and Cabernet Sauvignon★★, under 20 Barrels and Visión labels, are excellent, as are the Visión Riesling★★, Gewürztraminer★ and Viognier★. Isla Negra is a budget label.

CH. LA CONSEILLANTE★★ *Pomerol AC, Bordeaux, France* Elegant, exotic, velvety wine that blossoms beautifully after 5–6 years but can age much longer. Second wine: Duo de Conseillante (from 2007). Best years: 2010 09 08 **07** 06 **05** 04 03 02 01 00 **99** 98 96 95 90 89.

CONSTANTIA WO *South Africa* The historic heart of South African wine, covering much of Simon van der Stel's original 1685 land grant. Today 10 properties stretch along the Constantiaberg, from STEENBERG in the south to Beau Constantia in the north. Sauvignon Blanc thrust this cool-climate area into the limelight, and the increasing trend for Semillon-Sauvignon blends is realized in Constantia Uitsig's elegant, flavoursome Constantia White★ and Groot Constantia's poised, persistent Reserve White★. Wines such as the pure-fruited, supple Eagles' Nest Shiraz★★ and Steenberg's Merlot★ show reds too have a promising future. Cap Classique sparkling wines are also gaining in popularity. Best producers: BUITENVERWACHTING★, Constantia Glen★, Constantia Uitsig★, Eagles' Nest★, Groot Constantia (since 2004), High Constantia, KLEIN CONSTANTIA★, STEENBERG★★. Best years: (whites) **2011** 10 09 08 07 06 05 04 03.

ALDO CONTERNO *Barolo DOCG, Piedmont, Italy* One of BAROLO's finest traditionalist producers. He makes good Dolcetto d'Alba★, excellent BARBERA D'ALBA Conca Tre Pile★★, a barrique-aged LANGHE Nebbiolo Il Favot★★, red blend Quartetto★★ and 2 Langhe Chardonnays: unoaked Printaniè and Bussiador★, fermented and aged in new wood. Pride of the range, though, are his Barolos from the hill of Bussia. In top vintages he produces Vigna Colonnello★★★, Vigna Cicala★★★ and excellent Granbussia★★★, as well as a regular Barolo called Bussia Soprana★★. All these Barolos, though accessible when young, need several years to show their true majesty, but retain a remarkable freshness. Best years: (Barolo) (2011) (10) (09) 08 **07** 06 **04** 01 **99** 98 97 96 95 90 89 88.

GIACOMO CONTERNO *Barolo DOCG, Piedmont, Italy* Aldo's late elder brother Giovanni, now followed by his son Roberto, took an even more traditional approach to winemaking. The flagship wine is BAROLO Monfortino★★★ (only released after some 5 or 6 years in large oak barrels), but Barolo Cascina Francia★★★ is also superb. Excellent traditional BARBERA D'ALBA★★. Best years: (Monfortino) (2011) (10) (09) (08) 07 06 04 **02** 01 **00** 99 98 97 96 95 90 89 88 85 82 71.

CONTINO *Rioja DOCa, Rioja, Spain* An estate on some of the finest RIOJA land, half-owned by CVNE but run with passion and skill as a boutique operation. Beautifully balanced Reserva★★, a scented single-vineyard Viña del Olivo★★ (sometimes ★★★) and a remarkable, piercing Graciano★★. These wines all age beautifully. Also white Rioja★. Best years: (Reserva) (2007) 06 05 **04** 03 02 01 00 99 98 96 95 94 86 85.

CONTUCCI *Tuscany, Italy* The Contucci family has been making wines for 1000 years, long before it was called VINO NOBILE. Arch-traditionalists, favouring long-macerated wines with protracted aging in large barrels, they hold court in a *palazzo* in the medieval town of Montepulciano. Top Vino Nobile is Riserva★★ followed by crus Mulinvecchio★★ and Pietra Rossa★★, but even the basic Vino Nobile★ has great purity of fruit.

COONAWARRA *South Australia* A cigar-shaped ridge of terra rossa soil over limestone, Coonawarra can produce sublime Cabernet with leafy blackcurrant flavours yet real depth, and spicy Shiraz that can age for years. Riesling, Sauvignon and Merlot can be good too. Massive expansion outside the terra rossa strip has caused inconsistency and many poor wines bearing the Coonawarra label, but this has spurred the owners of the terra rossa land to redouble their efforts to produce some of Australia's best wine. Best producers: BALNAVES★★, Bowen, BRAND'S★★, Hollick★, KATNOOK★★, Ladbroke Grove, Leconfield★, LINDEMAN'S★★, MAJELLA★★★, Murdock, Orlando/JACOB'S CREEK★★, PARKER★★, PENLEY★★, PETALUMA★, WYNNS★★★, Zema★★. Best years: (Cabernet Sauvignon) (2010) 09 08 **06 05 04 03 02 01 99 98 97 96 94 91** 90.

COOPERS CREEK *Auckland, North Island, New Zealand* Successful HAWKES BAY Swamp Reserve Chardonnay★ and tangy MARLBOROUGH Sauvignon Blanc★. GISBORNE Arneis★, Marlborough Riesling★ and Late Harvest Riesling★ are also good. A smart range of Reserve reds from Hawkes Bay includes powerful Syrah★ and complex Merlot★ and Cabernet Sauvignon blends★. Best years: (Chardonnay) **2010 09 07 06 04**.

FRANCIS FORD COPPOLA *Rutherford AVA, California, USA* Movie director Francis Ford Coppola splits his winemaking activities between luxury and lifestyle brands, with volume approaching 1 million cases. The historic Inglenook Niebaum winery had been renamed Rubicon Estate, but in 2011 Coppola bought the trademarked Inglenook name and gave the estate back its original name. Rubicon★, a BORDEAUX blend, lacked grace in early vintages and is still a bit thick-set for my taste. Also Cask Cabernet★★, Edizione Pennino★ (Zinfandel), RC Reserve Syrah★ and tiny amounts of Merlot★★ and Cabernet Franc★★, as well as white blend Blancaneaux★. Coppola also owns the former Chateau Souverain winery at Geyserville (renamed as the Francis Ford Coppola Winery and turned into an elaborate tourist destination), where brands include Sofia bubblies and good-value Coppola Diamond Collection varietals. Best years: (Rubicon) 2008 **07 06 05 04 03 02 01 00 99 97 96 95 94** 91.

CORBIÈRES AC *Languedoc, France* Huge region, with its cru of Boutenac, producing some of LANGUEDOC's best reds, with juicy fruit and a whiff of wild hillside herbs. Excellent young, but wines from the best estates can age for years. White Corbières can be tasty for drinking young. Best producers: (reds) Baillat★, La Baronne★, Bel-Evêque★, Caraguilhes★, Cascadais★, CLOS DE L'ANHEL★, Embrès-et-Castelmaure★, Étang des Colombes★, Fontsainte★, Grand Crès★, Grand Moulin★, Haut-Gléon★, Hélène★, l'Ille★, Lastours★, Mansenoble★, Ollieux★, Ollieux-Romanis★, les Palais★, St-Auriol★, Voulte-Gasparets★. Best years: (reds) (2011) **10 09 08 07 06 05**.

CORISON *Napa Valley AVA, California, USA* Cathy Corison is one of NAPA VALLEY's best Cabernet producers, steering clear of the heavily oaked, over-extracted style favoured by many Napa newcomers. The straight Cabernet★★ and Kronos Vineyard Cabernet★★ are gorgeous, age-

worthy wines. She also makes ANDERSON VALLEY Gewurztraminer★. Best years: (Kronos) 2008 **07 06 05 04** 03.

CORLISS ESTATES *Columbia Valley AVA, Washington State, USA* Michael and Lauri Corliss produce a bold mineral Syrah★★, a complex BORDEAUX-style red★★, and an ageworthy Cabernet Sauvignon★★ that ranks with the top in Washington. Wines are released after significant bottle-aging, adding complexity and balance. Best years: (2010) (09) 08 **07 06** 05.

CORNAS AC *Rhône Valley, France* Pure Syrah wines with clearer fruit and balance in the past 10 years, including a remarkable 2010; attractive alternatives to pricey neighbours HERMITAGE and CÔTE-RÔTIE. When young, the wines are dark red, with brooding dark fruit aromas; the fruit comes with a mineral tang. Best producers: ALLEMAND★★★, F Balthazar★★, CLAPE★★★, COLOMBO★★, du Coulet★, Courbis★★, DELAS★, E & J Durand★★, Equis, JABOULET, J Lemenicier★, J Michel★, V Paris★★, TAIN co-op★, Tardieu-Laurent★★, Tunnel★, A Voge★★. Best years: (2011) 10 09 **07 06 05 04 03 01 00 99 98 97 96 95 94 91 90 89 88 85.**

CORSE AC, VIN DE *Corsica, France* Overall AC for CORSICA with 5 superior sub-regions: Calvi, Coteaux du Cap Corse, Figari, Porto Vecchio and Sartène. Ajaccio and Patrimonio are entitled to their own ACs. The most distinctive wines, mainly red, come from local grapes: Nielluccio (thought to be related to Sangiovese) and Sciacarello for reds, Vermentino (known locally as Vermentinu or Malvasia) for whites. There are some rich sweet Muscats, especially from Muscat du Cap Corse AC. Best producers: ARENA★, Canarelli★, Clos d'Alzeto★, Clos Capitoro, Clos Culombu▲, Clos Landry▲, Clos Nicrosi▲, Gentile, Leccia, Maestracci★, Comte Peraldi★, Renucci★, Saparale, Signadore, Torraccia★.

CORSICA *France* This Mediterranean island has continued its trend toward quality, reaping the benefits of investment in equipment and planting. Syrah, Merlot, Cabernet Sauvignon and Mourvèdre for reds, and Chardonnay and Sauvignon Blanc for whites, are used to complement the local reds Nielluccio, Sciacarello, Aleatico, and whites Barbarossa and Vermentino. Whites and rosés are pleasant for drinking young; reds are more exciting and can age for 3–4 years. See also CORSE AC.

CORTES DE CIMA *Alentejo, Portugal* Good modern Portuguese reds. Blends of Aragonez (Tempranillo) and Syrah with Portuguese grapes such as Trincadeira and Touriga Nacional are used for spicy, fruity Chaminé, oaked red Cortes de Cima★ and a splendid dark, smoky Reserva★★. Also aromatic varietal Touriga Nacional★★ and Incógnito★★, a gutsy, black-fruited blockbuster Syrah. Best years: 2009 **08 05 04 03 01 00.**

CORTESE White grape variety of south-eastern PIEDMONT in Italy; it can produce good, zesty, fairly acidic, dry whites. Sometimes labelled simply as Cortese Piemonte DOC, its main purpose is as the sole grape in GAVI.

CORTON AC *Grand Cru, Côte de Beaune, Burgundy, France* The only red Grand Cru in the CÔTE DE BEAUNE; the best examples have some of the perfumed class of fine CÔTE DE NUITS. Too much land was classified as Grand Cru and some does not deserve it. Best wines are from Bressandes, Clos du Roi, Le Corton and Le Rognet. New excitement with participation of Dom. de la ROMANÉE-CONTI from 2009. Very little white Corton. Best producers: B Ambroise★★, d'Ardhuy★★, Bonneau du Martray★★, CHANDON DE BRIAILLES★★, Croix★★, Dubreuil-Fontaine★★, FAIVELEY★★★, Follin-Arbelet★, Camille Giroud★★, Guyon★★, JADOT★★★, Dom. LEROY★★★, MEO-CAMUZET★★★, Dom. du Pavillon/Bichot★★, J Prieur★★, Senard★, TOLLOT-BEAUT★. Best years: (reds) (2011) 10 09 08 **07 06 05 03 02 01 99 98 96 95 90.**

CORTON-CHARLEMAGNE AC *Grand Cru, Côte de Beaune, Burgundy, France* Corton-Charlemagne, on the west and south-west flanks and at the top of the famous CORTON hill, is the largest of Burgundy's white Grands

Crus. It can produce some of the most impressive white Burgundies –
richly textured yet with a fine mineral quality. The best should show their
real worth only at 10 years or more. Best producers: H Boillot★, Bonneau du
Martray★★★, BOUCHARD PÈRE ET FILS★★, Champy★★, COCHE-DURY★★★,
DROUHIN★★, FAIVELEY★★, V GIRARDIN★★★, JADOT★★★, P Javillier★★, Louis
LATOUR★★, J Prieur★★, Rapet★★, M Rollin★★, ROUMIER★★, TOLLOT-
BEAUT★★, VOUGERAIE★★. Best years: (2011) 10 09 08 **07 06** 05 **04 02 00 99**.

CH. COS D'ESTOURNEL★★★ *St-Estèphe AC, 2ème Cru Classé, Haut-Médoc,*
🍷 *Bordeaux, France*   One of the leading châteaux of BORDEAUX. The wine is
classically made for aging and usually needs 10 years to show really well.
Used to have a high proportion of Merlot (around 40%) but from 2007
Cabernet Sauvignon has been on the increase (65–85%). Recent vintages
have been dark, brooding, powerful and, but for a wobble in 1998 and 99,
of the highest order. Small production of white from 2005 and new state-
of-the-art winery in 2008. Second wine: les Pagodes de Cos. Best years:
2010 09 08 07 06 05 **04 03 02 01 00 96 95 94 90 89 88**.

DOM. COSSE-MAISONNEUVE *Cahors AOP, South-West France*   Cult
🍷 biodynamic producers of CAHORS, combining the best of the traditional
and modern styles. From the fruity Le Combal★, move up through Le
Petit Sid★★ to Les Laquets★★ and finally Le Sid★★, which reflects the
iron that underlies the soil. Best years: (2011) 10 09 **06 05 04 01**.

COSTANTI *Brunello di Montalcino DOCG, Tuscany, Italy*   One of the original
🍷 Montalcino estates, making fine BRUNELLO★★ (Riserva★★) and ROSSO DI
MONTALCINO★, as well as Vermiglio★, a partially barrique-aged
Sangiovese, and 'international' style Merlot-Cabernet blend Calbello★.
Best years: (Brunello) (2011) (10) (09) (08) 07 06 **04 01 99 97 95 90 88 85 82**.

COSTERS DEL SEGRE DO *Cataluña, Spain*   DO in western CATALUÑA, with
🍷🍷 an array of grape varieties, generally good quality and moderate prices.
Best producers: Castell del Remei★, Celler de Cérvoles★★, Tomás Cusiné★,
RAÏMAT★. Best years: (reds) (2010) 09 **08 07 06** 05 **04 03 01**.

COSTIÈRES DE NÎMES AC *Rhône Valley, France*   Underestimated quality
🍷🍷 region west of Avignon. Reds are bright, spicy, chewy, perfumed, the best
substantial; rosés are good young gluggers; whites are tasty, rich versions
of Marsanne and Roussanne. Best producers: l'Amarine★, Amphoux, Grande
Cassagne★, Lamargue, Mas des Bressades★, Mas Carlot, Mas Neuf, Mourgues du
Grès★, Nages★, d'Or et de Gueules★, la Patience, Roubaud★, Tardieu-Laurent,
la Tour de Beraud★, la Tuilerie, Vieux-Relais★. Best years: **2010 09 07**.

CÔTE DE BEAUNE *Côte d'Or, Burgundy, France*   Southern part of the CÔTE
🍷 D'OR: beginning at the hill of CORTON, north of the town of BEAUNE, the
Côte de Beaune progresses south as far as MARANGES. Mostly red, but
whites dominate MEURSAULT, PULIGNY and CHASSAGNE.

CÔTE DE BEAUNE AC *Côte de Beaune, Burgundy, France*   Small AC, high on
🍷 the hill above the town of Beaune, named to ensure confusion with the
title of the region. Lean but attractive reds and whites. Best producers:
DROUHIN★, Giboulot, VOUGERAIE★. Best years: (red) (2011) 10 **09 08 05**.

CÔTE DE BEAUNE-VILLAGES AC *Côte de Beaune, Burgundy, France*   Red
🍷 wine AC covering 16 villages, such as AUXEY-DURESSES, LADOIX, MARANGES.
Blends from several villages are sold as Côte de Beaune-Villages. It can
also cover the red wine production of mainly white wine villages such as
MEURSAULT. Best producers: DROUHIN★, JADOT★. Best years: (2011) 10 **09 08 05**.

CÔTE DE BROUILLY AC *Beaujolais, Burgundy, France*   Wine from the slopes
🍷 of Mont Brouilly, a small, abrupt volcanic mountain in the south of the
BEAUJOLAIS Crus area. The wine is deeper in colour and fruit and has more

intensity than that of BROUILLY. Best producers: Lagneau (Vieilles Vignes★),
Ch. Thivin★ (La Chapelle★★, Les Sept Vignes★★). Best years: (2011) **10** 09.

CÔTE CHALONNAISE See BOURGOGNE-CÔTE CHALONNAISE.

CÔTE DE NUITS *Côte d'Or, Burgundy, France* The northern part of the CÔTE
D'OR and *not* an AC. Almost entirely red wine country, the vineyards start
in the southern suburbs of Dijon and continue south in a narrow swathe
to below the town of NUITS-ST-GEORGES. Some of the greatest wine names
in the world – GEVREY-CHAMBERTIN, VOUGEOT and VOSNE-ROMANÉE etc.

CÔTE DE NUITS-VILLAGES AC *Côte de Nuits, Burgundy, France* The wines
(mostly red) are often good, sourced from lesser villages north of GEVREY
and south of NUITS – not very deep in colour but with a nice cherry fruit.
Best producers: (reds) l'Arlot, D Bachelet★, BELLENE, Chopin-Groffier★, David
Clark★, J-J Confuron, de la Douaix★, Gille, JADOT, G Jourdan★, Loichet,
Millot★. Best years: (reds) (2011) 10 **09 08 07 06 05**.

CÔTE D'OR *Burgundy, France* Europe's most northerly great red wine area,
and also the home of some of the world's best dry white wines. The
name, meaning 'golden slope', refers to a 48km (30-mile) stretch
between Dijon and Chagny which divides into the CÔTE DE NUITS in the
north and the CÔTE DE BEAUNE in the south.

CÔTE ROANNAISE AC *Loire Valley, France* Small, improving AC in the
upper LOIRE producing Gamay reds and rosés; the best are of BEAUJOLAIS-
VILLAGES standard. Vin de pays whites can be good. Best producers:
A Baillon, V Giraudon, de la Paroisse, M Piat, R Sérol★.

CÔTE-RÔTIE AC *Rhône Valley, France* The Côte-Rôtie, or 'roasted slope',
produces one of France's finest red wines. On its steep, slippery slopes,
the Syrah balances full aromatic ripeness with freshness, and the small
amount of white Viognier sometimes included adds exotic or violet
fragrance. Lovely young, it is better aged for 5–8 years. Best producers:
G Barge★★, Bernard★, Billon, P & C Bonnefond★★, Bonserine★★,
B Burgaud★, CHAPOUTIER★, Clusel-Roch★★, CUILLERON★★, DELAS★,
Duclaux★★, Garon★, J-M Gérin★★, GUIGAL★★, JAMET★★★, P Jasmin★★,
Levet, S Ogier★★, Rosiers★, ROSTAING★★★, J-M Stéphan★, Tardieu-
Laurent★★, VIDAL-FLEURY★, F Villard★★, Vins de Vienne★. Best years: (2011)
10 09 **07 06 05 04 03 01 00 99 98 95 94 91 90 89**.

COTEAUX D'AIX-EN-PROVENCE AC *Provence, France* The first AC in
the south to allow Cabernet Sauvignon to enhance the traditional local
grape varieties Grenache, Cinsaut, Mourvèdre, Syrah and Carignan. The
reds can age. Some quite good fresh rosé. The whites, mostly traditionally
made, are merely pleasant. Best producers: Ch. Bas★, les Bastides★, les
Béates★★, Beaupré★, Calissanne★, d'EOLE★, Fonscolombe, Revelette★,
Valdition, Vignelaure★. Best years: (reds) (2011) 10 **09 08 07 06 05 04 03**.

COTEAUX DE L'ARDÈCHE, VIN DE PAYS DES *Rhône Valley, France*
Increasingly good, lively red wines made from Cabernet Sauvignon,
Syrah, Merlot or Gamay, and dry, fresh whites from Chardonnay,
Viognier or Sauvignon Blanc. Best producers: Vignerons Ardéchois,
Colombier, DUBOEUF, G Flacher, Grangeon, Louis LATOUR★, Mas de Libian
(Viognier), Pradel, Romaneaux-Destezet★, Vigier.

COTEAUX DE L'AUBANCE AC *Loire Valley, France* Smallish AC north of
COTEAUX DU LAYON AC for sweet or semi-sweet white wines made from
Chenin Blanc. Top sweet wines are labelled Sélection de Grains Nobles,
as in ALSACE. Best producers: Bablut★★/Daviau, Dittière, Giraudières, Haute
Perche★, Montgilet★★, Princé, Richou★★, Rochelles★/J-Y Lebreton. Best
years: (2011) 10 09 **07 06 05 04 03 02 01 99 97 96**.

COTEAUX BOURGUIGNONS AC *Burgundy, France* New AC replacing BOURGOGNE Grand Ordinaire from 2011. It will also be possible to reclassify BEAUJOLAIS under this new name. Why? Ask the politicians.

COTEAUX CHAMPENOIS AC *Champagne, France* Still wines from Champagne. Fairly acid, with a few exceptions, notably from Bouzy and Aÿ. The best age for 5 years or more. Best producers: Paul Bara★, BOLLINGER★, Egly-Ouriet★, Geoffroy★, H Goutorbe, Benoît Lahaye★, LAURENT-PERRIER, Joseph PERRIER, Ch. de Saran★/MOËT & CHANDON. Best years: 2009 08 **04**.

COTEAUX DU GIENNOIS AC *Loire Valley, France* Small appellation near SANCERRE for white wines made from Sauvignon Blanc, reds from Pinot Noir or Gamay, and rosés made from a blend of both red grapes. Best producers: Balland-Chapuis, C Bardin, J-M Berthier★★, H BOURGEOIS★, M Langlois, J Mellot★, de Montbenoit★, Quintin, Florian Roblin, Thibault.

COTEAUX DU LANGUEDOC AC *Languedoc, France* Large region between Nîmes and Narbonne, producing around 50 million bottles of beefy red, tasty rosé and surprisingly characterful whites. Quality is improving year by year. Was due to be replaced from April 2011 by the larger AC Languedoc, which covers Roussillon as well, but now delayed until 2017. A number of 'crus' were historically allowed to append their names to the AC – these are in the process of being delineated by climate and soil type, with the introduction of the categories of grand vin and cru du Languedoc. All is in a state of flux. See also LANGUEDOC-ROUSSILLON. Best producers: l'Aiguelière★, Aupilhac★, Calage★, Clavel★, CLOS MARIE★, la Coste★, Grès St-Paul★, Lacroix-Vanel★, Mas Cal Demoura, Mas des Chimères★, Mas Jullien★, Mas de Martin, Montcalmès, PEYRE ROSE★, Poujol★, PRIEURE DE ST-JEAN DE BÉBIAN★★, Puech-Haut★, St-Martin de la Garrigue★, Terre Megère★. Best years: (2011) **10 09 08 07 06 05**.

COTEAUX DU LAYON AC *Loire Valley, France* Sweet wine from the Layon Valley, south of Angers. The wine is made from Chenin Blanc grapes that, ideally, are attacked by noble rot or, for intense but fresher styles, dried by warm, autumnal breezes that concentrate grape sugars. In great years like 2007, and from a talented grower, this can be one of the world's exceptional sweet wines. Six villages are entitled to use the Coteaux du Layon-Villages AC, which requires lower yields; the village name appears on the label. Three sub-areas, BONNEZEAUX, QUARTS DE CHAUME (both regarded as Grand Cru sites) and Chaume (regarded as Premier Cru), have their own ACs. Best producers: P Aguilas★★, P Baudouin★★, Baumard★★, Bergerie★★, Cady★★, P Delesvaux★★, Dom. F L, Forges★, de Juchepie★, OGEREAU★★, Passavant★, PIERRE-BISE★★★, Pithon-Paillé★, Quarres★, J Renou★★, Roulerie★★, Sablonnettes★★, Sauveroy★, Soucherie★★. Best years: (2011) 10 09 **07** 06 05 04 03 02 01 99 97 96 95 90.

COTEAUX DU LOIR AC See JASNIÈRES AC.

COTEAUX DU LYONNAIS AC *Beaujolais, Burgundy, France* Good, light, BEAUJOLAIS-style reds and a few whites and rosés from scattered vineyards between Villefranche and Lyon. Drink young.

COTEAUX DU QUERCY AOP *South-West France* Cabernet Franc-based area south of CAHORS. Fruity food-friendly wines of originality and character, best kept for 3–4 years. Best producers: d'Ariès, Ganapes, la Garde, Merchien★. Best years (2011) (10) 09 08 **06 05** 04.

COTEAUX DU TRICASTIN See GRIGNAN-LES-ADHÉMAR.

COTEAUX VAROIS-EN-PROVENCE AC *Provence, France* Improving area north of Toulon and stretching inland, where it is notably cooler than the coast, with new plantings of classic grapes. Best producers: Alysses★,

Calisse★, Deffends★, Fontlade, Garbelle, Margüi★, Miraval★, Routas★, St-Estève, St-Jean-le-Vieux, Triennes★. Best years: (2011) 10 09 08 **07 06**.

CÔTES DE BERGERAC AOP See BERGERAC.

CÔTES DE BORDEAUX AC See BLAYE, CADILLAC, CASTILLON, FRANCS.

CÔTES DE BOURG AC *Bordeaux, France* The best red wines are earthy but blackcurranty and can age for 6–10 years. A little dry but dull white. Best producers: Brulesécaille★, Bujan★, Civrac, FALFAS★, Fougas, Guerry★, Haut-Guiraud★, Haut-Macô★, Haut-Mondésir★, Macay, Mercier, Nodoz★, ROC DE CAMBES★★, Tayac, Tour de Guiet★. Best years: 2010 **09 08 05 03 02 01 00.**

CÔTES DU BRULHOIS AOP *South-West France* A bunch of rapidly improving winemakers clustered round the city of Agen and led by a rather good co-op, Les Vignerons du Brulhois. Quality independents include Ch. La Bastide, Bois de Simon, Coujetou-Peyret, Pountet and Dom. des Thermes. The reds will age. Best years: (2011) 10 **09 08 06 05.**

CÔTES CATALANES, IGP DES *Roussillon, France* Covering much the same area as the CÔTES DU ROUSSILLON AC; co-ops dominate production but there is a growing number of talented individual producers, especially in the Fenouillèdes hills, benefiting from outside investment. Warm, rich, spicy reds, often from old-vines Grenache Noir and Carignan, plus Syrah; full-bodied minerally whites from Grenache Blanc and Gris, and Macabeo. Best producers: la CASENOVE, CAZES, GAUBY/le Soula, l'Horizon, Jones, Matassa, Pertuisane, Olivier Pithon, Préceptorie de Centenach, Soulanes.

CÔTES DE DURAS AC *South-West France* South of BERGERAC, using traditional BORDEAUX grapes, a hot spot for mostly organic growers seeking to establish an identity away from other vineyards of the South-West. The vanguard is led by domaines Haut Lavigne, Hauts de Riquets, Mont Ramé★, Mouthes-le-Bihan★★ and Petit Malromé★. More traditional estates include des Allegrets, Chater★, Condom-Perceval (sweet white★★) and Laulan★. Best years: (reds) (2011) 10 **09 08 06 05.**

CÔTES DE GASCOGNE, IGP DES *South-West France* Tangy-fresh, fruity, mostly white, wine-bar wines that outsell everything else from the South-West put together. Drink young. Best producers: Arton, Brumont★, Cassagnoles, Chiroulet★, de Joÿ, Lauroux, Millet★, Mont Milan, Pellehaut★, PLAIMONT★, San de Guilhem★, Sédouprat, TARIQUET★.

CÔTES DU JURA AC *Jura, France* This AC includes a variety of ageworthy wines, including specialities *vin jaune* and *vin de paille*. Savagnin makes strong-tasting whites, often sherry-like; some Chardonnay is made in this style, while others are dry and mineral, reminiscent of good CÔTE CHALONNAISE. Distinctive reds and rosés from local Poulsard and Trousseau and also from Pinot Noir. See also CRÉMANT DU JURA AC. Best producers: Ch. d'Arlay, Badoz, Baud★, Berthet-Bondet★, Boilley, Bourdy★, Ganevat★★, Grand, A Labet★★, J Macle★, Pignier★★, Reverchon, Rijckaert★★, A & M Tissot★. Best years: 2010 **09 08 07 05.**

CÔTES DU MARMANDAIS AOP *South-West France* The northern gateway of Gascony. Grapes such as Abouriou, Cot, Fer Servadou, Gamay and Syrah are added to conventional BORDEAUX-style Merlot and Cabernet blends to give the red wines from this blossoming area a distinctive southern twist. Best producers: Beaulieu★, Beyssac, Boissonneau, Bonnet & Laborde, ELIAN DA ROS★★, Lassolle. Best years: (reds) (2011) (10) **09 08 06 05.**

CÔTES DE PROVENCE AC *Provence, France* Large AC mainly for fruity reds and rosés to drink young. Three new sub-appellations show that producers are taking regional differences more seriously, especially Côtes de Provence-Ste Victoire – producing wines with fresh minerality

and good aging ability – and Côtes de Provence-La Londe, for wines with salty-mineral acidity, mainly rosés but also rich, fruity reds. Whites have improved. Best producers: Barbanau★, Bastide Neuve, la Bernarde★, Clos d'Alari, Clos de la Procure, Commanderie de Peyrassol★, la Courtade★, Coussin Ste-Victoire★, Cressonnière★, de la Croix★, d'ESCLANS, Féraud★, Galoupet, Gavoty★, Houchart★, Jale, Malherbe, Mauvanne★, Minuty★, Ott★, Pourcieux, Réal Martin★, RICHEAUME★, Rimauresq★★, Roquefort★, St-Albert, St-André de Figuière, Sarrins★, SORIN★, Élie Sumeire★, Les Valentines.

CÔTES DU RHÔNE AC *Rhône Valley, France* AC for the whole RHÔNE VALLEY. Over 90% is red and rosé, mainly Grenache, with some Cinsaut, Syrah, Carignan and Mourvèdre to add warm southern personality. Modern winemaking has improved many wines, which are generally juicy, spicy and easy to drink, ideally within 5 years. Most wine is made by co-ops. Best producers: (reds) Amouriers★, d'Andézon★, les Aphillanthes★, A Brunel★, Charvin★, CLAPE★, Clos des Grillons, Co Ho La, COLOMBO★, Coudoulet de BEAUCASTEL★★, Cros de la Mûre★, Dauvergne Ranvier, DELAS, Espiers★, Estézargues co-op★, Fonsalette★★, FONT DE MICHELLE★, Gramenon★★, Grand Moulas★, Grand Prébois★, GUIGAL★, Hugues★, JABOULET★, JAMET★, la Janasse★, J-M Lombard★, la Manarine, Mas de Libian★, Montfaucon★, la Mordorée★, la RÉMÉJEANNE★, M Richaud★, Romarins, Rouge Garance, St-Estève d'Uchaux, St-Etienne, ST-GAYAN, Ste-Anne★, Santa Duc★, Tardieu-Laurent★, Texier★★ (Brézème), Tours★, Vieille Julienne★, Vieux-Chêne★; (whites) Cassan, Coudoulet de BEAUCASTEL★, P Gaillard★, la RÉMÉJEANNE★, St-Maurice, Ste-Anne★, Texier★★. Best years: (reds) 2010 09.

CÔTES DU RHÔNE-VILLAGES AC *Rhône Valley, France* AC covering 17 villages in the southern CÔTES DU RHÔNE that have traditionally made superior wine (especially CAIRANNE, Laudun, Massif d'Uchaux, Séguret, Valréas, Sablet, Visan). Some exciting, good value wines. Best are spicy, racy-fruited, food-friendly reds that can age well. Best producers: Achiary★, Amouriers★, Beaurenard★, Boissan★, Bramadou, Bressy-Masson★, Brugalière, de Cabasse★, Cabotte★, Chapoton★, D Charavin★, la Charbonnière★, Chaume-Arnaud★, Combe★, Coriançon★, Coste Chaude, Cros de la Mûre★, J David, Durieu, Espigouette★, Estézargues co-op★, Florane, Fourmente★, les Goubert, Gourt de Mautens★★, Gramenon★, Grand Moulas★, Grand Veneur★, Gravennes, la Janasse★★, Jérôme★, Lucena, Mourchon★, Pélaquié★, Piaugier★, Pique Basse★, Rabasse-Charavin★, Rasteau co-op★, la RÉMÉJEANNE★, Roche-Audran, ST-GAYAN★, St-Maurice, St-Pierre, St-Siffrein, Ste-Anne★, Saladin, la Soumade★, Trapadis★, Valériane, Viret★. Best years: (reds) 2010 09 07 06 05.

CÔTES DU ROUSSILLON AC *Roussillon, France* ROUSSILLON's catch-all AC, dominated by co-ops. It's a hot area, and much of the wine is baked and dull. But there's a lively bunch of estates making exciting reds and doing surprisingly good things with whites. Best producers: (reds) la CASENOVE★★, Vignerons Catalans, CAZES★, Chênes★, Ferrer-Ribière★, Força Réal, Joliette, Laporte★, Mas Crémat★, Mossé, Olivier Pithon★, Rivesaltes co-op, Sarda-Malet★. Best years: (reds) (2011) 10 09 08 07 06 05.

CÔTES DU ROUSSILLON-VILLAGES AC *Roussillon, France* Wines from the best sites in the northern CÔTES DU ROUSSILLON, one of the liveliest wine areas in the south of France. Villages Caramany, Latour-de-France, Lesquerde and Tautavel may add their own name. Best producers: Calvet-Thunevin, Vignerons Catalans, CAZES★, Chênes★, Clos des Fées★, CLOT DE L'OUM★, Fontanel★, Força Réal, Gardiés★, GAUBY★★, Jau, Mas Amiel★, Mas Cremat★, Piquemal, Reveille, Roc des Anges, Schistes★. Best years: (reds) (2011) **10 09 08 07 06 05.**

CÔTES DE THONGUE, IGP DES *Languedoc, France* Zone north-east of Béziers, where some dynamic estates are producing excellent results, with intriguing blends as well as varietal wines. Best producers: l'Arjolle★, les Chemins de Bassac, La Croix Belle, Magellan, Monplézy.

CÔTES DU VIVARAIS AC *Rhône Valley, France* Southern Rhône grapes (Grenache, Syrah, Cinsaut, Carignan) from hilly vineyards produce simple-fruited, fresh reds and rosés for drinking young. Whites from Marsanne and Grenache Blanc. Uneven quality. Best producers: Vignerons Ardéchois, Gallety★, Vigier.

QUINTA DO CÔTTO *Douro DOC and Port DOC, Douro, Portugal* Unfortified DOURO wine expert. Quinta do Côtto red and creamy Paço de Teixeró white are good, and Grande Escolha★★ can be excellent: oaky and powerful when young, rich and cedary when mature. Best years: (Grande Escolha) **2007 01 00 97 95 94 90 87 85.**

VIGNOBLES DE LA COULÉE-DE-SERRANT *Savennières AC, Loire Valley, France* Nicolas Joly is biodynamics' most vocal proponent and, with his winemaker daughter Virginie, produces powerfully concentrated, distinctive and ageworthy SAVENNIÈRES wines with atypically high degrees of alcohol. Eponymous top cuvée hails from monopole Clos de la Coulée de Serrant★★, a steep, walled 7ha (17-acre) vineyard with its own sub appellation. Also impressive Savennières Clos de la Bergerie★★ and Les Vieux Clos★. Best years: (2009) **08 07 06 05 04 03 02 01 00 97 96 95 90 89.**

PIERRE COURSODON *St-Joseph AC, Rhône Valley, France* Family-owned 16ha (40-acre) domaine producing rocking, rich ST JOSEPH★ from old vines. Reds need up to 4 years to show their magnificent cassis, truffle and violet richness, especially La Sensonne★★, aged in new oak, and le Paradis St Pierre★. Food-friendly whites, especially Paradis St Pierre★ from Marsanne. Best years: (reds) (2011) **10 09 07 06 05 04 03 01 00 99 98.**

COUSIÑO MACUL *Maipo, Chile* Established in 1856 and now run by the sixth generation of the Cousiño family. The old Macul winery and cellars near the city of Santiago are a draw for tourists, but the wines are now made in a modern facility further south. Best known for Antiguas Reservas★ and premium wines such as Lota★ and Finis Terrae★, but they also make an unusual Sauvignon Gris and a Riesling.

CH. COUTET★★ *Barsac AC, 1er Cru Classé, Bordeaux, France* BARSAC's largest Classed Growth property; on great form in recent years, and with its finesse and balance it is once again a classic Barsac. Extraordinarily intense Cuvée Madame★★★ is made in exceptional years. Best years: **2010 09 07 06 05 04 03 02 01 00 99 98 97 96 95 90 89.**

CRAGGY RANGE *Hawkes Bay and Martinborough, North Island, New Zealand* Ambitious winery whose style becomes more attractive and refined with each vintage. Premium HAWKES BAY wines include stylish Les Beaux Cailloux Chardonnay★★, a bold Cabernet blend called The Quarry★★, a rich, butch Merlot blend known as Sophia★★ and the flagship Le Sol Syrah★★. Also elegant Gimblett Gravels Chardonnay★, Syrah★★ and Merlot★ from Hawkes Bay; fine Te Muna Road Pinot Noir★★ and Riesling★ from MARTINBOROUGH; restrained yet intense Avery Sauvignon Blanc★ and tangy Rapaura Road Riesling★ from MARLBOROUGH. Best years: (Syrah) **2010 09 08 07 06 04.**

QUINTA DO CRASTO *Douro DOC and Port DOC, Douro, Portugal* Well-situated property with good Vintage★ PORT, massively enjoyable juicy reds Crasto★ and Crasto Superior★, complex Reserva Old Vines★★, oaky but excellent Touriga Nacional★★ and Tinta Roriz★★, and flagship reds Vinha da Ponte★★★ and Maria Teresa★★★. Austere Xisto★ red is a venture with Jean-Michel Cazes of Ch. LYNCH-BAGES. Also pleasant spicy Crasto white★. Best years: (Vintage port) 2007 **04 03 00 99 97 95 94**; (Ponte) **2007 04 00**; (Maria Teresa) 2009 **07 05 03 01 98**.

CRÉMANT D'ALSACE AC *Alsace, France* Good traditional-method sparkling wine from ALSACE, usually made from Pinot Blanc and/or Pinot Gris. Reasonable quality, if not great value for money. Best producers: J-B ADAM★, P Blanck★, Cave de Cleebourg, Dopff & Irion, Dopff au Moulin★, J Gross★, Kuentz-Bas, MURÉ★, OSTERTAG★★, Pfaffenheim co-op, P Sparr★, A Stoffel★, TURCKHEIM co-op★.

CRÉMANT DE BOURGOGNE AC *Burgundy, France* Most Burgundian Crémant is white and is made either from Chardonnay alone or blended with Pinot Noir. The result, especially in ripe years, can be full, soft, almost honey-flavoured – but needs 2–3 years' aging for mellowness to develop. Best producers: L Bouillot, A Delorme, Simonnet-Febvre, A Sounit, Veuve Ambal; (co-ops) Bailly (rosé★), Lugny★, St-Gengoux-de-Scissé, Viré.

CRÉMANT DE DIE AC *Rhône Valley, France* Traditional-method fizz made entirely from the Clairette Blanche grape. Crisper, less aromatic and musky than CLAIRETTE DE DIE. Best producers: Jacques Faure, J-C Raspail★.

CRÉMANT DU JURA AC *Jura, France* AC for fizz from all over Jura, which accounts for nearly a quarter of the region's production. Largely Chardonnay-based; Poulsard, a pale red grape, is dominant in the pinks. Best producers: Fruitière Vinicole d'Arbois, Ch. de l'Étoile★, Grand★, La Maison des Vignerons (Marcel Cabelier), Montbourgeau★, Rolet★, A & M Tissot★★.

CRÉMANT DE LIMOUX AC *Languedoc, France* Sparkling wine made from a blend of Chardonnay, Chenin Blanc, Mauzac and Pinot Noir; the wines generally have more complexity than BLANQUETTE DE LIMOUX. Drink young. Best producers: l'Aigle★, Antech, Delmas, Fourn, Guinot, Laurens★, Martinolles★, Rives-Blanques, SIEUR D'ARQUES.

CRÉMANT DE LOIRE AC *Loire Valley, France* Sparkling wine made by the *méthode traditionnelle* from grapes from Anjou, Saumur and Touraine. Aged for at least 12 months, wines are generally finer than those of VOUVRAY and SAUMUR MOUSSEUX; increasingly Chardonnay is added to Loire stalwarts Chenin Blanc and Cabernet Franc, giving fresh, elegant fruit. Drink young. Best producers: l'Aulée, Baumard★, Bouvet-Ladubay★, Brizé★, Fardeau★, Gratien & Meyer, Langlois-Château★, des Liards★/Berger, Michaud★, Nerleux★, Passavant★, Richou★, St-Just★, Varinelles★.

CRIOTS-BÂTARD-MONTRACHET AC See BÂTARD-MONTRACHET AC.

CROFT *Port DOC, Douro, Portugal* Owned by the Fladgate Partnership (along with TAYLOR'S and FONSECA) since 2001, these wines are showing distinct improvements, especially at basic level. Vintage ports★★ have traditionally been elegant, rather than thunderous. Single-quinta Quinta da Roêda★ is pretty good in recent vintages. Also good pink. Best years: (Vintage) 2009 **07 04 03 00 94 91 77 70 66 63 55**; (Roêda) 2008 **05 04 97 95**.

CROZES-HERMITAGE AC *Rhône Valley, France* The largest of the northern Rhône ACs. Ideally, the pure Syrah reds should have a strong, clear, black fruit flavour. You can drink them young, but in ripe years from a hillside site the fine-textured, red-fruited wine improves greatly for 2–5 years. In lesser years, too much clumsy oak on the more expensive wines can obscure the fruit. The best whites (2010 for instance) can age for 3–5 years. Best producers: (reds) A Belle★★, Bruyères★★, CHAPOUTIER★, Y Chave★, Colombier★ (Cuvée Gaby★★), Combier★ (Clos des Grives★★), E Darnaud★★, DELAS★ (Le Clos★★, Dom. des Grands Chemins★★), O Dumaine★, Entrefaux★, Fayolle Fils & Fille★★, Ferraton★, GRAILLOT★★, Paul JABOULET, P & V Jaboulet★, Lises★, Murinais★, Pavillon-Mercurol★, Pochon★, Remizières★★, G Robin★, Rousset (Picaudières★★), TAIN co-op, Tardieu-Laurent★, Vins de Vienne★; (whites) Y Chave★, Colombier★, Combier★, Dard & Ribo★★, DELAS, O Dumaine★, Entrefaux★, Fayolle Fils & Fille★★, Ferraton★, GRAILLOT★, Mucyn★, Pochon★ (Ch. Curson★★), Remizières★, M Sorrel★★. Best years: (reds) **(2011)** 10 09 07 06 05 03 01 99.

CRUZ DE PIEDRA *Mendoza, Argentina* Founded by the Alonso family in the early 1970s to champion single-variety wines. The appointment of wine-maker Daniel Ekkert in 2007 brought a real upturn in quality. Deliciously bright varietal wines under the Tiasta label. The more serious Umbral de los Tiempos Malbec★ and Cabernet Sauvignon★, from 30-year-old vines, are plush, concentrated and expressive.

YVES CUILLERON *Condrieu AC, Rhône Valley, France* With wines like Cuilleron's, you can understand CONDRIEU's fame and high prices. Les Chaillets★★★, from old vines, is rich and sensual, with perfumed honey and apricot aromas. La Petite Côte★★ and 18-month-aged Vertige★★ are also exceptional, and the late-harvest Ayguets★★★ is an extraordinary sweet whirl of dried apricots, honey and barley sugar. Cuilleron also makes red and white ST-JOSEPH★★, ST-PERAY★ and limited amounts of ripe, dark, oaked, spicy CÔTE-RÔTIE★★. A joint venture, les Vins de Vienne, with Pierre Gaillard and François Villard, produces COLLINES RHODANIENNES Sotanum★★ (100% Syrah) and Taburnum★ (100% Viognier). Best years: (Condrieu) **(2011)** 10 09 08 07 06 05 04.

CULLEN *Margaret River, Western Australia* One of the original MARGARET RIVER vineyards, established by Diana and Kevin Cullen and now run by their winemaker daughter Vanya. Kevin John Chardonnay★★★ is complex and satisfying; Sauvignon-Semillon★★ marries nectarines with melon and nuts. Diana Madeline Cabernet Sauvignon-Merlot★★★ is gloriously soft, deep and scented. Mangan Malbec-Petit Verdot-Merlot★★ is wild and delicious. Best years: (Cabernet Sauvignon-Merlot) (2011) 10 09 08 07 05 04 03 02 01 00 99 98 97 96 95 94.

CURICÓ *Chile* Most of the big producers here have planted Cabernet Sauvignon, Merlot, Carmenère, Chardonnay and Sauvignon Blanc. It's a bit warm for whites, except in the east by the Andes, but the long growing season provides good fruit concentration for reds. Best producers: Echeverría★, SAN PEDRO★, Miguel TORRES★, VALDIVIESO★.

CUVELIER LOS ANDES *Mendoza, Argentina* The Argentine outpost of Bordeaux's Ch. LÉOVILLE-POYFERRÉ, producing profound wines on this 115ha (285-acre), extreme-altitude Uco Valley estate, helped by enologist Michel Rolland. Colección★, originally a Malbec-based blend exhibiting indulgent, violet-scented fruit, has been joined by Malbec, Cabernet and Merlot bottlings. The Grand Vin★★ is an opulent, layered and ageworthy blend, while Grand Malbec★★ is intense and perfumed – both need time but repay the wait. Best years: (2009) 08 **07** 06 05.

CVNE *Rioja DOCa, Rioja, Spain* Compañía Vinícola del Norte de España is the full name of this firm, usually known as 'coonay'. Viña Real★ is one of RIOJA's few remaining well-oaked whites. Viña Real Reserva★ (sometimes ★★) and Gran Reserva★ reds can be rich and meaty, and easily surpass the rather commercial Crianzas. Imperial Reserva★ (can be ★★) is balanced and delightful; Gran Reserva★★★ is long-lived and impressive. Top of the range is red Real de Asúa★. Best years: (Reservas) 2005 04 **03 02** 01 98 96 95 94 91 90 89 87 86 85.

DIDIER DAGUENEAU *Pouilly-Fumé AC, Loire Valley, France* This much-needed innovator died in 2008 and is succeeded by his son, Louis-Benjamin. The range starts with Blanc Fumé★★ and moves up through flinty Buisson Renard★★ to barrel-fermented Silex★★ and Pur Sang★★ to Asteroïde★★, which is made in tiny quantities from ungrafted vines. Also a SANCERRE★★ from the precipitous Les Monts Damnés. Wines benefit from 4–5 years' aging. Since 2004, also making Jurançon Les JARDINS DE BABYLONE★. Best years: (2011) 10 09 **08 07** 06 05 04 03 02 01.

ROMANO DAL FORNO *Valpolicella DOC, Veneto, Italy* VALPOLICELLA Superiore★★ from Monte Lodoletta vineyard, outside the Valpolicella Classico area, is a model of power and grace; AMARONE★★★ and RECIOTO DELLA VALPOLICELLA★★★, from the same source, are even more voluptuous. Best years: (Amarone) (2011) (10) (09) 08 **07** 06 04 03 01 00 99 97 96 95.

DALLA VALLE *Napa Valley AVA, California, USA* Stunning hillside winery, producing some of NAPA's most irresistible Cabernets. Maya★★★ is a magnificent blend of Cabernet Sauvignon and Cabernet Franc; the straight Cabernet Sauvignon★★★ is almost as rich and brilliantly balanced. The wines drink well at 10 years, but will keep for 20 or more.

DÃO DOC *Beira Alta, Portugal* Dão has steep slopes ideal for vineyards, and a great climate for local grape varieties. Now it is producing characterful, scented, austerely satisfying red and white wines. Best producers: (reds) ALIANCA (Quinta da Garrida★), Boas Quintas (Quinta Fonte do Ouro★), Quinta de Cabriz★, Fontes da Cunha (Munda)★, Quinta das Maias★, Pape★★, Quinta da Pellada★★, Quinta do Perdigão, Quinta da Ponte Pedrinha, Quinta dos ROQUES★★, Quinta de Sães★, Caves SÃO JOÃO★, SOGRAPE★ (Quinta dos Carvalhais★), Quinta da Vegia★★; (whites) Quinta de Cabriz, Quinta das Maias★, Quinta dos ROQUES★, Quinta de Sães★, SOGRAPE★. Best years: (reds) (2009) **08 05** 04 03 01 00 99 97 96 95.

D'ARENBERG *McLaren Vale, South Australia* As this family winery celebrates its centenary year, Chester Osborn continues to make blockbuster Dead Arm Shiraz★★, Ironstone Pressings Grenache-Shiraz-Mourvèdre★★, Custodian Grenache★, Coppermine Road Cabernet Sauvignon★★ and numerous other blends from low-

yielding old vines. These are big, brash, character-filled wines, and are continually being joined by new ideas. While others were cautious in difficult times, Osborn was steadily buying up plots of ancient vines around the Vale. Stellar but expensive single-vineyard Grenache (Beautiful View★★, Blewitt Springs★★). Whites mustn't be overlooked: Money Spider★ (Roussanne) and Hermit Crab★★ (Viognier-Marsanne) are lush and waxy. Best years: (Dead Arm Shiraz) (2010) 08 **06** 05 04 03 02 01 00 97 96 95.

VINCENT DAUVISSAT *Chablis, Burgundy, France* CHABLIS at its most complex – refreshing, seductive and beautifully structured, with the fruit balancing the subtle influence of mostly older oak. Look for La Forest★★, the more aromatic Vaillons★★★ and the powerful Les

Clos★★★. He also makes one red IRANCY. Best years: (2011) 10 09 08 **07 06 05** 02 00 99 95.

MARCO DE BARTOLI *Sicily, Italy* The winery is most noted for a dry, unfortified MARSALA-style wine called Vecchio Samperi – the late Marco De Bartoli's idea of what Marsala was before the English merchant John Woodhouse first fortified it for export. Particularly fine is the 20-year-old Ventennale★★: dry, intense and redolent of candied citrus peel, dates and raisins. Also excellent MOSCATO PASSITO DI PANTELLERIA Bukkuram★★.

DE BORTOLI *Riverina, New South Wales/Yarra, Victoria, Australia* Large, family-owned company producing large amounts of good basic wine as well as some starry stuff, including YARRA VALLEY Sauvignon★, Chardonnay★★, Syrah★★, Cabernet★, Pinot Noir★, and three Melba★ Cabernet blends. The RIVERINA winery first gained prominence for its world-class botrytized Semillon (Noble One★★★), but is now equally well known for the quality of its budget labels – Sacred Hill, Deen and Montage. VICTORIA-based Sero, Windy Peak and Gulf Station quaffers can be good too. Best years: (Noble One) (2011) 10 09 08 04 03 02 00 98 96 95 94 93 90.

DE LOACH *Russian River Valley AVA, California, USA* Revitalized under new owner BOISSET of France and run by Jean-Charles Boisset, this property makes an array of stylish Pinot Noirs★★ and soft nutty Chardonnays★ from estate fruit. The winery has just released its first wines (three Pinot Noirs and a Chardonnay) from Marin County, all from the 2009 vintage. Best years: (Pinot Noir) 2010 09 08 07 06 05 04 03.

DE MARTINO *Maipo, Chile* Old-established winery enjoying a renaissance, producing primarily robust but not over-concentrated red wines. Single Vineyard wines – Alto de Piedras Carmenère★★ (from MAIPO), El León Carignan★★ from old vines in MAULE and Quebrada Seca Chardonnay★★ from LIMARI – are among Chile's best examples of these grapes; Familia Cabernet Sauvignon★★ is dense and complex. Viejas Tinajas, from unirrigated old-vine Cinsault, is vinified in the traditional Chilean way, in old earthenware amphorae (*tinajas*)

DE TRAFFORD *Stellenbosch WO, South Africa* David Trafford's barrel-fermented Chenin Blanc★, from venerable Helderberg vines, is rich and ageworthy; the Straw Wine★★ is honey-tinged and succulent. Spicy-rich yet elegant Syrah 393★★ heads the reds. Cabernet Sauvignon★ and Merlot★, alone and with Shiraz in Elevation 393★, are classically styled and built to age. Sijnn, a new venture at the mouth of the Breede River, shows promise. Best years: (reds) 2010 **09 08 07 06 05 04 03 02 01 00**.

DEHLINGER *Russian River Valley AVA, California, USA* Outstanding Pinot Noir★★★ from vineyards in the cool RUSSIAN RIVER VALLEY, best at 5–10 years old. Also mouthfilling Chardonnay★★ and bold, peppery Syrah★★. Recent vintages of Cabernet Sauvignon★★ reflect a surge in quality. Best years: (Pinot Noir) 2009 **08 07 06 05 04 03 02**.

MARCEL DEISS *Alsace AC, Alsace, France* Jean-Michel Deiss is fanatical about *terroir* and, controversially for ALSACE, his top wines are now blends, named according to the vineyard – Grands Crus Altenberg, Mambourg and Schoenenbourg are all ★★★. These are outstanding wines of huge character, often with some residual sugar. Pinot Noir Burlenburg★★ is vibrant and delicious. Basic Riesling and Pinot Blanc are delightful. Best years: (Grand Cru blends) (2011) 10 **09 08 07 05 04 03 02 01 00**.

DELAS FRÈRES *Rhône Valley, France* Upmarket, extremely reliable merchant (owned by ROEDERER) selling wines from the whole RHÔNE VALLEY, but with its own vineyards in the northern Rhône. Single-vineyard wines include dense, powerful red HERMITAGE (Dom. des Tourettes★★, Les Bessards★★★), which needs a decade or more to reach its peak, perfumed CÔTE-RÔTIE La Landonne★★ and complex, *terroir*-specific ST-JOSEPH Ste-Épine★★; CROZES-HERMITAGE Le Clos★★ is good, too. Classy, aromatic CONDRIEU Clos Boucher★★ and decent VACQUEYRAS★ red and TAVEL rosé. Best years: (premium reds) (2011) 10 09 **07 06 05 04 03 01 00 99 98 97 96 95 94 91 90 89 78**.

DELEGAT *Henderson, Auckland, North Island, New Zealand* Family-run winery, getting larger by the second as Oyster Bay becomes a major brand (Sauvignon Blanc, delicate Chardonnay, gently fruity Pinot Noir and sparkling wines from MARLBOROUGH, plus soft-textured HAWKES BAY Merlot). Delegat Chardonnay Reserve★, Merlot Reserve★ and Cabernet are from Hawkes Bay. Best years: (Oyster Bay Sauvignon Blanc) **2011 10 09 06**.

DELILLE CELLARS *Columbia Valley AVA, Washington State, USA* BORDEAUX-style wines from some of the better vineyards in YAKIMA VALLEY. Chaleur Estate red★★ is a powerful, ageworthy Cabernet-Merlot blend. Chaleur Estate Blanc★★ (Semillon-Sauvignon Blanc) has a GRAVES-like character. The second wine, D2★★, is an early-drinking red. Doyenne Syrah★★ shows great potential. Best years: (Chaleur Estate Red) (2010) 09 **08 07 06 05 04**.

DENBIES *Surrey, England* Impressive single vineyard with 107ha (265 acres) of vines, planted on chalky slopes outside Dorking. Wines are variable in quality, although with veteran Australian John Worontschak now in charge of winemaking, things should look up. Ortega★ and Juniper Hill★ still whites and sparkling Greenfields★ and Cubitt Reserve★.

JEAN-LOUIS DENOIS *Pays d'Oc IGP, Languedoc, France* Maverick producer based in LIMOUX, who can't see a rule without breaking it. His Chloé★ is made from Merlot and Cabernet, without any of the 'Mediterranean' varieties obligatory in Limoux; it mixes the flavours of BORDEAUX with a bit of southern warmth. Also red and white Grande Cuvée★ and good fizz★.

DEUTZ *Champagne AC, Champagne, France* This small company has been owned by ROEDERER since 1993. The non-vintage Brut★★ is now regularly one of the best in CHAMPAGNE, often boasting a cedary scent, while the top wines are the classic Blanc de Blancs★★, the weightier Cuvée William Deutz★★ and the de luxe vintage blanc de blancs Amour de Deutz★★. Deutz collaborates with Pernod Ricard in New Zealand to produce sparkling wine. Best years: 2006 05 04 **02 00 99 98 96 95 90 89 88**.

D F J VINHOS *Portugal* Owned by one of Portugal's most innovative winemakers, José Neiva. The large range includes off-dry Pink Elephant rosé, Segada red and white from LISBOA and Pedras do Monte from PENINSULA DE SETÚBAL. At the top end are the Grand'Arte reds, including fruity, peppery Trincadeira★ and beefy Alicante Bouschet★, the DFJ range (Alvarinho-Chardonnay★, Tinta Roriz-Merlot, Touriga Nacional-Touriga Franca★) and prestige wines from the DOURO (Escada★), ALENQUER (Francos Reserva) and LISBOA (Consensus).

DIAMOND CREEK *Napa Valley AVA, California, USA* Small Diamond Mountain estate specializing in Cabernet: Gravelly Meadow★★, Red Rock Terrace★★, Volcanic Hill★★★. Traditionally huge, tannic wines: now showing less tannin, and wonderful perfume and balance even in their youth. Best years: 2009 08 07 **06 05 04 03 02 01 00 99 98 97 96 95 94 92 91**.

SCHLOSSGUT DIEL *Burg Layen, Nahe, Germany* Armin Diel is one of the leading producers of classic-style Rieslings. Spätlese and Auslese from Dorsheim's top sites (Burgberg, Goldloch, Pittermännchen) are regularly ★★. Good Sekt★ too. Best years: (2011) 10 09 **08 07 06 05 04 02**.

DISTELL *Stellenbosch, South Africa* South Africa's largest wine company; some of the allied wineries – such as Stellenzicht and Durbanville Hills★ – perform consistently. The Fleur du Cap★ range is showing exciting improvement; Noble Late Harvest★★ botrytized dessert wine is an annual standout. Two wineries in PAARL, Nederburg★ and Plaisir de Merle★, are run separately. There has been admirable progress across Nederburg's wide range; Ingenuity White★ is a harmonious blend of 8 varieties; the Red★ is a vibrant mix of Sangiovese and Barbera with Nebbiolo. Botrytized Edelkeur★ is sold only through an annual auction.

DOGLIANI DOCG *Piedmont, Italy* Used to be called Dolcetto di Dogliani, and despite the name change is still 100% Dolcetto. Considered the king of Dolcettos, Dogliani can be aged in bottle (unlike most Dolcetto) when from the best producers. Best producers: M & E Abbona★, Ca' Viola, Chionetti★★, Luigi Einaudi★★, Pecchenino★★. Best years: (2011) 10 **09 08** 07.

CH. DOISY-DAËNE★★ *Sauternes AC, 2ème Cru Classé, Bordeaux, France* Owned by enologist Denis Dubourdieu (see Ch. REYNON), a consistently good property in BARSAC (although it uses the SAUTERNES AC). Principally Sémillon, with a splash of Sauvignon Blanc. It ages well for 10 years or more. The extra-rich Extravagant★★★ is produced in exceptional years. Doisy-Daëne Sec★ is a perfumed, barrel-fermented dry white; drink young. Best years: (sweet) 2010 09 **07 06 05** 04 03 02 01 99 98 97 96.

CH. DOISY-VÉDRINES★★ *Sauternes AC, 2ème Cru Classé, Bordeaux, France* Next door to DOISY-DAËNE (and also using the SAUTERNES AC), Doisy-Védrines is a richly botrytized wine, fatter and more syrupy than most BARSAC. Best years: (sweet) 2010 09 **07 05** 04 03 02 01 99 98 97 96 95 90 89 88.

DOLCETTO One of Italy's most charming grapes, producing, for the most part, purple wines bursting with fruit. Virtually exclusive to PIEDMONT and LIGURIA, it boasts several DOCs and 3 DOCGs (Dogliani, Diano d'Alba and Ovada) in Piemonte, with styles ranging from intense and rich in Alba, Ovada and Diano d'Alba, to lighter, more perfumed in Acqui and Asti. Many of the most serious wines are from Alba. Usually best drunk within 1–2 years, a few traditionally vinified wines can last 10 years. A tiny bit in California and Australia. Best producers: (Alba) Alario★★, ALTARE★★, Boglietti★★, Bongiovanni★★, Bricco Maiolica★, Bricco Rosso★, Brovia★, Elvio Cogno★★, Aldo CONTERNO★, Conterno-Fantino★★, B Marcarini★, B MASCARELLO★, G MASCARELLO★★, Paitin★, Pelissero★★, PRUNOTTO★, RATTI★, Albino Rocca★★, SANDRONE★★, Vajra★★, Vietti★, Gianni Voerzio★, Roberto VOERZIO★.

DÔLE *Valais, Switzerland* Red wine from the VALAIS made from at least 51% Pinot Noir, the rest being Gamay. Dôle is generally a light wine – the deeper, richer (100% Pinot Noir) styles may call themselves Pinot Noir. Most should be drunk young and lightly chilled. Best producers: G Clavien, Faye, Jean-René Germanier, A Mathier, Provins, G Raymond.

DOMAINE CARNEROS *Carneros AVA, California, USA* Very successful TAITTINGER-owned sparkling wine house. The vintage Brut might match Taittinger's Champagne if it were made a little drier. Far classier are vintage Le Rêve★★ (100% Chardonnay) and attractive Pinot Noirs★★. The winery also makes a small amount of a white from Pinot Noir grapes.

DOMAINE CHANDON *Yarra Valley, Victoria, Australia* MOËT & CHANDON's Aussie offshoot makes fine Pinot Noir-Chardonnay fizz: non-vintage Brut★ and Cuvée Riche, vintage Brut★★, Rosé★★, Blanc de Blancs★,

Blanc de Noirs★, ZD★★ (Zero Dosage), YARRA VALLEY Brut★★ and a Tasmanian Cuvée★★, plus sparkling red Pinot-Shiraz★. Table wines, often of ★★ quality, under the Green Point label, with Reserve Shiraz★★ standing out and Chardonnay increasingly impressive. The Green Point name is also used on fizz for export markets.

DOMAINE CHANDON *Napa Valley AVA, California, USA* California's first French-owned (MOËT & CHANDON) sparkling wine producer majors in reasonable price, but doesn't match the quality of Moët's subsidiaries in Australia or Argentina. Reserve bottlings can be rich and creamy. Étoile★ is an aged de luxe wine, also made as a flavourful Rosé★.

DOMAINE DROUHIN OREGON *Willamette Valley AVA, Oregon, USA* Burgundy wine merchant Robert DROUHIN bought 40ha (100 acres) in OREGON in 1987. The regular Pinot Noir★ (can be ★★) is lean but can be delightfully scented. The de luxe Pinot Noir Laurène★★ is supple and voluptuous when not overoaked. Pinot Noir Louise★★ is a selection of the finest barrels in the winery. Also very good Chardonnay Arthur★★. Best years: (Pinot Noir) (2010) 09 **08 07 06 05**.

DOMAINE SERENE *Willamette Valley AVA, Oregon, USA* Ken and Grace Evenstad named the property after their daughter, Serene. The full-bodied Pinot Noir Evenstad Reserve★★ is aged in French oak and has striking black cherry and currant flavours. Single-vineyard Pinot Noirs are a focus of the winery (Mark Bradford Vineyard★★, Jerusalem Hill Vineyard★). The Chardonnay Clos du Soleil★★, made from Dijon clones, has a rich apple and hazelnut character. Best years: (Pinot Noir) (2010) 09 **08 07 06 05**.

DOMINIO DEL PLATA *Mendoza, Argentina* Superstar winemaker Susana Balbo crafts exquisite wines in the shadow of the Andes. The emphasis is firmly on Malbec and Cabernet Sauvignon, but it is in the blending that she excels. Top wine Nosotros★★ is a lush blockbuster but not typical of the estate. Susana Balbo Malbec★★ is elegant and delicious. Brioso★★, a BORDEAUX-style blend, is structured and pure; BenMarco Malbec★ and Cabernet Sauvignon★ are extremely good. The lower-priced Crios range (Torrontés★) is exceptional value for money.

DOMINUS★★ *Napa Valley AVA, California, USA* Owned by Christian MOUEIX, director of Bordeaux superstar PETRUS. Wines are based on Cabernet Sauvignon, with leavenings of Merlot and Cabernet Franc. Early releases were excessively tannic, but recent wines are mellow and delicious. Best years: 2009 08 07 **06 05 04 03 02** **01 00** 99 97 96 95 94 91 90.

DOÑA PAULA *Mendoza, Argentina* Doña Paula performs brilliantly with both red and white wines. The top wine, Selección de Bodega Malbec★★, continues to beat the drum for the estate. The Estate Malbec★★ exhibits beautiful violet-edged fruit. The intense, tropical and perfumed Estate Sauvignon Blanc★★ demonstrates the talent of winemaker Edy del Popolo. Further down the ladder, the sharp, fresh Los Cardos Sauvignon Blanc★ and new varietal range, Paula, are great value.

DONAULAND See WAGRAM.

DÖNNHOFF *Oberhausen, Nahe, Germany* Helmut Dönnhoff is the quiet winemaking genius of the NAHE, conjuring from a string of top sites some of the most mineral dry and naturally sweet Rieslings in the world. The very best are the subtle, long-lived wines from the Niederhäuser Hermannshöhle★★★ and Oberhäuser Brücke★★★ vineyards. Eiswein★★★ is equally exciting. Best years. (Hermannshöhle Grosses Gewächs) (2011) 10 09 08 **07 06 05 04**.

DOURO DOC *Douro, Portugal* As prices soar for the best wines, deciding whether to use top grapes for unfortified Douro wine or PORT has become much harder for Douro producers. Quality can be superb when the lush, scented fruit is not smothered by new oak. Reds may improve for 10 years or more. Whites from higher-altitude vineyards have improved, but best drunk young. Best producers: (reds) ALIANÇA (Quinta dos Quatro Ventos★★), Altano★, Barca Velha★★★, Maria Doroteia Serôdio Borges (Fojo★★), Casal de Loivos★★, Chryseia★★, Conceito, Quinta do CÔTTO (Grand Escolha★★), Quinta do CRASTO★★, Quinta da Gaivosa★ (Abandonado★★), Vinha de Lordelo★★), Quinta da Leda★★, Quinta de Macedos★, Quinta da Manuela★, Muxagat, NIEPOORT★★, Quinta do NOVAL★★, Quinta da Padrela★, Quinta do Passadouro★, Pintas★★, Poeira★★, Quinta do Portal★, RAMOS PINTO★, Quinta da Romaneira★, Quinta de la ROSA★, SOGRAPE★, Quinta do Vale Dona Maria★★, Quinta do Vale Meão★★, Quinta do Vallado★, Quinta de VESÚVIO★★, Xisto★. Best years: (reds) (2011) **09 08 07 05 04 03 01 00 97 95**.

DOW'S *Port DOC, Douro, Portugal* The grapes for Dow's Vintage PORT★★ come mostly from the Quinta do Bomfim – also the name of the excellent single quinta★★. Dow's ports are relatively dry compared with GRAHAM's and WARRE's (other major brands belonging to the Symington family). Good Crusted★ and some excellent aged tawnies★★. Quinta Senhora da Ribeira★★ has made impressive ports since 1998, released 'en primeur'. Best years: (Vintage) 2007 **03 00 97 94 91 85 83 80 77 70 66 63 60 55**; (Bomfim) (2009) **06 99 98 95 92 87 86**; (Senhora da Ribeira) (2009) **08 06 05 04 99 98**.

JOSEPH DROUHIN *Beaune, Burgundy, France* Beaune-based merchant with substantial holdings in CHABLIS as well as DOMAINE DROUHIN OREGON. Flagship CÔTE D'OR whites include BEAUNE Clos des Mouches★★★ and MONTRACHET Marquis de Laguiche★★★. Finer still are the graceful perfumed reds such as CHAMBOLLE-MUSIGNY Premier Cru★★ and Grands Crus Grands-ÉCHÉZEAUX★★★, MUSIGNY★★, etc. Good-value cheaper wines too. Best years: (top reds) (2011) 10 09 08 07 05 **02 99 96 95**.

PIERRE-JACQUES DRUET *Bourgueil AC, Loire Valley, France* A passionate producer, Druet's BOURGUEILS les Cent Boisselées★, Grand Mont★★ and Vaumoreau★★ are subtly different, spicy expressions of Cabernet Franc that attain wonderful purity with age – keep for at least 3–5 years. Also small quantities of CHINON (Clos de Danzay★★). Best years: (top cuvées) (2011) 10 09 08 **07 06 05 04 03 02 01 00 99 97 96**.

DRY CREEK VALLEY AVA *Sonoma, California, USA* Best known for Sauvignon Blanc, Zinfandel and Cabernet Sauvignon, this valley runs parallel and west of ALEXANDER VALLEY AVA, and similarly becomes hotter moving northward. Best producers: DRY CREEK VINEYARD★, Duxoup★, FERRARI-CARANO★, GALLO (Zinfandel★, Cabernet Sauvignon★), Lambert Bridge★, Michel-Schlumberger★, NALLE★, Pezzi King★, Preston★, Quivira★, Rafanelli (Zinfandel★★), RIDGE (Lytton Springs★★), SEGHESIO★. Best years: (reds) (2010) 09 08 **07 06 05 03 02 01 00**.

DRY CREEK VINEYARD *Dry Creek Valley AVA, California, USA* An early advocate of Fumé Blanc★, Dry Creek remains faithful to the brisk racy style. Fumé Blanc DCV3★ (sometimes ★★) is from the original (1972)

Dry Creek Valley vineyard and displays subtle notes of fig and herb. A drink-young Chardonnay (Reserve★) is attractive, but the stars here are a superb Dry Chenin Blanc★★, red Meritage★, Merlot★ and Old Vine Zinfandel★★. Best years: (Old Vine Zin) (2009) 08 **07 06** 05 03 02 01 00.

DRY RIVER *Martinborough, North Island, New Zealand* Low yields and an uncompromising attitude to quality at this tiny winery have created some of the country's top Gewurztraminer★★★, Pinot Gris★★★, powerful, long-lived Craighall Riesling★★★, sleek Chardonnay★★ and intense, ultra-ripe yet mineral Pinot Noir★★★. Excellent Syrah★★ is made in tiny quantities. Now owned by a wealthy American; founder Neil McCallum recently resigned as chief winemaker. Best years: (Craighall Riesling) 2011 **10 09 08 06** 03 01; (Pinot Noir) (2011) **10 09 08 07 06** 03 01.

GEORGES DUBOEUF *Beaujolais, Burgundy, France* Duboeuf is responsible for more than 10% of the wine produced in BEAUJOLAIS. Given the size of his operation, the quality of the wines is reasonable. His BEAUJOLAIS NOUVEAU is usually reliable, but his top wines are those he bottles for independent growers, particularly Jean Descombes★ in MORGON, and Clos des Quatre Vents★ and la Madone★ in FLEURIE. Duboeuf also makes wine from the MÂCONNAIS, the southern RHÔNE VALLEY and the LANGUEDOC.

DUCKHORN *Napa Valley AVA, California, USA* The influence of New Zealand winemaker Bill Nancarrow shows in Merlot★ and Cabernet★ – much more charming than they used to be – along with tasty Sauvignon Blanc. Paraduxx★ is a Zinfandel-Cabernet blend; Decoy is the budget line. The company's Pinot Noir project is Goldeneye★ in ANDERSON VALLEY with lower-priced offshoot, Migration. Best years: (Merlot) 2009 **08 07 06** 05 03.

CH. DUCRU-BEAUCAILLOU★★★ *St-Julien AC, 2ème Cru Classé, Haut-Médoc, Bordeaux, France* Traditionally the epitome of ST-JULIEN, mixing charm and austerity, fruit and firm tannins. Flawed from mid-1980s to 1990; back on form since 95, more luscious since 03. Second wine: la Croix de Beaucaillou. Best years: 2010 09 08 07 06 05 **04 03 02** 01 00 99 98 96.

CH. DUHART-MILON★ *Pauillac AC, 4ème Cru Classé, Haut-Médoc, Bordeaux, France* Property adjacent to and owned by LAFITE-ROTHSCHILD. A healthy portion of Merlot (35%) adds flesh to the steely Pauillac character. Rising quality since 2005. Prices have risen on the back of Asian interest in Lafite. Best years: 2010 09 08 07 06 05 **04 03 02** 01 00.

DUJAC *Morey-St-Denis, Côte de Nuits, Burgundy, France* The Seysses family estate is based in MOREY-ST-DENIS, with some choice vineyards elsewhere in the CÔTE DE NUITS. The wines are perfumed and elegant, including a small quantity of white Morey-St-Denis★, but the outstanding bottlings are the Grands Crus – ÉCHÉZEAUX★★★, CLOS DE LA ROCHE★★★, BONNES-MARES★★★ and CLOS ST-DENIS★★★, with CHAMBERTIN★★★ and ROMANÉE-ST-VIVANT★★★ since 2005. All need to age for a decade or more. Son Jeremy makes *négociant* cuvées under Dujac Fils et Père label. Best years: (Grands Crus) (2011) 10 09 08 06 05 **03 02 01 00** 99 98 96 95 90 89.

DUNHAM CELLARS *Columbia Valley AVA, Washington State, USA* Family-owned winery in a remodelled airplane hangar near the Walla Walla airport. Wines were powerful and extracted, including Cabernet Sauvignon★★, Syrah★, Lewis Vineyard Syrah Reserve★★, Trutina★ (BORDEAUX-style blend), Three Legged Red (named after a winery dog) and 'Shirley Mays' Chardonnay. Best years: (reds) (2010) 09 **08 07 06**.

DUNN VINEYARDS *Howell Mountain AVA, California, USA* Austere, concentrated, hauntingly perfumed, long-lived Cabernet Sauvignon★★ from HOWELL MOUNTAIN; NAPA VALLEY Cabernets★★ are less powerful but still scented. Thankfully, Randy Dunn has resisted the move toward high alcohol, and his wines' ability to age impressively is evidence of this. Best years: 2000 07 06 05 **03 01 01 00 99 97 96 95 94 93 92 91 90 88 87.**

DURBANVILLE WO *South Africa* Tucked into the folds of the Tygerberg Hills, Durbanville borders Cape Town's northern suburbs. Cool breezes from both the Atlantic Ocean and False Bay suit Sauvignon Blanc: wines often show invigorating minerality. Semillon also does well. Merlot shows promise both on its own and blended with Cabernet Sauvignon, though the latter sometimes struggles to ripen. **Best producers:** De Grendel★, Diemersdal★, Durbanville Hills★, Meerendal★, Nitida★.

DURIF See PETITE SIRAH.

DUTTON GOLDFIELD *Russian River Valley AVA, California, USA* Racy, elegant and deeply flavoured Chardonnays★, Pinot Noirs★★, Zinfandels★★ and a superb cool-climate Syrah★★ from long-time cool-climate winemaker Dan Goldfield. Most of the fruit, grown by Steve Dutton, is from RUSSIAN RIVER. The superb Freestone Hill Pinot Noir★★★ is from one of the coldest parts of SONOMA COUNTY. Goldfield also makes wine from fruit grown in even-cooler Marin County. Most wines take years to reach their peak. **Best years:** (Pinot Noir) 2010 09 **08 07 06 05 04 01 99.**

JOHN DUVAL *Barossa Valley, South Australia* John Duval was the winemaker for Penfolds GRANGE from 1986 to 2002. He started his family label in 2003, specializing in Shiraz and blends sourced from old-vine BAROSSA fruit. Shiraz-Grenache-Mourvèdre blend Plexus★★ is plush, vibrant, deeply flavoured and approachable; white Plexus★★ is a round, waxy RHÔNE-style blend; Entity Shiraz★★ combines elegance, finesse and approachability with concentrated flavour and power; ultra concentrated Eligo Shiraz★★ is made from the best parcels from the vintage. He also consults in WASHINGTON STATE, Chile and elsewhere in Australia.

DUVAL-LEROY *Champagne AC, Champagne, France* Run by Carol Duval-Leroy since 1991, this is one of the largest family-owned producers in CHAMPAGNE, with 170ha (420 acres) of vineyards. While its entry-level non-vintage styles are unremarkable, its vintage★ wines, prestige cuvée Femme★★ and wines under the Authentis★ label are well worth seeking out. **Best years:** 2005 04 03 **02 99 96 95.**

ÉCHÉZEAUX AC *Grand Cru, Côte de Nuits, Burgundy, France* The Grands Crus of Échézeaux and the smaller and more prestigious Grands-Échézeaux are sandwiched between the world-famous CLOS DE VOUGEOT and VOSNE-ROMANÉE. Look for subtlety, intricacy, delicacy from Échézeaux and a little more weight, deepening over the years to a gamy, chocolaty richness, from the 'Grands' version. **Best producers:** Arnoux-Lachaux★★, BOUCHARD PÈRE & FILS★★, Cacheux-Sirugue★★, Clos Frantin/Bichot★★, DROUHIN★★, D Duband★★, DUJAC★★, Eugénie★★ (formerly Engel), GRIVOT★★★, A-F GROS★★★, Jayer-Gilles★★, F Lamarche★★, LIGER-BELAIR★★★, MUGNERET-GIBOURG★★★, Perdrix★★, J Prieur★★, Dom. de la ROMANÉE-CONTI★★★, E Rouget★★★. **Best years:** (2011) 10 09 08 **07 06 05 03 02 01 99 98 96 95 93 90.**

EDEN VALLEY See BAROSSA, pages 76–7.

CH. L'ÉGLISE-CLINET★★★ *Pomerol AC, Bordeaux, France* A tiny 5.5ha (13-acre) domaine with a very old vineyard – one of the reasons for the depth and elegance of the wines. The other is the winemaking ability of owner Denis Durantou. The wine can be enjoyed young, though the best vintages should be cellared for 10 years or more. Second wine: La Petite Église. **Best years:** 2010 09 08 **07 06 05 04 03 02 01 00 99 98 96 95 90 89.**

ELGIN WO *South Africa* High-lying district where summer cloud helps to keep temperatures reasonable, creating good conditions for pure-fruited, structured and fresh Sauvignon Blanc, Chardonnay, Riesling and Pinot Noir. Best producers: Almenkerk, Paul CLUVER★★, Neil ELLIS★★, Iona★, Catherine Marshall, Oak Valley★, Shannon★, THELEMA★.

DOM. ELIAN DA ROS *Côtes du Marmandais AOP, South-West France* Elian's eclectic wines show influences from ALSACE, BURGUNDY and the LOIRE (with his use of Cabernet Franc). Top wines are Chante Coucou★ and Clos Baquey★★; they need aging. Also a varietal from the Abouriou grape★. Best years: (2011) (10) **09 08 06 05 04 02 01**.

ELK COVE *Willamette Valley AVA, Oregon, USA* Back in 1974, Elk Cove was one of the pioneers of the WILLAMETTE VALLEY. Today the Campbell family produces Pinot Gris★, Pinot Blanc★, Riesling and a Riesling-based dessert wine called Ultima. Basic Pinot Noir★★ frequently outclasses the more expensive single-vineyard Pinot Noirs (Roosevelt, Windhill★, La Bohème★). Best years: (Pinot Noir) (2010) **09 08 07 06**.

NEIL ELLIS *Stellenbosch WO, South Africa* Winemaker and *négociant*, renowned for invigorating Groenekloof Sauvignon Blanc★★ and STELLENBOSCH reds (blackcurranty Cabernet Sauvignon★★, supple Cabernet-Merlot★). Single-vineyard Syrah★ and Cabernet★ (both from Jonkershoek Valley fruit), a subtly delicious Chardonnay★★ from cool ELGIN and old-vine Grenache from Piekenierskloof confirm his versatility. Best years: (Cabernet) 2009 **08 07 06 05 04 03 01**.

ELQUI *Chile* Chile's northernmost wine region (though the nascent Huasco is even further north), close to the Atacama desert, with steep, arid valleys, cooling winds and exceptional clarity of light (some of the world's finest space observatories are located here), and high-altitude vineyards, some as high as 2000m (6500ft) above sea level. Syrah, in an elegant, fragrant style, excels in this cool, sunny climate, along with crisp Sauvignon Blanc and fresh Chardonnay. Best producers: FALERNIA★ (reds★★), Mayu★ (reds★★), SAN PEDRO★ (Castillo de Molina Sauvignon Blanc★★).

ERNIE ELS *Stellenbosch WO, South Africa* Now under the sole ownership of golfer Ernie Els, with Louis Strydom as MD and winemaker. The enlarged range includes whites, but the flagships remain Ernie Els Signature★★, a dark, serious BORDEAUX blend, and the rich, international style Proprietor's Blend★, combining the Bordeaux grapes, with Shiraz. Best years: (Ernie Els Signature) 2009 **08 07 06 05 04 03**.

EMILIA-ROMAGNA *Italy* Emilia and Romagna are two parts of a very heterogeneous wine region. Romagna, from Bologna east to the Adriatic, closely follows the Tuscan pattern of wines, with reds from Sangiovese and Trebbiano whites. Emilia on the other hand, while producing some serious still wines, makes a speciality of frothing reds (and whites), not just LAMBRUSCO but also Barbera, Bonarda, Malvasia and others. See also COLLI PIACENTINI, ROMAGNA.

EMILIANA *Colchagua, Chile* Venture from the Guilisasti family, main shareholders at CONCHA Y TORO, with leading winemaker Alvaro Espinoza contributing his biodynamic and organic approach to viticulture. Adobe is the good entry-level range; Novas★★ range is significantly better; and red blend Coyam★★ (sometimes ★★★) is one of Chile's most fascinating wines. Gê★★, a 'Super Coyam', is a dense, powerful long-distance runner. Best years: (Coyam) (2010) **09 08 07 06 05 03 01**.

EMRICH-SCHÖNLEBER *Monzingen, Nahe, Germany* Although Monzingen is not the most prestigious of NAHE villages, Werner Schönleber has steadily brought his 17ha (42-acre) property into the front ranks. His vigorous, spicy Rieslings are consistently ★★ to ★★★ and his Eisweins are ★★★. Best years: (2011) 10 09 08 **07 06 05 04 02**.

ENATE *Somontano DO, Aragón, Spain* Barrel-fermented Chardonnay★ is rich, buttery and toasty; Gewürztraminer★ is exotic and convincing. International grape varieties also feature in the red Crianza, Reserva★ (100% Cabernet Sauvignon), Reserva Especial★★ (Cabernet-Merlot) and blockbuster Merlot-Merlot and Syrah-Shiraz. Best years: (reds) 2009 **07 06 05 04 03 01 00 99 98**.

ENTRAYGUES-ET-DU-FEL AOP, ESTAING AOP *South-West France* Two diminutive appellations in the hills above the Lot Valley. Notable for tingling crisp dry whites from Chenin Blanc (Dom. Méjanassère★) and tangy reds from Dom. Laurent Mousset★. Drink young. Note also vins de pays/IGPs from nearby Nicolas Carmarans and, overlooking Conques Abbey, Patrick Rols.

ENTRE-DEUX-MERS AC *Bordeaux, France* This large AC between the rivers Garonne and Dordogne increasingly represents some of the freshest, snappiest dry white wine in France. In general, drink the latest vintage, though better wines will last a year or two. Most of Bordeaux's basic red wine under the Bordeaux AC comes from here too. Sweet wines are sold as PREMIÈRES CÔTES DE BORDEAUX, CADILLAC, LOUPIAC and STE-CROIX-DU-MONT. Best producers: Beauregard-Ducourt, BONNET★, Castenet Greffier, de Fontenille★, Landereau★, Marjosse★, Nardique la Gravière★, Ste-Marie★, Tour de Mirambeau★, Toutigeac★, Turcaud★.

DOM. D'EOLE *Coteaux d'Aix-en-Provence AC, Provence, France* Top wines from this organic estate are rosé Cuvée Caprice★ and red Cuvée Léa★★, a powerful 50:50 blend of Syrah and Grenache. Best years: (2011) **10 09 08 07 06 05 03**.

ERBACH *Rheingau, Germany* Erbach's famous Marcobrunn vineyard is one of the top spots for Riesling along the Rhine. The village wines are elegant while those from Marcobrunn more powerful. Best producers: Jakob Jung★, Langwerth von Simmern★★, SCHLOSS REINHARTSHAUSEN★★, Schloss Schönborn★★. Best years: (2011) 10 09 08 **07 06 05 04 02**.

ERDEN *Mosel, Germany* Middle MOSEL village with the superb Prälat and Treppchen vineyards. Wines are rich and succulent with a strong mineral character. Best producers: Christoffel★★, Erbes, Dr Hermann★, Dr LOOSEN★★★, MOLITOR★, Mönchhof★, Pauly-Bergweiler★, Dr Weins-Prüm★. Best years: (2011) 10 09 08 **07 06 05 04 02**.

ERRÁZURIZ *Aconcagua, Chile* One of Chile's oldest family-run wineries (founded in 1870), rapidly modernizing under dynamic Eduardo Chadwick. Its portfolio includes the Arboleda range, Seña★★, a ripe, dense Cabernet-based blend from western ACONGAGUA, and Viñedo Chadwick★★★, a single-vineyard Cabernet Sauvignon from Puente Alto, a high-quality area of MAIPO. The classic label is Don Maximiano Founder's Reserve★★ (sometimes ★★★), a Cabernet Sauvignon-based red from Aconcagua, also the source of La Cumbre Syrah★, rich, perfumed Kai Carmenère★ and dense red The Blend★. Also very good

Wild Ferment Chardonnay★★ and Pinot Noir★★ from CASABLANCA. New cool-climate Manzanar vineyard in coastal Aconcagua is exciting, especially for Sauvignon★★ and Syrah★★. Best years: (reds) (2010) (09) **08 07 06 05 04 03 01**.

CH. D'ESCLANS *Côtes de Provence AC, Provence, France* Sacha Lichine has created what is claimed to be the 'most expensive rosé in the world', Garrus, an explosive, wood-aged blend of old-vine Grenache and Rolle. For lesser mortals, there are Les Clans, Esclans and the sweeter Whispering Angel. Best years: (2011) **10 09 08 07**.

ESPORÃO *Alentejo DOC, Portugal* Huge estate in the heart of the ALENTEJO, where Australian David Baverstock makes a broad range of wines. Principal labels are Esporão (red★ and white★ Reservas), Vinha de Defesa, Monte Velho and Alandra. Also some delightful varietals: Trincadeira★, Aragonês, Touriga Nacional★, Syrah★, Alicante Bouschet★ and Verdelho★. Best years: (reds) **2008 07 05 04 01 00**.

ESTAING AOP See ENTRAYGUES-ET-DU-FEL.

CH. DES ESTANILLES *Faugères AC, Languedoc, France* Michel Louison sold the property to financier Julien Seydoux in 2009, so watch this space as planned improvements take shape. The best site is the Clos du Fou★★, with its steep schistous slope planted with Syrah. Grande Cuvée★★ includes a little Mourvèdre and Grenache. Also a wood-fermented and aged rosé, plus characterful white★. Best years: (reds) (2011) **10 09 08 07 06**.

ETNA DOC *Sicily, Italy* Sicily's still-active volcano is clad with vines (Nerello Mascalese and Nerello Cappuccio for reds, Carricante for whites) for over half of its circumference and up to 1000m (3300ft). In the 19th century the wines were much in demand for their perfume and elegance, but in the 20th century demand fell away. They are making a storming comeback and being likened – especially the reds – to fine Burgundy. Best producers: Benanti★★, Il Cantante★★, Cottanera★★, Nicosia, Passopisciaro, Russo, Terre Nere★★, Barone di Villagrande. Best years: (2011) (10) 09 08 **07 06 04 01**.

L'ÉTOILE AC *Jura, France* A tiny area within the CÔTES DU JURA that has its own AC for whites, mainly Chardonnay with some Savagnin, and for *vin jaune* and *vin de paille*. Best producers: Ch. de l'Étoile, Geneletti★, Montbourgeau★★, P Vandelle★. Best years: 2010 **09 08 07 05**.

CH. L'ÉVANGILE★★ *Pomerol AC, Bordeaux, France* A neighbour to PETRUS and CHEVAL BLANC, this estate has been wholly owned and managed by the Rothschilds of LAFITE-ROTHSCHILD since 1999. The wine is quintessential POMEROL – rich, fat and exotic. Recent vintages have been very good (2009 and 2010 were ★★★), but expect further improvement as the Rothschild effect intensifies. Second wine: Blason de l'Évangile. Best years: 2010 09 08 **07 06 05 04 03 02 01 00 99 98 95 90 89**.

EVENING LAND *Willamette Valley AVA, Oregon, USA* An investment group created this ambitious project, buying respected vineyards in California and Oregon and hiring Dominique LAFON to oversee winemaking. The WILLAMETTE VALLEY Blue Label Pinot Noir★ is a complex, blueberry-scented red. Vineyard-specific Gold Label Pinot Noir★★ is among America's best Pinot Noirs, and the Gold Label Chardonnay★★ could easily be mistaken for a Premier Cru white Burgundy. Also good Celebration Gamay Noir★. Best years: (Pinot Noir) (2010) 09 **08 07**.

FABRE MONTMAYOU *Mendoza and Patagonia, Argentina* Engaging French owners Hervé and Diane Joyaux Fabre are among the original foreign investors in Argentina, in the early 1990s. In an old area of MENDOZA called Luján de Cuyo, the estate is famous for Malbec, especially the dense damson and plum Grand Vin★★. Recent arrival of young superstar Argentine winemaker Matias Riccitelli has added another layer of excellence. Wines under the Viñalba★ label, particularly Malbec, are perhaps the best in Argentina at the price point, with remarkable purity of fruit, concentration and freshness. A PATAGONIA winery produces attractive wines under the Phebus label (also in Mendoza).

FAIRVIEW *Paarl WO, South Africa* Owner Charles Back believes South Africa's strength, especially in warmer areas, lies with Rhône varieties. These are expressed in the 'Goats' range: Goat-Roti★, Goats do Roam, etc. Complementing these is Bored Doe, a classic BORDEAUX-style blend. Fine Shiraz★★ (Eenzaamheid★★, The Beacon★★, Jakkalsfontein★★), Pinotage★ (Primo★★), Pegleg Carignan★, Merlot★ and Cabernet Sauvignon★. Good whites include Oom Pagel Semillon★★, Viognier★ and outstanding sweet wine La Beryl★★★. Back also owns SPICE ROUTE. Best years: (Shiraz) 2010 **09 08 07 06 05 04 03**.

JOSEPH FAIVELEY *Nuits-St-Georges, Côte de Nuits, Burgundy, France* There's been a revolution in this famous house since Erwan Faiveley took the helm in 2005. Gone are the dry-as-dust tannic reds, replaced by vibrant fruit and a great sense of *terroir* from vineyards such as CORTON★★★, CHAMBERTIN-Clos-de-Bèze★★★ and Mazis-Chambertin★★, as well as a range of less expensive wines from MERCUREY★, among others. Recent expansion into the CÔTE DE BEAUNE in PULIGNY★★ – with the remarkable acquisition of more than 1ha (2.5 acres) of Grand Cru – and MEURSAULT★. Best years: (top reds) (2011) 10 09 08 **07**; (whites) (2011) 10 09 **08 07**.

FALERNIA *Elqui, Chile* Established in 1998 when Italian immigrants Aldo Olivier and his brother-in-law Giorgio Flessati forsook Piedmont for the stunning ELQUI valley and swiftly made a name for themselves with Alta Tierra Reserva Syrah★★ from vines at up to 2000m (6500ft). Carmenère★★ also excellent. Mayu wines are from the same stable.

FALESCO *Lazio, Italy* Property of the Cotarella brothers: Renzo is ANTINORI's technical director (responsible for SOLAIA, TIGNANELLO, etc.); Riccardo is a high-profile consultant enologist, working all over Italy, from Piedmont to Sicily. Located at Montefiascone, their Poggio dei Gelsi★ is considered the best of the Est! Est!! Est!!! wines, but they are better known for their Merlot Montiano, the essence of smooth if somewhat soulless modernity. Best years: (Montiano) (2011) (10) 09 08 **07 06 04 01 00**.

CH. FALFAS★ *Côtes de Bourg AC, Bordeaux, France* Biodynamic estate making concentrated, structured wine that needs 4–5 years to soften. Le Chevalier★ is an old-vines cuvée. Best years: 2010 **09 08 06 05 04 03**.

FALUA See João Portugal RAMOS.

CH. DE FARGUES★★ *Sauternes AC, Bordeaux, France* Property run by the Lur-Saluces family, who until 1999 also owned Ch. d'YQUEM. The quality of this fine, rich wine is more a tribute to their commitment than to the inherent quality of the vineyard. Best years: 2010 09 **07 06 05 04 03 02 01 99 98 97 96 95 90 89 88**.

BY FARR *Geelong, Victoria, Australia* Gary Farr, ex-BANNOCKBURN, is now making wine with his son, Nick, from his 4.8ha (12-acre) family vineyard. Three single-vineyard Pinot Noirs express their different soils and aspects: Farrside★★ is complex yet ethereal; Sangreal★★ shows elegance with power; the close-planted Tout Pres★★★ is dense, fleshy and ageworthy. The Shiraz★★ is meaty, minerally, dry and firm; Viognier★ is heady, complex and alluring; Chardonnay★ austere yet tangy and elegant. Nick Farr makes more moderately priced wines under the Farr Rising label, including classy Chardonnay, dry Saignée (a Pinot rosé), and Pinot Noirs from GEELONG★ and MORNINGTON.

GARY FARRELL *Russian River Valley, California, USA*   Pioneering producer of fine Pinot Noir★★ and Chardonnay★★ from the RUSSIAN RIVER VALLEY, along with very tasty Zinfandel★★. The winery has a new owner, which has pledged to bring renewed focus to the small-lot, vineyard-focused winemaking. Best years: (Pinot Noir) 2009 **08 07 06 05 04 03 02 01 00**.

FAUGÈRES AC *Languedoc, France*   The schistous hills north of Béziers in the Hérault produce red wines whose ripe, plummy flavour marks them out from other LANGUEDOC reds. Best producers: Abbaye Sylva Plana★, Alézon★, Jean-Michel ALQUIER★, l'Ancienne Mercerie, Léon Barral★, Cébène★, Chenaie★, ESTANILLES★, Les Fusionels, Haut Lignières, la Liquière★, Ollier-Taillefer (Castel Fossibus★), Saint-Antonin, Trinités. Best years: (2011) 10 **09 08 07 06 05.**

FAUSTINO *Rioja DOCa, País Vasco and Rioja, and Cava DO, Spain*   Family-owned and technically very well equipped, this RIOJA company makes fair Reserva V and Gran Reserva I red Riojas, as well as a more modern, oak-aged red, Faustino de Autor, and fruit-driven Faustino de Crianza. But they should try harder. New top-end Faustino 9 Mil★ is ambitious and convincing. Best years: (reds) 2007 **06 05 04 03 01 99 98 96 95 94**.

FEILER-ARTINGER *Rust, Neusiedlersee, Burgenland, Austria*   Kurt Feiler makes sumptuous Ausbruch dessert wines★★: the finest are labelled Essenz★★★. Also dry whites★ and reds: Solitaire★★ is a suave blend of Merlot with Blaufränkisch and Cabernet Sauvignon. Best years: (sweet whites) (2011) 10 09 08 07 06 **05 04 02 01**; (Solitaire) (2011) (10) (09) 08 **07 06 05 04 03.**

LIVIO FELLUGA *Colli Orientali del Friuli DOC, Friuli-Venezia Giulia, Italy*   A younger generation has continued the great work of Livio Felluga at this prestigious Friuli estate. Top billing goes to Sossó★★ Rosso Rosazzo Riserva, a blend of native Refosco and Pignolo with Merlot. Terre Alte★★ is a white blend (Friulano, Pinot Bianco and Sauvignon) at a similar

level. Illivio★ is a tasty blend of Pinot Bianco, Chardonnay and Picolit; well-made varietals include Pinot Grigio, Sauvignon and Friulano. Recent vintages have all been good to excellent.

FATTORIA DI FELSINA *Chianti Classico DOCG, Tuscany, Italy*   Full, chunky CHIANTI CLASSICO★★ wines which improve with several years' bottle age. Quality is good to outstanding; most notable are the single-vineyard Riserva Rancia★★★ and (under the regional IGT Toscana) Sangiovese Fontalloro★★★. Also good Cabernet Maestro Raro★ and Chardonnay I Sistri★. Best years: (Fontalloro) (2011) (10) (09) **08 07 06 04 01 99**.

FELTON ROAD *Central Otago, South Island, New Zealand*   Runaway success with vineyards in the old goldfields of Bannockburn. Intensely fruity, seductive Pinot Noir★★ is surpassed by very limited quantities of concentrated, complex Block 3★★★ and Block 5★★★. Intense and spicy Calvert★★★ and fleshy, scented Cornish Point★★ are from separate vineyards. Three classy Rieslings (all ★★) range from dry (sometimes ★★★) to sweet. Mineral, citrus unoaked Elms Chardonnay★★ can be one of New Zealand's best; barrel-fermented Chardonnay★★ is funky and delicious; limited edition Block 2★★★ is sensational. Best years: (Pinot Noir) **2010 09 08 07 06 05 03 02 01**.

FENDANT *Valais, Switzerland* Chasselas wine from the steep slopes of the VALAIS. It should be slightly *spritzig*, with a nutty character, but many are thin and virtually characterless. Drink very young. Best producers: Chappaz, Jean-René Germanier, A Mathier, Simon Maye, D Mercier, Dom des Muses.

FER SERVADOU With its many aliases (Braucol in GAILLAC, Mansois in MARCILLAC, Pinenc in MADIRAN), this grape is a mainstay of many regions in South-West France. According to *terroir*, it can give fragrantly fruity or earthily rustic wine.

FERNGROVE *Great Southern, Western Australia* Ambitious winery founded in 1998, based in Frankland River and now with a cellar door in MARGARET RIVER. The quality potential in sunny yet cool Frankland River is unquestioned. Lack of water is a limiting factor, but that also means yields are naturally limited and flavours intensified. I've noticed a slight coarsening of flavours recently in basic wines, but top labels are on song: plush, brambly Majestic Cabernet★★ is often one of the state's finest, King Malbec★★ is scented and lush, Cossack Riesling★★ and Diamond Chardonnay★★ are also very good. Sauvignon-Semillon★ is tangy and Cabernet-Merlot★ rich and eucalyptusy. The flagship Stirlings Shiraz-Cabernet blend★ is pretty good, though I'd like less oak.

FERRARI *Trento DOC, Trentino, Italy* Founded in 1902, the firm is a leader for *metodo classico* sparkling wine. Consistent, classy wines include Ferrari Brut★, Maximum Brut★, Perlé★, Rosé★ and vintage Giulio Ferrari Riserva del Fondatore★★, aged 8 years on its lees and an Italian classic.

FERRARI-CARANO *Dry Creek Valley AVA, California, USA* Full-bodied Chardonnay: the regular bottling★ has apple-spice fruit, while the Reserve★ is deeply flavoured with more obvious oak. Fumé Blanc★ is also good. Red wines include Trésor★★ (a BORDEAUX blend), Siena★★ (based on Sangiovese), Syrah★, Merlot★ and Zinfandel★, with a new line of premium reds called PreVail (Back Forty Cabernet★★). Best years: (reds) 2009 08 **07** 06 05 03 02 01 00 99.

FERREIRA *Port DOC and Douro DOC, Douro, Portugal* Old PORT house owned by SOGRAPE. Best known for excellent tawny ports: creamy, nutty Quinta do Porto 10-year-old★ and Duque de Bragança 20-year-old★★. The Vintage★★ is increasingly good. Ferreira's unfortified wine operation, known as Casa Ferreirinha, produces Portugal's most sought-after red, Barca Velha★★★ (sometimes); made from DOURO grape varieties (mainly Tinta Roriz), it is produced only in the finest years – just 15 vintages since 1953. Marginally less good years are sold as Reserva Especial★. Quinta da Leda reds★ are also fine. Best years: (Vintage) **2003 00 97 95** 94 91 85 83 82 78 77 70 66 63; (Barca Velha) 2000 99 95 91 85 83 82 81 78.

CH. FERRIÈRE★★ *Margaux AC, 3ème Cru Classé, Haut-Médoc, Bordeaux, France* Ferrière was bought by the Merlaut family, owners of Ch. CHASSE-SPLEEN, in 1992 and is now owned and managed by Claire Villars. The ripe, rich and perfumed wines are among the best in MARGAUX AC. Best years: 2010 09 08 **07** 06 05 04 03 02 01 00 99 98 96.

FETZER *Mendocino County, California, USA* Important winery that has never fulfilled its potential. Locals swear by the quality of the cellar door releases, but we never see these in the outside world. Basic wines are OK, with tasty Gewürztraminer, Riesling and Syrah★. Bargain-priced Valley Oaks line is decent value. A leader in organic viticulture with slowly improving Bonterra range: Chardonnay, Viognier, Roussanne, Merlot,

Zinfandel, Cabernet Sauvignon and Sangiovese. Sold in 2011 to Chile's CONCHA Y TORO. So the future vintages should be interesting.

FIANO Exciting, distinctive, low-yielding southern Italian white grape variety originating in CAMPANIA and spreading now to PUGLIA and SICILY. Best producers: (Molise) Di Majo Norante; (Campania) Colli di Lapio★, Feudi di San Gregorio★★, La Guardiense★, L Maffini (Kràtos★★), MASTROBERARDINO★, Terredora di Paolo★, Vadiaperti★; (Puglia) Polvanera★; (Sicily) PLANETA (Cometa★★), Settesoli (Inycon★); (Australia) Coriole, Fox Gordon, Oliver's Taranga, Rutherglen Estates, Witches Falls.

CH. DE FIEUZAL *Pessac-Léognan AC, Cru Classé de Graves, Bordeaux, France* Under new ownership since 2001; the objective is to recapture the form of the 1980s when Fieuzal was the most exotic of all PESSAC-LÉOGNANS. With help from the owner of ANGÉLUS, it's beginning to work. The red★ is juicy and drinkable almost immediately, but ages well. The white★★, gorgeous, perfumed (and ageworthy), is the star performer. Second wine (red and white): l'Abeille de Fieuzal. Best years: (reds) 2010 09 08 **07 06 01 00 98 96 95 90 89**; (whites) **2010** 09 08 07 06 05 02 01 00.

CH. FIGEAC★★ *St-Émilion Grand Cru AC, 1er Grand Cru Classé, Bordeaux, France* The wine traditionally has a delightful fragrance and gentleness of texture. An unusually high percentage (70%) of Cabernets Franc and Sauvignon make it more structured than other ST-ÉMILIONS. Somewhat erratic in the late 1980s, but since 1996 is again the lovely Figeac of old: consistent in style and quality. Long-time owner Thierry Manoncourt (63 vintages) died in 2010. Second wine: la Grange Neuve de Figeac. Best years: 2010 09 08 **07** 06 05 **04 03 02 01 00 99 98 96 95 90 89**.

FINGER LAKES AVA *New York State, USA* Cool region in upstate NEW YORK STATE, where some winemakers are establishing a regional style for dry (and sweet) Riesling. Chardonnay and sparkling wines also star. Pinot Noir and Cabernet Franc are the best reds, but encouraging experiments with Blaufränkisch, Teroldego and even Syrah and Saperavi. Wineries around Seneca and Cayuga lakes can now use those smaller designations on their labels. Best producers: ANTHONY ROAD★, Casa Larga (Ice Wine), Chateau Lafayette Reneau★, FOX RUN★, Dr Konstantin FRANK★, Heron Hill, King Ferry, LAMOREAUX LANDING★, Martini-Reinhardt, Ravines, Red Newt, Sheldrake Point★, Swedish Hill, Wagner, Hermann J WIEMER★.

FITOU AC *Languedoc, France* After success in the 1980s, quality slumped, but with the innovative MONT TAUCH co-op taking the lead, Fitou is once again a great place for dark, herb-scented reds. Best producers: Abelanet, Bertrand-Bergé★★, Lerys★, Milles Vignes, MONT TAUCH★, Nouvelles★, Rochelière, Rolland, Roudène★, Wiala. Best years: (2011) **10** 09 **08** 07 06 05.

FIXIN AC *Côte de Nuits, Burgundy, France* Although it's next door to GEVREY-CHAMBERTIN, Fixin rarely produces anything really magical. The wines are often sold as CÔTE DE NUITS-VILLAGES. Best producers: Charlopin★, Coillot, Galeyrand★, Pierre Gelin★, Alain Guyard★, Joliet/Clos de la Perrière★★, MORTET★. Best years: (reds) (2011) 10 09 **08 07 06 05 03 02 99**.

LA FLEUR DE BOÜARD★ *Lalande-de-Pomerol AC, Bordeaux, France* Hubert de Boüard (of ANGÉLUS) acquired this property in 1998 and it's since become arguably the AC's most famous property. The wines are as rich and sensuous as good POMEROL. A super-cuvée, Le Plus★, aged in new oak barrels for 33 months, is both challenging and expensive. My only worry is the amount of oak used. Best years: 2010 09 **08 07 06 05 04 02 01 00**.

CH. LA FLEUR-PÉTRUS★★ *Pomerol AC, Bordeaux, France*   Like the better-known PETRUS and TROTANOY, this is owned by the dynamic MOUEIX family. Unlike its stablemates, it is situated entirely on gravel soil and tends to produce tighter wines with less immediate fruit but considerable elegance and cellar potential. Among POMEROL's top dozen properties. Best years: 2010 09 08 06 **05 04 03 02 01 00 99 98 96 95 94 90 89**.

FLEURIE AC *Beaujolais, Burgundy, France*   The best-known BEAUJOLAIS Cru, Fleurie can reveal heady perfumes and a delightful juicy fruit. But demand has meant that many wines are overpriced and dull. Best producers: Ch. de Beauregard (Colonies de Rochegrès★), Coquard★, DUBOEUF (la Madone★, Quatre Vents★), L Lardy (Les Roches★), la Madone/Despres★, Y Métras★, Métrat★, Point du Jour★, Villa Ponciago★. Best years: (2011) 10 09.

FLORA SPRINGS *Napa Valley AVA, California, USA*   Best known for red wines such as Merlot★★, Cabernet Sauvignon★★ and BORDEAUX-blend Trilogy★★. Barrel-fermented Chardonnay★★ and Soliloquy Vineyard Sauvignon Blanc★ top the whites. Also Italian varieties, including weighty Pinot Grigio★ and lightly spiced Sangiovese★, available only at the winery. Best years: (Trilogy) (2009) 08 07 **06 05 04 03 02 01 00 99 96**.

FLOWERS *Sonoma Coast AVA, California, USA*   Small producer whose estate vineyard, Camp Meeting Ridge, a few miles from the Pacific, yields delicate wines of great intensity. Camp Meeting Ridge Pinot Noir★★★ and Chardonnay★★ are usually made with native yeasts and offer beautifully restrained, subtly balanced aromas and flavours. Andreén-Gale★★ are full-flavoured barrel selections. Also SONOMA COAST★★ wines from purchased fruit. Best years: (Chardonnay) **2009 08 07 06 05 04 03 01**; (Pinot Noir) 2009 **08 07 06 05 04 03 01 00 99**.

AMBROGIO & GIOVANNI FOLONARI *Tuscany, Italy*   A few years ago the Folonari family, owners of the giant RUFFINO, split asunder and this father and son team went their own way. Their properties/brands include Cabreo (Sangiovese-Cabernet Il Borgo, Chardonnay La Pietra) and Nozzole (powerful, long-lived Cabernet Il Pareto★★) in CHIANTI CLASSICO, plus VINO NOBILE estate TorCalvano-Gracciano, Campo al Mare in BOLGHERI and BRUNELLO producer La Fuga.

FONSECA *Port DOC, Douro, Portugal*   Owned by the same group as TAYLOR's (Fladgate Partnership), Fonseca makes ports in a rich, densely plummy style. Vintage★★★ is magnificent, the aged tawnies★★ superb. Guimaraens★★ is the 'off-vintage' wine. Crusted★ and Late Bottled Vintage★★ are among the best examples of their styles, as is the Terra Prima★ organic port. Quinta do Panascal is the single quinta vintage. Best years: (Vintage) 2009 **07 03 00 97 94 92 85 83 77 75 70 66 63 55**.

JOSÉ MARIA DA FONSECA *Península de Setúbal, Portugal*   A huge range of wines, from fizzy Lancers Rosé to serious reds. Best include Hexagon★★, Vinya★ (Syrah-Aragonez), Domingos Soares Franco Private Collection★, and Garrafeiras with codenames like RA★★ and TE★★. Periquita is the mainstay, with Clássico★ made only in the best years. Also SETÚBAL made mainly from the Moscatel grape: 5-year-old★ and 20-year-old★★. Older vintage-dated Setúbals are rare but superb.

DOM. FONT DE MICHELLE *Châteauneuf-du-Pape AC, Rhône Valley, France*   CHÂTEAUNEUF-DU-PAPE reds★★, in particular Cuvée Étienne Gonnet★★, with richness and southern herb fragrance – and great value for money. Fresh, accomplished whites★★. Successful new Gonnet Selection range (VENTOUX red★). Best years: (Étienne Gonnet red) (2011) 10 09 **07 06 05 04 03 01 00 99 98 97 95 90**.

FONTANAFREDDA *Barolo DOCG, Piedmont, Italy* Large property, formerly the hunting lodge of the King of Italy. Under new management, basic BAROLO Serralunga d'Alba★ is improving; also single-vineyard Barolos La Rosa★★, La Villa★★ and La Delizia★★★. Add to this a range of good PIEDMONT varietals, a lot of ASTI and a tasty dry sparkler, Contessa Rosa. Best years: (Barolo) (2011) (10) (09) 08 **07** 06 **04**.

CASTELLO DI FONTERUTOLI *Chianti Classico DOCG, Tuscany, Italy* This estate has belonged to the Mazzei family since the 15th century, though the wine style is modern/international. Good CHIANTI CLASSICO Riserva★★, along with excellent Siepi★★★ (Sangiovese-Merlot). Belguardo★ is a more recent venture in the MAREMMA, with IGT and MORELLINO DI SCANSANO wines.

FONTODI *Chianti Classico DOCG, Tuscany, Italy* The Manetti family has built this superbly sited estate into one of the most admired in CHIANTI CLASSICO, with fine Chianti Classico★★ and Riserva Vigna del Sorbo★★. Flaccianello della Pieve★★★, from a selection of best bunches, remains IGT although 100% Sangiovese. Pinot Nero and Syrah★ are made under the Case Via label. Best years: (Flaccianello) (2011) (10) 09 **08** 07 06 **04 01**.

FORADORI *Teroldego Rotaliano DOC, Trentino, Italy* Producer of dark, spicy, berry-fruited wines from Teroldego grapes, including TEROLDEGO ROTALIANO★ and a couple of crus, Morei★★ and Sgarzon★★. Best years: (Sgarzon) (2011) (10) 09 08 **07 06 04**.

FORST *Pfalz, Germany* Village with outstanding vineyard sites, including the Ungeheuer or 'Monster', which can show marvellous mineral intensity and richness. Equally good are the Kirchenstück, Jesuitengarten, Freundstück and Pechstein. Best producers: BASSERMANN-JORDAN★★, von BUHL★★, BÜRKLIN-WOLF★★, MOSBACHER★★, E Müller, Spindler, Wolf★★. Best years: (2011) 10 09 **08 07 06 05 04 03 02**.

O FOURNIER *Argentina, Chile, Spain* Exciting Tempranillo and Malbec from old vines in the La Consulta area of MENDOZA's Uco Valley. Alfa Crux★★ (a Tempranillo-Malbec-Merlot blend) is top of the line, while Alfa Crux Malbec★★ is an excellent, juicy expression of Argentina's flagship red grape. Also very good Syrah★. B Crux★ is the lighter, but delicious, second label. An operation in Chile produces excellent Centauri Sauvignon Blanc★★ from the Leyda Valley and Centauri★★ red blend of old-vine Carignan, Cabernet and Merlot, plus a range of other exciting MAULE reds. O Fournier also has a venture in RIBERA DEL DUERO, Spain, with O Fournier★, Alfa Spiga★ and less oaky Spiga★★ cuvées.

FOX CREEK *McLaren Vale, South Australia*
Impressive, opulent, superripe MCLAREN VALE reds. Reserve Shiraz★★ and Reserve Cabernet Sauvignon★★ have wowed the critics; JSM (Shiraz-Cabernets)★★ is rich and succulent; Merlot★★ is a little lighter, but still concentrated and powerful. Vixen sparkling Shiraz★ is also lip-smacking stuff.

FOX RUN *Finger Lakes AVA, New York State, USA* A leader in dry Riesling★, Fox Run has teamed up with Red Newt and ANTHONY ROAD wineries to produce Tierce★, aiming to define a regional style for Riesling. Fox Run also produces elegant Reserve Chardonnay★, spicy, attractive Pinot Noir, Merlot and Cabernet Franc★, and a complex, fruit-forward red Meritage.

FRAMINGHAM *Marlborough, South Island, New Zealand* Small winery owned by SOGRAPE. Much of Framingham's success is thanks to the thoughtful and uncompromising approach of English winemaker Dr Andrew Hedley. Aromatic grape varieties do well, particularly Riesling: Select★★, off-dry Classic★ and Dry★. Pure, spicy Gewürztraminer★★ with its ALSACE-style big brother F-Series★★, and sleek, ethereal Pinot Gris★★ are among New Zealand's best. In favourable years sweet wines★★★ can be truly outstanding. Best years: (Riesling) (2011) **10 09 07 06**.

FRANCIACORTA DOCG *Lombardy, Italy* *Metodo classico* fizz made from Pinot and Chardonnay grapes. Still whites from Pinot Bianco and Chardonnay and reds from Cabernet, Barbera, Nebbiolo and Merlot are all DOC with the appellation Curtefranca. Best producers: BELLAVISTA★★, Fratelli Berlucchi★, Guido Berlucchi★, CA' DEL BOSCO★★, Castellino★, Cavalleri★, La Ferghettina★, Enrico Gatti★, Monte Rossa★, Il Mosnel★, Ricci Curbastro★, San Cristoforo★, Uberti★, Villa★.

FRANCISCAN *Napa Valley AVA, California, USA* Consistently good wines at fair prices: the Cuvée Sauvage Chardonnay★★ is a blockbusting, savoury mouthful, and the Cabernet Sauvignon-based meritage Magnificat★ is very attractive. Part of Constellation.

FRANCS-CÔTES DE BORDEAUX AC *Bordeaux, France* Tiny area east of ST-ÉMILION for reds and a little white; previously known as Bordeaux-Côtes de Francs but part of Côtes de Bordeaux AC since 2008; the top wines are good value. The Thienpont family (Ch. Puygueraud) is the driving force. Best producers: les Charmes-Godard★, Franc-Cardinal, Francs★, Laclaverie★, Marsau★, Nardou★, Pelan★, la Prade★, le Priolat, Puygueraud★★, Vieux Saule. Best years: 2010 **09 08 05 04 03**.

DR KONSTANTIN FRANK *Finger Lakes AVA, New York State, USA* The good doctor was a pioneer of *vinifera* grapes in the FINGER LAKES region in the 1960s. Now under the direction of his grandson Fred, the winery continues to spotlight the area's talent with Riesling★ and Rkatsiteli★, an obscure but delightful Georgian white grape. There's also some nice Chateau Frank fizz.

FRANKEN *Germany* 6060ha (15,000-acre) wine region specializing in dry wines – recognizable by their squat Bocksbeutel bottles (familiar because of the Portuguese wine Mateus Rosé). Silvaner is the traditional variety, although Müller-Thurgau is more widely planted. The most famous vineyards are on slopes around WÜRZBURG, RANDERSACKER, IPHOFEN and Escherndorf.

FRANSCHHOEK WO *South Africa* Huguenot refugees settled in this picturesque valley, encircled by breathtaking mountain peaks, in the 17th century. Many wineries and other landmarks still bear French names. The valley is recognized for its whites – Semillon is a local speciality (a few vines are over 100 years old) – though reds are establishing a reputation. Best producers: BOEKENHOUTSKLOOF★★, CAPE CHAMONIX★★, La Motte★, La Petite Ferme, Landau du Val, L'Ormarins, Solms-Delta★, Stony Brook. Best years: (reds) 2010 **09 08 07 06 05 04 03**.

FRASCATI DOC *Lazio, Italy* Once one of Italy's most famous whites, and still Rome's quaffing wine. It may be made from Trebbiano or Malvasia or any blend thereof; the better examples have a higher proportion of Malvasia. There's much mediocre stuff, but Frascati Superiore DOCG is worth seeking out, as is the sweet Cannellino DOCG. Other light, dry Frascati-like wines come from neighbouring DOCs in the hills of the

Castelli Romani and Colli Albani, including Marino, Montecompatri, Velletri and Zagarolo. Best producers: Casale Marchese★, Castel de Paolis★, Colli di Catone★, Piero Costantini/Villa Simone★, Fontana Candida★, Zandotti★.

FREESTONE VINEYARDS *Sonoma Coast AVA, California, USA* The Napa Valley's Joseph PHELPS planted 40ha (100 acres) of Chardonnay and Pinot Noir in 3 parcels at Freestone on the SONOMA COAST. The first releases were in 2006 and the lushness of the Chardonnay★★ and the rich yet scented fruit of the Pinot Noir★ made an immediate impact. Good second label Fogdog★ and top Chardonnay Ovation★★.

FREIXENET *Cava DO, Cataluña, Spain* The second-biggest Spanish sparkling wine company (after CODORNÍU) makes the famous Cordon Negro Brut CAVA in a vast network of cellars in Sant Sadurní d'Anoia. Freixenet also owns a number of other Cava brands (including Castellblanch and Segura Viudas) as well as PENEDÈS winery René Barbier and international interests in Champagne, California, Australia, Argentina and Bordeaux.

FRESCOBALDI *Tuscany, Italy* Ancient Florentine company selling large quantities of blended CHIANTI, but from its own vineyards (some 1000ha/ 2470 acres in Tuscany) it produces good to very good wines at Castello di Nipozzano (CHIANTI RUFINA Nipozzano Riserva★★, Montesodi★★ and the BORDEAUX-blend Mormoreto★★), Castello di Pomino★ (Benefizio Chardonnay★) and Castelgiocondo (BRUNELLO DI MONTALCINO★), where Sangiovese for Brunello and Merlot for the 'super-Tuscan' Luce are grown. Frescobaldi owns several other estates in Tuscany including, since 2005, a majority stake in the famous Bolgheri estate, ORNELLAIA. Best years: (premium reds) (2011) (10) 09 **08** 07 06 **04 01**.

FRIULANO Friulano (formerly Tocai Friulano) is a north-east Italian grape producing dry, nutty, oily whites of great character in COLLIO and COLLI ORIENTALI. Friuli producers have now, under pressure from the Hungarians, removed the name Tocai. Best producers: Borgo del Tiglio★, Livio FELLUGA★, Edi Keber★★, Miani★★, Princic★, Ronco del Gelso★★, Russiz Superiore★★, SCHIOPETTO★★, Le Vigne di Zamò★★, Villa Russiz★.

FRIULI GRAVE DOC *Friuli-Venezia Giulia, Italy* DOC in western Friuli covering multiple wine types, mostly varietal. Good affordable Merlot, Refosco, Chardonnay, Pinot Grigio, Traminer and Friulano. Best producers: Borgo Magredo★, Di Lenardo★, Le Fredis★, Orgnani★, Pighin★, Pittaro★, Plozner★, Pradio★, Russolo★, Scarbolo, Vigneti Le Monde★, Villa Chiopris★, Vistorta★. Best years: (whites) (2011) 10 **09 08 07** 06.

FRIULI ISONZO DOC *Friuli-Venezia Giulia, Italy* Classy southern neighbour of COLLIO with wines of outstanding value. The DOC covers numerous styles, the best being whites: Chardonnay, Pinot Grigio and Sauvignon. There are some decent reds too (Merlot does well). Best producers: (Isonzo DOC) Borgo San Daniele★, Colmello di Grotta★, Sergio & Mauro Drius★★, Lis Neris★★, Masùt da Rive★, Pierpaolo Pecorari★★, Giovanni Puiatti★, Ronco del Gelso★★, Vie di Romans★★, Villanova★; (Carso DOC) Castelvecchio, Edi Kante★★. Best years: (whites) (2011) (10) 09 08 **07 06**.

FRIULI-VENEZIA GIULIA *Italy* North-east Italian region bordering Austria and Slovenia. The hilly DOC zones of COLLIO and COLLI ORIENTALI produce some of Italy's finest whites from Chardonnay, Pinot Bianco, Pinot Grigio, Sauvignon and Friulano (Tocai), and good reds mainly from Cabernet,

Merlot and Refosco. Good-value wines from the DOCs of Friuli Aquileia, FRIULI ISONZO, Friuli Latisana and FRIULI GRAVE, in the rolling hills and plains.

FROMM *Marlborough, South Island, New Zealand* Small winery where low-yielding vines and intensively managed vineyards are the secret behind a string of winning white wines, including fine Burgundian-style Clayvin Vineyard Chardonnay★★, German-style Riesling Spätlese★ and Riesling Auslese★★. Despite its success with whites, Fromm is perhaps best known for intense, long-lived reds, including Clayvin Vineyard Pinot Noir★★★, Fromm Vineyard Pinot Noir★★ and a powerful, peppery Syrah★. Best years: (Pinot Noir) 2010 09 07 06 05 04 03 02.

FRONSAC AC *Bordeaux, France* Small area west of POMEROL making good-value Merlot-based wines. The top producers have taken note of the feeding frenzy in neighbouring Pomerol and sharpened up their act accordingly, with finely structured wines, occasionally perfumed, and better with at least 5 years' age. Best producers: Carles (Haut-Carles★), Chadenne, Dalem★, la Dauphine★, Fontenil★, la Grave, Magondeau Beau-Site, Mayne-Vieil (Cuvée Aliénor★), Moulin Haut-Laroque★, Richelieu★, la Rivière★, la Rousselle★, Tour du Moulin, les Trois Croix★, la Vieille Cure★, Villars★. Best years: 2010 09 08 06 05 03 01 00 98.

FRONTON AOP *South-West France* From north of Toulouse, some of the most distinctive and improving reds – silky, with hints of violets and licorice – of South-West France. Négrette is the chief grape, but most producers blend in Cabernet and/or Syrah. Best producers: Baudare★, Bellevue-la-Forêt★, Bouissel★, Boujac, Caze★, Joliet, Laurou, PLAISANCE★, le Roc★, Viguerie de Belaygues★. Best years: (2011) 10 09.

FUMÉ BLANC See SAUVIGNON BLANC, pages 284–5.

FÜRST *Bürgstadt, Franken, Germany* Fürst's dry Rieslings★★ are unusually elegant for a region where white wines can be earthy, with Burgundian-style Spätburgunder (Pinot Noir) reds★★ and barrel-fermented Weissburgunder (Pinot Blanc) whites★★ are some of Germany's best. Sensual, intellectual wines with excellent aging potential. Best years: (dry Riesling) (2011) 10 09 08 07 06 05 04; (reds) (2010) 09 08 07 06 04.

JEAN-NOËL GAGNARD *Chassagne-Montrachet, Côte de Beaune, Burgundy, France* Run since 1989 by Gagnard's daughter Caroline Lestimé, who consistently makes some of the best wines of CHASSAGNE-MONTRACHET, particularly Premiers Crus Caillerets★★★ and Morgeot★★. Top wine is rich, toasty BÂTARD-MONTRACHET★★★. All whites are capable of extended cellaring. Reds★ are good, but not in the same class. Best years: (whites) (2011) 10 09 08 06 05 04 02 00 99.

GAILLAC AOP *South-West France* A huge variety of wines: whites, mainly from Mauzac and Len de l'El, range from dry to ultra-sweet. Reds and rosés are from local grapes too – Braucol, Duras – and sometimes Syrah. Some reds are matured in wood and can be kept. Sparkling Gaillac usually has no added yeasts or sugar. Best producers: Bourguet, Brin, CAUSSE MARINES★★, Escausses★, Labarthe★, Mas Pignou, Palvié★★, Peyres Roses★, Pialentou, PLAGEOLES★★, la RAMAYE★★, Rotier★. Best years: (reds) (2011) 10 09 08 06 05; (sweet whites) (2011) 10 09 07 06 05.

GAJA *Barbaresco DOCG, Piedmont, Italy* Angelo Gaja was instrumental in bringing about the transformation of PIEDMONT from an old-fashioned region to a world-class area of sophistication and high price, thus giving other Piedmont growers the chance to get a decent return for their labours. Into this fiercely conservative area, full of fascinating grape varieties but proudest of the native Nebbiolo, he introduced French grapes like Cabernet Sauvignon (Darmagi★★), Sauvignon Blanc (Alteni di Brassica★) and Chardonnay (Gaia & Rey★★). He has also renounced the Barbaresco and Barolo DOCGs for his best wines! Gaja's traditional strength has been in single-vineyard wines from the BARBARESCO region: his Sorì San Lorenzo★★★, Sorì Tildìn★★★ and Costa Russi★★★, sold under the LANGHE Nebbiolo DOC, which permits 15% of other grapes in the blend, are often cited as Barbaresco's best of the modern style, although they tend to be more 'Gaja' than 'Barbaresco'. Only one 100% Nebbiolo bottling of Barbaresco DOCG★★★ is now made. His outstanding Sperss★★★ and Conteisa★★★ (from BAROLO) are sold as Langhe Nebbiolo. Gaja has also invested in BRUNELLO DI MONTALCINO (Pieve Santa Restituta) and BOLGHERI (Ca' Marcanda). Best years: (Barbaresco) (2011) (10) 09 08 **07** 06 **04 01** 99 98 97 96 95 90 89 88 85.

GALICIA *Spain* Up in Spain's hilly, verdant north-west, Galicia is renowned for its Albariño whites. There are 5 DOs: RÍAS BAIXAS can make excellent, fragrant Albariño, with modern equipment and serious wine-making; Ribeiro DO has also invested heavily in new equipment, and better local white grapes such as Treixadura are now being used; it's a similar story with the Godello grape in the mountainous Valdeorras DO, where producers such as the young Rafael Palacios, from the ubiquitous Rioja-based family, are reaching new heights for ageworthy, individual whites. Some ambitious reds from the Mencía grape are also made there and in the Ribeira Sacra DO. Monterrei DO has found a showcase estate in Quinta da Muradella★, with Raúl PÉREZ as the consulting winemaker. An increasing number of ageworthy whites and reds are now produced.

GALLO *Central Valley, California, USA* Gallo, the world's largest family-owned wine company – and for generations a byword for cheap, drab wines – has made a massive effort to change its reputation since the mid-1990s. This began with the release of Sonoma Estate Chardonnay and Cabernet Sauvignon. The emphasis is still on Sonoma Chardonnay and Cabernet Sauvignon, with Zinfandel and Cabernet Sauvignon from DRY CREEK VALLEY and ALEXANDER VALLEY. New SONOMA COAST vineyards are in a very cool area south of Santa Rosa, with stylish single-vineyard Two Rock Chardonnay. Vineyards in RUSSIAN RIVER VALLEY and the Sonoma Coast have been planted to Pinot Noir and Pinot Gris (some of it to make the premium MacMurray wines). Even so, Gallo continues to produce oceans of ordinary wine. Turning Leaf isn't going to turn many heads, but the company has taken Rancho Zabaco upscale and added a parallel brand, Dancing Bull, in which Sauvignon Blanc★ and Zinfandel★ are budding stars. Gallo also owns historic Louis M Martini in NAPA VALLEY, with its famed Monte Rosso vineyard, as well as Barefoot Cellars (a fast-growing brand), Frei Brothers, William Hill, Mirassou and CENTRAL COAST's Bridlewood.

GAMAY The only grape allowed for red BEAUJOLAIS. In general Gamay wine is rather rough-edged and quite high in raspy acidity, but in Beaujolais, so long as the yield is not too high, it can achieve a wonderful, juicy-fruit gluggability, almost unmatched in the world of wine. Elsewhere in France, it is successful in the Ardèche, Savoie and the Loire (sometimes blended with Pinot Noir) and less so in the Mâconnais. In Switzerland it is blended with Pinot Noir to create DÔLE and Goron. There are occasional plantings in Canada, Brazil, New Zealand, Australia, South Africa and Italy.

GANTENBEIN *Fläsch, Graubünden, Switzerland* Since 1982 Daniel Gantenbein has focused on producing intense and powerful versions of the Burgundian varieties, and has won a fine reputation above all for his Pinot Noir★★, as well as Chardonnay★ and Riesling★. Best years: (Pinot Noir) (2011) (10) 09 **08 07 06 05 04**.

GARD, IGP DU *Languedoc, France* Mainly reds and rosés from the western side of the RHÔNE delta. Most red is light, spicy and attractive. Some fresh young rosés and whites have been improved by modern winemaking. Best producers: des Aveylans★, Cantarelles, Coste Plane, Grande Cassagne★, Guiot★, Mas des Bressades★.

GARNACHA BLANCA See GRENACHE BLANC.

GARNACHA TINTA See GRENACHE NOIR.

GATTINARA DOCG *Piedmont, Italy* Nebbiolo-based red from north-central PIEDMONT that consistently disappoints Barolo-lovers, having an earthier character than its famous rival, i.e. Barolo! – but I quite like it. Best producers: Antoniolo★, Anzivino, Nervi★, Travaglini★.

DOM. GAUBY *Côtes du Roussillon-Villages AC, Roussillon, France* Gérard Gauby, and now his son Lionel, can make marvellously concentrated and balanced wines. Highlights include powerful CÔTES DU ROUSSILLON-VILLAGES Vieilles Vignes★★, Muntada★★, red and white les Calcinaires★, as well as a gorgeously seductive white CÔTES CATALANES Coume Gineste★. Best years: (reds) (2011) 10 09 08 07 06 05.

GAVI DOCG *Piedmont, Italy* This fashionable and rapidly improving Cortese-based steely, lemony white can age up to 5 years, providing it starts life with enough fruit. Mainly still, occasionally sparkling. Best producers: Battistina★, Bergaglio★, Broglia★, La Chiara★, Chiarlo★, FONTANAFREDDA, La Giustiniana★★, Pio Cesare, San Pietro★, La Scolca★, Tassarolo★, Villa Sparina★.

CH. GAZIN★★ *Pomerol AC, Bordeaux, France* Large château in POMEROL, situated next to the legendary PETRUS. The wine, traditionally a succulent, sweet-textured Pomerol, seemed to lose its way in the 1980s but has now got much of its character back under owner Nicolas de Bailliencourt. Best years: 2010 09 08 **07 06 05** 04 03 02 01 00 99 98 96 95 90 89.

GEELONG *Victoria, Australia* Cool-climate, maritime-influenced region revived in the 1960s after destruction by phylloxera in the 19th century. Can be brilliant – potentially a match for the YARRA VALLEY. Impressive Pinot Noir, Chardonnay, Riesling, Sauvignon and Shiraz. Best producers: Austin's★, BANNOCKBURN★★, Clyde Park, By FARR★★, Lethbridge★, Scotchmans Hill★.

GEROVASSILIOU *Macedonia AO, Greece* Bordeaux-trained Evángelos Gerovassiliou has 40ha (100 acres) of vineyards and a modern winery in Epanomi in northern Greece. High-quality fruit results in Syrah-dominated Gerovassiliou red★ and some fresh, modern whites, including fabulously scented Malagousia★★, Viognier★, barrel-fermented Chardonnay, Fumé, and Assyrtiko-Malagousia blend Gerovassiliou★ white.

GEVREY-CHAMBERTIN AC *Côte de Nuits, Burgundy, France* A new generation of growers has restored the reputation of Gevrey as a source of well-coloured, firmly structured, powerful, perfumed wines that become rich and gamy with age. Village wines should be kept for at least 5 years, Premiers Crus and the 9 Grands Crus for 10 years or more, especially CHAMBERTIN and Clos-de-Bèze. The Premier Cru Clos St-Jacques is worthy of promotion to Grand Cru, with Cazetiers and Combottes not far behind. Best producers: D Bachelet★★, Louis Boillot★, A Burguet★★, B CLAIR★★, Confuron-Cotetidot★, P Damoy★★, DROUHIN★, C Dugat★★★, B Dugat-Py★★, S Esmonin★★, FAIVELEY★★, J-M Fourrier★★, Geantet-Pansiot★★, Harmand-Geoffroy★, JADOT★★, Denis MORTET★★★, Perrot-Minot★★, Rossignol-Trapet★★, J Roty★★, ROUSSEAU★★★, Sérafin★★, J & J-L Trapet★★, C Tremblay★★, VOUGERAIE★. Best years: (2011) 10 09 08 **07** 06 05 **03 02 01 99 98 96 95 93 90.**

GEWÜRZTRAMINER *Gewürz* means spice, and typically the wine is spicy, exotically perfumed with rose petals and lychees, and low in acidity. It is thought to have originated in the village of Tramin, in Italy's ALTO ADIGE, and the name Traminer is used by many producers. It makes an appearance in many wine-producing countries; quality is mixed and styles vary enormously, from the fresh, light, florally perfumed wines produced in Alto Adige to the rich, luscious, late-harvest ALSACE Vendange Tardive. Best in Alsace and also good in Austria's Styria (STEIERMARK), southern Germany, Croatia, California, Chile and New Zealand. Small amounts in South Africa and Australia.

GIACONDA *Beechworth, Victoria, Australia* In spite of (or perhaps because of) Giaconda's tiny production, Rick Kinzbrunner is one of Australia's most influential winemakers. Following on from his success, BEECHWORTH has become one of the country's most exciting viticultural regions. His tightly structured, minerally, savoury Chardonnay★★★ is one of Australia's best – as are both the serious and beautiful Pinot Noir★★★ (a Beechworth-YARRA blend) and the deep, gamy, HERMITAGE-style Warner Vineyard Shiraz★★★. The Cabernet★ is ripe, deep and complex; Aeolia Roussanne and Nantua Les Deux (Chardonnay-Roussanne) are complex and textural. Look for the estate vineyard Shiraz and joint venture with CHAPOUTIER, Ergo Sum Shiraz. Best years: (Chardonnay) (2011) (10) 08 07 **06** **05** 04 02 00 99 98 96 93.

BRUNO GIACOSA *Barbaresco DOCG, Piedmont, Italy* One of the great winemakers of the LANGHE hills, indeed of Italy, still basically a traditionalist, though he has reduced maturation time for his BARBARESCOS and BAROLOS to a maximum of 4 years. Superb Barbarescos Asili★★★, Santo Stefano★★★ and Rabajà★★★, and Barolos including Rocche del Falletto★★★ and Falletto★★. Excellent BARBERA D'ALBA★, Dolcetto d'Alba★, Roero ARNEIS★, MOSCATO D'ASTI★★ and sparkling Extra Brut★★. Giacosa suffered a stroke in 2006 but he is back in business, having sold his 2006s in bulk, even though others consider 06 a great year. Best years: (2011) (10) 09 08 **07 04 01 00 99 98 97 96 95 90 89 88 85 82.**

GIGONDAS AC *Rhône Valley, France* Gigondas red wines are mainly Grenache, plus Syrah and, increasingly, Mourvèdre. They offer big, spiced southern flavours and good value; most drink well with 5 years' age, but will happily age for much longer. Best producers: P Amadieu★★, la Bouïssière★★, Brusset★★, Cassan★★, Cayron★, Clos des Cazaux★★, Clos du Joncuas★, Cros de la Mûre★★, DELAS★, Espiers★★, Font-Sane★, la Fourmone★, les Goubert★, Gour de Chaulé★, Grand Bourjassot, Grapillon d'Or★★, GUIGAL★, Paul JABOULET, Longue-Toque★, Montvac★★, Moulin de la Gardette★★, les Pallières★★, Famille Perrin★, Pesquier★★, Piaugier★, Raspail-Ay★★, Redortier★, Roubine★, St-Cosme★★, ST GAYAN★★, Santa Duc★★, Tardieu-Laurent★★, la Tourade★, Tourelles★★, Trignon★. Best years: (2011) **10 09 08 07 06 05 04 03 01 00 99 98 95**.

CH. GILETTE★★ *Sauternes AC, Bordeaux, France* These astonishing wines are stored in concrete vats as opposed to the more normal wooden barrels. This virtually precludes any oxygen contact, and it is oxygen that ages a wine. Consequently, when released at up to 20 years old, they are bursting with life and lusciousness. Best years: **1989 88 86 85 83 82 81 79 78 76 75 71 70 67 61 59 55 53 49**.

GIPPSLAND *Victoria, Australia* Diverse wineries along the southern VICTORIA coast, all tiny but with massive potential. Results are erratic, occasionally brilliant. Nicholson River's exotic, hedonistic Chardonnay sometimes hits ★★, Shiraz can be ★★★. Bass Phillip Pinot Noirs (Reserve★★★, Premium★★★) are among the best in Australia, with a cult following. McAlister★ is a tasty red BORDEAUX blend. Best producers: Bass Phillip★★★, William Downie★★, McAlister★, Nicholson River★★.

VINCENT GIRARDIN *Santenay, Côte de Beaune, Burgundy, France* A grower in SANTENAY who developed a thriving *négociant* business in MEURSAULT, but is now concentrating on a significantly enhanced domaine, specializing in whites from CHASSAGNE (Caillerets★★) and PULIGNY★. Good reds too: Santenay Gravières★★. Best years: (whites) (2011) 10 09 **08 07 06 05**.

GISBORNE *North Island, New Zealand* Gisborne, with its hot, humid climate and fertile soils, delivers both quality and quantity. Christened (by local growers) 'The Chardonnay Capital of New Zealand', although the focus is rapidly shifting to Pinot Gris, while Gewürztraminer and Chenin Blanc are also a success. Good reds, however, are hard to find. Cancellation of big company contracts has caused a crisis growers are fighting hard to resolve. Best producers: MILLTON★★, Vinoptima★★. Best years: (Chardonnay) 2010 **09 07 05**.

GIVRY AC *Côte Chalonnaise, Burgundy, France* Important CÔTE CHALONNAISE village. The reds have an intensity of fruit and ability to age that are unusual in the region. There are some attractive, fairly full, nutty whites, too. Best producers: Bourgeon★, Chofflet-Valdenaire★, Clos Salomon★, Joblot★★, F Lumpp★★, Ragot★, Sarrazin★. Best years: (reds) (2011) 10 **09 08 07 05**; (whites) (2011) **10 09**.

GLAETZER *Barossa Valley, South Australia* Colin Glaetzer is one of the BAROSSA VALLEY's most enthusiastic and successful winemakers. He made his reputation working for other people, and now he and his son Ben make tip-top Barossa wines for the family label. There is fleshy Wallace Shiraz-Grenache★, rich, superripe Bishop Shiraz★★ (from 30–60-year-old vines), the opulent, succulent and velvety Amon-Ra Shiraz★★ and Anaperenna★★, a deep, dense Shiraz-Cabernet blend. Ben also makes reds and whites for the Heartland label using fruit from vineyards in Langhorne Creek and LIMESTONE COAST, but recent releases have lost their initial zip. Best years: (Bishop Shiraz) 2010 08 **06 05 04 02 01 99 98 96**.

GLEN CARLOU *Paarl WO, South Africa* Started by the Finlaysons in the 1980s; now owned by Californian businessman Donald Hess. Rich but elegant Chardonnay★ and single-vineyard Quartz Stone Chardonnay★★

lead the whites. Reds, with rather more New World panache, feature sweet-textured Pinot Noir★, deep, dry Syrah★, concentrated Gravel Quarry Cabernet★ and Grand Classique★, a red BORDEAUX blend with good aging potential. Best years: (Chardonnay) 2011 **10 09 08 07 06 05 04 03**.

CH. GLORIA★ *St-Julien AC, Haut-Médoc, Bordeaux, France* An interesting property, created out of tiny plots of Classed Growth land scattered all round ST-JULIEN. Generally very soft and sweet-centred, the wine nonetheless ages well. Same owner as Ch. ST-PIERRE. Second wine: Peymartin. Best years: 2010 09 08 **07 06 05 04 03 01 00 99 98 95 90 89**.

GODELLO See VERDELHO.

GONZÁLEZ BYASS *Jerez y Manzanilla DO, Andalucía, Spain* Tio Pepe★ fino is the world's biggest-selling sherry. The old sherries are superb: intense, dry Amontillado del Duque★★★; rich, complex sweet Oloroso Matusalem★★ and Palo Cortado Apóstoles★★; treacly Noé Pedro Ximénez★★★. One step down is the Alfonso Dry Oloroso★. The firm pioneered the rediscovery of single-vintage (non-solera) dry olorosos★★ and palos cortados★★. Outstanding new Palmas★★★ range of three unfiltered 'En Rama' finos and an amontillado.

GOSSET *Champagne AC, Champagne, France* Gosset, the oldest wine producer in CHAMPAGNE, based in the Grand Cru of Aÿ, makes a complex, rich Grande Réserve Brut★★, a three-vintage blend that has 5 years' aging before release. The more austere top wines – Celebris★★, also produced in rosé★★ and Blanc de Blancs★★ styles – need extra time to show at their best. Best years: (2003) (02) 00 99 **98 96 95 90**.

GRAACH *Mosel, Germany* Important Middle MOSEL wine village with 4 vineyard sites, the most famous being Domprobst (also the best) and Himmelreich. The wines have an attractive fullness to balance their steely acidity, and great aging potential. Best producers: Kees-Kieren★, von Kesselstatt★, Dr LOOSEN★★, MOLITOR★★, JJ PRUM★★, SA PRUM★, M F RICHTER★, Willi SCHAEFER★★★, SELBACH-OSTER★★, Dr Weins-Prüm★. Best years: (2011) 10 09 **08 07 06 05 04 02 01 99 98**.

GRACIANO Rare, low-yielding but excellent Spanish grape, traditional in RIOJA, NAVARRA and Extremadura. It makes dense, highly structured, fragrant reds, and its high acidity adds life when blended with low-acid Tempranillo. In Portugal it is called Tinta Miúda. Also grown by BROWN BROTHERS and others in Australia.

GRAHAM'S *Port DOC, Douro, Portugal* Part of the Symington empire, making rich, florally scented Vintage Port★★★, sweeter than DOW'S and WARRE'S, but with the backbone to age. In non-declared years makes a fine vintage wine called Malvedos★★. Six Grapes★ is one of the best premium rubies, and Crusted★★ and 10-year-old★ and 20-year-old★★ tawnies are consistently good. Best years: (Vintage) **2007 03 00 97 94 91 85 83 80 77 75 70 66 63 60**; (Malvedos) 2009 **05 01 99 98 95 92 90**.

ALAIN GRAILLOT *Crozes-Hermitage AC, Rhône Valley, France* Excellent family estate producing concentrated, rich, fruity Syrah reds. The top wine is the classy, long-lived CROZES-HERMITAGE la Guiraude★★; the regular Crozes-Hermitage★★ is wonderful too, and great for early drinking, as are the ST-JOSEPH★★ and a fragrant white Crozes-Hermitage★. Keep top reds for at least 5 years. Son Max has promising Dom. des Lises estate and Equis brand (also CORNAS, ST-JOSEPH). Best years: (la Guiraude) (2011) **10 09 07 06 05 04 03 01 00 99 95**.

GRAMERCY CELLARS *Walla Walla Valley AVA, Washington State, USA* Gramercy produces a fine Syrah Lagniappe★★ with mineral notes, and a version from Walla Walla Valley★★. Their Cabernet Sauvignon★★ ranks among the top in the state. Also Tempranillo Inigo Montoya★ and Syrah-Grenache L'Idiot du Village★★. Best years: (2010) 09 **08 07**.

GRAMPIANS AND PYRENEES *Victoria, Australia* Two adjacent cool-climate regions in central western VICTORIA, producing some of Australia's most characterful Shiraz, distinguished Riesling, subtle Pinot Gris and savoury Chardonnay. Best producers: BEST'S★★, Blue Pyrenees, Dalwhinnie★★, MOUNT LANGI GHIRAN★★, Redbank★, SEPPELT★★, The Story★★, Summerfield★, Taltarni★. Best years: (Shiraz) (2010) 09 07 **06 05 04 03 02 01 99 98 97 96 94 91 90**.

CH. GRAND-PUY-DUCASSE★ *Pauillac AC, 5ème Cru Classé, Haut-Médoc, Bordeaux, France* Form dipped in the early 90s but recovered again after 95. Greater regularity since 2005. Approachable after 5 years, but the best vintages can improve for considerably longer. Second wine: Artigues-Arnaud. Best years: 2010 09 08 **07** 06 05 04 03 02 00 96 95 90.

CH. GRAND-PUY-LACOSTE★★ *Pauillac AC, 5ème Cru Classé, Haut-Médoc, Bordeaux, France* Classic PAUILLAC, with lots of blackcurrant and cigar-box perfume. It begins fairly dense, but as the wine develops, the flavours mingle with the sweetness of new oak to become one of Pauillac's most memorable taste sensations. Second wine: Lacoste-Borie. Best years: 2010 09 08 07 06 05 04 **03** 02 01 00 **99** 98 96 95 94 90 89 88.

GRANDS-ÉCHÉZEAUX AC See ÉCHÉZEAUX AC.

GRANGE★★★ *Barossa Valley, South Australia* In 1950, Max Schubert, chief winemaker at PENFOLDS, visited Europe and came back determined to make a wine that could match the great BORDEAUX reds. Undeterred by a lack of Cabernet Sauvignon grapes and French oak barrels, he set to work with BAROSSA Shiraz and barrels made from the more pungent American oak. Initially ignored and misunderstood, Schubert eventually achieved global recognition for his wine, a stupendously complex, thrillingly rich red that only begins to reveal its magnificence after 10 years in bottle – but is even better after 20. Best years: (2010) (08) 06 05 04 02 **01** 99 98 96 94 92 91 90 88 86 84 83 80 76 71 66 62 53.

DOM. DE LA GRANGE DES PÈRES *IGP de l'Hérault, Languedoc, France* Meticulously crafted unfiltered red★★, a blend of Syrah, Mourvèdre and Cabernet Sauvignon; only 500 cases are produced each year. The white★★, based on Roussanne, with Marsanne and Chardonnay, is made in even smaller quantities. Best years: (red) 2010 09 **08 07** 06 05 04.

GRANGEHURST *Stellenbosch WO, South Africa* Boutique winery known for modern Pinotage★, Cabernet-Merlot★★ with Bordeaux-ish appeal, and Nikela★, a polished blend of all three varieties with Shiraz. Also two Cabernets (Reserve★) and Shiraz-Cabernet Reserve★. All mature well for several years and are deliberately held back with later-than-normal release times. Best years: **2007** 06 05 04 03 01 00.

GRANS-FASSIAN *Leiwen, Mosel, Germany* LEIWEN owed its reputation initially to Gerhard Grans. Both sweet and dry Rieslings have gained in sophistication over the years: Spätlese★★ and Auslese★★ from

TRITTENHEIMER Apotheke are particularly impressive. Eiswein is ★★★ in good vintages. Best years: (2011) 10 09 **08 07 06 05 04 02**.

ALFRED GRATIEN *Champagne AC, Champagne, France* This small company makes some of my favourite CHAMPAGNE. Its wines are made in wooden casks, which is very rare nowadays. The non-vintage★★ blend is usually 4 years old when sold, rather than the normal 3 years, and can age further. The vintage★★★ is deliciously ripe and toasty when released, but can age for another 10 years. New 2007 vintage Blanc de Blancs★. The prestige cuvée, Cuvée Paradis★★, is non-vintage. Best years: 2000 99 **98 97 96 95 91 90 89 88 85 83**.

GRAVES AC *Bordeaux, France* The Graves region covers the area south of the city of Bordeaux to Langon, but the villages in the northern half broke away in 1987 to form the PESSAC-LEOGNAN AC. In the southern Graves, a new wave of winemaking has produced plenty of clean, bone-dry white wines with lots of snappy freshness, as well as more complex soft, nutty, barrel-aged whites, and some juicy, quick-drinking reds. Sweet white wines take the Graves Supérieures AC; the best make a decent substitute for the more expensive SAUTERNES. Best producers: Archambeau★, Ardennes★, Brondelle★, Chantegrive★, Clos Floridène★★, Crabitey★, Ferrande, Fougères★, Haura★, l'Hospital, Léhoul★, Magence, Magneau★, Rahoul★, Respide (Callipyge★), Respide-Médeville★, St-Robert (cuvée Poncet Deville★), Seuil, Toumilon, Venus, Vieux-Ch.-Gaubert★, Villa Bel-Air★; (sweet) Brondelle, Léhoul. Best years: (reds) 2010 **09 08 05 04 01 00 98 96 95**; (dry whites) (2011) **10 09 08 07 06 05 04 02 01 00**.

GRAVNER *Friuli-Venezia Giulia, Italy* Josko Gravner is seen as a revolutionary or a fanatic – his wines brilliant or undrinkable. In recent years he has taken to fermenting his white wines in open-top amphorae dug into the winery floor, leaving them exposed to oxygen to ferment, macerate and clarify, with no intervention for months. Gravner is phasing out all white grapes except Ribolla Gialla. On the red side he limits himself to the indigenous Pignolo, which is not released for 10 years post-production.

GREAT SOUTHERN *Western Australia* A vast, cool-climate region encompassing the sub-regions of Frankland River, Denmark, Mount Barker, Albany and Porongurup. Frankland River is particularly successful with Riesling, Shiraz and Cabernet; Denmark with Chardonnay and Pinot Noir; Mount Barker with Riesling and Shiraz; Albany with Pinot Noir; Porongurup with Riesling and Pinot Noir. Plantings have boomed in recent years, especially in Frankland River. Best producers: Alkoomi, Castelli, Castle Rock★★, CHERUBINO★★, FERNGROVE★, Forest Hill★★, Frankland Estate★, Gilberts★, HAREWOOD★★, HOUGHTON★★, HOWARD PARK★★, Lake House, Marchand & Burch★★, Matilda's Estate, PLANTAGENET★★, Three Drops★, West Cape Howe★, Wignalls, Willoughby Park.

GRECHETTO Italian grape centred on UMBRIA; the main component of ORVIETO DOC, also making tasty, anise-tinged dry white varietals. Occasionally used in VIN SANTO in TUSCANY. Best producers: Antonelli, Barberani★, Caprai★, FALESCO★, Palazzone, Castello della Sala.

PATRICIA GREEN CELLARS *Willamette Valley AVA, Oregon, USA* Patty Green and Jim Anderson aim to produce wines that reflect the specific *terroirs* of the Willamette Valley: there are many different bottlings of Pinot Noir from vineyards in Ribbon Ridge, the Dundee Hills, the Chehalem

Mountains and the Eola Hills. Highlights include Croft Vineyard★★, Eason Vineyard★, Balcombe Vineyard★, Notorious★★ and Pinot Noir Reserve★. Fine Sauvignon Blanc★ and a CHABLIS-like Chardonnay are worth seeking out. Best years: (Pinot Noir) (2010) 09 **08** 07 06.

GRENACHE BLANC An underrated white grape in the south of France, with a rapidly growing band of admirers. It can make light anise and pear-scented young whites, or heroically dense, oily mouth-fillers. Low-yield examples take surprisingly well to oak. Generally best within a year of the vintage, although the odd old-vine example can age impressively (Château RAYAS is half Grenache Blanc). Grown as Garnacha Blanca in Spain, where it's now producing some stunning examples in PRIORAT, Terra Alta and RIOJA. A few old vines are contributing to some characterful blends and varietal wines in South Africa and California.

GRENACHE NOIR Among the world's most widely planted red grapes – the bulk of it in Spain, where it is called Garnacha Tinta. It is a hot-climate grape and in France it reaches its peak in the southern RHÔNE, especially in CHÂTEAUNEUF-DU-PAPE, where it combines great alcoholic strength with rich yet refined raspberry fruit and a perfume hot from the herb-strewn hills. It is generally given more tannin, acid and structure by blending with Syrah, Mourvèdre, Cinsaut or other southern French grapes. With Cinsaut, it can make wonderful rosé in TAVEL, LIRAC and CÔTES DE PROVENCE, as well as in NAVARRA in Spain. It makes lovely juicy reds and pinks in Aragón's CALATAYUD, CAMPO DE BORJA and CARINENA, and forms the backbone of the impressive reds of PRIORAT; in RIOJA it adds weight to the Tempranillo. It is also the basis for the *vins doux naturels* of RASTEAU in the southern Rhône and BANYULS and MAURY in the ROUSSILLON. In SARDINIA, as Cannonau, it produces deep, tannic reds and lighter, modern wines, although traditional sweet and fortified styles can still be found. Produced in VENETO's Colli Berici DOC as Tai (was Tocai) Rosso. Also grown in CALIFORNIA and SOUTH AUSTRALIA, where it is finally being accorded respect as imaginative winemakers realize there is a great resource of century-old vines capable of making wild and massively enjoyable reds, either alone or with Syrah and/or Mourvèdre. More is being planted in South Africa, where it is a popular component in Rhône-style wines.

GRÈS DE MONTPELLIER *Grand Vin du Languedoc, AC Languedoc, France* Sprawling area in the hinterland of Montpellier with sub-zones St Georges d'Orques, Méjanelle, St Christol, St Drézery. Some good reds from Grenache and Syrah. Whites are COTEAUX DU LANGUEDOC. Best producers: Clavel, Prose★★, St Martin de la Garrigue★. Best years: (2011) 10 **09** 08 07 06 05.

GRGICH HILLS ESTATE *Rutherford AVA, California, USA* Mike Grgich makes classic NAPA VALLEY and CARNEROS Chardonnay★★, which can age for at least a decade, as well as tasty Fumé Blanc★, ripe, rich Cabernet★, plummy Merlot★ and a huge, old-style Zinfandel★. Best years: (Chardonnay) 2009 08 07 06 05 04 03.

GRIGNAN-LES-ADHÉMAR AC *Rhône Valley, France* Change of name from Coteaux du Tricastin after recent clumsy publicity about the local nuclear plant hit this mid-Rhône region. Direct, sometimes full, spice-pepper reds and rosés with juicy fruit. Nutty dry white. Drink young, unless from old vines. Best producers: Décelle, Grangeneuve★, Lônes, Montine, St-Luc★, la Tour d'Elyssas, Vieux Micocoulier. Best years: 2010 09 07.

GRIOTTE-CHAMBERTIN AC See CHAMBERTIN AC.

JEAN GRIVOT *Vosne-Romanée, Côte de Nuits, Burgundy, France* Étienne Grivot settled into a successful stride from 1995 and has raised his game from 2004 with increasingly ripe yet always fine and complex wines from a host of VOSNE-ROMANÉE Premiers Crus (Beaux Monts★★★) as well as fine CLOS DE VOUGEOT★★★ and RICHEBOURG★★★. Best years: (2011) 10 09 08 **07 06 05 04 03 02 01 99 98 96 95.**

GROS *Côte de Nuits, Burgundy, France* Brilliant CÔTE DE NUITS wines from various members of the family, especially Anne Gros, Michel Gros, Gros Frère et Soeur and Anne-Françoise Gros. Look out for CLOS DE VOUGEOT★★★, ÉCHÉZEAUX★★★ and RICHEBOURG★★★ as well as good-value HAUTES-CÔTES DE NUITS★. Best years: (2011) 10 09 08 **07 06 05 03 02 99 96.**

GROS MANSENG see PETIT MANSENG.

GROSSET *Clare Valley, South Australia* Jeffrey Grosset is a perfectionist, crafting tiny quantities of hand-made wines. A Riesling specialist, he sources single-vineyard Watervale★★★ and Polish Hill★★★ from his own properties; both are supremely good and age well. New is a thrilling Off-dry Riesling★ from an estate vineyard at Watervale's highest elevation. Cabernet blend Gaia★★ is smooth and seamless. Also outstanding ADELAIDE HILLS wines: Piccadilly Chardonnay★★★, very fine Pinot Noir★★ and one of Australia's finest, tautest Semillon-Sauvignon★★. Best years: (Riesling) 2011 10 09 **06 05 04 03 02 01 00 99.**

CH. GRUAUD-LAROSE★★ *St-Julien AC, 2ème Cru Classé, Haut-Médoc, Bordeaux, France* One of the largest ST-JULIEN estates. Until the 1970s the wines were classic, cedary St-Juliens; since the early 80s, they have been darker, richer and coated with new oak, yet inclined to exhibit an unnerving feral quality. Recent vintages have mostly combined considerable power with finesse, despite disappointments in 2002 and 03. On great form since 2008 and still relatively good value. Second wine: Sarget de Gruaud-Larose. Best years: 2010 09 08 **07 06 05 04 01 00 99 98 96 95 90.**

GRÜNER VELTLINER Austrian grape, also grown in the Czech Republic, Slovakia, Hungary, Italy, New Zealand and California. It is at its best in Austria's KAMPTAL, KREMSTAL and the WACHAU and in ALTO ADIGE's Eisacktal, where the soil and cool climate bring out all the lentilly, white-peppery aromas. Styles vary from light and tart to savoury, mouthfilling yet appetizing wines equalling the best in Europe.

GUIGAL *Côte-Rôtie AC, Rhône Valley, France* Marcel Guigal is the most internationally famous name in the RHÔNE, producing wines from his own big spread of vineyards in CÔTE-RÔTIE under the Ch. d'Ampuis★★ label as well as Dom. de Bonserine★ (La Garde★★, La Viallière★), VIDAL-FLEURY and the Guigal range from domaine and purchased grapes. Côte-Rôtie Brune et Blonde is ★★. The big-flavoured La Mouline, La Turque and La Landonne all rate ★★★ in most critics' opinions – and sometimes in mine. CONDRIEU★★ (la Doriane★★★) is opulent and fragrant. Red and white HERMITAGE★★ and Ermitage Ex-Voto★★ are also good, and ST-JOSEPH★★ (red and white) is improving, as are the top-value red, white and rosé CÔTES DU RHÔNE★, chunky GIGONDAS★ and bright, full TAVEL rosé. Best years: (top reds) (2011) 10 09 07 **06 05 04 03 01 00 99 98 97 95 94 91 90 89 88 85 83 82 78.**

CH. GUIRAUD★★ *Sauternes AC, 1er Cru Classé, Bordeaux, France* High price
reflects the fact that only the best grapes are selected and fermentation
takes place in 100% new oak barrels. New ownership from 2006. Keep
best vintages for 10 years or more. Second wine: Petit Guiraud (from
2005). Also dry white G de Guiraud. Best years: 2010 09 **07 06 05 04 03
02 01** 99 98 97 96 95 90 89 88.

GUNDERLOCH *Nackenheim, Rheinhessen, Germany* Sensationally concentrated
and luscious Beerenauslese★★ and Trockenbeerenauslese★★★ dessert
Rieslings are expensive but worth it. However, dry and off-dry Rieslings,
at least ★, are good value. Late-harvest Spätlese and Auslese are ★★ year
in, year out. Best years: (2011) 10 09 **08 07** 06 05 04 03 02.

GUNDLACH BUNDSCHU *Sonoma Valley AVA, California, USA* Family-owned
winery, founded in 1858. From the Rhinefarm estate vineyards come
outstanding juicy, fruity Cabernet Sauvignon★★, rich yet tightly
structured Merlot★★, Zinfandel★ and Pinot Noir★. Whites include
Chardonnay★, attractive Riesling and dramatic dry Gewürztraminer★★.
The Bundschu family also operates the boutique winery Bartholomew
Park, which specializes in Cabernet blends.

GUSBOURNE *Kent, England* Newcomer to the UK wine scene, producing
very impressive wines: sparkling Blanc de Blancs★ and Brut Reserve★.

FRITZ HAAG *Brauneberg, Mosel, Germany* MOSEL grower with vineyards in the
BRAUNEBERGer Juffer and Juffer Sonnenuhr. Pure, elegant Rieslings at least
★★ quality, with Auslese and above often reaching ★★★. Best years:
(2011) 10 09 08 **07 06** 05 04 02 01 99.

REINHOLD HAART *Piesport,
Mosel, Germany* Theo Haart
produces sensational Rieslings
– with blackcurrant, peach and
citrus aromas – from the great
PIESPORTer Goldtröpfchen
vineyard. Ausleses are often
★★★. Wines from his vine-
yards in Wintrich can be
bargains. Best years: (2011) 10 09 08 **07 06** 05 04 02 01 99.

HAMILTON RUSSELL VINEYARDS *Hemel en Aarde Valley WO, South Africa*
A pioneer in the WALKER BAY region. Delicately scented Pinot Noir★★ has
an uninterrupted history since 1981, the taut, minerally Chardonnay★★
since 1983. Under the Ashbourne label, intriguing Pinotage★ and subtle
Sauvignon Blanc-based Sandstone★. Southern Right Sauvignon Blanc★
is zingy and easy-drinking. Best years: (Pinot Noir) (2011) **10 09 08 07 06
05 04 03**; (Chardonnay) 2011 **10 09 08 07 06 05 04 03 02 01.**

HANDLEY *Mendocino County, California, USA* Serious producer of sparkling
wines, including one of California's best Brut Rosés★. Aromatic
Gewürztraminer★★ and Riesling★★, and two bottlings of Chardonnay
(DRY CREEK VALLEY★ and ANDERSON VALLEY★), are worth seeking out. The
Anderson Valley estate Pinot Noirs (regular★, Reserve★★) are in a
lighter, more subtle style. Syrah★ is excellent.

HANGING ROCK *Macedon Ranges, Victoria, Australia* Highly individual, gutsy
sparkling wine Macedon Cuvée XII★★ (stunning late-disgorged
Cuvée★★) stands out at John and Ann (née TYRRELL) Ellis's ultra-cool-
climate vineyard high in the Macedon Ranges. Tangy estate-grown 'The
Jim Jim' Sauvignon Blanc★★ is mouthwatering stuff, while HEATHCOTE
Shiraz★ is the best red. Good-value new Odd One Out label.

HARAS DE PIRQUE *Maipo, Chile* Located in Pirque, a sub-region of MAIPO in the foothills of the Andes. Dense, spicy Elegance Cabernet Sauvignon★★ leads the portfolio; Cabernet-based Character★ is equally impressive, and more approachable. Savoury Cabernet-Carmenère blend Albis is a joint venture with Italy's ANTINORI.

HARDYS *McLaren Vale, South Australia* Owned by Accolade (formerly Constellation), the basic wines under the Hardy labels do no honour to the great family tradition. Varietals (especially Shiraz and Grenache) under the Nottage Hill label are more reliable. Top of the tree are the Eileen Hardy Shiraz★★ and Thomas Hardy Cabernet★★, both dense reds for hedonists. Eileen Hardy Chardonnay★★ is more elegant, tightly structured and focused than it used to be. Best years: (Eileen Hardy Shiraz) (2010) (08) **06 05 04 03 02 01 00 98 97 96 95 93**.

HAREWOOD ESTATE *Great Southern, Western Australia* One of Denmark's finest vineyards, owned by James Kellie (ex-HOWARD PARK). The portfolio shows evidence of Kellie's skill and knowledge of the GREAT SOUTHERN, especially with powerful Cabernet Sauvignon★, gutsy yet silky smooth Frankland River Shiraz★, intense, zesty Riesling★★, tangy Sauvignon-Semillon and elegant single-vineyard Denmark Chardonnay★★.

HARLAN ESTATE★★★ *Oakville AVA, California, USA* One of California's most sought-after reds, a full-bodied and robustly tannic BORDEAUX blend offering layers of ripe black fruits and heaps of new French oak. Dense but thrilling upon release, the wine is built to develop for 10 years. Bond★ is a cheaper label from locally grown fruit.

HARTENBERG ESTATE *Stellenbosch WO, South Africa* Shiraz is the prime performer at this Bottelary Hills winery. Regular Shiraz★ is fleshy and accessible, while The Stork★ and single-vineyard Gravel Hill★★ reflect the soils they grow in. Merlot and Cabernet also perform well, topped by The Mackenzie★★ (Cabernet-Merlot). Whites include two Chardonnays (standard★ and refined, complex The Eleanor★), off-dry Riesling and crunchy Sauvignon. Best years: (top reds) 2009 **08 07 06 05 04 03**.

HARTFORD FAMILY *Russian River Valley AVA, California, USA* Chardonnays and Pinot Noirs from RUSSIAN RIVER and SONOMA COAST bear the Hartford Court label: most have textbook cool-climate intensity and acidity. Pinot Noirs include Arrendell Vineyard★★, Land's Edge★★★, Fog Dance★★★, Far Coast★★, Seascape★★; Chardonnays include Four Hearts★, Stone Côte★, Seascape★★. Hartford label old-vine Zinfandels include Russian River Valley★, Fanucchi-Wood Road★★ and Highwire★★. Owned by Jackson Family Wines.

HARTWELL *Stags Leap District AVA, Napa Valley, California, USA* Wine collector Bob Hartwell has been producing a gloriously fruity and elegant Cabernet Sauvignon★★ from his small vineyard in the STAGS LEAP DISTRICT since 1993. Now joined by an equally supple Merlot★★ and lower-priced Misté Hill Cabernet Sauvignon★. Best years: (Cabernet Sauvignon) 2008 **07 06 05 03 02 01 00 99 98 97**.

HATTENHEIM *Rheingau, Germany* RHEINGAU village with 13 vineyard sites, including the celebrated Steinberg, a monopoly of Kloster Eberbach★. Best producers: Barth★, Lang, Langwerth von Simmern★, Ress, SCHLOSS REINHARTSHAUSEN★★, Schloss Schönborn★. Best years: (2011) 10 09 **08 07 06 05 04 02**.

CH. HAUT-BAGES-LIBÉRAL★ *Pauillac AC, 5ème Cru Classé, Haut-Médoc, Bordeaux, France* Little-known PAUILLAC property that has quietly been gathering plaudits for some years now: loads of unbridled delicious fruit, a positively hedonistic style – and its lack of renown keeps the price just about reasonable. The wines will age well, especially the latest vintages. Best years: 2010 09 08 **07** 06 **05 04 03 02 01 00 99 98 96 95** 90.

CH. HAUT-BAILLY★★ *Pessac-Léognan AC, Cru Classé de Graves, Bordeaux, France* Traditionally one of the softest and most charming of the PESSAC-LÉOGNAN Classed Growths, and on good form during the 1990s. New ownership from 1998 has gradually returned Haut-Bailly to a leading role, no longer always soft and silky, but increasingly full of personality and style. On a winning streak since 2005. Second wine: la Parde-de-Haut-Bailly. Best years: 2010 09 08 **07** 06 **05 04 02 01 00** 98 96 95 90 89 88 86.

CH. HAUT-BATAILLEY★ *Pauillac AC, 5ème Cru Classé, Haut-Médoc, Bordeaux, France* This estate has produced too many wines that are light, attractively spicy, but rarely memorable. Owner François-Xavier Borie of GRAND-PUY-LACOSTE is changing this and from 2005 the wines have shown much improvement, becoming distinctly more substantial. Best years: 2010 09 08 **07** 06 **05 04 03 02 01 00** 98 96 95.

CH. HAUT-BRION *Pessac-Léognan AC, 1er Cru Classé, Graves, Bordeaux, France* This property's excellent gravel-based vineyard is now part of Bordeaux's suburbs. The red wine★★★ is one of Bordeaux's most subtle, with a magical ability to age. There is a small amount of white★★★ which, at its best, is memorably rich yet marvellously dry, blossoming over 5–10 years. Second wine: (red) le Clarence de Haut-Brion (from 2007), previously Bahans Haut Brion. Best years: (red) 2010 09 00 07 06 05 **04 03 02 01 00** **99 98 97 96 95 90 89**; (white) 2010 **09 08 07 06 05 04 03 02 01 00**.

CH. HAUT-MARBUZET★★ *St-Estèphe AC, Haut-Médoc, France* Impressive ST-ESTÈPHE wine worthy of classification with great, rich, mouthfilling blasts of flavour and lots of new oak. Best years: 2010 09 08 06 **05 04 03 02 01 00 99 98 96 95 90** 89.

HAUT-MÉDOC AC *Bordeaux, France* The finest gravelly soil is here in the southern half of the MEDOC peninsula; this AC covers all the decent vineyard land not included in the 6 village ACs (MARGAUX, MOULIS, LISTRAC, ST-JULIEN, PAUILLAC and ST-ESTÈPHE). Wines vary in quality and style. Best producers: d'Agassac★, Belgrave★, Belle-Vue★, Bernadotte★, Cambon la Pelouse★, Camensac, CANTEMERLE★, Charmail★, Cissac★, Citran★, Coufran, la LAGUNE★, Lanessan★, Malescasse★, Maucamps★, Peyrabon★, Sénéjac★, SOCIANDO-MALLET★★, la Tour-Carnet★, Tour-du-Haut-Moulin★, Villegeorge. Best years: 2010 09 **08 06 05 04 03 02 01 00 96 95**.

HAUTES-CÔTES DE BEAUNE AC See BOURGOGNE-HAUTES-CÔTES DE BEAUNE AC.
HAUTES-CÔTES DE NUITS AC See BOURGOGNE-HAUTES-CÔTES DE NUITS AC.

HAWKES BAY *North Island, New Zealand* New Zealand's second largest and one of its most prestigious wine regions. Plenty of sunshine, moderately predictable weather during ripening and a complex array of soils make it ideal for a range of wine styles. Traditionally known for Cabernet Sauvignon and, particularly, Merlot, it has recently produced some superb Syrahs. Whites can be very good too, especially Chardonnay. Free-draining Gimblett Gravels is the outstanding area, followed by The Bridge Pa Triangle. Best producers: Alpha Domus★, Bilancia★, CHURCH ROAD★★, Clearview★, COOPERS CREEK★, CRAGGY RANGE★★, Elephant Hill★★, Esk Valley★★★, Matariki★, MATUA VALLEY★, Mission★, Moana Park★, MORTON ESTATE★, Newton Forrest★ (Cornerstone★★), NGATARAWA★, C J PASK★, Sacred Hill★★, Stonecroft★, Te Awa★, TE MATA★★, TRINITY HILL★★, Unison★, Vidal★★, VILLA MARIA★★. Best years: (top reds) 2010 **09 08 07** 06 04.

HdV *Carneros AVA, California, USA* A joint venture between Hyde Vineyards of Napa Valley and Aubert & Pamela de Villaine of Burgundy. Known for its minerally, Burgundian-style Chardonnay★★, the winery also makes small amounts of Cabernet Sauvignon, Syrah and BORDEAUX blend Belle Cousine. Best years: (Chardonnay) (2009) **08 07 06 05 04 03 02**.

HEATHCOTE *Central Victoria, Australia* This wine region's unique feature is the deep russet Cambrian soil, formed more than 600 million years ago, which is found on the best sites and is proving ideal for Shiraz. BROWN BROTHERS and TYRRELL'S have extensive recent plantings. Best producers: BROWN BROTHERS★★, Greenstone, Heathcote Estate★★★, Heathcote Winery★★, Jasper Hill★★★, Red Edge★, Sanguine★★, Shelmerdine, TYRRELL'S★ (Rufus Stone★★), Wild Duck Creek★. Best years: (Shiraz) 2010 09 08 **06 05 04 03 02 01 00 97 96 95 94 91 90**.

HEDGES FAMILY ESTATE *Columbia Valley AVA, Washington State, USA* Top wines are Cabernet-Merlot blends using fruit from prime Red Mountain AVA vineyards: Three Vineyards★ is powerful and ageworthy, with bold tannins but plenty of cassis fruit; Red Mountain Reserve★ shows more polish and elegance. Red CMS★ (Cabernet-Merlot-Syrah) and crisp white CMS (Chardonnay-Marsanne-Sauvignon) form the bulk of the production. Best years: (top reds) (2010) 09 **08** 07 06.

DR HEGER *Ihringen, Baden, Germany* Joachim Heger specializes in powerful, dry Weissburgunder (Pinot Blanc)★★ and Spätburgunder (Pinot Noir)★★, with Riesling a sideline in this warm climate. Winklerberg Grauburgunder★★ is also serious stuff, while his ancient Yellow Muscat vines deliver powerful dry wines★ and rare but fabulous TBAs★★. Best years: (white) (2011) 10 09 **08 07 05 04 02**.

CHARLES HEIDSIECK *Champagne AC, Champagne, France* Charles Heidsieck is the most consistently fine of all the major houses, with vintage★★★ Champagne declared only in the very best years. The non-vintage★★ is regularly of vintage quality; these age well for at least 5 years. Best years: **2000 96 95 90 89 88 85 82**.

HEITZ CELLAR *Napa Valley AVA, California, USA* Star attraction here is the Martha's Vineyard Cabernet Sauvignon★★. Many believe that early bottlings of Martha's Vineyard are among the best wines ever produced in CALIFORNIA. After 1992, phylloxera forced replanting; although bottling only resumed in 1996, the 1997 vintage was exceptional and set the tone for

the modern era. Heitz also produces Trailside Vineyard Cabernet★, Bella Oaks Vineyard Cabernet★ and a NAPA Cabernet★, as well as scented Sauvignon Blanc★. Dry Grignolino Rosé★ is a snappy picnic delight. Best years: (Martha's Vineyard) 2007 06 **05 04 03 02** 97 96 92 91 86.

HENRIOT *Champagne AC, Champagne, France* In 1994 Joseph Henriot bought back the name of his old-established family company. Henriot CHAMPAGNES have a limpid clarity, and no Pinot Meunier is used. The range includes non-vintage Brut Souverain★, Blanc de Blancs★ and Rosé Brut★; vintage Brut★★ and Rosé; and de luxe Cuvée des Enchanteleurs★★. Best years: 2003 02 **00 98 96 95 90 89 88 85**.

HENRIQUES & HENRIQUES *Madeira DOC, Madeira, Portugal* The wines to look for are the 10-year-old★★ and 15-year-old★★ versions of the classic varieties. Vibrant Sercial and Verdelho, and rich Malmsey and Bual are all fine examples of their styles. Henriques & Henriques also has vintage Madeiras★★★ of extraordinary quality.

HENRY OF PELHAM *Niagara Peninsula VQA, Ontario, Canada* A pioneer of *vinifera* wines in the Niagara Peninsula. Best are Riesling Icewine★, Speck Family Reserve Riesling★, Chardonnay★ and Cabernet-Merlot.

HENSCHKE *Eden Valley, South Australia* Fifth-generation winemaker Stephen Henschke and his viticulturist wife Prue make some of Australia's grandest reds from old vines: stunning HILL OF GRACE★★★, Mount Edelstone Shiraz★★★, Tappa Pass Shiraz★★, Cyril Henschke Cabernet★★, Johann's Garden Grenache★, and Shiraz blends Henry's Seven★ and Keyneton Estate★. Whites are led by perfumed Julius Riesling★★ and toasty yet fruity Louis Semillon★★. ADELAIDE HILLS plantings at Lenswood yield waxy, toasty Croft Chardonnay★, scented Giles Pinot Noir★★ and impressive Abbotts Prayer Merlot-Cabernet★★. Best years: (Mount Edelstone) (2010) (08) 07 06 05 **04 02 01 99 96 94 92 91 90 88 86**.

HÉRAULT, IGP DE L' *Languedoc, France* A huge region, covering the entire Hérault *département*. Red wines predominate, based on Carignan, Grenache and Cinsaut, and most of the wine is sold in bulk. But things are changing. There are lots of hilly vineyards with great potential, and MAS DE DAUMAS GASSAC followed by GRANGE DES PÈRES and Gérard Depardieu's Référence have made waves internationally. Whites are improving, too. The better-known OC is often used in preference to Hérault. Best producers: Capion★, GRANGE DES PÈRES★★, Marfée, Mas Conscience, MAS DE DAUMAS GASSAC★, Mas Gabriel, Poujol.

HERMITAGE AC *Rhône Valley, France* Great Hermitage, from a steep, largely granite vineyard above the town of Tain l'Hermitage in the northern RHÔNE, is revered throughout the world as a rare, rich red wine – expensive, memorable and classic. The best growers, with mature Syrah vines, can create superbly original wine, needing 5–10 years' aging even in a light year and a minimum of 15 years in a ripe, very sunny vintage. White Hermitage, from Marsanne plus Roussanne, is less famous, but the best – wonderfully rich wines, made by traditionalists – can outlive the reds, sometimes lasting as long as 40 years. Best producers: A Belle★, CHAPOUTIER★★, J-L CHAVE★★★, Y Chave★, Colombier★, COLOMBO★, DELAS★★, B Faurie★★, Fayolle Fils & Fille★, Ferraton★, GUIGAL★★, Paul JABOULET, Nicolas Perrin, Remizières★, J-M Sorrel★, M Sorrel★★★, TAIN co-op★, Tardieu-Laurent★★, les Vins de Vienne★. Best years: (reds) (2011) 10 09 07 **06** 05 **04** 03 01 00 99 98 97 96 95 94 91 90 89 88 85 83 78.

HESSISCHE BERGSTRASSE *Germany* A small (440ha/1086-acre), warm region near Darmstadt. Riesling occupies half the vineyards. Lovely Eiswein★★ is made by the Domäne Bergstrasse. Simon-Bürkle★ is reliable too.

HEYMANN-LÖWENSTEIN *Winningen, Mosel, Germany* A leading estate in WINNINGEN in the Lower MOSEL. Its dry Rieslings are unusually full-bodied for the region; those from the Röttgen and Uhlen sites often reach ★★. Also powerful Auslese★★. Best years: (2011) 10 09 **08 07 06 05 04**.

HIDALGO *Jerez y Manzanilla DO, Andalucía, Spain* Hidalgo's Manzanilla La Gitana★★ is deservedly one of the best-selling manzanillas in Spain. Hidalgo is family-owned, and only uses grapes from its own vineyards. Brands include Amontillado Napoleon★★, Jerez Cortado Wellington★★ and rich but dry Oloroso Viejo★★.

HILL OF GRACE★★★ *Eden Valley, South Australia* This stunning Shiraz with
dark, exotic flavours celebrated its 50th vintage in 2012. It is regarded by
many as sharing the pinnacle of Australian winemaking with Penfolds
GRANGE. It is made by HENSCHKE from a single vineyard which stands
opposite the Gnadenberg (or Hill of Grace) Lutheran Church. The
vineyard was first planted in the 1860s, and the old vines produce a
powerful, structured wine with superb ripe fruit, chocolate, coffee, earth,
leather and the rest. Can be cellared for 20 years or more. Best years:
(2010) (08) 07 06 05 04 02 01 **99 98 97 96 95 94 93 92 91 90 88 86.**

HILLTOP *Neszmély, Hungary* Winemaker Akos Kamocsay produces fresh,
bright wines, especially white. Indigenous varieties such as Irsai Olivér
and Cserszegi Füszeres line up with Gewürztraminer, Sauvignon
Blanc★, Pinot Gris and Chardonnay. Good but controversial TOKAJI.

HILLTOPS *New South Wales, Australia* High-altitude cherry-growing region
with a small but fast-growing area of vineyards around the town of Young.
Good potential for reds from Cabernet Sauvignon and Shiraz, plus bright,
tangy Riesling. Moppity's budget-priced Lock & Key range offers some
of the best value in the country. Best producers: Chalkers Crossing★★,
Freeman★, Grove Estate, MCWILLIAM'S/Barwang★, Moppity★, Woodonga Hill.

FRANZ HIRTZBERGER *Wachau, Niederösterreich, Austria* Highly consistent
quality for many years. The finest wines are the concentrated, elegant
Smaragd Rieslings from Singerriedel★★★ and Hochrain★★. The best
Grüner Veltliner comes from Honivogl★★★. Best years: (Riesling Smaragd)
(2011) 10 09 **08 07 06 05 04 03 02 01 99.**

HOCHHEIM *Rheingau, Germany* Village best known for having given the
English the word 'Hock' for Rhine wine, but it has good individual
vineyard sites, especially Domdechaney, Hölle (hell!) and Kirchenstück.
Best producers: Joachim Flick★, Franz KUNSTLER★★, Werner★. Best years:
(2011) 10 09 **08 07 06 05 04 03 02.**

HORTON VINEYARDS *Virginia, USA* Horton's Viognier★ established
VIRGINIA's potential as a wine region and ignited a rush of wineries
wanting to make the next CONDRIEU. Innovations include a sparkling
Viognier and varietals such as Tannat, Petit Manseng and Rkatsiteli.
The Cabernet Franc★ is among the best red wines of the eastern US.

DOM. DE L'HORTUS *Pic St-Loup AC, Languedoc, France* One of PIC ST-LOUP's
pioneering estates. Bergerie de l'Hortus★, a ready-to-drink unoaked
Syrah-Mourvèdre-Grenache blend, has delightful flavours of herbs,
plums and cherries. Big brother Grande Cuvée★★ needs time for the
fruit and oak to come into harmony. The white Grande Cuvée★ is a
Chardonnay-Viognier-Roussanne blend. Best years: (Grande Cuvée red)
(2011) 10 09 **08 07 06 05.**

HOSPICES DE BEAUNE *Côte de Beaune, Burgundy, France* Scene of
theatrical auction on the third Sunday in November each year, now
under the auspices of Christie's, the Hospices is an historic foundation
which sells the wine of the new vintage from its holdings in the CÔTE D'OR
to finance its charitable works. Pricing reflects charitable status rather
than common sense, but the auction trend is regarded as an indicator of
which way the market is heading. Much depends on the Hospices'
winemaking, which has been variable, as well as on the maturation and
bottling, which are in the hands of the purchaser of each lot.

CH. L'HOSPITALET *La Clape AC, Languedoc, France* Gérard Bertrand is now
a major vineyard owner in the Languedoc. Best wines are red and white
La CLAPE★ and red and white Pays d'OC, Cigalus★★. He also has

vineyards in MINERVOIS La Liviniere (Laville-Bertrou), CORBIÈRES Boutenac (Villemajou), TERRASSES DU LARZAC (la Sauvageonne) and LIMOUX. Best years: (2011) 10 **09 08 07 06 05**.

HOUGHTON *Swan District, Western Australia* WESTERN AUSTRALIA's biggest winery, owned by Accolade (formerly Constellation), sources fruit from throughout the estate. The budget-priced 'Stripe' range includes the flavoursome White Classic★. Moondah Brook Cabernet Sauvignon★ and Shiraz★ are a step up in quality. The regional Wisdom range has a GREAT SOUTHERN Riesling★★, Shiraz★★ from Frankland River, a MARGARET RIVER Cabernet★★, as well as sublime funky Chardonnay★★ and pure, taut Sauvignon Blanc★★ from PEMBERTON. Opulent, dense yet elegant Gladstones Cabernet★★ from Margaret River and powerful, lush Jack Mann Cabernet Sauvignon★★ from Frankland River.

HOWARD PARK *Margaret River, Western Australia* Howard Park has vineyards in MARGARET RIVER and GREAT SOUTHERN. Top-quality Abercrombie Cabernet Sauvignon (sometimes ★★★), plus zesty, floral Riesling★★ and classy Chardonnay★★. Good Scotsdale Shiraz★ and Leston Cabernet★. Affordable MadFish label is good for Riesling★, Shiraz, Sauvignon-Semillon★ and unwooded Chardonnay★. Marchand & Burch label has exquisite Chardonnay★★, Pinot Noir★★ (rare Gibraltar Rock★★★) and Shiraz★, as well as tiny quantities of Burgundy (yes, French Burgundy). Best years: (Cabernet) (2011) 10 09 08 07 **05 04 03 02** 01 99 96 94 92 91 90 88 86; (Riesling) 2011 10 09 **08 06 05 04 03 02 01 97 95 92 91 89**.

HOWELL MOUNTAIN AVA *Napa Valley, California, USA* NAPA's north-eastern corner is noted for powerhouse Cabernet Sauvignon and Zinfandel, as well as exotic, full-flavoured Merlot. Best producers: BERINGER (Merlot★★), Cade★, Cakebread★, DUNN★★, La Jota★★, Ladera★★, Liparita★, O'Shaughnessy★, PINE RIDGE (Cabernet Sauvignon★), VIADER★★, White Cottage★★. Best years: (reds) 2009 08 07 **06 05 03 02 01 00 99 98 97 96 95 94 91 90**.

HUBER *Malterdingen, Baden, Germany* For two decades Bernhard Huber has been crafting full-bodied Chardonnay★★ and increasingly sophisticated Pinot Noir★★. Over-oaked in the past, now more fleshy and balanced. Charming Muskateller★ too. Best years: (red) (2010) 09 00 **07 06 05 04**.

HUET *Vouvray AC, Loire Valley, France* Complex, traditional VOUVRAY that can age for decades. Biodynamic methods are bringing into even sharper focus the individual traits of its 3 excellent sites – le Haut-Lieu, Clos du Bourg and le Mont. These yield dry★★, medium-dry★★★ or sweet★★★ and Pétillant★★ or Mousseux★★ sparkling wines, depending on the vintage. Cuvée Constance *liquoreux*, made in exceptional years, is a blend of parcels. Best years: (sec, demi-sec) (2011) **10 07 06**; (moelleux) (2011) 10 09 05 04 **03 02 01 00 99 98 97 96 95 90 89**.

HUGEL *Alsace AC, Alsace, France* Basic Gentil cuvée is gluggable but fairly featureless, but Jubilee Riesling is a reliable ★★. Best sweet wines are Vendange Tardive★★ and Sélection de Grains Nobles★★★. Despite owning some Grand Cru land, Hugel continues to ignore the system for labelling purposes. Patriarch Jean Hugel died in 2009, but quality has, if anything, improved under the leadership of his nephew Etienne. Best years: (Jubilee dry Riesling) (2011) (10) 09 08 **07 05 03 01 00**.

HUNTER VALLEY *New South Wales, Australia* NEW SOUTH WALES' oldest wine zone overcomes a tricky climate to make fascinating, ageworthy Semillon and rich, buttery Chardonnay. Shiraz is the mainstay for reds, aging well but nowadays fresh and drinkable young; Cabernet is occasionally successful. Premium region is the Lower Hunter Valley; the Upper Hunter has few wineries but extensive vineyards in between the coal mines. Best producers: Allandale★, Audrey Wilkinson, BROKENWOOD★★★, Capercaillie, De Iuliis★, Hope★, Lake's Folly★, Margan Family, Mount Pleasant★★/MCWILLIAM'S, MEEREA PARK★, Oakvale, Scarborough, THOMAS★★, TOWER★, Tulloch, Keith Tulloch★, TYRRELL'S★★★. Best years: (Shiraz) 2011 10 09 07 **06 04 03 02 00 99 98 97 96 94 91**.

HUNTER'S *Marlborough, South Island, New Zealand* One of MARLBOROUGH's stars, with fine, if austere, Sauvignon★, savoury Burgundian Chardonnay★, vibrant long-lived Riesling★ and sophisticated Pinot Noir★. Attractive Miru Miru fizz★. Best years: (Chardonnay) (2011) **10 09 07 06 05**.

CH. DU HUREAU *Saumur-Champigny AC, Loire Valley, France* Philippe Vatan barely uses oak; his SAUMUR-CHAMPIGNY are particularly lifted and silky. The basic red, Tuffe★ is deliciously bright and fruity; Fours à Chaux★ from an early-ripening site shows elegant structure, while special cuvées Lisagathe★★ and Fevettes★★ need a bit of time. Jasmine-scented white SAUMUR★ is exceptional in top years. Decent fizz and occasional sweet Coteaux de Saumur. Best years: (top reds) (2011) 10 **09 08 06 05 04 03 02**.

INNISKILLIN *Niagara Peninsula VQA, Ontario, Canada* One of Canada's leading wineries, with good Pinot Noir★ and Cabernet Franc, well-rounded Chardonnay★ and rich Vidal Icewine★★, Cabernet Franc Icewine★, Riesling Icewine★ and Sparkling Vidal Icewine★. Another Inniskillin winery is in the OKANAGAN VALLEY in British Columbia. Best years: (Vidal Icewine) **2009 08 07 05 04 03 02 00 99**.

IPHOFEN *Franken, Germany* Important wine town in FRANKEN for dry Riesling and Silvaner. Both are powerful, with a pronounced earthiness. Best producers: JULIUSSPITAL★, Johann Ruck★, Hans Wirsching★. Best years: (2011) 10 09 **08 07 06 05 04 03 02 01**.

IRANCY AC *Burgundy, France* This northern outpost of vineyards, just south-west of CHABLIS, is an unlikely champion of the clear, pure flavours of the Pinot Noir grape. But red Irancy can be delicate, lightly touched by the ripeness of plums and strawberries, and can age well. Best producers: Colinot, DAUVISSAT, Goisot, Richoux. Best years: (2011) 10 **09 07 06 05 03**.

IRON HORSE VINEYARDS *Sonoma County, California, USA* A pioneer of the Green Valley AVA, part of the RUSSIAN RIVER VALLEY. Outstanding sparkling wines with vintage Brut★★ and Blanc de Blancs★★ delicious on release but highly suitable for aging. The Brut LD★★★ (Late Disgorged) is a heavenly mouthful – yeasty and complex. Wedding Cuvée★ Blanc de Noirs and Brut Rosé★ have been joined by Ultra Brut★ and Joy!★★, which is aged for 10–15 years before release. Still wines include a lovely Pinot Noir★★, stunningly fresh, crisp Rued Clone Chardonnay★★ and a seductive Viognier★★.

IROULÉGUY AOP *South-West France* The only French Basque wines. Tannat, usually blended with Cabernet Franc, gives fascinating, robust reds that are softer than MADIRAN. Whites are mainly from Petit Courbu. Best producers: Ameztia★, ARRETXEA★★, Brana★, Ilarria★, Irouléguy co-op (red Mignaberry★, dry white Xuri d'Ansa★), Mourguy. Best years: (reds) (2011) (10) 09 08 **06 05 04**.

ISOLE E OLENA *Chianti Classico DOCG, Tuscany, Italy* Paolo De Marchi has long been one of the pacesetters in CHIANTI CLASSICO. His Chianti Classico★★, characterized by clean, elegant and spicily perfumed fruit, excels in every vintage. The elegant Cepparello★★★, made from

100% Sangiovese, is the top wine. Excellent Syrah★★, Cabernet Sauvignon★★★, Chardonnay★★ and VIN SANTO★★★. Best years: (Cepparello) (2011) (10) 09 08 **07 06 04 03 01 99 98 97 95 90 88**.

CH. D'ISSAN★★ *Margaux AC, 3ème Cru Classé, Haut-Médoc, Bordeaux, France*
This lovely moated property pulled its socks up in the 1990s. When successful (there's been a rising crescendo through the 2000s), the wine can be one of the most delicate and scented in the MARGAUX AC. Best years: 2010 09 08 **07** 06 **05** 04 03 02 01 00 99 98 96 95 90 89.

J VINEYARDS *Sonoma County, California, USA* Established as a sparkling wine house by Judy Jordan. The J★ fizz is an attractive mouthful; J also makes a series of top-notch RUSSIAN RIVER Pinot Noirs★★ including excellent vineyard designates, as well as a small amount of tasty Pinotage★.

PAUL JABOULET AÎNÉ *Rhône Valley, France* During the 1970s, Jaboulet led the way in raising the world's awareness of the great quality of RHÔNE wines. Although some of the wines are still good, they have risen in price and are no longer the star in any appellation. Best wines are top red HERMITAGE La Chapelle (this was a ★★★ wine in its heyday) and whites La Chapelle★ and Chevalier de Stérimberg★. Also CROZES-HERMITAGE Dom. de Thalabert, Dom. de Roure★ and Mule Blanche★ (white), attractive CORNAS Dom. de St-Pierre★, ST-JOSEPH Le Grand Pompée★, reliable CÔTES DU RHÔNE Parallèle 45, good-value VENTOUX★ and sweet, perfumed MUSCAT DE BEAUMES-DE-VENISE★★. In 2006, Jaboulet was bought by Swiss financier Jean-Jacques Frey, owner of Ch. la LAGUNE. Best years: (La Chapelle) 2010 09 **07 05 01 99 98 97 96 95 94 91 90 89 88 78**.

JACKSON ESTATE *Marlborough, South Island, New Zealand* Sauvignon Blanc is showing a little more traditional zip after a couple of sweaty vintages; barrel-fermented Grey Ghost Sauvignon Blanc★★ can improve with a little age. Restrained Chardonnay and powerful Vintage Widow Pinot Noir★. Best years: (Pinot Noir) 2010 **08 06 05 04**.

JACKSON-TRIGGS *Okanagan Valley VQA, British Columbia, Canada* Top-flight reds include Gold Series Merlot★ and single-vineyard Gold Series Sun Rock Shiraz★. Also good Riesling Icewine★ and Entourage★ fizz. There's another Jackson-Triggs estate in NIAGARA PENINSULA. Osoyoos Larose★★ is an excellent BORDEAUX blend made for a joint-venture partnership between Canadian giant Vincor and French Groupe Taillan.

JACOB'S CREEK *Barossa Valley, South Australia*
Australia's leading export brand, with more consistent quality than its rivals, especially its Riesling★, Grenache-Shiraz★ and Blanc de Blancs fizz★. Jacob's Creek Reserve and Limited Release wines can be ★★. Top-end wines include Steingarten Riesling★★★, St Hugo Cabernet Sauvignon★★ from
COONAWARRA, Centenary Hill Shiraz★★ from the BAROSSA, plus well-established Orlando Jacaranda Ridge Cabernet Sauvignon★ from Coonawarra and Orlando Lawson's Shiraz★ from PADTHAWAY. New super-premiums Johann Shiraz-Cabernet★★ and Reeves Point Chardonnay★★ are well worth a look. Best years: (St Hugo) (2010) 09 08 **05 04 03 02 01 00 99 98 96 94 91 90 88 86**.

JACQUESSON *Champagne AC, Champagne, France* The non-vintage is an austerely-styled one-off that changes each year to produce the best possible blend. Cuvée No. 735★★ (the eighth version made), based on the 2007 harvest, was released in October 2011. Superb single-vineyard, single-cru and single grape variety Champagnes from Avize Champ Caïn (Chardonnay)★★, Ay Vauzelle Terme (Pinot Noir)★★ and Dizy Corne Bautray (Chardonnay)★★, and a saignée pink fizz, Dizy Terres Rouges Rosé★★. Best years: 2002 **00 97 96 95 93 90 89 88 85**.

LOUIS JADOT *Beaune, Côte de Beaune, Burgundy, France* Ambitious merchant which has been expanding southward, especially in MOULIN-À-VENT (Ch. des Jacques★) and POUILLY-FUISSÉ (Clos des Prouges, Ferret★★). Top domaine whites from the CÔTE D'OR include PULIGNY-MONTRACHET Folatières★★ and CHEVALIER-MONTRACHET les Demoiselles★★★, while the reds range from attractive BEAUNE Premiers Crus★★ through to sumptuous Bonnes Mares★★★ and MUSIGNY★★★. Best years: (top reds) (2011) 10 09 08 **07 06** 05 03 99 90; (whites) (2011) 10 09 **08 07 06** 05 04.

JAMET★★★ *Côte-Rôtie AC, Rhône Valley, France* A domaine in top form; Jean-Paul and Jean-Luc Jamet are two of the most talented growers of CÔTE-RÔTIE, with excellent vineyards on vertiginous slopes above the Rhône. The full-bodied, intricate wines, led by the marvellous Côte Brune★★★, age beautifully for well over a decade. Superb CÔTES DU RHÔNE★★ and COLLINES RHODANIENNES Syrah★★. Best years: (2011) 10 09 **08 07 06** 05 04 03 01 99 98 97 96 95 91 90 89 88.

JANUIK *Columbia Valley AVA, Washington State, USA* Experience as head winemaker at CHATEAU STE MICHELLE allows Mike Januik to source fruit from exceptional sites. His Cold Creek Chardonnay★★ is among the top in the state. Lewis Vineyard Syrah★★ is rich, earthy and bold, and Cabernet Sauvignons (Champoux Vineyard★★, Ciel du Cheval★★) are chocolaty, complex and ageworthy. Best years: (reds) (2010) 09 **08 07 06**.

JARDIN See JORDAN, South Africa.

JARDINS DE BABYLONE *Jurançon AOP, South-West France* Louis-Benjamin DAGUENEAU makes exquisitely elegant, understated wines from this micro-vineyard: sweet★★★ from Gros Manseng and dry★★ blend that includes rare Camaralet and Lauzet grapes. Best years: (sweet) (2010) 09 **08 07 04**.

JASNIÈRES AC *Loire Valley, France* Tiny AC north of Tours. Reputation for long-lived, bone-dry whites from Chenin Blanc, though new movers and shakers here and in neighbouring appellation Coteaux du Loir (which additionally makes delicate Pineau d'Aunis and Gamay reds) are picking Chenin riper. Sweet wine may be made in good years. Best producers: Bellivière★★, le Briseau★, J Gigou★★, Les Maisons Rouges★, J P Robinot★. Best years: (2011) 10 09 **08 07 05** 04 03 02 01.

JEREZ Y MANZANILLA DO/SHERRY See pages 186–7.

JERMANN *Friuli-Venezia Giulia, Italy* Silvio Jermann produces a range of non-DOC whites and reds, including Chardonnay★, Sauvignon Blanc★, Pinot Bianco★ and Pinot Grigio★. Vinnae★ is based on Ribolla and long-lived Vintage Tunina★★ uses Sauvignon, Chardonnay, Ribolla, Malvasia and Picolit. Capo Martino★ is also a blend of local varieties.

JOHANNISBERG *Rheingau, Germany* Probably the best known of all the Rhine wine villages, with 10 vineyard sites, including the famous Schloss Johannisberg. Best producers: Prinz von Hessen★, Johannishof★★, SCHLOSS JOHANNISBERG★★, Trenz. Best years: (2011) 10 09 **08 07 06** 05 04 03.

JORDAN *Alexander Valley AVA, Sonoma County, California, USA* Ripe, fruity Cabernet Sauvignon★ with a cedar character rare in California. The winery has recently moved toward greater use of mountain-grown Cabernet. Chardonnay★ from RUSSIAN RIVER VALLEY fruit is nicely balanced. Best years: (Cabernet) (2008) 07 **06** 02 01 **97** 95 94.

JORDAN *Stellenbosch WO, South Africa* Meticulous attention to detail in both the multi-aspected hillside vineyards and the cellar ensure consistent quality. Chardonnays (creamy/limy regular★★; dense, nutty, balanced Nine Yards★★) and delicious peppery Chenin★★ head a strong white range. Syrah★★, Cabernet Sauvignon★, Merlot★ and BORDEAUX-blend Cobblers Hill★★ are beautifully balanced for aging. Sophia★★, a barrel selection of Cobblers Hill, is sold only at auction. Sold under the Jardin label in the USA. Best years: (Chardonnay) 2011 **10 09 08 07 06 05 04 03 02**; (Cobblers Hill) 2009 **08 07 06 05 04 03**.

TONI JOST *Bacharach, Mittelrhein, Germany* Peter Jost was the grower who put the MITTELRHEIN on the map. From the Bacharacher Hahn site come some delicious, racy Rieslings★; Auslese★★ adds creaminess without losing that pine-needle scent. Best years: (2011) 10 09 **08 07 06 05 04 01**.

JULIÉNAS AC *Beaujolais, Burgundy, France* Juliénas is attractive, 'serious' BEAUJOLAIS, which can be big and tannic enough to develop in bottle. Best producers: B Broyer★, Coquard★, D Desvignes★, DUBOEUF (Ch. des Capitans★), Ch. de Juliénas★, Matray (Vieilles Vignes★), Pelletier★, B Santé★, M Tête★. Best years: (2011) 10 09.

JULIUSSPITAL *Würzburg, Franken, Germany* A 16th-century charitable foundation, with 170ha (420 acres) of vineyards, known for its dry wines – especially from IPHOFEN and WÜRZBURG. Look out for the Würzburger Stein wines, especially the grapefruit Silvaners★★ and petrolly Rieslings★★. Best years: (2011) 10 09 **08 07 06 05 04**.

JUMILLA DO *Murcia and Castilla-La Mancha, Spain* Jumilla's reputation is for brutal alcoholic reds, but dense, serious yet balanced reds from Monastrell (Mourvèdre) show the region's potential. Very few whites. Best producers: Carchelo, Casa Castillo★★, Casa de la Ermita, Juan Gil★, Luzón★, El Nido★. Best years: 2010 09 **08 07 06 05 04 01**.

JURA See ARBOIS, CHÂTEAU-CHALON, CÔTES DU JURA, CRÉMANT DU JURA, l'ÉTOILE.

JURANÇON AOP, JURANÇON SEC AOP *South-West France* The sweet white wine made from late-harvested grapes can be heavenly, with floral, spicy, apricot-quince flavours. The lemony dry wine can be just as age-worthy. Best producers: Bellegarde★, Bordenave★, Castera★, CAUHAPÉ★★, Clos Guirouilh★, Clos Thou★, Guirardel, JARDINS DE BABYLONE★★★, LAPEYRE★★, Larrédya★, SOUCH★★, Uroulat★★. Best years: (sweet) (2011) (10) 09 07 05 04 01 00 97.

K VINTNERS *Walla Walla Valley AVA, Washington State, USA* K Vintners opened its doors in 2001 and made a splash with its bold black and white labels, each with a different font of 'K' designating a unique Syrah or Syrah blend. The focus is on fruit from two growing areas, the Wahluke Slope and Walla Walla Valley. The big chewy wines are hard to find as they sell out rapidly, but look out for The Creator★, a Cabernet-Syrah blend, and K Syrah Morrison Lane★. Best years: (reds) (2010) 09 **08 07 06**.

KAISERSTUHL *Baden, Germany* A 4000ha (10,000-acre) volcanic stump rising to 600m (2000ft) and overlooking the Rhine plain. Pinot varieties excel. Best producers: BERCHER★★, Gleichenstein★, Dr HEGER★★, Karl H Johner★, Franz Keller★★, Koch, Salwey★★, Schneider★★. Best years: (dry whites) (2011) 10 09 **08 07 06 06 04**.

KAMPTAL *Niederösterreich, Austria* 4000ha (10,000-acre) wine region centred on the town of Langenlois, making some impressive dry Riesling and Grüner Veltliner. Best producers: BRÜNDLMAYER★★★, Ehn★★, Eichinger★, Hiedler★, Hirsch★★, Jurtschitsch★, Fred Loimer★★, Schloss Gobelsburg★★, Topf. Best years: (2011) 10 09 **08 07 06 05 04**.

JEREZ Y MANZANILLA DO/SHERRY

Andalucía, Spain

The Spanish now own the name outright – at least in the EU, where the only wines that can be sold as sherry come from the triangle of vineyard land between the Andalusian towns of Jerez de la Frontera (inland), and Sanlúcar de Barrameda and Puerto de Santa María (by the sea). Australia, South Africa and California have traditionally made fortified sherry-style wines; South Africa has agreed to drop the label term 'sherry' and Australia is replacing the term 'sherry' with 'apera', but California has yet to reach agreement with the EU and producers may still use the term 'sherry' for wines sold locally.

The best sherries can be spectacular. Three main factors contribute to the high-quality potential of wines from this region: the chalky-spongy albariza soil where the best vines grow, the Palomino Fino grape – unexciting for table wines but potentially great once transformed by the sherry-making processes – and a natural yeast called *flor*. All sherry must be a minimum of 3 years old, but fine sherries age in barrel for much longer. Sherries must be blended through a solera system. About a third of the wine from the oldest barrels is bottled, and the barrels topped up with slightly younger wine from another set of barrels and so on, for a minimum of 3 sets of barrels. The idea is that the younger wine takes on the character of older wine, as well as keeping the blend refreshed.

MAIN SHERRY STYLES

Fino and manzanilla Fino sherries derive their extraordinary, tangy, pungent flavours from *flor*. Young, newly fermented wines destined for these styles of sherry are deliberately fortified very sparingly to just 15–15.5% alcohol before being put in barrels for their minimum of 3 years' maturation. The thin, soft, oatmeal-coloured mush of *flor* grows on the surface of the wines, protecting them from the air (and thereby keeping them pale) and giving them a characteristic sharp, pungent tang. The addition of younger wine each year feeds the *flor*, maintaining an even layer. Manzanillas are fino-style wines that have matured in the cooler seaside conditions of Sanlúcar de Barrameda, where the *flor* grows thickest and the fine, salty tang is most accentuated.

Amontillado True amontillados are fino sherries that have continued to age after the *flor* has died (after about 5 years) and so finish their aging period in contact with air. These should all be bone dry and taste of raisins and buttered brazils. Medium-sweet amontillados are concoctions in which the dry sherry is sweetened with mistela, a blend of grape juice and alcohol.

Oloroso This type of sherry is strongly fortified after fermentation to deter the growth of *flor*. Olorosos, therefore, mature in barrel in contact with the air, which gradually darkens them while they remain dry, but develop rich, intense, nutty and raisiny flavours.

Other styles Manzanilla pasada is aged manzanilla, with greater depth and nuttiness. Palo cortado is an unusual, deliciously nutty, dry style somewhere in between amontillado and oloroso. Sweet oloroso creams and pale creams are almost without exception enriched solely for the export market. Sweet, syrupy varietal wines are made from sun-dried Pedro Ximénez or Moscatel grapes.

See also individual producers.

BEST PRODUCERS AND WINES

Argüeso (Manzanilla San León, Manzanilla Fina Las Medallas).

BARBADILLO (Manzanilla Eva, Manzanilla En Rama, Manzanilla Solear, Amontillado Príncipe, Amontillado de Sanlúcar, Palo Cortado Obispo Gascón, Oloroso Seco Cuco).

Delgado Zuleta (Manzanilla Pasada La Goya).

El Maestro Sierra.

Equipo Navazos (La Bota de…)

Fernando de Castilla.

Garvey (Amontillado Tio Guillermo, Palo Cortado, Pedro Ximénez Gran Orden).

M Gil Luque.

GONZÁLEZ BYASS (Tio Pepe Fino, 'En Rama' Palmas range, Amontillado del Duque, Apóstoles Palo Cortado, Matusalem Oloroso, Vintage Oloroso, Noé Pedro Ximénez).

HIDALGO (Manzanilla La Gitana, Manzanilla Pasada Pastrana, Amontillado Napoleon, Jerez Cortado Wellington, Oloroso Viejo).

LUSTAU (Almacenista single-producer wines, Puerto Fino, Fino La Ina, East India Solera).

OSBORNE (Fino Quinta, Amontillado 51-1A, Amontillado Coquinero, Oloroso Bailén, Oloroso Sibarita, Oloroso Solera India, Pedro Ximénez).

Sánchez Romate (Pedro Ximénez Cardenal Cisneros).

Tradición.

VALDESPINO (Fino Inocente, Amontillado Coliseo, Amontillado Tio Diego, Palo Cortado Cardenal, Oloroso Don Gonzalo, Pedro Ximénez Niños).

Valdivia (Sacromonte).

Williams & Humbert (Alegría Manzanilla).

KANONKOP *Stellenbosch WO, South Africa* Pinotage and Kanonkop are synonymous: the black label Pinotage★★ is made in minuscule quantities from one of the oldest blocks still extant in South Africa, planted in 1953; standard Pinotage★★, now from younger vines, is equally stylish. Muscular, savoury BORDEAUX-blend Paul Sauer★★ really does mature for 10 years or more. A straight Cabernet Sauvignon★★ is very good too. Best years: (Paul Sauer) 2009 **08 07 06 05** 04 03 02 01 00 99 98 97.

KARTHÄUSERHOF *Trier, Mosel, Germany* Ruwer estate at the top of its game. Rieslings combine aromatic extravagance with racy brilliance. Most wines, including some dry styles, are now ★★, some Auslese and Eiswein ★★★. Best years: (2011) 10 09 08 **07 06 05 04 03 02** 01.

KATNOOK ESTATE *Coonawarra, South Australia* Chardonnay★★ is the best of the fairly expensive whites, though Riesling★ and Sauvignon★★ are very tasty. Well-structured Cabernet Sauvignon★ and treacly Shiraz★ lead the reds, with Odyssey Cabernet Sauvignon★★ and Prodigy Shiraz★★ mixing power with indulgence. Owned by FREIXENET. Best years: (Odyssey) (2011) (10) 09 08 06 05 04 03 02 01 00 99 98 97 96 94 92 91.

KÉKFRANKOS See BLAUFRÄNKISCH.

KELLER *Flörsheim-Dalsheim, Rheinhessen, Germany* Klaus Keller and son Klaus-Peter are the leading winemakers in the hill country of RHEINHESSEN, away from the Rhine riverbank. They produce a stunning range of varietal dry wines and naturally sweet Rieslings, as well as extra-special dry Grosses Gewächs Rieslings★★★ from three sites. Astonishing TBA★★★ from Riesling and Rieslaner. Best years: (2011) 10 09 **08 07 06 05 04 03** 02.

KENDALL-JACKSON *Sonoma County, California, USA* The late Jess Jackson founded KJ in 1982; it now produces about 4 million cases. KJ's volume leader, Vintner's Reserve Chardonnay (2 million cases) is made entirely from estate-grown fruit. Now joined by a fresh, neutral-oaked Chardonnay called Avant. Higher levels of quality are found in the Grand Reserve reds and whites, the vineyard-based Highland Estates★ series and the top-of-the-range red BORDEAUX blend Stature★★.

KENWOOD *Sonoma Valley AVA, California, USA* This winery – bought by BANFI in 2012 – has always represented very good quality at reasonable prices. The Sauvignon Blanc★ has floral and melon flavours with a slightly earthy finish. Long-lived Artist Series Cabernet Sauvignon★★ is the flagship, Jack London Zinfandel★★ is impressive, and RUSSIAN RIVER VALLEY Pinot Noir★ is fine value. Best years: (Zinfandel) 2009 **08 07 06 05** 04.

KIEDRICH *Rheingau, Germany* Top vineyard here is the Gräfenberg, for long-lived, mineral Rieslings. Sandgrub and Wasseros are other good sites. Best producer: WEIL★★. Best years: (2011) 10 09 **08 07 06 05 04** 02.

KING ESTATE *Oregon, USA* Over 400ha (1000 acres) are certified organic at the King Estate vineyard in Lorane, far south of the more popular WILLAMETTE VALLEY. The Pinot Gris★ is first-rate. The Pinot Noirs have taken time to perfect, but the Signature Collection Pinot Noir★ is a powerful currant- and cassis-flavoured wine, and the Domaine★ is a fine example of Oregon Pinot Noir. Best years: (reds) (2010) 09 **08 07** 06.

CH. KIRWAN★ *Margaux AC, 3ème Cru Classé, Haut-Médoc, Bordeaux, France* This MARGAUX estate has shown considerable improvement since the mid-1990s. Investment in the cellars, more attention to the vineyards and the advice of consultant Michel Rolland (until 2007) have produced wines of greater depth and power, but less perfume. Now working on bringing the elegance back. Second wine: Les Charmes de Kirwan. Best years: 2010 09 08 **07** 06 **05** 04 03 01 00 99 98 96 95.

KISTLER *Sonoma Valley AVA, California, USA* One of California's trail-blazing Chardonnay producers, with wines from individual vineyards: Kistler Vineyard, Durell Vineyard and Dutton Ranch can be ★★★; McCrea Vineyard and ultra-cool-climate Camp Meeting Ridge Vineyard★★. All possess great complexity with good aging potential. Also a number of single-vineyard Pinot Noirs (some ★★) that go from good to very good. Best years: (Kistler Vineyard Chardonnay) 2009 **08 07 06 05 04**.

KLEIN CONSTANTIA *Constantia WO, South Africa* All change at this showpiece estate in 2011: the Jooste family sold to a couple of investment bankers and winemaker Adam Mason moved to MULDERBOSCH. 'The heritage remains,' insist the new owners. That includes crisp Sauvignon Blanc★ (occasional vibrant Perdeblokke★★), good Chardonnay, attractive piquant dry Riesling★, excellent barrel-fermented white blend Madame Marlbrook★★, bright Cabernet-led BORDEAUX blend Marlbrook, and Vin de Constance★★ (recent vintages ★★★), a thrilling Muscat dessert wine based on the 18th-century Constantia. Best years: (Vin de Constance) 2007 **06 05 04 02 01 00 99 98 97 96 95 94**.

KNAPPSTEIN *Clare Valley, South Australia* Three outstanding single vineyard wines from mature vines: Ackland Riesling★★★, Enterprise Cabernet★★ and Yertabulti Shiraz★★. The regular Riesling★★ is reliably good and Three★ intriguingly combines Gewürztraminer with Riesling and Pinot Gris. The Enterprise Brewery★ (established 1878) has been re opened with refreshing results. Best years: (Enterprise Cabernet Sauvignon) (2010) 09 08 06 **05 04 03 02 01 00 99 98**.

KNIPSER *Laumersheim, Pfalz, Germany* Brothers Werner and Volker produce a wide range of wines, including rarities (for Germany) such as Sauvignon Gris and Syrah. Their most convincing wines, though, are dry Rieslings★★ and perfumed Spatburgunder (Pinot Noir)★★. Best years. (2011) 10 09 **08 07 06 05**.

EMMERICH KNOLL *Wachau, Niederösterreich, Austria* Since the late 1970s, some of the greatest Austrian dry white wines. The rich, complex Riesling and Grüner Veltliner are packed with fruit and invariably ★★ quality, with versions from the Loibenberg, Kellerberg and Schütt sites often ★★★. They repay keeping for 5 years or more. Best years: (Riesling Smaragd) (2011) 10 09 **08 07 06 05 04 03 02 01 99**.

KOEHLER-RUPRECHT *Kallstadt, Pfalz, Germany* Powerful, concentrated dry Rieslings★★★ from the Kallstadter Saumagen site, oak-aged botrytized Elysium★ and Burgundian-style Spätburgunder (Pinot Noir)★. Best years: (Saumagen Riesling) (2011) (10) 09 08 **07 06 05 04 03 02 01**.

KOLLWENTZ *Neusiedlersee-Hügelland, Burgenland, Austria* Expert in both white and red wines. Fine Chardonnays★★ and Sauvignon Blanc★ are matched by Austria's best Cabernet Sauvignon★ and spicy red blends such as Steinzeiler★★ (Blaufränkisch, Cabernet, Zweigelt) and Eichkogel★ (Blaufränkisch, Zweigelt). Fine TBAs★★ too. Best years: (reds) (2011) (10) 09 **08 06 05 04 03**.

KOOYONG *Mornington Peninsula, Victoria, Australia* Under the same ownership as the nearby Port Phillip Estate. From 1995, 30ha (74 acres) at Kooyong were planted to Pinot Noir (Haven★★★, Ferrous★★ and Meres★ Vineyards) and Chardonnay (Faultline★★ and Farrago★★ Vineyards). The Kooyong Estate Chardonnay★★ is structured, complex and restrained and the Estate Pinot Noir★★ needs time to show its seductive best, while entry-level Clonale Chardonnay★★ and Massale Pinot Noir★ show real personality, as well as pure varietal character.

ALOIS KRACHER *Illmitz, Burgenland, Austria* Unquestionably Austria's greatest sweet wine maker until his untimely death in 2007. Son Gerhard is following ably in his footsteps. Nouvelle Vague wines are aged in new barriques while Zwischen den Seen wines are aged in steel tanks. The Grande Cuvée and TBAs from Scheurebe, Welschriesling and Chardonnay are all ★★★. Best years: (whites) (2011) (10) 09 **08 07 06 05 04 02 01 99**.

KREMSTAL *Niederösterreich, Austria* 2600ha (6420-acre) wine region around Krems, producing some of Austria's best whites. From 2007 the DAC appellation can be used for dry Riesling and Grüner Veltliner. Best producers: Malat★★, Mantlerhof★, Sepp Moser★, NIGL★★, NIKOLAIHOF★★, Proidl★, Salomon★★, Stadt Krems★. Best years: (2011) 10 09 **08 07 06 05 04**.

KRUG *Champagne AC, Champagne, France* Owned by luxury goods behemoth LVMH, this is a serious CHAMPAGNE house, making seriously expensive wines. The non-vintage Grande Cuvée★★ is deservedly regarded as one of the leading de luxe super-brands, though recent releases have become a little more international in style. Also an impressive vintage★★, rosé★★ and an ethereal, outrageously expensive, single-vineyard Clos du Mesnil★★★ Blanc de Blancs. Best years: 2000 98 **96 95 90 89 88 85 82 81 79**.

KRUTZLER *Deutsch-Schützen, Südburgenland, Austria* Perwolff★★, one of Austria's finest red wines, is a generously oaked Blaufränkisch-based blend with a little Cabernet Sauvignon. The Blaufränkisch Reserve★ is almost as fine. Best years: (2011) (10) 09 08 **07 06 05 04 03 02**.

PETER JAKOB KÜHN *Oestrich, Rheingau, Germany* A brilliant grower and winemaker, Kühn makes substantial dry Rieslings and thrilling nobly sweet wines, all usually★★ and occasionally★★★. Best years: (2011) 10 09 **07 06 05 04 03**.

KUMEU/HUAPAI *Auckland, North Island, New Zealand* A small but significant viticultural area north-west of Auckland. The 11 wineries profit from their proximity to New Zealand's largest city, but most make little or no wine from grapes grown in their home region due to the heavy clay soils and erratic weather patterns. Best producers: COOPERS CREEK★, KUMEU RIVER★★, MATUA VALLEY★, West Brook. Best years: (Chardonnay) 2010 **09 07 06 05**.

KUMEU RIVER *Kumeu, Auckland, North Island, New Zealand* This family winery has been transformed by New Zealand's first Master of Wine, Michael Brajkovich, with adventurous, high-quality wines: a big, complex Chardonnay★★★ and three single-vineyard Chardonnays – Maté's★★★, Coddington★★ and Hunting Hill★★ – plus a complex oak-aged Pinot Gris★. Only Pinot Noir disappoints so far. Best years: (Chardonnay) 2010 **09 07 06 05**.

KUNDE ESTATE *Sonoma Valley, California, USA* The Kunde family have grown wine grapes in SONOMA COUNTY for more than 100 years; in 1990 they started producing wines, with spectacular results. Impressive Chardonnay★ (Reserve★★), zesty Magnolia Lane Sauvignon Blanc★★ and explosively fruity Viognier★★. The Century Vines Zinfandel★★ gets rave reviews, as does the peppery Syrah★★. Best years: (Zinfandel) 2008 **07 06 05 02 01 00**.

KÜNSTLER *Hochheim, Rheingau, Germany* Gunter Künstler makes some of the best dry Rieslings★★ in the RHEINGAU – powerful, mineral wines. Also powerful, earthy and pricey Pinot Noir. Best years: (2011) 10 09 **08 07 06 05 04 03**.

KWV *Paarl WO, South Africa* Continued improvement at this industry giant, mainly from new The Mentors range (Semillon★★, Grenache Blanc★) which focuses on *terroir*, with individual vineyard selection the next goal. The huge range of South African spirits and wine, to be rationalized, includes the flagship Cathedral Cellar range, led by bright-fruited, well-oaked Cabernet-based Triptych★, and tangy Sauvignon Blanc★. Single-vineyard Perold is an ultra-ripe international-style Shiraz lavishly adorned with new American oak. Port-style and Muscadel fortifieds remain superb value.

DOM. LABRANCHE-LAFFONT *Madiran AOP, South-West France* Christine Dupuy is a rare female vigneronne in this rugby-playing appellation Superb MADIRAN★ (Vieilles Vignes★★) and excellent PACHERENC★★ (both sweet and dry). Best years: (red) (2011) 10 09 **08 06 05**; (sweet white) 2010 **09 06 05**.

LADOIX AC *Côte de Beaune, Burgundy, France* Most northerly village in the CÔTE DE BEAUNE. The best vineyards are included in Grands Crus CORTON and CORTON-CHARLEMAGNE, but otherwise most used to be sold off as CÔTE DE BEAUNE-VILLAGES. That's starting to change with some decent Ladoix reds on the lower slopes and exotic whites above. Best producers: (reds) Cachat-Ocquidant★, Chevalier★, E Cornu★, M Mallard★ (Les Joyeuses★★); (whites) R & R Jacob★, S Loichet★. Best years: (reds) (2011) 10 09 08 **07 05 03 02 99**.

MICHEL LAFARGE *Volnay, Côte de Beaune, Burgundy, France* These are not easy wines to understand, and I've been disappointed as often as I've been thrilled. Some outstanding red wines, notably Volnay Clos des Chênes★★, Volnay Clos du Château des Ducs★★ (a monopole) and less fashionable BEAUNE Grèves★★. BOURGOGNE Rouge★ is good value. Top wines may seem a little lean at first, but are expected to blossom after 10 years or more aging. Best years: (top reds) (2011) 10 09 08 **07 06 05 03 02 99 98 97 96 95 91 90**.

CH. LAFAURIE-PEYRAGUEY★★ *Sauternes AC, 1er Cru Classé, Bordeaux, France* Took off in the 1980s and is now one of the most consistent SAUTERNES properties: sumptuous and rich when young, and marvellously deep and satisfying with age. Occasionally close to YQUEM in body and flavour. Best years: 2010 09 **07 06 05 04 03 02 01 99 98 97 96 95 90 89 88 86 85 83**.

CH. LAFITE-ROTHSCHILD★★★ *Pauillac AC, 1er Cru Classé, Haut-Médoc, Bordeaux, France* This property was bought by the Rothschild banking family in 1868 and they still own it today. A PAUILLAC First Growth, Lafite is frequently cited as the epitome of elegance, indulgence and expense (the Chinese are certainly doing their bit to ensure the latter!). Since the late 1990s vintages have been superb, with added depth and body to match the wine's traditional finesse. Second wine: les Carruades de Lafite-Rothschild. Best years: 2010 09 08 **07 06 05 04 03 02 01 00 99 98 97 96 95 94 90 89 88 86 85 82**.

CH. LAFLEUR★★★ *Pomerol AC, Bordeaux, France* Using some of POMEROL's most traditional winemaking, this tiny estate can seriously rival the great PETRUS for texture, flavour and aroma. But a high percentage (50%) of Cabernet Franc makes this a more elegant wine. Second wine: Pensées de Lafleur. Best years: 2010 09 08 07 06 05 04 **03 02 01 00 99 98 96 95 90 89**.

L LAFON

LAFON *Meursault, Côte de Beaune, Burgundy, France* One of Burgundy's current superstars, with prices to match. Early exponent of biodynamics for brilliant MEURSAULT (Clos de la Barre★★, Charmes★★★, Perrières★★★), le MONTRACHET★★★ and exciting long-lived reds from VOLNAY (Santenots-du-Milieu★★★, Champans★★). Also Héritiers Lafon★ in the Maconnais (Clos du Four★, Clos de la Crochette★, VIRÉ-CLESSÉ★) and from 2008 Dominique Lafon label for Meursault, Beaune, Volnay, Puligny Champsgains★★. Best years: (whites) (2011) 10 09 08 **07** 06 05 **04 02**; (reds) (2011) 10 09 08 **07** 06 05 **03 02** 99 98 96 90.

CH. LAFON-ROCHET★ *St-Estèphe AC, 4ème Cru Classé, Haut-Médoc, Bordeaux, France* Good-value, affordable Classed Growth claret. Recent vintages have seen an increase of Merlot, making the wine less austere but still structured. Delicious and blackcurranty after 10 years. Best years: 2010 09 08 06 05 **04 03 02** 01 00 99 98 96 95 94 90 89.

ALOIS LAGEDER *Alto Adige DOC, Trentino-Alto Adige, Italy* Among the leading independents in ALTO ADIGE, making good, medium-priced varietals and pricey estate and single-vineyard wines such as Löwengang Cabernet★ and Chardonnay★★, Sauvignon Lehen★★, Cabernet Cor Römigberg★, Pinot Noir Krafuss★, Pinot Bianco Haberle★ and Pinot Grigio Benefizium Porer★. Also owns the historic Casòn Hirschprunn estate: white Contest★★ is based on Pinot Grigio and Chardonnay with Viognier; the red Casòn★★ is Merlot-Cabernet based.

CH. LAGRANGE★★ *St-Julien AC, 3ème Cru Classé, Haut-Médoc, Bordeaux, France* Good fruit and perfume, meticulous winemaking and consistently fine quality mark out this large estate owned by Japanese company Suntory, an occasional surfeit of tannin being the only cautionary note. Dry white les Arums de Lagrange since 1997. Second wine: les Fiefs de Lagrange. Best years: 2010 09 08 06 05 **04 03 02** 01 00 98 96 95 90 89.

LAGREIN Black grape of ALTO ADIGE, producing deep-coloured, brambly, chocolaty reds and full-bodied, attractively scented rosés. Brazil produces a bit. Best producers: Colterenzio co-op (Cornell★), Glögglhof, Gries co-op★, Hofstätter★, LAGEDER★, Laimburg★, Muri-Gries★, J Niedermayr★, I Niedriest★, Plattner-Waldgries★, Hans Rottensteiner★, Terlano co-op★★, Thurnhof★★, TIEFENBRUNNER★★, Zemmer★.

CH. LA LAGUNE★ *Haut-Médoc AC, 3ème Cru Classé, Haut-Médoc, Bordeaux, France* The closest MÉDOC Classed Growth to Bordeaux city. The soils are sandy-gravel and the wines round and elegant in style. Took a dip in the late 1990s but new investment from 2000 has improved things without adding any real personality. Second wine: Moulin de la Lagune. Best years: 2010 09 08 06 **05 04 03 02** 00 98 96 95 90 89.

LALANDE-DE-POMEROL AC *Bordeaux, France* To the north of its more famous neighbour POMEROL, this AC produces ripe, plummy wines with an unmistakable mineral edge that are very attractive to drink at 4–5 years old, but age reasonably well too. Even though they lack the concentration of top Pomerols, the wines are not particularly cheap. Best producers: Annereaux★, Bertineau St-Vincent★, Chambrun★, La Croix des Moines★, la Croix-St-André★, les Cruzelles★, La FLEUR DE BOÜARD★, Garraud★, Grand Ormeau★, Haut-Chaigneau, les Hauts Conseillants, Jean de Gué★, Laborderie-Mondésir★, Perron (La Fleur★), Sergant, la Sergue★, Siaurac★, Tournefeuille★. Best years: 2010 09 **08** 06 05 04 03 02 00 98 96 95.

LAMBRUSCO *Emilia-Romagna, Italy* 'Lambrusco' refers to a heterogeneous family of black grape varieties, grown in 3 DOC zones on the plains of EMILIA and 1 in LOMBARDY. Today the cheap and cheerful stuff of the 1980s is all but forgotten, but there is genuine quality Lambrusco (especially Lambrusco di Sorbara and Grasparossa di Castelvetro), frothing, acidic and dry or off-dry, ideal as a partner to the rich local foods. Best producers: Barbieri, Barbolini, F Bellei★, Casali, Cavicchioli★, Chiarli, Vittorio Graziano★, Oreste Lini, Stefano Spezia, Venturini Baldini.

LAMOREAUX LANDING *Finger Lakes AVA, New York State, USA* One of the most versatile and consistently good wineries in the FINGER LAKES. Its Chardonnay Reserve★ is a regular medal winner, and the Pinot Noir★ is arguably the region's best. Merlot★ and Cabernet Franc★ are also attractive, as are Dry Riesling★ and good, quaffable fizz.

LANDMARK *Sonoma County, California, USA* This producer concentrates on Chardonnay and Pinot Noir. Chardonnays include Overlook★★ and the oakier Damaris Reserve★★ and Lorenzo★★. Tropical-fruited Courtyard Chardonnay★ is lower-priced. Pinot Noir from Kastania Vineyard★★ (SONOMA COAST) is beautifully focused. The winery has replanted its estate Chardonnay vineyard in Sonoma Valley to Rhône varieties, and first sightings of Viognier, Grenache and Syrah are impressive.

LANGHE DOC *Piedmont, Italy* Important DOC covering blends (Rosso, Bianco) and varietals from the Langhe hills around Alba; the 'varietals' crucially allow 15% of other grapes, thus allowing people like GAJA to sell as Langhe what he used to sell as Barbaresco and Barolo. Best producers: (reds) ALTARE★★, Boglietti (Buio★★), Bongiovanni (Falletto★★), Ceretto★★, Chiarlo★, Cigliuti★★, CLERICO★★, Aldo CONTERNO★★, Conterno-Fantino (Monprà★★), Luigi Einaudi★, GAJA★★★, A Ghisolfi★★, Marchesi di Gresy (Virtus★★), F Nada (Seifile★★), Oberto★★, Parusso (Bricco Rovella★★), Rocche dei Manzoni (Quatr Nas★), Vajra★, Gianni Voerzio (Serrapiu★★), Roberto VOERZIO★★. Best years: (reds) (2011) (10) 09 08 **07** 06 **04** 01 99.

CH. LANGOA-BARTON★★ *St-Julien AC, 3ème Cru Classé, Haut-Médoc, Bordeaux, France* Owned by the Barton family since 1821, Langoa-Barton is usually less scented and elegant, though often richer than its ST-JULIEN stablemate LÉOVILLE-BARTON, but it is still extremely impressive and excellent value. Drink after 7 or 8 years, although it may improve for 15–20. Second wine: Réserve de Léoville-Barton (a blend from the young vines of both Barton properties). Best years: 2010 09 08 **07** 06 **05** 04 03 02 01 00 99 98 96 95 90 89 88.

LANGUEDOC-ROUSSILLON *France* This vast area of southern France, running from Nîmes to the Spanish border and covering the *départements* of the GARD, HÉRAULT, Aude and Pyrénées-Orientales, is still a source of undistinguished cheap wine, but is also one of France's most exciting wine regions. The transformation is the result of reviving ancient vineyards, better grape varieties, modern winemaking and ambitious producers, from the heights of GRANGE DES PÈRES to very good local co-ops. The best wines are the reds, particularly those from CORBIÈRES, MINERVOIS, FAUGÈRES, ST-CHINIAN and PIC ST-LOUP, and some new-wave Cabernets, Merlots and Syrahs, as well as the more traditional *vins doux naturels*, such as BANYULS, MAURY and MUSCAT DE RIVESALTES; but we are now seeing exciting whites as well, particularly as new plantings of Chardonnay, Marsanne, Roussanne, Viognier, Vermentino (Rolle) and Sauvignon Blanc mature. An all-embracing appellation, called simply Languedoc AC, was agreed in 2007 and covers all of COTEAUX DU

LANGUEDOC, plus Corbières, Minervois and the ROUSSILLON appellations. Coteaux du Languedoc AC is now set to disappear in May 2017. See also BLANQUETTE DE LIMOUX, CABARDÈS, COLLIOURE, CÔTES DU ROUSSILLON, CÔTES CATALANES, CÔTES DE THONGUE, FITOU, GRÈS DE MONTPELLIER, LIMOUX, MUSCAT DE FRONTIGNAN, MUSCAT DE ST-JEAN-DE-MINERVOIS, OC, PÉZENAS, PICPOUL DE PINET, RIVESALTES, TERRASSES DU LARZAC.

LANSON *Champagne AC, Champagne, France* Non-vintage Lanson Black Label★ is reliably tasty and, like the rosé★ and vintage★ wines, especially de luxe Noble Cuvée★★, improves greatly with aging. Also three new Extra Aged multi-vintage blends in rosé, regular and Blanc de Blancs styles. Best years: **1999 98 97 96 95 93 90 89 88 85 83 82**.

LAPEYRE *Jurançon AOP, South-West France* Jean-Bernard Larrieu, fervent Gascon and fiercely organic, produces a fine range of JURANÇON wines, ranging from dry, especially from older vines (Vitatge Vielh★) through to ever sweeter gems such as Magendia★ and Vent Balaguer★★. Both sweet and dry wines age well. Best years: (sweet) 2010 **07 05 04** 03.

LAPOSTOLLE *Rapel, Chile* Owned by Marnier-Lapostolle of France, with consultancy from BORDEAUX winemaker Michel Rolland. Cuvée Alexandre Merlot★★, from the acclaimed Apalta area in COLCHAGUA, was its first hit back in 1994, now eclipsed by red blend Clos Apalta★★★. Even so, Cuvée Alexandre Cabernet★★ and Syrah★★ are tremendously tasty. Good Pinot Noir★, rich, creamy Chardonnay★ and delightful, juicy Casa Carmenère★. Parts of the Apalta estate are now biodynamic.

DOM. LAROCHE *Chablis, Burgundy, France* Significant CHABLIS domaine with associated *négociant*, plus interests in Languedoc, Chile and South Africa, merged in 2009 with larger Jeanjean operation, retaining minority share. Should not change wine styles noticeably.

LAS MORAS *San Juan, Argentina* Highly successful winery in SAN JUAN, producing consistently attractive wines at all price levels, from a wide range of grape varieties. Famed for its 3 Valleys Gran Shiraz★, powerful, spicy, laden with blackberry and licorice flavours with a lovely floral edge. Mora Negra★, an aromatic Malbec-Bonarda blend, is also classy stuff.

CH. LASCOMBES★ *Margaux AC, 2ème Cru Classé, Haut-Médoc, Bordeaux, France* One of the great underachievers in the MARGAUX AC and little worth drinking in the 1980s and 90s, but new American ownership and investment and the advice of consultant enologist Michel Rolland have begun to make an occasional difference; the 2005 and 2009 are the best for a generation, 2010 wasn't. Now owned by a French insurance company (since 2011). Best years: 2009 08 **07 06 05 04 03 01 00 96 95**.

CH. LATOUR★★★ *Pauillac AC, 1er Cru Classé, Haut-Médoc, Bordeaux, France* Latour's reputation is based on powerful, long-lasting classic wines. Strangely, in the early 1980s there was an attempt to make lighter, more fashionable wines, with mixed results. The late 80s saw a return to classic Latour, much to my relief. Its reputation for making fine wine in less successful vintages is well deserved. Spanking new cellars from 2004 have helped take the quality and precision even higher. Second wine: les Forts de Latour. Best years: 2010 09 08 07 06 05 **04 03 02 01 00 99 98 97 96 95 94 90 89 88 86**.

LOUIS LATOUR *Beaune, Burgundy, France* Merchant almost as well known for his COTEAUX DE L'ARDÈCHE Chardonnays as for his Burgundies. Latour's white Burgundies are much better than the reds, although the red CORTON-Grancey★★ can be very good. Latour's oaky CORTON-

CHARLEMAGNE★★, from his own vineyard, is his top wine, but there is also good CHEVALIER-MONTRACHET★★, BÂTARD-MONTRACHET★★ and le MONTRACHET★★. Even so, as these are the greatest white vineyards in Burgundy, there really should be more top performances; there are some signs of a revival. Best years: (top whites) (2011) 10 09 **08 07 06 05 02**.

CH. LATOUR-MARTILLAC *Pessac-Léognan AC, Cru Classé de Graves, Bordeaux, France* The vineyard here is strictly organic, and has many ancient vines. The deep, dark, well-structured reds★ have been fairly consistent since the late 1990s. Whites★ are thoroughly modern and of good quality. Good value as well. Best years: (reds) 2010 09 08 **06 05 04 03 02 01 00 98 96 95 90**; (whites) 2010 09 08 07 06 05 04 02 01 00.

CH. LATOUR-À-POMEROL★ *Pomerol AC, Bordeaux, France* Directed by Christian MOUEIX of PETRUS fame, this property makes luscious wines with loads of gorgeous fruit and enough tannin to age well. Best years: 2010 09 08 07 06 05 04 03 02 01 00 99 98 95 90 89.

LATRICIÈRES-CHAMBERTIN AC See CHAMBERTIN AC.

LAUREL GLEN *Sonoma Mountain AVA, California, USA* Cabernet-only mountaintop winery, long famous for restrained, cedary, ageworthy wines. Laurel Glen★★ is ripe but dry, with deep fruit flavours, aging after 6–10 years to a perfumed, complex BORDEAUX style. Counterpoint★ is an excellent second label. Vineyard sold in 2011 but former owner/winemaker Patrick Campbell will continue to make Zinfandel-based Reds from Lodi-grown fruit, and Terra Rosa (Malbec) from MENDOZA, Argentina, under the umbrella of his Tierra Divina wine company. Best years: 2009 08 **06 05 02 01 99 98 97 96 95 94**.

LAURENT-PERRIER *Champagne AC, Champagne, France* Large, family-owned CHAMPAGNE house, offering flavour and quality at reasonable prices. Non-vintage is light and savoury; the vintage★ is good, and the top wine, Grand Siècle★★ (sometimes★★★) can be among the finest Champagnes of all. Non-vintage rosé★ is good, vintage Alexandra Rosé★★★ is excellent. Best years: 2002 00 99 97 96 95 90 88 85 82.

L'AVENIR *Stellenbosch WO, South Africa* French-owned (by the LAROCHE/Jeanjean group), but strictly South African in focus, the refined range is headed by Chenin Blanc and Pinotage. Three Pinotages, from cheerfully fruity, via well-oaked Platinum, to ageworthy Grand Vin Pinotage★★, are echoed by a stylish trio of Chenin Blancs (Platinum★, Grand Vin★★). Promising Chardonnay★, Cabernet★ and BORDEAUX-blend Stellenbosch Classic★. Best years: (Pinotage) 2010 **09 08 07 06 05 04 03**.

CH. LAVILLE-HAUT-BRION★★★ *Pessac-Léognan AC, Cru Classé de Graves, Bordeaux, France* One of the finest white PESSAC-LÉOGNANs, with a price tag to match. Fermented in barrel, it needs 10 years or more to reach its savoury but luscious peak. Renamed la-MISSION-HAUT-BRION *blanc* from the 2009 vintage. Best years: **2008 07 06 05 04 03 02 01 00 96 95 94 93 90 89**.

DOMAINE COSTA LAZARIDI *Drama, Greece* State-of-the-art, Bordeaux-inspired winery making good use of indigenous and international varieties. Fresh gooseberry Amethystos white★ (Sauvignon Blanc, Sémillon and Assyrtiko); a fascinatingly intense Viognier★ with a stunning, oily, peach kernel finish; tasty Château Julia Chardonnay★; and fine Amethystos Cava★, an oak-aged Cabernet from very low yields.

LAZIO *Italy* The nation's political centre is not famous for wine, being able to boast not much more than glugging whites based on Trebbiano and Malvasia, such as Est! Est!! Est!!! di Montefiascone and FRASCATI. The region's most interesting wines are reds based on Cesanese, an up and coming variety. **Best producers:** Casale del Giglio★, Castel de Paolis (Quattro Mori★★), Cerveteri co-op (Tertium★), FALESCO, Giuliani Marcella★, Paola di Mauro (Vigna del Vassallo★★), l'Olivella★, Pietra Pinta★, Trappolini★, Villa Santa★.

L'ECOLE No 41 *Walla Walla Valley AVA, Washington State, USA* Velvety and deeply flavoured Seven Hills Vineyard Merlot★, good Cabernet Sauvignon★ and lush Syrah★★; a BORDEAUX blend called Apogee★ from the Pepper Bridge vineyard in WALLA WALLA VALLEY is dark and challenging. The best wines are the barrel-fermented Semillons: a nutty COLUMBIA VALLEY★★ version and Luminesce Seven Hills Vineyard★★. The Chardonnay★★ is very attractive and oatmealy. **Best years:** (top reds) (2010) 09 **08 07** 06.

LEEUWIN ESTATE *Margaret River, Western Australia*
MARGARET RIVER's perennial high flier, with pricey, supremely balanced Art Series Chardonnay★★★ that gets Burgundy lovers drooling. Art Series Cabernet Sauvignon★★ (sometimes ★★★) exhibits superb blackcurrant and cedar balance. Art Series Riesling★★ is complex and fine, and Shiraz★★ is now exceptional. Prelude (Chardonnay★★) and Siblings (Sauvignon Blanc-Semillon★) give Leeuwin pleasure at lower prices. **Best years:** (Art Series Chardonnay) (2011) (10) 09 08 **07 06 05** 04 02 01 00 99 98 97.

DOM. LEFLAIVE *Puligny-Montrachet, Côte de Beaune, Burgundy, France* Famous white Burgundy producer with extensive holdings in some of the greatest vineyards of PULIGNY-MONTRACHET (les Pucelles★★★), Chevalier-MONTRACHET★★★, BÂTARD-MONTRACHET★★★ and a tiny slice of le MONTRACHET★★★. Anne-Claude Leflaive has taken the family domaine right back to the top using biodynamic methods. These extraordinarily fine wines can age for 20 years and are understandably expensive. More reasonably priced Mâcon-Verzé★. **Best years:** (2011) 10 09 08 **07 06 05** 03 02.

OLIVIER LEFLAIVE *Puligny-Montrachet, Côte de Beaune, Burgundy, France*
Négociant Olivier Leflaive specializes in crisp, modern white wines from the CÔTE D'OR and the CÔTE CHALONNAISE, mostly for early drinking. Lesser ACs – ST-ROMAIN★, MONTAGNY★, MERCUREY★, ST-AUBIN★, RULLY★ – offer good value, but the rich, oaky BÂTARD-MONTRACHET★★ is the star turn. **Best years:** (top whites) (2011) 10 **09 08 07**.

PETER LEHMANN *Barossa Valley, South Australia* BAROSSA doyen Lehmann buys grapes from many local growers and owns the superb Stonewell vineyard, which contributes its fruit and name to his great Shiraz★★★. The 1885 Shiraz★★★ from the Ebenezer vineyard is another stunner. Juicy, fruit-packed reds include Grenache-Shiraz★, Mentor Cabernet★★ and Eight Songs Shiraz★★. The top whites have been consistently sublime in recent years: impeccably balanced Wigan Eden Valley Riesling★★★ and rich, pure, zesty, unwooded Margaret Semillon★★★ from Barossa Valley old vines. Also lemony Semillon★★ and Chenin★, and dry, long-lived Eden Valley Riesling★★. Owned by California-based Donald Hess since 2003. Befuddling array of budget lines – but the quality is holding up so far. **Best years:** (Stonewell Shiraz) (2011) (10) (09) 08 06 **05 04 03 02** 01 99 98 96 94 93 90 89.

JOSEF LEITZ *Rüdesheim, Rheingau, Germany* Some of the RHEINGAU's best dry
and off-dry Rieslings, especially from the Berg Rottland★★ and Berg
Schlossberg★★ sites, whose recent vintages go from strength to strength.
Best years: (2011) 10 09 **08 07 06 05 04 02**.

LEIWEN *Mosel, Germany* In the 1990s this village became a hotbed of the
MOSEL Riesling revolution, as a number of estates made the most of
Leiwen's unrealized potential. Still a source of excellent, reasonably priced
Rieslings. Best producers: GRANS-FASSIAN★★, Carl Loewen★★, Josef Rosch★,
ST URBANS-HOF★★. Best years: (2011) 10 09 **08 07 06 05 04**.

LEMBERGER See BLAUFRÄNKISCH.

LENZ WINERY *Long Island, New York State, USA* A leading LONG ISLAND winery
focused on BORDEAUX varietal reds, exclusively from estate fruit. The
Estate Merlot★★ is elegant and powerful with soft, balanced tannins; dry
Gewurztraminer★ is spicy and tasty; Chardonnay★ can be good.
Sparkling wines are limited in quantity though not in quality.

LEONETTI CELLAR *Walla Walla Valley AVA, Washington State, USA* WALLA
WALLA VALLEY's first winery opened in 1977. Today it produces highly
sought-after, rich and velvety Cabernet Sauvignon★★ and Merlot★★
aged in a combination of French and American oak; dense and powerful
Reserve★★★. Sangiovese★★ has very fine texture and lots of new wood.
Most of the fruit is now estate grown. Best years: (2010) 09 **08 07 06 05**.

CH. LÉOVILLE-BARTON★★★ *St-Julien AC, 2ème Cru Classé, Haut-Médoc,
Bordeaux, France* A traditionalist's delight, made by Anthony Barton,
whose family has run this ST-JULIEN property since 1826. Dark, dry and
tannic, and not overly oaked, the wines are often underestimated, but
over 10–20 years they achieve a lean yet sensitively proportioned beauty
rarely equalled in Bordeaux. Second wine: Réserve de Léoville-Barton.
Best years: 2010 09 **08 07 06 05 04 03 02 01 00 99 96 95 94 93 90 89 88**.

CH. LÉOVILLE-LAS-CASES★★★ *St-Julien AC, 2ème Cru Classé, Haut-Médoc,
Bordeaux, France* The largest of the three Léoville properties, making
wines of startlingly deep, dark concentration. I now find them so dense
and thick in texture that it is difficult to identify them as ST-JULIEN but they
still achieve the highest of all the St-Julien prices. Second wine: Le Petit
Lion (since 2007), previously Clos du Marquis. Best years: 2010 09 08 07
06 05 **04 03 02 01 00 99 98 96 95 94 93 90 89 88 86**.

CH. LÉOVILLE-POYFERRÉ★★★ *St-Julien AC, 2ème Cru Classé, Haut-Médoc,
Bordeaux, France* Since the 1986 vintage Didier Cuvelier has gradually
increased the richness of the wine without wavering from its reserved and
elegant style. A string of excellent wines in the 90s and 00s frequently
show more classic ST-JULIEN style than those of neighbour LEOVILLE-LAS-CASES
and have resulted in a considerable increase in popularity and reputation.
Second wine: Moulin-Riche. Best years: 2010 09 08 **07** 06 05 **04 03 02 01
00 99 98 96 95 90 89 86**.

DOM. LEROY *Vosne-Romanée, Côte de Nuits, Burgundy, France* In 1988 Lalou
Bize-Leroy bought the former Dom. Noëllat in VOSNE-ROMANEE,
renaming it Domaine Leroy. It should not be confused with her *négociant*
house, Maison Leroy, which contains stocks of great mature vintages, or
her personal estate, Dom. d'Auvenay. Here she produces fiendishly
expensive, though fabulously concentrated, wines with biodynamic
methods and almost ludicrously low yields from top vineyards such as
CHAMBERTIN★★★, CLOS DE VOUGEOT★★★, MUSIGNY★★★, RICHEBOURG★★★
and ROMANÉE-ST-VIVANT★★★. Best years: (top reds) (2011) 10 09 08 **07** 06 05
03 02 01 00 99 96 90 89.

LEYDA See SAN ANTONIO.

VIÑA LEYDA *San Antonio, Chile* Pioneering winery founded in 1997 that led to the creation of the exciting coastal appellation Leyda Valley in 2002. Famed for its Pinot Noirs (Cahuil★★, Las Brisas★★, Lot 21★★) and Sauvignon Blanc★★ from the Garuma vineyard. Also makes lovely unoaked Chardonnay★★, Riesling★, Sauvignon Gris★, Pinot Noir Rosé★ and a potentially thrilling, cool, scented Syrah★.

LIGER-BELAIR *Côte de Nuits, Burgundy, France* Louis-Michel Liger-Belair makes stylish, perfumed wines under the Comte Liger-Belair label in VOSNE-ROMANÉE, including serious aux Reignots★★, scented ECHÉZEAUX★★★ and the monopoly of la ROMANÉE★★★ itself. His cousin Thibault Liger-Belair makes rich, plump wines from his NUITS-ST-GEORGES base, including Premier Cru les St-Georges★★ and Grands Crus RICHEBOURG★★ and CLOS DE VOUGEOT★★. Best years: (Comte) (2011) 10 09 08 **07** 06 05 **03 02**; (Thibault) (2011) 10 09 08 **07** 06 05 **02**.

LIGURIA *Italy* Thin coastal strip of north-west Italy, running from the French border at Ventimiglia to the Tuscan border. Best grape: Vermentino (try Lambruschi★). Best wines, mostly drunk by natives or tourists, are the Cinqueterre, Colli di Luna, Riviera Ligure di Ponente and Rossese di Dolceacqua DOCs.

LIMARÍ *Chile* During the past decade this valley – 400km (250 miles) north of Santiago – has shown that its cold ocean influence, long sunshine hours and chalky/clay soils can produce world-class wines. Chardonnay and Syrah are the top performers, both expressing fresh, vibrant flavours and subtle yet clear minerality. Also some salty Sauvignons from the coastal region. Best producers: DE MARTINO★, Maycas del Limarí★/CONCHA Y TORO, TABALÍ★, Tamaya.

LIMESTONE COAST *South Australia* Zone for south-east of South Australia, including COONAWARRA, PADTHAWAY, Mount Benson, Robe, Wrattonbully and Mount Gambier. New vineyards in this far-flung area have Coonawarra-like terra rossa soil with great potential. Big boys Pernod Ricard, Treasury and YALUMBA are all involved, as well as private estates.

LIMOUX AC *Languedoc, France* The first AC in the LANGUEDOC to allow Chardonnay and Chenin Blanc, which must be vinified in oak. Production is dominated by the SIEUR D'ARQUES co-op. Red Limoux is made from Merlot and Cabernet with local varieties. Best producers: d'Antugnac★, Bégude★, Mouscaillo, Rives-Blanques★, SIEUR D'ARQUES★. See also BLANQUETTE DE LIMOUX, CRÉMANT DE LIMOUX.

LINDEMAN'S *Murray Darling, Victoria, Australia* Large, historic company, part of Treasury Wine Estates. Underperforming for some years – indeed Lindeman's is now a 'global' brand, sourcing wines from wherever they choose – but the Bin range, especially Bin 65 Chardonnay, and the Cawarra wines, show some signs of emphasizing a bit of quality again. Traditionally strong in COONAWARRA, where the best wines are the minerally St George Cabernet★★, spicy Limestone Ridge Shiraz-Cabernet★★ and red BORDEAUX-blend Pyrus★★. Best years: (Coonawarra reds) 2010 09 08 **06 05** 04 01 99 98 96 94 91 90.

LINDEN VINEYARDS *Virginia, USA* For nearly three decades, Jim Law has quietly farmed a hillside vineyard called Hardscrabble, about an hour's drive west of Washington DC. He crafts European-styled wines of impressive concentration and finesse. He is leading Virginia's charge up steep slopes as the best sites for new vineyard plantings. Best wines are the Hardscrabble red blend★ of BORDEAUX varieties and Hardscrabble Chardonnay★. He also makes minerally Sauvignon Blanc.

LIRAC AC *Rhône Valley, France* Underrated AC between TAVEL and CHÂTEAUNEUF-DU-PAPE. Reds have the spice of Châteauneuf without the richness or the intensity, and are helped by Mourvèdre. They age over 8–10 years but are good, if stony, young. Refreshing rosé has lovely strawberry fruit; whites can be good and have the body to match full southern flavours. Best producers: Aquéria, Beaumont★, Boucarut★, Bouchassy★, Clos de Sixte★, Corne-Loup, Duseigneur★, la Genestière★, Alain Jaume★, Joncier★, Lafond-Roc-Épine★★, Lorentine★, Maby★, Mont-Redon★, la Mordorée★★, Pélaquié★, Roger Sabon★★, St-Roch★, Ségriès, Tavel co-op★. Best years: (reds) (2011) **10 09 07 06 05 04 03**.

LISBOA *Portugal* This used to be called Estremadura, and is Portugal's most productive region, occupying the western coastal strip, with an increasing number of clean, characterful wines. The leading area is ALENQUER DOC and there are eight other DOC regions; however, much of the region's best wine is simply labelled as Vinho Regional Lisboa. Spicy, perfumed reds are often based on Castelão, but Aragonez (Tempranillo), Cabernet Sauvignon, Syrah and Touriga Nacional contribute to top examples, which can benefit from 4 or 5 years' aging. Top producers also make fresh, aromatic whites. Best producers: Quinta de Chocapalha★, Quinta da Cortezia★, D F J VINHOS, Quinta dos Loridos (Loridos Chardonnay Extra Brut★), Quinta do Monte d'Oiro★★, Companhia Agricola do Sanguinhal, Quinta de Sant'Ana, Casa SANTOS LIMA★. See also BUCELAS. Best years: (reds) **2008 07 05 04 03 01 00**.

LISTRAC-MÉDOC AC *Haut-Médoc, Bordeaux, France* Set back from the Gironde and away from the best HAUT-MÉDOC gravel ridges, Listrac wines can be good but never thrilling, and are marked by solid fruit, a slightly coarse tannin and an earthy flavour. More Merlot and warmer vintages are now producing softer wines. Best producers: Cap Léon Veyrin, Clos des Demoiselles, CLARKE★, Ducluzeau, Fonréaud, Fourcas-Dupré★, Fourcas-Hosten★, Mayne-Lalande★, Reverdi, Saransot-Dupré. Best years: 2010 09 **08 06 05 03 01 00 96 95**.

LLANO ESTACADO *Texas High Plains AVA, Texas, USA* Texas' largest premium winery, in the western part of the state. Llano produces a wide array of wines at consistent quality and reasonable prices. Nice unoaked Chardonnay and exotically perfumed white blend Viviana★.

LOIRE VALLEY *France* The Loire river cuts right through the heart of France. The middle reaches are the home of world-famous SANCERRE and POUILLY-FUMÉ. The region of TOURAINE makes good Sauvignon Blanc and Gamay, while at VOUVRAY and MONTLOUIS-SUR-LOIRE Chenin Blanc makes some pretty good fizz and scintillatingly fresh, minerally still whites, ranging from sweet to very dry. The Loire's best reds are made in CHINON, BOURGUEIL, ST-NICOLAS-DE-BOURGUEIL and SAUMUR-CHAMPIGNY mainly from Cabernet Franc, with ANJOU-VILLAGES improving fast. Anjou is famous for rosé, but the best wines are white Chenin Blanc, either sweet from the Layon Valley or dry from SAVENNIÈRES and ANJOU, where a new generation of producers are making richer, barrel-fermented and aged wines. Near the mouth of the river around Nantes is MUSCADET. See also BONNEZEAUX, CABERNET D'ANJOU, CHEVERNY, CÔTE ROANNAISE, COTEAUX DE L'AUBANCE, COTEAUX DU GIENNOIS, COTEAUX DU LAYON,

CRÉMANT DE LOIRE, JASNIÈRES, MENETOU-SALON, POUILLY-SUR-LOIRE, QUARTS DE CHAUME, QUINCY, REUILLY, ROSÉ DE LOIRE, SAUMUR, SAUMUR MOUSSEUX, VAL DE LOIRE.

LOMA LARGA *Casablanca, Chile* One of Chile's leaders in cool-climate reds, specializing in crunchy Cabernet Franc★, Malbec★, Pinot Noir★ and Syrah★ made by a French winemaker hailing from the Loire region. Whites are also good. Excellent second label, Lomas del Valle.

LOMBARDY *Italy* Lombardy, whose capital is Milan, is a larger consumer than producer, though OLTREPÒ PAVESE does produce a lot of grapes, many of them used in Italy's *spumante* industry. There are some interesting wines from Oltrepò; also from VALTELLINA, Valcalepio and Garda's LUGANA. FRANCIACORTA makes top-quality sparklers.

LONG ISLAND *New York State, USA* Long Island encompasses 3 AVAs: the Hamptons, North Fork, and the broader Long Island AVA. People have likened growing conditions to BORDEAUX, and the long growing season, combined with a maritime influence, does produce similarities. Certainly Merlot and Cabernet Franc are the best reds, with Chardonnay the best white. Best producers: BEDELL★, CHANNING DAUGHTERS★, LENZ★, Macari, Martha Clara, Palmer★, Paumanok★, Pellegrini★, Pindar, Raphael, Shinn Estate, WÖLFFER★. Best years: (reds) (2010) (09) **08 07 06 02 01**.

LONG SHADOWS VINTNERS *Columbia Valley AVA, Washington State, USA* A series of partnerships, led by Allen Shoup, encompassing several wineries in the COLUMBIA VALLEY. It includes Pedestal★★ with Michel Rolland, Feather★ with Randy DUNN, Poet's Leap★ with Armin Diel of Schlossgut DIEL, Saggi★ with Ambrogio and Giovanni FOLONARI, Sequel★★ with John DUVAL, and Chester-Kidder★ with Allen Shoup and Gilles Nicault, the group's head winemaker. Best years: (reds) (2010) 09 **08 07 06**.

DR LOOSEN *Bernkastel, Mosel, Germany* Loosen's estate has portions of some of the MOSEL's most famous vineyards: Treppchen and Prälat in ERDEN, Würzgarten in ÜRZIG, Sonnenuhr in WEHLEN, Himmelreich in GRAACH and Lay in BERNKASTEL. Most of the wines achieve ★★, and Spätlese and Auslese from Wehlen, Ürzig and Erden frequently ★★★. Even the most basic Rieslings are excellent, year in year out. A joint venture with CHATEAU STE MICHELLE in Washington revolutionized Riesling production in that state. Best years: (2011) 10 09 **08 07 06 05 04 02 01 99**.

LÓPEZ DE HEREDIA *Rioja DOCa, Rioja, Spain* Family-owned RIOJA company, still aging wines in old oak casks. Younger red wines are called Viña Cubillo★, and mature wines Viña Tondonia★★ and Viña Bosconia★★. Good, oaky whites, including Viña Gravonia★★, and white wines are a different world, sometimes ★★★ in their idiosyncratic way. Best years: (Viña Tondonia) 2001 00 99 98 96 95 94 93 91 87 86 85.

LOUPIAC AC *Bordeaux, France* A sweet wine area across the Garonne river from BARSAC. The wines are attractively sweet without being gooey. Drink young in general, though the best can age. Best producers: Clos Jean★, Cros★, Loupiac-Gaudiet, Noble★, Ricaud, les Roques★. Best years: **2010 09 07 05 03 02 01 99**.

CH. LA LOUVIÈRE *Pessac-Léognan AC, Bordeaux, France* The star of PESSAC-LÉOGNAN's non-classified estates, its reputation almost entirely due to owner André Lurton. Well-structured reds★ and fresh, Sauvignon-based whites★★ are excellent value. Best years: (reds) 2010 09 08 **06 05 04 02 01 00 99 98**; (whites) **2010** 09 08 07 06 05 04 03 02 01 00.

LUBÉRON AC *Rhône Valley, France* Production is dominated by the co-ops east of Avignon along the Durance Valley; their light wines drink young. Domaine wines (Grenache, Syrah) have more body. Whites are often oaked. Best producers: Bonnieux co-op, la Canorgue, la Citadelle★, Fontenille★, de l'Isolette★, St-Estève de Néri★, la Tour-d'Aigues co-op, des Tourettes, Val Joanis★, la Verrerie. Best years: **2010 09.**

STEFANO LUBIANA *Tasmania, Australia* One of the stars of the Tasmanian wine scene. Vintage★★, non-vintage★ and Prestige★ (10 years on lees) sparkling wines rank with the best in Australia. Chardonnay★ is restrained and elegant, Sauvignon Blanc★ shows greengage and passionfruit characters, while the Pinot Noir★ has weight, concentration and a velvety texture. Entry-level 'Primavera' Pinot Noir is pretty tasty.

LUGANA DOC *Lombardy, Italy* Dry white (occasionally sparkling) from the Trebbiano di Lugana grape (aka Verdicchio) grown on the southern shores of Lake Garda. Well-structured wines from the better producers can develop excitingly over a few years. Best producers: Ca' dei Frati★★, Ottella★, Provenza★, Visconti★, Zenato★, Zeni.

LUIGI BOSCA *Mendoza, Argentina* Old family-owned winery that constantly delights with the unexpected, whether red, white, sparkling or dessert wine. The La Linda range offers excellent value for everyday drinking. At estate level the Malbec★, sparkling Brut Nature★, Pinot Noir and Riesling are the pick of the bunch. At the top end, the white blend Gala 3★★ is among Argentina's best whites, and Icono★★, a Malbec-Cabernet Sauvignon blend, is a hedonist's dream. Seriously old-vine field blends plus old-vine Chardonnay under the Los Nobles★★ label are gorgeous. Side project Viña Alicia★★ for exceptional, tiny production reds, mainly Malbec but also Nebbiolo, Petit Verdot and Cabernet Sauvignon.

LUIS FELIPE EDWARDS *Colchagua, Chile* Progressive family-owned winery that combines commercial winemaking with innovation and investment in new locations. Latest development is the LFE900 project, a stunning series of vineyards at 500–900m (1600–3000ft) above the Colchagua Valley floor – Cabernet, Syrah, Carmenère and Malbec, but also Mourvèdre, Grenache, Roussanne and Marsanne. New Marea de Leyda range (Sauvignon Blanc★★, Pinot Noir★). Also good Gran Reserva★ reds and Cabernet-dominant Doña Bernarda★.

DOM. LUNEAU-PAPIN *Muscadet Sèvre-et-Maine, Loire Valley, France* Pierre Luneau-Papin and his son, eighth-generation vigneron Pierre-Marie, make a thrilling range of seven 'cru' Muscadets from the region's rich smörgåsbord of soils: micaschist and gneiss (Pierre de la Grange★), serpentite (Terre de Pierre★), schist (Les Pierres Blanches★, Clos des Allées★, Excelsior Schistes de Goulaine★★), gneiss and granite with two micas (Le L d'Or★★), schist and micaschist (Pueri Solis★★). With age Excelsior, Pueri Solis and Le L d'Or take on a Burgundian complexity. Best years (Le L d'Or): 2010 **09** 07 05 03 99 95.

LUNGAROTTI *Torgiano DOC, Umbria, Italy* Leading, nearly sole, producer of the fine, black-cherry-flavoured Torgiano DOC. The Torgiano Riserva (Vigna Monticchio★★) is DOCG. Also makes red San Giorgio★ (Cabernet-Sangiovese) and Chardonnay Palazzi.

LUSSAC-ST-ÉMILION AC *Bordeaux, France* Much of the wine from this AC, which tastes like a lighter ST-ÉMILION, is made by the first-rate local co-op and should be drunk within 4 years of the vintage; certain properties are worth seeking out. Best producers: Barbe-Blanche★, Bel-Air,

Bellevue★, Courlat★, la Grenière, Lussac★, Lyonnat★, Mayne Blanc, La Rose Perrière. Best years: 2010 **09 08 05 03**.

LUSTAU *Jerez y Manzanilla DO, Andalucía, Spain* Specializes in supplying ♀ 'own-label' wines to supermarkets. It acquired the La Ina Fino★ brand in 2008. Quality is generally good, especially the Almacenista★★ range: very individual sherries from small, private producers.

CH. LYNCH-BAGES *Pauillac AC, 5ème Cru Classé, Haut-Médoc, Bordeaux, France* 🍷 I am a great fan of Lynch-Bages red★★★, with its almost succulent richness, its gentle texture and its starburst of flavours: all butter, blackcurrants and mint – and it is now one of PAUILLAC's most popular wines. Sadly, its price is rapidly approaching the stratospheric. Impressive at 5 years, beautiful at 10 and irresistible at 20. Second wine: Echo de Lynch-Bages (since 2008), previously Haut-Bages-Averous. Also a small amount of white wine, Blanc de Lynch-Bages★. Best years: (reds) 2010 09 08 **07** 06 05 **04 03** 02 01 **00 99 98 96 95 94 90 89**.

LYNMAR *Russian River Valley AVA, California, USA* Small producer of superb 🍷 Chardonnay★★ and Pinot Noir★★, using largely estate-grown fruit from its Quail Hill Vineyard. The gracious, supple Pinots age well. Also a peppery, cold-climate Syrah★ and elegant Pinot Noir rosé★.

FRÉDÉRIC MABILEAU *St-Nicolas-de-Bourgueil AC, Loire Valley, France* 🍷 Meticulous attention to detail and a gentle handling regime yield ST-NICOLAS-DE-BOURGUEIL (Les Rouillères★, Les Coutures★★, Éclipse★★) and BOURGUEIL (Racines★) of startling fruit purity and finesse. A white SAUMUR★★ and ANJOU BLANC (maiden vintages 2007 and 2009) attest to Frédéric's passion for Chenin Blanc. ANJOU Cabernet Sauvignon also new in 2007. Certified organic with effect from 2009. Best years: (top reds) (2011) 10 **09 08 07** 06 05 **04 03** 02 01

LE MACCHIOLE *Bolgheri, Tuscany, Italy* The late Eugenio Campolmi made 🍷 this one of the leading quality estates of the new Tuscany, and his widow Cinzia is keeping up high standards. Mainstay is Paleo Rosso★★, a pure Cabernet Franc. Best known wine is the Merlot Messorio★★, while Scrio★★ is one of the best Syrahs in Italy. Best years: (2011) (10) 09 08 **07 06 04 03 01 00 99**.

MÂCON AC *Mâconnais, Burgundy, France* The basic Mâconnais AC, but most 🍷 whites in the region are labelled under the superior MÂCON-VILLAGES AC. Rarely exciting. Mâcon Blanc, especially, is a rather expensive basic quaffer. Drink young.

MÂCON-VILLAGES AC *Mâconnais, Burgundy, France* There is a sea of ♀ modestly priced and often modest wines under this appellation, which covers 26 villages. Co-ops still dominate production, but these days a handful of growers make more exciting wines from individually named villages such as Mâcon-Lugny and Mâcon la Roche Vineuse. Best villages: Bussières, Chaintré, Chardonnay, Charnay, Clessé, Cruzille, Davayé, Igé, Lugny, Prissé, la Roche Vineuse, Uchizy, Verzy. Best producers: D & M Barraud★★, A Bonhomme★★, Bret Brothers★★, Deux Roches★, la Greffière★★, Guffens-Heynen★★, A & J Guillot★★, Guillot-Broux★★, LAFON★, Maillet★, Jean Manciat★, O Merlin★★, Michel★, Pauget★, Rijckaert★, Robert-Denogent★★, Saumaize-Michelin★, Valette★, VERGET★★, J-J Vincent★. Best years: (2011) 10 **09**. See also VIRÉ-CLESSÉ.

MACULAN *Breganze DOC, Veneto, Italy* Fausto Maculan makes an impressive 🍷 range under the BREGANZE DOC, led by Cabernet-Merlot blend Fratta★★ and Cabernet Palazzotto★, along with excellent reds★★ and whites★★ from the Ferrata vineyards. Even more impressive are sweet

Torcolato★★ and outstanding Acininobili★★★, made mainly from botrytized Vespaiolo grapes.

MADEIRA DOC *Madeira, Portugal* The holiday island of Madeira seems an unlikely place to find a serious wine. However, Madeiras are very serious wines indeed and the best can survive to a great age. Modern Madeira was shaped by the oïdium epidemic of the 1850s, which wiped out the vineyards, and phylloxera, which struck in the 1870s. Replantation was with hybrid, non-*vinifera* vines greatly inferior to the 'noble' and traditional Malvasia (or Malmsey), Boal (or Bual), Verdelho and Sercial varieties. There are incentives to replant the hybrids with European varieties, but progress is slow, and most of the replantations are of the red Tinta Negra Mole. The typically burnt, tangy taste of inexpensive Madeira comes from *estufagem* (heating in huge vats), but modern controls give better flavours than used to be possible. The best wines are aged naturally in the subtropical warmth. All except dry wines are fortified early on and may be sweetened with fortified grape juice before bottling. Basic 3-year-old Madeira is made mainly from Tinta Negra Mole, whereas higher-quality 10-year-old, 15-year old and vintage wines (from a single year, aged

in cask for at least 20 years) tend to be made from 1 of the 4 'noble' grapes. Colheita is an early-bottled vintage Madeira, which can be released after 5 years in wood (7 years for Sercial). Best producers: BARBEITO, Barros e Souza, H M Borges, HENRIQUES & HENRIQUES, Justino's Madeira Wines, MADEIRA WINE COMPANY, Pereira d'Oliveira.

MADEIRA WINE COMPANY *Madeira DOC, Madeira, Portugal* This company (now back under the control of the Blandy family) ships more than half of all Madeira exported in bottle, under brand names such as Blandy's, Cossart Gordon, Leacock's. Big improvements have taken place in 5-, 10- and 15-year-old wines, including a tasty 5-year-old (a blend of Malvasia and Bual) called Alvada★. Vintage wines★★★ are superb. Specially blended 'early release' colheita wines are tangy and complete.

MADIRAN AOP *South-West France* The tannic Tannat grape is the mainstay of this macho appellation, whose growers are at last coming to terms with the market demand for easier, fruity reds. Several producers use new oak and micro-oxygenation, or *microbullage* – bubbling tiny amounts of oxygen through the wine, either during fermentation or during barrel aging – to soften their wines. Best producers: AYDIE★★, Barréjat★, BERTHOUMIEU★★, Bouscassé★★, Capmartin★★, Chapelle Lenclos★★, Clos Baste★★, du Crampilh★, LABRANCHE-LAFFONT★★, Laffitte-Teston★, MONTUS★★, Pichard★, PLAIMONT, Viella★. Best years: (2011) 10 09 08 **06 05 04 02 01**.

VINOS DE MADRID DO *Madrid region, Spain* The southern part of the Madrid region has sprung to life with some well-equipped wineries that have pioneered the rediscovery of old, unappreciated vineyards, particularly on the granite soils of the Gredos mountains to the west, with Garnacha and the white Albillo Real grapes, but also on the limestone hills to the east, with Garnacha and the white Malvar. Best producers: 4 Monos, VinosAmbiz, Ricardo Benito, Bernabeleva★, Comando G★, Jeromín★, Licinia, Marañones★★, El Regajal★, El Rincón★, Tagonius.

CH. MAGDELAINE★ *St-Émilion Grand Cru AC, 1er Grand Cru Classé, Bordeaux, France* Dark, rich, aggressive wines, yet with a load of luscious fruit and oaky spice. In lighter years the wine has a gushing, easy, tender fruit and can be enjoyed at 5–10 years. Owned by the quality-conscious company of MOUEIX. Best years: 2010 09 08 **06 05 04 03 01 00 99 98 96 95 90**.

MAIPO *Chile* Historic heart of the Chilean wine industry and increasingly encroached upon by Chile's capital, Santiago. Cabernet is king and many premium-priced reds come from here, but warming conditions are pushing vineyards higher into the Cordilleras. Best producers: ALMAVIVA★★★, Antiyal★★, CARMEN★★, CONCHA Y TORO★★, COUSIÑO MACUL★, DE MARTINO★★, Domus Aurea (Peñalolén★), HARAS DE PIRQUE★★, PÉREZ CRUZ★, SANTA CAROLINA★, SANTA RITA★, UNDURRAGA★, Viñedo Chadwick★★★.

MAJELLA *Coonawarra, South Australia* The Lynn family are long-term grapegrowers turned successful winemakers. A trademark lush, sweet vanillin oakiness to the reds is always balanced by dense, opulent fruit. The profound Malleea★★★ (Cabernet-Shiraz) is the flagship, while the Cabernet Sauvignon★★★ (a succulent, fleshy cassis bomb) and Shiraz★★ are almost as good and very reasonably priced; the Musician★★ (Cabernet-Shiraz) is rich but deliciously drinkable.

MÁLAGA DO *Andalucía, Spain* A curious blend of sweet wine, alcohol and juices; production is dwindling. The best are intensely nutty, raisiny and caramelly. A 'sister' appellation, Sierras de Málaga, includes non-fortified wines. Best producers: Cortijo Los Aguilares★★, Gomara★, López Hermanos★★, Jorge Ordóñez★★, Telmo RODRIGUEZ★, Friedrich Schatz★.

CH. MALARTIC-LAGRAVIÈRE★★ *Pessac-Léognan AC, Cru Classé de Graves, Bordeaux, France* A change of ownership in 1997 and massive investment in the vineyard and cellars have seen a considerable improvement here since the 98 vintage. Now one of Pessac-Léognan's most reliable properties. The tiny amount of white★★ is made from a majority of Sauvignon Blanc (80%) and is immediately delicious, and then softens after 3–4 years into a lovely nutty wine. Best years: (reds) 2010 09 08 **07 06 05 04 03 02 01 00 99 98**; (whites) 2010 09 08 07 06 05 04 03 02 01.

MALBEC A red grape, rich in tannin and flavour, from South-West France. The major ingredient in CAHORS wines, where it is also known as Auxerrois or Cot; it is also planted in the LOIRE, as Cot. Successful in Chile and especially in Argentina, where it produces lush-textured, ripe, perfumed, damsony reds. In California and New Zealand it sometimes appears in BORDEAUX-style blends. In South Africa and Australia it is used both in blends and for varietal wines.

CH. MALESCOT ST-EXUPÉRY★★ *Margaux AC, 3ème Cru Classé, Haut-Médoc, Bordeaux, France* Once one of the most scented, exotic reds in Bordeaux, a model of perfumed MARGAUX. In the 1980s Malescot lost its reputation and some vintages (1985 excepted) were pale, dilute and uninspired, but since 2000 it has rediscovered that glorious cassis and violet perfume which makes it one of Bordeaux's most delightful reds. Best years: 2010 09 08 **07 06 05 04 03 02 01 00 99 98 96**.

HERDADE DA MALHADINHA NOVA *Alentejo DOC, Portugal* 2003 arrival on the ALENTEJO wine scene, owned by the Soares family (who also have an Algarve wine-shop chain). Ultra-modern winery and wines, making Monte da Peceguinha red★, white and rosé, and top wines, Malhadinha Tinto★★, Malhadinha Branco★ and Marias da Malhadinha★★.

MALVASIA This grape, of Greek origin, is widely planted, especially in Italy, and is found in many guises, both white and red. In Friuli and in Croatia, as Malvasia Istriana, it produces light, mildly fragrant wines of considerable youthful charm, while in TUSCANY, UMBRIA and the rest of central Italy it is widely used to make innocuous dry and sweet whites. On the islands, Malvasia is used in rich dry or sweet wines in Bosa and Cagliari (in SARDINIA) and in Lipari off the coast of SICILY to make really tasty, apricotty sweet wines. As a black grape, Malvasia Nera is blended with Negroamaro in PUGLIA and occasionally with Sangiovese in CHIANTI. Variants of Malvasia grow in Spain's CATALUÑA and CANARY ISLANDS and mainland Portugal. On the island of MADEIRA it produces sweet fortified wine, usually known by its English name, Malmsey.

MAN O'WAR *Waiheke Island, Auckland, North Island, New Zealand* Wealthy businessman John Spencer is the largest vineyard (and land) owner on WAIHEKE ISLAND; almost 90 small pockets of vines are spread over his 1800ha (4500-acre) estate. After a slow start they're now making some cracking wines, including tangy, salty Sauvignon★, a heroic Valhalla Chardonnay★★ and even more powerful Ironclad Cabernet★, plus strong, spicy Dreadnought Syrah★★. Expect some ★★★ in the near future. Best years: (reds) 2010 09 08 07.

LA MANCHA DO *Castilla-La Mancha, Spain* Spain's vast central plateau is Europe's biggest delimited wine area. Since 1995, DO regulations have allowed for irrigation and the planting of higher quality grape varieties, including Macabeo (Viura), Verdejo, Chardonnay, Cabernet Sauvignon, Petit Verdot, Merlot and Syrah – and also banned new plantings of the white Airén grape. Whites are rarely exciting but are often fresh and attractive (see AIRÉN). Reds can be light and fruity, or richer. Best producers: Ayuso, Campos Reales★, Vinícola de Castilla (Castillo de Alhambra, Señorío de Guadianeja), Finca Antigua★, Fontana★, Muñoz (Blas Muñoz★), Casa de la Viña.

MANCHUELA DO *Castilla-La Mancha, Spain* Higher, hillier, cooler than its huge neighbour La MANCHA. The international recognition gained since 2000 by Finca Sandoval has helped a small band of private producers and quality-conscious co ops to get a foothold in foreign markets. Best producers: Altolandón★, Cien y Pico★, Finca Sandoval★★, Monegrillo, Ponce★★, San Antonio Abad, Vega Tolosa, Vitis Natura, Vitivinos.

DOM. ALBERT MANN *Alsace AC, Alsace, France* Powerful, flavoursome and ageworthy wines from a range of Grand Cru vineyards, including intense, mineral Rieslings from Furstentum★★ and Schlossberg★★ and rich Furstentum Gewurztraminer★★. Impressive range of Pinot Gris culminates in some astonishingly concentrated Sélections de Grains Nobles★★★. Basic wines are stylish and reliable. Best years: (Grand Cru Riesling) (2011) (10) (09) 08 07 05 01 00 98 97.

MANZANILLA See Jerez y Manzanilla.

MARANGES AC *Côte de Beaune, Burgundy, France* AC right at the southern tip of the CÔTE DE BEAUNE. Slightly tough red wines of medium depth which are rightly mainly sold as CÔTE DE BEAUNE-VILLAGES. Some growers are beginning to show their mettle. Less than 5% of production is white. Best producers: Bachelet-Monnot, Chevrot★, Contat-Grangé★, Cyrot-Buthiau★, DROUHIN. Best years: (reds) (2011) 10 09 08 07 05 03 02.

MARCASSIN *Sonoma County, California, USA* Helen Turley focuses on cool-climate Chardonnay and Pinot Noir of incredible depth and restrained power. Single-vineyard Chardonnays (Alexander Mountain Upper Barn,

Three Sisters Vineyard, Marcassin Vineyard) and Pinot Noirs (Marcassin Vineyard, Three Sisters Vineyard, Blue Slide Vineyard) are very difficult to obtain but can rank ★★★.

MARCHE *Italy* Adriatic region best known for VERDICCHIO but producing increasingly good reds from Montepulciano and Sangiovese, led by CONERO/ROSSO CONERO and ROSSO PICENO, and also from the curiously aromatic, indigenous Lacrima di Morro d'Alba. Good international varietals such as Cabernet, Chardonnay and Merlot under the Marche IGT or Esino DOC, as well as blends with the native grapes. Best of the reds are Boccadigabbia's Akronte★★ (Cabernet), Oasi degli Angeli's Kurni★★ (Montepulciano), Monte Schiavo's Adeodato★★ (Montepulciano), Umani Ronchi's Pelago★★ (Montepulciano-Cabernet-Merlot), La Monacesca's Camerte★★ (Sangiovese-Merlot) and Le Terrazze's Chaos★★ (Montepulciano-Merlot-Syrah).

MARCILLAC AOP *South-West France* Curranty, dry red wines (and a little rosé), made from a local grape, Mansois. The reds are rustic but full of soft fruit flavour and should be drunk at 2–5 years old. Best producers: Costes★, Cros/Philippe Teulier★, Marcillac-Vallon co-op, Jean-Luc Matha★.

MAREMMA TOSCANA *Tuscany, Italy* IGT Maremma Toscana, which covered varietals like Sangiovese and Merlot in the province of Grosseto, has recently been upgraded to DOC. Historically Maremma was a loose geographical term for the parts of Tuscany mainly, but not necessarily, southern that lie on the coast.

MARGARET RIVER *Western Australia* Planted on the advice of agronomist John Gladstones from the late 1960s, this coastal region quickly established its name as a leading area for Cabernet, with marvellously deep, BORDEAUX-like structured reds. Now Chardonnay, concentrated and opulent, vies with Cabernet for top spot, but there is also fine grassy Semillon, often blended with citrus-zest Sauvignon. Increasingly popular Shiraz provides the occasional gem. Best

producers: Amelia Park★, Arlewood, Ashbrook★, Brookland Valley★★, CAPE MENTELLE★★★, Chapman Grove, Clairault★, CULLEN★★★, Devil's Lair★★, Edwards, Evans & Tate★★, Fermoy Estate★, Fraser Gallop★★, Gralyn★, HOWARD PARK★★, Juniper Estate★★, LEEUWIN ESTATE★★★, Lenton Brae★, McHenry Hohnen★, MOSS WOOD★★★, PIERRO★★, SANDALFORD★★, Stella Bella★★, VASSE FELIX★★★, VOYAGER ESTATE★★, Watershed, Woodlands★★, Woodside Valley★, Xanadu★★. Best years: (Cabernet-based reds) 2010 09 **08 07** 05 **04** 03 01 **00** 99 98 96 95.

MARGAUX AC *Haut-Médoc, Bordeaux, France* AC centred on the village of Margaux. Gravel banks dotted through the vineyards mean the wines are rarely heavy and should have a divine perfume after 7–12 years. Best producers: (Classed Growths) Boyd-Cantenac★, BRANE-CANTENAC★★, Cantenac Brown★, Dauzac★, FERRIÈRE★★, Giscours★, ISSAN★★, KIRWAN★, LASCOMBES★, MALESCOT ST-EXUPÉRY★★, MARGAUX★★★, PALMER★★★, PRIEURÉ-LICHINE★, RAUZAN-SEGLA★★, Tertre★; (others) ANGLUDET★, Deyrem Valentin, Eyrins★, la Gurgue★, Labégorce-Zédé★, Monbrison★, SIRAN★, Vincent. Best years: 2010 09 08 06 **05 04** 02 01 **00** 98 96 95.

CH. MARGAUX★★★ *Margaux AC, 1er Cru Classé, Haut-Médoc, Bordeaux, France*
Frequently the most seamless, flawless wine in the Médoc, so much so that I occasionally pine for a few faults to add a little frisson of unpredictability. Also some delicious white, Pavillon Blanc★★, from Sauvignon Blanc (100%), but it must be the most expensive BORDEAUX AC wine by a mile. Second wine: Pavillon Rouge★★. Best years: (reds) 2010 09 08 07 06 05 **04** 03 02 01 00 99 98 96 95 90 89 88 86; (whites) **2010 09 08 07 06 05 04 02 01 00.**

MARIAH *Mendocino Ridge AVA, Mendocino County, California, USA* Boutique Zinfandel producer with a vineyard at 600m (2000ft) overlooking the Pacific Ocean. The wines have cherry fruit and naturally high acidity. Mariah Vineyard Zinfandel★★ is the flagship. A tiny amount of fruit-forward Syrah★. Best years: (Zinfandel) (2008) 07 **06 05 02 01 00.**

MARIMAR ESTATE *Sonoma County, California, USA* The sister of Spanish winemaker Miguel TORRES has established her own winery in the cool Green Valley region of RUSSIAN RIVER VALLEY, only a few miles from the Pacific Ocean. She specializes in Chardonnay and Pinot Noir, the best of which are from the Don Miguel Vineyard: the Chardonnay★★ is intense but restrained in a European way, and likely to age gracefully to fascinating maturity at 10 years old. Acero★★ is a fine, minerally, unoaked version. Recent vintages of full-flavoured Pinot Noir★★ are the best yet. Best years: (Pinot Noir) (2009) **08 07 06 05 03 02 01.**

MARLBOROUGH *South Island, New Zealand* This spectacularly successful wine region only planted its first commercial vines in 1973. Marlborough is now home to well over half the country's vines. Its 2 main vineyard areas are Wairau Valley and AWATERE VALLEY, and its long, cool and relatively dry ripening season, cool nights and free-draining stony soils are the major assets. Its snappy, aromatic Sauvignon Blanc first brought the region fame worldwide. Fine-flavoured Chardonnay, steely Riesling, elegant traditional-method fizz and luscious botrytized wines are other successes. Pinot Noir is now establishing a strong regional identity. Best producers: ASTROLABE★★, BRANCOTT★, CLOUDY BAY★★, The Crossings★, Dog Point★★, Drylands★, Forrest★, Foxes Island★, FRAMINGHAM★★, FROMM★★, HUNTER'S★, JACKSON ESTATE★, Lawson's Dry Hills★, Mahi★, MORTON ESTATE★, Mount Riley★, Nautilus★, SAINT CLAIR★, SERESIN★★, Stoneleigh★, VILLA MARIA★★, WITHER HILLS, YEALANDS★. Best years: (Chardonnay) **2010 09 07 06 05;** (Pinot Noir) **2010 07 06 05 04;** (Sauvignon Blanc) (2011) **10 09 07 06 05.** See also AWATERE VALLEY.

MARQUÉS DE CÁCERES *Rioja DOCa, Rioja, Spain* Crisp, aromatic, modern whites★ and rosés★, and fleshy, fruity reds (Reservas★) with the emphasis on aging in bottle, not barrel. There is also a luxury red, Gaudium★. Best years: (reds) (2008) 07 **06 05 04 03** 01 99 98 96 95 94 92.

MARQUÉS DE GRIÑÓN *Castilla-La Mancha, Spain* From his estate at Malpica, near Toledo, now with its own Dominio de Valdepusa DO, Carlos Falcó (the eponymous Marqués) produces some impressive if superripe wines: the basic Caliza, Dominio de Valdepusa Cabernet Sauvignon★, Petit Verdot★, Syrah★ and Eméritus★★, a blend of the 3 varieties. AAA★★, the estate's top wine, changes varietal make-up depending on the vintage. Best years: (Eméritus) 2005 04 **03 02** 01 00 99 98.

MARQUÉS DE MURRIETA *Rioja DOCa, Rioja, Spain* This RIOJA bodega faithfully preserves the traditional style of long aging, but typical time in barrel has been reduced by a third. The ornately labelled Castillo Ygay

Gran Reserva★★ is less forbidding than in the past. There's a more international-styled, oaky cuvée, Dalmau★★. Whites are dauntingly oaky but age brilliantly; reds are packed with savoury mulberry fruit. Best years: (reds) 2007 **06** 05 **04** 03 01 00 99 96 95 94 92 91 89 87 85.

MARQUÉS DE RISCAL *Rioja DOCa, País Vasco and Rueda DO, Castilla y León, Spain* A producer that has restored its reputation for classic pungent RIOJA reds (Reserva, Gran Reserva★★). Expensive Barón de Chirel★★, with significant Cabernet content, is made only in selected years. Attractively aromatic RUEDA whites★. Best years: (Barón de Chirel) **2006** 01 96 95 94.

MARSALA DOC *Sicily, Italy* Fortified wines, once as esteemed as sherry or Madeira. A taste of an old Vergine (unsweetened) Marsala, fine and complex, will show why. Today most is sweetened and used for cooking, though some are fighting back, notably DE BARTOLI★★, Florio (Baglio Florio★, Terre Arse★), Pellegrino (Soleras★, Riserva 1962★).

MARSANNAY AC *Côte de Nuits, Burgundy, France* Village almost in Dijon, originally known for its pleasant but quite austere rosé. Reds are much better: light, but frequently one of Burgundy's more fragrant wines. Whites mostly dull. Best producers: Audoin★, P Charlopin★★, B CLAIR★★, Fournier★★, Geantet-Pansiot★★, JADOT★, MÉO-CAMUZET★, D MORTET★★, Pataille★★, J & J-L Trapet★. Best years: (reds) (2011) 10 **09** 08 05.

MARSANNE Undervalued white grape yielding rich, honeysuckle-scented, nutty wines in the northern Rhône (notably HERMITAGE, CROZES-HERMITAGE, ST-JOSEPH and ST-PÉRAY), often with the more scented, lively Roussanne. Generally drink young, except the Hermitage, which can mature for decades. Also increasingly successful in southern Rhône, PIC ST-LOUP and other LANGUEDOC wines, and performs well in California and Australia, especially at Mitchelton and TAHBILK. As Ermitage, it produces some good wines, sweet as well as dry, in Swiss VALAIS.

MARTINBOROUGH/WAIRARAPA *North Island, New Zealand* A cool, dry climate, free-draining soil and a passion for quality are this region's greatest assets. Mild autumn weather promotes intense flavours balanced by good acidity: top Pinot Noir and complex Chardonnay, intense Cabernet blends in favourable years, full Sauvignon Blanc and honeyed Riesling. Best producers: (Martinborough) ATA RANGI★★, CRAGGY RANGE★★, DRY RIVER★★, Escarpment★★, Gladstone★★, Kusuda★★, MARTINBOROUGH VINEYARD★★, Murdoch James★, Nga Waka★, PALLISER ESTATE★★; (Wairarapa) Johner★, Matahiwi★, Schubert★★. Best years: (Pinot Noir) (2011) 10 **09** 08 07 06 03.

MARTINBOROUGH VINEYARD *Martinborough, North Island, New Zealand* Famous for Pinot Noir★★ but also makes impressive Chardonnay★, spicy Riesling★, creamy Pinot Gris★ and luscious botrytized styles★★ when vintage conditions allow. Good vineyard sites and sensitive winemaking have produced a string of very elegant wines. Best years: (Pinot Noir) (2011) 10 **09** 08 07 06 03.

MARTÍNEZ BUJANDA *Rioja DOCa, País Vasco, Spain* This family-owned firm, known for producing some of the best modern RIOJA, was split in two in 2007: Jesús Martínez-Bujanda keeps the Valdemar winery in Rioja, while Carlos and Pilar Martínez-Bujanda retain the Finca Valpiedra and Finca Antigua estates and the Cosecheros y Criadores wine company. Valpiedra wines are revitalized since 2006 vintage, with crisp whites and rosés, lush young-vines red Cantos★ and scented, refined Reserva★★.

MARYLAND *USA* Maryland's Boordy Vineyards was the pioneer in French hybrid varieties, but the state fell behind its neighbour VIRGINIA in growth and quality, despite sharing a similar moderate climate and benefits of the Blue Ridge Mountains. However, things have improved dramatically since the turn of the century as new wineries have implemented rigorous vineyard standards. Boordy replanted nearly 20ha (50 acres) of vines in a bold move to boost quality – the first fruits of this effort were harvested in 2010. Best producers: Black Ankle, Boordy, Knob Hill, Slack, Sugarloaf Mountain.

DOM. DU MAS BLANC *Banyuls AC, Roussillon, France* Run by the Parcé family, this estate makes great traditional BANYULS, specializing in the *rimage* (early-bottled vintage) style (La Coume★★). Also Banyuls Hors d'Age★★ from a solera laid down in 1955, plus a range of Jean-Michel Parcé COLLIOURES★★. Best years: (2011) 10 09 08 **07 06 05 04**.

MAS BRUGUIÈRE *Pic St-Loup AC, Languedoc, France* L'Arbouse★ has rich, spicy Syrah character, while La Grenadière★★ develops buckets of black fruit and spice after 3 years. Super-cuvée Le Septième★★ (seventh generation) blends Mourvèdre with some Syrah. Calcadiz is an easy-drinking red; aromatic, fruity, refreshing white Les Mûriers★ is based on Roussanne. Best years: (reds) (2011) 10 **09 08 07 06 05**.

MAS LA CHEVALIÈRE *IGP Pays d'Oc, Languedoc, France* State-of-the-art winery created by Chablis producer LAROCHE in the early 1990s. Wines include La Croix Chevalière★, a blend of Syrah, Merlot and Grenache, and Mas la Chevalière Rouge★ from the estate vineyard. Now part of the Jeanjean group. Best years: (2011) **10 09 08 07 06 05**.

MAS DE DAUMAS GASSAC *IGP de l'Hérault, Languedoc, France* Aimé Guibert and now his son Samuel have proved over 20 years that the HÉRAULT, previously associated with cheap table wine, can produce fine, ageworthy wines. Others have now overtaken his quality. The lush, scented white★★ (Viognier-Chardonnay-Petit Manseng-Chenin) is best of all; Cabernet Sauvignon-based red★ is firm and tannic, with more concentrated Cuvée Emile Peynaud★★. Good cheaper blend Grande Réserve de Gassac. Sweet Vin de Laurence★★ is a triumph. Best years: (reds) 2010 09 08 **07 06 05 04 03 02 01 00**.

MAS DOIX *Priorat DOCa, Cataluña, Spain* The Doix and Llagostera families own some extraordinary old Garnacha and Cariñena vineyards, which provide the grapes for some equally impressive wines. Doix Vinyes Velles★★★ is probably the first of the new generation PRIORATS to reach the heights of the pioneers such as CLOS ERASMUS, CLOS MOGADOR and Alvaro PALACIOS' L'Ermita. Best years: (2009) 08 07 **06** 05 **04 03 02 01**.

BARTOLO MASCARELLO *Barolo DOCG, Piedmont, Italy* Run by the late Bartolo Mascarello's daughter Maria Teresa since the early 1990s. The BAROLO★★★ remains a blend of vineyards in the traditional manner. The Dolcetto★ and Barbera★ can need a little time to soften. Best years: (Barolo) (2011) (10) (09) 08 **07 06 04 01 00 99 98 97 96 95 90 89 88 86 85**.

GIUSEPPE MASCARELLO *Barolo DOCG, Piedmont, Italy* The old house of Giuseppe Mascarello (now run by grandson Mauro) is renowned for dense, vibrant Dolcetto d'Alba (Bricco★), intense Barbera (Codana★★) and fine LANGHE Nebbiolo★, but the pride of the house is BAROLO from the superb south-west-facing Monprivato★★★ vineyard in Castiglione Falletto. A little is now produced as a Riserva, Cà d'Morissio★★★, in top years. Villero★ is a lesser but still important cru. Best years: (Monprivato) (2011) (10) (09) 08 07 06 **04 01 00 99 98 97 96**.

MASI *Veneto, Italy* Large private firm, one of the driving forces in VALPOLICELLA. Campofiorin★ (effectively if not legally a *ripasso* Valpolicella) is worth looking out for, as is AMARONE (Mazzano★★, Campolongo di Torbe★★). Valpolicella's Corvina grape is also used in red blend Toar★; Osar★ is made from a local grape, Oseleta, rediscovered by Masi. The wines of Serègo Alighieri★ are also produced by Masi. Best years: (Amarone) (2011) (10) 09 **08 07 06 04 03 01 00 97**.

MASTROBERARDINO *Campania, Italy* For many years this family firm flew the flag almost alone for CAMPANIA in southern Italy, though it has now been joined by numerous others. Best known for red TAURASI★★ and white Greco di Tufo★ and Fiano di Avellino★. Best years: (Taurasi Radici) (2011) (10) (09) 08 07 **06 05 04 01 99 97 96 95 90**.

MATANZAS CREEK *Bennett Valley AVA, Sonoma County, California, USA* Complex, zesty Sauvignon Blanc★ is taken seriously here; Chardonnay★★ is rich and toasty. Merlot★★ has silky, mouthfilling richness. Journey Chardonnay★★ and Merlot★★ are opulent but pricey. Owned by Jackson Family Wines. Best years: (Chardonnay) (**2009**) 08 07 06 05 04 03 02; (Merlot) (2008) **07 06 05 04 03 02 00 99**.

MATETIC VINEYARDS *San Antonio, Chile* Matetic has been making high-quality organic wines from SAN ANTONIO – especially under the EQ label – since it burst on to the scene in 2001. Exceptional, concentrated and scented Syrah★★ is the star, but there's also a fleshy Pinot Noir★, juicy Sauvignon Blanc★ and refreshing Coastal Sauvignon★.

MATUA VALLEY *Auckland, North Island, New Zealand* Once exciting winery; more commercial since becoming part of Foster's (now Treasury). Top wines have dramatically improved with the release of classy Single Vineyard Wairau Sauvignon Blanc★ from MARLBOROUGH, Dartmoor Chardonnay★★ and Matheson Merlot★, Cabernet Sauvignon★ and Grenache-Syrah-Viognier★ from HAWKES BAY, Cromwell and Bannockburn Pinot Noir★ from CENTRAL OTAGO. Second label: Shingle Peak. Best years: (Hawke's Bay reds) 2010 **09 08 07 04**.

CH. MAUCAILLOU★ *Moulis AC, Haut-Médoc, Bordeaux, France* Maucaillou shows that you don't have to be a Classed Growth to make high-quality claret. Expertly made by the Dourthe family, it is soft but classically flavoured. It is accessible early on but ages well for 10–12 years. Best years: 2010 **09 08 06 05 04 03 02 00 98 96 95 90**.

MAULE *Chile* The most southerly region of Chile's CENTRAL VALLEY, with wet winters and a large day/night temperature difference. Nearly 30% of Chile's vines are planted here, with nearly 10,000ha (25,000 acres) of Cabernet Sauvignon. Merlot does well on the cool clay soils, and there is some tasty Carmenère, Cabernet Franc and Syrah. Whites are mostly Chardonnay and Sauvignon Blanc. A new community of producers has recently been redefining the region's identity, especially using old-vine Carignan in the Cauquenes sub-region, and there's a general feeling that Maule's old 'bulk' mentality is giving way to a belief that it has some of Chile's best mature vineyards, just waiting to be discovered. An association called Vigno was formed in 2011 to promote non-irrigated Carignan wines from Maule. Best producers: J Bouchon, CONCHA Y TORO★,

DE MARTINO★★, O FOURNIER★★, Gillmore★★, La Reserva de Caliboro★★, Odfjell★, Palo Alto, TORRES★★, VALDIVIESO★.

MAURICIO LORCA *Mendoza, Argentina* Mauricio Lorca is making groundbreaking, frequently oak-free wines from serious *terroir* in MENDOZA. The Opalo★ (can be ★★) range, all unoaked, are intensely pure *terroir* expressions. The Fantasía★ varietal range, especially Malbec, is fresh and perfumed. The pioneering Malbrontes★ label blends Malbec with Torrontés into a scented, fruit bomb.

MAURO *Castilla y León, Spain* Mariano García made his name as VEGA SICILIA's winemaker for 30 years and now successfully leads his family's estate. Wines include Crianza★★, Vendimia Seleccionada★★ and Terreus★★★. Best years: (2009) 08 07 **06** 05 **04** 03 02 01 00 99 98 97 96 95 94.

MAURY AC *Roussillon, France* A *vin doux naturel*, mainly from Grenache Noir. It can be made in either a young, fresh style (vintage) or the locally revered and delicious old *rancio* style. Maury Sec is a new appellation for table wines. Best producers: la Coume du Roy/Maurydoré★, Mas Amiel★★, Maury co op★, Pla del Fount★★, la Pléiade★.

MAUZAC The traditional basis of white GAILLAC and BLANQUETTE DE LIMOUX. Fresh and green-appley when picked early, it loses its acidity on the vine and can then produce luscious sweet wines.

MAXIMIN GRÜNHAUS *Grünhaus, Mosel, Germany* Great wine estate, with two top vineyards, Abtsberg and Herrenberg, both of monastic origin. Dr Carl von Schubert makes chiefly dry and medium-dry wines of great subtlety. In good vintages the Ausleses and other top wines are ★★★ and are among the most long-lived white wines in the world. Best years: (2011) 10 09 08 **07 06** 05 **04** 03 02 99 97 95 94 93.

MAZIS-CHAMBERTIN, MAZOYÈRES-CHAMBERTIN See CHAMBERTIN AC.

McLAREN VALE *South Australia* Sunny maritime region south of Adelaide, producing superb full-bodied wines from Shiraz, Grenache and Cabernet. White Fiano, Savagnin, Marsanne, Roussanne, Verdelho and Viognier are now making their mark, along with chubby Chardonnay. More than 60 small wineries, plus big boys Accolade (formerly Constellation) and Treasury. Best producers: Cascabel, CHAPEL HILL★★, CLARENDON HILLS★★, Coriole★, D'ARENBERG★★, FOX CREEK★★, Gemtree★, HARDYS★★, Kangarilla Road★, Maxwell★, Geoff MERRILL★, Mitolo, Noon★, Oliver's Taranga★★, S C PANNELL★★, Paxton, Pirramimma, PRIMO ESTATE★★, RockBare, Scarpantoni, Shingleback★, Tatachilla★, Ulithorne★, Willunga 100★, WIRRA WIRRA★★, Woodstock.

McWILLIAM'S *Riverina, New South Wales, Australia* Large family winery, with interests right across Australia. HUNTER VALLEY offers classic bottle-aged Mount Pleasant Semillons (Elizabeth★★, Lovedale★★★), buttery Chardonnays★ and Shiraz from Rosehill★, Old Paddock & Old Hill★★ and Maurice O'Shea (★★★ in best years). Classy sweet Morning Light Botrytis Semillon★★ and Liqueur Muscat★★ from RIVERINA, and good table wines from HILLTOPS Barwang★ vineyard. McWilliam's also owns Lillydale in the YARRA VALLEY (Chardonnay★★), BRAND'S in COONAWARRA, and Evans & Tate in MARGARET RIVER. Best years: (Lovedale Semillon) (2011) (10) (09) (08) **07** 06 05 **04** 03 02 01 00 99 98 97 96 95 94 87 86 84 83.

MÉDOC AC *Bordeaux, France* The Médoc peninsula north of Bordeaux on the left bank of the Gironde river produces a good fistful of the world's most famous reds. These are all situated in the HAUT-MEDOC, the southern, more gravelly half of the area. The Médoc AC, for reds only, covers the northern part. The best vineyards are on gravel outcrops from the ever-present clay and, with global warming, are producing increasingly attractive, earthy but juicy wines. Best at 3–5 years old. **Best producers: Bournac★, Cardonne, Escurac★, Goulée★, les Grands Chênes★, Greysac★, L'Inclassable★, Labadie, Loudenne, Lousteauneuf★, les Ormes-Sorbet★, Patache d'Aux★, POTENSAC★★, Preuillac★, Ramafort★, Rollan de By★, la Tour de By★, la Tour Haut-Caussan★, Tour St-Bonnet★, Vieux-Robin★. Best years: 2010 09 08 06 05 04 03 01.**

MEEREA PARK *Hunter Valley, New South Wales, Australia* Brothers Rhys and Garth Eather specialize in single-vineyard, old-vine HUNTER VALLEY Semillon and Shiraz; they are helping breathe new life into the region. Hell Hole Semillon★★ is vibrant, lemony and restrained when young, gently toasty, mineral and delicious with age. Alexander Munro Shiraz★★ seamlessly integrates fruit, oak and tannins, and pure brambly flavours.

MEERLUST *Stellenbosch WO, South Africa* Venerable estate on the up. Cabernet★★ is supple yet vibrant, Merlot★ plush and finely textured; together with Cabernet Franc they achieve harmony and complexity in Rubicon★, one of the Cape's first BORDEAUX blends (first vintage in 1980). Pure, silky Pinot Noir★ completes the red range. Also elegant, fresh Chardonnay★. **Best years: (Rubicon) 2008 07 06 05 04 03 01; (Chardonnay) 2011 10 09 08 07 06 05.**

ALPHONSE MELLOT *Sancerre AC, Loire Valley, France* Biodynamic producer with an equal focus on white and red SANCERRE, made with obsessive attention to detail by Alphonse 'Junior', the 19th generation of the family. Other than unoaked white cuvée La Moussière★, wines come exclusively from old vines and show a fine balance of fruit and oak. Satellite★★ is from 60-year-old vines. White Edmond★★ and red and white Génération XIX★★ are outstanding and reward keeping. Also makes IGP Les Pénitents: aromatic, fruity but fine Chardonnay and increasingly serious Pinot Noir★. **Best years: (Edmond white) (2011) 10 09 08 07 06 05 04 03 02 01.**

CHARLES MELTON *Barossa Valley, South Australia* Leading light in hand-crafted Shiraz, Grenache and Mourvèdre in the BAROSSA. Fruity Grenache rosé Rose of Virginia★★ is arguably Australia's best; RHÔNE-blend Nine Popes★★, heady, sumptuous Grenache★★, smoky Shiraz★★ and Sparkling Red★★ have all attained cult status. Cabernet Sauvignon is ★★ at best. Two single-site Shiraz: fleshy, blackberry-pastille Grains of Paradise★★ from the Barossa Valley, and fragrant, elegant, brambly Voices of Angels★★ from the Eden Valley. **Best years: (Nine Popes) (2010) 09 05 04 03 02 01 99 98 96 95 94 91 90.**

MENCIA Known as Jaen in Portugal's DÃO, this Iberian grape gives characterful, intensely fruity, dense, attractively funky red wines in Spain's emerging BIERZO, Ribeira Sacra and Valdeorras (GALICIA) regions. **Best producers: (Spain) Castro Ventosa, Dominio do Bibei, Descendientes de J Palacios, Lusia, Raúl PÉREZ, Picos de Cabariezo, Pittacum, Dominio de Tares, Tilenus, D Ventura; (Portugal) Quinta das Maias.**

MENDEL *Mendoza, Argentina* The core of this estate is an 80-year-old 25ha (60-acre) vineyard planted to Malbec, Cabernet Sauvignon and Petit Verdot; non-estate fruit is sourced for some cuvées. Mendel Malbec★ is deep, fresh and perfumed; Finca Remota★★ Malbec seamlessly combines power and elegance; the top cuvée Unus★★ (Cabernet Sauvignon-Malbec) is fine boned, glossy and intense. An old-vine Semillon★ is magical and intriguing. Best years: (reds) 2009 08 **07 06**.

MENDOCINO COUNTY *California, USA* The northernmost county of the North Coast AVA. It includes cool-climate ANDERSON VALLEY, excellent for sparkling wines and a little Pinot Noir, and the warmer Redwood Valley AVA, with good Zinfandel and Cabernet. Coro is a stylish Zinfandel-based blend made by numerous Mendocino wineries. Best producers: Black Kite★, Brutocao★, Claudia Springs★, FETZER, Goldeneye★, Graziano, HANDLEY★★, Husch, Lazy Creek★, Littorai★, McDowell Valley★, NAVARRO★★★, Pax★, ROEDERER ESTATE★★, Saracina★, SCHARFFENBERGER CELLARS★. Best years: (reds) 2009 **07 06 05 04 03 01 00**.

MENDOCINO RIDGE AVA *California, USA* One of the most unusual AVAs in California. Mendocino Ridge starts at an altitude of 365m (1200ft) on the timber-covered mountaintops of western MENDOCINO COUNTY. Because of the topography, the AVA is non-contiguous: rising above the fog, the vineyards are commonly referred to as 'islands in the sky'. Currently only 30ha (75 acres) are planted, primarily with Zinfandel. Best producers: Edmeades★, Greenwood Ridge★, MARIAH★, STEELE★★.

MENDOZA *Argentina* The most important wine province in Argentina, accounting for around 80% of the country's wine. Situated in the eastern foothills of the Andes, Mendoza's bone-dry climate produces powerful, high-alcohol reds.The region is complex and vast. Altitude is the key: the higher the vineyards the higher the quality, so the Uco Valley, especially Tupungato, hard against the Andes, has the freshest whites and the raciest reds. Ancient areas to the south and west of Mendoza city, including Vistalba, Agrelo, Perdriel, Luján de Cuyo and Las Compuertas, are famed for profound, intense, structured reds. Best producers: ACHAVAL FERRER★★, Alpamanta★, ALTOS LAS HORMIGAS★, Andeluna, Bressia★★, CATENA★★, Clos de Chacras★, Clos de los Siete★, COBOS★★, CUVELIER LOS ANDES★★, DOMINIO DEL PLATA★★, DOÑA PAULA★★, FABRE MONTMAYOU★, Finca Sophenia, O FOURNIER★★, Kaiken★, Krontiras★, LUIGI BOSCA★, Lurton★, MAURICIO LORCA★, MENDEL★★, NORTON★, PASCUAL TOSO★, PULENTA★, Salentein, TERRAZAS DE LOS ANDES★★, TRAPICHE★★, ZUCCARDI★.

MENETOU-SALON AC *Loire Valley, France* Attractive, chalky-clean Sauvignon whites and cherry-fresh Pinot Noir reds and rosés from west of SANCERRE. Best producers: R Champault, Chatenoy★, Chavet★, J-P Gilbert★, N Girard, P Jacolin, J Mellot, H Pellé★, J-M Roger★, J Teiller★, Tour St-Martin★.

MÉO-CAMUZET *Vosne-Romanée, Côte de Nuits, Burgundy, France* Super quality estate. New oak barrels and luscious, rich fruit combine in superb wines, which age well. CLOS DE VOUGEOT★★★, RICHEBOURG★★★ and CORTON★★ are grandest, along with the VOSNE-ROMANÉE Premiers Crus (aux Brulées★★★, Cros Parantoux★★★, les Chaumes★★). Fine NUITS-ST-GEORGES aux Boudots★★ and aux Murgers★★; also some less expensive *négociant* wines. Best years: (2011) 10 09 08 **07** 06 05 **03 02** 01 99 96 95 91.

MERCUREY AC *Côte Chalonnaise, Burgundy, France* The red from this village is usually pleasant and strawberry-flavoured, sometimes rustic, and can take some aging. Not much white, but I like its buttery, even spicy, taste. Best at 3–4 years old. Best producers: (reds) FAIVELEY★, Hasard★, M Juillot★, Lorenzon★★, F Raquillet★, Rodet★, de Suremain★★, Theulot-Juillot★, de Villaine★★; (whites) Ch. de Chamirey★, FAIVELEY (Clos Rochette★), M Juillot★, O LEFLAIVE★. Best years: (reds) (2011) 10 **09 08 07 05**.

213

MERLOT See pages 216–17.

GEOFF MERRILL *McLaren Vale, South Australia* Geoff Merrill makes a nicely judged bottle-aged Reserve Cabernet★ in a light, early-picked style, Reserve Shiraz★ (Henley★★), Chardonnay★ (Reserve★★) and moreish unoaked, yet ageworthy, Bush Vine Grenache★★.

MERRYVALE *Napa Valley AVA, California, USA* A Chardonnay powerhouse (Silhouette★★, CARNEROS★★, Starmont★★), but reds are not far behind, with BORDEAUX-blend Profile★★ and juicy NAPA VALLEY Merlot★★. Best years: (Chardonnay) **2009 08 07 06 05 04 03 02 01**.

MEURSAULT AC *Côte de Beaune, Burgundy, France* The biggest and most popular white wine village in the CÔTE D'OR. There are no Grands Crus, but a whole cluster of Premiers Crus, of which Perrières, Charmes and Genevrières stand out. The general standard is better than in neighbouring PULIGNY and village Meursault from named vineyard sites (such as Tesson, Tillets) is particularly exciting and good value. These pale gold wines are lovely to drink young, but ought to age for 5–8 years. Virtually no Meursault red is now made. Best producers: M Ampeau★★, P Boisson★★, BOUCHARD PÈRE & FILS★★, M Bouzereau★★, V Bouzereau★, Boyer-Martenot★★, Coche-Bizouard★★, COCHE-DURY★★★, Darnat★, Deux MONTILLE★, DROUHIN★★, A Ente★★★, J-P Fichet★★, Henri Germain★, GIRARDIN★★, Grux★, JADOT★★, P Javillier★★, Antoine Jobard★★, Rémi Jobard★★, LAFON★★★, Latour-Labille★, Matrot★★, Mikulski★★, P MOREY★★, J Prieur★★, ROULOT★★★. Best years: (2011) 10 09 **08 07 06 05 04 02**.

MEYER-NÄKEL *Dernau, Ahr, Germany* Of the handful of top growers in the AHR, Werner Näkel has the best track record for structured yet elegant Spätburgunder (Pinot Noir)★★ from 3 Grosses Gewächs sites. Consistent if pricey wines. Best years: (2010) 09 08 **07 06 05 04 03**.

CH. MEYNEY★ *St-Estèphe AC, Haut-Médoc, Bordeaux, France* One of the most reliable ST-ESTÈPHEs, producing broad-flavoured wine with dark, plummy fruit. Second wine: Prieur de Meyney. Best years: 2010 09 08 **06 05 04 03 02 01 00 99 98 96 95 94 90 89**.

PETER MICHAEL WINERY *Sonoma County, California, USA* British-born Sir Peter Michael has turned a country retreat into an impressive winery known for its very expensive small-batch wines. Les Pavots★★ is the estate red BORDEAUX blend (L'Espirit des Pavots★★ is also good). Top Chardonnays include Mon Plaisir★★, Cuvée Indigène★, Ma Belle-Fille★★ and La Carrière★. Also Le Caprice Pinot Noir★. Best years: (Les Pavots) (2009) 08 **07 06 05 04 03 02 01 00 99 97 96 95 94 91 90**.

MILLTON *Gisborne, North Island, New Zealand* Biodynamic vineyard whose top wines include the powerful Clos de Ste Anne Chardonnay★, lush Riverpoint Viognier★, Opou Vineyard Riesling★ and complex barrel-fermented Chenin Blanc★★. Chardonnays and Rieslings both age well. Deliciously savoury Syrah★★ and good, gentle Pinot Noir★. Excellent Clos Samuel sweet Viognier★★. Best years: (whites) **2010 09 07 05**.

MINER FAMILY VINEYARDS *Oakville AVA, California, USA* Dave Miner has 32ha (80 acres) planted on a ranch 300m (1000ft) above the OAKVILLE valley floor. Highlights include yeasty, full-bodied Chardonnay★ (Oakville Ranch★★, Wild Yeast★★) as well as intense Merlot★★ and Cabernet Sauvignon★★ that demand a decade of aging. Also a stylish Viognier★★ and a striking Rosé★ from purchased fruit.

MINERVOIS AC *Languedoc, France* Attractive, mostly red wines from north-east of Carcassonne, made mainly from Syrah, Carignan and Grenache. The local co-ops produce good, juicy, quaffing wine at reasonable prices, but the best wines are made by the estates: full of ripe, red fruit and pine-dust perfume, for drinking young. It can age, especially if a little new oak has been used. A village denomination and Cru du Languedoc, La Livinière, covering 6 superior communes, can be appended to the Minervois label. These wines can be particularly scented and fine, if not overripened. Overripening, however, is a concern. Best producers: (reds) Aires Hautes★, Ch. Bonhomme★, Borie de Maurel★, CLOS CENTEILLES★, Pierre Cros★, Fabas★, la Grave, Oupia, Oustal Blanc★, Primo Palatum, Pujol, St-Jacques d'Albas, Ste-Eulalie★, Senat★, TOUR BOISEE★, Villerambert-Julien★. Best years: (2011) **10 09 08 07 06 05 04**.

CH. LA MISSION-HAUT-BRION★★★ *Pessac-Léognan AC, Cru Classé de Graves, Bordeaux, France* 2008 was the year I finally accepted the true brilliance of La Mission. In the past I had often found the wine long on power but short on grace, but the owners laid on a vertical tasting reaching way back into the 1920s and the general quality level was majestic, with the vintages since 1990 actually outshining the admittedly beautiful earlier wines. Muscularity and richness combined with depth and fragrance is quite a challenge, but La Mission meets it triumphantly. Best years: (reds) 2010 09 08 07 06 05 **04 03 02 01 00 98 96 95 94 90 89 88 85**; (whites) 2010 **09** (formerly LAVILLE-HAUT-BRION).

MISSION HILL *Okanagan Valley VQA, British Columbia, Canada* The winery has expanded its operations and hired consultant Michel Rolland to help Kiwi winemaker John Simes – not that he needed any help – craft some of the most noteworthy wines from the OKANAGAN VALLEY. Excellent Perpetua Chardonnay★★, SLC Sauvignon-Semillon★ and Pinot Blanc Reserve★ are joined by SLC Merlot★ and Reserve Cabernet Sauvignon, Pinot Noir and Shiraz★, and a red BORDEAUX-style blend, Oculus★★.

MITCHELL *Clare Valley, South Australia* Jane and Andrew Mitchell turn out ageworthy Watervale Riesling★★ and a classy barrel-fermented Semillon★★. GSM★ (Grenache-Sangiovese-Mourvedre) is an unwooded, heady fruit bomb. Peppertree Shiraz★★ and Sevenhill Cabernet Sauvignon★ are plump, chocolaty and satisfying. Aged release McNicol Riesling★ and Shiraz★★ show the cellaring potential of CLARE's best.

MITTELRHEIN *Germany* Small 460ha (1135-acre) wine region, adjoining the RHEINGAU. Two-thirds of the wine here is Riesling, but the vineyard area is shrinking as the sites are steep and difficult to work. The best growers (like Toni JOST★, Müller★, Ratzenberger★ and Weingart★★), clustered around Bacharach and Boppard, make wines of a striking mineral tang and dry, fruity intensity. Best years: (2011) **10 09 08 07 06 05**.

MOËT & CHANDON *Champagne AC, Champagne, France* Owned by LVMH, Moët & Chandon dominates the CHAMPAGNE market (more than 25 million bottles a year), and has become a major producer of sparkling wine in California, Argentina, Brazil and Australia too. Non-vintage exhibits distressing unreliability – some barely acceptable recent releases. The vintage rosé★★ can show a rare Pinot Noir floral fragrance. The de luxe cuvée, Dom Pérignon★★★, can be one of the greatest Champagnes of all, but you've got to age it for a number of years after release or you're wasting your money; but, of course, most of the people who drink it have a different view of money to you or me. The winemaker changed in 2005, but so far I don't see any great change in quality or consistency. Best years: 2004 **03 02 00 99 98 96 95 90 88 86 85 82**.

MERLOT

Red wine without tears. That's the reason Merlot has vaulted from being merely Bordeaux's red wine support act, well behind Cabernet Sauvignon in terms of class, to being the red wine drinker's darling, planted like fury all over the world. It is able to claim some seriousness and pedigree, but – crucially – can make wine of a fat, juicy character mercifully low in tannic bitterness, which can be glugged with gay abandon almost as soon as the juice has squirted from the press. Yet this doesn't mean that Merlot is the jelly baby of red wine grapes. Far from it. Some of Bordeaux's greatest wines are based on it.

WINE STYLES

Bordeaux Merlot The great wines of Pomerol and St-Émilion, on the right bank of the Dordogne, are largely based on Merlot and the best of these – for example, Château Pétrus, which is virtually 100% Merlot – can mature for 20–30 years. In fact, there is more Merlot than Cabernet Sauvignon planted throughout Bordeaux, and I doubt if there is a single red wine property that does not have some growing, because the variety ripens early, can cope with cool conditions and is able to bear a heavy crop of fruit. In a cool, damp area like Bordeaux, Cabernet Sauvignon cannot always ripen, so the soft, mellow character of Merlot is a fundamental component of the blend, even in the best Cabernet-dominated Médoc estates, imparting a supple richness and approachability to the wines. Go-ahead areas like Blaye and Castillon depend on it.

Other European regions The south of France has briskly adopted the variety, producing easy-drinking, fruit-driven wines, but in the hot Languedoc the grape often ripens too fast to express its full personality and can seem a little simple, even raw-edged, unless handled well. Italy has long used very high-crop Merlot to produce light quaffers in the north, particularly in the Veneto, though today Friuli and Alto Adige make fuller styles. There are some impressive examples from Tuscany, and it can be found as far south as Sicily. The Swiss canton of Ticino is often unjustly overlooked for its intensely fruity, oak-aged versions. Eastern Europe has the potential to provide fertile pastures for Merlot: so far the most convincing, juicy styles have come from Croatia, Hungary and Bulgaria; the younger examples are almost invariably better than the old. In Spain, Merlot only really succeeds in cool sites.

New World Youth is also important in the New World, nowhere more so than in Chile. Chilean Merlot, often blended with Carmenère, has leapt to the front of the pack of New World examples with gorgeous garnet-red wines of unbelievable crunchy fruit richness that cry out to be drunk virtually in their infancy. California Merlots often have more serious pretensions, but the nature of the grape is such that its soft, juicy quality still shines through. Cooler sites in Washington State have produced some impressive wines, and the east coast of the US has good examples from places such as Long Island. In South Africa, Merlot on the right sites is showing improvement, and in New Zealand the warm, dry conditions of Hawkes Bay and Waiheke Island are producing classic styles. Australia seems to find Merlot problematic (winemakers believe things will improve as better clones become more widespread), but there are some fine exceptions from cooler areas, including some surprisingly good fizzes – red fizzes, that is!

BEST PRODUCERS

France

Bordeaux (St-Émilion) ANGELUS, BEAU-SEJOUR BECOT, CANON, Clos Fourtet, La Mondotte, PAVIE, PAVIE-MACQUIN, TERTRE-ROTEBOEUF, TROPLONG-MONDOT, VALANDRAUD; *(Pomerol)* le BON PASTEUR, Clinet, la CONSEILLANTE, l'EGLISE-CLINET, l'EVANGILE, la FLEUR-PETRUS, GAZIN, Hosanna, LATOUR-A-POMEROL, PETRUS, le PIN, TROTANOY; *(Languedoc)* Magellan.

Other European Merlots

Italy (Friuli) Livio FELLUGA; *(Tuscany)* Castello di AMA (l'Apparita), Castelgiocondo (Lamaione), Le MACCHIOLE (Messorio), ORNELLAIA (Masseto), Petrolo, San Giusto a Rentennano, TUA RITA (Redigaffi); *(Lazio)* FALESCO; *(Sicily)* PLANETA.

Spain (Vino de la Tierra de Castilla) Pago del Ama.

Switzerland Gialdi (Sassi Grossi), Daniel Huber, Stucky, Tamborini, Christian Zündel.

New World Merlots

USA (California) ARROWOOD, BERINGER, CHATEAU ST JEAN, MATANZAS CREEK, MERRYVALE, NEWTON, Pahlmeyer, SHAFER; *(Washington)* ANDREW WILL, LEONETTI, LONG SHADOWS (Pedestal), WOODWARD CANYON; *(New York)* BEDELL, LENZ.

Australia BRAND'S, CLARENDON HILLS, COLDSTREAM HILLS, Elderton, Irvine, PARKER COONAWARRA ESTATE, TAPANAPPA, Tatachilla, YALUMBA (Heggies).

New Zealand CRAGGY RANGE, Esk Valley, FROMM, C J PASK, Sacred Hill (Broken Stone), TRINITY HILL, VILLA MARIA.

South Africa Bein, Shannon, THELEMA, VEENWOUDEN, VERGELEGEN.

Chile CARMEN, CASABLANCA (Nimbus Estate), CONCHA Y TORO, CONO SUR (20 Barrels), Gillmore, LAPOSTOLLE (Cuvée Alexandre).

MARKUS MOLITOR *Bernkastel-Wehlen, Mosel, Germany* Dynamic estate with fine vineyards throughout Middle MOSEL. Brilliant Riesling Auslesen, often ★★★, and probably the best, if costly, Spätburgunder (Pinot Noir)★ from the Mosel. Best years: (2011) 10 09 **08 07 06 05 04 03 02**.

MONBAZILLAC AOP *South-West France* BERGERAC's best-known sweet wine, nowadays seriously rivalling all but the best SAUTERNES and at a fraction of the price. They can age for 10 years and more. Best producers: l'ANCIENNE CURE★★, Bélingard (Blanche de Bosredon★), Grande Maison★★, Haut-Bernasse★, Haut-Montlong (Grande Cuvée), les Hauts de Caillevel★★, Pécoula, La Rayre, Theulet★, TIRECUL LA GRAVIÈRE★★★, VERDOTS★★. Best years: (2011) 10 **07 06 05 04 03 00**.

CH. MONBOUSQUET★ *St-Émilion Grand Cru AC, Grand Cru Classé, Bordeaux, France* Gérard Perse, owner of Ch. PAVIE, transformed this struggling estate into one of ST-ÉMILION's 'super-crus'. The reward was promotion to Grand Cru Classé in 2006. Rich, voluptuous and very expensive, the wine is drinkable from 3–4 years but will age longer. Also a plush white Monbousquet★ (BORDEAUX AC). Best years: 2010 09 **08 07 06 05 04 03 02 01 00 99 98 96**.

ROBERT MONDAVI *Napa Valley, California, USA* A Californian institution, best known for regular Cabernet Sauvignon, Reserve Cabernet★ and dense, gravelly To Kalon★★ Cabernet. Regular★ and Reserve★★ Pinot Noir are velvety smooth, supple wines. For many years the Mondavi signature white was Fumé Blanc★ (Sauvignon Blanc), but in recent years Chardonnay★ (Reserve★★) has overtaken it. The Robert Mondavi Winery is now part of Constellation's Icon Estates portfolio; Mondavi's lower-priced 'lifestyle' lines, Private Selection and Woodbridge (from Lodi in the CENTRAL VALLEY), are promoted separately. Recent vintages of Cabernet Sauvignon have become far weightier than any that ever appeared under the late Bob Mondavi's stewardship. Best years: (Cabernet Sauvignon Reserve) 2008 **07 06 05 04 03 02 01 00 99 98 97 96**.

MONSANTO *Chianti Classico DOCG, Tuscany, Italy* Fabrizio Bianchi, with his daughter Laura, makes a range of Sangiovese-based wines topped by the CHIANTI CLASSICO Riserva Il Poggio★★★, a traditional-style single-vineyard cru, remarkable for its discreet austerity and need of bottle age. Chianti Classico Riserva★★★ is equally excellent. Best years: (2011) (10) (09) **08 07 06 04 01 99**.

MONT TAUCH *Fitou AC, Languedoc-Roussillon, France* A big, quality-conscious and pioneering co-op producing a large range of wines, from good gutsy FITOU★ and CORBIÈRES to rich MUSCAT DE RIVESALTES★, MAURY and light but gluggable vin de pays. Top wines: Les Quatre★, Les Douze★. Best years: (Les Douze) (2011) **10 09 08 07 06**.

MONTAGNE-ST-ÉMILION AC *Bordeaux, France* A ST-ÉMILION satellite with rather good red wines. The wines are normally ready to drink in 4 years but age quite well in their slightly earthy way. Best producers: Beauséjour★, Calon★, La Couronne, Croix Beauséjour★, Faizeau★, Gachon★, Haut Bonneau, Maison Blanche, Montaiguillon★, Rocher Corbin★, Roudier, Teyssier, Vieux-Ch.-St-André★. Best years: 2010 **09 08 05 03 01**.

MONTAGNY AC *Côte Chalonnaise, Burgundy, France* Wines from this CÔTE CHALONNAISE village can be rather lean, but are greatly improved now that some producers are giving their wines a touch of new oak. Generally best with 2–3 years' bottle age. Best producers: S Aladame★, BOUCHARD PÈRE ET FILS★, BUXY★, Davenay★, FAIVELEY, Louis LATOUR★, O LEFLAIVE★, A Roy★, J Vachet★. Best years: (2011) 10 **09**.

MONTALCINO See BRUNELLO DI MONTALCINO DOCG.

MONTANA See BRANCOTT.

MONTECARLO DOC *Tuscany, Italy* Distinctive reds (Sangiovese with Syrah) and whites (Trebbiano with Sémillon and Pinot Grigio) from Lucca. Also non-DOC Cabernet, Merlot, Pinot Bianco, Roussanne and Vermentino. Best producers: Buonamico★, Carmignani★, Montechiari★, La Torre★, Wandanna★. Best years: (reds) (2011) (10) 09 **08 07 06 04**.

MONTEFALCO DOC *Umbria, Italy* Good Sangiovese-based Montefalco Rosso is outclassed by dense, massive Sagrantino di Montefalco DOCG (dry) and glorious sweet red Sagrantino Passito from dried grapes. Best producers: Adanti★, Antonelli★, Caprai★★ (25 Anni★★★), Colpetrone★★, Perticaia★★, Scacciadiavoli★★. Best years: (Sagrantino) (2011) (10) (09) 08 07 06 **04 01 00 99 98 97**.

MONTEPULCIANO Grape grown mostly in eastern Italy (unconnected with TUSCANY's Sangiovese-based wine VINO NOBILE DI MONTEPULCIANO). In ABRUZZO, can produce deep-coloured, fleshy, brambly, spicy wines with moderate tannin and acidity, which also helps to keep the rosé wines (called Cerasuolo) fresh. Besides Montepulciano d'Abruzzo DOC, it is used in CONERO DOCG and ROSSO PICENO DOC in the MARCHE and also in UMBRIA, Molise and PUGLIA. Best producers: (Montepulciano d'Abruzzo) Cataldi Madonna★, Contesa★★, Cornacchia★, Filomusi Guelfi★, Illuminati★, Marramiero★★, Masciarelli★★, Montori★, Umani Ronchi★, La Valentina★, Valentini★★★. Best years: (2011) 10 **09 07 06 04 01**.

MONTEREY COUNTY *California, USA* Large CENTRAL COAST county south of San Francisco in the Salinas Valley, boasting a mix of small estates and vast plantations (one even has a drag strip in the middle of it). The most important AVAs are Monterey, Arroyo Seco, Chalone, Carmel Valley and Santa Lucia Highlands. Best grapes are Chardonnay, Riesling and Pinot Blanc, with some good Cabernet Sauvignon and Merlot in Carmel Valley and superb Pinot Noir in the Santa Lucia Highlands in the cool middle of the county. Best producers: Belle Glos★★, Bernardus★★, Capiaux★, Chalone★, Estancia★, Jekel★, Joullian★★, Mer Soleil★, MORGAN★★, Roar★, TALBOTT★★, Testarossa★, Ventana★★.

MONTES *Colchagua, Chile* One of Chile's pioneering wineries in the modern era, notable for development of top-quality vineyard land on the steep Apalta slopes of COLCHAGUA and the virgin country of Marchíhüe out toward the Pacific. Chardonnay★ (Alpha★★) and Sauvignon Blanc★ (Leyda★★) are good and fruit-led; all the reds are more austere and need bottle age. Top-of-the-line Cabernet-based Montes Alpha M★★ is consistently good. The most impressive reds, however, are Montes Alpha Syrah★★, Montes Folly★★ and a vibrant, scented Carmenère called Purple Angel★★. The Outer Limits range includes Sauvignon Blanc★ and Pinot Noir★ from a new cool-climate estate on the ACONCAGUA coast near picturesque Zapallar. Also Outer Limits CGM (Carignan-Grenache-Mourvèdre) from Apalta vineyards in Colchagua.

MONTEVERTINE *Tuscany, Italy* Based in the heart of CHIANTI CLASSICO, Montevertine is famous for its non-DOC wines, particularly Le Pergole Torte★★★. This was among the first of the so-called 'super-Tuscans' made solely with Sangiovese, and it remains one of the best. A little Canaiolo is included in the excellent Montevertine Riserva★★. Best years: (Le Pergole Torte) (2011) (10) 09 08 **07 06 04 01 00 99 97 95**.

MONTHELIE AC *Côte de Beaune, Burgundy, France* Attractive, mainly red wine village lying halfway along the CÔTE DE BEAUNE behind MEURSAULT and VOLNAY. The wines generally have a lovely cherry fruit and make pleasant drinking at a good price. Best producers: BOUCHARD PÈRE ET FILS, COCHE-DURY★, Darviot-Perrin★, P Garaudet★, R Jobard★, LAFON★★, G ROULOT★★, de Suremain★. Best years: (reds) (2011) 10 **09 07 06 05**.

MONTILLA-MORILES DO *Andalucía, Spain* Sherry-style wines that used to be sold almost entirely as lower-priced sherry substitutes. However, the wines *can* be superb, particularly the top dry amontillado, oloroso and rich Pedro Ximénez styles. Best producers: Alvear★★, Aragón, Gracia Hermanos, Pérez Barquero★★, Toro Albalá★★.

DOM. DE MONTILLE *Côte de Beaune, Burgundy, France* Brought to fame by *Mondovino* star Hubert de Montille, and now run by son Étienne. Consistent producer of stylish reds that demand aging, from VOLNAY (especially Mitans★★, Champans★★, Taillepieds★★) and POMMARD (Pezerolles★★, Rugiens★★). Also top PULIGNY-MONTRACHET Le Cailleret★★★. Expensive. From 2005 outstanding VOSNE-ROMANÉE Malconsorts★★★. Étienne and his sister have also started a *négociant* business, Deux Montille★. Best years: (red) (2011) 10 09 08 **07** 05 **03 02 99 96 90 88**.

MONTLOUIS-SUR-LOIRE AC *Loire Valley, France* On the opposite bank of the Loire to VOUVRAY, Montlouis makes similar styles (dry, medium, sweet and CHAMPAGNE-style fizz). New blood is injecting a healthy dose of ambition. Non-dosage gently sparkling *pétillant originel* wines are well worth seeking out. Still wines ideally need 3–5 years, particularly the sweet *moelleux*. Best producers: Alex-Mathur★, L Chatenay★, F CHIDAINE★★, Delétang★, L & B Jousset★, des Liards★/Berger, Le Rocher des Violettes★, F Saumon★, Taille aux Loups★★/BLOT. Best years: (sec) (2011) 10 **08 07**; (moelleux) 2011 **09 05 04 03 02 01 99 97 96**.

MONTRACHET AC *Côte de Beaune, Burgundy, France* This world-famous Grand Cru straddles the boundary between the villages of CHASSAGNE-MONTRACHET and PULIGNY-MONTRACHET. Wines have a unique combination of concentration, finesse and perfume: white Burgundy at its most sublime. Chevalier-Montrachet, immediately

above it on the slope, yields slightly leaner wine that is less explosive in its youth, but good examples become ever more fascinating with age. Best producers: BOUCHARD★★★, M Colin★★★, DROUHIN (Laguiche)★★★, LAFON★★★, Louis LATOUR★★, Dom. LEFLAIVE★★★, LEROY★★★, Prieur★★★, RAMONET★★★, Dom. de la ROMANÉE-CONTI★★★, SAUZET★★, Thénard★★. Best years: (2011) 10 09 08 07 06 05 **04 02 00 99 97 95 92 90 89**.

MONTRAVEL AOP *South-West France* All styles and colours can be found here at the western end of the BERGERAC region. Crisp and dry whites, medium-sweet whites from Côtes de Montravel AOP and ultra-sweet from Haut-Montravel AOP. Montravel reds are in a modern oak-aged style while less ambitious reds from the area are sold as Bergerac or Côtes de Bergerac. Best producers: du Bloy★★, Jonc Blanc★★, Laulerie, Libarde, Mallevieille, Masburel★, Moulin Caresse★, Pique-Sègue, Puy-Servain★★, le Raz. Best years: (sweet) 2010 **07 06 05 04 03 00**; (red) (2011) 10 09 **06 05 04 02**.

CH. MONTROSE★★ *St-Estèphe AC, 2ème Cru Classé, Haut-Médoc, Bordeaux, France* A leading ST-ESTÈPHE property, once famous for its dark, brooding wine that would take around 30 years to reach its prime. In the late 1970s and early 80s the wines became lighter, but Montrose has now returned to a powerful style, though softer than before. Recent vintages have been extremely good. Sold in 2006; lots of investment and greater precision in the wines. Second wine: la Dame de Montrose. Best years: 2010 09 08 07 06 05 **04 03 02 01 00 99 98 96 95.**

CH. MONTUS *Madiran AOP, South-West France* Alain Brumont clings to a precarious lead in MADIRAN, largely because of his media-flair, his keen ambition and his ability to dodge all manner of financial disasters. He is said to own 15% of the entire Madiran *vignoble*. His all-Tannat, hefty oak-aged reds Montus (Prestige★★) and Bouscassé (Vieilles Vignes★★) have white counterparts: PACHERENC DU VIC-BILH★★, dry and in varying degrees of sweetness. Best years: (red) (2011) 10 09 **06 05 04 01 00**; (sweet white) (2010) 09 **07 06 05.**

MORELLINO DI SCANSANO DOCG *Tuscany, Italy* Morellino is the local name for Sangiovese in the south-west of TUSCANY. The wines, which used to be agreeable gluggers, are becoming more serious under DOCG, not necessarily to their advantage. Best producers: E Banti★, Belguardo★/ FONTERUTOLI, Cecchi★, Lohsa★/POLIZIANO, Il Macereto★, Mantellassi★, Morellino di Scansano co-op★, Moris Farms★★, Podere 414★, Poggio Argentaria★★, Le Pupille★★. Best years: (2011) (10) 09 **08 07 06 04 01 00 99.**

MOREY *Chassagne-Montrachet, Côte de Beaune, Burgundy, France* Albert, Bernard, Jean-Marc, Marc, Michel Morey-Coffinet, Thomas and Vincent – how do you sort them out? Try CHASSAGNE-MONTRACHET Premiers Crus Baudines (Thomas), Embrazées (Vincent), Chenevottes (Jean-Marc) or Virondot (Marc), all ★★. There's also Pierre Morey for excellent MEURSAULT★★ and Pierre-Yves COLIN-Morey.

MOREY-ST-DENIS AC *Côte de Nuits, Burgundy, France* Morey has 5 Grands Crus (CLOS DES LAMBRAYS, CLOS DE LA ROCHE, CLOS ST-DENIS, CLOS DE TART and a share of BONNES-MARES) as well as some very good Premiers Crus. Basic village wine is sometimes unexciting, but from a quality grower the wine has good fruit and acquires an attractive depth as it ages. A tiny amount of startling nutty white wine is also made. Best producers: Pierre Amiot★, Arlaud★★, Dom. des Beaumont★, CLAIR★★, David Clark★, DUJAC★★, A Jeanniard★★, Dom. des Lambrays★★, H Lignier★★★, Lignier-Michelot★★, H Perrot-Minot★★, Ponsot★★, ROUMIER★★, ROUSSEAU★★, Sérafin★★, Taupenot-Merme★★. Best years: (2011) 10 09 08 **07** 06 05 **03 02 00 99 98 96 95 90.**

MORGAN *Monterey County AVA, California, USA* Founded in 1982 by Dan Morgan Lee and his wife Donna, this Santa Lucia Highlands pioneer specializes in Pinot Noir and Chardonnay. The winery's single-vineyard Pinots from the Double L★★, Rosella's★★ and Garys'★★ vineyards combine ripe fruit, structure and elegance. The winery also makes a fresh, appealing unoaked Chardonnay called Metallico★. Best years: (Pinot Noir) 2010 09 **08 07 06 05 04.**

MORGENHOF *Stellenbosch WO, South Africa* A 300-year-old Cape farm grandly restored and run with French flair by owner Anne Cointreau. The range spans Cap Classique sparkling to PORT styles. Best are a well-oaked, muscular Chenin Blanc★, structured Merlot and the dark-berried, supple Morgenhof Estate★, a BORDEAUX-style blend.

MORGON AC *Beaujolais, Burgundy, France* The longest-lasting of BEAUJOLAIS Crus, wines that – at their best – have delightful cherry fruit and the structure to age. Named sub-zones like Côte du Py and Javernières are considered to be the source of many of the best Morgons. There are, however, many more Morgons, made in a commercial style for early drinking, which are nothing more than a pleasant, fruity – and pricey – drink. Best producers: J-P Brun/Terres Dorées★, Domaine J-M Burgaud (Côte du Py★★), D Desvignes★, L-C Desvignes (Côte du Py★★, Voûte St Vincent★), DUBOEUF (Jean Descombes★), J Foillard★★, M Lapierre★★. Best years: (2011) **10 09**.

MORNINGTON PENINSULA *Victoria, Australia* Exciting cool-climate maritime region dotted with small vineyards. Chardonnay runs the gamut from honeyed to leafy, but increasing numbers are oatmealy and scented; Pinot Noir can be very stylish in warm years, especially from vineyards in the mild Moorooduc area. Best producers: Crittenden★, Dexter, Eldridge, Hurley★, KOOYONG★★, Main Ridge★★, Montalto, Moorooduc★★, Paradigm Hill★, PARINGA ESTATE★★, Port Phillip Estate★, Quealy, Scorpo, STONIER★, Ten Minutes by Tractor★★, T'Gallant★, Tuck's Ridge, Willow Creek★, Yabby Lake★★. Best years: (Pinot Noir) 2010 09 **08 07 06 05 04 03 02 01 00 99 98 97 95 94**.

MORRIS *Rutherglen, Victoria, Australia* Historic winery with an outstanding fortified wine portfolio. David Morris is the custodian of a store of aged fortifieds that have been with his family since 1859. He continues to make old favourites like Liqueur Muscat★★ and Tokay★★ (Old Premium★★★), 'ports', 'sherries' and robust table wines to high quality levels, especially ageworthy Durif.

DENIS MORTET *Gevrey-Chambertin, Côte de Nuits, Burgundy, France* Before his untimely death in 2006, Denis Mortet had built a brilliant reputation for his GEVREY-CHAMBERTIN (various cuvées, all ★★★) and tiny amounts of CHAMBERTIN★★★. Early vintages were deep coloured and powerful; recent years show increased finesse, a trend being continued by son Arnaud. Best years: (2011) 10 09 08 **07** 06 05 **03 02 96 95 93**.

MORTON ESTATE *Marlborough, Hawkes Bay, Bay of Plenty, Auckland, New Zealand* Founded in 1983 by Morton Brown, who built a distinctive Cape-style winery in Katikati. Now owned by John Coney, it is one of the country's larger wineries, making wine from all major regions. Top-of-the-line Black Label wines can be very good and include a full-bodied Chardonnay★★ and Merlot-Cabernet★ from HAWKES BAY, plus a stylish MARLBOROUGH Sauvignon Blanc★ and a rich, complex, vintage-dated sparkling wine. White Label wines offer excellent value, particularly Chardonnay and Pinot Gris★. Best years: (Chardonnay) **2010** 09 07 06.

GEORG MOSBACHER *Forst, Pfalz, Germany* This 18ha (45-acre) estate makes mostly dry white wines in the village of FORST. Best of all are the dry Rieslings★★ from the Forster Ungeheuer site, which are among the lushest in Germany. Delicious young, but worth cellaring. Best years: (2011) 10 09 **08 07 06 05 04 02**.

MOSCATO D'ASTI DOCG *Piedmont, Italy* Utterly beguiling, delicately scented, gently bubbling wine, made from Moscato Bianco grapes grown in the hills between Acqui Terme, Asti and Alba in north-west Italy. The DOCG is the same as for ASTI, but only select grapes go into this wine, which is frizzante (semi-sparkling) rather than fully sparkling. Drink while they're bubbling with youthful fragrance. Best producers: Araldica/Alasia★, Ascheri★, Bava★, Bera★★, Braida★, Cascina Castlèt★, La Caudrina★★, Michele Chiarlo, Giuseppe Contratto★, Coppo★, Cascina Fonda★,

Forteto della Luja★, Bruno GIACOSA★★, Icardi★, Marenco★, Beppe Marino★, La Morandina★, Marco Negri★, Perrone★★, Cascina Pian d'Or★, Saracco★★, Scagliola★, La Spinetta★★, I Vignaioli di Santo Stefano★, Gianni Voerzio★.

MOSCATO PASSITO DI PANTELLERIA DOC *Sicily, Italy* Powerful dessert wine made from the Muscat of Alexandria, or Zibibbo, grape. Pantelleria is a small island south-west of SICILY, closer to Africa than it is to Italy. The grapes are picked in mid-August and laid out in the hot sun to shrivel for a couple of weeks. They are then crushed and fermented to give an amber-coloured, intensely flavoured sweet Muscat. The wines are best drunk within 5–7 years of the vintage. Best producers: Benanti★, D'Ancona★, DE BARTOLI★★, Donnafugata (Ben Ryé★), Murana★, Nuova Agricoltura co-op★, Pellegrino.

MOSEL *Germany* A collection of vineyard areas on the Mosel and its tributaries, the Saar and the Ruwer, amounting to 9000ha (22,230 acres). The Mosel river rises in the French Vosges before forming the border between Germany and Luxembourg. In its first German incarnation in the Upper Mosel, the light, tart Elbling grape holds sway, but with the Middle Mosel begins a series of villages responsible for some of the world's very best Riesling wines: LEIWEN, TRITTENHEIM, PIESPORT, BRAUNEBERG, BERNKASTEL, GRAACH, WEHLEN, ÜRZIG and ERDEN. The wines have tremendous slatiness and an ability to blend the greenness of citrus leaves and fruits with the golden warmth of honey. Great wines are rarer between Erden and Koblenz, although WINNINGEN and Pünderich are islands of excellence. The Saar can produce wonderful, piercing wines in villages such as Serrig, Ayl, Ockfen and Wiltingen. Ruwer wines are slightly softer yet equally long-lived; the estates of MAXIMIN GRUNHAUS and KARTHÄUSERHOF are world class. Since 2007 only the name 'Mosel' is permitted on labels in place of the region's former name Mosel-Saar-Ruwer.

MOSHIN VINEYARDS *Russian River Valley, California, USA* Retired mathematics professor Rick Moshin spent 4½ years building his RUSSIAN RIVER winery, which crushed its first grapes in 2005. Today, Moshin has a strong, almost cultish, following for his brilliant Pinot Noirs★★ and a handful of other wines (Zinfandel★, Petite Sirah★, Merlot★) made in small quantities. Best years: (Pinot Noir) 2009 **08 07 06 05 04 03 02 01**.

MOSS WOOD *Margaret River, Western Australia* Seminal MARGARET RIVER winery at the top of its form. From its home vineyard come heavenly scented Cabernet★★★ needing at least 5 years to blossom, classy Chardonnay★★, pale, fragrant Pinot Noir★ and crisp, fruity but ageworthy Semillon★★. Range is expanding with excellent Ribbon Vale★★ wines (from a nearby single vineyard owned by Moss Wood), very good Cabernet-based Amy's★ and a MORNINGTON PENINSULA Pinot, added from 2008 to allow the winemakers to work with a cool-climate expression of the variety. Best years: (Cabernet) (2011) (10) 09 08 07 05 04 03 01 **00 99 98 96 95 94 91 90 85**.

J P MOUEIX *Bordeaux, France* The Moueix family runs a thriving merchant business specializing in the wines of the Right Bank, particularly POMEROL and ST-ÉMILION. Generally high quality. Also owns PETRUS, la FLEUR-PETRUS, BELAIR-MONANGE, MAGDELAINE, TROTANOY, Hosanna and others.

MOULIN-À-VENT AC *Beaujolais, Burgundy, France* Potentially the greatest of the BEAUJOLAIS Crus, taking its name from an ancient windmill that stands above Romanèche-Thorins. The granitic soil yields a majestic wine that with time can transform into a rich Burgundian style more characteristic of the Pinot Noir than the Gamay. Best producers: J-P Brun/Terres Dorées★, DUBOEUF, H Fessy, Ch. des Jacques★/JADOT, O Merlin★, Richard Rottiers (Climat Champ de Cour★), B Santé★, La Tour du Bief★/V GIRARDIN. Best years: (2011) **10 09**.

MOULIS AC *Haut-Médoc, Bordeaux, France* Small AC within the HAUT-MÉDOC. Much of the wine is excellent – delicious at 5–6 years old, though good examples can age 10–20 years – and not overpriced. Best producers: Anthonic, Biston-Brillette★, Branas-Grand-Poujeaux★, Brillette★, CHASSE-SPLEEN★, Duplessis, Dutruch-Grand-Poujeaux, Gressier-Grand-Poujeaux, MAUCAILLOU★, Moulin-à-Vent, POUJEAUX★. Best years: 2010 09 **08 06 05 03 02 01 00 96 95 90**.

MOUNT HORROCKS *Clare Valley, South Australia* Stephanie Toole has transformed this label into one of the CLARE VALLEY's best, with taut, minerally, limy Riesling★★★ from a single vineyard in Watervale; waxy, cedary Semillon★★; complex, savoury Shiraz★; velvety-textured Cabernet★ with a pure core of blackcurrant; and one of Australia's most delicious stickies (dessert wine), the Cordon Cut Riesling★★★, which shows zingy fruit character with a satisfying lush texture.

MOUNT LANGI GHIRAN *Grampians, Victoria, Australia* Part of the Rathbone group. Quintessential cool-climate Shiraz★★★ with remarkable dark plum, chocolate and pepper spice, dark, intriguing Cabernet Sauvignon★★, delightful Riesling★ and honeyed Pinot Gris★. Less expensive Cliff Edge★ and Billi Billi★. Best years: (Shiraz) (2011) (10) (09) 08 07 06 05 **04 03 99 98 97 96 95 94 93**.

MOUNT MARY *Yarra Valley, Victoria, Australia* Classic YARRA VALLEY property, using only estate-grown grapes. Dry white Triolet★★ is blended from Sauvignon, Semillon and Muscadelle; red Quintet★★ (★★★ for keen Francophiles), from Cabernet Sauvignon and Franc, Merlot, Malbec and Petit Verdot, ages beautifully. The Pinot Noir★★ is equally as good. Best years: (Quintet) (2010) 08 07 **06 05 03 01 00 99 98 97 96 95 94 93 92 91 90 88 86**.

MOUNT VEEDER AVA *Napa Valley, California, USA* Small south-west NAPA AVA with impressive, rough-hewn Cabernet Sauvignon and Zinfandel. Best producers: Chateau Potelle★, Robert Craig★★, Hess Collection★, Lagier Meredith★★, Lokoya★★, Mayacamas Vineyards, Mount Veeder Winery★, Rubissow★★. Best years: (Cabernet) 2009 08 **07 06 05 04 02 01**.

MOURVÈDRE The variety originated in Spain, where it is called Monastrell. It dominates the JUMILLA DO and also Alicante, Bullas and Yecla. It needs lots of sunshine to ripen, which is why it performs well on the Mediterranean coast at BANDOL. It is increasingly important as a source of body and tarry, pine-needle flavour in the wines of CHÂTEAUNEUF-DU-PAPE, GIGONDAS and parts of LANGUEDOC-ROUSSILLON. It is making quite a reputation in California (J Lohr Gesture and Villicana in PASO ROBLES) and Australia – where it is sometimes known as Mataro (Caillard, Hewitson, Teusner, Spinifex) – and is also starting to make its presence felt in South Africa and Chile. Best producers: (Spain) Rafael Cambra, Castaño, Casa Castillo, Juan Gil, El Nido, El Sequé.

MOUTON-CADET *Bordeaux AC, Bordeaux, France* The most widely sold red BORDEAUX in the world was created by Baron Philippe de Rothschild in the 1930s. Blended from the entire Bordeaux region, the wine has always been undistinguished – and never cheap – but I have to admit quality is on the up. Also a bright breezy white, rosé, and Réserve GRAVES, MÉDOC, ST-EMILION and SAUTERNES.

CH. MOUTON-ROTHSCHILD★★★ *Pauillac AC, 1er Cru Classé, Haut-Médoc, Bordeaux, France* Baron Philippe de Rothschild died in 1988, having raised Mouton from a run-down Second Growth to its promotion to First Growth in 1973, and a reputation as one of the greatest wines in the world. It can still be the most magnificently opulent of the great MÉDOC reds, but inexcusable inconsistency frequently makes me want to downgrade it. Recent vintages (since 2004) have been back on top form. When young, it is rich and indulgent on the palate, aging after 15–20 years to a complex bouquet of blackcurrant and cigar box. There is also a white wine, Aile d'Argent. Second wine: Le Petit-Mouton. **Best years:** (red) 2010 09 08 **07** 06 05 04 **03 02 01 00 99 98 97 96 95 90 89 88**.

MOVI *Chile* Movimiento de Viñateros Independientes is a group of some of the smallest, independent, *terroir*-focused winemakers in Chile, representing a trend toward a more *garagiste* philosophy that not long ago was an anathema in Chile. Quality varies hugely but some members, such as Bravado, Gillmore, Erasmo, Polkura and VON SIEBENTHAL, have real style and potential.

MUDGEE *New South Wales, Australia* Small region neighbouring HUNTER VALLEY, with a higher altitude and marginally cooler temperatures. Proximity to the famous Hunter meant its wines were long overlooked, or trucked to the Hunter when needed. More carefully-sited new plantings are giving it a fresh lease of life and producers are beginning to make the best use of very good fruit. **Best producers:** Abercorn, Farmer's Daughter, Logan, Lowe Family, Miramar, Oatley★, Robert Stein.

MUGA *Rioja DOCa, Rioja, Spain* Traditional family winery making high-quality, rich red RIOJA★ (Gran Reserva Prado Enea★★). It is the only bodega in Rioja where every step of red winemaking is still carried out in oak containers. The modern Torre Muga Reserva★★ marks a major stylistic change. Top cuvée is Aro★★. Whites★★ are excellent and rosés★ are good. **Best years:** (Torre Muga Reserva) 2007 06 05 **04 03 01 99 98 96 95**.

MUGNERET-GIBOURG *Vosne-Romanée, Côte de Nuits, Burgundy, France* Great wines in a beautifully balanced, elegant red fruit style from the daughters of the late Dr Georges Mugneret. Look out for ECHÉZEAUX★★★, Ruchottes-CHAMBERTIN★★ and various NUITS cuvées, especially les Chaignots★★.

J-F MUGNIER *Chambolle-Musigny, Côte de Nuits, Burgundy, France* Since giving up his other career as an airline pilot in 1998, Frédéric Mugnier has produced beautifully crafted wines at the Ch. de Chambolle-Musigny, especially from les Amoureuses★★ and Grand Cru MUSIGNY★★★. In 2004 the 9ha (23-acre) NUITS-ST-GEORGES Clos de la Maréchale★★ vineyard came back under his control; first vintages are very stylish and a small section has been grafted over to white wine production. **Best years:** (2011) 10 09 08 **07** 06 05 **02 01 00** 99 98 96 93 90 89.

MULDERBOSCH *Stellenbosch WO, South Africa* Now under ownership of Charles Banks, former owner of California cult winery, SCREAMING EAGLE; the rest of the new team includes winemaker, Adam Mason, ex-KLEIN CONSTANTIA. The core range will focus on Sauvignon Blanc★★,

Chardonnay (regular★, barrel-fermented★★) and especially Chenin Blanc (Small Change★, oak-brushed Steen op Hout★) from old bush vine fruit. Faithful Hound, a BORDEAUX-style blend and Cabernet Sauvignon Rosé will be retained. Best years: (barrel-fermented Chardonnay) **2010 09 08 07 06 05 04 03 02.**

MÜLLER-CATOIR *Neustadt-Haardt, Pfalz, Germany* This PFALZ producer makes wine of a piercing fruit flavour and powerful structure rarely surpassed in Germany, including Riesling, Scheurebe, Rieslaner, Gewürztraminer, Muskateller and Pinot Noir – all ★★. BA and TBA are invariably ★★★. Best years: (2011) 10 **09 08 07 06 05 04 03 02 01.**

EGON MÜLLER-SCHARZHOF *Scharzhofberg, Mosel, Germany* Some of the world's greatest – and most expensive – sweet Rieslings are this perfectionist estate's Auslese, Beerenauslese, Trockenbeerenauslese and Eiswein: all usually rating ★★★. Regular Kabinett and Spätlese wines are pricey but classic. Best years: (2011) 10 09 08 07 **06 05 04 03 02 01 99 97 95.**

MÜLLER-THURGAU The workhorse grape of Germany, with around 13% of the country's vineyards. When yields are low it produces pleasant floral wines, but this is rare since modern clones are all super-productive. It is occasionally better in England – and a few good examples, with a slightly green edge to the grapy flavour, come from Switzerland (here known as Riesling-Sylvaner), Luxembourg (as Rivaner) and Italy's TRENTINO and ALTO ADIGE, which latter boasts one of Europe's highest vineyards in TIEFENBRUNNER's Feldmarschall at 1000m (3280ft).

G H MUMM *Champagne AC, Champagne, France* Mumm's top-selling non-vintage brand, Cordon Rouge, disappointing in the 1990s, improved when Dominique Demarville took over as winemaker in 1998, although he left in 2006 to join VEUVE CLICQUOT. His efforts at improving quality were confirmed by the 2005 release of Mumm Grand Cru★ and elegant de luxe Cuvée R Lalou★★. Encouraging to see release of fine Mumm de Verzenay★ blanc de noirs, to go with their traditionally excellent Mumm de Cramant★. Best years: 2004 02 **99 98 96 95 90 89 88 85 82.**

MUMM NAPA *Napa Valley AVA, California, USA* The California offshoot of Champagne house MUMM has always made good bubbly, and after a slight dip is now back on form. Brut Prestige★ is a fair drink; Brut Rosé★ is better than most pink Champagnes. Elegant vintage-dated Blanc de Blancs★★ and flagship DVX★★. Part of Pernod Ricard.

RENÉ MURÉ *Alsace AC, Alsace, France* The pride and joy of this domaine's fine vineyards are the Clos St-Landelin, a parcel within the Grand Cru Vorbourg. The Clos is the source of lush, concentrated wines, with particularly fine Riesling★★ and Pinot Gris★★. The Muscat Vendange Tardive★★ is rare and remarkable, as is the opulent old-vine Sylvaner Cuvée Oscar★. The Vendange Tardive★★ and Sélection de Grains Nobles★★★ wines are among the best in Alsace. Best years: (Clos St-Landelin Riesling) (2011) (10) **09 08 07 06 05 04 02 01 00 97 96.**

ANDREW MURRAY VINEYARDS *Santa Barbara County, California, USA* Working with RHÔNE varieties, winemaker Andrew Murray has created an impressive array of wines. Rich, aromatic Viognier★ and Roussanne★★ whites, as well as several Syrahs (Roasted Slope★★, Hillside Reserve★★). Espérance★ is a spicy blend patterned after a serious CÔTES DU RHÔNE. Best years: (Syrah) 2009 08 **07 06 05 04 03 02 01.**

MUSCADET AC *Loire Valley, France* AC for the region around Nantes in
north-west France; the simplest wines are best drunk young and fresh as
an apéritif or with the local seafood. Wines from 3 better-quality zones
(Muscadet Coteaux de la Loire, Muscadet Côtes de Grand-Lieu and
Muscadet Sèvre-et-Maine) are typically labelled *sur lie*. They must be
matured on the lees for a maximum of 12 months and show greater depth
of flavour and more fruit. The three new *crus communaux* (with a further
four in the pipeline) are from vineyards planted in some of the region's
best soils (granite, gneiss, quartz, sandstone and schist), but are not
permitted to use a 'sur lie' label, despite a minimum of 17 months' lees
aging. The rich flavours of aged styles can take on white meats as well as
fish and shellfish. **Best producers:** Bonhomme★, Bonnet-Huteau★, de la
Chauvinière/J Huchet★, Chéreau-Carré★, Choblet/Herbauges★, Clisson,
Bruno Cormerais★, Dorices★, l'Ecu★, Gadais★, Jacques Guindon★,
Landrons★, LUNEAU-PAPIN★, Metaireau★, le Pallet, de la Pépière, RAGOTIERE★,
Sauvion★, la Touche★. **Best years:** (sur lie) 2011 **10 08 07 05**.

MUSCAT See pages 228–9

MUSCAT OF ALEXANDRIA This grape rarely shines in its own right but
performs a useful job worldwide, adding sultry perfume and fleshy fruit
to what would otherwise be dull, neutral white wines. It is common for
sweet and fortified wines throughout the Mediterranean basin (in Sicily,
and especially on the island of Pantelleria, it is called Zibibbo) and in
South Africa (where it is also known as Hanepoot), as well as being a
fruity, perfumed bulk producer there and in Australia, where it is also
known as Gordo Blanco or Lexia.

MUSCAT DE BEAUMES-DE-VENISE AC *Rhône Valley, France* *Vin doux
naturel* (fortified) from the southern Rhône. It has a fruity acidity and a
bright fresh feel, and is best drunk young – as an apéritif or dessert wine –
to get all that lovely grapy perfume and bright honeyed fruit at its peak.
Becomes very rich and concentrated when aged. **Best producers:**
Beaumalric★, Beaumes-de-Venise co-op, Bernardins★★, DELAS★, Durban★★,
Fenouillet★, Paul JABOULET★★, Pigeade★★, VIDAL-FLEURY★.

MUSCAT BLANC À PETITS GRAINS See MUSCAT, pages 228–9.

MUSCAT DE FRONTIGNAN AC *Languedoc, France* Muscat *vin doux
naturel* on the Mediterranean coast. Quite impressive but can be a bit
cloying. Muscat de Mireval AC, a little further inland, can have a touch
more acid freshness and quite an alcoholic kick. Also Muscat de Lunel
further east. **Best producers:** (Frontignan) Mas Rouge, la Peyrade★, Stony,
(Lunel) Mas de Bellevue★; (Mireval) la Capelle★, Mas des Pigeonniers, Moulinas.

MUSCAT DE LUNEL, MUSCAT DE MIREVAL See MUSCAT DE FRONTIGNAN.

MUSCAT DE RIVESALTES AC *Roussillon, France* Made from both Muscat
Blanc à Petits Grains and Muscat of Alexandria, the wine can be very
good from go-ahead producers who keep the aromatic skins in the juice
for longer periods to gain extra perfume and fruit. Most delicious when
young. **Best producers:** Baixas co-op (Dom. Brial★, Ch. les Pins★), la
CASENOVE★, CAZES★★, Chênes★, Corneilla, Fontanel★, Força Réal★, l'Heritier,
Jau★, Laporte★, MONT TAUCH★, de Nouvelles★, Piquemal★, des Vents.

MUSCAT DE ST-JEAN-DE-MINERVOIS AC *Languedoc, France* AC in the
remote Minervois hills for fortified Muscat. Less cloying, more tangerine
and floral than some Muscats from the plains. **Best producers:** Barroubio,
Clos Bagatelle, Clos du Gravillas, Vignerons de Septimanie.

MUSCAT

It's strange, but there's hardly a wine grape in the world which makes wine that actually tastes of the grape itself. Yet there's one variety which is so joyously, exultantly grapy that it more than makes up for all the others – the Muscat, generally thought to be the original wine vine. In fact, there seem to be about 200 different branches of the Muscat family worldwide, but the noblest of these and the one that always makes the most exciting wine is called Muscat Blanc à Petits Grains (the Muscat with the small berries). These berries can be crunchily green, golden yellow, pink or even brown – as a result Muscat has a large number of synonyms. The wines they make may be pale and dry, rich and golden, sparkling or still, subtly aromatic or as dark and sweet as treacle.

WINE STYLES

France Muscat is grown from the far north-east right down to the Spanish border, yet it is rarely accorded great respect in France. This is a pity, because the dry, light, hauntingly grapy Muscats of Alsace are some of France's most delicately beautiful wines. It pops up sporadically in the Rhône Valley, especially in the sparkling wine enclave of Die. Mixed with Clairette, the Clairette de Die Tradition is a fragrant, grapy, honest fizz that deserves to be better known. Muscat de Beaumes-de-Venise is a delicious manifestation of the grape, this time fortified, musky and sweet. Its success has encouraged the traditional fortified winemakers of Languedoc-Roussillon to make fresher, more perfumed wines as well as unfortified late-harvest wines and, especially around Rivesaltes, dry vins de pays/IGPs. In Provence it is cropping up more often as an aromatic off-dry aperitif-style wine.

Italy Various types of Muscat are grown in Italy. In the north-west, especially Piedmont, Moscato Bianco/Moscato di Canelli makes the fragrantly sweet sparklers called Asti or (less bubbly) Moscato d'Asti; the same grape makes Tuscany's Moscadello di Montalcino. Orange Muscat (Moscato Giallo/Goldmuskateller) is used in the north-east for making passito-style dessert (or occasionally dry) wines, while Muscat of Alexandria prevails in the south, especially in relation to the great passitos of Pantelleria. Italy also has red varieties: Moscato Nero for rare sweet wines in Lazio, Lombardy and Piedmont; Moscato Rosa/Rosenmuskateller for delicately sweet wines in Trentino-Alto Adige and Friuli-Venezia Giulia.

Other regions Elsewhere in Europe, Muscat is a component of some Tokajis in Hungary, Crimea has shown how good it can be in the Massandra fortified wines, and the rich golden Muscats of Samos and Patras are among Greece's finest wines. As Muskateller in Austria and Germany, it makes primarily dry, subtly aromatic wines. In Spain, Moscatel de Valencia is sweet, light and sensational value, Moscatel de Grano Menudo is on the resurgence in Navarra and Castilla-La Mancha and it has also been introduced in Mallorca. Portugal's Moscatel de Setúbal is also wonderfully rich and complex. California grows Muscat, often calling it Muscat Canelli (and the Muscat category is one of the fastest-growing in the US), but South Africa and Australia make better use of it. With darker berries, and called Muscadel in South Africa and Brown Muscat in Australia, it makes some of the world's sweetest and most luscious fortified wines, especially in the north-east Victoria regions of Rutherglen and Glenrowan in Australia.

BEST PRODUCERS

Sparkling Muscat
France (*Clairette de Die*) Achard-Vincent, Clairette de Die co op, Jean-Claude Raspail.

Italy (*Asti*) G Contratto, Gancia; (*Moscato d'Asti*) Bera, Braida, La Caudrina, Saracco, La Spinetta, Gianni Voerzio.

Brazil Courmayeur, Monte Paschoal, Salton.

Dry Muscat
Austria (*Muskateller*) Gross, Lackner-Tinnacher, POLZ, TEMENT.

France (*Alsace*) J-M Bernhard, Paul Buecher, Dirler-Cadé, Kientzler, Kuentz Bas, OSTERTAG, Rolly Gassmann, SCHOFFIT, Bruno Sorg, TRIMBACH, WEINBACH, ZIND-HUMBRECHT.

Germany (*Muskateller*) BERCHER, Dr HEGER, HUBER, MULLER-CATOIR, REBHOLZ.

Spain (*Alicante*) Bocopa co-op; (*Málaga*) Jorge Ordóñez; (*Penedès*) TORRES (Viña Esmeralda).

Italy (*Goldmuskateller*) LAGEDER.

Sweet Muscat
Australia (*Liqueur Muscat*) All Saints, Baileys of Glenrowan, BROWN BROTHERS, Buller, Campbells, CHAMBERS, John Korovich, MCWILLIAM'S, MORRIS, Pfeiffer, Seppeltsfield, Stanton & Killeen, Talijancich, YALUMBA.

France (*Alsace*) Ernest Burn, René MURÉ, Rolly Gassmann, SCHOFFIT; (*Beaumes-de-Venise*) Bernardins, Durban, Paul JABOULET, Pigeade; (*Frontignan*) la Peyrade; (*Lunel*) Lacoste/Mas de Bellevue; (*Rivesaltes*) CAZES, Jau.

Greece SAMOS co-op.

Italy (*Goldmuskateller*) Viticoltori Caldaro, Thurnhof; (*Moscato Passito di Pantelleria*) DE BARTOLI, Murana.

Portugal (*Moscatel de Setúbal*) BACALHÔA, J M da FONSECA.

South Africa KLEIN CONSTANTIA.

Spain (*Navarra*) Camilo Castilla, CHIVITE; (*Valencia*) Gandía; (*Alicante*) Gutiérrez de la Vega, Enrique Mendoza, Primitivo Quiles; (*Jumilla*) Silvano García; (*Sierras de Málaga*) Jorge Ordóñez, Telmo RODRIGUEZ.

229

MUSIGNY AC *Grand Cru, Côte de Nuits, Burgundy, France* One of a handful of
truly great Grands Crus, combining power with an exceptional depth of
fruit and lacy elegance – an iron fist in a velvet glove. **Best producers:**
DROUHIN★★★, JADOT★★★, Dom. LEROY★★★, J-F MUGNIER★★★, J Prieur★★,
ROUMIER★★★, VOGÜÉ★★★, VOUGERAIE★★★. **Best years:** (2011) 10 09 08 07 06
05 **03** 02 **01 00** 99 98 96 95 93 90 89.

NAHE *Germany* 4155ha (10,260-acre) wine region named after the River
Nahe, which rises below Birkenfeld and joins the Rhine by BINGEN, opposite
RÜDESHEIM in the RHEINGAU. The Rieslings from this geologically complex
region are often among Germany's best. The finest vineyards are those of
Niederhausen and SCHLOSSBÖCKELHEIM, situated in the dramatic, rocky Upper
Nahe Valley, and at Dorsheim and Münster in the lower Nahe.

CH. NAIRAC★★ *Barsac AC, 2ème Cru Classé, Bordeaux, France* An established
name in BARSAC which, by dint of enormous effort, produces a sweet wine
sometimes on a par with the First Growths. The influence of aging in
new oak casks, adding spice and even a little tannin, means this can age
for 10–15 years. **Best years:** 2010 09 **07** 06 05 04 03 02 01 99 98 97 96.

NALLE *Dry Creek Valley AVA, California, USA* This family-owned winery
specializes in juicy, spicy, berryish Zinfandels★★ with refreshingly low
alcohol levels. The wines are delicious when young, but they can improve
with age. **Best years:** 2009 08 **07** 06 05.

NAPA VALLEY AVA *California, USA* An AVA that covers virtually all the
wines made in Napa County and one that is strenuously promoted as
California's premier wine region by a highly efficient trade organization,
the Napa Valley Vintners. Sub-AVAs have been and are being created.
There are a significant number that, over a generation or so, have proved
that their wines do have a particular personality; among them, I'd include
CARNEROS, STAGS LEAP, HOWELL MOUNTAIN, Diamond Mountain, SPRING
MOUNTAIN, MOUNT VEEDER, OAKVILLE and RUTHERFORD. See also pages 232–3.

NAVARRA DO *Navarra, Spain* Vineyards planted to Cabernet Sauvignon,
Merlot, Tempranillo, Garnacha, Chardonnay and Moscatel (Muscat),
producing juicy reds, barrel-fermented whites and modern sweet Muscats,
but quality is haphazard. **Best producers:** Artazu★, Azul y Garanza★, Camino
del Villar★, Camilo Castilla (Capricho de Goya Muscat★★), CHIVITE★
(Arínzano★★), Bodega del Jardin★, Iñaki Núñez★★, Inurrieta★, Lezaun★,
Domaines Lupier★, Castillo de Monjardin★, Nekeas co-op★, Ochoa, Señorío
de Sarria, Emilio Valerio★. **Best years:** (reds) 2010 09 **08** 07 06 05 04 03 01.

NAVARRO VINEYARDS *Anderson Valley AVA, California, USA* Small, family-
owned producer of sensational Gewürztraminer★★★, Pinot Gris★★,
Riesling★★, Dry Muscat★★ and late-harvest Riesling★★★, perfectly
balanced Pinot Noir★★ and a dozen other stellar wines.

NEBBIOLO The grape variety responsible for the majestic wines of BAROLO
and BARBARESCO. Its name may derive from the Italian for fog, *nebbia*,
because it ripens late when the hills are shrouded in autumn mists. It
needs a thick skin to withstand this fog, so often gives very tannic wines
that need years to soften. When grown in the limestone soils of the
Langhe hills around Alba, Nebbiolo produces wines that are only
moderately deep in colour but have a wonderful array of perfumes and an
ability to develop great complexity with age. Barolo is usually considered
the best and longest-lived of the Nebbiolo wines; the best Barolos now

reach a plateau within 10 years and then subtly mature for decades. Barbaresco also varies widely in style between the traditional and the new. The variety is used for NEBBIOLO D'ALBA and ROERO, and for barrique-aged blends, often with Barbera and/or Cabernet, sold under the LANGHE DOC. Nebbiolo is also the principal grape for reds of Carema on the VALLE D'AOSTA border as well as of northern PIEDMONT's GATTINARA and Ghemme, where it is called Spanna. In LOMBARDY it is known as Chiavennasca and is used in the Valtellina DOC and VALTELLINA SUPERIORE DOCG wines. Outside Italy, rare examples are made in Australia (S C PANNELL is outstanding; Arrivo, Joseph/PRIMO ESTATE, Longview, Luke Lambert, Pizzini and Tar & Roses are very good), California, Virginia, Brazil and South Africa.

NEBBIOLO D'ALBA DOC *Piedmont, Italy* Nebbiolo grown in the hills around Alba, but excluding the BAROLO and BARBARESCO zones. Two styles – for drinking young and, Barolo-like, for keeping. Best producers: Alario★, Bricco Maiolica★★, Burlotto★, Ceretto, Cascina Chicco★, Correggia★★, GIACOSA★, Giuseppe MASCARELLO▲, Pio Cesare★, BRUNOTTO★ RATTI★, SANDRONE★, Vietti★. Best years: (2011) (10) 09 **08** 07 06 04.

NELSON *South Island, New Zealand* Nelson is made up of a series of small hills and valleys with a wide range of mesoclimates, separated from MARLBOROUGH by mountains at the northern end of South Island. Pinot Noir, Chardonnay, Riesling and Sauvignon Blanc do well. Best producers: Brightwater★, Greenhough★★, Himmelsfeld, Kina Beach, NEUDORF★★★, Rimu Grove★, Seifried★, Waimea★. Best years: (whites) (2011) **10 09 07** 06.

NERO D'AVOLA The name of SICILY's great red grape derives from the town of Avola near Siracusa, although it is now planted all over the island. Its deep colour, high sugars and acidity make it useful for blending, especially with the lower-acid Nerello Mascalese, but also with Cabernet, Merlot and Syrah. On its own, and from the right soils, it can be brilliant, with a soft, ripe, spicy blackberry and damson character. Examples range from simple quaffers to many of Sicily's top reds.

NEUCHÂTEL *Switzerland* Swiss canton with high-altitude vineyards, mainly Chasselas whites and Pinot Noir reds and rosé. Best producers: Ch. d'Auvernier, Chambleau, Châtenay-Bouvier, Gerber.

NEUDORF *Nelson, South Island, New Zealand* Some of New Zealand's most stylish and sought-after wines, including gorgeous, creamily textured Chardonnay★★★, rich but scented Pinot Noir★★ (sometimes ★★★), Sauvignon Blanc★★, Riesling★★ and Pinot Gris★. Best years: (Chardonnay) (2011) **10 09** 08 06 05 04; (Pinot Noir) 2010 **09** 07 06 05 03.

NEW SOUTH WALES *Australia* Australia's most populous state is responsible for about 29% of the country's grape production. The largest centres of production are the irrigated areas of RIVERINA, and Murray Darling, Swan Hill and Perricoota on the Murray River, where better viticultural and winemaking practices and lower yields have led to significant quality improvement. Smaller premium-quality regions include the old-established HUNTER VALLEY, Cowra, higher-altitude MUDGEE and, especially, ORANGE and HILLTOPS. CANBERRA is an area of tiny vineyards and great potential at chilly altitudes, as is Tumbarumba at the base of the Snowy Mountains.

NAPA VALLEY

California, USA

 From the earliest days of California wine, and through all its ups and downs, the Napa Valley has been the standard-bearer for the whole industry and the driving force behind quality and progress. The magical Napa name – derived from an Indian word for plenty – applies to the fertile valley itself, the county in which it is found and the AVA for the overall area, but the region is so viticulturally diverse that the appellation is virtually meaningless.

The valley was first settled by immigrants in the 1830s, and by the late 19th century Napa, and in particular the area around the communities of Rutherford and Oakville, had gained a reputation for exciting Cabernet Sauvignon. Despite the long, dark years of Prohibition, this reputation survived and when the US interest in wine revived during the 1970s, Napa was ready to lead the charge.

GRAPE VARIETIES

Most of the classic French grapes are grown, but Cabernet is the one that sells best and is most widely recognized. In Napa, Cabernet is king, and Napa's strongest reputation is for varietal Cabernet and Bordeaux-style (or meritage) blends, usually Cabernet-Merlot. Pinot Noir and Chardonnay, for both still and sparkling wines, do best in the south, from Yountville down to Carneros. Zinfandel is grown mostly at the north end of the valley. Syrah, Viognier, Sangiovese and Malbec are relatively new here.

SUB-REGIONS

The most significant vine-growing area is the valley floor running from Calistoga in the north down to Carneros, below which the Napa River flows out into San Pablo Bay. It has been said that there are more soil types in Napa than in the whole of France, but much of the soil in the valley is heavy, clayish, over-fertile, difficult to drain and really not fit to make great wine. Some of the best vineyards are tucked into the mountain slopes at the valley sides or in selected spots at higher altitudes.

There is as much as a 10°C temperature difference between torrid Calistoga and Carneros at the mouth of the valley, cooled by Pacific fog and a benchmark for US Pinot Noir and cool-climate Chardonnay. Fifteen major sub-areas have been identified along the valley floor and in the mountains, although there is much debate over how many have a real claim to individuality. Rutherford, Oakville and Yountville in the mid-valley produce Cabernet redolent of dust, dried sage and ultra-ripe blackcurrants. Softer flavours come from Stags Leap to the east. The higher-altitude vineyards of Diamond Mountain, Spring Mountain and Mount Veeder along the Mayacamas mountain range to the west produce deep Cabernets, while Howell Mountain in the north-east also has stunning Zinfandel and Merlot.

See also CARNEROS AVA, HOWELL MOUNTAIN AVA, MOUNT VEEDER AVA, NAPA VALLEY AVA, OAKVILLE AVA, RUTHERFORD AVA, SPRING MOUNTAIN AVA, STAGS LEAP DISTRICT AVA; and individual producers.

Shafer
2005
Napa Valley
Stags Leap District
HILLSIDE
SELECT

BEST YEARS

(2010) 09 08 **07 06 05 04 01 99 95 94 91 90**

BEST PRODUCERS

Cabernet Sauvignon and meritage blends
Altamura, Anderson's Conn Valley, ARAUJO, Barnett (Rattlesnake Hill), Bennett Lane, BERINGER, Bryant Family, Buccella, Burgess Cellars, Cafaro, Cain, Cakebread, CAYMUS, Chappellet, CHATEAU MONTELENA, Chateau Potelle (VGS), CHIMNEY ROCK, Cliff Lede, CLOS DU VAL, Clos Pegase, Colgin, CORISON, Cosentino, Robert Craig, DALLA VALLE, Darioush, Del Dotto, DIAMOND CREEK, DOMINUS, DUNN, Eisele, Elyse, Far Niente, FLORA SPRINGS, Forman, Freemark Abbey, Frog's Leap, Grace Family, Groth, HARLAN ESTATE, HARTWELL, HEITZ, Honig, Jarvis, Jones Family, Leo Joseph, Krupp Brothers, Ladera, La Jota, Lang & Reed, Lewis Cellars, Livingston Moffett, Lokoya, Long Meadow Ranch, Long Vineyards, Markham, Mayacamas Vineyards, MERRYVALE, Peter MICHAEL, MINER, MONDAVI, Monticello, Mount Veeder Winery, NEWTON, Oakville Ranch, OPUS ONE, O'Shaughnessy, Pahlmeyer, Palladian, Paradigm, Robert Pecota, PHELPS, PINE RIDGE, Pride, Quintessa, Raymond, Rubicon/COPPOLA, Rubissow, Rudd Estate, Saddleback, St Clement, ST SUPÉRY, SCREAMING EAGLE, Seavey, SHAFER, SILVER OAK, SILVERADO, SPOTTSWOODE, Staglin Family, STAG'S LEAP WINE CELLARS, Sterling, Swanson, Terra Valentine, The Terraces, Titus, Turnbull, VIADER, Villa Mt Eden, Vine Cliff, Vineyard 29, Von Strasser, Whitehall Lane, ZD.

NEW YORK STATE *USA* Wine grapes were first planted on Manhattan Island in the mid-17th century, but it wasn't until the early 1950s that a serious wine industry began to develop in the state as *vinifera* grapes were planted to replace natives such as *Vitis labrusca*. Weather conditions, particularly in the north, can be challenging, but improved vineyard practices have made a good vintage possible in most recent years. The most important region is the FINGER LAKES in the north of the state, which is enjoying a surge of consumer interest in Riesling. The boom that had LONG ISLAND vintners atwitter at the turn of the century seems to have fizzled, though top producers still make serious BORDEAUX-styled reds and good Chardonnay. The Hudson River Region has a couple of good producers and a few upstarts are producing noteworthy wines amid the ocean of plonk along the shores of Lake Erie.

NEWTON *Napa Valley AVA, California, USA* Spectacular winery and steep vineyards high above St Helena, owned by French luxury giant LVMH. Cabernet Sauvignon★★, Merlot★★ and Claret★ are some of California's most pleasurable examples. Even better is the challenging, intellectual, single-vineyard Cabernet Sauvignon-based The Puzzle★★★. Newton pioneered the unfiltered Chardonnay★★ style, but the cheaper Red Label Chardonnay★ is also very attractive. Best years: (Cabernet Sauvignon) 2009 08 **07 06 05 03 02 01 00 99 97 96 95 94**.

NGATARAWA *Hawkes Bay, North Island, New Zealand* Established winemakers producing Chardonnay★, botrytized Riesling and Merlot-Cabernet under the premium Alwyn label. The Glazebrook range includes attractive Chardonnay★ and Cabernet-Merlot★, both of which are best drunk within 5 years. Best years: (reds) 2010 **09 08 07 06**.

NIAGARA PENINSULA *Ontario, Canada* Sandwiched between lakes Erie and Ontario, the Niagara Peninsula benefits from regular breezes off Lake Ontario, buffered by the Niagara escarpment. Icewine, from Riesling and Vidal, is the showstopper, with growing acclaim. Chardonnay and Riesling lead the dry whites, with promising reds from Pinot Noir, Merlot and Cabernet Franc. Best producers: Cave Spring★, Château des Charmes★, Le CLOS JORDANNE★, Flat Rock, HENRY OF PELHAM★, Hidden Bench★★, INNISKILLIN★, Southbrook★, Stratus★★, TAWSE★★, THIRTY BENCH★. Best years: (Icewine) **2009 08 07 05 04 03 02 00 99**.

NIEPOORT *Port DOC and Douro DOC, Douro, Portugal* Remarkable small wine and PORT producer of Dutch origin. Outstanding Vintage ports★★★, old tawnies★★★ and colheitas★★★. Complex, unfiltered LBVs★★ are among the best in their class. The Vintage port second label is Secundum★★. Niepoort also produces fine red, white and rosé DOURO Redoma★★, white Tiara★★, and red Vertente★★, Batuta★★★ and Charme★★. Best years: (Vintage) (2011) 09 08 **07 05 03 00 97 94 92 91 87 85 82 80 77 70 66 63**.

NIERSTEIN *Rheinhessen, Germany* The name of both a small town and a large Bereich, which includes the infamous Grosslage Gutes Domtal. The town boasts 23 vineyard sites and the top ones (Pettenthal, Brudersberg, Hipping, Oelberg and Orbel) are some of the best in the Rhine Valley. Best producers: GUNDERLOCH★★, Heyl zu Herrnsheim, Kühling-Gillot★, St Antony★, Schneider, Seebrich. Best years: (2011) 10 09 **08 07 06 05 04**.

NIGL *Senftenberg, Kremstal, Austria* Consistently fine and crystalline Riesling and Grüner Veltliner from this organic estate. Top vineyard is called Piri★ but each year Martin Nigl releases his best wines under the Privat★★ label. Best years: (2011) 10 09 **08 07 06 05 04**.

NIKOLAIHOF *Wachau, Niederösterreich, Austria* Biodynamic estate making
some of the best wines in the WACHAU as well as in nearby Krems-Stein in
KREMSTAL, including steely, intense Rieslings from the famous Steiner
Hund vineyard, always ★★. Best years: (2011) 10 09 **08 07 06 05 04 02**.

DOM. DE NIZAS *Pézenas, Languedoc, France* Owned by John Goelet, also
owner of NAPA-based CLOS DU VAL. Nizas makes an intense red PÉZENAS
(Mourvèdre-Carignan-Grenache), a spicy red LANGUEDOC and white
Languedoc from Roussanne, Rolle (Vermentino) and a drop of Viognier.
Entry-level Le Mas Pays d'Oc red is Cabernet Sauvignon-Syrah-based.
Best years: 2010 **09 08 07 06**.

NOBILO *Kumeu/Huapai, Auckland, North Island, New Zealand* Owned by
Constellation. Wines range from medium-dry White Cloud to premium
varietals. Restrained Sauvignon Blanc and a vibrant Chardonnay★ from
MARLBOROUGH, but most wines have a sweetish edge. Owns Selaks in
AUCKLAND and Drylands in Marlborough, with intense Drylands
Marlborough Sauvignon Blanc★, Chardonnay★ and Riesling★. Best
years: (Chardonnay) (2011) **10 09 07 06**.

NOEMÍA *Patagonia, Argentina* The partnership between Noemi Cinzano
(owner of Argiano in Tuscany) and famed winemaker Hans Vinding-
Diers discovered these precious few hectares of near-derelict, ancient
Malbec vineyards. A period of intensive care and conversion to
biodynamic practices has transformed the winery into one of the world's
top Malbec producers. Noemía★★★ is elegant, complex and ageworthy –
and expensive. Second wine J Alberto★★ is exceptional and its sibling,
A Lisa★, is glorious on release. Vinding-Diers has also finally realized his
dream of producing a 'Grand Vin' in the BORDEAUX tradition, with the
birth of the layered, precise Noemía '2'★★ (a Cabernet-Merlot blend) in
2007. Best years: (Noemía) 2009 **08 07 06 04**.

NORTON *Mendoza, Argentina* A Mendoza institution that, despite under-
performing in recent years, still produces an impressive range, where reds
outshine the whites. Enjoyable everyday wines under the Norton Reserva
label. Norton Privada★, a lush, chocolaty blend of Malbec, Cabernet and
Merlot, has been consistently fine and good value. The original Finca
Perdriel★ blend is dense with old-vine fruit, Quorum★ is a multi-
vintage, multi-varietal red, and the icon wine, Gernot Langhes★, is from
low-yielding old vines. Torrontés is best of the whites.

QUINTA DO NOVAL *Port DOC and Douro DOC, Douro, Portugal* Owned by
AXA-Millésimes, this property is the source of extraordinary Quinta do
Noval Nacional★★★, made from ungrafted vines – virtually unobtainable
except at auction. Other Noval ports (including Quinta do Noval
Vintage★★★ and Silval★) are excellent too. Also fine Colheita★★ and
stunning 40-year-old tawny★★★. Also DOURO red, Quinta do Noval
Tinto★★. Best years: (Nacional) (2007) **03 00 97 94 87 85 70 66 63 62 60
31**; (Vintage) 2008 **07 04 03 00 97 95 94 91 87 85 70 66 63 60 31**.

NUITS-ST-GEORGES AC *Côte de Nuits, Burgundy, France* This large AC is
one of the few relatively reliable 'village' names in Burgundy. Although it
has no Grands Crus, many of its Premiers Crus (it has 38!) are extremely
good. The red can be rather slow to open out, often needing at least 5
years, but it ages to a delicious, chocolaty, deep figs-and-prune fruit.
Minuscule amounts of white are made by Henri Gouges★, l'Arlot★,
Chevillon and RION. Best producers: l'Arlot★, Arnoux-Lachaux★★,
BELLENE★★, S CATHIARD★★, J Chauvenet★★, R Chevillon★★, J-J Confuron★★,
FAIVELEY★★, H Gouges★, GRIVOT★★, Jayer-Gilles★★, Lechenaut★★,

Comte LIGER-BELAIR★★, T LIGER-BELAIR★★, MEO-CAMUZET★★, A Michelot★, MUGNERET-GIBOURG★★, J-F MUGNIER★★, Perrot-Minot★★, RION★★, VOUGERAIE★★. Best years: (reds) (2011) 10 09 08 **07** 06 05 **03 02 99 98 96 95 90.**

NYETIMBER *West Sussex, England* England's largest sparkling wine producer with 177ha (438 acres) planted (but not yet all cropping) on eight sites, including 58ha (143 acres) on chalk downland in Hampshire. The Classic Cuvée★★ and 100% Chardonnay Blanc de Blancs★★ have been joined by an excellent Rosé★★. Best years: **2007 06 03.**

OAKRIDGE *Yarra Valley, Victoria, Australia* Outstanding boutique winery, showcasing the YARRA's strengths. Run by David Bicknell, one of Australia's most exciting winemaking talents. The 864 range includes complex, oatmealy Chardonnay★★★, impressive Pinot Noir★★, lush, structured Cabernet-Merlot★★ and seamless Syrah★★. The medium-priced Oakridge range (especially Chardonnay★ and Pinot Noir) and budget-priced Over the Shoulder range represent excellent value.

OAKVILLE AVA *Napa Valley, California, USA* This region is cooler than RUTHERFORD, which lies immediately to the north. Planted primarily to Cabernet Sauvignon, the area contains some of NAPA's best vineyards, both on the valley floor (MONDAVI, OPUS ONE, Paradigm, SCREAMING EAGLE) and hillsides (DALLA VALLE, HARLAN ESTATE, Oakville Ranch), producing wines that display lush, ripe black fruits and firm tannins. Best years: (Cabernet Sauvignon) (2010) 09 08 **07** 06 05 04 03 02 01 00 99 95 94 91 90.

OC, IGP DU PAYS D' *Languedoc-Roussillon, France* Important former vin de pays covering LANGUEDOC-ROUSSILLON. Overproduction and consequent underripeness have not helped its reputation, but an increasing number of fine reds and whites show what can be done. Best producers: l'Aigle★, Clovallon (Viognier★), Condamine Bertrand, Croix de St-Jean, J-L DENOIS★, l'HOSPITALET★, J & F Lurton★, MAS LA CHEVALIÈRE, Ormesson★, Pech-Céleyran, Quatre Sous★, Vignerons Val d'Orbieu (top reds★).

DOM. OGEREAU *Coteaux du Layon AC, Loire Valley, France* Vincent Ogereau's wines are sybaritic in concentration and purity of fruit yet beautifully tailored, especially COTEAUX DU LAYON Clos des Bonnes Blanches★★★. The modestly priced ANJOU-VILLAGES★ (Cabernet Franc) drinks young but develops beautifully over 15 years or more in great vintages. The leaner Côte de la Houssaye Anjou-Villages★ (Cabernet Sauvignon) takes 5 years to reveal its charms. Also Clos le Grand Beaupréau SAVENNIÈRES and Tutti Frutti, a botrytized Cabernet Sauvignon. Best years: (sweet) (2011) 10 09 **07** 05 03 02 01 00 97 96 95 90 89.

OKANAGAN VALLEY *British Columbia, Canada* The most important wine-producing region of British Columbia and first home of Canada's rich Icewine. The Okanagan Lake helps temper the bitterly cold nights, but October frosts can be a problem. Chardonnay, Pinot Blanc, Pinot Gris and Pinot Noir are the top performers. South of the lake, Cabernet, Merlot and Syrah are having some success. Adjacent Similkameen Valley has promising BORDEAUX blends and Syrah. Best producers: Blue Mountain★, Burrowing Owl★, CedarCreek★, INNISKILLIN, JACKSON-TRIGGS★, Joie Farm★, LaStella★, MISSION HILL★, Nk'Mip Cellars, Painted Rock★, Quails' Gate★, Sandhill, SUMAC RIDGE★, Le Vieux Pin★. Best years: (reds) 2009 08 **06 05 04 03 02.**

OLTREPÒ PAVESE DOC *Lombardy, Italy* Italy's main source of Pinot Nero, used mainly for sparkling wines, now upgraded to DOCG when made by the traditional method. The DOC covers still or frothing reds from Barbera and Bonarda, Pinot Nero red or blanc de noir, and whites from Pinot Bianco, Pinot Grigio, Riesling and Chardonnay among others.

Best producers: Cà di Frara★, Le Fracce★, Frecciarossa★, Castello di Luzzano/Fugazza, Mazzolino★, Monsupello★, Montelio★, Vercesi del Castellazzo★, Bruno Verdi★. Best years: (reds) (2011) 10 09 **08 07 06 04**.

OPUS ONE *Oakville AVA, California, USA* BORDEAUX-blend wine, a joint venture initially between Robert MONDAVI and Baron Philippe de Rothschild of MOUTON-ROTHSCHILD, now between Constellation and Baroness Philippine de Rothschild. Most Opus bottlings have been in the ★★ range, some achieving ★★★, in a beautifully cedary, minty manner whose balance and elegance can be a delight in modern-day NAPA. Best years: 2008 **07 06 05 04** 99 98 97 96 95 94 93 92 91 90.

ORANGE *New South Wales, Australia* Uniquely in Australia, the Orange region is defined by altitude: its grapes must be grown more than 600m (1900ft) above sea level. Orange is a relatively small, wonderfully picturesque vineyard region, established in the early 1980s. 60% red grapes, but the finest wines to date have been the whites, with Sauvignon Blanc, Chardonnay, Viognier and Riesling most impressive. Pinot Noir has made the most exciting reds, although Cabernet Sauvignon, Shiraz and blends have enormous potential. Best producers: Angullong, Bloodwood★, Cumulus, Logan★, Printhie, Philip SHAW★, Word of Mouth.

DOM. ORATOIRE ST-MARTIN *Côtes du Rhône-Villages AC, Rhône Valley, France* Careful fruit selection in a mature, high-terraced vineyard is the secret of Frédéric and François Alary's intense CAIRANNE reds and whites. Haut-Coustias white★ has peach and exotic fruit aromas, while the red★★ is a luscious mouthful of raspberries, herbs and spice. Top red Cuvée Prestige★★ from 100-year-old vines is deep and intense, with darkly spicy fruit. Best years: (Cuvée Prestige) (2011) 10 09 **07 06 05 04** 03 01.

OREGON *USA* Oregon shot to international stardom in the early 1980s following some perhaps overly generous praise of its Pinot Noir, but it is only with the release of a succession of fine recent vintages (2007 being an unfortunate exception) and some soul-searching by the winemakers about what style they should be pursuing that we can now begin to accept that some of the hype was deserved. Consistency is still a problem, however, with surprisingly warm weather now offering challenges along with the traditional ones of overcast skies and unwelcome rain. Chardonnay can be good in an austere, understated style. The rising star is Pinot Gris, which can be delicious, with surprising complexity. Pinot Blanc and Riesling are also gaining momentum. The WILLAMETTE VALLEY is considered the best growing region, although the more BORDEAUX-like climate of the Umpqua and Rogue Valleys can produce good Cabernet Sauvignon and Merlot. Best producers: (Rogue, Umpqua) ABACELA★, Bridgeview, Foris★, Henry Estate, Valley View.

TENUTA DELL'ORNELLAIA *Bolgheri, Tuscany, Italy* This beautiful property was developed by Lodovico ANTINORI, brother of Piero. Now owned by FRESCOBALDI-controlled Tenute di Toscana. Ornellaia★★, a Cabernet-Merlot blend, doesn't quite have the class of neighbouring SASSICAIA, but it is more lush; Masseto★★★ (Merlot) is superb. Second wine: Le Serre Nuove di Ornellaia★. Best years: (Ornellaia) (2011) (10) 09 08 **07 06 05 04** 03 01 00 99 98 97 96 95.

ORTENAU *Baden, Germany* A chain of granitic hills south of Baden-Baden, which produce elegant, generally dry Rieslings, and fragrant, medium-bodied Spätburgunder (Pinot Noir) reds. **Best producers:** Franckenstein★, Laible★★, Nägelsförst★, Schloss Neuweier★★, Wolff Metternich★.

ORVIETO DOC *Umbria, Italy* Traditionally a lightly sweet white wine made from a blend of grapes including Procanico (Trebbiano) and Umbria's native Grechetto, basic Orvieto is today usually dry. In the Classico zone, however, richer, more complex wines exist, especially in the Superiore category. Also some very good botrytis-affected sweet wines. **Best producers:** Barberani★ (dry Castagnolo★★, sweet Calcaia★★), La Carraia★, Decugnano dei Barbi★, Palazzone★ (dry Campo del Guardiano★★, sweet Muffa Nobilis★★), Castello della Sala★, Salviano★, Conte Vaselli★, Le Velette★.

OSBORNE *Jerez y Manzanilla DO, Andalucía, Spain* Spain's biggest drinks company. Osborne's sherry arm in Puerto de Santa María specializes in light Fino Quinta★. Amontillado Coquinero★, intense Bailén Oloroso★★ and Solera India Oloroso★★ are very good. It acquired Amontillado 51-1A★★★, Sibarita★★ and Venerable★★ soleras from defunct Domecq. Also a large estate at Malpica de Tajo in CASTILLA-LA MANCHA.

DOM. OSTERTAG *Alsace AC, Alsace, France* A biodynamic estate whose output is 50% Riesling, but which is more remarkable for Pinot Gris and Pinot Noir. The former is made in a Burgundian mode, using new oak barriques. This is so anathema to Alsace that the authorities have previously declassified their wines for their atypicality! The A360P Pinot Gris★★ has 50% new oak, and is stylish and rich. Fronholz Pinot Noir★★ is fragrant and complex but also ageworthy and serious. **Best years:** (a360p Pinot Gris) (2011) (10) **09 08 07 05 04 02 01 00**.

OWEN ROE *Columbia Valley AVA, Washington State, USA* David O'Reilly produces a broad range of wines in Washington and Oregon. Cabernet Sauvignon DuBrul Vineyard★★ is typically dense and powerful; Cabernet Sauvignon Red Willow 1973 Block★★ is made with fruit from one of the oldest vineyards in Washington State. Expressive Syrahs (Chapel Block★★, Ex Umbris★★) rank among the best in the state. **Best years:** (Cabernet Sauvignon) (2010) 09 **08 07 06**.

PAARL WO *South Africa* A great diversity of soil and climate favour everything from Cap Classique sparkling wines to sherry styles, but the fact that Paarl was famous for sherry tells you that it's fairly hot, and it is now big reds that are setting the quality pace, especially Shiraz. Its white RHÔNE counterpart, Viognier, solo and in white blends, is also performing well. Wellington, previously a ward within Paarl, is now a district in its own right. **Best producers:** Boschendal, DISTELL (Nederburg★, Plaisir de Merle★), FAIRVIEW★, GLEN CARLOU★, Rupert & Rothschild★, Scali★, Val de Vie, VEENWOUDEN★★, Vilafonté★; (Wellington) Diemersfontein★, Mont du Toit★. **Best years:** (premium reds) 2010 **09 08 07 06 05 04 03**.

PACHERENC DU VIC-BILH AOP *South-West France* MADIRAN's white wines, ranging from dry to sweet late-harvest styles. **Best producers:** AYDIE★, Barréjat, BERTHOUMIEU★★, Brumont (Bouscassé★, MONTUS★★), Capmartin★★, du Crampilh★, Damiens★, LABRANCHE-LAFFONT★★, Laffitte-Teston★★, PLAIMONT. **Best years:** (sweet) 2010 09 **07 06 05**.

PADTHAWAY *South Australia* This wine region has always been the alter ego of nearby COONAWARRA, growing whites to complement Coonawarra's reds: Chardonnay has been particularly successful. Nowadays there are some excellent reds, especially from Henry's Drive; Orlando's premium Lawson's Shiraz★★ is 100% Padthaway; even

GRANGE has included Padthaway grapes. Best producers: Browns of Padthaway, Henry's Drive★★, Orlando/JACOB'S CREEK★★, Padthaway Estate.

BRUNO PAILLARD *Champagne AC, Champagne, France* Bruno Paillard is one of the very few individuals to have created a new CHAMPAGNE house in the 20th century. Paillard still does the blending himself. Non-vintage Première Cuvée★ is lemony and crisp; Réserve Privée★ is a blanc de blancs; vintage Brut★★ is a serious wine. De luxe cuvée Nec Plus Ultra★★ is a barrel-fermented blend of Grands Crus made in top vintages. Best years: **1999 96 95 90 89 88**.

ALVARO PALACIOS *Priorat DOCa, Cataluña, Spain* After experience in Bordeaux and Napa, Alvaro Palacios launched his boutique winery in PRIORAT, in the rough hills of southern CATALUÑA, in the late 1980s. He is now one of the driving forces of the area's rebirth. His red wines (super-expensive, highly concentrated L'Ermita★★★, Finca Dofí★★ Les Terrasses Vinyes Velles★★, Gratallops Vi de la Vila★★ and affordable Camins del Priorat★) from old Garnacha vines and a dollop of Cabernet Sauvignon, Merlot, Cariñena and Syrah have won a cult following. Best years: (2009) 08 **07 06** 05 04 03 01 00 99 98 97 96 95.

PALETTE AC *Provence, France* Tiny AC just east of Aix-en-Provence. Even though the local market pays high prices, I find the reds and rosés rather tough and charmless. However, Ch. Simone manages to achieve a white wine of some flavour from mostly basic southern French grapes. Best producers: Crémade, Ch. Simone★.

PALLISER ESTATE *Martinborough, North Island, New Zealand* Winery producing some of New Zealand's best Sauvignon Blanc★★, as well as Riesling★, delightful Chardonnay★★ and Pinot Gris★, and impressive, rich-textured Pinot Noir★★. Good Méthode Traditionelle★ fizz, and exciting botrytized dessert wines in favourable vintages. Pencarrow is the tasty second label. Best years: (Pinot Noir) (2011) **10 09 08 07 06 03**.

CH. PALMER★★★ *Margaux AC, 3ème Cru Classé, Haut-Médoc, Bordeaux, France* This estate was named after a British major-general who fought in the Napoleonic Wars, and is one of the leading properties in MARGAUX AC. The wine is wonderfully perfumed, with irresistible plump fruit, and recent vintages have been some of the best ever (lots of Merlot). The very best vintages can age for 30 years or more. Second wine: Alter Ego★ (usually an excellent, scented red). Best years: 2010 09 08 **07 06 05 04 03 02 01 00 99 98 96 95 90 89 88 86 85**.

S C PANNELL *McLaren Vale, South Australia* Steve Pannell enjoyed corporate success as BRL HARDYS' chief red wine maker. Now, without vineyards or a winery, he specializes in producing MCLAREN VALE Shiraz and Grenache, and he has had equal success with ADELAIDE HILLS Sauvignon★. Lavishly concentrated Shiraz-Grenache★★ and complex Shiraz★★ show more restraint and elegance than is common locally, while Nebbiolo★★ (from Adelaide Hills) is some of the best you'll find outside BAROLO.

CH. PAPE-CLÉMENT *Pessac-Léognan AC, Cru Classé de Graves, Bordeaux, France* The expensive red wine★ has not always been as consistent as it should be – but things changed direction during the 1990s with the introduction of a deeper, darker style of wine: impressive, but difficult to recognize as PESSAC-LÉOGNAN. Recent vintages are more aromatic, but still very oaky, and may blossom to ★★ with a decade of aging. Also a small amount of fine, aromatic white wine★★. Second wine: (red) Clémentin. Best years: (reds) 2010 09 08 **07** 06 05 **04** 03 02 01 00 99 98 96 95 90 89; (white) 2010 **09 08 07 06 05 04 03 02 01 00**.

PARINGA ESTATE *Mornington Peninsula, Victoria, Australia* Teacher-turned-winemaker Lindsay McCall planted his suntrap site at Red Hill South in 1985. His attention to detail and flair has brought enormous success for his Pinot Noirs (entry-level Peninsula label, Estate★ and Reserve★★★), the best of which are ethereal with silky smooth texture, depth, power and finesse. Also multi-layered, intense, cool-climate Shiraz★★.

PARKER COONAWARRA ESTATE *Coonawarra, South Australia* Owned by the Rathbone family, who also own Yering Station, MOUNT LANGI GHIRAN and Xanadu. The top label, cheekily named First Growth★★ (sometimes ★★★) in imitation of illustrious BORDEAUX reds, is regularly one of COONAWARRA's most impressively balanced reds. It is released only in better years. Second-label Terra Rossa Cabernet Sauvignon★ is lighter and leafier. The Merlot★★ is among the best in Australia. Best years: (First Growth) (2010) 08 07 **06 05** 04 01 99 98 96 93 91 90.

PASCUAL TOSO *Mendoza, Argentina* Consultant winemaker Californian Paul Hobbs (who co-owns the boutique COBOS winery), has transformed Toso into a leading Malbec producer. The rich Reserve Malbec★ sets the house style. Alta Reserva Malbec★ (also Syrah★) is concentrated and floral, inky deep Finca Pedregal★★ is magical, and top cuvée Magdalena Toso★★ is powerful, dense and long lived. Best years: 2009 08 07 **06 05**.

C J PASK *Hawkes Bay, North Island, New Zealand* Chris Pask made the first wine in the now-famous Gimblett Gravels area of HAWKES BAY. Flagship Declaration label includes an intensely oaky Syrah★, rich Merlot and a powerful Cabernet-Merlot-Malbec blend. Mid-range wines under the Gimblett Road label. Best years: (reds) 2010 **09 08 07** 06 04 02.

PASO ROBLES AVA *California, USA* A large AVA at the northern end of SAN LUIS OBISPO COUNTY. Most famous for high-volume Cabernet and heady Zinfandel, there has been an influx of energetic, creative winemakers keen on Rhône varieties, led by the Perrin Brothers at TABLAS CREEK. The white and red Rhône varieties (Roussanne, Marsanne, Grenache, Syrah, Mourvèdre) are really proving their worth,

along with old-timers like Petite Sirah and newcomers like Sangiovese, Tannat, Tempranillo, Aglianico, Vermentino and even Pinot Noir. Serious Bordeaux blends include Petit Verdot and Malbec. Paso's getting on a roll. Expect fireworks. Best producers: 4 Vines★★, Adelaida★, Alta Colina★, Ancient Peaks★, Clavo★, Clayhouse★, Cypher★, Daou★, Eberle★, Eos★, Halter Ranch★, Hearst Ranch★★, Hope/Treana★, Justin★★, J Lohr★, Minassian-Young★, Niner★, Peachy Canyon★★, TABLAS CREEK★★, Villicana★, Vina Robles★, Wild Horse★.

PATAGONIA *Argentina* 750km (465 miles) south of MENDOZA lie the two wine-producing regions of northern Patagonia: Río Negro, with a 100-year history of wine production, and its neighbour to the west, Neuquén. Extreme day/night temperature differences and relentless southerlies are common to both, resulting in deeply coloured, intense and healthy wines. Racy Pinot Noirs, graphite-edged Malbecs, pure, round Merlot and tasty sparkling wines are the order of the day. Also plantings in Chabut further south and in the El Deserto project in La Pampa east of Neuquén on the Colorado river. Best producers: (Río Negro) Humberto Canale, Chacra★★, FABRE MONTMAYOU★, NOEMÍA★★; (Neuquén) Fin del Mundo, NQN★, Familia Schroeder★, Universo Austral.

LUÍS PATO *Beira Atlântico, Portugal* Leading modernist, passionately convinced of the Baga grape's ability to make great reds on chalky-clay soil. Wines such as the Vinhas Velhas★, Vinha Barrosa★★, Vinha Pan★★ and the flagship Quinta do Ribeirinho Pé Franco★★ (from ungrafted vines) rank among Portugal's finest modern reds: some can reach ★★★ with age. Good white, Vinha Formal★, is 100% Bical. Also good fizz. Daughter Filipa makes delightful reds and whites under Lokal★★ and Ensaios FP★ labels. Best years: (reds) (2009) **08 05 04 03 01 00 97 96 95 92.**

PAUILLAC AC *Haut-Médoc, Bordeaux, France* The deep gravel banks around the town of Pauillac in the HAUT-MÉDOC are the heartland of Cabernet Sauvignon. For many wine lovers, the king of red wine grapes finds its ultimate expression in the 3 Pauillac First Growths (LATOUR, LAFITE-ROTHSCHILD and MOUTON-ROTHSCHILD). The large AC also contains 15 other Classed Growths. The uniting characteristic of Pauillac wines is their intense blackcurrant fruit flavour, pencil-shavings perfume and undertow of graphite. These are the longest-lived of BORDEAUX's great red wines. Best producers: Armailhac★, BATAILLEY★, Bellegrave, Clerc-Milon★, DUHART MILON★, Fonbadet, GRAND-PUY-DUCASSE★, GRAND-PUY-LACOSTE★★, HAUT-BAGES-LIBERAL★, HAUT-BATAILLEY★, LAFITE-ROTHSCHILD★★★, LATOUR★★★, LYNCH-BAGES★★★, Lynch-Moussas, MOUTON-ROTHSCHILD★★★, Pibran★, PICHON-LONGUEVILLE★★★, PICHON-LONGUEVILLE-LALANDE★★★, PONTET-CANET★★. Best years: 2010 09 08 06 **05 04 03 02 01 00** 96 95 90 89 88 86.

CH. PAVIE★★ *St-Émilion Grand Cru AC, 1er Grand Cru Classé, Bordeaux, France* The style of the wine may be controversial – dense, rich, succulent – and it has as many enemies as friends, but there's no doubting the progress made at Pavie since Gérard Perse acquired the property in 1998. The price has also soared. Pavie-Decesse★ and MONBOUSQUET★ are part of the same stable. Best years: 2010 09 08 07 06 05 **04 03 02 01 00** 99 98 90.

CH. PAVIE-MACQUIN★★ *St-Émilion Grand Cru AC, 1er Grand Cru Classé, Bordeaux, France* This has become one of the stars of the ST-ÉMILION GRAND CRU since the 1990s, with promotion to Premier Grand Cru Classé in 2006. Rich, firm and reserved, the wines need 7–8 years and will age longer. Best years: 2010 09 08 07 06 05 **04 03 02 01 00** 99 98 96.

PÉCHARMANT AOP *Bergerac, South-West France* The iron-rich soil here is called 'tran' and it gives the wines their distinctive minerally style and keeping qualities. Best producers: Bertranoux, Chemins d'Orient★, Clos les Côtes★, Grand Jaure, Haut-Pécharmant★★, La Métairie, Terre Vieille★, la Tilleraie, Tiregand★★. Best years: (2011) (10) 09 **06 05 04 01 00**

PECORINO Relatively recently rescued from near-extinction, this is ABRUZZO's finest white grape variety, capable (also in LE MARCHE) of making dry sappy whites of considerable complexity. Best producers: Cataldi Madonna★, Citra★, Contesa★★, Marramiero★, Montori★, Pasetti★, San Lorenzo★, Terra d'Aligi★, Tiberio★★, La Valentina★★.

PEGASUS BAY *Canterbury, South Island, New Zealand* Matthew Donaldson and Lynnette Hudson make lush, mouthfilling Chardonnay★★, an almost chewy Pinot Noir★★ and its even richer big sister Prima Donna Pinot Noir★★, powerful, idiosyncratic Sauvignon Blanc-Semillon★★, all kinds of very stylish Riesling★★ (sometimes ★★★) and an occasional heavenly Gewurztraminer★★★. These are some of the most original wines in New Zealand, and all will age well. Best years: (Pinot Noir) (2011) **09 08 07 06 03.**

PEMBERTON *Western Australia* Exciting emergent cool-climate region, deep in the Karri forests of the south-west. So far, white varieties have done best, especially taut, tangy Sauvignon Blanc and thrilling, minerally Chardonnay. Occasional superb examples of Riesling, Viognier, Semillon and Marsanne, as well as Western Australia's only distinguished sparkling wine. Best of the reds so far is Pinot Noir, with Shiraz rewarding patience in its best (warmest) vintages, and occasional BORDEAUX blends. HOUGHTON leads the way with Wisdom range. Best producers: Bellarmine★, HOUGHTON★★, Lillian, Pemberley★★, Picardy★, Salitage.

PENEDÈS DO *Cataluña, Spain* The booming CAVA industry is based in Penedès, and the majority of the still wines are white, made from the Cava trio of Parellada, Macabeo and Xarel-lo, clean and fresh when young, but never exciting. Better whites are made from Chardonnay. The reds are variable, the best made from Cabernet Sauvignon and/or Tempranillo and Merlot. Best producers: Albet i Noya★, Can Feixes★, Can Ràfols dels Caus★★, Gramona★, Cavas Hill, Jané Ventura★, Jean León★, Marques de Monistrol, Masía Bach★, Albert Milá i Mallofré★, Puig & Roca★, Sot Lefriec★, TORRES★, Vallformosa.

PENFOLDS *Barossa Valley, South Australia* Penfolds' performance as part of the Foster's/Treasury group has been uneven, particularly at the lower end. It still makes the country's most famous red wine, GRANGE★★★, and other superb reds such as RWT Shiraz★★★, Magill Estate★★, St Henri★, Bin 707 Cabernet★★, Bin 389 Cabernet-Shiraz★, Bin 28 Kalimna★ and Bin 128 Coonawarra Shiraz. Its Cellar Reserve wines are difficult to find but outstanding, and occasional releases of Special Bin reds are among Australia's best. However, further down the range they need to reverse a dispiriting blandness which has entered into previously reliable wines like Koonunga Hill and Rawson's Retreat. Whites are led by expensive but excellent Yattarna Chardonnay★★★, stunningly good Reserve Bin Chardonnay★★★ and impressive cool-climate Bin 311 Chardonnay★★; there's also citrus Bin 51 Eden Valley Riesling★ and decent Rawson's Retreat Riesling. Thomas Hyland Cabernet, Shiraz and Chardonnay are pretty good. Best years: (top reds) 2010 08 **06 04 02 99 98 96 94 91 90.**

PENÍNSULA DE SETÚBAL *Portugal* Warm, maritime area south of Lisbon. Vinho Regional has some decent whites and good reds; the best reds are from old Castelão vines, often under the Palmela DOC. SETÚBAL DOC produces sweet fortified wine. Best producers: (reds) BACALHÔA★★, Herdade da Comporta, D F J VINHOS★, Ermelinda Freitas★, José Maria da FONSECA★★, Pegões co-op, Pegos Claros★, Soberanas. Best years: **2008 07 05 04 03 01 00 99 97 96 95.**

PENLEY ESTATE *Coonawarra, South Australia* Kym Tolley, a member of the PENFOLD family, launched Penley Estate in 1991. Cabernet Sauvignon★★★ is outstanding. Chardonnay and Hyland Shiraz can reach ★★; Gryphon Merlot★ and fizz★ are good, too. Best years: (Cabernet Reserve) (2010) (09) 08 07 **06 05 04 02 00 99 98 96 94 93 92 91.**

PENNSYLVANIA *USA* Pennsylvania has seen its wine industry blossom over the last two decades, to about 150 wineries today. The state boasts the two highest elevation vineyards in the US east of the Rocky Mountains. Native and French hybrid grapes are common, with *vinifera* making inroads. Best producers: Allegro, CHADDSFORD, Presque Isle, Stargazers.

PEPPER BRIDGE WINERY *Walla Walla Valley AVA, Washington State, USA*
This estate's vineyards, Pepper Bridge and Seven Hills, are two of WASHINGTON STATE's best. The Cabernet Sauvignon★ is powerful and requires aging to show its potential; Merlot★ is a muscular version of the variety; BORDEAUX-style blend Reserve★★ is produced in very small amounts. Best years: (2010) 09 **08** 07 06.

RAÚL PÉREZ *Bierzo DO, Castilla y León and Ribeira Sacra DO, Galicia, Spain* The affable, BIERZO-born Pérez has taken the wine world by storm with his ultra-natural, elegant wines – not only those he produces in north-western Spain (Ultreia de Valtuille★★★, El Pecado★★★), but also those from wineries where he consults elsewhere in the country.

PÉREZ CRUZ *Maipo, Chile* Modern winery in the Alto Maipo, with 150ha (370 acres) of red vines in a unique microclimate close to the Andes foothills. Noted for its minty Cabernet Sauvignon★, Cot★ (Malbec), Syrah★ and Liguai★★ (Syrah-Cabernet Sauvignon Carmenère).

PERNAND-VERGELESSES AC *Côte de Beaune, Burgundy, France* The little-known village of Pernand-Vergelesses contains a decent chunk of the great Corton hill, including much of the best white CORTON-CHARLEMAGNE Grand Cru vineyard. As no one ever links Pernand with the heady heights of Corton-Charlemagne, the whites sold under the village name can be a bargain. The wines can be a bit lean and dry to start with but fatten up beautifully after 2–4 years in bottle. The red wines sold under the village name are attractive when young, with a nice raspberry pastille fruit and a slight earthiness, and will age for 6–10 years. Best vineyard: Île des Vergelesses. Best producers: (reds) Champy★, CHANDON DE BRIAILLES★★, C Cornu★, Denis Père et Fils★, Dubreuil-Fontaine★; (whites) Dubreuil-Fontaine★, A Guyon, JADOT★, J-M Pavelot★, Rapet★, Rollin★. Best years: (reds) (2011) 10 09 **08** 07 05 03 02 99; (whites) (2011) 10 09 **00** 07 06 **05**.

ANDRÉ PERRET *Condrieu AC, Rhône Valley, France* A top CONDRIEU grower, with 2 standout cuvées: Clos Chanson★★ is mineral and dashing; Chéry★★★, made with some later-picked Viognier, is gloriously musky, floral and rich. Impressive white and red ST-JOSEPH★★ (Les Grisières★★ from old Syrah vines). Very good COLLINES RHODANIENNES Syrah and Marsanne. Best years: (Condrieu Chéry) **2011** 10 09 08 07 06 05 04.

JOSEPH PERRIER *Champagne AC, Champagne, France* The vintage Blanc de Blancs★★ and vintage Rosé★★ are classy and the NV Cuvée Royale★ is biscuity and creamy. Prestige Cuvée Josephine★★ has length and complexity, but the much cheaper Cuvée Royale Vintage★★ is the best deal. Best years: 2004 **02** 99 98 96 95 90 89 88 85 82.

PERRIER-JOUËT *Champagne AC, Champagne, France* Perrier-Jouët has had three owners in the past 10 years (it's now owned by Pernod Ricard). This doesn't help consistency, but Perrier-Jouët had fallen so low during the 1990s that the latest change must be positive. Certainly the NV is now a decent drink once more, the Blason Rosé★ is charming and the de luxe vintage cuvée Belle Époque★ (known as Fleur de Champagne in the US) reasonably classy. Best years: 2004 **02** 99 98 96 95 90 89 85 82.

PESQUERA *Ribera del Duero DO, Castilla y León, Spain* Tinto Pesquera reds, 100% Tempranillo, richly coloured, firm, fragrant, plummy-tobaccoey, have long been among Spain's best. Sold as Crianza★ and Reserva★; Gran Reserva★★ and Janus★★★ are made in the best years. The firm owns another RIBERA DEL DUERO estate, Condado de Haza★ (Alenza★★), plus ventures in Zamora (Dehesa La Granja★) and La MANCHA (Vínculo). Best years: (Pesquera Crianza) (2010) 09 **07** 06 05 **04** 01 99 96 95 94 93 92 91.

243

PESSAC-LÉOGNAN AC *Bordeaux, France* AC created in 1987 for the northern (best) part of the GRAVES and including all the Classed Growths. The supremely gravelly soil tends to favour red wines over the rest of the Graves. Thanks to cool fermentation and the use of new oak barrels, this is also one of the most exciting areas of France for top-class white wines. Best producers: (reds) Carbonnieux★, les Carmes Haut-Brion★, Dom. de CHEVALIER★★, Couhins-Lurton★, FIEUZAL★, HAUT-BAILLY★★, HAUT-BRION★★★, Larrivet-Haut-Brion★, LATOUR-MARTILLAC★, la LOUVIÈRE★, MALARTIC-LAGRAVIÈRE★★, la MISSION-HAUT-BRION★★★, PAPE-CLEMENT★, SMITH-HAUT-LAFITTE★★; (whites) Brown★, Carbonnieux★, Dom. de CHEVALIER★★, Couhins-Lurton★★, FIEUZAL★★, la Garde★, HAUT-BRION★★★, LATOUR-MARTILLAC★, LAVILLE-HAUT-BRION★★★, la LOUVIÈRE★★, MALARTIC-LAGRAVIÈRE★★, PAPE-CLEMENT★★, Rochemorin★, SMITH-HAUT-LAFITTE★★. Best years: (reds) 2010 09 08 **06** 05 04 02 01 00 99 98; (whites) (2011) **10** 09 08 07 06 05 04 02 01 00.

PETALUMA *Adelaide Hills, South Australia* Founded by Brian Croser, probably Australia's most influential winemaker (see TAPANAPPA) – now owned by brewer Lion Nathan. CHAMPAGNE-style Croser★ is stylish and fruitier than before. COONAWARRA★ (Cabernet-Merlot) and Chardonnay★ are consistently good and Hanlin Hill Riesling★★ from the CLARE VALLEY is at the fuller end of the spectrum and matures well. Best years: (Coonawarra) (2010) 09 08 **07** 06 05 04 03 02 01 00 99 97 94 91 90.

PETIT MANSENG Petit and Gros Manseng are an increasingly important pair of grapes in the far south-west of France. Left late to overripen naturally on the vines (their skins are too thick to allow development of noble rot), the sweetness of the juice is balanced by a refreshing acidity, the hallmark of JURANÇON and PACHERENC.

PETIT VERDOT A rich, tannic variety, grown mainly in Bordeaux's HAUT-MÉDOC to add depth, colour and violet fragrance to top wines. Late ripening and erratic yield limit its popularity, but warmer-climate plantings in Australia, California, Virginia, South Africa, Chile, Argentina, Israel, Spain, Portugal and Italy are giving exciting results, often from including only a few per cent in blends. Increasingly, varietal Petit Verdot wines are now made in Spain.

CH. PETIT-VILLAGE★ *Pomerol AC, Bordeaux, France* This POMEROL used to be rather dry and dense, but has considerably softened up in recent vintages. New cellar and even better quality from 2006. Generally worth aging for 8–10 years. Best years: 2010 09 08 **07** 06 **05** 04 03 02 01 00 99 98.

PETITE ARVINE A Swiss grape variety from the VALAIS, Petite Arvine has a bouquet of peach and apricot, and develops a spicy, honeyed character. Dry, medium or sweet, the wines have good aging potential. Also found in VALLE D'AOSTA in Italy. Best producers: Chappaz★, R Favre, A Mathier★, Maye, Dom. du Mont d'Or★, Rouvinez★, Varone.

PETITE SIRAH Once used primarily as a blending grape in California, this variety is identical to the obscure Rhône blender Durif. Some 500 or more California wineries now make a varietal Petite Sirah. At its best, it is almost black but surprisingly scented and sweet-fruited, though it can be tannic and unfriendly. Australian, Mexican and Israeli examples are generally softer though still hefty, and can also occasionally develop a floral scent and blackberry fruit. It has a limited presence in South Africa. Best producers: (California) Alta Colina★★, Clayhouse, Cypher★★, Jessie's Grove, J Lohr★, Loma Linda★, RAVENSWOOD★, RIDGE★★, Ripken★, Rosenblum, Stags' Leap Winery★★, TURLEY★★; (Australia) Campbells, DE BORTOLI, Nugan Estate, Rutherglen Estates★, Stanton & Killeen, WESTEND★; (Mexico) L A CETTO★; (Chile) CARMEN.

CH. PÉTRUS★★★ *Pomerol AC, Bordeaux, France* The powerful, concentrated wine (one of the most expensive red wines in the world) is the result of the caring genius of Pétrus' owners, the MOUEIX family, who have maximized the potential of the vineyard of almost solid clay, although the impressive average age of the vines has been much reduced by recent replantings. Drinkable for its astonishingly rich, dizzying blend of fruit and spice flavours after a decade, but top years will age for much longer, developing exotic scents of tobacco and chocolate and truffles. Best years: 2010 09 08 07 06 05 04 **03 02 01 00 99 98 96 95 90 89 88 86.**

DOM. PEYRE ROSE *Grès de Montpellier AC, Languedoc, France* Organic viticulture, ultra-low yields, lengthy aging, but total absence of oak are hallmarks of Marlène Soria's wines. Syrah is the dominant grape in both the raisin- and plum-scented Clos des Cistes★ and the dense, velvety Cuvée Léone★★. Marlène No 3 is a blend of Syrah and Grenache with Carignan. Best years and current vintages: 2003 02.

CH. DE PEZ★ *St-Estèphe AC, Haut-Médoc, Bordeaux, France* One of ST-ESTÈPHE's leading non Classed Growths, de Pez makes mouthfilling, satisfying claret with sturdy fruit. Slow to evolve, good vintages often need 10 years or more. Owned by Champagne house ROEDERER. Best years: 2010 09 08 **07 06 05 04 03 02 01 00 99 98 96 95 90 89.**

PÉZENAS *Grand Vin du Languedoc, Languedoc AC, France* From vineyards around the town of Pézenas, mainly from Syrah, Grenache, and Mourvèdre. White and pink wines are COTEAUX DU LANGUEDOC or LANGUEDOC AC. Best producers: Aurelles★, Conte des Floris★, NIZAS★, PRIEURÉ DE ST-JEAN DE BÉBIAN★★, Ste-Cecile du Parc★. Best years: (reds) (2011) 10 **09 08 07 06 05.**

PFALZ *Germany* This immense, 23,460ha (58,000-acre) wine region makes a lot of mediocre wine, but the quality estates can match the best that Germany has to offer. The northern area (the Mittelhaardt) can produce profound full-bodied Riesling, especially round the villages of Bad Dürkheim, WACHENHEIM, FORST and Deidesheim; Freinsheim, Kallstadt, Ungstein, Ruppertsberg, Gimmeldingen and Haardt also produce fine Riesling as well as Scheurebe, Rieslaner and Pinot Gris. In the Südliche Weinstrasse, the warm climate makes the area ideal for Spät-, Weiss- and Grauburgunder (aka Pinots Noir, Blanc and Gris), as well as Chardonnay, Gewürztraminer, Scheurebe, Muscat and red Dornfelder, the last often dark and tannic, sometimes with oak influence.

JOSEPH PHELPS *Napa Valley AVA, California, USA* Phelps' BORDEAUX-blend Insignia★★ is usually one of California's top reds, strongly fruit-driven with a lively spicy background. Cabernets include Napa Valley★ and huge Backus Vineyard★★, beautifully balanced with solid ripe fruit. The Napa Merlot★ is ripe and elegant, with layers of fruit. Phelps was the first California winery to successfully major on RHÔNE varietals, and makes an intense Viognier★ and complex Syrah★. See also FREESTONE. Best years: (Cabernet) 2008 **07 06 05 04 02 01 00 99 96 95 94 91.**

PHILIPPONNAT *Champagne AC, Champagne, France* Quality across the whole range has improved over the past 5 years. The non-vintage★ is (now) one of the best in Champagne, vintage★ is very good too, while single-vineyard Clos des Goisses★★★, from an extremely steep, south-facing vineyard, is some of the purest, ripest and longest-lasting wine in the whole of Champagne. Best years: 2004 02 **00 99 98 96 95 90**.

CH. DE PIBARNON *Bandol AC, Provence, France* One of BANDOL's leading properties, with excellently located vineyards. The reds★★, extremely attractive when young, develop a truffly, wild herb character with age. Ripe, strawberryish rosé. Best years: (2011) 10 09 **08 07 06 05 03 01**.

PIC ST-LOUP *Grand cru du Languedoc AC, Languedoc, France* Will be Pic St-Loup AC from 2013. One of the coolest growing zones in the Midi, to the north of Montpellier, and, along with la CLAPE, produces some of the best reds in the Languedoc. Syrah is the dominant variety, along with Grenache and Mourvèdre. Whites, usually IGP, from Marsanne, Roussanne and Rolle are showing promise. Best producers: Cazeneuve★, CLOS MARIE★, Ermitage du Pic St-Loup, l'Euzière★, l'HORTUS★, Lancyre★, Lascaux★, Lavabre★, MAS BRUGUIERE★, Mas de Mortiès★, Valflaunès. Best years: (reds) (2011) **10 09 08 07 06 05**.

FRANZ X PICHLER *Wachau, Niederösterreich, Austria* One of Austria's most famous producers of dry wines; 'FX', as he is known, is handing the reins to his son Lucas. Grüner Veltliner and Riesling 'M'★★★ (for monumental) and Riesling Unendlich★★★ (endless) – alcoholically potent but balanced – are amazing. So are the Riesling Steinertal★★★ and the Grüner Veltliner Kellerberg★★★. Best years: (2011) 10 09 08 **07 06 05 04 03 02**.

RUDI PICHLER *Wachau, Niederösterreich, Austria* Pichler has steadily made his way into the top tier of WACHAU producers. Riesling Achleiten and Grüner Veltliner Kollmütz and Hochrain are regularly ★★. Best years: (2011) 10 09 **08 07 06 05 04 02**.

CH. PICHON-LONGUEVILLE★★★ *Pauillac AC, 2ème Cru Classé, Haut-Médoc, Bordeaux, France* Despite its superb vineyards, Pichon-Longueville (called Pichon-Baron until 1988) wines were 'also-rans' for a long time. In 1987 the property was bought by AXA and Jean-Michel Cazes of LYNCH-BAGES took over the management. The improvement was immediate and thrilling. Cazes has now left, but many recent vintages have been of First Growth standard, with firm tannic structure and rich dark fruit. Cellar for at least 10 years, although it is likely to keep for 30. Second wine: les Tourelles de Longueville. Best years: 2010 09 08 **07** 06 05 **04 03 02 01 00 99 98 96 95 91 90 89 88 86**.

CH. PICHON-LONGUEVILLE-LALANDE★★★ *Pauillac AC, 2ème Cru Classé, Haut-Médoc, Bordeaux, France* The inspirational figure of May de Lencquesaing forged the modern reputation of this property. It's now (since 2007) controlled by Champagne house ROEDERER with Sylvie Cazes (LYNCH-BAGES connection) as MD. Divinely scented and lush at 6–7 years, the wines usually stay gorgeous for 20 at least. Recent years have been excellent. Second wine: Réserve de la Comtesse. Best years: 2010 09 08 **07** 06 05 **04 03 02 01 00 99 98 96 95 91 90 89 88 86 85**.

PICPOUL DE PINET *Grand Vin du Languedoc, Languedoc AC, France* Fresh salty, pithy white wine made from Picpoul Blanc grown around the village of Pinet near the Etang de Thau. Drink as young as possible. Quality greatly improved in recent vintages. Best producers: Félines-Jourdan★, Pinet co-op, Pomerols co-op, St Martin de la Garrigue★.

PIEDMONT *Italy* The most important Italian region for the tradition of quality wines. In the north, there is Carema, Ghemme and GATTINARA. To the south, in the LANGHE hills, there's BAROLO and BARBARESCO, both masterful examples of the Nebbiolo grape, and other wines from Dolcetto and Barbera grapes. In the Monferrato hills, in the provinces of Asti and Alessandria, the Barbera, Moscato and Cortese grapes hold sway. The broad DOCs of Langhe and Monferrato, backed by the region-wide Piemonte DOC (the region does not admit IGT at all), are designed to classify all wines of quality from a great range of grape varieties. See also ASTI, GAVI, MOSCATO D'ASTI, NEBBIOLO D'ALBA, ROERO.

PIEROPAN *Veneto, Italy* The estate that single-handedly preserved SOAVE's reputation for quality for many years still produces exceptionally good Soave Classico★ and, from 2 single vineyards, outstanding Calvarino★★ and La Rocca★★★. Excellent RECIOTO DI SOAVE Le Colombare★★ and opulent Passito della Rocca★★, a barrique-aged blend of Sauvignon, Riesling Italico (Welschriesling) and Trebbiano di Soave. Single-vineyard Soaves can improve for 5 years or more, as can the sweet styles.

CH. PIERRE-BISE *Coteaux du Layon AC, Loire Valley, France* Claude Papin has a professorial grasp of *terroir*. His COTEAUX DU LAYON vineyard is divided into over 20 mini parcels based on factors like soil depth, topography, and wind and sun exposure that help him analyse optimum ripeness. And the results are sublime: rich, yet pure-fruited and precise Coteaux du Layon★★★ and QUARTS DE CHAUME★★★ with a mineral undertow. Very good dry ANJOU BLANC★, SAVENNIÈRES★, ANJOU Gamay★ and ANJOU-VILLAGES★★. Best years: (sweet) (2011) 10 09 **07** 05 03 02 01 00 97 96 95 90 89.

PIERRO *Margaret River, Western Australia* Mike Peterkin doesn't make much Chardonnay★★★, yet it is a masterpiece of elegance and complexity. The Semillon-Sauvignon LTC★★ is full with just a hint of leafiness, while the Pinot Noir★ should approach ★★ as the vines mature. Dark, dense Cabernet Sauvignon-Merlot Reserve★★ is the serious, BORDEAUX-like member of the family, while LTCf is a more approachable example, with a little touch of Cabernet Franc. The Fire Gully range is from a vineyard next door to MOSS WOOD and is consistently good. Best years: (Chardonnay) (2011) 10 09 **08 07** 06 05 04 03 02.

MARGARET RIVER
CHARDONNAY
2008

PIERRO

Vintaged at Lewis River Vineyard in the Margaret River region of Australia
750 ml WINE OF AUSTRALIA 14.0% FROM MARGARET RIVER vol

PIESPORT *Mosel, Germany* Generic Piesporter Michelsberg wines, soft, sweet, forgettable, have nothing to do with the excellent Rieslings from the top Goldtröpfchen site. With intense peach and blackcurrant aromas they are unique among MOSEL wines. Best producers: GRANS-FASSIAN★★, J Haart★, Reinhold HAART★★, Kurt Hain★, von Kesselstatt★, Lehnert-Veit, ST URBANS-HOF★★. Best years: (2011) 10 09 **08 07** 06 05 04 02 01.

CH. LE PIN★★★ *Pomerol AC, Bordeaux, France* Now one of the most expensive wines in the world. The first vintage was 1979 and the wines, which are concentrated but elegant, sumptuous yet refined, are produced from 100% Merlot. The tiny 2ha (5-acre) vineyard lies close to those of TROTANOY and VIEUX-CHÂTEAU-CERTAN. Best years: 2010 09 08 07 06 05 **04 02** 01 00 99 98 96 95 94 90 89 88 86 85.

PINE RIDGE *Stags Leap District AVA, California, USA* Wines come from several NAPA AVAs, but its flagship Cabernet remains the supple, plummy STAGS LEAP DISTRICT★★. Andrus Reserve★★, a BORDEAUX blend, has more richness and power, while the HOWELL MOUNTAIN Cabernet★ offers intense fruit and structure for long aging. CARNEROS Merlot★ is spicy and cherry fruited, and Carneros Chardonnay★ looks good. Winemaker Michael Beaulac (formerly of ST SUPERY) also makes a nice Chenin Blanc-Viognier. Best years: (Stags Leap Cabernet) 2008 **07 06 05** 03 02 01 **00 99** 97 96 95.

DOMINIO DE PINGUS *Ribera del Duero DO, Castilla y León, Spain* Since 1995, Peter Sisseck's tiny vineyards and winery have produced Pingus★★★, a cult wine of extraordinary depth and character. Second wine Flor de Pingus★★ and third wine Psi★★ are also super. Best years: (Pingus) (2010) 09 08 07 **06** 05 **04 03 01 00 99** 96 95.

PINOT BIANCO See PINOT BLANC.

PINOT BLANC Wines have a clear, yeasty, appley taste, and good examples can age to a delicious honeyed fullness. In ALSACE it is the mainstay of most CRÉMANT D'ALSACE. Important in northern Italy as Pinot Bianco and especially in ALTO ADIGE where it reaches elevated levels of purity, complexity and longevity. Taken seriously in southern Germany and Austria (as Weissburgunder), producing imposing wines with ripe pear and peach fruit and a distinct nutty character. Also successful in Hungary, Slovakia, Slovenia and the Czech Republic and promising in California (notably from Robert Sinskey), Oregon's WILLAMETTE VALLEY and British Columbia, Canada.

PINOT GRIGIO See PINOT GRIS.

PINOT GRIS At its finest in ALSACE: with lowish acidity and a deep colour, the grape produces fat, rich dry wines that somehow mature wonderfully. It is very occasionally used in BURGUNDY (as Pinot Beurot) to add fatness to a wine. Italian Pinot Grigio, often boring, occasionally delicious, is currently so popular worldwide that New World producers are tending to use the Italian name in preference to the French version. Also successful in Austria and Germany as Ruländer or Grauburgunder, and as Malvoisie in the Swiss VALAIS. There are good Romanian, Croatian and Czech examples, as well as spirited ones in Hungary (where it may appear as Szürkebarát). In a crisp style, it can be successful in Oregon and is showing promise in California, Virginia and OKANAGAN VALLEY in Canada. Now fashionable in New Zealand and cooler regions of Australia in a spicy pear style. Starting to appear in Chile.

PINOT MEUNIER An important ingredient in CHAMPAGNE and English sparkling wine, along with Pinot Noir and Chardonnay. Occasionally found in the LOIRE and OREGON and also grown in Germany under the name of Schwarzriesling.

PINOT NERO See PINOT NOIR.
PINOT NOIR See pages 250–1.

PINOTAGE A Pinot Noir x Cinsaut cross, conceived in South Africa in 1925 and covering 6% of the country's vineyards. DeWaal's Top of the Hill is the oldest, planted in 1950 and still bearing. Highly versatile;

classic versions are full-bodied and well-oaked with ripe plum, spice and maybe some mineral, redcurrant, banana or marshmallow flavours. New Zealand, Israel (Barkan) and California have interesting examples. Graziano in MENDOCINO and J VINEYARDS in RUSSIAN RIVER VALLEY make stylish versions. Best producers: (South Africa) Ashbourne★, Graham BECK★, BEYERSKLOOF★★, DeWaal★ (Top of the Hill★★), Diemersfontein★, FAIRVIEW★ (Primo★★), GRANGEHURST★, Kaapzicht★, KANONKOP★★, Laibach★, L'AVENIR★, SIMONSIG★★, Tukulu; (New Zealand) Muddy Water★, Te Awa★.

PIPER-HEIDSIECK *Champagne AC, Champagne, France* They've put a big effort into restoring Piper's reputation: non-vintage★ is now gentle and biscuity, and the vintage★★ is showing real class. They've also launched a plethora of new cuvées: Sublime (demi-sec), Divin (blanc de blancs), Rosé Sauvage and Rare★★, a de luxe blend available in 2002, 1999, 98, 88 and 79 vintages. Best years: 2004 (02) **00 96 95 90 89 85 82**.

DOM. PLAGEOLES *Gaillac AOP, South-West France* Traditionalists and modernizers, Robert and Bernard Plageoles have revived 14 ancient Gaillac grape varieties, including Prunelart, Verdanel and the rare Ondenc, which goes into their lusciously sweet Vin d'Autan★★★, one of France's great stickies. Dry wines include a range from the Mauzac grape★ and bone-dry Mauzac Nature★ fizz. Reds include a remarkable varietal from the Duras★ grape.

PRODUCTEURS PLAIMONT *Madiran AOP, St-Mont AOP and IGP des Côtes de Gascogne, South-West France* This Gascon grouping is the largest, most reliable and most successful co-op in the South-West. The whites★, full of crisp fruit, are reasonably priced and are best drunk young. The reds, especially Ch. de Sabazan★, are very good too and at their best after 5 years or so.

CH. PLAISANCE *Fronton AOP, South-West France* Now fully organic, Marc Pénavayre's range includes a fruity quaffer named after the château★ and a lightly oaked cuvée Thibaut★★. Note too his 100% varietal from the Négrette grape★. Best years: (2011) **10 09**.

PLANETA *Sicily, Italy* Dynamic Sicilian estate. Chardonnay★★ is one of the best in southern Italy; Cabernet Sauvignon Burdese★★ and Merlot★★ are among Italy's most impressive; and rich, peppery Santa Cecilia★★ (Nero d'Avola) has star quality. The white Cometa★ is a fascinating Sicilian version of FIANO. Gluggable Cerasuolo di Vittoria★ and La Segreta red★ and white★ blends are marvellously fruity.

PLANTAGENET *Great Southern, Western Australia* The region's first and still among its most influential wineries. The spicy Shiraz★★ is among the best in WESTERN AUSTRALIA; limy Riesling★★ and classy Cabernet Sauvignon★ also impress. Omrah, from bought-in grapes, is a good second label: Sauvignon Blanc★, Chardonnay★ and Pinot Noir★ stand out. Best years: (Shiraz) (2011) (10) **09 08 07 05 04 03 02 01 99 98 97 95 93**.

PLUMPTON COLLEGE *East Sussex, England* The UK's only teaching establishment that covers vine growing and winemaking produces some good non-vintage sparkling wines, The Dean Brut★ and The Dean Blush Brut★.

IL POGGIONE *Brunello di Montalcino DOCG, Tuscany, Italy* Montalcino's third largest estate, setting the standard for traditional-style BRUNELLO DI MONTALCINO★★ (Riserva★★★) at a reasonable price. Also fine ROSSO DI MONTALCINO★ and Cabernet-Sangiovese blend San Leopoldo★. Best years: (2011) (10) (09) (08) 07 06 **04 01 99 98 97 95 90 88 85**.

PINOT NOIR

There's this myth about Pinot Noir that I think I'd better lay to rest. It goes something like this. Pinot Noir is an incredibly tricky grape to grow and an even more difficult grape to vinify; in fact Pinot Noir is such a difficult customer that the only place that regularly achieves magical results is the thin stretch of land known as the Côte d'Or, between Dijon and Chagny in France, where mesoclimate, soil conditions and 2000 years of experience weave an inimitable web of pleasure.

This just isn't so. The thin-skinned, early-ripening Pinot Noir is undoubtedly more difficult to grow than other great varieties like Cabernet or Chardonnay, but that doesn't mean that it's impossible to grow elsewhere – you just have to work at it with more sensitivity and seek out the right growing conditions. And although great red Burgundy is a hauntingly beautiful wine, it is not the only brilliant interpretation of this remarkable grape variety. The glorious thing about places like New Zealand, California, Oregon, Chile, Australia and Germany is that we are seeing an ever-increasing number of wines that are thrillingly different from anything produced in Burgundy, yet with flavours that are unique to Pinot Noir.

WINE STYLES

France All France's great Pinot Noir wines come from Burgundy's Côte d'Or. Rarely deep in colour, they should nonetheless possess a wonderful fruit quality when young – raspberry, strawberry, cherry or plum – that becomes more scented and exotic with age, the plums turning to figs and prunes, and the richness of chocolate mingling perilously with truffles and well-hung game. Strange, challenging, hedonistic. France's other Pinots – in north and south Burgundy, the Loire Valley, Jura, Savoie, Alsace and now occasionally in the south of France – are lighter and milder, and in Champagne its pale, thin wine is used to make sparkling wine.

Other European regions Since the 1990s, helped by good vintages, German winemakers have made considerable efforts to produce serious Pinot Noir (generally called Spätburgunder). Switzerland, where it is also called Blauburgunder, and Italy (as Pinot Nero) both have fair success, especially in Alto Adige. Austria and Spain have a couple of good examples. Romania, the Czech Republic and Hungary produce significant amounts of Pinot Noir, though of generally low quality.

New World Light, fragrant wines have given Oregon the reputation for being 'another Burgundy', but I get more excited about the sensual wines of the cool, fog-affected areas of California: the ripe, stylish Russian River Valley examples; the exotically scented wines of Carneros, Anderson Valley and Sonoma Coast; the startlingly original offerings from Santa Barbara County (notably Sta. Rita Hills) and Santa Lucia Highlands on east-facing slopes of western Monterey County.

New Zealand produces wines of thrilling fruit and individuality, most notably from Martinborough, Canterbury's Waipara, Marlborough and Central Otago. Cooler regions of Australia – including Yarra Valley, Mornington Peninsula, Adelaide Hills, Geelong, Beechworth and Tasmania – are equally good. Off a small base, new Burgundian clones are gaining ground and quality in cooler spots in South Africa. Chile's San Antonio/Leyda and Bío Bío areas are beginning to shine.

CRISTOM

Willamette Valley

Pinot Noir
Mt. Jefferson Cuvée
2009

PRODUCED AND BOTTLED BY CRISTOM VINEYARDS, INC., SALEM
ALCOHOL 14.0% BY VOL.   PRODUCT OF THE U.S.A.   UNFILTERED

BEST PRODUCERS

France (Burgundy) d'ANGERVILLE, l'Arlot, Comte Armand, D Bachelet, G Barthod, J-M Boillot, BOUCHARD, CATHIARD, CHANDON DE BRIAILLES, R Chevillon, CLAIR, J-J Confuron, DROUHIN, C Dugat, B Dugat-Py, DUJAC, FAIVELEY, GIRARDIN, GRIVOT, Anne GROS, JADOT, LAFARGE, LAFON, Dom. LEROY, LIGER-BELAIR, H Lignier, MÉO-CAMUZET, de MONTILLE, MORTET, J-F MUGNIER, Ponsot, J Prieur, RION, Dom. de la ROMANÉE-CONTI, E Rouget, ROUMIER, ROUSSEAU, Sérafin, de VOGÜÉ, VOUGERAIE.

Germany Becker, BERCHER, FÜRST, HUBER, Johner, KELLER, Kesseler, MEYER-NÄKEL, MOLITOR, REBHOLZ, Stodden.

Italy CA' DEL BOSCO, Franz Haas, Haderburg, Hofstätter, Nals-Margreid.

Spain Cortijo Los Agullares, TORRES.

Switzerland Adank, GANTENBEIN, Mathier.

New World Pinot Noirs
USA (California) ACACIA, Ancien, AU BON CLIMAT, CALERA, Clos Pepe, DE LOACH, DEHLINGER, DUTTON GOLDFIELD, Merry Edwards, Gary FARRELL, FLOWERS, HARTFORD FAMILY, KISTLER, LANDMARK, Littorai, LYNMAR, MARCASSIN, MORGAN, NAVARRO, Patz & Hall, RASMUSSEN, ROCHIOLI, SAINTSBURY, SANFORD, SEA SMOKE, Siduri, Talley, WILLIAMS SELYEM; *(Oregon)* ARGYLE, BEAUX FRERES, Cristom, DOMAINE DROUHIN, DOMAINE SERENE, EVENING LAND, Ken Wright.

Canada (British Columbia) Blue Mountain, Cedar Creek; *(Ontario)* Le CLOS JORDANNE, Flat Rock, INNISKILLIN.

Australia Ashton Hills, BANNOCKBURN, Bass Phillip, BAY OF FIRES, Bindi, Castle Rock, COLDSTREAM HILLS, Curly Flat, DE BORTOLI, Diamond Valley, By FARR, Freycinet, Gembrook Hill, GIACONDA, Giant Steps, Hurley, KOOYONG, Stefano LUBIANA, Marchand & Burch, Moorooduc, OAKRIDGE, Paradigm Hill, PARINGA, STONIER, Tamar Ridge, TARRA-WARRA, Ten Minutes by Tractor, Tomboy Hill, Yabby Lake.

New Zealand ATA RANGI, CRAGGY RANGE, DRY RIVER, Escarpment, FELTON ROAD, Foxes Island, FROMM, Greenhough (Hope Vineyard), MARTINBOROUGH VINEYARD, NEUDORF, PALLISER ESTATE, PEGASUS BAY, Peregrine, QUARTZ REEF, SAINT CLAIR, SERESIN, VAVASOUR.

South Africa BOUCHARD FINLAYSON, CAPE CHAMONIX, Paul CLUVER, HAMILTON RUSSELL, Newton Johnson.

Chile ANAKENA, CASA MARIN, CASAS DEL BOSQUE, CONO SUR (Ocio), Viña LEYDA.

251

POL ROGER *Champagne AC, Champagne, France* Non-vintage Brut Réserve★ (formerly known as White Foil) is biscuity and dependable rather than thrilling. New ultra-dry wine called Pure★. Pol Roger also produces a vintage★★, a vintage rosé★★ and a vintage Chardonnay★★. Its top Champagne, the Pinot-dominated Cuvée Sir Winston Churchill★★, is a deliciously refined drink. All vintage wines will improve with at least 5 years' keeping. Best years: (2002) **00 99 98 96 95 90 89 88 85 82**.

POLIZIANO *Vino Nobile di Montepulciano DOCG, Tuscany, Italy* A leading light in Montepulciano. VINO NOBILE★★ is smoother if more international than average, especially the Riserva Asinone★★. Le Stanze★★ (Cabernet Sauvignon-Merlot) can be outstanding – the fruit in part coming from owner Federico Carletti's other estate, Lohsa, in MORELLINO DI SCANSANO. Best years: (Vino Nobile) (2011) (10) 09 **08 07** 06 **04 01**.

POLZ *Steiermark, Austria* Aromatic dry white wines, mostly★, while Weissburgunder (Pinot Blanc), Morillon (Chardonnay), Muskateller and Sauvignon Blanc frequently deserve ★★ for their combination of intensity and elegance. Best years: (2011) 10 **09 08 07 06 05**.

POMEROL AC *Bordeaux, France* This AC includes some of the world's most sought-after red wines. Pomerol's unique quality lies in its deep clay (though gravel also plays a part in some vineyards) in which the Merlot grape flourishes. The result is seductively rich, almost creamy wine with wonderful mouthfilling fruit flavours: often plummy, but with blackcurrants, raisins and chocolate, too, and mint and minerals to freshen it up. Best producers: Beauregard★, le BON PASTEUR★★, Bonalgue, Certan-de-May★, Clinet★★, Clos l'Église★★, Clos René, la CONSEILLANTE★★, l'ÉGLISE-CLINET★★★, l'ÉVANGILE★★, Feytit-Clinet★, la FLEUR-PETRUS★★, GAZIN★★, Hosanna★★, LAFLEUR★★★, LATOUR-À-POMEROL★, Montviel, Nénin★, PETIT-VILLAGE★, PÉTRUS★★★, Le PIN★★★, Rouget★, TROTANOY★★, VIEUX-CHÂTEAU-CERTAN★★. Best years: 2010 09 08 **06 05 04 01 00 98 96 95 94 90 89**.

POMINO DOC See CHIANTI RUFINA.

POMMARD AC *Côte de Beaune, Burgundy, France* The first village south of Beaune. At their best, the wines should have full, round, beefy flavours, and plenty of tannins. Can age well, often for 10 years or more. There are no Grands Crus, but les Rugiens Bas and les Épenots (both Premiers Crus) are the best sites. Best producers: Aleth-Girardin★, Comte Armand★★★, J-M Boillot★★, de Courcel★★, Dancer★, M Gaunoux★, V GIRARDIN★★, Huber-Vereau★★, LAFARGE★★, Lejeune★, de MONTILLE★★, Parent★, Dom. du Pavillon/Bichot★, Ch. de Pommard★, Pothier-Riesset★. Best years: (2011) 10 09 08 **07** 06 05 03 **02 99 98 96 95 90**.

POMMERY *Champagne AC, Champagne, France* High-quality CHAMPAGNE house now owned by Vranken, who in recent years have launched 10 – yes 10 – non-vintage cuvées! Along with Brut Royal and Apanage★, the range now includes Summertime blanc de blancs, Wintertime blanc de noirs and Springtime rosé. Austere vintage Brut★ is delicious with maturity; the prestige cuvée Louise, both white★ and rosé★, is elegant when on form, but erratic. Best years: 2004 02 00 **99 98 96 95 92 90 89 88 85 82**.

PONDALOWIE *Bendigo, Victoria, Australia* Dominic and Krystina Morris are dynamic producers making a name for their red wines, including Shiraz★, Shiraz-Viognier★ and dramatic, opulent Tempranillo★.

CH. PONTET-CANET★★ *Pauillac AC, 5ème Cru Classé, Haut-Médoc, Bordeaux, France* This property's vineyards are near those of MOUTON-ROTHSCHILD and are run biodynamically. Since 2000 the wine has been on fine form: typically big, chewy, intense PAUILLAC that develops a beautiful blackcurrant fruit. It's one of the wines of the vintage in 2004, 2005 and 2009 – and that's saying something. Used to be great value but prices have climbed. Best years: 2010 09 08 **07** 06 05 **04 03 02 01 00 99 98 96 95 90** 89.

PONZI VINEYARDS *Willamette Valley AVA, Oregon, USA* Dick and Nancy Ponzi sold their first wine in 1974. Second-generation winemaker Luisa Ponzi is crafting exceptionally fine Pinot Gris★★, Pinot Blanc★ and Chardonnay★ – juicy whites for early drinking. The Pinot Noirs★ are developing in complexity and profile. Best years: (reds) (2010) 09 **08** 07 06.

PORT See pages 254–5.

NICOLAS POTEL *Burgundy, France* The eponymous Nicolas left the company in 2009 (see BELLENE). Inexpensive wines still being offered under the Nicolas Potel label, though without the man himself involved.

CH. POTENSAC★★ *Médoc AC, Bordeaux, France* Owned and run by the Delon family, of LÉOVILLE-LAS-CASES, Potensac's fabulous success is based on a rich, sturdy personality, consistency and value for money. The wine can be drunk at 4–5 years, but fine vintages will improve for between 10 and 20 years. Best years: 2010 09 08 **07** 06 05 04 03 02 01 00 99 98 96.

POUILLY-FUISSÉ AC *Mâconnais, Burgundy, France* The sexiest name in the MÂCONNAIS sometimes lives up to its billing for heady white Burgundy. But there is quite a difference in style from producers who vinify their wines simply in stainless steel to those who age them for up to 18 months in oak. The AC covers 5 villages: the richest wines come from Fuissé, the most mineral from Vergisson. Plans are afoot to designate Premier Cru vineyards. Best producers: D & M Barraud★★, Ch. de Beauregard★★, Bret Brothers★★, Cordier★★, Corsin★★, C & T Drouin★, J-A Ferret★★, Ch. Fuissé★★, Guffens-Heynen★★, R Lassarat★★, R Luquet★, O Merlin★★, Ch. des Rontets★★, J & N Saumaize★★, Saumaize-Michelin★★, Valette★★, VERGET★. Best years: (2011) 09 **08 07 06** 05.

POUILLY-FUMÉ AC *Loire Valley, France* Fumé means 'smoked' in French and a good Pouilly-Fumé has a pungent smell often likened to gunflint – as if you'd know. The grape is Sauvignon Blanc, and the extra smokiness comes from a flinty soil called silex. With a few notable exceptions, lacks something of the energy and ambition of SANCERRE. Best producers: F Blanchet★, Henri BOURGEOIS★, A Cailbourdin★, J-C Chatelain★, Chauveau★, Didier DAGUENEAU★★, Serge Dagueneau★, Ch. Favray, Fouassière★, Ladoucette★, Landrat-Guyollot★, Masson-Blondelet★, M Redde★, H Seguin, Tinel-Blondelet★, Ch. de Tracy★. Best years: 2011 10 **09** 08 07 06 05.

POUILLY-LOCHÉ AC See POUILLY-VINZELLES AC.

POUILLY-SUR-LOIRE AC *Loire Valley, France* Light appley wines from the tiny plantings (40ha/100 acres) of the Chasselas grape around Pouilly-sur-Loire, the town which gave its name to POUILLY-FUMÉ. Drink as young as possible. Best producers: Serge Dagueneau★, Landrat-Guyollot★.

POUILLY-VINZELLES AC *Mâconnais, Burgundy, France* With its neighbour Pouilly-Loché, this AC lies somewhat in the shadow of POUILLY-FUISSÉ. Most wines come through the co-op, but there are some good domaines. Best vineyard is Les Quarts. Best producers: Cave des Grands Crus Blancs★, DROUHIN★, la Soufrandière★★, Tripoz★, Valette★. Best years: (2011) 10 **09**.

CH. POUJEAUX★ *Moulis AC, Haut-Médoc, Bordeaux, France* Frequently Poujeaux is the epitome of MOULIS – beautifully balanced, gentle ripe fruit jostled by stony dryness – but just lacking that something extra to propel it to a higher plane. Attractive at 5–6 years old, good vintages can easily last for 10–20 years. Since 2007 same ownership as Clos Fourtet in ST-ÉMILION. Best years: 2010 09 08 **07** 06 05 04 03 02 01 00 99 98 96 95 90.

PORT DOC

Douro, Portugal

The Douro region in northern Portugal, where the grapes for port are grown, is wild and beautiful, and part is classified as a World Heritage Site. Steep hills covered in vineyard terraces plunge dramatically down to the Douro river. Grapes are one of the few crops that will grow in the inhospitable climate, which gets progressively drier the further inland you travel. But not all the Douro's grapes qualify to be made into port. A quota is established every year, and the rest are made into increasingly good unfortified Douro wines.

Red port grapes include Touriga Franca, Tinta Roriz, Touriga Nacional, Tinta Barroca, Tinta Cão and Tinta Amarela. Grapes for white port include Côdega, Gouveio, Malvasia Fina, Rabigato and Viosinho. The grapes are partially fermented, and then *aguardente* (grape spirit) is added, which fortifies the wine and stops the fermentation, leaving sweet, unfermented grape sugar in the finished port.

PORT STYLES

Vintage Finest of the ports matured in bottle, made from grapes from the best vineyards. Vintage port is not 'declared' every year (usually there are 3 or 4 declarations per decade), and only during the second calendar year in cask if the shipper thinks the standard is high enough. It is bottled after 2 years, and may be consumed soon afterwards, as is not uncommon in the USA; at this stage it packs quite a punch. The British custom of aging for 20 years or more can yield exceptional mellowness. Vintage port throws a thick sediment, so requires decanting.

Single quinta (Vintage) A single-quinta port comes from an individual estate; many shippers sell a vintage port under a quinta name in years which are not declared as a vintage. It is quite possible for these 'off vintage' ports to equal or even surpass the vintage wines from the same house.

Aged tawny Matured in cask for 10, 20, 30 or even 40 years before bottling, older tawnies have delicious nut and fig flavours. The age is stated on the label.

Colheita Tawny from a single vintage, matured in cask for at least 7 years – potentially the finest of the aged tawnies.

Late Bottled (Vintage) (LBV) Port matured for 4–6 years in cask and vat, then usually filtered to avoid sediment forming in the bottle. Traditional unfiltered LBV has much more flavour and requires decanting; it can generally be aged for another 5 years or more.

Crusted This is a blend of good ports from 2–3 vintages, bottled without filtration after 3–4 years in cask. A deposit (crust) forms in the bottle and the wine should be decanted. A gentler, junior type of 'vintage' flavour.

Reserve (most can be categorized as Premium Ruby) has an average of 3–5 years' age. A handful represent good value.

Ruby The youngest red port with only 1–3 years' age. Ruby port should be bursting with young, almost peppery, fruit, and there has been an improvement in quality of late, except at the cheapest level.

Tawny Cheap tawny is either an emaciated ruby, or a blend of ruby and white port, and is usually best avoided.

White Only the best taste dry and nutty from wood-aging; most are coarse and alcoholic, and best with tonic water and a slice of lemon.

BEST YEARS

2009 07 05 03 00 97 94 92
91 85 83 80 77 70 66 63 60
55 48 47 45 35 34 31 27 12
08 04 1900

BEST PRODUCERS

Vintage BURMESTER, CHURCHILL,
COCKBURN'S, CROFT, DOW'S,
FERREIRA, FONSECA, GRAHAM'S,
NIEPOORT, Quinta do NOVAL,
RAMOS PINTO, SMITH WOODHOUSE,
TAYLOR'S, WARRE'S.

Single quinta (Vintage)
CHURCHILL (Quinta da Gricha),
COCKBURN'S (Quinta dos
Canais), Quinta do CRASTO,
CROFT (Quinta da Roêda),
DOW'S (Quinta do Bomfim,
Quinta Senhora da Ribeira),
FONSECA (Guimaraens),
GRAHAM'S (Malvedos), Quinta do
Passadouro, Pintas, Quinta de la
ROSA, TAYLOR'S (Quinta de Terra
Feita, Quinta de Vargellas),
Quinta do Vale Dona Maria,
Quinta do Vale Meão, Quinta
do Vallado, Quinta do VESUVIO,
WARRE'S (Quinta da Cavadinha).

Aged tawny Barros,
BURMESTER, COCKBURN'S, DOW'S,
FERREIRA, FONSECA, GRAHAM'S,
Krohn, NIEPOORT, NOVAL,
RAMOS PINTO, SANDEMAN,
TAYLOR'S, WARRE'S.

Colheita Andresen, Barros,
BURMESTER, Cálem, Feist, Kopke,
Krohn, Messias, NIEPOORT,
NOVAL.

**Traditional Late Bottled
Vintage** Andresen, CHURCHILL,
Quinta do CRASTO, FONSECA,
Quinta do Infantado, NIEPOORT,
NOVAL, Poças, RAMOS PINTO,
Quinta de la ROSA, SMITH
WOODHOUSE, WARRE'S.

Crusted CHURCHILL, DOW'S,
FONSECA, GRAHAM'S.

Reserve Ruby COCKBURN'S,
FERREIRA, FONSECA, GRAHAM'S,
Quinta de la ROSA, SANDEMAN,
SMITH WOODHOUSE, TAYLOR'S,
WARRE'S.

White CHURCHILL, Dalva,
NIEPOORT.

PRAGER *Wachau, Niederösterreich, Austria* Toni Bodenstein is one of the
pioneers of the WACHAU, producing the elegant high-elevation Riesling
Wachstum★★★, other Rieslings from the Achleiten and Klaus vineyards
(often ★★★) and excellent Grüner Veltliners from Achleiten★★. Best
years: (2011) 10 09 **08 07 06 05 04 03 02 01**.

PREMIÈRES CÔTES DE BORDEAUX AC *Bordeaux, France* Part of the
hilly region opposite GRAVES and SAUTERNES (see CADILLAC-COTES DE
BORDEAUX). As of 2008 this AC designation is for sweet white wines only.
Mildly sweet in style; drink young. Best producers: Crabitan-Bellevue★,
Fayau★, du Juge, Suau. Best years: **2010** 09 07 05 03.

CH. PRIEURÉ-LICHINE★ *Margaux AC, 4ème Cru Classé, Haut-Médoc, Bordeaux,*
France Underachieving property that saw several false dawns before
being sold in 1999. Right Bank specialist Stéphane Derenoncourt (PAVIE-
MACQUIN, CANON-LA-GAFFELIERE) is now the consultant winemaker, and
some vintages have more fruit, finesse and perfume, especially the 2009.
Best years: 2009 08 **07 06 05 04 03 01 00 99 98 96**.

PRIEURÉ DE ST-JEAN DE BÉBIAN *Pézenas Grand Vin du Languedoc AC,*
Languedoc, France One of the pioneering estates in the Midi, producing
an intense, spicy, generous red★★, second wine La Chapelle de Bébian,
a barrel-fermented white★ and pink Bébian en rose. Sold in 2009 to
Russian investors, but winemaking team remains the same. Best years:
(reds) (2011) 10 09 08 **07 06 03 04**.

PRIMITIVO DI MANDURIA DOC *Puglia, Italy* The most important
appellation for PUGLIA's Primitivo grape, which has been enjoying a
renaissance since it was found to be almost identical to California's
Zinfandel. The best wines combine outstanding ripeness and
concentration with a knockout alcohol level. Good Primitivo is also sold
as Primitivo del Tarantino IGT and Gioia del Colle DOC. Best
producers: Felline★★, Pervini★, Giovanni Soloperto. Best years: (2011) (10) 09
08 07 06 05 04.

PRIMO ESTATE *McLaren Vale, South Australia* Joe Grilli is one of Australia's
most thoughtful and innovative winemakers; quality has been even higher
as he sources better vineyards, primarily in MCLAREN VALE. For his premium
label, Joseph, Grilli adapts the Italian AMARONE method for Moda
Cabernet-Merlot★★ (★★★ with 10 years' age) and makes a dense, eye-
popping, complex Joseph Red fizz★★. He also does a sensuous Botrytis
Riesling La Magia★★ and fine, powerful Nebbiolo★. Zesty dry white La
Biondina Colombard★, cherry-ripe Il Briccone Shiraz-Sangiovese★ and
bright, velvety Merlesco Merlot. Best years: (Moda Cabernet-Merlot) (2011)
10 09 08 07 **06 05 04 02 01 00 99 98 97 96 95 94 93 91**.

PRINCE EDWARD COUNTY *Ontario, Canada* A newly designated
viticultural area jutting into Lake Ontario, east of Toronto. Deep
limestone makes the region ideal for Pinot Noir, Chardonnay and
traditional method sparkling wine; the Chardonnays have positively
Burgundian oatmeal texture. Twenty-five wineries have opened since
2000. Best producers: Closson Chase★, Exultet Estates, Norman Hardie★,
Hinterland (sparkling), Huff Estates, Long Dog, Rosehall Run★.

PRIORAT DOCa *Cataluña, Spain* A hilly, isolated district with very low-
yielding vineyards planted on precipitous slopes of deep slate soil. Old-
style fortified *rancio* wines used to attract little attention. Then in the
1980s a group of young winemakers revolutionized the area, bringing in
state-of-the-art winemaking methods and grape varieties such as
Cabernet Sauvignon to back up the native Garnacha and Cariñena.

Their rare, expensive wines have taken the world by storm. Ready at 5 years old, the best will last much, much longer. Best producers: Bodegas B G (Gueta-Lupia★), Capafons-Ossó★, Cims de Porrera★★, CLOS ERASMUS★★★, CLOS MOGADOR★★★, Combier-Fischer-Gérin★★ (Trio Infernal 2/3★★), La Conreria d'Scala Dei★, Costers del Siurana (Clos de l'Obac★★), Gran Clos★, Ithaca★, Les Cousins Marc & Adrià★, Mas Alta★★, MAS DOIX★★★, Mas d'en Gil (Clos Fontà★, Como Vella★), Mas Martinet (Clos Martinet★), Nin★, Alvaro PALACIOS★★★, Pasanau Germans (Finca la Planeta★), TERROIR AL LIMÍT★★★, TORRES★★, VALL LLACH★★. Best years: (reds) (2010) 09 08 07 05 04 03 01 00 99 98 96 95 94 93.

PROSECCO DOC/DOCG *Veneto and Friuli-Venezia Giulia, Italy* Following years of misuse and abuse, the laws relating to this north-eastern Italian grape variety, and the slightly off-dry *spumante* or *frizzante* (occasionally still) wines derived from it, have been substantially revised. The grape has been renamed Glera. 'Prosecco', now that it's no longer a grape but a wine, may be produced only in designated areas of Veneto and Friuli, and only as DOCG or DOC. The DOCG applies only to the wines of the historic Veneto zones of Conegliano and Valdobbiadene, and to the sub zone of Valdobbiadene called Cartizze, usually considered the best. Best producers: Adami★, Biancavigna, Bisol★, Carpene Malvolti★, Le Colture★, Nino Franco★, La Riva dei Frati★, Ruggeri★, Vignarosa, Zardetto★.

PROVENCE *France* Provence is home to France's oldest vineyards, but the region has been better known for its beaches and arts festivals than for its wines. However, even Provence is caught up in the revolution sweeping through the vineyards of southern France. Most of the wine comes from the CÔTES DE PROVENCE, COTEAUX VAROIS-EN-PROVENCE, Coteaux de Pierrevert and COTEAUX D'AIX-EN-PROVENCE. There are 5 smaller ACs (BANDOL, les BAUX-DE-PROVENCE, BELLET, CASSIS and PALETTE), and the BOUCHES-DU-RHÔNE, Alpilles, Alpes-Maritimes and Var IGPs are becoming increasingly important. Reds can be good and there is a growing movement among producers throughout the region to develop and promote quality red wines. Two distinct styles are emerging: lighter aperitif wine and a wood-aged 'gastronomic' style. Opinions are divided as to whether the latter style is 'Provençal'. Whites have a way to go but top producers are making good wines from Rolle (Vermentino).

J J PRÜM *Bernkastel, Mosel, Germany* Estate making some of Germany's most exquisite Riesling in sites like the Sonnenuhr★★★ in WEHLEN, Himmelreich★★ in GRAACH and Lay★★ and Badstube★★ in BERNKASTEL. Slow to develop but they all have great aging potential. Best years: (2011) 10 09 08 07 06 05 04 03 02 01 99 97 95 94.

S A PRÜM *Wehlen, Mosel, Germany* There are a confusing number of Prüms in the MOSEL – the best known is J J PRÜM, but S A Prüm comes a decent second. The most interesting wines are Riesling from WEHLENer Sonnenuhr, especially Auslese★★; there's also good wine from sites in BERNKASTEL★, ÜRZIG★ and GRAACH★. Best years: (2011) 10 09 08 **07 06 05 04 03 02.**

PRUNOTTO *Barolo DOCG, Piedmont, Italy* One of the historic BAROLO producers, now ably run by Albiera, Piero ANTINORI's eldest daughter. Highlights include Barolo Bussia★★★ and Cannubi★★, BARBERA D'ALBA Pian Romualdo★★, BARBERA D'ASTI Costamiòle★★, BARBARESCO Bric Turot★★ and NEBBIOLO D'ALBA Occhetti★. Also good MOSCATO D'ASTI★, Barbera d'Asti Fiulot★ and Roero ARNEIS★. Best years: (Barolo) (2011) (10) (09) 08 07 06 **04 01 99 98 97 95 90.**

PUGLIA *Italy* This heel-of-the-boot region was once a prolific source of blending wines, but exciting progress has been made with native varieties: red Uva di Troia in CASTEL DEL MONTE; white Greco for characterful Gravina DOC, revived by Botromagno; and Verdeca and Bianco d'Alessano for Locorotondo DOC. The red Primitivo, led by examples from producers under the RACEMI umbrella, makes a big impact (whether under the PRIMITIVO DI MANDURIA DOC or more general IGTs). But it is the Negroamaro grape grown on traditional bush-trained or *alberello* vines in the Salento peninsula that provides the best wines, whether red or rosé. Outstanding examples include Vallone's Graticciaia★★, Candido's Duca d'Aragona★★, Azienda Monaci's le Braci★★ and Taurino's Patriglione★★. Brindisi and SALICE SALENTINO are good-value, reliable DOCs.

PUISSEGUIN-ST-ÉMILION AC *Bordeaux, France* Small ST-ÉMILION satellite. The wines are generally fairly solid but with an attractive chunky fruit, for drinking in 3–5 years. **Best producers:** Bel-Air, Branda, Durand-Laplagne★, Fongaban, Guibeau-la-Fourvieille, Laurets, la Mauriane★, Producteurs Réunis, Soleil★. **Best years:** 2010 **09 08 05 03 01**.

PULENTA ESTATE *Mendoza, Argentina* Brothers Hugo and Eduardo Pulenta established this 135ha (330-acre) Alto Agrelo estate in the early 1990s. The altitude and proximity to the Andes Mountains ensures purity, freshness and elegance. La Flor Malbec★ is juicy and full of fresh blue fruits; La Flor Sauvignon Blanc★ is a racy, tropical delight. The Estate range has expanded over time, including such oddities as Pinot Gris and late-harvest Cabernet Franc Tardío, but the Malbec★ and Cabernet Sauvignon★ are as supple and aromatic as ever. The sublime XI Gran Cabernet Franc★★ is packed with raspberry coulis richness and leaf freshness, and Gran Corte★★ red blend is dense and rich.

PULIGNY-MONTRACHET AC *Côte de Beaune, Burgundy, France* Puligny is one of the finest white wine villages in the world and adds the name of its greatest Grand Cru, le MONTRACHET, to its own. There are 3 other Grands Crus (BÂTARD-MONTRACHET, Bienvenues-BÂTARD-MONTRACHET and Chevalier-MONTRACHET) and 11 Premiers Crus. The flatter vineyards use the Puligny-Montrachet AC. Good vintages really need 5 years' aging, while Premiers Crus and Grands Crus should last 10 years or more. A few barrels of red wine are made. **Best producers:** H Boillot★★, J-M Boillot★★, CARILLON★★★, Chavy★, Deux MONTILLE★, DROUHIN★★, B Ente★, FAIVELEY★★, JADOT★★, Louis LATOUR★, Dom. LEFLAIVE★★★, O LEFLAIVE★, P Pernot★★, Ch. de Puligny-Montrachet★★, SAUZET★★. **Best years:** (2011) 10 09 08 **07 06 05 04 02 00 99**.

PYRENEES See GRAMPIANS AND PYRENEES.

QUARTS DE CHAUME AC *Loire Valley, France* The Chenin Blanc grape finds one of its most rewarding mesoclimates in this 40ha (100-acre) AC within the larger COTEAUX DU LAYON AC; steep, sheltered, schistous slopes favour optimal ripening and noble rot. The result is intense, sweet wines with a mineral backbone, which can last for longer than almost any in the world – although many can be drunk after 5 years. **Best producers:** P Baudouin★, Baumard★★, Bellerive★★, Bergerie★★, Laffourcade★, PIERRE-BISE★★★, Pithon-Paillé, Plaisance★, Joseph Renou★★, Suronde★★, la Varière★. **Best years:** (2011) 10 09 **07 06 05 03 02 01 99 97 96 95 90 89**.

QUARTZ REEF *Central Otago, South Island, New Zealand* Austrian-born winemaker/owner Rudi Bauer is one of the region's leading lights in winemaking innovation. Best known for its powerful, serious Pinot Noir★★ and sleek bottle-fermented sparkling wine★ (vintage★★).

Intensely-flavoured, minerally, almost chewy Pinot Gris★ is one of their lesser known stars. Best years: (Pinot Noir) **2010 09 08 07 06 05**.

QUEENSLAND *Australia* The Queensland wine industry – closely linked to tourism – is expanding fast. About 60 wineries perch on rocky hills in the main region, the Granite Belt, near the NEW SOUTH WALES border. New areas South Burnett (north-west of Brisbane), Darling Downs (around the town of Toowoomba) and Mount Tamborine in the Gold Coast hinterland are showing promise. Best producers: Barambah, BOIREANN★★, Robert Channon★, Clovely Estate, Heritage, Lucas Estate, Preston Peak★, Pyramids Road, Robinsons Family, Sirromet, Summit Estate, Witches Falls.

QUERCIABELLA *Chianti Classico DOCG, Tuscany, Italy* Modern Chianti producer with a gorgeously scented, rich-fruited CHIANTI CLASSICO★★. But the top wines are Burgundy-like white Batàr★★ (Pinot Bianco-Chardonnay) and tobaccoey, spicy Camartina★★★ (Sangiovese-Cabernet). Mongrana★, a juicy, smooth-but-serious blend of Sangiovese, Merlot and Cabernet Sauvignon, is from a new estate in MAREMMA. Best years: (Camartina) (2011) (10) 09 08 **07 06 04 01 99**.

QUILCEDA CREEK *Washington State, USA* One of America's top Cabernet Sauvignons★★★, a wine with intense concentration and exceptional character. It benefits from cellaring for 7-10 years. A less expensive Columbia Valley Red★★ offers a tantalizing glimpse of the winemaking style. Best years: (2010) 09 08 07 **06 05 04 03 02 01**.

QUINCY AC *Loire Valley, France* Appealingly aggressive gooseberry-flavoured, dry white wine from Sauvignon Blanc vineyards west of Bourges. Can age for a year or two. Best producers: Ballandors★, H BOURGEOIS, Chevilly★, B & L Lecomte★, Mardon★, A Pigeat★, J C Roux★, C Tremblay, Trotereau★.

QUINTARELLI *Valpolicella DOC, Veneto, Italy* Recently deceased Bepi Quintarelli was the great traditional winemaker of VALPOLICELLA. His philosophy was to grow the very best grapes and let nature do the rest. The Classico Superiore★★ is left in cask for about 4 years and the famed AMARONE★★★ and RECIOTO★★ for up to 7 years before release. Alzero★★ is a spectacular Amarone-style wine made from Cabernets Franc and Sauvignon. His daughter and family continue the tradition. Best years: (Amarone) (2010) (09) (08) 07 06 **04 03 01 99 97 95 93 90 88 85 83**.

QUPÉ *Santa Maria Valley AVA, California, USA* Owner/winemaker Bob Lindquist is focused on cooler-climate Syrahs with a peppery aroma and makes a savoury, tasty Bien Nacido Syrah★. His Reserve Chardonnay★ and Bien Nacido Cuvée★ (a Viognier-Chardonnay blend) have beguiling appley fruit and perfume. A leading exponent of red and white RHÔNE-style wines, including Viognier★, Marsanne★ and Roussanne★★. Best years: (Syrah) 2010 09 08 07 06 05 04 03 02 01 **00 99 98 97**.

RACEMI *Puglia, Italy* Premium venture run by Gregory Perrucci, scion of a long-established family of bulk shippers of basic Puglian wines. Modern-style reds, mainly from Primitivo and Negroamaro, under various producers' names: Felline (Vigna del Feudo★★), Pervini (PRIMITIVO DI MANDURIA Archidamo★★), Masseria Pepe (Dunico★★). Best years: (reds) (2011) 10 **09 08 07 06 04**.

CH. DE LA RAGOTIÈRE Muscadet Sèvre-et-Maine, Loire Valley, France The
Couillaud brothers are pioneers. M★★ is an old-vines wine matured *sur
lie* for more than 2 years. The standard Muscadet★ is elegant and built to
last, too; lighter ones come from the Couillauds' other property, Ch. la
Morinière. Vin de pays Chardonnay★ is a speciality and the Collection
Privée label includes a late-harvest Petit Manseng, Sauvignon Gris★ and
Viognier. Best years: (M) 2009 **06 01 99 97**.

RAÏMAT Costers del Segre DO, Cataluña, Spain Owned by CODORNÍU, this large,
irrigated estate makes pleasant and wines from Tempranillo, Cabernet
Sauvignon and Chardonnay. Lively 100% Chardonnay CAVA and upscale
red blend 4 Varietales. Best years: (reds) 2009 **08 07 06**.

DOM. DE LA RAMAYE Gaillac AOP, South-West France High-quality wines
from Michel Issaly: whites, mostly from Mauzac, include Les Cavaillés
Bas★★, sweeter Sous-Bois de Rayssac★★ and, in great years,
Quintessence★★★. Reds include La Combe d'Avès★★, a Duras-Braucol
blend, and Prunelard-based Le Grand Tertre★★. Best years: (2011) 10 09
08 06 05 04.

RAMEY WINE CELLARS Sonoma County, California, USA David Ramey is one
of the state's most creative winemakers (as well as a consultant for many
other wineries) and his marvellously savoury, primarily CARNEROS and
RUSSIAN RIVER-based Chardonnays★★ (Hyde★★, Ritchie★★), NAPA-
based Cabernet Sauvignons★★ and scented SONOMA-based Syrahs★★ are
highly sought-after. Best years: (Cabernet) (2009) 08 **07 06 05 01**.

RAMONET Chassagne-Montrachet, Côte de Beaune, Burgundy, France The
Ramonets (Noël and Jean-Claude) produce some of the most complex of
all white Burgundies from 3 Grands Crus (BÂTARD-MONTRACHET★★★,
Bienvenues-BÂTARD-MONTRACHET★★★, le MONTRACHET★★★) and Premiers
Crus (Ruchottes★★★, Caillerets★★★, Chaumées★★★, Boudriotte★★,
Vergers★★, Morgeot★★). To spare your wallet, try the ST-AUBIN★★ or
the village CHASSAGNE-MONTRACHET★★. Red Clos de la Boudriotte★★ is
excellent too. Best years: (whites) (2011) 10 09 08 **07 06 05 02 00 99**.

JOÃO PORTUGAL RAMOS Alentejo, Portugal João Portugal Ramos has
built his ALENTEJO, TEJO (Falua) and DOURO (Duorum) empire from
nothing. Excellent Vila Santa Trincadeira★, Aragonês (Tempranillo)★
and Syrah★, and intensely dark-fruited red blend Vila Santa Reserva★★.
Good Marquês de Borba reds, with brilliant red Reserva★★. Tagus
Creek is juicy and affordable. Best years: **2008 07 05 04 01 00 99 97**.

RAMOS PINTO Douro DOC and Port DOC, Douro, Portugal Innovative company
owned by ROEDERER. Full-bodied Late Bottled Vintage★ and aged tawny
ports (10-year-old Quinta de Ervamoira★, 20-year-old Quinta do Bom
Retiro★★). Vintage ports★★ are rich and early maturing. Consistently
good DOURO reds Duas Quintas (Reserva★, Reserva Especial★★) and
white Bons Ares★. Best years: (Vintage) 2007 **04 03 00 97 95 94 83**.

CASTELLO DEI RAMPOLLA Chianti Classico DOCG, Tuscany, Italy
Outstanding, if French-influenced, CHIANTI CLASSICO★★. Sammarco,
sometimes ★★★, is mostly Cabernet with some Sangiovese; Vigna
d'Alceo★★★ adds Petit Verdot to Cabernet Sauvignon. Best years:
(Sammarco) (2011) (10) 09 08 **07 06 04 01 00 99**; (Vigna d'Alceo) (2011) (10)
09 08 **07 06 04 01 00 99 98 97**.

RANDERSACKER Franken, Germany Village near WÜRZBURG, producing
excellent dry Riesling, dry Silvaner, spicy Traminer and piercingly intense
Rieslaner. Best producers: Bürgerspital, JULIUSSPITAL★, Schmitt's Kinder★,
Störrlein★, Trockene Schmitts. Best years: (2011) 10 09 **08 07 06 05 04**.

RAPEL *Chile* One of Chile's most exciting red wine regions, the cradle of Chilean Carmenère, Rapel covers both the Cachapoal Valley in the north and the COLCHAGUA Valley in the south. New CONCHA Y TORA coastal development Ucúquer is promising thrilling cool flavours. Best producers: Altaïr★★/SAN PEDRO, ANAKENA★, CASA SILVA★, Clos des Fous★★, CONCHA Y TORO★★, CONO SUR★, EMILIANA★★, Gracia★, La Rosa, LAPOSTOLLE★★, Los Vascos, Misiones de Rengo★, MONTES★★, MontGras, Neyen★★, VENTISQUERO★, Viu Manent★.

KENT RASMUSSEN *Carneros AVA, California, USA* Delicious, oatmealy Chardonnay★★ capable of considerable aging and a fascinating juicy but also long-lasting Pinot Noir★★ are made by ultra-traditional methods. Ramsay is the second label, for Pinot Noir★, Cabernet Sauvignon and Merlot. Best years: (Pinot Noir) 2009 **08 07 06 05 02 01 00 99 98.**

RASTEAU *Rhône Valley, France* The AC is both for the red wine and for fortified Grenache (red, white wine and a reviving *rancio* version which is left in barrel for 2 or more years). The red, robust and spicy, delivers big flavours, with some refinement. Best producers: E Balme, Beau Mistral★, Beaurenard★, Cave des Vignerons, Escaravailles★, Gourt de Mautum★★, Grand Nicolet, Perrin★, Rabasse-Charavin, ST GAYAN, Santa Duc★, la Soumade★, Trapadis★. Best years: (reds) (2011) **10 09 07 06 05 04 03.**

RENATO RATTI *Barolo DOCG, Piedmont, Italy* The late Renato Ratti was a leading modernist in the Alba area, with BAROLO and BARBARESCO of better balance, colour and richness and softer in tannins than the traditional models. Today his son Pietro produces sound Barolo Marcenasco★ and fine crus Conca★★ and Rocche★★ from the Marcenasco vineyards at La Morra, as well as good BARBERA D'ALBA Torriglione★, Dolcetto d'Alba Colombé★, NEBBIOLO D'ALBA Ochetti★ and Monferrato DOC Villa Pattono★, a Barbera-Cabernet-Merlot blend.

RAUENTHAL *Rheingau, Germany* Only a few producers make the best of this village's great Baiken and Gehrn sites for intense, spicy Rieslings. Best producers: Georg BREUER★★, Langwerth von Simmern★, Staatsweingut (Kloster Eberbach)★. Best years: (2011) **10 09 08 07 06 05 04 02.**

CH. RAUZAN-SÉGLA★★ *Margaux AC, 2ème Cru Classé, Haut-Médoc, Bordeaux, France* The purchase of the property by Chanel in 1994 followed by massive investment and astute management have propelled Rauzan-Ségla up the quality ladder. Now the wines have a rich plummy fruit, round, mellow texture, powerful woody spice and good concentration, though they rarely show typical MARGAUX scent. Second wine: Ségla. Best years: 2010 09 08 07 06 05 04 03 02 01 00 98 96 95 90 89 88.

DOM. RAVENEAU *Chablis, Burgundy, France* Jean Marie and Bernard Raveneau make beautifully nuanced CHABLIS from 3 Grands Crus (Blanchot★★★, les Clos★★★, Valmur★★★) and 4 Premiers Crus (Montée de Tonnerre★★★, Vaillons★★, Butteaux★★★, Chapelot★★), using a combination of mostly old oak and stainless-steel fermentation. The wines can age for a decade or more. Best years: (top crus) (2011) **10 09 08 07 06 05 02 00 99 95 90.**

RAVENSWOOD *Sonoma Valley AVA, California, USA* Zinfandel expert Joel Peterson established Ravenswood in 1976. Constellation bought the winery in 2001, but Peterson remains in charge. Large-volume Vintners Blend★ has greatly improved recently, and the old-vine Zinfandels (Sonoma★, Napa★, Lodi★) are tasty and characterful. Single-vineyard wines like Teldeschi can be ★★. Super-premium Icon★★ is a blend of Carignan, Petite Sirah, Zinfandel and other grapes from ancient vines.

CH. RAYAS *Châteauneuf-du-Pape, Rhône Valley, France* Emmanuel Reynaud produces exotically fragrant rich but subtle reds★★★ and whites★★ that age incredibly well. Methods are traditional, prices are high, but recent vintages are on top form – at its best Rayas is thrilling. The red is made entirely from low-yielding Grenache vines, while the white is a blend of Clairette, Grenache Blanc and a drop or two (so rumour has it) of Chardonnay. Second-label Pignan can also be impressive. CÔTES DU RHONE Ch. de Fonsalette★★ is usually wonderful in the same style as Rayas. Also fine VACQUEYRAS Ch. des Tours★.

Best years: (Châteauneuf-du-Pape) (2011) 10 09 08 07 06 05 **04 03 01 99 98 96 95 94 91 90 89 88 86**; (whites) (2011) 10 09 08 07 **06** 05 **04** 03 01 **00 99 98 97 96 95 94 91 90 89**.

REBHOLZ *Siebeldingen, Pfalz, Germany* Crystalline Riesling★★, Weissburgunder★★ (Pinot Blanc) and Grauburgunder★ (Pinot Gris), with vibrant fruit aromas. Top of the range are intensely mineral dry Riesling★★★ from the Kastanienbusch and Sonnenschein vineyards, and extravagantly aromatic dry Muskateller★★. The sparkling wine★★ is among Germany's most elegant. Also fine Chardonnay★★ and serious Spätburgunder★★ (Pinot Noir) reds. Best years: (whites) (2011) 10 09 **08 07 06 05 04 03 02**; (reds) (2011) (10) 09 **08 07 06 05 04**.

RECIOTO DELLA VALPOLICELLA DOCG *Veneto, Italy* The great sweet wine of VALPOLICELLA, made from grapes picked earlier than usual and left to dry on straw mats until February or March. The wines are deep in colour, with a rich, bitter-sweet cherryish fruit. Top wines age well for 10 years, but most are best drunk young. As with Valpolicella, the Classico tag is important, though not essential. Best producers: Accordini★, ALLEGRINI★★, Bolla (Spumante★), Brigaldara★, BUSSOLA★★★, Michele Castellani★★, DAL FORNO★★, MASI★, QUINTARELLI★★, Le Ragose★, Le Salette★, Serègo Alighieri★★, Speri★, Tedeschi★, Tommasi★, Villa Monteleone★★, VIVIANI★★. Best years: (2011) (10) 09 **08 06 05 04**.

RECIOTO DI SOAVE DOCG *Veneto, Italy* Sweet white wine made in the SOAVE zone from dried grapes, like RECIOTO DELLA VALPOLICELLA. Garganega grapes give wonderfully delicate yet intense wines that age well for up to a decade. One of the best, ANSELMI's I Capitelli★★, is sold as IGT Veneto. Best producers: Cà Rugate★, La Cappuccina★★, Coffele★★, Gini★★, PIEROPAN★★, Prà★, Bruno Sartori★, Tamellini★★. Best years: (2011) (10) 09 **08 06 04**.

RÉGNIÉ AC *Beaujolais, Burgundy, France* In good years this BEAUJOLAIS Cru is light, aromatic and enjoyable along the style of CHIROUBLES, but can be thin in lesser years. Best producers: Bulliats★, J-M Burgaud★, Coquard★, DUBOEUF (Dom. des Buyats★), Gilles Roux/de la Plaigne★. Best years: (2011) 10.

DOM. LA RÉMÉJEANNE *Côtes du Rhône AC, Rhône Valley, France* First-class property making a range of strikingly individual, punchy wines. CÔTES DU RHÔNE-VILLAGES les Genévriers★★ has the intensity, weight and texture of good CHÂTEAUNEUF-DU-PAPE, while CÔTES DU RHÔNE les Eglantiers★★ is superb. Both need at least 3–5 years' aging. Also good Côtes du Rhône les Chèvrefeuilles★ and les Arbousiers★ (red and white). Best years: (les Eglantiers) (2011) **10 09 07 06 05 04 03**.

REMELLURI *Rioja DOCa, País Vasco, Spain* Organic RIOJA estate producing red
🍷 wines with far more fruit than usual and good concentration for
aging – the best are ★★. There is also a delicate, barrel-fermented
white★★. As of 2010, Telmo RODRÍGUEZ is at the helm again. Best years:
(Reserva) 2007 **06 05 04 03 02 01 99 98 96 95 94**.

REUILLY AC *Loire Valley, France* Dry but attractive Sauvignon from west of
🍷🍷 SANCERRE. Some pale Pinot Noir red and Pinot Gris rosé. Best producers:
H Beurdin, G Bigonneau, D Jamain★, C Lafond, A Mabillot, J Rouzé, Les
Demoiselles Tatin, J Vincent.

CH. REYNON *Cadillac-Côtes de Bordeaux AC, Bordeaux, France* Property of
🍷 enology professor Denis Dubourdieu. Dry whites, particularly the fruity,
minerally Sauvignon Blanc★, are delightful (drink the most recent
vintage) and the red★ is good, too. The lovely white GRAVES Clos
Floridène★★ is vinified at Reynon. Best years: (reds) 2010 **09 08 07 06 05**.

RHEINGAU *Germany* 3125ha (7720-acre) wine region on a south-facing
stretch of the Rhine flanking the city of Wiesbaden, planted mostly with
Riesling and some Spätburgunder (Pinot Noir). At their best, the Rieslings
are racy and slow-maturing. Famous names are no longer a guarantee of top
quality, as a new generation of winemakers is producing many of the best wines.
See also ERBACH, HATTENHEIM, HOCHHEIM, JOHANNISBERG, KIEDRICH, RAUENTHAL,
RÜDESHEIM. Best years: (2011) 10 09 **08 07 06 05 04 01**.

RHEINHESSEN *Germany* 26,440ha (65,300 acre) wine region with a
number of famous top-quality estates, especially at Bodenheim, Nackenheim,
NIERSTEIN and Oppenheim. BINGEN, to the north-west, also has a fine vineyard
area along the left bank of the Rhine. Further away from the river a few
growers, such as KELLER, WITTMANN and Wagner-Stempel also make superlative
wines. Riesling accounts for only 14% of the vineyard area; Weissburgunder
(Pinot Blanc) is a rising star. Best years: (2011) 10 09 **08 07 05 04 03 02**.

RHÔNE VALLEY *France* The Rhône starts out as a river in Switzerland,
cruising through Lake Geneva before hurtling westward into France. In the
area south of Lyon, between Vienne and Avignon, the valley becomes one of
France's great wine regions. In the northern part precipitous granite slopes
overhang the river and the small amount of wine produced has remarkable
individuality and great finesse. The Syrah grape reigns here in CÔTE-RÔTIE and
on the great hill of HERMITAGE. ST-JOSEPH, CROZES-HERMITAGE and CORNAS also
make excellent reds, while the white Viognier grape yields perfumed, musky
wine at CONDRIEU and elegance at the tiny CHÂTEAU-GRILLET. In the southern part
the steep slopes give way to hot, wide, alluvial plains, with hills both in the
west and east. Most of these vineyards are either CÔTES DU RHONE or CÔTES DU
RHÔNE-VILLAGES reds, whites and rosés, but there are also specific ACs, the best
known being CHÂTEAUNEUF-DU-PAPE, GIGONDAS and the luscious golden dessert
wine, MUSCAT DE BEAUMES-DE-VENISE. See also BEAUMES-DE-VENISE, CAIRANNE,
CLAIRETTE DE DIE, COSTIÈRES DE NÎMES, COTEAUX DE L'ARDÈCHE, GRIGNAN-LES-ADHÉMAR,
LIRAC, LUBÉRON, RASTEAU, ST-PÉRAY, TAVEL, VACQUEYRAS, VENTOUX, VINSOBRES.

RÍAS BAIXAS DO *Galicia, Spain* The best of GALICIA's DOs. The magic
🍷 ingredient is the Albariño grape, making dry, fruity whites with a
glorious fragrance and citrus tang. In general drink young, but there are
now ageworthy whites and fragrant, Atlantic-cooled reds from native
grape varieties. Best producers: Agro de Bazán★★, Castro Martín, Martín

Códax★, Condes de Albarei★, Quinta de Couselo, Fillaboa★★, Forjas del Salnés★, Adegas Galegas★, Lagar de Besada★, Lagar de Fornelos★, La Val★, Gerardo Méndez★ (Do Ferreiro Cepas Vellas★★), Viña Nora★, Palacio de Fefiñanes★, Pazo de Barrantes★, Pazo de Señorans★★, Pazos de Lusco★★, Santiago Ruiz★, Terras Gauda★★, Valmiñor★.

RIBERA DEL DUERO DO *Castilla y León, Spain* Dark, mouthfilling reds, ideally with delightful dry blackcurrant fruit, from Tinto Fino (Tempranillo), sometimes with a little Cabernet Sauvignon or Merlot – generally richer and more concentrated than those of RIOJA. But excessive expansion of vineyards, increase in yields and excessive use of oak may threaten its supremacy. Best producers: AALTO★★, Alión★★, Alonso del Yerro★★, Arroyo, Arzuaga★, Los Astrales★, Dominio de Atauta★, Balbás★, Hijos de Antonio Barceló★, Briego, Felix Callejo, Cillar de Silos★, Convento San Francisco★, O FOURNIER★★, Hacienda Monasterio★★, Matarromera★, Montecastro★★, Emilio Moro★★, Pago de los Capellanes★★, Pago de Carraovejas★, Pedrosa/Pérez Pascuas★★, Peñafiel, PESQUERA★★, PINGUS★★★, Protos★, Rodero★, Telmo RODRIGUEZ★, Hermanos Sastre★★, Tarsus★, TORRES (Celeste★), Valdubón, Valduero★, Valtravieso, VEGA SICILIA★★★. Best years: (2009) 08 05 **04 03 01 00 99 96 95 94 91 90 89 86 85**.

BARONE RICASOLI *Chianti Classico DOCG, Tuscany, Italy* The estate (largest in CHIANTI CLASSICO) where guidelines for different styles of Chianti were set down by Baron Bettino Ricasoli in the mid-19th century. The flagship is Chianti Classico Castello di Brolio★★, named after the magnificent medieval castle of that name. Riserva Guicciarda★ is good value. Casalferro★★ is a Sangiovese-Merlot blend. Best years: (Casalferro) (2011) (10) 09 **08 07 06 04 01**.

DOM. RICHEAUME *Côtes de Provence AC, Provence, France* German-owned property, run on organic principles and producing impressively deep-coloured reds★; Les Terrasses★★ is from Syrah aged in new wood. Best years: (Terrasses) (2011) 10 09 08 07 **06 05 04**.

RICHEBOURG AC *Grand Cru, Côte de Nuits, Burgundy, France* Rich, fleshy wine from the northern end of VOSNE-ROMANÉE. Most domaine-bottlings are exceptional. Best producers: GRIVOT★★★, Anne GROS★★★, A-F GROS★★★, Hudelot-Noëllat★★, Dom. LEROY★★★, T LIGER-BELAIR★★, MÉO-CAMUZET★★★, Dom. de la ROMANÉE-CONTI★★★. Best years: (2011) 10 09 08 07 06 05 03 02 **01 00 99 98 96 95 93 91 90**.

MAX FERD RICHTER *Mülheim, Mosel, Germany* Modestly priced yet racy Rieslings from top sites in the MOSEL, including WEHLENer Sonnenuhr★★, BRAUNEBERGER Juffer★★ and GRAACHer Domprobst★. Richter's Mülheimer Helenenkloster vineyard produces a magical Eiswein★★★ virtually every year, unless wild boar eat the crop. Best years: (2011) 10 09 08 **07 06 05 04 02 01**.

RIDGE VINEYARDS *Santa Cruz Mountains AVA, California, USA* Trailblazing winery which produces some of California's most pleasing and original wines, with a particular emphasis on old vine fruit. Paul Draper's Zinfandels★★★, made with grapes from various sources, have great intensity and age wonderfully. Other reds, led by cool-climate Cabernet-based Monte Bello★★★, show impressive personality and require years, if not decades, to come around. Geyserville★★ is a fascinating blend of Zinfandel with old-vine Carignan, Syrah and Petite Sirah which is good young but better old. There's fine Chardonnay★★, too. Best years: (Monte Bello) (2009) 08 **07 06 05 03 02 01 00 99 98 97 95 94 93 92 91 90**.

RIDGEVIEW *West Sussex, England* Ridgeview has probably spread the gospel of English fizz more than any other producer. It produces a wide variety of cuvées, many of which, while younger than many other UK sparkling wines and missing yeasty richness, do show excellent fruit characteristics. Occasional aged examples – for example Grosvenor blanc de blancs – can be very good. The range includes the traditional three-variety blends Cavendish★ and Bloomsbury★; Knightsbridge★, a blanc de noirs; Grosvenor, a blanc de blancs★★; and Fitzrovia, a Chardonnay-Pinot Noir rosé★★. Best years: **2009 08**.

RIESLANER One of the few German grape crossings of real merit, Rieslaner resembles Riesling, but with greater breadth and even higher acidity. This makes it an ideal sweet wine grape, as MÜLLER-CATOIR (Pfalz), KELLER (Rheinhessen) and some Franken growers have demonstrated.

RIESLING See pages 266–7.

CH. RIEUSSEC★★★ *Sauternes AC, 1er Cru Classé, Bordeaux, France* Apart from the peerless Ch. d'YQUEM, Rieussec is often the richest, most succulent wine of SAUTERNES. Cellar for at least 10 years. Dry white 'R' is nothing special. Second wine: Carmes de Rieussec. Owned by LAFITE-ROTHSCHILD. Best years: 2010 09 **07 06 05 04 03 02 01 99 98 97 96 95 90 89 88**.

RIOJA DOCa *Rioja, Navarra, País Vasco and Castilla y León, Spain* Rioja, in northern Spain, is not all oaky, creamy white wines and elegant, barrel-aged reds, combining oak flavours with wild strawberry and prune fruit. Over half Rioja's red wine is sold young, never having seen the inside of a barrel, and as such is one of Spain's best glugging reds; the white is increasingly tasty and fresh. Wine quality, as could be expected from such a large region with more than 400 producers, is inconsistent, but a growing gang of ambitious new producers is taking quality seriously. Best producers: (reds) Alavesas, ALLENDE★★, Altanza, Altos de Lanzaga★/Telmo RODRIGUEZ, ARTADI★★★, Barón de Ley★, Bodegas Bilbaínas, Campillo★, CAMPO VIEJO, CONTINO★★, CVNE★★, FAUSTINO, Viña Ijalba, Lan (Culmen★), LÓPEZ DE HEREDIA★★, MARQUES DE CÁCERES★, MARQUES DE MURRIETA★★, MARQUES DE RISCAL★★, Marqués de Vargas★★, MARTÍNEZ BUJANDA★, Abel Mendoza★★, Montecillo★, MUGA★, Ostatu, Viñedos de Páganos★★, Palacios Remondo★, REMELLURI★, Fernando Remírez de Ganuza★★, La RIOJA ALTA★★, RIOJANAS★★, Roda★★, ROMEO★★, Sierra Cantabria★★, Señorío de San Vicente★★, Tobía, TORRES (Ibéricos★), Valdemar★, Valpiedra★, Ysios; (whites) ALLENDE★★, CAMPO VIEJO, CONTINO★, CVNE★, LÓPEZ DE HEREDIA★★, MARQUES DE CÁCERES★, MARQUES DE MURRIETA★, REMELLURI★★, RIOJANAS★, Valdemar★. Best years: (reds) (2009) **05 04 01 00 96 95 94 91 89 87 85**.

LA RIOJA *Argentina* Important region in Argentina. Not a source of fine wine, but producers here are astute and specialize in excellent quality, value-for-money wines. La Rioja is also home to the largest FairTrade winery in South America. Best producers: Chañarmuyo, La Riojana co-op (FairTrade), San Huberto, Valle de la Puerta.

LA RIOJA ALTA *Rioja DOCa, Rioja, Spain* Good, long-established RIOJA producer, making mainly Reservas and Gran Reservas. Its only Crianza, Viña Alberdi★, fulfils the minimum age requirements for a Reserva. Viña Arana★ and Viña Ardanza★★ Reservas age splendidly, and Gran Reservas 904★★ and 890★★ are among the very best of traditional Rioja. Barón de Oña★ and Áster★ are high-quality, modern, single-estate wines. Best years: (Gran Reserva 890) **1995 94 89 87 85 82 81**.

RIESLING

If you have tasted wines with names like Laski Riesling, Olasz Riesling, Welschriesling, Gray Riesling, Riesling Italico, Cape Riesling and the like and found them bland or unappetizing, do not blame the Riesling grape. These wines have filched Riesling's name, but have nothing whatsoever to do with the great grape itself.

Riesling is Germany's finest contribution to the world of wine – and herein lies the second problem. German wines fell to such a low level of general esteem through the proliferation of wines like Liebfraumilch during the 1980s that Riesling was dragged down with them.

So what is true Riesling? It is a very ancient German grape, probably the descendant of wild vines growing in the Rhine Valley. It certainly performs best in the cool vineyard regions of Germany's Rhine, Nahe and Mosel Valleys, and in Alsace and Austria. It also does well in Ontario in Canada, New Zealand and both warm and cool parts of Australia. Ironically, the Riesling revival is being led more by Australia than Germany. It is widely planted in Washington State and New York's Finger Lakes region, less so in northern Italy.

Young Rieslings often show a delightful floral perfume, sometimes blended with the crispness of green apples, often lime, peach, nectarine or apricot, sometimes even raisin, honey or spice depending upon the ripeness of the grapes. As the wines age, the lime often intensifies, and a flavour perhaps of slate, perhaps of petrol/kerosene, appears – or, in Australia, buttered toast! In general Rieslings may be drunk young, but top dry wines can improve for many years, and the truly sweet German styles can age for generations.

WINE STYLES

Germany These wines have a marvellous perfume and an ability to hold on to a piercing acidity, even at high ripeness levels, so long as the ripening period has been warm and gradual rather than broiling and rushed. German Rieslings can be bone dry, through to medium and lusciously sweet. Styles range from crisp elegant Mosels to riper, fuller wines from the Rheingau and Nahe, with rounder, fatter examples from the Pfalz and Baden regions in the south. The very sweet Trockenbeerenauslese (TBA) Rieslings are made from grapes affected by noble rot; for Eiswein (icewine), also intensely sweet, the grapes are picked and pressed while frozen.

Other regions In the valleys of the Danube in Austria, Riesling gives stunning dry wines that combine richness with elegance, but the most fragrant wines, apart from German examples, come from France's Alsace. The mountain vineyards of northern Italy and the cool vineyards of the Czech Republic and Slovakia can show a floral sharp style. Cool areas of South Australia, Tasmania, Victoria and Western Australia all offer superb – and different – examples typified by a citrus, mineral scent, and often challenging austerity. New Zealand's style is floral, fresh and frequently attractively off-dry, but with enough acidity to age. South Africa's best examples are sweet, but dry versions are appearing. Chile has some fragrant examples in San Antonio and Bío Bío. The USA has fragrant dry Rieslings from New York, mostly off-dry from the Pacific Northwest and slightly sweet styles from California. Drier Rieslings are becoming more common. Michigan and Ohio have excellent potential. Canada produces bone-dry Riesling to ultra-sweet Icewine.

FELTON ROAD
ESTABLISHED 1991

Block 1
RIESLING
CENTRAL OTAGO
2009

PRODUCED AND BOTTLED BY
FELTON ROAD WINES LTD
BANNOCKBURN

GRAPES GROWN AT THE ELMS BANNOCKBURN VINEYARD

Wine of New Zealand

Alc 8.5%

BEST PRODUCERS

Germany
Dry BASSERMANN-JORDAN, Georg BREUER, BÜRKLIN-WOLF, BUSCH, Christmann, HEYMANN-LÖWENSTEIN, KELLER, KOEHLER-RUPRECHT, KÜNSTLER, J LEITZ, REBHOLZ, SAUER, WITTMANN.

Non-dry DIEL, DÖNNHOFF, GUNDERLOCH, HAAG, HAART, HEYMANN-LÖWENSTEIN, KARTHÄUSERHOF, von Kesselstatt, KÜHN, KÜNSTLER, Dr LOOSEN, MAXIMIN GRÜNHAUS, MOLITOR, MÜLLER-CATOIR, Egon MÜLLER-SCHARZHOF, J J PRÜM, ST URBANS-HOF, Willi SCHAEFER, SCHÄFER-FRÖHLICH, SELBACH-OSTER, WEIL, ZILLIKEN.

Austria
Alzinger, BRÜNDLMAYER, Hiedler, HIRTZBERGER, J Högl, KNOLL, Loimer, Malat, NIGL, NIKOLAIHOF, F X PICHLER, Rudi PICHLER, PRAGER, Schloss Gobelsburg, Schmelz.

France
(Alsace) J-B ADAM, Léon Beyer, P Blanck, A Boxler, DEISS, Dirler-Cadé, HUGEL, Josmeyer, Kientzler, Kreydenweiss, A MANN, MURÉ, OSTERTAG, SCHOFFIT, TRIMBACH, WEINBACH, ZIND-HUMBRECHT.

Australia
Tim ADAMS, Jim BARRY, Bloodwood, Leo Buring (Leonay), Larry CHERUBINO, Crabtree, Eden Road, Forest Hill, Frankland Estate, Freycinet, Frogmore Creek, GROSSET, Heggies, HENSCHKE, HOUGHTON, HOWARD PARK, JACOB'S CREEK (Steingarten), Kerrigan & Berry, Kilikanoon, KNAPPSTEIN, KT, Peter LEHMANN, Mesh, MOUNT HORROCKS, PETALUMA, Pewsey Vale, SEPPELT (Drumborg), SKILLOGALEE, Three Drops.

Canada
(British Columbia) Cedar Creek, Quails' Gate; *(Ontario)* Château des Charmes (sweet), Flat Rock, HENRY OF PELHAM, TAWSE, THIRTY BENCH.

Chile CASA MARIN, CONO SUR (Visión).

New Zealand
CLOUDY BAY, DRY RIVER, FELTON ROAD, Foxes Island, FRAMINGHAM, FROMM, Mt Difficulty, Mount Edward, NEUDORF, PEGASUS BAY, VILLA MARIA.

South Africa Paul CLUVER (sweet).

USA
(Washington) CHATEAU STE MICHELLE (Eroica), LONG SHADOWS (Poet's Leap); *(New York)* ANTHONY ROAD, FOX RUN, Dr Konstantin FRANK, Hermann J WIEMER.

BODEGAS RIOJANAS *Rioja DOCa, Rioja, Spain* Quality winery producing Reservas and Gran Reservas in 2 styles – elegant Viña Albina★ and richer Monte Real★★ – plus refined Gran Albina★ and a more modern, more controversial, Monte Real Crianza. The Reservas can be kept for 5 years after release, Gran Reservas for 10 or more. Best years: (Monte Real Gran Reserva) 2001 **98 96 95 94 91 89 87 85**.

RION *Nuits-St-Georges, Côte de Nuits, Burgundy, France* Three related estates: Daniel, Armelle & Bernard, and the best-known, Michèle & Patrice. Patrice makes rich, concentrated BOURGOGNE Rouge★, CHAMBOLLE-MUSIGNY les Cras★★ and NUITS-ST-GEORGES Clos des Argillières★★ from his own vines, plus a small *négociant* range. Best years: (top reds) (2011) 10 09 08 07 **06** 05 **03** 02.

RIVERINA *New South Wales, Australia* Centred on the town of Griffith and irrigated by the waters of the Murrumbidgee River, the Riverina is an important source of reliable quaffing wines. Many of Australia's best-known brands, though not mentioning the Riverina on the label, are based on wines from here. Locally based companies such as DE BORTOLI (Deen, Montage, Sacred Hill), Berton, Casella (YELLOWTAIL, Yendah), MCWILLIAM'S (Hanwood, Inheritance), Nugan Estate★ (Cookoothama, Talinga Park) and WESTEND★ (Richland) have lifted quality at budget prices. Remarkable sweet wines, led by Noble One Botrytis Semillon★★★ from De Bortoli; others from Cookoothama★★, Lillypilly, McWilliam's★★, Westend (Golden Mist★).

RIVERLAND *Australia* This important irrigated region, responsible for about 20% of the national grape crush, lies along the Murray River in SOUTH AUSTRALIA near the border with VICTORIA. A great deal goes to cheap quaffers but an increased awareness of quality has seen inferior varieties replaced and yields lowered. Here and there, wines of real character are emerging, including some remarkable reds from the Petit Verdot grape. Although the 10-year drought was broken by the most serious flooding in decades, there are concerns about long-term water supply and the area under vines is likely to continue to be reduced. Best producers: Angove, Banrock Station, Kingston Estate, Renmano, YALUMBA (Oxford Landing).

RIVESALTES AC *Roussillon, France* *Vin doux naturel* from a large area around the town of Rivesaltes. Some of southern France's best fortified wines. Can be made from various grapes, mainly white Muscat (when it is called MUSCAT DE RIVESALTES) and Grenache Noir, Gris and Blanc. A *rancio* style ages beautifully. Best producers: Baixas co-op, la CASENOVE★, CAZES★★, Chênes★, Las Collas, Fontanel★, Força Réal★, GAUBY★, Joliette★, Laporte, Nouvelles★, Rivesaltes co-op, Sainte Barbe★★, Sarda-Malet★, Sisqueille★.

ROBERTSON WO *South Africa* Hot, dry inland area with lime-rich soils, uncommon in the Cape, that are ideal for vines. Chenin Blanc and Colombard are the major white varieties, though just over a quarter of all South Africa's Chardonnay also grows here, for both still and, increasingly, sparkling styles. Sauvignon can also be good. Muscadel (Muscat Blanc à Petits Grains) yields a benchmark fortified wine, usually unoaked and released young. A red revolution is under way: Shiraz, Merlot and Cabernet have made an excellent start. Best producers: Graham BECK★, Bon Courage, De Wetshof★, Quando, Robertson Winery, SPRINGFIELD ESTATE★, Van Loveren, Weltevrede, Zandvliet.

ROC DE CAMBES★★ *Côtes de Bourg AC, Bordeaux, France* François Mitjavile of TERTRE-RÔTEBOEUF has applied diligence and genius to this property since he acquired it in 1988. Full and succulent, with ripe dark fruit, this wine takes the CÔTES DE BOURG appellation to new heights. Best years: 2010 09 08 07 06 **05 04 03 02 01 00 99 98.**

DOM. DES ROCHES NEUVES *Saumur-Champigny AC, Loire Valley, France*   A shift to biodynamic methods and less new oak has elevated very good wines to a higher level. Fresh, pure and mineral, top cuvées Insolite SAUMUR★★ (Chenin Blanc) and Marginale SAUMUR-CHAMPIGNY★★ (Cabernet Franc) are excellent expressions of fruit and *terroir*. Generic Saumur-Champigny and Terres Chaudes★ are good value; Franc de Pied is from young, ungrafted vines. Bulles de Roche★ is a finely fruity sparkler. Best years: (Marginale) 2011 **09 08 06 05 04 03 02 01 00 99.**

ROCHIOLI *Russian River Valley AVA, California, USA*   Well-known grape growers, the Rochioli family are equally good at winemaking, offering silky, black cherry Pinot Noir★★ and a richer, dramatic West Block Reserve Pinot★★. Also a good Sauvignon Blanc and a range of cult Chardonnays★★. Best years. (Pinot Noir) 2009 **00 07 06 05 04 03 02 01 00.**

ROCKFORD *Barossa Valley, South Australia*   Robert O'Callaghan is a great respecter of the old vines so plentiful in the BAROSSA, who uses antique machinery to create wines of irresistible drinkability. Masterful Basket Press Shiraz★★, Riesling★★, slurpable Moppa Springs★ (Grenache-Shiraz-Mourvèdre), smoothly satisfying Rifle Range Cabernet★★ and Australia's best sparkling red, the stellar Black Shiraz★★★. Best years: (Basket Press Shiraz) (2010) (09) 08 **06 05 04 03 02 01 99 98 96 95 92 91 90.**

TELMO RODRÍGUEZ *Spain*   The son of REMELLURI's owner, who recently re-joined his father at the family estate, has formed a team of enologists and viticulturists that is active throughout Spain: it forms joint ventures with local growers and manages the winemaking. Top wines: Molino Real★ (Sierras de MÁLAGA), Matallana★ (RIBERA DEL DUERO), Altos de Lanzaga★ (RIOJA), Dehesa Gago Pago La Jara★★ (TORO), Viña 105 (Cigales), Basa★ (RUEDA).

LOUIS ROEDERER *Champagne AC, Champagne, France*   Renowned firm making some of the best, full-flavoured CHAMPAGNE around. As well as the excellent non-vintage★★ and pale vintage rosé★★, it also makes a big, exciting vintage★★, delicious vintage Blanc de Blancs★★ and the famous Roederer Cristal★★★ and Cristal Rosé★★★, de luxe cuvées which are nearly always magnificent. Both the vintage and Cristal can usually be aged for 10 years or more; the non-vintage benefits from a bit of aging too. Best years: 2006 **05 04 03 02 00 99 97 96 95 90 89 88 85.**

ROEDERER ESTATE *Anderson Valley AVA, California, USA*   Offshoot of Louis ROEDERER, whose wines show how suitable the ANDERSON VALLEY is for fizz. The Brut★★ (sold in the UK as Quartet) is savoury and impressive, and it will age beautifully; the top bottling, L'Ermitage★★★, is stunning. Also lovely rosé★★. Best years: (L'Ermitage) 2003 **02 00 99 97 96 94 92 91.**

ROERO DOCG *Piedmont, Italy*   The Roero hills lie across the Tanaro river from the LANGHE hills, home of BAROLO and BARBARESCO. Long noted as a source of supple, fruity Nebbiolo-based red wines to drink in 2–5 years, Roero has increasingly been turning out Nebbiolos of Barolo-like intensity from producers such as Correggia, Malvirà and Negro. Also very good dry white Roero ARNEIS. Best years: (2011) (09) 08 **07 06 04 01 00 99 98 97 96 95.**

ROMAGNA *Emilia-Romagna, Italy*   Historically a contender, with classic zones of Tuscany, for Italy's finest Sangiovese, Sangiovese di Romagna DOC (now simply Romagna DOC); in recent decades it has lost ground due to the industrialization of so much of the product. Producers have also followed the

Tuscans down the misguided trail of allowing 'international' (French) grapes into their blend. On the white side, Trebbiano rules in terms of quantity, and Albana (Romagna Albana DOCG) supposedly for quality, though it only achieves excellence when sweet. Best producers: (Sangiovese) Castelluccio (IGT), Drei Donà★★, San Patrignano co-op/Terre del Cedro★ (Avi★★), Zerbina★★.

LA ROMANÉE AC★★★ *Grand Cru, Côte de Nuits, Burgundy, France* Tiny Grand Cru of the highest quality, owned and now made (since 2002) by Comte LIGER-BELAIR. Best years: (2011) 10 09 08 07 06 05 **03 02**.

LA ROMANÉE-CONTI AC★★★ *Grand Cru, Côte de Nuits, Burgundy, France* For many extremely wealthy wine lovers this is the pinnacle of red Burgundy. It is an incredibly complex wine with great structure and pure, clearly defined fruit flavour, but you've got to age it 15 years to see what all the fuss is about. The vineyard, wholly owned by Dom. de la ROMANÉE-CONTI, covers only 1.8ha (4^1/$_2$ acres). Best years: (2011) 10 09 08 07 06 05 03 02 **00 99 98 97** 96 95 **93 90 89 88 85** 78.

DOM. DE LA ROMANÉE-CONTI *Vosne-Romanée, Côte de Nuits, Burgundy, France* This famous domaine owns a string of Grands Crus in VOSNE-ROMANÉE (la TÂCHE★★★, RICHEBOURG★★★, ROMANÉE-CONTI★★★, ROMANÉE-ST-VIVANT★★★, ÉCHÉZEAUX★★★ and Grands-Échézeaux★★★) as well as a small parcel of le MONTRACHET★★★. CORTON★★ since 2009. The wines are ludicrously expensive, especially at auction, but can be sublime: full of fruit when young, but capable of aging for 15 years or more to a marriage made in the heaven and hell of richness and decay. Best years: (reds) (2011) 10 09 08 07 06 05 03 02 **00** 99 **98 97** 96 **95** 93 90 89 85 78.

ROMANÉE-ST-VIVANT AC *Grand Cru, Côte de Nuits, Burgundy, France* The largest of VOSNE-ROMANÉE's 6 Grands Crus. At 10–15 years old the wines should reveal the keenly balanced brilliance of which the vineyard is capable, but a surly, rough edge sometimes gets in the way. Best producers: l'Arlot★, Arnoux-Lachaux★★★, S CATHIARD★★★, J-J Confuron★★★, DROUHIN★★★, Hudelot-Noëllat★★, JADOT★★★, LATOUR★★, Dom. LEROY★★★, Dom. de la ROMANÉE-CONTI★★★. Best years: (2011) 10 09 08 **07** 06 05 03 **02 01 00** 99 98 96 95 93 90.

CH. ROMANIN *Les Baux-de-Provence AC, Provence, France* Biodynamically run vineyard owned by Jean-Louis Charmolüe, former owner of Ch. MONTROSE in Bordeaux. Top wine is Le Coeur de Romanin★★ from Syrah, Mourvèdre, Cabernet Sauvignon and Grenache – the same mix as for the delightfully textured Château Romanin★★. La Chapelle de Romanin★ is a third label for good, herb-scented red. Best years: (Le Coeur) (2011) 10 09 **08 07 06 05 04** 03.

BENJAMIN ROMEO *Rioja DOCa, La Rioja, Spain* ARTADI's former winemaker launched his own estate with a collection of tiny old vineyards, and immediately caused a sensation with his superripe, dense, powerful, if rather atypical wines, Contador★★, La Viña de Andrés Romeo★★ and La Cueva del Contador★★; also tasty Macizo★ white from CATALUÑA. Best years: (2009) 08 07 06 05 **04 03 02 01 00**.

QUINTA DOS ROQUES *Dão DOC, Terras do Dão, Portugal* One of DÃO's finest producers, making wines from 2 quite different estates. Quinta dos Roques red★ is ripe and supple, while higher-altitude Quinta das Maias★ produces smoky, peppery reds. The top wines are the Roques Reserva★★, made from old vines and aged in 100% new oak, and Touriga Nacional★★. Both estates also have decent dry whites, especially Roques Encruzado★. Best years: (2009) **08 07 05 04 03 01 00 97 96**.

QUINTA DE LA ROSA *Douro DOC and Port DOC, Douro, Portugal* The Bergqvist family have transformed this property into a small but serious producer of both PORT and unfortified DOURO★ (Reserva★★) wines. The Vintage Port★★ is excellent, as is unfiltered LBV★★; Finest Reserve and Tonel No. 12, a 10-year-old tawny, are also good. Best years: (Vintage) **2007 05 04 03 00 97 96 95 94 92 91.**

ROSÉ DE LOIRE AC *Loire Valley, France* Dry rosé from ANJOU, SAUMUR and TOURAINE. It can be lovely, full of red berry fruits, but drink as young as possible, chilled. It's far superior to Rosé d'Anjou AC, which is usually sweetish. Best producers: Hautes Ouches, F MABILEAU, OGEREAU, Passavant.

ROSÉ DES RICEYS AC *Champagne, France* Still, dark pink wine made from Pinot Noir grapes in the southern part of the CHAMPAGNE region. Best producers: Alexandre Bonnet★, Devaux★, Guy de Forez, Morel..

ROSETTE AOP *Bergerac, South-West France* A small region producing rather exquisite off-dry aperitif-style wines from Sémillon. Drink young. Best producers: de Coutancie★, Ch. Romain★.

ROSSO CONERO DOC See CONERO DOCG/ROSSO CONERO DOC.

ROSSO DI MONTALCINO DOC *Tuscany, Italy* BRUNELLO DI MONTALCINO must age for at least 4 years before release onto the market, so this wine was devised for quicker return on investment and a more approachable style. Like Brunello, Rosso di Montalcino must be 100% Sangiovese – sinister moves to allow blending with other grapes (in this case Merlot) having been recently defeated. Best producers as for Brunello. Best years: (2011) (10) **09 08 07 06.**

ROSSO DI MONTEPULCIANO DOC See VINO NOBILE DI MONTEPULCIANO DOCG.

ROSSO PICENO DOC *Marche, Italy* Often considered a poor relative of CONERO DOCG/ROSSO CONERO, but it can be rich and seductive when the full complement (70%) of Montepulciano is used, and also when it comes from the more restricted Superiore zone. Best producers: Boccadigabbia★ (Villamagna★★), Le Caniette★, Laurentina★, Monte Schiavo★, Saladini Pilastri★, Velenosi★. Best years: **2011 10 09 08 07 06.**

RENÉ ROSTAING *Côte-Rôtie AC, Rhône Valley, France* Modern, lightly oaked, enormously fine wines with deep colour and softly elegant fruit flavours, from some of the most coveted sites in CÔTE-RÔTIE: classic Côte-Rôtie★, Côte Blonde★★ and la Landonne★★★. Be patient. There's a very good CONDRIEU La Bonnette★★ too. Best years: (top crus) (2011) **10 09 07 06 05 04 03 01 00 99 98 95 94 91 90 88.**

DOM. ROULOT *Meursault, Côte de Beaune, Burgundy, France* Jean-Marc Roulot quietly outperforms in the field of fine white Burgundy, whether it be Bourgogne Blanc★, village MEURSAULT such as Les Luchets★★ or the amazing Les Tessons Clos de Mon Plaisir★★, up to Premier Cru Bouchères★★ or Perrières★★★. Tuck in while the price is still relatively right.

GEORGES ROUMIER *Chambolle-Musigny, Côte de Nuits, Burgundy, France* Christophe Roumier is one of Burgundy's top winemakers, devoting as much attention to his vineyards as to cellar technique, believing in severe pruning, low yields and stringent grape selection. Roumier rarely uses more than one-third new oak. His best wine is often BONNES-MARES★★★; other

Grands Crus include MUSIGNY★★★, Ruchottes-Chambertin★★ and CORTON-CHARLEMAGNE★★. Best value are usually the village CHAMBOLLE★★ and an exclusively owned Premier Cru in MOREY-ST-DENIS, Clos de la Bussière★★. Best years: (reds) (2011) 10 09 08 **07** 05 **03 02** 01 99 98 96 95 90.

ROUSSANNE The RHÔNE VALLEY's best white grape, frequently blended with Marsanne to produce surprisingly fragrant, even salty, warm-climate whites. Roussanne is the more aromatic and elegant of the two, less prone to oxidation and with better acidity, but growers usually prefer Marsanne due to its higher yields and greater body. There is a great refinement in old vines Roussanne, such as at CHATEAUNEUF-DU-PAPE. Now being planted in LANGUEDOC-ROUSSILLON. There are some interesting examples in SAVOIE (where it is called Bergeron) and Australia. Off a tiny base, it is showing good potential in South Africa. While much of the Roussanne first planted in California has been identified as Viognier, there are a few true plantings that produce fascinating, complex, exotically fruited wines.

ARMAND ROUSSEAU *Gevrey-Chambertin, Côte de Nuits, Burgundy, France* Highly respected estate, with vineyards in CHAMBERTIN★★★, Clos-de-Bèze★★★, Mazis-Chambertin★★ and Charmes-Chambertin★★ as well as GEVREY-CHAMBERTIN Clos St-Jacques★★★ and CLOS DE LA ROCHE★★★. The long-lived wines are outstandingly harmonious, elegant, yet rich. Best years: (2011) 10 09 08 **07** 06 05 **03 02** 99 96 93 91 90 89 88.

ROUSSETTE DE SAVOIE AC *Savoie, France* AC for dry or off-dry, floral and mineral whites made from the Altesse grape variety. Best producers: Dupasquier★★, E Jacquin★, Lupin, Prieuré St-Christophe★★, Saint-Germain★. Best years: 2011 10 **09 08 07**.

ROUSSILLON *France* The snow-covered peaks of the Pyrenees form a spectacular backdrop to the sun-baked, wind-swept ancient region of Roussillon, now the Pyrénées-Orientales *département*. The vineyards produce a wide range of fairly priced wines, mainly red, from the ripe, raisin-rich *vins doux naturels* to light, fruity-fresh vins de pays/IGPs. Once dominated by co-operatives, there are now some really exciting wines being made, both white and red, especially by individual estates. See also BANYULS, COLLIOURE, CÔTES CATALANES, CÔTES DU ROUSSILLON, CÔTES DU ROUSSILLON-VILLAGES, LANGUEDOC-ROUSSILLON, MAURY, MUSCAT DE RIVESALTES, RIVESALTES.

RUBICON ESTATE See Francis Ford COPPOLA.
RUCHOTTES-CHAMBERTIN AC See CHAMBERTIN AC.
RÜDESHEIM *Rheingau, Germany* Village producing silky, aromatic wines from steep terraced vineyards high above the Rhine (Berg Schlossberg, Berg Rottland, Berg Roseneck and Bischofsberg). Best producers: Georg BREUER★★★, Johannishof★, Kesseler★★, Josef LEITZ★★, Ress, Schloss Schönborn★, WEGELER★. Best years: (2011) 10 09 08 **07** 06 05 04 03 02 01.
RUEDA DO *Castilla y León, Spain* The RIOJA firm of MARQUES DE RISCAL launched the reputation of this region in the 1970s, first by rescuing the almost extinct Verdejo grape, then by introducing Sauvignon Blanc. Fresh young whites have been joined by barrel-fermented wines aiming for a longer life, particularly at Belondrade y Lurton, Castilla La Vieja and Ossian – the latter uses VT Castilla y León rather than Rueda DO for its top cuvées Best producers: Alvarez y Diez★, Antaño (Viña Mocén★), Belondrade y Lurton★

Castelo de Medina★, Bodegas de Crianza Castilla La Vieja★, Cerrosol (Doña Beatriz), Viña Garedo, José Pariente★★, Hermanos Lurton, MARQUES DE RISCAL★, Naia★, Viñedos de Nieva★, Palacio de Bornos★, Javier Sanz★, Vinos Sanz★, Sitios de Bodega★, Angel Rodríguez Vidal (Martinsancho★).

RUFFINO *Tuscany, Italy* Huge operation, partly owned by American giant Constellation; production is still controlled by a branch of the FOLONARI family, and is increasingly oriented toward quality. Top wines include La Solatia★ (Chardonnay), Modus★ (Sangiovese-Cabernet-Merlot), Nero del Tondo★ (Pinot Noir) and Romitorio di Santedame★★ (Colorino-Merlot). Ruffino also owns VINO NOBILE estate Lodola Nuova, BRUNELLO Greppone Mazzi and Borgo Conventi in COLLIO.

RUINART *Champagne AC, Champagne, France* Ruinart has a surprisingly low profile given the quality of its wines. Non-vintage★ is very good, and better value than the Blanc de Blancs★, but the top wines here are the supremely classy Dom Ruinart Blanc de Blancs★★ and the Dom Ruinart Rosé★★. Best years: 2006 05 04 02 **00 98 96 95 90 88 85 83 82.**

RULLY AC *Côte Chalonnaise, Burgundy, France* Best known for white wines, often oak-aged. Reds are light, with a fleeting strawberry and cherry perfume. Most wines are reasonably priced. Best producers: (whites) d'Allaines★, J-C Brelière★, M Briday★, Devevey★, DROUHIN★, Dureuil-Janthial★★, Duvernay, FAIVELEY★, V GIRARDIN★, Hasard★, H & P Jacqueson★★, JADOT★, O LEFLAIVE★, Rodet★, de Villaine★; (reds) Dureuil-Janthial★★, la Folie, H & P Jacqueson★. Best years: (whites) 2010 **09**; (reds) 2010 **09 08.**

RUSSIAN RIVER VALLEY AVA *Sonoma County, California, USA* Beginning south of Healdsburg, this valley cools as it meanders toward the Pacific. In late 2011, the AVA was expanded by a whopping 5670ha (14,000 acres) in response to a controversial proposal by Gallo. Green Valley, a sub-AVA, is home to IRON HORSE, DUTTON GOLDFIELD and MARIMAR ESTATE. Along with SONOMA COAST and CARNEROS it is the leading producer of high-quality Pinot Noir and Chardonnay in north coast California. Best producers: ALYSIAN★, DE LOACH★★, DEHLINGER★★, DUTTON GOLDFIELD★★, Merry Edwards★★, Gary FARRELL★★, HARTFORD★★, IRON HORSE★★, Kosta Browne★★, LYNMAR★★, MARIMAR ESTATE★★, MOSHIN★, Papapietro Perry★, Patz & Hall★, RAMEY★★, ROCHIOLI★★, Siduri★★, SONOMA-CUTRER★, Rodney Strong★, Joseph SWAN★, WILLIAMS SELYEM★★, Wind Gap★★. Best years: (Pinot Noir) 2010 09 **08 07 06 05 04 03 02 01 00.**

RUST EN VREDE *Stellenbosch WO, South Africa* Big bold statement reds, in equally bold and unwelcome heavyweight packaging, include Single Vineyard Syrah★ and 1694 Classification★ (a Cabernet-Shiraz blend named for the year the property was granted). Rust en Vrede★, a Cabernet-Shiraz-Merlot blend, reflects the farm's *terroir*; Shiraz★, Merlot and Cabernet all show fine, soft tannins and fresh fruit. The Guardian Peak wines (all red) are ripe and powerful in style. Best years: (Rust en Vrede estate wine) 2009 **08 07 06 05 04 03 02 01.**

RUSTENBERG *Stellenbosch WO, South Africa* Top-notch wines led by big but classically structured single-vineyard Cabernet Peter Barlow★★ and bold Five Soldiers★★ (Chardonnay). Standard Chardonnay★ is more delicate, cheaper and equally good. There's also complex, layered BORDEAUX-style blend John X Merriman★★ and R M Nicholson★★, while RHÔNE-style wines are represented by a lean but scented Roussanne and intricate, refined Syrah★★. Straw Wine★ is an occasional luscious 'sticky'. Best years: (Peter Barlow) 2009 **08 07 06 05 04 03 01**; (Five Soldiers) 2010 **09 08 07 06 05 04 03 02.**

273

RUTHERFORD AVA *Napa Valley, California, USA* This viticultural area in mid-NAPA VALLEY has inspired endless argument over whether it has a distinct identity. Thankfully, producers have largely stopped pursuing ultra-ripeness and it *is* now possible to see a true Rutherford character. The heart of the area, the Rutherford Bench, does seem to be a prime Cabernet Sauvignon zone, and many traditional Napa Cabernets come from here and exhibit the 'Rutherford dust' flavour. Best producers: Beaulieu (Private Reserve★), Cakebread★, CAYMUS★★, FLORA SPRINGS★★, Freemark Abbey★ (Bosché★★), Frog's Leap★, Hall★, PINE RIDGE★, Quintessa★, Rubicon/COPPOLA★, ST SUPÉRY★, Sequoia Grove★, Staglin★★. Best years: (Cabernet) 2009 08 **07 06 05 04 03 02 01 00 99 95 94 93 91 90**.

RUTHERGLEN *Victoria, Australia* This region, established in the late 19th century, is the home of heroic reds from Shiraz, Cabernet and Durif (Petite Sirah), and luscious, world-beating fortifieds from Muscat and Tokay (now called 'Topaque'). These fortifieds are now classified in quality terms from regional (Rutherglen) to Classic, Grand and Rare. Good sherry- and port-style wines. Best producers: (fortifieds) All Saints★★, Buller★★, Campbells★★, CHAMBERS★★★, MORRIS★★★, Stanton & Killeen★★.

SAALE-UNSTRUT *Germany* Vines can only flourish in the folds of the river valleys in this bleak expanse of the former East Germany near Leipzig. This far north it is only just possible to ripen most grapes, yet 80 different varieties are now grown here, of which the most important are Riesling, Müller-Thurgau, Silvaner and Weissburgunder (Pinot Blanc). Only 685ha (1690 acres), mostly on limestone slopes, with a very dry, fragrant style being the most successful. Best producers: Böhme, Gussek, Lützkendorf★, Pawis★.

SACHSEN *Germany* 462ha (1140-acre) wine region centred on the cities of Meissen and Dresden along the Elbe Valley. At more than 50°N, grapes don't ripen easily, and frost is a constant hazard. Global warming is easing conditions, and some lovely, delicate dry Rieslings are beginning to appear, along with good Müller-Thurgau, Gewürztraminer, Silvaner and Weissburgunder (Pinot Blanc). Best producers: Schloss Proschwitz★, Vincenz Richter, Schwarz★, Klaus Zimmerling★.

SADIE FAMILY WINES *Swartland WO, South Africa* Eben Sadie's Ouwinger-dreeks (old vines) project focuses on specific sites of old vines (some over 100 years); he is expanding the initial range of six highly individual wines (just one red), made with minimum intervention, in tiny quantities. He crafts just slightly larger quantities of Columella★★★ (Syrah with a little Mourvèdre and Grenache), which combines richness and power, and Palladius★★, a generously textured, multi-varietal dry white featuring Chenin Blanc. A separate venture, Sequillo, produces a mineral-fresh Syrah-based red★★ and elegant barrel-fermented Chenin-based white★★. See also TERROIR AL LIMIT. Best years: (Columella) 2009 **08 07 06 05 04 03 02 01**.

ST-AMOUR AC *Beaujolais, Burgundy, France* The most northerly BEAUJOLAIS Cru, much in demand through the romantic connotation of its name. The granitic vineyards produce wines with great intensity of colour that may be initially harsh, needing a few months to soften. Best producers:

des Billards★, Coquard★, DUBOEUF★ (Dom. des Sablons★), des Duc★. Best years: (2011) **10 09 08**.

ST-AUBIN AC *Côte de Beaune, Burgundy, France* These days almost as good a source of white Burgundy (though in a less rich style) as its MONTRACHET neighbours, PULIGNY and CHASSAGNE, and much more affordable. En Remilly and Murgers Dents de Chien stand out as vineyards, along with Frionnes for pretty, perfumed Pinot Noir. Best producers: J-C Bachelet★★, F & D Clair★★, COLIN★★, P-Y COLIN-MOREY★★, Deux MONTILLE★, DROUHIN★, JADOT★, H Lamy★★, Lamy-Pillot★, Larue★★, O LEFLAIVE★, B MOREY★, Prudhon★, RAMONET★★. Best years: (reds) (2011) **09 07 06 05**; (whites) (2011) **10 09 08 07 06 05**.

ST-BRIS AC *Burgundy, France* Appellation near CHABLIS for Sauvignon Blanc; wines are less interesting than a decade ago. Drink young. Chardonnay and Pinot Noir wines in this area use the BOURGOGNE Côtes d'Auxerre AC. Best producers: Clotilde Davenne, J-H Goisot★★.

ST-CHINIAN AC *Languedoc, France* Large AC of hill villages, covering strong, spicy red wines with more personality and fruit than run-of-the-mill HÉRAULT. Roquebrun and Berlou are crus du Languedoc. Best producers: Berlou co-op, BORIE LA VITARÈLE★, CANET-VALETTE★, Cazal-Viel★, Clos Bagatelle★, la Dournie, Jougla★, Madura, Mas Champart★, Mas de Cynanque★, Maurel Fonsalade★, Moulin de Ciffre, Moulinier, Navarre, Rimbert★, Roquebrun co-op, Tabatau (Lo Tabataire★), les Terrasses de Gabrielle★, Terres Falmet. Best years: (2011) **10 09 08 07 06 05**.

SAINT CLAIR *Marlborough, South Island, New Zealand* Important player best known for its various bottlings of Sauvignon Blanc. Wairau Reserve★★ is impressively intense, plus single-vineyard Pioneer Block labels (my favourite is the tangy Bell★★). Excellent Reserve Chardonnay★★, tasty Riesling and Gewürztraminer★. Vicar's Choice is impressive entry-level label. Various Pinot Noirs★ (Pioneer Block Doctor's Creek★★) are becoming serious quality contenders and chocolaty Rapaura Reserve Merlot★ lead the reds. Best years: (Sauvignon Blanc) 2011 **10 09 07 06**.

ST-ÉMILION AC *Bordeaux, France* The scenic Roman hill town of St-Émilion is the centre of Bordeaux's most historic wine region. The finest vineyards are on the plateau and *côtes*, or steep slopes, around the town, although an area to the west, called the *graves*, contains 2 famous properties, CHEVAL BLANC and FIGEAC. It is a region of smallholdings, with over 1000 properties, and consequently the co-operative plays an important part. The dominant early-ripening Merlot grape gives wines with a 'come-hither' softness and sweetness rare in red BORDEAUX. St-Émilion is the basic generic AC, with 4 'satellites' (LUSSAC, MONTAGNE, PUISSEGUIN, ST-GEORGES) allowed to annex their name to it. The best producers, including the Classed Growths, are found in the more tightly controlled ST-ÉMILION GRAND CRU AC category but there are anomalies, e.g. La Mondotte★★. Best years: 2010 **09 08 05 01 00 98 96 95**.

ST-ÉMILION GRAND CRU AC *Bordeaux, France* ST-ÉMILION's top-quality AC, which includes the estates classified as Grand Cru Classé and Premier Grand Cru Classé (below). The classification is revised approximately every 10 years, most recently in 2012. This AC also includes many of the new wave of limited edition *vins de garage*. Best producers: (Grands Crus Classés) l'ARROSEE★, Balestard-la-Tonnelle★, Bellefont-Belcier, Bellevue★, Boutisse, CANON-LA-GAFFELIÈRE★★, Carteau, Clos la Madeleine, Clos de l'Oratoire★★, la Dominique★, Fleur Cardinale★, Grand Corbin-Despagne★, Grand Mayne★★, Grand Pontet★, Larcis-Ducasse★★,

Larmande★, MONBOUSQUET★, Pavie-Decesse★, la Tour Figeac★; (others) Faugères★, Fombrauge★, la Gomerie★, Gracia★, Moulin St-Georges★, Quinault l'Enclos★, Rol Valentin★, TERTRE-RÔTEBOEUF★★, Teyssier, VALANDRAUD★★. Best years: 2010 09 08 07 06 05 03 01 00 98 96 95 90 89.

ST-ÉMILION PREMIER GRAND CRU CLASSÉ *Bordeaux, France* The St-Émilion élite level, divided into 2 categories – 'A' and 'B' – with only the much more expensive CHEVAL BLANC and AUSONE in category 'A'. There are 13 'B' châteaux, with PAVIE-MACQUIN and TROPLONG MONDOT added from the 2006 Classification. Best producers: ANGELUS★★★, AUSONE★★★, BEAU-SÉJOUR BÉCOT★★, Beauséjour★, BELAIR-MONANGE★★, CANON★★, CHEVAL BLANC★★★, Clos Fourtet★, FIGEAC★★, la Gaffelière★, MAGDELAINE★, PAVIE★★, PAVIE-MACQUIN★★, TROPLONG-MONDOT★, Trottevieille★. Best years: 2010 09 08 06 05 04 03 02 01 00 98 96 95 90 89 88.

ST-ESTÈPHE AC *Haut-Médoc, Bordeaux, France* Large AC north of PAUILLAC with 5 Classed Growths. St-Estèphe wines have high tannin levels, but given time (10–20 years) those sought-after flavours of blackcurrant and cedarwood do peek out. More Merlot has been planted to soften the wines and make them more accessible at an earlier age. As vintages get drier and hotter, these wines are coming into their own. Best producers: Le Boscq★, CALON-SÉGUR★★, COS D'ESTOURNEL★★★, Cos Labory★, Le Crock★, HAUT-MARBUZET★★, LAFON-ROCHET★, Lilian-Ladouys★, MEYNEY★, MONTROSE★★, Ormes de Pez★, PEZ★, Phélan Ségur★, Tronquoy-Lalande★. Best years: 2010 09 08 06 05 04 03 02 01 00 96 95 90 89 88 86.

DOM. ST GAYAN *Gigondas AC, Rhône Valley, France* The Meffre family rely on very old vines, making and maturing their wines in vat and large barrels, which lend power to the chunky, long-lived GIGONDAS★ (★★ in top years). Other reds, such as RASTEAU, are also good value. Best years: (Gigondas) 2011 10 09 07 06 05 04 03 01 00 99 98 97 95 90.

ST-GEORGES-ST-ÉMILION AC *Bordeaux, France* The smallest satellite of ST-ÉMILION, with lovely, soft wines that can nevertheless age for 6–10 years. Best producers: Calon, Macquin St-Georges★, St-André Corbin★, Ch. St-Georges★, Tour-du-Pas-St-Georges★, Vieux-Montaiguillon. Best years: 2010 09 08 05 03 01.

ST HALLETT *Barossa Valley, South Australia* Owned by brewer Lion Nathan. Excellent quaffers Poacher's Blend★ (Semillon-Sauvignon), Game-keeper's Reserve★ (Shiraz-Grenache) and delicious easy-drinking Gamekeeper's Shiraz★. These and the EDEN VALLEY Riesling★ are performing pretty well; venerable Old Block Shiraz★★ is regaining top form and excellent Shiraz siblings Blackwell★ and Faith★ are deep and tasty. Best years: (Old Block) (2010) 09 08 06 04 03 02 98 96 94 93 91 90.

ST INNOCENT WINERY *Willamette Valley AVA, Oregon, USA* St Innocent produces a number of *terroir*-driven single-vineyard Pinot Noirs (Justice Vineyard★★, Zenith Vineyard★) as well as a blended Villages Cuvée★. White wines include stylish Chardonnay (Freedom Hill Vineyard), Pinot Gris (Vitae Springs★, Freedom Hill) and crisp, apple-scented Pinot Blanc. Best years: (Pinot Noir) (2010) 09 08 06 05.

ST-JOSEPH AC *Rhône Valley, France* Long hillside AC, up and down the opposite bank of the Rhône to HERMITAGE. Made from Syrah, the reds have mouthfilling fruit with irresistible blackcurrant richness. Brilliant at 1–2 years, they can last for at least 10. The white wines are usually pleasant and flowery to drink young, although an increasing number can age, as in 2010. Best producers: (reds) Boissonnet, CHAPOUTIER★, J-L CHAVE★★, Chêne★, L Chèze★, Courbis★, COURSODON★★, CUILLERON★★,

Dard & Ribo★, DELAS★★, E & J Durand★★, Faury★, P Gaillard★★, Gonon★★, GRAILLOT★★, B Gripa★★, GUIGAL★★, Paul JABOULET, P Jamet★, P Marthouret, Monier★, Monteillet★★, Paret★, A PERRET★★, C Pichon★, Richard (Nuelles ▲), TAIN co-op★, Tardieu-Laurent★★, Vallet★, G Vernay★, F Villard★★; (whites) CHAPOUTIER (Granits★★), Chêne★★, L Chèze★, Courbis★ (Royes★★), CUILLERON★★, DELAS★, Ferraton★, P Finon, G Flacher, P Gaillard★★, Gonon★★, B Gripa★, GUIGAL★★, Monteillet★, A PERRET★★, Villard★★. Best years: (reds) (2011) **10 09 07 06 05 03 01 00 99 98**; (whites) **2011 10 09 08 07 06 05 04**.

ST-JULIEN AC *Haut-Médoc, Bordeaux, France* For many, St-Julien produces perfect claret, with an ideal balance between opulence and austerity and between the brashness of youth and the genius of maturity. It is the smallest of the principal HAUT-MEDOC ACs but almost all is first-rate vineyard land and quality is high. Best producers: BEYCHEVELLE★★, BRANAIRE-DUCRU★★, DUCRU-BEAUCAILLOU★★★, GLORIA★, GRUAUD LAROSE★★, LAGRANGE★★, LANGOA-BARTON★★, LÉOVILLE-BARTON★★★, LÉOVILLE-LAS-CASES★★★, LÉOVILLE-POYFERRE★★★, ST-PIERRE★★, TALBOT★. Best years: 2010 09 08 06 **05** 04 03 02 01 00 99 98 96 95 94 90 89 88 86.

ST-MONT AOP *South-West France* Recently promoted former VDQS noted principally for whites, though there are red and rosé wines too, all based on local grape varieties. Producers PLAIMONT★ have a near-monopoly.

ST-NICOLAS-DE-BOURGUEIL AC *Loire Valley, France* An enclave within the larger BOURGUEIL AC, and similarly producing light wines from vineyards toward the river, sturdier bottles from up the hill. Almost all the wine is red and with the same piercing red fruit flavours of Bourgueil, and much better after 7–10 years, especially in warm vintages. Best producers: Y Amirault★★, Clos des Quarterons★/T Amirault, la Cotelleraie/ G Vallée★★, L & M Cognard-Taluau★, S David★★, F MABILEAU★★, J Taluau★. Best years: (2011) 10 09 **08 06 05** 04 03 01.

ST-PÉRAY AC *Rhône Valley, France* Small, mainly hillside appellation opposite Valence. Underrated white wines, mainly Marsanne, are fragrant and mineral on the finish. Also some rather hefty traditional-method fizz. Best producers: S Chaboud★, CHAPOUTIER★, CLAPE★, COLOMBO★, CUILLERON★, B Gripa★★, J Lemenicier★, TAIN co-op★, Tardieu-Laurent★, J L Thiers★, Tunnel★, Vins de Vienne, A Voge★ (Fleur de Crussol★ ★). Best years: **2011** 10 09 08 07 06 05.

CH. ST-PIERRE★★ *St-Julien AC, 4ème Cru Classé, Haut-Médoc, Bordeaux, France* Small ST-JULIEN property making wines that have become a byword for ripe, lush fruit wrapped round with the spice of new oak. Drinkable early, but top vintages can improve for 20 years. Best years: 2010 09 08 06 05 04 03 02 01 00 99 98 96 95 94 90 89 85.

ST-ROMAIN AC *Côte de Beaune, Burgundy, France* Red wines with a firm, bitter-sweet cherrystone fruit and flinty-dry whites. Usually good value by Burgundian standards, but take a few years to open out. There's talk of introducing Premiers Crus for best vineyards such as Sous le Château. Best producers: (whites) Bazenet★, H & G Buisson, Chassorney★, A Gras★★, O LEFLAIVE★, VERGET★; (reds) A Gras★. Best years: (whites) (2011) 10 **09** 07 06; (reds) (2011) 10 **09** 05.

ST SUPÉRY *Napa Valley, California, USA* This French-owned property in RUTHERFORD gets most of its fruit from its Dollarhide Ranch in Pope Valley to the east. Tangy Sauvignon Blanc★, Merlot★ and ripe, juicy Cabernet Sauvignon★★, as well as an excellent white Meritage blend called Virtú★★, with a substantial amount of Semillon, and Cabernet-based red Élu★★. Best years: (Cabernet) (2008) **07 06 05 03 02 01**.

277

ST URBANS-HOF *Leiwen, Mosel, Germany* Nik Weis's dynamic estate has two
strings to its bow: excellent vineyards in Piesport and from Ockfen and
Wiltingen in the Saar. Crystalline Spätlese and Auslese from both are ★
to ★★, while Ockfener Bockstein TBA is always ★★★. Best years: (2011)
2010 09 **08 07 06 05 04**.

ST-VÉRAN AC *Mâconnais, Burgundy, France* Often thought of as a POUILLY-
FUISSÉ understudy, this is gentle, fairly fruity, normally unoaked
Mâconnais Chardonnay. Overall quality is good and improving. Drink
young. Best producers: D & M Barraud★, Cordier★, Corsin★★, Croix
Senaillet, Deux Roches★, DUBOEUF★, R Lassarat★, O Merlin★, Poncetys★,
Saumaize-Michelin★, VERGET★, J-J Vincent★. Best years: (2011) **10 09**.

STE-CROIX-DU-MONT AC *Bordeaux, France* Best of the 3 sweet wine ACs
that gaze jealously at SAUTERNES and BARSAC across the Garonne river (the
others are CADILLAC and LOUPIAC). The wine is mellow and sweet rather
than splendidly rich. Top wines can age for at least a decade. Best
producers: Crabitan-Bellevue★, Loubens★, Lousteau-Vieil, Mailles, Mont,
Pavillon★, la Rame★. Best years: 2010 **09 07 05 03 02 01 99 98**.

SAINTSBURY *Carneros AVA, California, USA* Deeply committed CARNEROS
winery. Its Pinot Noirs★★ are brilliant examples of the perfume and fruit
quality of Carneros; vineyard-designated Pinots, led by the impressive
Brown Ranch★★, are deeper and oakier, while Garnet★ is a delicious
lighter style. The Chardonnays★★ are also impressive, best after 2–3
years, and new Syrah★ is tasty. Best years: (Pinot Noir) 2009 **08 07 06 05
04 03 02 01 00**.

DUCA DI SALAPARUTA *Sicily, Italy* Corvo is the brand name for the basic
range of Sicilian reds and whites, made from local grape varieties. There
are superior whites, like Kados★★ from the Grillo grape, and fine reds
like Duca Enrico★★ and Passo delle Mule★, both from Nero d'Avola,
red blend Triskelè★, and Lavico★ from the Nerello Mascalese grape.

SALICE SALENTINO DOC *Puglia, Italy* One of the better DOCs in the
Salento peninsula, using Negroamaro tempered with a dash of perfumed
Malvasia Nera for ripe, chocolatey wines that acquire hints of roast
chestnuts and prunes with age. Drink after 3–4 years, although they may
last as long again. The DOCs of Alezio, Brindisi, Copertino, Leverano,
Squinzano and others, plus various IGTs, are similar. Best producers:
Candido★, Casale Bevagna★, Leone de Castris★, Due Palme★, Taurino★,
Vallone★★, Conti Zecca. Best years: (reds) (2011) (10) **09 08 06 04 01**.

SALTA *Argentina* The vineyards of Salta province, 700km (435 miles)
north of MENDOZA, are concentrated along the Calchaquí Valley. The
most important location is Cafayate, at about 1750m (5750ft), where
most of the traditional producers are located. Colomé, further up the
valley, has been producing wine for nearly 200 years and its new
vineyards, at over 3000m (10,000ft), are the highest in the world. High
altitude, mostly sandy soils and almost no rain produce wines of intense
colour and high alcohol content, with scented white Torrontés and lush
inky Malbec. Best producers: (Cafayate) Amalaya★, Domingo Hermanos, El
Porvenir de los Andes, El Transito, Felix Lavaque, Michel Torino, Yacochuya★;
(Colomé) COLOMÉ★★.

SAMOS *Greece* The island of Samos has a centuries-old reputation for rich,
sweet, Muscat-based wines. The Samos co-op's wines include deep gold,
honeyed Samos Nectar★★, made from sun-dried grapes; apricotty
Palaio★, aged for up to 20 years; and seductively complex Samos
Anthemis★, fortified and cask-aged for up to 5 years.

SAN ANTONIO *Chile* A region of many parts, including the sub-region of Leyda. Water shortage is a problem, though much is pumped from the Maipo River several kms away to the south. Closeness to the Pacific Ocean and the icy Humboldt Current decides whether you are best at snappy Sauvignon Blanc and fragrant Pinot Noir, or scented, juice-laden Syrah. There are half a dozen estates here, but big companies like CONCHA Y TORO, CONO SUR, MontGras, SANTA RITA and MONTES are also making exciting wine from the region's fruit. Best producers: CASA MARÍN★★, Chocalán★, O FOURNIER★, Garcés Silva/Amayna★, Viña LEYDA★★, LUIS FELIPE EDWARDS★, MATETIC★, MONTES★.

SAN JUAN *Argentina* The second largest wine-producing region in Argentina, lying 2 hours' drive north of MENDOZA. Three transverse valleys, Pedernal, Tulum and the Zonda, make up the lunar landscape. It's hot and dry here, so it's no surprise to see varieties like Shiraz and Viognier performing well. Like most areas in Argentina, altitude is key to quality. Thus the Pedernal Valley at about 1300m (4260ft) above sea level is being planted extensively and attracting interest from major Mendoza producers. Watch this space. Best producers: Antigua, Callia, Casa Montes, Graffigna, LAS MORAS★, Manos Negras★, Xumek.

SAN LEONARDO *Trentino, Italy* Marchese Carlo Guerrieri Gonzaga, a former winemaker at SASSICAIA, together with Tuscan consultant Carlo Ferrini, has established his Cabernet-Merlot blend San Leonardo★★★ as the northern equivalent of the famous Tuscan. Villa Gresti★ is Merlot-based. Best years: (2011) (10) 09 08 **07 06 04 01 00 99 97 96 95**.

SAN LUIS OBISPO COUNTY *California, USA* CENTRAL COAST county best known for Chardonnay, Pinot Noir, a bit of old-vine Zinfandel, Syrah and Cabernet Sauvignon. There are 5 AVAs: Edna Valley, PASO ROBLES, SANTA MARIA VALLEY (shared with SANTA BARBARA COUNTY), Arroyo Grande Valley and York Mountain. Best producers: ALBAN★★, Claiborne & Churchill★, Edna Valley★★, Laetitia, Meridian★, Norman★, Saucelito Canyon★, Savannah-Chanelle★, Talley★★, Tolosa Estate. Best years: (reds) 2009 08 **07 06 05 04 03 02 01 99 98 97 95 94**.

SAN PEDRO *Curicó, Chile* The group counts 10 wineries among its subsidiaries, including 2 in Argentina (Tamarí and Finca la Celia). Prominent among the Chilean operations is the quality-focused Viña LEYDA in SAN ANTONIO. After a shaky start, Cachapoal-based Altaïr★★ has found its stride since the excellent 2005 vintage. Under the San Pedro label, Castillo de Molina Reservas★★ are outstanding, especially the Sauvignon Blanc from ELQUI. Cabernet-based Cabo de Hornos★ is deep and concentrated. Look out for exciting reds from MAULE and Elqui, and single-vineyard wines under the 1865★★ label.

SANCERRE AC *Loire Valley, France* From a good grower, white Sancerre perfectly captures the bright green tang of the Sauvignon grape. Stony calcareous soils (*les caillottes*) produce the most forward, aromatic styles, while clay and limestone (*terre blanches*) and flint (*silex*) make for more ageworthy wines. Some growers produce a richer style using new oak. Pinot Noir reds from top producers are now a serious proposition, while Pinot Noir rosé is delicate and refreshingly dry. The wines are more consistent than those of neighbouring POUILLY. Prices reflect the appellation's popularity.

Best producers: F & J Bailly-Reverdy★, G Boulay★★, H BOURGEOIS★★, H Brochard★, R Champault★, D Chotard★, F Cotat★★, F Crochet★★, L Crochet★, Delaporte★, A Dezat★, Gitton★, P Jolivet, Serge Laloue★, Serge Laporte★, Y & P Martin★, A MELLOT★★, J Mellot★, Mollet-Maudry★, H Natter★, V Pinard★, P Prieur★, J Reverdy★, P & N Reverdy★, C Riffault★, J-M Roger★, Thomas-Labaille★★, VACHERON★★, André Vatan★. Best years: 2011 **10 09 08 07 06 05**.

SANDALFORD *Swan Valley, Western Australia* Pioneering WESTERN AUSTRALIA winery with 4 wine ranges: flagship Prendiville (Cabernet★★★, Shiraz★★), Estate Reserve (dark, classically ripe, fleshy Shiraz★★, Cabernet Sauvignon★★), Margaret River and budget-priced Element, which offers quality at fair prices. Whites – Sauvignon Blanc-Semillon★, Verdelho★ and Chardonnay★ – are also attractive. Best years: (Cabernet Sauvignon) (2011) 10 09 **08 07** 05 **04 03 02 01 00**.

SANDEMAN *Port DOC, Douro, Portugal, and Jerez y Manzanilla DO, Spain* The PORT operation is now owned by SOGRAPE and run by George Sandeman (7th-generation descendant of the founder). Excellent aged tawnies: 20-year-old★ and 30-year-old★★. Vintage ports are better recently. Vau Vintage★ is good second label, for early drinking. Sandeman sherry brands have been made by Garvey until recently. Best years: (Vintage) **2007 03 00 97 94 66 63 55**.

LUCIANO SANDRONE *Barolo DOCG, Piedmont, Italy* Luciano Sandrone has become one of PIEDMONT's leading wine stylists, renowned for his BAROLO Cannubi Boschis★★★ and Le Vigne★★★, as well as BARBERA D'ALBA★★ and Dolcetto d'Alba★★, which rank with the best.

SANFORD *Sta. Rita Hills AVA, California, USA* Richard Sanford planted the great Sanford & Benedict vineyard in the Santa Ynez Valley in 1971, thus establishing SANTA BARBARA as a potentially top-quality vineyard region. He subsequently planted an estate vineyard in the STA. RITA HILLS, an area that has burst onto the Pinot Noir scene with some spectacular wines (sharply focused, dark-fruited Pinot Noir★★, Chardonnay★★). Richard Sanford left in 2005 to found high-quality Alma Rosa label. Best years: (Pinot Noir) 2010 09 **08 07 06 05** 04 02 01 00 99.

DOM. LE SANG DES CAILLOUX *Vacqueyras AC, Rhône Valley, France* Top VACQUEYRAS estate with big, firmly fruited, peppery red wines. Cuvée de Lopy★★, from old-vine Grenache and Syrah, bursts with fruit over 10 or more years. The traditional cuvée★, restrained but full, is named Azalaïs, Doucinello or Floureto, changing every vintage. Also big, rich white Vacqueyras★. Best years: 2011 10 **09 07 06 05 04 03 01 00 99 98**.

SANGIOVESE Sangiovese, the most widely planted grape variety in Italy, reaches its greatest heights in central TUSCANY, especially in Montalcino, whose BRUNELLO is supposed to be 100% varietal. This grape has produced a wide range of sub-varieties, plus a growing number of 'improved' clones, which makes generalization difficult. Much care is being taken when replanting, whether in CHIANTI CLASSICO, Brunello di Montalcino, VINO NOBILE DI MONTEPULCIANO or elsewhere. Styles range from pale, lively and cherryish, through vivacious mid-range Chiantis, to excellent Riservas and top Tuscan blends; the dense red fruit often has a sweet-sour streak, a whiff of herbs and the scratch of raw earth. Some fine examples in ROMAGNA. California producers including Robert Pepi, Vino Noceto, Ortman and SEGHESIO are having a go at taming the grape, without much success, though it does quite well in the SIERRA FOOTHILLS. Australia has good examples from King Valley in VICTORIA (Crittenden, Greenstone, Pizzini), MCLAREN VALE (CHAPEL HILL, Coriole), BAROSSA (the Kalimna vineyard, source of GRANGE, has some) and MUDGEE (Oatley make a very snappy rosé). Also grown in Argentina, Chile, South Africa and New York.

SANTA BARBARA COUNTY *California, USA* CENTRAL COAST county, northwest of Los Angeles, known for Chardonnay, Riesling, Pinot Noir and Syrah. Main AVAs are STA. RITA HILLS, Santa Ynez Valley and most of SANTA MARIA VALLEY (the remainder is in SAN LUIS OBISPO COUNTY), all top areas for Pinot Noir. Best producers: AU BON CLIMAT★★, Babcock, BECKMEN★★, Brander★, Hitching Post★★, Longoria★, Melville★, Andrew MURRAY★★, Ojai★★, Fess Parker★, QUPE★, Zaca Mesa★. Best years: (Pinot Noir) 2009 **08 07 06 05 04 03 02 01 00.**

SANTA CAROLINA *Maipo, Chile* One of Chile's oldest wineries, whose ancient cellars are within Santiago's urban sprawl; recognized as a National Monument in 1973, although much had to be rebuilt after the 2010 earthquake. This large and improving winery has vineyards in all of Chile's major wine regions, and an extensive range under the direction of chief winemaker Andrés Caballero. Top wine VSC★★ is a Cabernet-based blend. Recently launched 'icon' Carmenère Herencia★★.

SANTA CRUZ MOUNTAINS AVA *California, USA* A sub-region of the CENTRAL COAST AVA. Notable for long-lived Chardonnays and Cabernet Sauvignons, including the stunning Monte Bello from RIDGE. Also small amounts of robust Pinot Noir. Best producers: BONNY DOON★★, David Bruce★★, Clos La Chance★, Thomas Fogarty★, Kathryn Kennedy★★, Mount Eden Vineyards★★, RIDGE★★★, Santa Cruz Mountain Vineyard★.

SANTA MARIA VALLEY AVA *Santa Barbara County and San Luis Obispo County, California, USA* This cool valley is a prime source of Chardonnay, Pinot Noir and Syrah. Look for wines from Bien Nacido and Sierra Madre vineyards. Best producers: AU BON CLIMAT★★, Belle Glos★★, Byron★★, Cambria, Foxen★★, Lane Tanner (Pinot Noir★★), QUPE★★.

SANTA RITA *Maipo, Chile* Long-established MAIPO giant. Red blends such as superb Triple C★★ (Cabernet Franc-Cabernet Sauvignon-Carmenère) show real flair. Floresta wines – Leyda Sauvignon Blanc★★ and Apalta Cabernet Sauvignon★★ – are tremendous. Cabernet-based Casa Real★ is expensive and – at last – gradually modernizing itself.

STA. RITA HILLS AVA *Santa Barbara County, California, USA* This small AVA lies at the western edge of the Santa Ynez Hills in SANTA BARBARA COUNTY. Fog and wind from the Pacific keep temperatures reasonably cool. Pinot Noir is the primary grape (along with small amounts of Syrah and Chardonnay) and the wines have deeper colour, greater varietal intensity and higher acidity than others in the region – they have pretty high alcohols, too. Best producers: Babcock, Brewer-Clifton★★, Clos Pepe★★, Fiddlehead★★, Foley★★, Lafond★, Melville★, SANFORD★★, SEA SMOKE★★.

SANTENAY AC *Côte de Beaune, Burgundy, France* Red Santenay wines often promise good ripe flavour, though they don't always deliver it, but are worth aging for 4–6 years in the hope that the wine will open out. Many of the best wines, both red and white, come from les Gravières Premier Cru on the border with CHASSAGNE-MONTRACHET. Best producers: (reds) R Belland★, Chevrot★, F & D Clair★, M COLIN★, J-N GAGNARD★, J Girardin★, V GIRARDIN★★, Monnot★, MOREY★★, L Muzard★★, Pousse d'Or★, J-M Vincent★★; (whites) V GIRARDIN★, Jaffelin, René Lequin-Colin★. Best years: (reds) (2011) 09 **07** 05 02.

CASA SANTOS LIMA *Alenquer DOC, Lisboa, Portugal* A beautiful estate with a wide range: fruity, tasty Espiga reds and whites; spicy red★ and creamy, perfumed white Palha Canas; red and white Quinta das Setencostas★. Also varietal Touriga Nacional★, Touriga Franca★, Trincadeira★, Tinta Roriz★ and peachy, herby Chardonnay★.

CAVES SÃO JOÃO *Beira Atlântico, Portugal* A pioneer of cool-fermented, white BAIRRADA, and makes rich, oaky Cabernet Sauvignon from its own vines. Rich, complex traditional reds and whites include outstanding Frei João★ (Reserva★★) from Bairrada and Porta dos Cavaleiros★★ from DÃO – they demand at least 10 years' age to show their quality.

SARDINIA *Italy* Grapes of Spanish origin, like the white Vermentino and Torbato and the red Monica, Cannonau and Carignano, dominate production on this huge, hilly Mediterranean island, but they vie with a Malvasia of Greek origin and natives like Nuragus and Vernaccia. The cooler northern part (Gallura) favours whites, especially Vermentino, while the southern and eastern parts are best suited to reds from Cannonau and Monica, with Carignano dominating in the south-west. The wines used to be powerful, alcoholic monsters, but the current trend is for a lighter, modern, more international style. Foremost among those in pursuit of quality are ARGIOLAS, Capichera, Còntini, Cantina Gallura, Alberto Loi, Santadi and Sella & Mosca. See also CARIGNANO DEL SULCIS.

SASSICAIA DOC★★★ *Tuscany, Italy* Legendary Cabernet Sauvignon-Cabernet Franc blend. Vines were planted in 1944 to satisfy the Marchese Mario Incisa della Rocchetta's thirst for fine red Bordeaux, which was in short supply during the war. The wine remained purely for family consumption until nephew Piero ANTINORI and winemaker Giacomo Tachis persuaded the Marchese to refine production practices and to release several thousand bottles from the 1968 vintage. Since then, under Mario's son Niccolò, Sassicaia's fame has increased as it proved itself to be one of the world's great Cabernets, combining a blackcurrant power of elegance and intensity with a heavenly scent of cigars.

Since 1995 it has its own DOC within the BOLGHERI appellation. Best years: (2011) (10) 09 08 **07** 06 **04** 01 99 98 97 95 90 88 85.

HORST SAUER *Escherndorf, Franken, Germany* Horst Sauer shot to stardom in the late 1990s. His dry Rieslings★★ and Silvaners★ are unusually juicy and fresh for a region renowned for blunt, earthy wines. His late-harvest wines are frequently ★★★; they will easily live a decade, sometimes much more. Best years: (dry Riesling, Silvaner) (2011) 10 09 **08 07** 06 05 04.

SAUMUR AC *Loire Valley, France* Dry white wines, mainly from Chenin Blanc, with up to 20% Chardonnay; the best combine bright fruit with a mineral seam. The reds are lighter than those of SAUMUR-CHAMPIGNY and new Saumur Puy-Notre-Dame AC. Also dry to off-dry Cabernet rosé, and sweet Coteaux de Saumur in good years. Best producers: Château-Gaillard★, Clos Rougeard★★, Collier★, Filliatreau★, Fosse-Seche★, Guiberteau★, HUREAU★, Langlois-Château★, R-N Legrand★, F MABILEAU★★,

Mélaric, la Paleine★, ROCHES NEUVES★★, St-Just★, Saumur co-op, VILLENEUVE★★, Yvonne★★. Best years: (whites) 2011 **10 09 08 07 06 05**.

SAUMUR-CHAMPIGNY AC *Loire Valley, France* Saumur's best red wine. Cabernet Franc is the main grape and, on Saumur's soft limestone soils, produces among the Loire's most seductively perfumed, silky examples. Delicious young, it can age for 6–10 years, top cuvées even longer. Best producers: Clos Cristal★, Clos Rougeard★★, de la Cune, B Dubois★, Filliatreau★, HUREAU★★, R-N Legrand★, Nerleux★, Pas Saint-Martin, la Perruche★, Retiveau-Rétif★, ROCHES NEUVES★★, St-Vincent★/Patrick Vadé, A Sanzay★, Saumur co-op, VILLENEUVE★★, Yvonne★. Best years: (2011) 10 **09 08 06 05 04 03 02 01**.

SAUMUR MOUSSEUX AC *Loire Valley, France* Reasonable CHAMPAGNE-method sparkling wines, mainly from Chenin Blanc. Adding Chardonnay and Cabernet Franc makes the wine softer and more interesting. Usually non-vintage. Small quantities of rosé are also made. Best producers: Ch. de Beauregard, Bouvet-Ladubay★, Gratien & Meyer★, Grenelle★, la Paleine★, la Perruche★, Saumur co-op, Veuve Amiot.

SAUSSIGNAC AOP *Bergerac, South-West France* Slightly more minerally than the sweet wines of neighbouring MONBAZILLAC. Best after about 3 years, but will age well. Best producers: Clos d'Yvigne★, Miaudoux★, La Maurigne★, Richard★.

SAUTERNES AC *Bordeaux, France* The name Sauternes is synonymous with the best sweet wines in the world. Sauternes and BARSAC both lie on the banks of the little river Ciron and are 2 of the very few areas in France where noble rot occurs naturally. Production of these intense, sweet, luscious wines from botrytized grapes is a risk-laden and extremely expensive affair, and the wines are never going to be cheap. From good producers the wines are worth their high price – as well as 14% alcohol, they have a richness full of flavours of pineapples, peaches, syrup and spice. Good vintages should be aged for 5–10 years and can last two or three times as long. Best producers: Bastor-Lamontagne★, Clos Haut-Peyraguey★★, Cru Barréjats★, DOISY-DAËNE★★, DOISY-VÉDRINES★★, FARGUES★★, GILETTE★★, GUIRAUD★★, Haut-Bergeron★, les Justices★, LAFAURIE-PEYRAGUEY★★, Lamothe-Guignard★, Laville, Malle★, Rabaud-Promis★, Raymond-Lafon★★, Rayne-Vigneau★, RIEUSSEC★★★, Sigalas Rabaud★★, SUDUIRAUT★★★, la TOUR BLANCHE★★, YQUEM★★★. Best years: (2011) 10 09 **07 05 03 02 01 99 98 97 96 95 90 89 88 86 83**.

SAUVIGNON BLANC See pages 284–5.

SAUZET *Puligny-Montrachet, Côte de Beaune, Burgundy, France* A producer with a reputation for rich, full-flavoured white Burgundies, but recently showing more classical restraint. Prime sites in PULIGNY-MONTRACHET★ with a great range of Premiers Crus, especially Combettes★★★, as well as small parcels of BÂTARD-MONTRACHET★★★ and Bienvenues-BÂTARD-MONTRACHET★★★. Best years: (2011) 10 09 **08 07 06 05 04 02**.

SAVENNIÈRES AC *Loire Valley, France* Wines from Chenin Blanc, produced on steep vineyards south of Anjou. Usually steely and dry, although some richer wines are being produced by a new generation using new oak and malolactic fermentation. The top wines usually need at least 8 years to mature, and can age for longer. Two vineyards have their own ACs: la Coulée de Serrant and Roche aux Moines. Best producers: Baumard★★, Bergerie, Closel★★, La COULÉE-DE-SERRANT★★, Épiré★★, Dom. F L★, Gué d'Orger, Damien Laureau★, aux Moines★, Eric Morgat★, OGEREAU, PIERRE-BISE★, Taillandier★. Best years: (2011) 09 08 **07 06 05 04 03 02 01 99 97 96**.

SAUVIGNON BLANC

Of all the world's grapes, the Sauvignon Blanc is leader of the 'love it or loathe it' pack. It veers from being wildly fashionable to totally out of favour, depending upon where it is grown and which country's wine writers are talking. But you, the consumers, love it – and so do I. Sauvignon is always at its best when full rein is allowed to its very particular talents, because this grape does give intense, sometimes shocking flavours, and doesn't take kindly to being put into a straitjacket. Periodically, producers lose confidence in its fantastic, brash, tangy personality and try to calm it down. Don't do it. Let it run free – it's that lip-smacking, in-yer-face nettles and lime zest and passionfruit attack that drinkers love. There's no more thirst-quenching wine than a snappy, crunchy young Sauvignon Blanc. Let's celebrate it.

WINE STYLES

Sancerre-style Sauvignon Although it had long been used as a blending grape in Bordeaux, where its characteristic green tang injected a bit of life into the blander, waxier Sémillon, Sauvignon first became trendy as the grape used for Sancerre, a bone-dry Loire white whose green gooseberry fruit and slightly smoky perfume inspired the winemakers of other countries to try to emulate, then often surpass, the original model.

The range of styles Sauvignon produces is as wide as, if less subtly nuanced than, those of Chardonnay. It is highly successful when picked slightly underripe, fermented cool in stainless steel, and bottled early. This is the New Zealand model and they in turn adapted and improved upon the Sancerre model from France. New Zealand is now regarded as the top Sauvignon country, and many new producers in places like Australia, South Africa, southern France, Hungary, Spain, Argentina and Chile are emulating this powerful mix of passionfruit, gooseberry and lime. South African and Chilean examples, from the coolest coastal regions, with tangy fruit and mineral depth, challenge New Zealand for quality.

Using oak Sauvignon also lends itself to fermentation in barrel and aging in new oak, though less happily than does Chardonnay. This is the model of the Graves region of Bordeaux, although generally here Sémillon would be blended in with Sauvignon to good effect.

New Zealand again excels at this style, and there are good examples from California (sometimes known as Fumé Blanc), Australia and northern Italy. The mix, usually led by Sémillon, is becoming a classy speciality of South Africa's coastal regions. In Austria, producers in southern Styria (Steiermark) make powerful, aromatic versions, sometimes with a touch of oak. In all these regions, the acidity that is Sauvignon's great strength should remain, with a nectarine fruit and a spicy, biscuity softness from the oak. These oaky styles are best drunk either within about a year, or after aging for 5 years or so, and can produce remarkable, strongly individual flavours.

Sweet wines Sauvignon is also a crucial ingredient in the great sweet wines of Sauternes and Barsac from Bordeaux, though it is less susceptible than its partner Sémillon to the sweetness-enhancing 'noble rot' fungus, botrytis.

Sweet Sauvignon-Semillon blends from elsewhere in the world range from the interesting to the outstanding – but the characteristic green tang of the Sauvignon should be found even at ultra-sweet levels.

Marea *de* **Leyda**

SAUVIGNON BLANC

Leyda Valley Chile
2010

BEST PRODUCERS

France
Pouilly-Fumé J-C Chatelain, Didier DAGUENEAU, Ladoucette, Masson-Blondelet, de Tracy; *Sancerre* G Boulay, H BOURGEOIS, F Cotat, F Crochet, A MELLOT, VACHERON; *Pessac-Léognan* Dom. de CHEVALIER, Couhins-Lurton, FIEUZAL, HAUT-BRION, la LOUVIÈRE, MALARTIC-LAGRAVIERE, SMITH-HAUT-LAFITTE; *Graves* Clos Floridène.

Other European Sauvignons
Austria Gross, Lackner-Tinnacher, POLZ, E Sabathi, Sattlerhof, TEMENT.

Italy Colterenzio, Peter Dipoli, Edi Kante, LAGEDER, SCHIOPETTO, Vie di Romans, Villa Russiz.

Spain (Rueda) Alvarez y Diez (Mantel Blanco), MARQUES DE RISCAL, Palacio de Bornos, Javier Sanz, Sitios de Bodega; *(Penedès)* TORRES (Fransola).

New Zealand
ASTROLABE, Blind River, CLOUDY BAY, Forrest Estate, Greywacke, Lawson's Dry Hills, MATUA VALLEY, Mudhouse, NEUDORF, PALLISER, PEGASUS BAY, SAINT CLAIR, Sea Level, SERESIN, Stoneleigh, TE MATA, VAVASOUR, VILLA MARIA, YFALANDS.

Australia
Angullong, BANNOCKBURN, Bird in Hand, Brookland Valley, Larry CHERUBINO, DE BORTOLI (Yarra Valley), HANGING ROCK, HOUGHTON (Wisdom), Karribindi, KATNOOK ESTATE, Lenton Brae, Logan, Longview, Nepenthe, S C PANNELL, Philip SHAW, SHAW & SMITH, Stella Bella, Tamar Ridge, Geoff WEAVER, Word of Mouth.

USA
ARAUJO, Brander, Coquerel, DRY CREEK (DCV3), FLORA SPRINGS (Soliloquy), GRGICH HILLS, HEITZ, Honig, KENWOOD, KUNDE, MATANZAS CREEK, MONDAVI, ST SUPÉRY, SPOTTSWOODE.

Chile
CASA MARÍN, CASAS DEL BOSQUE, CONCHA Y TORO (Terrunyo), CONO SUR (20 Barrels), ERRAZURIZ, O FOURNIER, Viña LEYDA, LUIS FELIPE EDWARDS, MONTES (Leyda), SAN PEDRO (Castillo de Molina), SANTA RITA (Floresta), UNDURRAGA (T.H.).

South Africa
Graham BECK (Pheasants' Run), CAPE POINT, Constantia Glen, Neil ELLIS, Flagstone, Fleur du Cap, Fryer's Cove, Hermanuspietersfontein, KLEIN CONSTANTIA, MULDERBOSCH, Oak Valley, Quoin Rock, SPRINGFIELD, STEENBERG, THELEMA, VERGELEGEN.

285

SAVIGNY-LÈS-BEAUNE AC *Côte de Beaune, Burgundy, France* Large village with reds dominating; usually dry and lean, they need 4–6 years to open out. Top Premiers Crus, such as Lavières, Peuillets and La Dominode, are more substantial. The white wines show a bit of dry, nutty class after 2–3 years. The wines are generally reasonably priced. Best producers: Belin★, BELLENE★, S Bize★★, Camus-Bruchon★, Champy★, CHANDON DE BRIAILLES★, Chenu★, B CLAIR★★, M Écard★, J J Girard★, Guyon★, L Jacob★★, Dom. LEROY★★, J-M Pavelot★. Best years: (reds) (2011) 10 09 08 **07** 05 02.

SAVOIE *France* Savoie's high Alpine vineyards produce fresh, snappy white wines from the local Jacquère, Chasselas (to drink young), and the more interesting Altesse (see ROUSSETTE DE SAVOIE) and Bergeron grapes (aka Roussanne, grown only in Chignin). There are attractive light reds and rosés, too, from Gamay or Pinot and, in warm years, some positively Rhône-like reds from the Mondeuse grape (related to Syrah). The 16 best villages can add their own name to the label; these include Apremont, Abymes, Chignin and Arbin, near Chambéry, and Jongieux near Aix-les-Bains, along with Crépy and Ripaille growing Chasselas near Lac Léman (Geneva). Seyssel has its own AC for sparkling and dry whites. One important producer, Domaine des Ardoisières, is outside the appellation area. Best producers: Belluard★, G Berlioz★, Berthollier★, Dupasquier★, Giachino, l'Idylle★, E Jacquin★, Magnin★, Maillet, J Masson, Prieuré St-Christophe★★, A & M Quenard★★, J-P & J-F Quenard, P & A Quénard★, Ch. de Ripaille, Saint-Germain★, Trosset★.

SAXENBURG *Stellenbosch WO, South Africa* In-demand red wines, led by dense, burly Private Collection Shiraz★★ and even richer, bigger Shiraz Select★★, plus excellent Cabernet★★ and Merlot★. Private Collection Sauvignon Blanc★★ and Chardonnay★ head the white range. Reds will improve for 5–8 years. Best years: (top reds) 2009 **08 07 06 05 04** 03 02.

WILLI SCHAEFER *Graach, Mosel, Germany* Classic MOSEL wines: Riesling Spätlese and Auslese from the GRAACHER Domprobst vineyard have a balance of piercing acidity and lavish fruit that is every bit as dramatic as Domprobst's precipitous slope. Extremely long-lived, they're frequently ★★★, as are the sensational Beerenauslese and Eiswein Schaefer produces in good vintages. Even his QbA wines are ★. Best years: (Riesling Spätlese, Auslese) (2011) 10 09 08 **07 06 05 04 03 02** 01 99.

SCHÄFER-FRÖHLICH *Bockenau, Nahe, Germany* From vineyards in SCHLOSSBOCKELHEIM and the more obscure Bockenau, Tim Fröhlich has since 2003 been producing racy dry Rieslings★★ and sumptuous nobly sweet wines★★★. Best years: (2011) 10 09 **08 07 06** 05 04.

SCHARFFENBERGER CELLARS *Anderson Valley AVA, California, USA* The quality trailblazer in the chilly ANDERSON VALLEY, now owned by top-performing neighbour ROEDERER. Non-vintage Brut★★, with lovely toasty depth, exuberant Rosé★★ and excellent vintage Blanc de Blancs★★.

SCHEUREBE Silvaner x Riesling crossing found in Germany's PFALZ and RHEINHESSEN. In Austria it is sometimes labelled Sämling 88. At its best in Trockenbeerenauslese and Eiswein. When ripe, it has a marvellous flavour of honey, exotic fruits and the pinkest of pink grapefruit.

SCHILCHER Rosé and sparkling wine from the Blauer Wildbacher grape, a speciality of the West STEIERMARK in Austria. Its high acidity means you either love it or detest it. Best producers: Prinz Liechtenstein, Strohmeier.

SCHIOPETTO *Friuli-Venezia Giulia, Italy* The late Mario Schiopetto pioneered the development of scented varietals and high-quality, intensely concentrated white wines from COLLIO. Outstanding are Friulano★★, Pinot Bianco★★ and Sauvignon★★, plus white blends Blanc des Rosis and Mario Schiopetto Bianco.

SCHLOSS JOHANNISBERG *Johannisberg, Rheingau, Germany* This historic 35ha (86-acre) estate has not always lived up to its reputation. A new director has refined and greatly improved the winemaking. TBA★★★ has long been outstanding (and costly), but drier styles of Riesling (can be ★★) are now vigorous and spicy. Best years: (2011) 10 09 08 07 06 05.

SCHLOSS LIESER *Lieser, Mosel, Germany* Since Thomas Haag (son of Wilhelm, of the Fritz HAAG estate) took over the winemaking in 1992 (and then bought the property in 97), this small estate has shot to the top. MOSEL Rieslings★★ marry richness with great elegance. Best years: (2011) 10 09 08 07 06 05 04 03.

SCHLOSS REINHARTSHAUSEN *Erbach, Rheingau, Germany* Estate formerly owned by the Hohenzollern family, rulers of Prussia. Top sites include the great ERBACHer Marcobrunn. Much improved under new management since 2003. Good Rieslings★★ in all styles and Sekt★. Best years: (2011) 10 09 08 07 06 05 04 01.

SCHLOSSBÖCKELHEIM *Nahe, Germany* This village's top sites are the Felsenberg and Kupfergrube; good wines also come from Mühlberg and Königsfels. Best producers: Dr Crusius★, DÖNNHOFF★★★, Gut Hermannsberg, SCHÄFER-FRÖHLICH★★. Best years: (2011) 10 09 08 07 06 05 04 02.

SCHNAITMANN *Württemberg, Germany* A rising star, with varietal red and white wines of equal excitement. Rainer Schnaitmann trained in New Zealand, and his Sauvignon Blanc★ is one of Germany's best. Fine Spätburgunder★★ and Lemberger★. Best years: (2011) 10 09 08 07 06 05.

DOM. SCHOFFIT *Alsace AC, Alsace, France* One of the two main owners of the outstanding Rangen Grand Cru vineyard, also making deliciously fruity non cru wines. Top-of-the-tree Clos St-Théobald wines from Rangen are often ★★★. Gewürztraminer and Pinot Gris will improve for at least 5–6 years after release, Rieslings for even longer. The Cuvée Alexandre range is essentially declassified ALSACE Vendange Tardive. Best years: (Clos St-Théobald Riesling) (2011) (10) (09) 08 07 06 04 02 01 00 99 98 97

SCHRAMSBERG *Napa Valley AVA, California, USA* The first California winery to make really excellent CHAMPAGNE-style sparklers from the classic grapes. These wines are generally among California's best, and as good as fine Champagne. The Crémant★ is an attractive, slightly sweetish sparkler; the Blanc de Noirs★★ and the Blanc de Blancs★ are more classic. Bold, powerful J Schram★★ is rich and flavoursome and increasingly good. Top of the line is the Reserve Brut★★. Vintage-dated wines can be drunk with up to 10 years' age and can achieve ★★★ quality. A rosé sparkler★★ is a superb summer quaffer. The J Davies Cabernet Sauvignon★★, from Diamond Mountain, is named in honour of the late founder, Jack Davies. The winery has just launched a line of vineyard-designated still Pinot Noir wines under the Davies Vineyards brand.

SCREAMING EAGLE *Oakville AVA, California, USA* First produced a Cabernet Sauvignon from OAKVILLE valley floor vineyard in 1992. Made in very limited quantities, Screaming Eagle★★★ is one of California's most sought-after Cabernets each vintage – a huge, brooding wine that displays all the lush fruit of Oakville. The vineyard has been replanted and a new winery built, but a change in style is not expected.

SEA SMOKE *Sta. Rita Hills AVA, California, USA* This boutique Pinot star is scaling back a bit on its rich, ripe style in favour of slightly lower alcohol levels. The Botella★ is the most approachable, followed by the more complex Southing★★ and blockbuster Ten★★. The winery makes just a splash of elegant Chardonnay★. New fresh, low-dosage sparkler called Sea Spray. Best years: 2009 08 07 05 04 03 02 01.

SEGHESIO *Sonoma County, California, USA* Bought by Napa's Crimson Wine Group in 2011. Having grown grapes in SONOMA COUNTY for a century, the Seghesio family became known for its own Zinfandel. All bottlings, from Sonoma County★★ to the single-vineyard San Lorenzo★★ and Cortina★★, display textbook black fruit and peppery spice. Sangiovese★ from 1910 vines is one of the best in the state. Also look for fascinating Aglianico★ and crisp Italian whites such as Pinot Grigio★ and Arneis★.

SELBACH-OSTER *Zeltingen, Mosel, Germany* Johannes Selbach is one of the MOSEL's new generation of stars, producing pure, elegant Riesling★★ from the Zeltinger Sonnenuhr site. Also fine wine from WEHLEN, GRAACH and BERNKASTEL. Best years: (2011) 10 09 08 07 06 05 04 03 02.

SELVAPIANA *Chianti Rufina DOCG, Tuscany, Italy* This estate has always produced excellent CHIANTI RUFINA. But since 1990 it has vaulted into the top rank of Tuscan estates, particularly with single-vineyard cru Bucerchiale Riserva★★★ and 'super-Tuscan' IGT Fornace★★. Very good VIN SANTO★★. Best years: (Bucerchiale) (2011) (10) 09 08 07 06 04 01 99 98 95 91 90 88 85.

SÉMILLON Found mainly in South-West France, especially in the sweet wines of SAUTERNES, BARSAC, MONBAZILLAC and SAUSSIGNAC, because it is prone to noble rot (*Botrytis cinerea*). Also blended for its waxy texture with Sauvignon Blanc to make dry wine – almost all the great PESSAC-LÉOGNAN whites are based on this blend and exhibit vivid nectarine fruit and custardy softness. Good in Australia on its own (the accent over the é is dropped on New World labels) – aged Semillon from the HUNTER, BAROSSA and CLARE VALLEY can be wonderful: bone-dry, lime zesty yet toasty – or as a blender with Chardonnay. Semillon is also blended with Sauvignon in Western Australia, New Zealand, California (including ST SUPÉRY's Virtu) and Washington State. In cooler regions of South Africa it is producing some outstanding results, often barrel-fermented (Ghost Corner★★ from Elim); also in flagship blends with Sauvignon.

SEPPELT *Grampians, Victoria, Australia* Controversially, Foster's sold Seppeltsfield (the BAROSSA base of Seppelt and its entire fortified resources) to a group centring on the CLARE VALLEY producer, Kilikanoon. From its GRAMPIANS base, Seppelt continues to excel with its flagship St Peters Shiraz★★, the definitive Show Sparkling Shiraz★★★ and the Original Sparkling Shiraz★. The sparkling whites appear to be suffering from a lack of focus. Drumborg Riesling★ and Drumborg Pinot Gris★ from the super-cool Henty region of south-western VICTORIA stand out, and there are some excellent budget-priced table wines.

SERESIN *Marlborough, South Island, New Zealand* Film producer Michael Seresin's MARLBOROUGH winery, with a range of stylish organic/biodynamic wines. Intense Sauvignon Blanc★★ is full of youthful exuberance. Creamy Reserve Chardonnay★★, succulent Pinot Gris★ and several labels of rich, oaky Pinot Noir★★, some single-vineyard, the best of which will age for up to 7 years. Best years: (Pinot Noir) 2010 09 07 06.

SETÚBAL DOC *Portugal* Fortified wine from the Setúbal Peninsula south of Lisbon, called 'Moscatel de Setúbal' when made from at least 85% Moscatel, and 'Setúbal' when it's not. **Best producers:** BACALHÔA★★, José Maria da FONSECA★★.

SEYVAL BLANC Hybrid grape whose disease resistance and ability to continue ripening in a damp autumn make it a useful variety in England, Quebec, NEW YORK STATE and other areas in the eastern US. Gives clean, sappy, grapefruit-edged wines that with age can sometimes give a very passable imitation of bone-dry CHABLIS.

SHAFER *Stags Leap District AVA, California, USA* One of the best NAPA wineries, run by the erudite and thoughtful Doug Shafer, and making unusually fruity One Point Five Cabernet★★ and stunning, focused Reserve-style Hillside Select★★★ that ages to a cedary beauty over a generation. Merlot★★ is also exciting. Relentless★ is made from estate-grown Syrah. Red Shoulder Ranch Chardonnay★★★ is classic full-bodied but scented CARNEROS style. **Best years:** (Hillside Select) 2007 06 05 04 03 02 01 00 99 98 97 96 95 94 93 91 90.

SHARPHAM *Devon, England* Beautiful vineyard on a bend in the river Dart with a stylish range of still and sparkling wines, including white Bacchus★ and Madeleine Angevine-based Estate Selection and Sharpham Pinot Noir. Also makes great cheese.

PHILIP SHAW *Orange, New South Wales, Australia* Philip Shaw is one of Australia's winemaking giants, now a major influence on the ORANGE region. He was at the winemaking helm guiding the rise of commercial giant Rosemount in the 1990s, and moved to Orange to build a family wine business around the picturesque Koomooloo vineyard, which he had planted in 1989. The No 19 Sauvignon Blanc★★ is pristine, tight and zesty; the No 11 Chardonnay★ powerful, rich and minerally; and the No 5 Cabernet Sauvignon★ fleshy, weighty yet elegant.

SHAW & SMITH *Adelaide Hills, South Australia* Influential winery run by cousins Martin Shaw and Michael Hill Smith. They now source much of their fruit from their M3 and Balhannah vineyards and the wines are showing the benefit of this. Tangy Sauvignon Blanc★★ has been a runaway success since its first vintage in 1989; increasingly brilliant single-vineyard M3 Chardonnay★★★; and impressive, fleshy, cool-climate Shiraz★★. Delightful Riesling★ and Pinot Noir★ (expect these to be ★★ soon). **Best years:** (M3 Chardonnay) 2010 09 08 07 06 05 04 03 02.

SHERRY See JEREZ Y MANZANILLA DO, pages 186–7.

SHIRAZ See SYRAH, pages 302–3.

SICILY *Italy* The Mediterranean's largest island is a historically prolific producer of good wine, with sweet Malvasias from the Eolian islands and Zibibbos (see MOSCATO PASSITO DI PANTELLERIA) joining the fortified brews from MARSALA and elegant table wines from the Nerello (black) and Carricante (white) varieties in the north-east (ETNA and Messina's Faro), not to mention the powerful Nero d'Avolas and delicate Frappatos of the south-east. In the late 20th and early 21st centuries there has been a flurry of enological activity. Nero d'Avola has spread all over the island, varietally or blended, now with Frappato, now with Syrah. Marsala, not so long ago a laughing stock, is beginning to command respect again (see DE BARTOLI), and the high slopes of Etna are for the first time since the 19th century bringing forth the bottles that have had them compared with fine Burgundy. Co-ops like Settesoli – with attractive budget label Inycon and top-end Mandrarossa (often ★★) – are doing a tremendous job on the large-scale commercial front, and modern-thinking wineries, using both native and international grapes, are mushrooming. Best producers: Abbazia Santa Anastasia★★, Avide★, Benanti★★, Il Cantante★★, Ceuso★★, COS★, Cottanera★★, Cusumano★, Donnafugata★★, Firriato★, Florio★, Gulfi★★, Morgante★★, Palari★★★, PLANETA★★, Duca di SALAPARUTA★, TASCA D'ALMERITA★★.

SIERRA FOOTHILLS AVA *California, USA*   The key word here is foothills, since valley floor locations 130km (80 miles) east of San Francisco tend to be warmer and less likely to produce fine wine. Some of the state's oldest Zinfandel is here. The region also does well with Italian varieties like Sangiovese and Barbera, and some old-vine Petite Sirahs are superb, long-lived brutes. Best producers: Granite Springs★, Latcham, Lava Cap★, Perry Creek★, Sobon Estate, Twisted Oak★, Vino Noceto.

SIEUR D'ARQUES, LES VIGNERONS DU *Limoux AC, Languedoc, France*   This modern co-op makes around 80% of the still and sparkling wines of LIMOUX. The BLANQUETTE DE LIMOUX and CRÉMANT DE LIMOUX are reliable, but the real excitement comes with the Toques et Clochers Chardonnays★. The co-op also makes a range of Pays d'OC wines.

SILVER OAK CELLARS *Napa Valley, California, USA*
Only Cabernet Sauvignon is made here, with bottlings from ALEXANDER VALLEY★★ and NAPA VALLEY★ grapes. Forward, generous, fruity wines, impossible not to enjoy young, yet with great staying power. Twomey is the owners' other winery, which started out making only Merlot but has expanded to include Pinot Noir from several AVAs as well as Sauvignon Blanc. Best years: (Napa Valley) 2007 **06 05 04 03 02 01 00 99 97 96 95 94 93 92 91 90 86**.

SILVERADO VINEYARDS *Stags Leap District AVA, California, USA*   The estate Cabernet Sauvignon★ has intense fruit and is drinkable fairly young; Limited Reserve★★ (not made every year) has more depth and is capable of aging; Solo★, from STAGS LEAP DISTRICT, displays the cherry fruit and supple tannins of this AVA. Also a fruity Merlot★, refreshing Sauvignon Blanc★ and Chardonnay★ with soft, inviting fruit and a silky finish. Best years: (Limited Reserve) **2005 02 01 99 95 94 91 90**.

SIMONSIG *Stellenbosch WO, South Africa*   Family-run property with broad range of styles. Reds include regular Mr Borio's Shiraz and lavishly oaked Merindol Syrah★; a delicious unwooded Pinotage★★ and well-oaked old-vine Redhill Pinotage★★; dense, powerful Frans Malan Reserve★, a Cape blend of Pinotage, Cabernet Sauvignon and Merlot; and Cabernet-led BORDEAUX-blend, Tiara★, since 2007 more powerful, tannic. Whites are sound, if less exciting. Cap Classique sparklers, Kaapse Vonkel and Cuvée Royale★, are biscuity and creamy. Best years: (premium reds) 2009 **08 07 06 05 04 03 02**.

CH. SIRAN★ *Margaux AC, Haut-Médoc, Bordeaux, France*   Owned by the same family since 1848, this estate produces consistently good claret – increasingly characterful, approachable young, but with enough structure to last for as long as 20 years. Second wine: S de Siran. Best years: 2010 09 **08 07 06 05 04 03 02 01 00 99 98 96 95 90 89**.

SKILLOGALEE *Clare Valley, South Australia* Good range from some of CLARE VALLEY's coolest vineyards: a stony Riesling★ typical of the region and an attractive lemony Gewürztraminer★. Reds include full, fresh Shiraz★★ and minty Cabernet Sauvignon★. Also a rich, raisiny Liqueur Muscat★★.

CH. SMITH-HAUT-LAFITTE *Pessac-Léognan AC, Cru Classé de Graves, Bordeaux, France* A change of ownership in 1990 heralded a decade of hard graft, resulting in massively improved quality. The reds, traditionally lean, now have much more fruit and perfume and can approach ★★. The white is a shining example of modern white Bordeaux and at best is ★★★. Second wine (red and white): Les Hauts de Smith. Also Le Petit Haut Lafitte (Cabernet Sauvignon-based red since 2007). Best years: (reds) 2010 09 08 **07 06 05 04 03 02 01 00 99 98 96 95**; (whites) **2010 09 08 07 06 05 04 02 01 00 99 98**.

SMITH WOODHOUSE *Port DOC, Portugal* Underrated but consistently satisfying PORT from this shipper in the Symington group. Good Vintage★★ and single-quinta Madalena★. Late Bottled Vintage★ is the rich and characterful, figgy, unfiltered type. Best years: (Vintage) **2007 03 00 97 94 92 91 85 83 80 77 70 63**; (Madalena) (2001) **99 96 95**.

SOAVE DOC *Veneto, Italy* In the hilly Soave Classico zone near Verona, the Garganega and Trebbiano di Soave (aka Verdicchio) grapes can produce smooth, nutty, scented wines. The blend may include 30% Chardonnay or Pinot Bianco, but while there are good examples of this style they tend to lack the personality of those made without resort to French grapes. Soave Superiore is DOCG, but the top private producers ignore it in protest at the anomalous rules governing the denomination: top wines nearly all remain Soave Classico DOC or, with screw cap, plain Soave DOC. Best producers: Bertani★, Ca' Rugate★, La Cappuccina★, Cecilia Beretta★, Coffele★★, Fattori★★, Gini★★, Inama★, MASI★, PIEROPAN★★★, Portinari★, Prà★★, Suavia★★, Tamellini★. See also ANSELMI, RECIOTO DI SOAVE.

CH. SOCIANDO-MALLET★★ *Haut-Médoc AC, Haut-Médoc, Bordeaux, France* It wasn't classified in 1855, but every single vintage nowadays outshines many properties that were. The wines massively repay 10–20 years' aging, but exhibit classic Bordeaux flavours from as early as 5 years old. Best years: 2010 09 08 06 **05 04 03 02 01 00 98 96 95 90 89 88**.

SOGRAPE *Portugal* Portuguese giant; Mateus Rosé is still the company's golden egg, but Sogrape makes good to very good VINHO VERDE (Quinta de Azevedo★), DOURO (Reserva Tinto★) and ALENTEJO (Vinha do Monte, Herdade do Peso★). A high-tech winery in DÃO produces Duque de Viseu★ and the Quinta dos Carvalhais range, with promising varietal Encruzado★ (white) and Touriga Nacional★ (red); Reserva★★ and Único★★★ reds are further steps up. Callabriga★ reds from Douro, Alentejo and Dão are based on Aragonez (Tempranillo), blended with local varieties. Subsidiaries FERREIRA, SANDEMAN and Offley provide top-flight ports. Also owns Finca Flichman in Argentina, FRAMINGHAM in New Zealand and Viña Los Boldos in Chile.

SOLAIA★★★ *Tuscany, Italy* One of ANTINORI's 'super-Tuscans', Solaia is a blend of Cabernet Sauvignon, Sangiovese and Cabernet Franc. Intense, with rich black fruit and a classic structure, it is not produced in every vintage. Best years: (2011) (10) 09 08 07 06 **04 01 99 98 97 95 94 93 91 90 88 86 85**.

SOMONTANO DO *Aragón, Spain* Erratic but eternally promising region in the Pyrenean foothills, with a mixture of international and local grapes. Chardonnay and Gewürztraminer are successful whites. Rosés are generally fresh and flavourful, while reds, particularly from the native Parraleta and Moristel or old-vine Garnacha, can be quite impressive. But the excessive dependence on international varieties, initially its strength, is now hurting it in the marketplace. Best producers: Otto Bestué, Blecua★★, ENATE★★, Fábregas, Irius★, Lalanne★, Laus★, Pirineos★, VIÑAS DEL VERO★ (Secastilla★★). Best years: (reds) 2009 07 **05 04 03 01 99 98**.

SONOMA COAST AVA *California, USA* A huge appellation, defined on its western boundary by the Pacific Ocean, that attempts to bring together the coolest regions of SONOMA COUNTY. It encompasses the Sonoma part of CARNEROS and overlaps parts of SONOMA VALLEY and RUSSIAN RIVER. The heart of the appellation are vineyards on the high coastal ridge only a few miles from the Pacific. Vintners and growers along the coastline have formed an association called the West Sonoma Coast Vintners to distinguish themselves from producers farther inland. Intense Chardonnays and Pinot Noirs are the focus. Best producers: Capiaux★, COBB★★, DUTTON GOLDFIELD★★, FLOWERS★★, FREESTONE★★, HARTFORD FAMILY★★, KISTLER★★, Kosta Browne★, LANDMARK★, Littorai★★, MARCASSIN★★, Patz & Hall★, Siduri★★, W H Smith★★, Sonoma Coast Vineyards★★ (Balistreri Vineyard★★★), Sean Thackrey★★.

SONOMA COUNTY *California, USA* Sonoma's vine-growing area is big and sprawling – some 25,500ha (63,000 acres) – with dozens of soil types and mesoclimates, from the fairly warm SONOMA VALLEY and ALEXANDER VALLEY regions to the cool Green Valley, lower RUSSIAN RIVER VALLEY and SONOMA COAST. The best wines are from Chardonnay, Sauvignon Blanc, Cabernet Sauvignon, Pinot Noir and Zinfandel. Often the equal of rival NAPA in quality and originality of flavours. See also CARNEROS, DRY CREEK VALLEY.

SONOMA-CUTRER *Russian River Valley AVA, Sonoma County, California, USA* Rich, oaky, popular Chardonnays. Single-vineyard Les Pierres★★ is the most complex and richest; Cutrer★★ can also have a complexity worth waiting for; Founders Reserve★★ is made in very limited quantities; Russian River Ranches★ is improved in recent releases. Pinot Noir★ is tasty stuff. Best years: (Chardonnay) 2010 **09 08 07 06 05 04 03 02 01 00**.

SONOMA VALLEY AVA *California, USA* The oldest wine region north of San Francisco, Sonoma Valley is on the western side of the Mayacamas Mountains, which separate it from NAPA VALLEY. Best varieties are Chardonnay and Zinfandel, with Cabernet and Merlot from hillside sites also good. Best producers: ARROWOOD★★, CHATEAU ST JEAN★, B R Cohn, Fisher★, GUNDLACH BUNDSCHU★★, KENWOOD★, KUNDE★★, LANDMARK★★, LAUREL GLEN★★, MATANZAS CREEK★★, Moon Mountain★★, RAVENSWOOD★, St Francis★, Sebastiani★, Three Sticks★, Wind Gap★★. Best years: (Zinfandel) 2010 09 08 **07 06 05 04 03 01**.

DOM. SORIN *Bandol AC, Provence, France* As well as red and rosé BANDOL★, Luc Sorin makes various CÔTES DE PROVENCE wines, including a mouthwatering white blend of Rolle and Sémillon★ and a crisp pink grapefruit- and cranberry-flavoured rosé Terra Amata★. Best years: (red Bandol) (2011) 10 09 **08 07 06 05 03 01**.

SOTER VINEYARDS *Willamette Valley AVA, Oregon, USA* Tony Soter founded Etude Wines (NAPA VALLEY) in 1982. When he sold the business, he followed his passion for Pinot Noir and moved to Oregon, planting his first Pinot Noir in 2002. The Mineral Springs Pinot Noir★★ is outstanding, with *terroir*-driven flavours showing from a very young site. North Valley★ is the basic cuvée. Small amounts of sparkling wine★★. Best years: (2010) 09 **08 07 06**.

DOM. DE SOUCH *Jurançon, South-West France* Legendary wines from
♀ veteran Yvonne Hégoburu, star of the film *Mondovino*. Fully organic, her
range runs from dry through to ultra-sweet, including Cuvée Marie
Kattalin★★, which, as it ages, develops unmistakeable notes of black
truffles. Best years: (sweet) (2010) **07 05 03**.

SOUTH AUSTRALIA Australia's biggest grape-growing state, with some
70,000ha (173,000 acres) of vineyards and almost half the country's total
production. Covers many wine styles, from bulk wines to the very best.
Established regions are ADELAIDE HILLS, Adelaide Plains, CLARE, BAROSSA and
Eden Valleys, MCLAREN VALE, Langhorne Creek, COONAWARRA, PADTHAWAY and
RIVERLAND. Newer regions creating excitement include Mount Benson, Robe,
Wrattonbully and Mount Gambier in the LIMESTONE COAST zone, Southern
Flinders Ranges, Southern Fleurieu, Currency Creek and Kangaroo Island.

SOUTH-WEST FRANCE South-West France has many lesser-known and
rapidly improving AOPs and IGPs, over 10 *départements* from the Massif
Central to the Pyrenees. Bordeaux grapes (Cabernet Sauvignon, Merlot,
Cabernet Franc for reds, Sauvignon Blanc, Sémillon, Muscadelle for whites)
play their part in the various BERGERAC appellations, but away from there you
will find interesting local varieties such as Fer Servadou, Tannat (in MADIRAN),
Gros and Petit Manseng (in Gascony and JURANÇON), Mauzac, Duras and Len
de l'El (in GAILLAC) and Négrette (in FRONTON). See also CAHORS, COTEAUX DU
QUERCY, CÔTES DE DURAS, CÔTES DE GASCOGNE, CÔTES DU BRULHOIS, CÔTES DU
MARMANDAIS, ENTRAYGUES-ET-DU-FEL, ESTAING, IROULÉGUY, MARCILLAC, MONBAZILLAC,
MONTRAVEL, PACHERENC DU VIC-BILH, PECHARMANT, SAINT-MONT, TURSAN.

SPÄTBURGUNDER See PINOT NOIR.

SPICE ROUTE *Swartland WO, South Africa* Owned by Charles Back of
🍷 FAIRVIEW. Ripe, well-oaked Flagship Syrah★★ and polished, Shiraz-based
Malabar★★ head the pack. Whites include flavoursome Viognier, rich,
barrel fermented Chenin Blanc★ and pure, spirited Sauvignon Blanc★
from Darling. Best years: (top reds) 2010 **09 08 07 06 05 04 03 02 01**.

SPOTTSWOODE *Napa Valley AVA, California, USA* Replanted in the mid-
🍷 1990s, this beautifully situated 16ha (40-acre) vineyard west of St Helena
has not missed a beat since the winery opened in 1982. Deep, blackberry-
and cherry-fruited Cabernet Sauvignon★★★ is wonderful to drink early,
but is best at 5–10 years. Sauvignon Blanc★★ (blended with a little
Semillon and barrel fermented) is a sophisticated treat. Best years:
(Cabernet) (2009) 08 **07** 06 05 04 03 02 01 00 99 98 97 96 95 94 91.

SPRING MOUNTAIN AVA *Napa Valley, California, USA* Divided by the
🍷 Mayacamas Mountains road that winds west, this rugged, forested area
has some odd exposures that make superb Cabernet Sauvignons and even
Chardonnays, as well as Sauvignon Blanc and Riesling. Best producers:
Barnett, Cain★, Newton★★, Pride★, Smith-Madrone★, Spring Mountain
Vineyard★, Terra Valentine★★.

SPRING VALLEY VINEYARD *Walla Walla Valley AVA, Washington State, USA*
🍷 Located amid wheat fields north-east of Walla Walla, Spring Valley
Vineyard was planted in 1993 and today the estate includes Merlot,
Cabernet Sauvignon, Cabernet Franc, Petit Verdot, Syrah and Malbec;
quality keeps improving. Named in tribute to family members, the wines
include Merlot-based Uriah★, Nina Lee Syrah★ and Frederick★, a
Cabernet Sauvignon-dominant blend. Best years: (2010) 09 **08** 07 06.

SPARKLING WINES OF THE WORLD —

Made by the Traditional (Champagne) Method

Although Champagne is still the benchmark for top-class sparkling wines all over the world, the Champagne houses themselves have taken the message to California, Australia and New Zealand via wineries they've established in these regions. However, Champagne-method fizz doesn't necessarily have to feature the traditional Champagne grape varieties (Chardonnay, Pinot Noir and Pinot Meunier), and this allows a host of other places to join the party. Describing a wine as Champagne method is strictly speaking no longer allowed (only original Champagne from France is officially sanctioned to do this), but the use of a phrase like Traditional or Classic Method should not distract from the fact that these wines are painstakingly produced using the complex system of secondary fermentation in the bottle itself.

STYLES OF SPARKLING WINE

France The best examples have great finesse and include appley Crémant d'Alsace, produced from Pinot Blanc and Pinot Gris, sometimes with a little Chardonnay; often inexpensive yet eminently drinkable Crémant de Bourgogne and Crémant du Jura, based mainly on Chardonnay; and some stylish Chenin-based examples from the Loire Valley, notably in Saumur, Montlouis-sur-Loire and Vouvray. The Rhône has dry St-Péray and deliciously grapy Clairette de Die Tradition. Gaillac, and Blanquette and Crémant de Limoux are good dry sparklers. Limoux, Gaillac and the Loire also make a little fizz by an older method using the unfinished primary fermentation to create bubbles in the bottle; this may be called *méthode ancestrale* or *gaillacoise* or, in the Loire, *pétillant originel*.

Rest of Europe Franciacorta DOCG is a success story for Italy. Most *metodo classico* sparkling wine is confined to the north, where ripening conditions are closer to those of Champagne, but a few good examples do pop up in unexpected places – Sicily, for instance. Asti, Lambrusco and Prosecco are not usually Champagne-method wines. In Spain, Cava offers an affordable style for everyday drinking, while top producers are developing a new style of long-lived Cava based on the native Xarel-lo grape. German Sekt comes in two basic styles: one made from Riesling grapes, the other using Champagne varieties. Producers in Austria and Portugal are having increasing success with both local varieties and the classic Champagne grapes. England is proving naturally suited to growing grapes for top-quality sparkling wine.

Other regions Australia has a wide range of styles. Blends are still being produced using fruit from many areas, but regional characters are starting to emerge. Chilly Tasmania is the star performer, making some top fizz from Chardonnay and Pinot Noir. Red sparklers, notably those made from Shiraz, are an irresistible Australian curiosity with an alcoholic kick. Cool-climate New Zealand is now producing some world-class examples difficult to tell from good Champagne; as in Australia, some have Champagne connections. Sparkling Sauvignon Blanc (mostly carbonated) is a recent development.

In California, some magnificent examples are produced – the best ones using grapes from Carneros or the Anderson Valley. Quality has been transformed by the efforts of French Champagne houses. Oregon is also a contender in the sparkling stakes, as is Canada.

Cap Classique is the South African name for the Champagne method; the best are very good. Brazil makes South America's best sparklers and Chile has some good examples.

BEST PRODUCERS

Australia *white* BROWN BROTHERS, Cope-Williams, DOMAINE CHANDON (Green Point), Freycinet (Radenti), HANGING ROCK, Heemskerk, House of Arras, Stefano LUBIANA, PETALUMA (Croser), Pipers Brook (Kreglinger), Taltarni (Clover Hill), YALUMBA (Jansz), Yarrabank, Yellowglen (Perle); *red* Peter LEHMANN (Black Queen), Charles MELTON, PRIMO ESTATE, ROCKFORD, SEPPELT, Ulithorne.

France *Alsace* OSTERTAG, TURCKHEIM co-op; *Burgundy* Bailly co-op, Louis Bouillot, Lugny co-op, Albert Sounit; *Gaillac* PLAGEOLES; *Crémant de Loire* Langlois-Château; *Saumur* Bouvet-Ladubay, Gratien & Meyer; *Vouvray* CLOS NAUDIN, HUET; *St-Péray* Chaboud, J-L Thiers.

Germany *Nahe* DIEL; *Pfalz* von BUHL, REBHOLZ; *Rheingau* Barth, BREUER, Solter, WEGELER; *Rheinhessen* Raumland.

Italy *Franciacorta* BELLAVISTA, CA'DEL BOSCO; *Trento* FERRARI; *Sicily* TASCA D'ALMERITA; *Piedmont* GIACOSA; *Friuli* Puiatti.

New Zealand CLOUDY BAY (Pelorus), DEUTZ, HUNTER'S, No. 1 Family Estate, PALLISER, QUARTZ REEF.

South Africa Ambeloui, Graham BECK, Bon Courage, High Constantia, SIMONSIG (Cuvée Royale), STEENBERG, Twee Jonge Gezellen, VILLIERA.

Spain Can Ràfols dels Caus, CODORNÍU, FREIXENET, Gramona, Parxet, Recaredo, Signat, Agustí Torelló.

UK BALFOUR, BREAKY BOTTOM, CAMEL VALLEY, COATES & SEELY, DENBIES, GUSBOURNE, NYETIMBER, RIDGEVIEW, STANLAKE PARK.

USA *California* DOMAINE CARNEROS, DOMAINE CHANDON, Gloria Ferrer, HANDLEY, IRON HORSE, J VINEYARDS, Laetitia, MUMM NAPA, ROEDERER ESTATE, SCHARFFENBERGER CELLARS, SCHRAMSBERG; *Oregon* ARGYLE.

Canada *British Columbia* Blue Mountain, SUMAC RIDGE, Summerhill; *Ontario* HENRY OF PELHAM, Huff Estates; *Nova Scotia* L'Acadie, Benjamin Bridge.

SPRINGFIELD ESTATE *Robertson WO, South Africa* Abrie Bruwer's approach is strictly hands-off in his efforts to capture his vineyard's *terroir*. Méthode Ancienne Chardonnay★ is barrel fermented with vineyard yeasts and bottled without fining or filtration. Not every vintage makes it! Cabernet Sauvignon is also made as Méthode Ancienne★. The unwooded Wild Yeast Chardonnay★ and flinty, lively Life from Stone Sauvignon Blanc★★ are also notably expressive. Work of Time★ is a Cabernet Franc-Merlot-based blend. Best years: (Sauvignon Blanc) **2011** 10 09.

STAGS LEAP DISTRICT AVA *Napa County, California, USA* One of California's best-defined appellations. Located in south-eastern NAPA VALLEY, it is cooler than OAKVILLE or RUTHERFORD to the north, and the red wines have a recognizably mellow, balanced character. A little Sauvignon Blanc and Chardonnay are grown, but the true stars are Cabernet Sauvignon and Merlot. Best producers: Balducci★, CHIMNEY ROCK★★, Cliff Lede★, CLOS DU VAL★, HARTWELL★★, PINE RIDGE★★, SHAFER★★★, SILVERADO★, Robert Sinskey★, STAG'S LEAP WINE CELLARS★★, Stags' Leap Winery★.

STAG'S LEAP WINE CELLARS *Stags Leap District AVA, California, USA* Cabernet Sauvignon can be stunning, particularly the SLV★★★ from estate vineyards and the Fay★★; the Cask 23 can be very good (sometimes★★★). After a dip in quality, recent vintages are back on form. A lot of work has gone into the Chardonnay★ (Arcadia Vineyard★★) and the style is one of NAPA's most successful. Sauvignon Blanc★ (Rancho Chimiles★) is intensely flavoured, with brisk acidity. Founder Warren Winiarski sold the property (excepting Arcadia Vineyard) in 2007 to CHATEAU STE MICHELLE and ANTINORI of Italy. Best years: (Cabernet) 2008 **07 06 05 04 03 02 01 00 99 98 97 96 95 94 91 90**.

STANLAKE PARK *Berkshire, England* This 10ha (25-acre) vineyard has, over the past 25 years, produced many stunning wines, including Pinot Noir, Bacchus and King's Fumé still wines and non-vintage sparkling Brut★.

STEELE *Lake County, California, USA* Owner/winemaker Jed Steele is a master blender. He sources grapes from all over California and Washington and shapes them into exciting wines, usually featuring vivid fruit with supple mouthfeel. He also offers single-vineyard wines and has, in current release, 4–6 Chardonnays, most ★★. His Zinfandels★★ and Pinot Noirs★★ (CARNEROS, SANTA MARIA VALLEY) are usually very good. Shooting Star label provides remarkable value in a ready-to-drink style.

STEENBERG *Constantia WO, South Africa* The oldest farm in CONSTANTIA, part of the Graham BECK stable, produces some of South Africa's best and most consistent Sauvignon Blanc: smoky, flinty Reserve★★ is brilliantly tangy, but it also ages well; straight Sauvignon★★ is pure upfront fruit. Barrel-fermented Semillon★★ (sometimes pushing ★★★) and complex, ageworthy Magna Carta★★ Sauvignon Blanc-Semillon blend. Reds include Cabernet-Merlot blend Catharina★★, smoky Shiraz★★ and Merlot★. Steenberg Brut 1682★ Cap Classique fizz is elegant and biscuity. Best years: (whites) 2011 **10 09 08 07 06 05 04 03 02 01**.

STEIERMARK *Austria* 4400ha (10,870-acre) region (Styria in English) in south-east Austria is divided into 3 areas: Südoststeiermark, Südsteiermark (the most important) and Weststeiermark. Technically it is the warmest of the Austrian wine regions, but the best vineyards are on cool, high-altitude slopes. The tastiest wines are Morillon (Chardonnay, often unoaked), Sauvignon Blanc and Gelber Muskateller (Muscat). For many growers, Steierische Klassik on the label indicates wines vinified without oak. Best producers: Gross★★, Lackner-Tinnacher★, POLZ★★, E Sabathi★, Sattlerhof★★, Walter Skoff, TEMENT★★, Winkler-Hermaden★, Wohlmuth★.

STELLENBOSCH WO *South Africa* District with the greatest concentration of wineries in the Cape; the vineyards straddle valley floors and stretch up the mountain slopes. Climates, soils and wine styles are diverse; smaller units of origin – wards – are now being demarcated to more accurately reflect this diversity. The renowned reds are matched by some excellent Sauvignon Blanc and Chardonnay, as well as modern Chenin Blanc and Semillon. Best producers: Bein★, BEYERSKLOOF★, De Toren★, DE TRAFFORD★★, DeWaal★, Edgebaston★, Neil ELLIS★★, Ernie ELS★★, Ken Forrester★, The Foundry★, GRANGEHURST★★, HARTENBERG★, Haskell★, JORDAN★★, Kaapzicht★, KANONKOP★★, Kleine Zalze★, Laibach★, L'AVENIR★★, Le Riche★★, MEERLUST★, Meinert★, MORGENHOF★, Morgenster★, MULDER-BOSCH★★, Quoin Rock★, Reyneke★, RUST EN VREDE★, RUSTENBERG★★, SAXENBURG★★, SIMONSIG★, Spier★, Stark-Condé★, Stellenzicht★, THELEMA★★, Tokara★★, VERGELEGEN★★, VILLIERA★, WARWICK★, Waterford★★, Waterkloof.

STONIER *Mornington Peninsula, Victoria, Australia* The peninsula's biggest winery and one of its best, though brewing group Lion Nathan, via PETALUMA, has a controlling interest. KBS Vineyard★★ and Reserve Chardonnay★★, and Windmill Vineyard★★ and Reserve Pinot Noir★★★ are outstanding. Some fine standard bottlings in warm vintages.

STONY HILL *Napa Valley AVA, California USA* Founded by Fred and Eleanor McCrea in 1953, the first winery in NAPA VALLEY after Prohibition, this tiny rock-strewn hillside produces sublime, minerally Chardonnay★★, dry Riesling★ and Gewurztraminer. The McCreas' son Peter and his wife Willinda now run the property with long-time winemaker Mike Chelini. Followers swear that the Chardonnays improve for decades. The first estate Cabernet Sauvignon was released from the 2008 vintage.

STONYRIDGE *Waiheke Island, Auckland, North Island, New Zealand* The leading winery on WAIHEKE ISLAND, Stonyridge specializes in reds. The top label, Larose★★★, is a remarkably BORDEAUX-like red of real intensity; Pilgrim★★ is a sexy, sultry CHÂTEAUNEUF-DU-PAPE lookalike. Best years: (Larose) 2010 **09 08 07 05 02.**

CH. SUDUIRAUT★★★ *Sauternes AC, 1er Cru Classé, Bordeaux, France* Together with RIEUSSEC, Suduiraut is regarded as a close runner-up to d'YQUEM. Although the wines are delicious at only a few years old, the richness and excitement increase enormously after a decade or so. Seemed to be under-performing in the 1980s and mid-90s, but owners AXA (see PICHON-LONGUEVILLE) have put it back on irresistible song. Best years: 2010 **09 07 06 05 04 03 02 01 99 98 97 96 95 90 89 86.**

SUMAC RIDGE *Okanagan Valley VQA, British Columbia, Canada* Excellent Sauvignon Blanc★ and Gewürztraminer Private Reserve★, fine Pinot Blanc (oaked and unoaked) and one of Canada's best CHAMPAGNE-method fizzes, Steller's Jay Brut★. Top reds include Black Sage Vineyard Cabernet Sauvignon, Cabernet Franc and Merlot, plus white Meritage★. Owned by Constellation Brands.

SWAN DISTRICT *Western Australia* The original WESTERN AUSTRALIA wine region, spread along the fertile silty flats of Perth's Swan River. It used to specialize in fortified wines, but SOUTH AUSTRALIA and north-east VICTORIA do them better. Modern whites and reds are fresh and generous but unmemorable. Best producers: Paul Conti, Faber★, Heafod Glen, HOUGHTON★, John Kosovich, Lamont★, Oakover, Pinelli, SANDALFORD★, Sittella, Upper Reach★.

SWEET WINES OF THE WORLD

Great sweet wines, which tend to cost a good deal, generally use the intense sweetness of their own grapes – rather than having any sweetness added. But it's not easy to grow grapes with enough sweetness. The classic way to gain sweetness is through 'noble rot' or botrytis.

MAIN SWEET WINE STYLES

Botrytis Traditionally there were only a very few areas of the world where good summers would ripen the grape, and then as autumn set in, a mixture of warm sunshine and fog or mists would cause the grapes to rot. Obviously rot will usually destroy crops, but there is a type of fungal infection called 'noble rot' that actually concentrates the sugars and acids in the grapes, so that the juice becomes more and more like a ridiculously sweet syrup. These grapes are then harvested late in the season, often berry by berry. They're so sweet that they have an enormous potential alcohol (alcohol is created by the transformation of sugar into alcohol by yeast action), but yeasts can only operate up to 15–16% alcohol, at which point they die. Any remaining sugar stays in the wine as sweetness.

Conditions for noble rot appear fairly regularly in Sauternes, Barsac and Monbazillac in South-West France, famous for luscious syrupy wines with intense flavours of peach and pineapple, barley sugar spices and beeswax honey. The main grape varieties are Sémillon and Sauvignon. Sauternes in particular has been taken as the model for ambitious winemakers around the world. Nearby parts of South-West France make similar wines, often from locally specific grape varieties, without benefit of noble rot, but by leaving the grapes to shrivel naturally on the vine: a method called *passerillage*.

The Loire Valley is France's other main sweet wine area, getting noble rot in its Chenin Blanc, particularly in Bonnezeaux, Coteaux du Layon, Quarts de Chaume and Vouvray. Orvieto in Italy can make wines with *muffa nobile* (noble rot). Tokaji in Hungary also gets regular botrytis.

Germany also has a great sweet wine tradition: when conditions are right, the Riesling grape manages to combine high acidity with stratospheric sugar levels. The wines are normally labelled Beerenauslese or Trockenbeerenauslese. Austria makes similar, though weightier styles, while Alsace makes equivalents called Sélection de Grains Nobles from not just Riesling, but also Pinot Gris and Gewurztraminer.

Semillon, Sauvignon and Riesling grapes are used in parts of Australia, New Zealand, the USA and South Africa to make botrytized sweet wines.

Eiswein This is a German and, occasionally, Austrian rarity, made from frozen Riesling grapes picked in the depth of winter, which manages a thrilling marriage of fierce acidity and unctuous sweetness. Canada has made a speciality of Icewine (both still and sparkling) using Riesling, Vidal or Cabernet Franc grapes, and China has released its first examples.

Muscat The Mediterranean countries – in particular France, Spain and Greece – as well as Portugal, Australia and South Africa have a variety of sweet Muscat wines, many of them fortified.

Late harvest Throughout the world, many fairly sweet wines are made from late-harvested (therefore very ripe) but not botrytis-infected grapes.

See also ALSACE, BARSAC, BANYULS, BORDEAUX WHITE WINES, COMMANDARIA, COTEAUX DU LAYON, JEREZ/SHERRY, MADEIRA, MÁLAGA, MARSALA, MAURY, MONBAZILLAC, MONTILLA-MORILES, MUSCAT, ORVIETO, PORT, RECIOTO DELLA VALPOLICELLA, RECIOTO DI SOAVE, SAUTERNES, SETÚBAL, TOKAJI, VIN SANTO, VOUVRAY; and individual producers.

Château Suduiraut
PREMIER CRU CLASSÉ EN 1855
SAUTERNES
2007

BEST PRODUCERS

France *Alsace* HUGEL, WEINBACH, ZIND-HUMBRECHT; *Bordeaux* CLIMENS, Clos Haut-Peyraguey, COUTET, DOISY-DAENE, DOISY-VEDRINES, FARGUES, GILETTE, GUIRAUD, LAFAURIE-PEYRAGUEY, NAIRAC, Raymond-Lafon, RIEUSSEC, Sigalas-Rabaud, SUDUIRAUT, la TOUR BLANCHE, YQUEM; *Loire* Bablut, Baumard, F CHIDAINE, CLOS NAUDIN, Fesles, HUET, Montgilet, OGEREAU, PIERRE-BISE, Taille aux Loups/BLOT, la Varière; *South-West* (Monbazillac) l'ANCIENNE CURE, Grande Maison, TIRECUL LA GRAVIÈRE, VERDOTS; (Saussignac) Clos d'Yvigne; (Jurançon) CAUHAPE, JARDINS DE BABYLONE, LAPEYRE, de SOUCH; (Pacherenc du Vic-Bilh) AYDIE, BERTHOUMIEU, LABRANCHE-LAFFONT, MONTUS; (Gaillac) PLAGEOLES, RAMAYE.

Italy ANSELMI, AVIGNONESI (Vin Santo), Barberani (ORVIETO Muffa Nobile), Dri (Ramandolo), MACULAN (Torcolato), PIEROPAN.

Germany DÖNNHOFF, EMRICH-SCHÖNLEBER, GUNDERLOCH, KELLER, KÜHN, DR LOOSEN, MÜLLER-SCHARZHOF, J J PRÜM, Horst SAUER, Willi SCHAEFER, SCHÄFER-FRÖHLICH, SCHLOSS JOHANNISBERG, Robert WEIL

Austria FEILER-ARTINGER, KRACHER, Opitz, Schröck, Tschida, VELICH.

Hungary Tokaji DISZNÓKŐ, Chateau Megyer, Chateau Pajzos, Royal Tokaji, Szepsy, Tokaj Kereskedőház.

Australia BROWN BROTHERS (Noble Riesling), Cookoothama, DE BORTOLI (Noble One), MCWILLIAM'S (Morning Light), MOUNT HORROCKS (Cordon Cut Riesling), PRIMO ESTATE (La Magia), WESTEND (Golden Mist)

New Zealand FELTON ROAD, Forrest, FRAMINGHAM, PEGASUS BAY, VILLA MARIA.

USA ANTHONY ROAD, BERINGER (Nightingale), Casa Larga (Ice Wine), Far Niente (Dolce), NAVARRO (Cluster Select Late Harvest Riesling).

Canada Château des Charmes, HENRY OF PELHAM, INNISKILLIN, JACKSON-TRIGGS.

South Africa Paul CLUVER, Fleur du Cap, KLEIN CONSTANTIA, Nederburg.

JOSEPH SWAN VINEYARDS *Russian River Valley AVA, California, USA* The late Joseph Swan made legendary Zinfandel in the 1970s and was one of the first to age Zinfandel★★ in French oak. In the 1980s he turned to Pinot Noir★ which is made in a rather old-fashioned but satisfying way. Also some old-style Syrah. Best years: (Zinfandel) **2007 06 05 02 01 00**.

SWARTLAND WO *South Africa* Warm inland district running up the west coast, and very much *the* wine area of the moment. Grape varieties are headed by Syrah for reds, Chenin Blanc, much from old vines, for whites; both appear solo and in blends. The Swartland Independent comprises around a dozen cutting-edge producers, intent on expressing the Swartland in their wines. The Mullineux Schist Syrah★★, rich and structured, and Granite Syrah★★, expressive and fresh, illustrate just how distinctive the different soils can be. Best producers: Badenhorst Family Wines★★, Lammershoek★, Mullineux★★, Porseleinberg★, SADIE FAMILY★★.

SYNCLINE *Columbia Valley AVA, Washington State, USA* The focus here is on Rhône-style wines. COLUMBIA VALLEY Syrah★ shows game and mineral flavours; single-vineyard McKinley Springs Syrah★ has intriguing coffee bean aromas; also earthy Mourvèdre★, crisp, refreshing Viognier★, Roussanne★ with pear and stone fruit notes, and a zesty Rosé★★ with a haunting similarity to a BANDOL rosé. Best years: (2010) 09 **08** 07 06.

SYRAH See pages 302–3.

TABALÍ *Limarí, Chile* Winery set up in the LIMARÍ valley in 1993 by one of Chile's wealthiest industrialists, Guillermo Luksic, along with SAN PEDRO – now independent. Best wines are the Reserva Especial Syrah★★ and Reserva Especial Chardonnay★★. New Caliza vineyard close to the ocean is producing thrilling Reserva Especial Sauvignon Blanc★★.

TABLAS CREEK VINEYARD *Paso Robles AVA, California, USA* This joint venture between the Perrin Brothers (of Ch. de BEAUCASTEL in Châteauneuf-du-Pape) and the Haas Family of Vermont is putting Rhône varieties on the map in SAN LUIS OBISPO COUNTY. The elegant, cherry-scented Esprit de Beaucastel★★ and the Côtes de Tablas★★ (red and white) are especially impressive. Best years: (reds) 2009 08 **07** 06.

LA TÂCHE AC★★★ *Grand Cru, Côte de Nuits, Burgundy, France* Along with la ROMANÉE and la ROMANÉE-CONTI, the greatest of the great VOSNE-ROMANÉE Grands Crus, owned by Dom. de la ROMANÉE-CONTI. The wine provides layer on layer of flavours; keep it for 10 years or you'll only experience a fraction of the pleasure you paid big money for. Best years: (2011) 10 09 08 07 06 05 03 02 **01 00** 99 96 **95** 93 90 89 88.

TAHBILK *Goulburn Valley, Central Victoria, Australia* Wonderfully old-fashioned family company established in 1860, making traditional big, gumleafy/minty red wines, matured largely in old wood. 1860 Vines Shiraz★, Eric Stevens Purbrick Shiraz and Eric Stevens Purbrick Cabernet are full of sturdy character, and need years of cellaring. White Marsanne★★ is rich and perfumed, as is a floral-scented Viognier★. Best years: (Eric Stevens Purbrick Shiraz) 2011 10 09 08 06 05 04 **03** 02 01 00 99 98 97 96 94.

CAVE DE TAIN *Hermitage, Rhône Valley, France* Large, progressive co-op offering good-value wines from the northern Rhône. Greatly improved quality. Impressive CROZES-HERMITAGE les Hauts du Fief★, fine CORNAS★, red ST-JOSEPH★, white St-Joseph Terre d'Ivoire★ and HERMITAGE★. Topping the range are an old-vine red Hermitage Gambert de Loche★★, a classy white Hermitage Au Coeur des Siècles★★ and a deliciously rich Vin de Paille★★ from Marsanne. Also still and sparkling ST-PÉRAY★. Best years: (top reds) 2011 10 09 **07 06 05 04 03 01 00** 99 98 97 95.

TAITTINGER *Champagne AC, Champagne, France* The top wine, Comtes de Champagne Blanc de Blancs★★★, can be memorable for its creamy, foaming pleasures; the Comtes de Champagne rosé★★ is elegant and oozing class. Prélude is an attractive, fuller-bodied non-vintage style made from 4 Grands Crus and aged for 4 years before release. Non-vintage Les Folies de la Marquetterie is from a steeply sloping single vineyard. Best years: 2005 **04 03 02 00 99 98 96 95 90 89 88 85 82**.

CH. TALBOT★ *St-Julien AC, 4ème Cru Classé, Haut-Médoc, Bordeaux, France* Chunky, soft-centred but sturdy, capable of aging well for 10–20 years and produced in abundance (100ha/250-acre vineyard). This isn't classic, cedary St-Julien but is consistently full-bodied and well priced. Also a tasty white wine, Caillou Blanc de Talbot★. Second wine: Connétable de Talbot. Best years: 2010 09 08 05 **04 03 02 01 00 99 98 96 95 90 89**.

TALBOTT *Monterey County, California, USA* Estate known for its Chardonnays: Sleepy Hollow Vineyard★★ (from the Santa Lucia Highlands), Cuvée Cynthia★★ and Diamond T★★ are all packed with ripe tropical fruit and ample oak. Kali Hart Chardonnay★ gives a taste of the style on a budget. Also Chardonnay and Pinot Noir under the Logan label.

TAMAYA *Limarí, Chile* 160ha (400-acre) estate started in 1997 in the LIMARÍ Valley. Easy-drinking, unoaked Carmenère★ and top-grade Winemaker's Selection Syrah★★ and Chardonnay★★.

TANNAT Its name implies high tannic content, but when fully ripe it is dark and dense yet delightfully scented, especially in parts of California, Brazil, Argentina and Chile. It is widely planted in Uruguay owing to its thick skin's ability to withstand wet weather. Important (either on its own or blended) in MADIRAN, TURSAN and IROULÉGUY in South-West France.

TAPANAPPA *Adelaide Hills, South Australia* The partnership of the families of Brian Croser (formerly of PETALUMA), Arnould d'Hautefeuille (BOLLINGER) and Jean-Michel Cazes (LYNCH-BAGES) explores the notion of *terroir*. Sublime Chardonnay from the Tiers Vineyard★★★ in the ADELAIDE HILLS; supremely elegant Cabernet-Shiraz and Merlot from the mature Whalebone Vineyard★★ at Wrattonbully; and increasingly ethereal Pinot Noir from Foggy Hill Vineyard★★ on the Southern Fleurieu Peninsula.

TARIQUET *Côtes de Gascogne IGP, South-West France* Brand name of the Grassa family, who produce some of France's snappiest, fruitiest, affordable dry wines (e.g. Côté★, a Sauvignon-Chardonnay blend) on their 900ha (2200-acre) estate. Also oak-aged★ and late-harvest★ styles.

TARRAWARRA *Yarra Valley, Victoria, Australia* Founder Marc Besen wanted to make a MONTRACHET, and hang the expense. The winemakers are doing well, and all fruit is now from estate vineyards. Reserve Chardonnay★★ is deep and multi-faceted; Reserve Pinot Noir★★ has almost CÔTE DE NUITS flavour and concentration. Under the Estate label there is an easy-drinking Chardonnay, a Marsanne-Roussanne-Viognier blend and a delicious Pinot Noir. Best years: (Pinot Noir) 2010 08 **06 04 03 02 01 98 97 96**.

TASCA D'ALMERITA *Sicily, Italy* This estate in the highlands of central SICILY has long made some of southern Italy's best wines. Native grape varieties give excellent Rosso del Conte★★ (based on Nero d'Avola) and white Nozze d'Oro★ (based on Inzolia), but there are also Chardonnay★★ and Cabernet Sauvignon★★ of extraordinary intensity and elegance. Almerita Brut★ (Chardonnay) is a fine CHAMPAGNE-method sparkler. Relatively simple Regaleali Bianco and Rosé are good value.

SYRAH/SHIRAZ

Syrah now produces world-class wines in France, Australia – where as Shiraz it produces some of the New World's most remarkable reds – Chile, New Zealand, California and, increasingly, South Africa, Argentina and Washington State. And wherever it appears it trumpets a proud and wilful personality based on loads of flavour and unmistakable originality.

When Syrah is grown in the coolest, most marginal areas for full ripening, such as France's Côte-Rôtie or New Zealand, it produces scented, elegant blackberryish wines. Syrah's heartland – Hermitage and Côte-Rôtie in the northern Rhône Valley – comprises a mere 365ha (900 acres) of steeply terraced, often granite, vineyards producing barely enough wine to spread the word to new drinkers. This may be one reason for its relatively slow uptake by growers in other countries, who simply had no idea as to what kind of flavour the Syrah grape produced, so didn't copy it. But Syrah's popularity in both the warm and the reasonably cool wine regions of the world becomes more evident with every vintage.

WINE STYLES

French Syrah Traditional Syrah had a savage, almost coarse, throaty roar of a flavour. And from the very low-yielding Hermitage vineyards, it sometimes took decades for the flavours to come together. But improved winemaking and a mix of scented new clones with the haughty old vines have revealed Syrah with a majestic depth of fruit – blackberry and damson, loganberry and plum – some quite strong tannin, occasionally bacon smoke and potato skins, but also a warm creamy aftertaste, and a promise of chocolate and occasionally a scent of violets. These characteristics have made Syrah popular throughout southern France as an 'improving' variety for traditional red wines, and it is now a major red variety in Provence, often combined with Grenache and/or Mourvèdre.

Australian Shiraz Australia's most widely planted red variety has become, in many respects, its premium varietal – especially in the Barossa, Clare, Eden Valley and McLaren Vale regions of South Australia. A diverse range of high-quality examples is also coming from Victoria's high country and cool-climate vineyards, increasingly elegant examples from New South Wales' Hunter Valley, and exciting, more restrained styles from Western Australia, Victoria's Yarra Valley and South Australia's Adelaide Hills, as well as patches of Canberra and Queensland. Just about everywhere, really. (A rare Tasmanian example won Australia's most prestigious trophy, the Jimmy Watson, in 2011.) Flavours range from rich, intense, thick sweet fruit coated with chocolate and seasoned with leather, herbs and spice, to fragrant, floral and flowing with damson and blackberry fruit.

Other regions Washington State is turning out superb Rhône-style blends as well as varietal Syrahs, while California's Syrahs are mostly high-octane, though occasionally beautifully restrained. Canada makes two styles: lush and fruity in British Columbia's desert conditions, and northern Rhône-style in cooler Ontario. Chile's coastal regions produce a string of exciting new offerings every vintage. Elegant examples are emerging from South Africa's warmer and cooler regions. New Zealand's cool-climate offerings are thrillingly different – light yet lush, green-streaked, florally scented yet succulent. Italy, Spain, Portugal, Switzerland and Argentina are beginning to shine, as are Israel, Lebanon and Morocco.

BEST PRODUCERS

France

Rhône ALLEMAND, F Balthazar, G Barge, A Belle, CHAPOUTIER, J-L CHAVE, Y Chave, CLAPE, Clusel-Roch, COLOMBO, Courbis, COURSODON, CUILLERON, DELAS, Duclaux, E & J Durand, B Faurie, Gaillard, J-M Gérin, Gonon, GRAILLOT, Gripa, GUIGAL, JAMET, P Jasmin, S Ogier, V Paris, ROSTAING, M Sorrel, Tardieu-Laurent, G Vernay, F Villard; *Languedoc* Jean-Michel ALQUIER, ESTANILLES, GAUBY, PEYRE ROSE.

Other European Syrah

Italy (Piedmont) Bertelli; *(Tuscany)* Stefano Amerighi, d'Alessandro, FONTODI, Fossi, ISOLE E OLENA, Le MACCHIOLE; *(Sicily)* Cottanera, PLANETA. *Spain* Casa Castillo, Finca Sandoval, Pago del Ama, Pago de Vallegarcía.

New World Syrah/Shiraz

Australia Tim ADAMS, JIM BARRY, BEST'S, Rolf BINDER, BROKENWOOD, Grant BURGE, CHAPEL HILL, CLARENDON HILLS, CLONAKILLA, Craiglee, Dalwhinnie, D'ARENBERG, DE BORTOLI, Dutschke, John DUVAL, FOX CREEK, GLAETZER, HARDYS (Eileen Hardy), Henry's Drive, HENSCHKE, Hewitson, Jasper Hill, Peter LEHMANN, MAJELLA, Charles MELTON, MOUNT LANGI GHIRAN, PANNELL, PENFOLDS, PLANTAGENET, ROCKFORD, SEPPELT, SHAW & SMITH, TORBRECK, Turkey Flat, TYRRELL'S, WENDOUREE, The Willows, WIRRA WIRRA (RSW), YALUMBA, Yering Station (Reserve), Zema.

New Zealand Bilancia, CRAGGY RANGE, DRY RIVER, Esk Valley, FROMM, MAN O'WAR, MILLTON, Passage Rock, Stonecroft, Te Awa, TE MATA, TRINITY HILL, Vidal, VILLA MARIA.

South Africa BOEKENHOUTSKLOOF, DE TRAFFORD, Eagles' Nest, FAIRVIEW, The Foundry, HARTENBERG, Mullineux, SADIE FAMILY, SAXENBURG, SPICE ROUTE.

USA (California) ALBAN, ARAUJO, BECKMEN, BONNY DOON, Cline Cellars, DEHLINGER, DUTTON GOLDFIELD, Krupp Brothers, Lagier Meredith, LYNMAR, Andrew MURRAY, Pax, QUPE, RAMEY, Sean Thackrey, Tor, Truchard, Wind Gap; *(Washington)* CAYUSE, GRAMERCY.

Canada (British Columbia) Church & State, JACKSON-TRIGGS, Painted Rock; *(Ontario)* Creekside, Flat Rock.

Chile CASA MARÍN, DE MARTINO, ERRAZURIZ, FALERNIA, LOMA LARGA, MATETIC, Maycas del Limarí, MONTES, TABALÍ, TAMAYA, UNDURRAGA (T.H.).

303

TASMANIA *Australia* Tasmania may be a minor state viticulturally, with around 1400ha (3460 acres) of vines, but the island has a diverse range of mesoclimates. The generally cool climate has always attracted seekers of greatness in Pinot Noir and Chardonnay, and good results are becoming more consistent as the vines mature and viticultural know-how spreads. Riesling, Gewürztraminer and Pinot Gris perform well, but the real star is fabulous premium fizz. Best producers: Apsley Gorge, BAY OF FIRES★★, Bream Creek, Domaine A, Freycinet★★, Frogmore Creek★, Heemskerk★, House of Arras★★, Jansz★★/YALUMBA, Stefano LUBIANA★, Moorilla★, Pipers Brook, Pirie, Pressing Matters★, Providence, Stoney Rise. Best years: (Pinot Noir) 2010 **07** 06 05 03 02 01 00 99 98 97 95 94.

TAURASI DOCG *Campania, Italy* MASTROBERARDINO created Taurasi's reputation; now the great potential of the Aglianico grape is being exploited by others, both within this DOCG and elsewhere in CAMPANIA. Drink at 5–10 years. Best producers: A Caggiano★★, Feudi di San Gregorio★★, MASTROBERARDINO★★, S Molettieri★, Struzziero, Luigi Tecce, Terredora di Paolo★. Best years: (2011) (10) 09 08 **07** 06 04 01.

TAVEL AC *Rhône Valley, France* Rosé from north-west of Avignon, in two styles: aromatic-aperitif or chunky and heady. The latter style needs food. Best producers: Aquéria, Genestière★, GUIGAL, Lafond Roc-Épine★, Maby★, de Manissy, Montézargues★, la Mordorée★, Moulin-la-Viguerie★, Rocalière★, Vignerons de Tavel, Trinquevedel★★.

TAWSE WINERY *Niagara Peninsula VQA, Ontario, Canada* One of Canada's best wineries. Top-notch Robyn's Block Chardonnay★★, Carly's Block Riesling★ and Cherry Avenue Pinot Noir★.

TAYLOR'S *Port DOC, Douro, Portugal* The aristocrat of the PORT industry, founded in 1692. Now part of the Fladgate Partnership, along with FONSECA and CROFT. Its Vintage★★ (sold as Taylor Fladgate in the USA) is superb; Quinta de Vargellas★★ is an elegant, cedary, single-quinta vintage port made in the best of the 'off-vintages'. Quinta de Terra Feita★★, the other main component of Taylor's Vintage, is also often released as a single-quinta. Taylor's 20-year-old★★ is a very fine aged tawny. First Estate is a successful premium ruby. Best years: (Vintage) (2009) 07 **03 00** 97 94 92 85 83 80 77 75 70 66 63 60 55 48 45 27; (Vargellas) (2009) 08 05 04 **01** 99 98 96 95 91 88 87 86 82 78 67 64 61.

TE MATA *Hawkes Bay, North Island, New Zealand* HAWKES BAY's glamour winery, best known for Coleraine★★★ and Awatea★, based on Cabernet Sauvignon with Merlot and Cabernet Franc. Also toasty Elston Chardonnay★★ (sometimes ★★★). Top vintages of all 3 wines might age for 5–10 years. Scented, peppery, elegant Bullnose Syrah★★, delicious Cape Crest Sauvignon Blanc★★ and Zara Viognier★. Trailblazing Woodthorpe single-vineyard range includes fine Syrah★★ and gorgeous, crunchy Gamay★. Best years: (Coleraine) 2010 **09 08 07** 06 04 02 00.

TEJO *Portugal* Portugal's second-largest wine region straddles the river Tagus (Tejo). Hotter and drier than LISBOA to the west, vineyards in the fertile flood plain are being uprooted in favour of less vigorous soils away from the river. Best producers: (reds) Quinta da Alorna, Quinta do Alqueve, Casa Cadaval★, Quinta do Casal Branco★ (Falcoaria★), D F J VINHOS★, Caves Dom Teodósio, Quinta do Falcão, Falua/J P RAMOS (Reserva★), Quinta da Lagoalva da Cima★, Companhia das Lezírias, Quinta da Ribeirinha (Vale de Lobos), Vale d'Algares.

TEMENT *Südsteiermark, Austria* Austria's best Sauvignon Blanc★★ (single-site Zieregg★★★) and Morillon (Chardonnay)★★. Both varieties are fermented and aged in oak, giving power, depth and subtle oak character. The Gelber Muskatellers are unusually racy – perfect aperitif wines. Red Arachon★★ is a joint venture with F X PICHLER and Szemes in BURGENLAND. Best years: (2011) 10 09 **08 07 06 05**.

TEMPRANILLO Spain's best native red grape can deliver wonderful wild strawberry and spicy, tobaccoey flavours. It is important in RIOJA, PENEDÈS (as Ull de Llebre), RIBERA DEL DUERO (as Tinto Fino or Tinta del País), La MANCHA and VALDEPEÑAS (as Cencibel), TORO (as Tinta de Toro), NAVARRA, SOMONTANO and UTIEL-REQUENA. In Portugal it is found in the ALENTEJO (as Aragonez) and in the DOURO, DÃO and LISBOA (as Tinta Roriz). Wines can be deliciously fruity for drinking young, but Tempranillo also matures well, and its flavours blend happily with oak. Good examples are now appearing in Argentina, California (Justin, Twisted Oak, VIADER, Kenneth Volk), Oregon (ABACELA), Washington (CAYUSE), Australia (Tim ADAMS, Gemtree, La Linea, Mayford, Nepenthe, PONDALOWIE, Running with Bulls/YALUMBA, Sanguine, Tar & Roses, Willunga 100), New Zealand (Elephant Hill, TRINITY HILL) and South Africa.

TEROLDEGO ROTALIANO DOC *Trentino-Alto Adige, Italy* Teroldego is a TRENTINO grape variety, producing mainly deep-coloured, leafy, blackberry-flavoured wine from gravel soils of the Rotaliano plain. Best producers: Barone de Cles★, M Donati★, Dorigati★, Endrizzi★, FORADORI★★, Conti Martini★, Mezzacorona (Riserva★), Cantina Rotaliana★, A & R Zeni★. Best years: (2011) (10) 09 08 **07 06 04 01**.

TERRAS DA BEIRA *Portugal* The interior of the former Beiras wine region, including Beira Interior DOC. Cool, high-altitude region, making bright, fresh reds and whites. Best producers: Quinta do Cardo★, Quinta dos Currais, Figueira de Castelo Rodrigo co-op, Rogenda, Quinta dos Termos.

TERRASSES DU LARZAC *Languedoc, France* Northern part of the Languedoc, recognized for its cooler climate, higher altitudes and fresher wines. Stretches from Lake Salagou towards Aniane. Best producers: Clos du Serres, Mas Cal Demoura, Mas de l'Ecriture, Mas Jullien, Montcalmès. Best years: (reds) (2011) 10 **09 08 07 06 05**.

TERRAZAS DE LOS ANDES *Mendoza, Argentina* Owned by LVMH. Reds and whites from high-altitude vineyards around Luján de Cuyo in MENDOZA. Top reds are Afincado Malbec★★ and Cabernet Sauvignon★★ (heading for ★★★). A joint venture with CHEVAL BLANC of ST-ÉMILION has yielded Cheval des Andes★★★, a stunning Cabernet Sauvignon-Malbec blend. Best years: (Cheval des Andes) (2008) 07 06 **05 03 02**.

CASTELLO DEL TERRICCIO *Tuscany, Italy* Estate in the Pisan hills. Top red Lupicaia★★ (Cabernet-Merlot) and less pricey Tassinaia★★ (Sangiovese-Cabernet-Merlot). Syrah-based Castello del Terriccio can be scented and exciting, potentially ★★★. White wines are Rondinaia★★ (Chardonnay) and Con Vento★ (Sauvignon Blanc). Best years: (Lupicaia) (2011) (10) 08 **06 04 01 00 98 97**.

TERROIR AL LÍMIT *Priorat DOCa, Cataluña, Spain* South Africa's Eben SADIE and his German partner Dominik Huber have revolutionized PRIORAT by making extraordinarily complex wines in a lighter, more elegant style than the norm, from old Garnacha and Cariñena vineyards. Top wines: Les Tosses★★★, Les Manyes★★★, Dits del Terra★★, Arbossar★★.

TERTRE-RÔTEBOEUF★★ *St-Émilion Grand Cru AC, Bordeaux, France*
ST-ÉMILION's most exceptional unclassified estate. The richly seductive, Merlot-based wines sell at the same price as the Premiers Grands Crus Classés – and so they should. Same ownership as the outstanding ROC DE CAMBES. Best years: 2010 09 08 07 **06** 05 04 03 02 01 00 99 98 96 95 90.

TEXAS *USA* Texas has enjoyed the tremendous wine industry growth that has hit the USA since the turn of the century, with the number of wineries soaring to 215 and counting. The state has 8 AVAs, with the Texas High Plains the most significant. Mediterranean grapes such as Grenache, Tempranillo, Syrah and Sangiovese have risen in favour over the traditional Cabernets and Chardonnay. Thunderstorms are capable of destroying entire crops in minutes. Best producers: Becker★, Fall Creek, Flat Creek, Haak, LLANO ESTACADO★, McPherson★, Messina Hof.

THELEMA *Stellenbosch WO, South Africa* With maturing vineyards in ELGIN, as well as on the home farm, now undergoing conversion to organics, output has increased in recent years. A pair of Cabernet Sauvignons – blackcurranty regular★★ and self-descriptive The Mint★★ – ripe fleshy Merlot★ (Reserve★★), spicy, accessible Shiraz★, barrel-fermented Chardonnay★★, vibrant Sauvignon Blanc★★ and citrus Riesling★ are among the leaders. From Elgin, minerally Sauvignon★ and citrussy, oatmealy Chardonnay★. Best years: (Cabernet Sauvignon) 2009 **08 07 06 05 04 03 01 00**; (Chardonnay) 2011 **10 09 08 07 06 05 04 03 02 01**.

THERMENREGION *Niederösterreich, Austria* Warm 2450ha (6050-acre) region south of Vienna, taking its name from the spa towns of Baden and Bad Vöslau. Gumpoldskirchen, near Vienna, has rich white wines from local varieties Zierfandler and Rotgipfler. The red wine area around Baden produces improving Pinot Noir and Cabernet. Best producers: Alphart, Biegler, Fischer★, Piriwe, Reinisch★, Schellmann, Stadlmann★, Zierer. Best years: (reds) (2011) (10) 09 **08 07 06 04**.

THIRTY BENCH *Niagara Peninsula VQA, Ontario, Canada* Thirty Bench is known for its excellent Rieslings★★, very good BORDEAUX-style red blends★ and a fine barrel-fermented Chardonnay★.

THOMAS *Hunter Valley, New South Wales, Australia* Andrew Thomas produces exemplary Semillon and Shiraz from individual vineyards: Braemore Semillon★★ is a traditional, ageworthy HUNTER white, while The OC Semillon★ is a delicious early-drinking style. Kiss Shiraz★★, from old vines, is ripe, powerful and velvety, and Shiraz from DJV, Motel Block and Sweetwater vineyards look set to enhance Thomas's cult status.

THREE CHOIRS *Gloucestershire, England* This 30ha (74-acre) estate makes a large range of good-value still and sparkling wines. Varietals Bacchus★ and Siegerrebe★, plus blends Coleridge Hill, off-dry Willow Brook, Rosé and white New Release to take on Beaujolais Nouveau.

TICINO *Switzerland* Italian-speaking canton. More than 80% of production is Merlot, usually soft and gluggable, but can be more serious with some oak barrel-aging. Best producers: Brivio, Delea★, Gialdi, Huber★, Werner Stucky★, Tamborini★, Terreni alla Maggia★, Valsangiacomo, Christian Zündel★.

TIEFENBRUNNER *Alto Adige DOC, Trentino-Alto Adige, Italy* Herbert Tiefenbrunner began his career at this castle (Schloss Turmhof) as a teenager in 1943. In his 80s, he still helps son Christof in the winery, producing 20-plus wines, mostly under the ALTO ADIGE DOC. Exceptionally pure, varietally focused whites are best, especially Chardonnay Linticlarus★★ and Müller-Thurgau Feldmarschall★★, grown at 1000m (3280ft). Best years: (Feldmarschall) (2011) (10) 09 08 **07 06 04**.

TIGNANELLO★★★ *Tuscany, Italy* In the early 1970s, Piero ANTINORI employed the almost unheard-of practice of aging in small French oak barrels and used Cabernet Sauvignon (20%) in the blend with Sangiovese. The quality was superb, and Tignanello's success sparked off the 'super-Tuscan' movement. Best years: (2011) (10) 09 08 **07** 06 **04** 01 00 **99 98 97 95 93 90 88 85**.

TINTA RORIZ See TEMPRANILLO.

CH. TIRECUL LA GRAVIÈRE *Monbazillac AOP, South-West France* Generally considered the best (and most expensive) of MONBAZILLAC wines, and comparable with top SAUTERNES, with a high proportion of Muscadelle and unusually regular benefit from botrytization. The top wine, Cuvée Madame★★★, is world class. Best years (2010) **09 07 05 04 03**.

TOCAI FRIULANO See FRIULANO.

TOKAJI *Hungary* Hungary's classic, liquorous wine of historic reputation, with its unique, sweet-and-sour, sherry-like tang, comes from 28 villages on the Hungarian–Slovak border. Mists from the Bodrog river ensure that noble rot on the Furmint, Hárslevelü and Muscotaly (Muscat Ottonel) grapes is a fairly common occurrence. Degrees of sweetness are measured in *puttonyos*. Discussions continue about traditional oxidized styles versus fresher modern versions. Best producers: Disznókö★★, Château Megyer★★, Oremus★, Château Pajzos★★, Royal Tokaji Wine Co★★, Istvan Szepsy★★, Tokaj Kereskedöház★ Best years: 2006 05 **03** 00 99 97 93.

TOLLOT-BEAUT *Chorey-lès-Beaune, Burgundy, France* Traditionally very fruity with seductive oak texture, I've recently noted an unwelcome aggressive oak style in many of them. The village-level ALOXE-CORTON★ is good, but the top BEAUNE Premier Crus★ are better. Whites are more variable, but at best delicious. Best years: (reds) (2011) 10 09 08 **07** 06 05 02 **99**.

TORBRECK *Barossa Valley, South Australia* Dave Powell specializes in opulent, well-structured reds from 60–120-year-old Shiraz, Grenache and Mataro (Mourvèdre) vines. Made in minute quantities, the flagship RunRig★★★, single-vineyard Descendant★★ and Factor★★ are all richly concentrated, powerful Shiraz. The Steading★ and the unoaked Juveniles★★ are Grenache-Mataro-Shiraz blends, while the Woodcutter's Semillon and Shiraz are lightly oaked, mouth-filling quaffers.

TORO DO *Castilla y León, Spain* Mainly robust red wines, full of colour and tannin. The main grape, Tinta de Toro, is a variant of Tempranillo, and there is some Garnacha. In the late 1990s, the arrival of some of Spain's top wineries gave the sleepy area a major boost. Best producers: Viña Bajoz, Dominio del Bendito★, Campo Eliseo★★, Fariña★, Frutos Villar (Muruve★), Garanza, Matarredonda, Maurodos★★, Numanthia-Termes★★, Pintia★★/VEGA SICILIA, Telmo RODRIGUEZ★★, Sobreño, Teso La Monja★★, Toresanas/Bodegas de Crianza Castilla La Vieja★, Valpiculata★, Vega Saúco, Villaester.

TORRES *Penedès DO, Cataluña, Spain* Iconic family winery based in CATALUÑA. Pink and white quaffers Viña Sol★, grapy, spicy Viña Esmeralda★, classic, barrel-fermented Fransola★★ (Sauvignon Blanc with some

Parellada) and delicate Milmanda★ Chardonnay. Reds include oaky Gran Coronas★ (Tempranillo-Cabernet), perfumed Mas Borràs (Pinot Noir) and raisiny Atrium★ (Merlot). The top reds are Grans Muralles★★, from Catalan grapes, BORDEAUX-blend Reserva Real★★ and Mas La Plana★★ (Cabernet Sauvignon). A new PRIORAT winery produces distinguished red, Perpetual★★. The family also owns wineries in RIBERA DEL DUERO (Celeste★), RIOJA (Ibéricos★), Chile and California (MARIMAR ESTATE). Best years: (Mas La Plana) 2007 06 05 **04 03 01 00 99 98 97 96 95 94.**

MIGUEL TORRES Curicó, Chile   TORRES' Chilean operation, which began in the early 1970s, is now producing its best ever wines, under the personal direction of Miguel Torres Junior. Snappy Sauvignon Blanc★; grassy, fruity, organic Santa Digna Cabernet Sauvignon rosé★; exciting, sonorous old-Carignan Cordillera★★; weighty, blackcurranty Manso de Velasco Cabernet★★; and Conde de Superunda★★, a tremendous, dense red blend (Cabernet, Carmenère, Tempranillo). Also Santa Digna Estelado rosé, a sparkling wine made from the País grape. Best years: (Manso de Velasco) 2007 06 **05 04 03 02 01.**

TORRONTÉS   Intensely aromatic white grape variety widely planted in Argentina – some 8500ha (21,000 acres). Torrontés has had a difficult history, but in recent years lower yields and cool fermentation in stainless steel have resulted in dry, fresh whites with lovely tropical fruit salad flavours, juicy acidity and a floral fragrance. The best wines tend to come from the northern province of SALTA. Best producers: (Salta): COLOMÉ, Domingo Hermanos, DOMINIO DEL PLATA, El Porvenir de Los Andes, Etchart, Michel Torino; (Mendoza): Alta Vista, DOÑA PAULA, Monteviejo.

CH. LA TOUR BLANCHE★★ Sauternes AC, 1er Cru Classé, Bordeaux, France   This estate regained top form in the 1980s with the introduction of new oak barrels for fermentation, lower yields and greater selection. Full-bodied, rich and aromatic, it now ranks with the best of the Classed Growths. Second wine: Les Charmilles de Tour Blanche. Best years: 2010 09 07 06 05 04 03 02 01 99 98 97 96 95 90 89 88.

DOM. TOUR BOISÉE Minervois AC, Languedoc, France   Top wines here are the red Jardin Secret★, Cuvée Marie-Claude★, aged for 12 months in barrel, the fruity Cuvée Marielle et Frédérique, and the white Cuvée Marie-Claude★, with a hint of Muscat Blanc à Petits Grains for added aroma. Best years: (reds) (2011) 10 **09 08 07 06.**

CH. TOUR DES GENDRES Bergerac AOP, South-West France   Luc de Conti makes his modern BERGERAC with as much sophistication as top BORDEAUX. Generously fruity Moulin des Dames★ and the more serious la Gloire de Mon Père★★ reds are mostly Cabernet Sauvignon. Full, fruity and elegant Moulin des Dames★★ white is a blend of Sémillon, Sauvignon Blanc and Muscadelle. His entry-level range includes some of the best-value wines in Bergerac. Best years: (reds) (2011) (10) 09 **06 05.**

TOURAINE AC Loire Valley, France   General AC in the central LOIRE; largely everyday wines to drink young, though an ambitious minority are making more ageworthy wines, many of which are labelled Vin de Pays du VAL DE LOIRE or even Vin de France. Most reds are from Gamay and, in hot years, can be juicy, rustic-fruited wines. There is a fair amount of red from Cabernets Sauvignon and Franc too, and some good Côt (Malbec). Best whites are Sauvignon Blanc, which can be a good substitute for SANCERRE at half the price, and the rare Romorantin; decent Chenin and

Chardonnay. White and rosé sparkling wines are made by the traditional method but rarely have the distinction of the best VOUVRAY and CRÉMANT DE LOIRE. Best producers: Brulée, La Chapinière, F CHIDAINE★, Clos de la Briderie★, Clos Roche Blanche★, Clos Roussely, Clos du Tue-Boeuf★, Corbillières★, J Delaunay★, Robert Denis★, de la Garrelière★, L Gosseaume★, L & B Jousset, J-C Mandard, Marcadet★, Henry Marionnet★, Marteau, J-F Merieux★, Michaud★, A & B Minchin, Octavie★, Pré Baron★, J Preys★, Ricard★, Sauvète. Best years: (reds) (2011) 10 **09 08 06 05 04 03**.

TOURIGA NACIONAL High-quality red Portuguese grape, rich in aroma and fruit. It contributes deep colour and tannin to PORT, and is rapidly increasing in importance for powerful black plum and violet-scented table wines throughout the country. Several producers in Spain have now planted it (it is native to GALICIA's Ribeiro DO under the name Carabuñeira). Small but important plantings in South Africa enhance some of the impressive port styles emerging across the country. Australia, Brazil and California are starting to test its potential for scented dry reds.

TOWER ESTATE *Hunter Valley, New South Wales, Australia* This syndicate, founded by the late, great Len Evans, focuses on sourcing top-notch grapes from their ideal regions. So, there is powerful, stylish COONAWARRA Cabernet★★, top-flight BAROSSA Shiraz★★, fine floral CLARE Riesling★★, fruity ADELAIDE HILLS Sauvignon Blanc★ and classic Semillon★★, Shiraz★ and Chardonnay★ from the HUNTER VALLEY.

TRAPICHE *Mendoza, Argentina* The fine wine arm of Peñaflor, Argentina's biggest wine producer, under chief winemaker Daniel Pi since 2002. Medalla Cabernet Sauvignon★★ is dense and satisfying, Malbec-Merlot blend Iscay★★ is solid and rich, and the annual trio of single-vineyard Malbecs★★★ are stunning expressions of how good the grape can be. The Finca Las Palmas★ range introduces Pi's genius at accessible prices, while the Trapiche varietal range offers impressive quality and great value for money.

TREBBIANO The most widely planted white Italian grape variety. As Trebbiano Toscano, it is the base for numerous neutral, dry white wines, as well as much VIN SANTO. Better grapes also masquerade under the Trebbiano name, notably the Trebbianos from SOAVE, LUGANA (Verdicchio) and ABRUZZO – grapes capable of full-bodied, fragrant wines. Called Ugni Blanc in France, where it is primarily used for distilling, but it makes decent CÔTES DE GASCOGNE whites and is used in small quantities (around 10%) to provide essential acidity for Rolle in Provençal whites.

TRENTINO *Italy* Wines from this northern Italian region rarely have the verve or perfume of ALTO ADIGE examples, but can make up for this with riper, softer flavours, where vineyard yields are restricted. The Trentino DOC covers numerous different styles of wine, including whites Pinot Bianco and Grigio, Chardonnay, Moscato Giallo, Müller-Thurgau and Nosiola, and reds Lagrein, Marzemino and Cabernet. Trento Classico is a DOC for traditional-method fizz. Best producers: N Balter★, N Bolognani★, La Cadalora★, Castel Noarna★, Cavit co-op, Cesconi★★, De Tarczal★, Dorigati, FERRARI★★,

Graziano Fontana★, FORADORI★★, Letrari★, Longariva★, Conti Martini★, Maso Cantanghel★★, Maso Furli★, Maso Roveri★, Mezzocorona, Pojer & Sandri★, Pravis★, SAN LEONARDO★★★, Simoncelli★, E Spagnolli★, Vallarom★, La Vis co-op. See also TEROLDEGO ROTALIANO.

DOM. DE TRÉVALLON *Provence, France* Iconoclastic Eloi Dürrbach makes brilliant reds★★ (at best ★★★) – a tradition-busting blend of Cabernet Sauvignon and Syrah, mixing herbal wildness with a sweetness of blackberry, blackcurrant and black, black plums – and a tiny quantity of white★★★. The reds age well, but are intriguingly drinkable in their youth. From 2009 to be IGP des Alpilles. Best years: (reds) (2011) 10 09 **08 07 06 05 04 03 01**.

TRIMBACH *Alsace AC, Alsace, France* An excellent grower/merchant whose trademark is beautifully structured, emphatically dry, subtly perfumed elegance. Top wines are Gewurztraminer Cuvée des Seigneurs de Ribeaupierre★★, Riesling Cuvée Frédéric Émile★★ and Riesling Clos Ste-Hune★★★. Also very good Vendange Tardive★★ and Sélection de Grains Nobles★★. Best years: (Clos Ste-Hune) (2011) (10) 09 08 **07 05 04 03 02 01 00 99 98 97 96 95 93 92 90**.

TRINITY HILL *Hawkes Bay, North Island, New Zealand* Passionate owner/winemaker John Hancock produces many top wines from the Gimblett Gravels area, including flagship Homage Syrah★★★ (co-fermented with a small amount of Viognier), an irresistibly soft yet peppery Syrah★★, impressive Merlot★★, gutsy long-lived Cabernet Sauvignon-Merlot blend The Gimblett★★, plus a big and complex Chardonnay★★. Trinity also makes a good job of less mainstream styles such as Montepulciano★, Tempranillo★, Arneis and Viognier★★. Also sweet Noble Viognier★★. Best years: (reds) 2010 **09 08 07 06 04 02 00**.

TRITTENHEIM *Mosel, Germany* Important village with some excellent vineyard sites, notably the Apotheke (pharmacy) and Leiterchen (little ladder). The wines are sleek, with crisp acidity and plenty of fruit. Best producers: A Clüsserath★, Clüsserath-Eifel, Clüsserath-Weiler★, Eifel★, GRANS-FASSIAN★★, Josef Rosch★★. Best years: (2011) 10 09 **08 07 06 05 04**.

CH. TROPLONG MONDOT★ *St-Émilion Grand Cru AC, 1er Grand Cru Classé, Bordeaux, France* Owner Christine Valette has been producing dense, concentrated wines at this property since the mid-1980s. Her reward – elevation to Premier Grand Cru Classé in 2006. Frankly, I find the wines just too much of a good thing, but they are certainly powerfully structured and mouthfillingly textured. Best years: 2009 08 **07 06 05 04 03 02 01 00 99 98 96 95 90 89**.

CH. TROTANOY★★ *Pomerol AC, Bordeaux, France* This POMEROL estate (like PÉTRUS and LATOUR-À-POMEROL) has benefited from the brilliant touch of the MOUEIX family. Had a dip in the mid-1980s (due to lots of replanting) but top form ever since. Best years: 2010 09 08 **07** 06 05 **04 03 02 01 00 98 96 95 90 89**.

TUA RITA *Tuscany, Italy* This estate in the commune of Suvereto, near BOLGHERI, has established itself at the top of the Italian Merlot tree with Redigaffi★★★; Cabernet-Merlot blend Giusto di Notri★★ is almost as renowned. Best years: (2011) (10) (09) 08 **07 06 05 04 01 00 99 98**.

CAVE DE TURCKHEIM *Alsace AC, Alsace, France* Important co-op with good basics (Réserve★) in all varieties. Consistent CRÉMANT D'ALSACE★. Brand★, Hengst★★ and Ollwiller★ bottlings are rich and concentrated. Best years: (Grand Cru Gewurztraminer) (2011) **10 09 07 05 04 02 01**.

TURLEY *Napa Valley AVA, California, USA* Larry Turley's ultra-ripe Zinfandels★★, from a number of old vineyards, are either praised for their profound power and depth or damned for their tannic, high-alcohol, PORT-like nature. Petite Sirah★★ is similarly built. Best years: (Zins) 2010 09 08 **07** 06 05 04 03 02 01 00.

TURSAN AOP *South-West France* From vineyards between Bordeaux and the Spanish border. Reds are Tannat-based blends with the Cabernets. Crisp, refreshing whites, mainly from the local Baroque grape. All for drinking young. Best producers: Baron de Bachen★, Dulucq★, Tursan co-op.

TUSCANY *Italy* Tuscany's rolling hills, clad with vines, olive trees and cypresses, have produced wine since at least Etruscan times. Today, its many DOC/DOCGs are based on the red Sangiovese grape and are led by CHIANTI CLASSICO, BRUNELLO DI MONTALCINO and VINO NOBILE DI MONTEPULCIANO, as well as famous 'super-Tuscans' like ORNELLAIA and TIGNANELLO. The term super-Tuscan was coined in the 1980s by journalists, who applied it to wines which, despite their superior quality and use of expensive equipment in the winery, did not satisfy the restrictive local DOC regulations (usually Chianti) and therefore had to be labelled Vino da Tavola. In the 1990s the wine laws changed and the majority of super-Tuscans are now sold under the regionwide IGT Toscana. White wines, despite sweet VIN SANTO and the occasional excellent Chardonnay and Sauvignon, do not figure highly. See also BOLGHERI, CARMIGNANO, MAREMMA, MONTECARLO, MORELLINO DI SCANSANO, ROSSO DI MONTALCINO, SASSICAIA, SOLAIA, VERNACCIA DI SAN GIMIGNANO.

TYRRELL'S *Hunter Valley, New South Wales, Australia* Top-notch family-owned company with prime HUNTER vineyards celebrated its 150th anniversary in 2008. It is expanding into COONAWARRA, MCLAREN VALE and HEATHCOTE, with impressive results. Comprehensive range, from good-value quaffers (Old Winery★, Lost Block★) to excellent Vat 47 Chardonnay★★★ and Vat 8 Shiraz★. Semillon is the speciality, with single-vineyard wines (all at least ★★) – Stevens, Belford and the rare HVD – and, best of all, the superb Vat 1★★★. Best years: (Vat 1 Semillon) (2011) (10) (09) 07 **05** 04 03 02 99 98 97 96 95 94 93 92 91 90 89 87; (Vat 47 Chardonnay) (2011) (10) 09 **08** 07 06 05 04 03 02 00.

UGNI BLANC See TREBBIANO.

UMATHUM *Frauenkirchen, Neusiedlersee, Burgenland, Austria* Resisting the trend in Austria toward heavily oaked blockbuster reds (thank goodness), Josef Umathum emphasizes finesse and sheer drinkability. The single-vineyard Ried Hallebühl★★ is usually his top wine, but the St Laurent Vom Stein★ and the Zweigelt-dominated Haideboden★ sometimes match it in quality. Best years: (reds) (2011) (10) 09 **08** 07 06 04.

UMBRIA *Italy* ORVIETO accounts for almost 70% of DOC wines in Umbria, but there are characterful reds from Torgiano DOC and MONTEFALCO DOC. International-style reds are made by consultant Riccardo Cotarella at estates such as La Carraia (Fobiano★★) and Lamborghini (Campoleone★★).

UNDURRAGA *Maipo, Chile* A long-established family winery; new management in 2008 has brought an injection of quality. Wines in the T.H.★★ (Terroir Hunter) and Sibaris ranges are transforming the reputation of the winery, aided by the consultancy of Alvaro Espinoza. There has been considerable investment in sparkling wine production.

ÜRZIG *Mosel, Germany* Middle MOSEL village with the famous red slate Würzgarten (spice garden) vineyard tumbling spectacularly down to the river and producing marvellously spicy and long-lived Riesling. **Best producers:** JJ Christoffel★★, Jos. Christoffel★★, Erbes★, Dr LOOSEN★★★, MOLITOR★★, Mönchhof★, Pauly-Bergweiler★, S A PRÜM★, Dr Weins-Prüm. **Best years:** (2011) 10 09 08 **07 06 05 04 03 02**.

UTIEL-REQUENA DO *Valencia, Spain* Renowned for its rosés, mostly from the Bobal grape. Reds, with Tempranillo often complementing Bobal, are on the up. The groundbreaking Mustiguillo★★ winery now has its own appellation, DO Terrerazo. **Best producers:** Coviñas, Gandía, Murviedro, Palmera (L'Angelet★), Sierra Norte, Torre Oria, Dominio de la Vega.

DOM. VACHERON *Sancerre AC, Loire Valley, France* This biodynamic domaine is reputed for its elegant Pinot Noir SANCERRE, now benefiting from less extraction and no new oak. Flagship wines Belle Dame★★ red and the flinty Les Romains★★ white have been joined by two single-site whites, Le Paradis★★ and Les Grands Champs★★ from limestone soils. The basic Sancerres – a cherryish red★ and a grapefruity white★ – have reserves of complexity that set them above the crowd. **Best years:** (Belle Dame) (2011) **09 08 07 06 05 04 03 02 01 99**.

VACQUEYRAS AC *Rhône Valley, France* Red wines, mainly Grenache, account for 95% of production; they have a warm, spicy bouquet and a rich deep flavour that seems infused with the herbs and pine dust of the south and its plateau vineyards. Lovely, if robust, to drink at 2–3 years, though good wines will age for 10 years. **Best producers:** Amouriers★, Burle, la Charbonnière★, Clos de Caveau, Clos des Cazaux★★, Couroulu★★, DELAS★, Font de Papier★, la Fourmone★, la Garrigue★, Paul JABOULET★, Alain Jaume,

Monardière★★, Montirius★★, Montmirail★, Montvac★, Ondines, Famille Perrin, Roucas Toumba★, SANG DES CAILLOUX★★, Tardieu-Laurent★★, la Tourade★, Ch. des Tours★. **Best years:** 2011 **10 09 07 06 05 04 03 01 99 98**.

VAL DE LOIRE, IGP *Loire Valley, France* Regional denomination that covers all 14 designated wine-producing regions of the LOIRE VALLEY – over 7,300ha (18,000 acres), accounting for around 600,000hl of wine. Key whites are Sauvignon Blanc, Chardonnay and Chenin Blanc, with some Grolleau Gris, Melon de Bourgogne, Folle Blanche and Pinot Blanc. The focus for reds is Gamay, Cabernets Franc and Sauvignon, with some Pinot Noir. It is increasingly a refuge for ambitious producers whose wines punch well above the weight of their appellation, especially in TOURAINE. **Best producers:** Ampelidae★, M Angeli/Sansonnière★★, C Battais, S Bernaudeau, l'Ecu★, Ch. Gaillard, de la Garrelière, La Grange aux Belles, H Marionnet★, A MELLOT★, J-F Merieau★, RAGOTIÈRE★★, Ricard, Robinot★.

VALAIS *Switzerland* Swiss canton flanking the Rhône. Between Martigny and Sierre the valley turns north-east, creating an Alpine suntrap, and this short stretch of terraced vineyard land provides many of Switzerland's most individual wines from Fendant (Chasselas), Johannisberger (Silvaner), Pinot Noir and Gamay, and several stunning examples from Syrah, Chardonnay, Ermitage (Marsanne) and Petite Arvine. **Best producers:** Bonvin★, Chappaz★, Cina★, G Clavien★, Cottagnoud★, Dorsaz★, Jean-René Germanier★, Adrian Mathier★, S Maye★, Mercier★, Dom. du Mont d'Or★, Provins, Rouvinez★, M Zufferey★.

CH. VALANDRAUD★★ *St-Émilion Grand Cru AC, Bordeaux, France* The progenitor of the 'garage wine' sensation in ST-ÉMILION, a big, rich, extracted wine from low yields, from grapes mainly grown in different parcels around St-Émilion. The core of the wine has been a top-quality limestone-based property and we can now see an impressive, consistent Valandraud style developing. Also a white Blanc de Valandraud from 2003. Best years: 2010 09 08 **07** 06 **05** 04 03 02 01 00 99 98 96 95.

VALDEPEÑAS DO *Castilla-La Mancha, Spain* Valdepeñas offers some of Spain's best inexpensive oak-aged reds, but there is an increasing number of unoaked, fruit-forward reds as well. In fact, there are more whites than reds, at least some of them modern, fresh and fruity. Best producers: Miguel Calatayud, Los Llanos, Luís Megía, Real, Félix Solís, Casa de la Viña.

VALDESPINO *Jerez y Manzanilla DO, Andalucía, Spain* Owned by Grupo Estévez (Marqués del Real Tesoro, Tío Mateo), probably the quality leader in Jerez today. Fino Inocente★★ (can be ★★★), Palo Cortado Cardenal★★★, Pedro Ximénez Niños★★★ and dry Amontillado Coliseo★★★ are stunning examples of sherry's different styles.

VALDIVIESO *Curicó, Chile* Varietals are attractive and direct, Reservas from cooler regions a definite step up, and Single Vineyard Chardonnay★ and Malbec★ are quite impressive. Multi-varietal, multi-vintage blend Caballo Loco★ (mad horse) is always fascinating and unpredictable, and Eclat★★, based on old Carignan, is chewy and rich.

VALENCIA *Spain* The best-known wines from Valencia DO are the inexpensive, sweet, grapy Moscatels. Simple, fruity whites, reds and rosés are also good. Alicante DO to the south produces a little-known treasure, the Fondillón dry or semi-dry fortified wine, as well as a cluster of wines made by a few quality-conscious modern wineries. Monastrell (Mourvèdre) is the main red grape variety. Best producers: (Valencia) J Belda, Rafael Cambra★, Cherubino Valsangiacomo (Marqués de Caro), Enguera, Gandía, Los Pinos★, Murviedro, Celler del Roure★; (Alicante) Bernabé Navarro★, Bocopa★, Heretat de Cesilia★, Gutiérrez de la Vega (Casta Diva Muscat★★), Laderas de Pinoso★, Enrique Mendoza★★, Salvador Poveda★, Primitivo Quiles★. See also UTIEL-REQUENA.

VALL LLACH *Priorat DOCa, Spain* This tiny winery, owned by Catalan folk singer Lluís Llach, produces powerful reds★★ dominated by old-vine Cariñena. Best years: 2007 06 05 **04** 03 01 00 99 98.

VALLE D'AOSTA *Italy* Tiny Alpine valley sandwiched between PIEDMONT and the Alps in northern Italy. The regional DOC covers around 20 wine styles, referring either to a specific grape variety (like Gamay or Pinot Nero) or to a delimited region like Donnaz (light red from steep Nebbiolo vineyards). Perhaps the finest wine from this valley is the sweet Chambave Moscato. Best producers: R Anselmet★, C Charrère/Les Crêtes★, La Crotta di Vegneron★, Grosjean, Institut Agricole Regional★, Onze Communes co-op, Ezio Voyat★.

VALLE CENTRAL See CENTRAL VALLEY, Chile.

VALPOLICELLA DOC *Veneto, Italy* Styles range from a light, cherryish red to dense, burly AMARONE and rich, PORT-like RECIOTO (both DOCG). Most of the better table wines are Valpolicella (Classico) Superiore from the hills north of Verona and are made predominantly from Corvina and Corvinone grapes, plus Rondinella. The most concentrated, ageworthy wines are made either from a particular vineyard, or by refermenting the

313

wine on the skins and lees of the Amarone, a style called *ripasso*, or by using a portion of dried grapes. **Best producers:** Accordini★, ALLEGRINI★★★, Bertani★, Brigaldara★, Brunelli★, BUSSOLA★★★, Michele Castellani★, Cecilia Beretta★, Valentina Cubi★, DAL FORNO★★★, Guerrieri-Rizzardi★, MASI★, Mazzi★, Morandina, C S Negrar★, QUINTARELLI★★★, Le Ragose★, Le Salette★, Serègo Alighieri★, Speri★★, Tedeschi★, Villa Monteleone★, VIVIANI★★, Zenato★, Zeni★. **Best years:** (Valpolicella Superiore) (2011) (10) **08 06 04 01 00.**

VALTELLINA SUPERIORE DOCG *Lombardy, Italy*   Red wine produced on the steep slopes of northern LOMBARDY. There is a basic light Valtellina DOC red, made from at least 90% Nebbiolo (here called Chiavennasca), but the best wines are Valtellina Superiore DOCG from sub-zones like Grumello, Inferno, Sassella and Valgella. From top vintages the wines are attractively perfumed and approachable. Sfursat or Sforzato is a high-alcohol AMARONE-like red made from semi-dried grapes. **Best producers:** La Castellina★, Enologica Valtellinese★, Fay★, Nino Negri★, Nera★, Rainoldi★, Conti Sertoli Salis★, Triacca★. **Best years:** (2011) (10) **09 08 07 06 04 01.**

VAN VOLXEM *Wiltingen, Mosel, Germany*   Roman Niewodniczanski bought this estate, with its great old vineyards in Scharzhofberg and Wiltinger Gottesfuss, in 2000. His style, off-dry and opulent, is atypical and controversial, but often ★★. **Best years:** (2011) 10 09 **08 07 06 05 04.**

CH. VANNIÈRES *Bandol AC, Provence, France*   Leading BANDOL estate, owned by the Boisseaux family since the 1950s. Wines are bottled unfiltered, and Mourvèdre makes up to 90–95% of the red Bandol★★. Also CÔTES DE PROVENCE and IGP wines. **Best years:** (2011) 10 09 **08 07 06 05 03 01.**

VASSE FELIX *Margaret River, Western Australia*   MARGARET RIVER's first vineyard and winery (planted in 1967). New vineyards have been added and the winery is clearly focused on what Margaret River does best: Cabernet, Chardonnay and Semillon-Sauvignon. Even 20-year-old Shiraz vines have been ripped up. The flagship Heytesbury Chardonnay★★★ is tighter, leaner and finer than before, while the powerful Cabernet-blend red Heytesbury★★★ shows greater elegance. There's a decadently rich Cabernet Sauvignon★ and oak-led Shiraz★, and the regular Chardonnay★ is pleasurable drinking for a modest price. **Best years:** (Heytesbury red) (2011) (10) 09 08 **07 05 04 01 99 97 96 95.**

VAUD *Switzerland*   The Vaud's main vineyards border Lake Geneva (Lac Léman), with 4 sub-regions: la Côte, Lavaux, CHABLAIS, Côtes de l'Orbe-Bonvillars. Fresh light white wines are made from Chasselas; at Dézaley it gains depth. Reds from Gamay and Pinot Noir. **Best producers:** Henri Badoux, Louis Bovard★, la Chenalettaz, Conne, Cruchon, Dubois, Obrist, Pinget★, J & P Testuz★.

VAVASOUR *Marlborough, South Island, New Zealand*   First winery in Marlborough's AWATERE VALLEY, now enjoying spectacular success. One of New Zealand's best Chardonnays★★, a fine, lush Pinot Noir★★ and palate-tingling, oak-tinged Sauvignon Blanc★★. Second-label Dashwood is also top stuff, particularly the tangy Sauvignon Blanc★★. **Best years:** (Sauvignon Blanc) 2011 **10 09 07 06.**

VEENWOUDEN *Paarl WO, South Africa*   Sumptuous, well-oaked Merlot Reserve★★, firm, silky-fruited BORDEAUX-blend Veenwouden Classic★★ and expressive, supple-tannined Syrah★. Also a tiny quantity of fine Chardonnay★. **Best years:** (Merlot Reserve, Classic) 2008 **07 06 05 04 03.**

VEGA SICILIA *Ribera del Duero DO, Castilla y León, Spain*   Among Spain's most expensive wines – rich, fragrant, complex and very slow to mature, and by no means always easy to appreciate. This estate was the first in Spain to introduce French varieties, and almost a quarter of the vines are now Cabernet Sauvignon, along with Tempranillo, Malbec and Merlot. Unico★★★ – the top wine – is aged in wood for 5 or 6 years. Second wine: Valbuena★★. A subsidiary winery produces the more modern Alión★, and the Pintia winery makes hefty wines in TORO. Makes good dry Furmint★ at Oremus winery in Hungary. Best years: (Unico) 2000 99 96 95 94 91 90 89 87 86 85 83 82 81 80 79 76 75 74 70 68.

VELICH *Neusiedlersee, Burgenland, Austria* Heinz Velich makes Austria's most mineral and sophisticated Chardonnay★★ from old vines in the Tiglat vineyard. Also spectacular ★★ and ★★★ dessert wines. Best years: (Tiglat Chardonnay) (2011) (10) 09 **08 07 06**; (sweet) (2011) (10) 09 **08 07 06 05 04**.

VENETO *Italy* Usually the most prolific wine region in Italy, a major source of Pinot Grigio and the home of VALPOLICELLA, BARDOLINO and SOAVE as well as DOCs from Garda (e.g. BIANCO DI CUSTOZA) in the west via BREGANZE and the PROSECCO zones of Conegliano and Valdobbiadene to Piave on the border with FRIULI GRAVE. Pretty well every wine style is covered somewhere in Veneto, from a variety of native and international grapes. With its port of Venice and crossroads-cities like Verona linking it with points south and north, Veneto has become the most cosmopolitan of regions, though it retains more than its share of local peculiarities such as the dried-grape method of producing so-called *vini da meditazione*. See also AMARONE, RECIOTO DELLA VALPOLICELLA and RECIOTO DI SOAVE.

VENTISQUERO *Maipo, Chile* State-of-the-art, ecologically friendly winery started in the late 1990s. Flagship wine in the Ventisquero range is the Grey Syrah★. Also a rapidly improving range under the Yali label. Pangea★★, from the Apalta region of COLCHAGUA, is a joint venture wine with the Australian John DUVAL (who made Penfolds GRANGE famous). New ultra-northern Huasco Valley promises tingling whites and reds.

VENTOUX AC *Rhône Valley, France* Vineyards spread out around the southern and western slopes of Mt Ventoux. When well made, the red wines have lovely juicy fruit or, in the case of Paul JABOULET and Pesquié, some real stuffing. Good, fresh rosés. Best producers: Anges★, Brusset, Cascavel★, Cave Courtoise★, La Croix des Pins★, Fenouillet, Font-Sane, Gonnet★, Paul JABOULET★, Cave de Lumières★, la Martinelle★, le Murmurium, Pesquié★★, Cave Terraventoux, Unang, Valcombe★, VIDAL-FLEURY★, la Vieille Ferme★. Best years: (reds) (2011) **10 09** 07.

VERDELHO Best known as the grape that produces an off dry style of MADEIRA fortified wine. Called Gouveio, it is used for white PORT. In Spain, as Godello, it was almost extinct in the early 1970s, but was progressively recovered in the Valdeorras (GALICIA) and BIERZO regions, where it makes fragrant, dry, often ageworthy whites. WESTERN AUSTRALIA and NEW SOUTH WALES make big, sometimes oily, dry whites from it.

VERDICCHIO DEI CASTELLI DI JESI, VERDICCHIO DI MATELICA DOC *Marche, Italy* Verdicchio, grown in the hills near the Adriatic around Jesi and in the Apennine foothills enclave of Matelica, has blossomed into one of central Italy's most promising white varieties. Usually fresh and fruity, but some Verdicchio can age into a white of surprising depth of flavour. A few producers, notably Garofoli with Serra Fiorese★★, age it in oak, but even without wood it can develop an almost Burgundy-like complexity. A little is made sparkling. **Best producers:** (Jesi) Brunori★, Bucci★★, Colonnara★, Coroncino★★, Fazi Battaglia★, Garofoli★★, Mancinelli★, Monte Schiavo★, Santa Barbara★, Sartarelli★★, Tavignano★, Terre Cortesi Moncaro★, Umani Ronchi★, Fratelli Zaccagnini★; (Matelica) Belisario★, Bisci★, Mecella★, La Monacesca★★.

VIGNOBLE DES VERDOTS *Bergerac AOP and Monbazillac AOP, South-West France* David Fourtout makes all kinds of BERGERACs, from the everyday, good-value Clos des Verdots★ range to Château les Tours des Verdots★ (barrique-aged), to the top of the tree Verdots★★ and Le Vin★★. Outstanding MONBAZILLAC★★. **Best years:** (reds) (2011) 10 **09 06 05 04**.

VERGELEGEN *Stellenbosch WO, South Africa* This historic farm's Sauvignon Blancs are considered benchmarks: the regular bottling★★ is aggressive and racy, streaked with tropical fruit; the single-vineyard Reserve★★ is flinty, dry and fascinating. White Vergelegen★★, a barrel-fermented Semillon- or Sauvignon-led blend, depending on vintage, ages superbly for at least 8 years. Also a ripe-textured, stylish Chardonnay Reserve★★. Of the reds, BORDEAUX blend Vergelegen★★★ shows classic mineral intensity, and Merlot★★ and Cabernet Sauvignon★★ are often among South Africa's best. Single-vineyard Cabernet Sauvignon-based 'V'★★ is an attention-grabbing individual. **Best years:** (premium reds) (2009) **08 07 06** 05 04 03 02 01.

VERGET *Mâconnais, Burgundy, France* *Négociant* house run by Jean-Marie Guffens-Heynen, with outstanding Premiers Crus and Grands Crus from CHABLIS and the CÔTE D'OR, notably PULIGNY-MONTRACHET Sous le Puits★★. Guffens-Heynen also has his own domaine, with excellent MÂCON-VILLAGES★★ and POUILLY-FUISSÉ★★. But take note, the wines are made in a very individualistic style. **Best years:** (2011) 10 **09 08 06**.

VERMENTINO The best dry white wines of SARDINIA generally come from the Vermentino grape. The best examples – full-bodied and flavoursome – are from the north-east of the island, where the Vermentino di Gallura DOCG zone is located. Vermentino di Sardegna DOC is lighter, less interesting. Vermentino is also grown in coastal areas of LIGURIA and TUSCANY, and in CORSICA. It is believed to be the same as Rolle, found in many blends in PROVENCE and the LANGUEDOC, and increasingly as varietal wines. Starting to appear in California and Australia. **Best producers:** (Sardinia) ARGIOLAS★, Capichera★★, Cherchi★, Contini★, Gallura co-op★★, Giogantinu★, Piero Mancini★, Pedra Majore★, Mura★, Santadi co-op★, Sella & Mosca, Vermentino co-op★★; (Tuscany) ANTINORI; (Provence) La Courtade★, Sarrins★; (Australia) YALUMBA.

VERNACCIA DI SAN GIMIGNANO DOCG *Tuscany, Italy* Famous Tuscan white wine: dry, variable and generally underwhelming, made from the Vernaccia grape grown in the hills around the town of San Gimignano. Up to 10% other grapes, e.g. Chardonnay, are allowed. There is a San Gimignano DOC for the zone's reds, though the best are sold as IGT Toscana. **Best producers:** Cà del Vispo★, Le Calcinaie★, Casale-Falchini★, V Cesani★, Guicciardini Strozzi★, La Lastra (Riserva★), Melini (Le Grillaie★),

Montenidoli★, G Panizzi★, Il Paradiso★, Pietrafitta★, La Rampa di Fugnano★, Teruzzi & Puthod (Terre di Tufi★★), Casa alle Vacche★, Vagnoni★.

QUINTA DO VESÚVIO★★ *Port DOC, Douro, Portugal* Top vintage PORT (and DOURO wine★★) from the Symington stable that appears only when the high quality can be maintained. Best with at least 10 years' age. **Best years:** (Vintage) (2009) 08 **07 06 05 04 03 01 00 99 97 96 95 94 92 91 90.**

VEUVE CLICQUOT *Champagne AC, Champagne, France* Owned by the LVMH luxury goods group, with a high-quality reputation but erratic standards. The non-vintage is full, toasty and satisfyingly weighty, or lean and raw, depending on your luck; the vintage used to be reliably impressive. Look out for Veuve Clicquot Cave Privée★★, recent releases of top older vintages. The de luxe Grande Dame★★★ is both powerful and elegant. Grande Dame Rosé★★★ is exquisite. **Best years:** 2004 **02 00 99 98 96 95 90 89 88 85 82.**

VIADER *Howell Mountain AVA, California, USA* Established in 1986 by Delia Viader. Excellent limited-production reds, including the signature Viader★★, an elegant, structured blend of Cabernets Sauvignon and Franc. Good Tempranillo★ and a dry rosé★ under the DARE label.

VICTORIA *Australia* Despite its relatively small area, Victoria has arguably a wider variety of land suited to quality grape-growing than any other state in Australia, with climates ranging from hot Murray Darling and Swan Hill on the Murray River to cool MORNINGTON PENINSULA and GIPPSLAND in the south. The range of flavours is similarly wide and exciting. With more than 500 wineries, Victoria leads the boutique winery boom, particularly in Mornington Peninsula. See also BEECHWORTH, BENDIGO, CENTRAL VICTORIA, GEELONG, GRAMPIANS AND PYRENEES, HEATHCOTE, RUTHERGLEN, YARRA VALLEY.

VIDAL-FLEURY *Rhône Valley, France* GUIGAL-owned, recently reinvigorated CÔTE-RÔTIE producer (classy La Chatillonne★★) and Rhône merchant; quality moving up fast. Old favourites MUSCAT DE BEAUMES-DE-VENISE★ and red VENTOUX★ now joined by red and white★ CÔTES DU RHÔNE, CAIRANNE and GIGONDAS★. **Best years:** (reds) 2011 **10 09 07.**

VIEUX-CHÂTEAU-CERTAN★★ *Pomerol AC, Bordeaux, France* Slow-developing, tannic but delightful red with up to 30% Cabernet Franc and 10% Cabernet Sauvignon in the blend, which after 15–20 years finally resembles more a fragrant, refined MÉDOC than a hedonistic POMEROL. **Best years:** 2010 09 08 **07 06 05 04 02 01 00 99 98 96 95 90 89 88 86 85.**

DOM. DU VIEUX TÉLÉGRAPHE *Châteauneuf-du-Pape AC, Rhône Valley, France* The vines are some of the oldest in CHÂTEAUNEUF and the Grenache-based red★★ (sometimes ★★★) is among the best, most complex wines of the RHÔNE VALLEY, and lives for 20 years. There is a small amount of white★★, which is rich and heavenly when very young but ages well. Good second wine, when not over-ripened, Télégramme. Also owns improving, well-fruited la Roquète★ in Châteauneuf and very fine les Pallières★★ in GIGONDAS. **Best years:** (reds) 2011 **10 09 08 07 06 05 04 03 01 00 99 98 97 96 95 90 89 88.**

VILLA MARIA *Auckland and Marlborough, New Zealand* Founder Sir George Fistonich also owns Esk Valley and Vidal (both in HAWKES BAY). Villa Maria Reserve Merlot-Cabernet★★★, Reserve Merlot★★, Esk Valley The Terraces★★★ and Vidal Merlot-Cabernet★ are superb. Syrahs are among New Zealand's best: Esk Valley, Villa Maria Reserve and Vidal Legacy, all ★★. Reserve Chardonnay from Vidal★★ and Villa Maria★★

are suave and serious. The Villa Maria range includes various MARLBOROUGH Sauvignon Blancs, with Clifford Bay Reserve★★, Wairau Reserve★★ and Taylors Pass★★ outstanding. Also from Marlborough, impressive Pinot Noir Reserve★★, Seddon Pinot Gris★, Reserve Riesling★★ and stunning botrytized Noble Riesling★★★. Best years: (Hawkes Bay reds) 2010 **09 08 07 06 04 02**.

CH. DE VILLENEUVE *Saumur-Champigny AC, Loire Valley, France* Low yields and fully ripe fruit produce first-class SAUMUR-CHAMPIGNY★, with concentrated, mineral Vieilles Vignes★★ and le Grand Clos★★. Barrel-fermented white Saumur Les Cormiers★★ develops Burgundian complexity with age. Best years: (2011) 10 **09 08 06 05 04 03 02 01 97 96**.

VILLIERA *Stellenbosch WO, South Africa* The speciality is Cap Classique sparklers: rich, biscuity Monro Brut★★ with 5 years on lees; additive-free Brut Natural Chardonnay★. Still whites include Sauvignon Blanc (Bush Vine★), a consistent Riesling and 2 delicious oaked Chenin Blancs★. Monro, a structured Merlot-led BORDEAUX blend, is best among the reds. Fired Earth★ is a tasty Late Bottled PORT style. Also 'mentor' to neighbouring M'hudi project (Pinotage★, Sauvignon Blanc★).

VIN SANTO *Tuscany, Italy* TUSCANY's 'holy wine' can be one of the world's great sweet wines – but the term has been wantonly abused (happily the *liquoroso* version, made by adding alcohol to partially fermented must, is no longer recognized as a legitimate style). Made from dried white or occasionally red grapes, fermented and aged in small barrels (*caratelli*) for between 3 and 10 years, the wines should be nutty, gently oxidized, full of the flavours of dried apricots and crystallized orange peel, concentrated and long. Vin Santo from red grapes (Sangiovese) is called Occhio di Pernice. Best producers: Castello di AMA★, AVIGNONESI★★★, Fattoria di Basciano★★, Bindella★★, Cacchiano★, Capezzana★★, Fattoria del Cerro★★, Corzano e Paterno★★, FONTODI★★, ISOLE E OLENA★★★, Romeo★★, San Felice★★, San Gervasio★★, San Giusto a Rentennano★★★, SELVAPIANA★★, Villa Sant'Anna★★, Villa di Vetrice★, VOLPAIA★.

VIÑAS DEL VERO *Somontano DO, Aragón, Spain* Minerally unoaked Chardonnay and its toasty barrel-fermented counterpart★ are joined by more original whites such as Clarión★, a blend of Chardonnay, Gewürztraminer and Macabeo. Top reds are Secastilla★★ (old-vines Garnacha with some Syrah), Gran Vos★ (Merlot-Cabernet-Pinot Noir) and the red blend made by its subsidiary Blecua★★.

VINHO VERDE DOC *Minho and Douro Litoral, Portugal* 'Vinho Verde' can be red or white – 'green' only in the sense of being young. The whites are the most widely seen outside Portugal and range from medium-sweet but acidic to aromatic, flowery and fruity, often with a slight spritzy tingle. Some that fall outside the DOC regulations are sold as Vinho Regional Minho (Quinta do CÔTTO's Paço de Teixeiró). Best producers: Quinta de Alderiz, Quinta do Ameal★★, Quinta da Aveleda★, Quinta de Azevedo★, SOGRAPE, Quinta da Baguinha★, Encostas dos Castelos, Quinta de Gomariz★, Quinta da Lixa, Quinta de Lourosa, Quintas de Melgaço, Anselmo Mendes (Muros Antigos★, Muros de Melgaço★), Palácio de Brejoeira, Casa de Sezim★, Quinta de Simães, Quinta de Soalheiro★★, Quinta do Tamariz★, Casa de Valle★.

VINO NOBILE DI MONTEPULCIANO DOCG *Tuscany, Italy* The 'noble wine' from the hills around the town of Montepulciano is made from the Sangiovese grape, known locally as Prugnolo Gentile, with the help of little Canaiolo and Mammolo (and increasingly, Merlot). At its best, i combines the power and structure of BRUNELLO DI MONTALCINO with the finesse and complexity found in top CHIANTI. Improvement since the 1990s has been impressive. The introduction of what is essentially a second wine, Rosso di Montepulciano DOC, has certainly helped. Best producers: AVIGNONESI★★, Bindella★, BOSCARELLI★★, La Braccesca★★ (ANTINORI), Le Casalte★, La Ciarliana★, CONTUCCI★★, Dei★★, Del Cerro★★, Fassati★★, Gracciano★, Il Macchione★, Nottola★★, Palazzo Vecchio★★, POLIZIANO★★, Redi★, Romeo★, Salcheto★★, Trerose★ (Simposio★★), Valdipiatta★. Best years: (2011) (10) (09) 08 **07** 06 **04 01 00 99 97**.

VINSOBRES AC *Rhône Valley, France* Southern RHÔNE village whose hallmark is clear fruit. A good, fresh area for Syrah, which goes into the blend with Grenache. Best producers: Chaume-Arnaud★, Constant-Duquesnoy, Coriançon★, Deurre★, Jaume★, Moulin★, Famille Perrin★, Rouanne, la Vinsobraise co-op. Best years: (reds) 2011 **10 09 07 06 05 03**.

VIOGNIER Traditionally grown only in the northern RHÔNE VALLEY, most famously for the rare and expensive wines of CONDRIEU, Viognier is traditionally a poor yielder, prone to disease and difficult to vinify. But the wine can be delicious: pear-fleshy, apricotty with a soft, almost waxy texture, usually a fragrance of spring flowers and sometimes a taste like crème fraîche. New, higher-yielding clones that limit its opulence are now being grown in LANGUEDOC-ROUSSILLON, Ardèche and the southern Rhône as well as in Spain, Portugal, Switzerland, Italy, Austria, the USA (Virginian Viognier can be world class), Argentina, Chile, Australia, New Zealand and South Africa. Traditionally used in parts of CÔTE-RÔTIE to co-ferment with Syrah (Shiraz); this practice is now becoming popular in other parts of the world. It is also increasingly being used as a blender with more neutral white varieties to inject perfume, texture and fruit.

VIRE-CLESSE AC *Mâconnais, Burgundy, France* Appellation created in 1998 out of 2 of the best MÂCON-VILLAGES. Originally, the rules outlawed wines with residual sugar, thus excluding Jean Thévenet's extraordinary cuvées, but common sense has prevailed. Best producers: A Bonhomme★★, Bret Brothers★, Cave de Viré★, Chaland★★, E Gillet★, Héritiers LAFON★, J-P Michel★, Roally★, Thévenet★★. Best years: (2011) 10 **09 08 07**.

VIRGINIA *USA* Virginia's surging wine industry has surpassed 200 wineries in 6 AVAs. Aromatic Viognier has already produced some world-class examples and earthy Cabernet Franc is promising, while varietal Petit Verdot produces some enticingly aromatic reds. Many growers continue to tinker with other varieties such as Petit Manseng, Nebbiolo and Tannat, which can be surprisingly good. Increasing emphasis on vineyard-designated red blends grown on densely planted steep hillsides has paid off in quality. Virginia is also producing some distinguished fizz. Best producers: BARBOURSVILLE★, Boxwood, Breaux★, Chrysalis, Glen Manor, HORTON★, Keswick★, King Family, LINDEN★, Pearmund★, Pollak, RdV★, Michael Shaps★, Veritas★, Williamsburg.

VIVIANI *Valpolicella DOC, Veneto, Italy* Claudio Viviani's 9ha (22-acre) site is turning out some beautifully balanced VALPOLICELLA. The top AMARONE, Casa dei Bepi★★★, is a model of enlightened modernity, and the Valpolicella Classico Superiore Campo Morar★★ and RECIOTO★★ are of a similar quality. Best years: (2011) (10) 09 **08 06 04 01**.

ROBERTO VOERZIO *Barolo DOCG, Piedmont, Italy* One of the best, and most expensive, of the new wave of BAROLO producers. Dolcetto (Priavino★) is successful, as is Vignaserra★★ – barrique-aged Nebbiolo with a little Cabernet – and the outstanding BARBERA D'ALBA Riserva Pozzo dell'Annunziata★★. Barriques are also used for Barolos, but they don't overwhelm the quality and concentration of fruit. Single-vineyard examples made in the best years include Brunate★★, Cerequio★★★, La Serra★★ and Riserva Capalot★★★. Best years: (Barolo) (2011) (10) (09) 08 07 06 **04 01 00 99 98 97 96 95 93 91 90 89** 88 85.

COMTE GEORGES DE VOGÜÉ *Chambolle-Musigny, Côte de Nuits, Burgundy, France* De Vogüé owns substantial holdings in 2 Grands Crus, BONNES-MARES★★★ and MUSIGNY★★★, as well as in Chambolle's top Premier Cru, les Amoureuses★★★ epitomizing the silky style of great Burgundy. It is the sole producer of minute quantities of Musigny Blanc★★, but because of recent replanting the wine is currently being sold as (very expensive) BOURGOGNE Blanc. Best years: (Musigny) (2011) 10 09 08 07 06 05 03 **00 99 98 96 93 91** 90.

VOLNAY AC *Côte de Beaune, Burgundy, France* Elegant CÔTE DE BEAUNE reds: attractive when young, good examples can age well. Top Premiers Crus: Caillerets, Champans, Clos des Chênes, Santenots, Taillepieds. Best producers: M Ampeau★★, d'ANGERVILLE★★★, BELLENE★, H Boillot★, J-M Boillot★★, COCHE-DURY★★, V GIRARDIN★★, LAFARGE★★, LAFON★★★, Matrot★★, MONTILLE★★, Pousse d'Or★★, J Prieur★★, N Rossignol★★, J Voillot★★. Best years: (2011) 10 09 08 **07** 05 **02 99 96 95 91** 90.

CASTELLO DI VOLPAIA *Chianti Classico DOCG, Tuscany, Italy* One of the first great estates to emerge into quality production in the 1970s, making elegant, perfumed reds from high, steep, south-facing vineyards. CHIANTI CLASSICO★ is light, intense, exceeded by the fine Riserva★★, Coltassala★★ (95% Sangiovese, 5% Mammolo) and Balifico★★ (Sangiovese-Cabernet). Good VIN SANTO★. Riccardo Cotarella (see FALESCO) is consultant enologist.

VON SIEBENTHAL *Aconcagua, Chile* Tiny boutique winery founded by Swiss lawyer Mauro von Siebenthal, who fell in love with the region. Eclectic range, with consistently good Carabantes★ (Syrah), Montelìg★ (Cabernet) and Parcela #7★★ (Cabernet-Merlot-Cabernet Franc). Toknar★★ is a rich and vibrant 100% Petit Verdot.

VOSNE-ROMANÉE AC *Côte de Nuits, Burgundy, France* The greatest village in the CÔTE DE NUITS, with 6 Grands Crus and 13 Premiers Crus (notably les Malconsorts, aux Brûlées and les Suchots) that are often as good as other villages' Grands Crus. The quality of Vosne's village wine is also high. In good years the wines need at least 6 years' aging, but 10–15 would be better. Best producers: Arnoux-Lachaux★★★, Cacheux-Sirugue★★, S CATHIARD★★★, B Clavelier★★, Confuron-Cotetidot★★, Eugénie★★ (formerly Engel), GRIVOT★★, Anne GROS★★★, A-F GROS★★, M GROS★★★, F Lamarche★★, Dom. LEROY★★★, Comte LIGER-BELAIR★★, MÉO-CAMUZET★★★, MUGNERET-GIBOURG★★, Dom. de la ROMANÉE-CONTI★★★, E Rouget★★★. Best years: (2011) 10 09 08 **07** 06 **05** 03 02 01 **00 99** 98 96 95 93 90.

VOUGEOT AC *Côte de Nuits, Burgundy, France* Outside the walls of CLOS DE VOUGEOT there are only 11ha (27 acres) of Premier Cru and 5ha (12 acres) of other vines. Clos Blanc de Vougeot was first planted with white grapes in 1110. Best producers: Bertagna★, Chopin★★, C Clerget★, VOUGERAIE★★. Best years: (reds) (2011) 10 09 08 **07** 06 05 **03** 02 00 99.

DOM. DE LA VOUGERAIE *Côte de Nuits, Burgundy, France* An estate created by Jean-Claude BOISSET in 1999 out of the numerous vineyards that came with Burgundy merchant houses acquired during his rise to prominence since 1964. Wines have been generally outstanding, notably Clos Blanc de VOUGEOT★★★ white, and le MUSIGNY★★★ and Vougeot les Cras★★ reds. Best years: (reds) (2011) 10 09 08 **07** 06 05 03 02.

VOUVRAY AC *Loire Valley, France* Dry, medium-dry, sweet and sparkling wines from Chenin grapes east of Tours. The dry wines acquire beautifully rounded flavours after 6–8 years. Medium-dry wines, when well made from a single domaine, are worth aging for 20 years or more, but avoid cheap examples. Spectacular noble-rot-affected sweet wines can be produced when conditions are right. The fizz, Mousseux and Pétillant (bottled at lower pressure), is some of the LOIRE's best. Best producers: Aubuisières★★, Bourillon Dorléans★★, C & P Breton, Champalou★★, F CHIDAINE★★, CLOS NAUDIN★★, la Fontainerie★, Gaudrelle★, Gautier★★, P Gendron★, Haute Borne/V Carême★, HUET★★, Pichot★, F Pinon★★, Taille aux Loups★★/BLOT, Vigneau Chevreau★. Best years: (dry) (2011) 10 08 07 06; (sweet) (2011) 09 04 03 02 01 99 97 96 95 90 89.

VOYAGER ESTATE *Margaret River, Western Australia* Originally planted in 1978, owned since 1992 by mining magnate Michael Wright and now run by his daughter, Alex. Impressive cellar-door complex. Stellar, oatmealy Chardonnay★★★, vibrant, zingy Sauvignon Blanc-Semillon★★★ and Cabernet Sauvignon-Merlot★★ are regularly some of WESTERN AUSTRALIA's best. Shiraz★ and Sauvignon★ are good.

WACHAU *Niederösterreich, Austria* This stunning 1400ha (3460-acre) stretch of the Danube is Austria's top region for dry whites, from Riesling and Grüner Veltliner. Best producers: Alzinger★★, Gritsch★, F HIRTZBERGER★★★, Högl★★, Jamek★, KNOLL★★★, NIKOLAIHOF★★, F X PICHLER★★★, Rudi PICHLER★★, PRAGER★★, Schmelz★★, Domäne Wachau★. Best years: (2011) 10 09 **08** 07 06 05 04 02 01 00 99.

WACHENHEIM *Pfalz, Germany* Wine village made famous by the BÜRKLIN-WOLF estate, its best vineyards can produce rich yet beautifully balanced Rieslings. Best producers: Josef Biffar, BÜRKLIN-WOLF★★, Karl Schaefer★, J L Wolf★. Best years: (2011) 10 09 **08** 07 05 04 03 02.

WAGRAM *Niederösterreich, Austria* 2800ha (7000-acre) wine region on both banks of the Danube, stretching north-west of Vienna towards St Pölten. Previously known as Donauland – the name changed in 2007 – Wagram is the source of fine Grüner Veltliners and a steadily improving band of red wines from Zweigelt and even Pinot Noir. Best producers: J Bauer★, K Fritsch★, Leth★, Bernhard Ott★★, Wimmer-Czerny★.

WAIHEKE ISLAND *North Island, New Zealand* Island in Auckland harbour with vines since the early 1980s; it is now home to over 30 wineries. Hot, dry ripening conditions make high-quality Cabernet-based reds that sell for high prices. Chardonnay, Sauvignon and Pinot Gris are now appearing, together with commercial plantings of stunning Syrah and Viognier. Best producers: Destiny Bay★★, MAN O'WAR★★, Mudbrick★, Obsidian★, Passage Rock★, STONYRIDGE★★★, Te Whau★. Best years: (reds) 2010 **08** 07 05.

WALKER BAY WO *South Africa* Maritime district on the south coast, home to a mix of grape varieties, but the holy grail of most producers is Pinot Noir, with the hub of activity in the Hemel en Aarde (heaven and earth) Valley. Also steely Sauvignon Blanc, minerally Chardonnay, refined Pinotage and intense Syrah. Best producers: Ashbourne★, Ataraxia★★, Beaumont★, BOUCHARD FINLAYSON★, Brunia★, Creation, HAMILTON RUSSELL★★, Hermanuspietersfontein★★, Newton Johnson★. Best years: (Pinot Noir) 2011 **10 09 08 07 06 05 04 03**.

WALLA WALLA VALLEY AVA *Washington State, USA* Walla Walla has over 100 of WASHINGTON's wineries, but 55 have only been producing wine since 1999. Similarly, vineyard acreage, although less than 5% of the state total, has trebled since 99 – and is still growing. If you think there's a gold-rush feel about this exciting area you wouldn't be far wrong. Best producers: ABEJA★, CAYUSE VINEYARDS★★, DUNHAM CELLARS★, K VINTNERS★, L'ECOLE NO. 41★★, LEONETTI CELLAR★★★, LONG SHADOWS VINTNERS★, Northstar★, PEPPER BRIDGE WINERY★, Reininger★, SPRING VALLEY VINEYARD★, WOODWARD CANYON★★.

WARRE'S *Port DOC, Douro, Portugal* Part of the Symington group, with top-quality Vintage PORT★★★ and a fine 'off-vintage' port from Quinta da Cavadinha★★. LBV★★ is in the traditional, unfiltered style. Warrior★ is a reliable ruby and Otima a solid 10-year-old tawny; Otima★ 20-year-old is much better. Best years: (Vintage) (2009) **07 03 00 97 94 91 85 83 80 77 70 66 63**; (Cavadinha) 2001 **99 98 96 95 92 90 88 87 86 82 78**.

WARWICK *Stellenbosch WO, South Africa* Warwick produces the complex Trilogy★ BORDEAUX-style blend and a refined, fragrant Cabernet Franc★. The Three Cape Ladies★ red blend includes Pinotage along with Cabernet Sauvignon, Merlot and 'fourth' lady, Shiraz. Whites are represented by an unwooded Sauvignon Blanc and full-bodied, lightly-oaked Chardonnay★. Best years: (Trilogy) 2009 **08 07 06 05 04 03 02**.

WASHINGTON STATE *USA* The second-largest premium wine-producing state in the US (after California), with more than 740 wineries. The chief growing areas are in irrigated high desert, east of the Cascade Mountains, where the COLUMBIA VALLEY AVA encompasses the smaller AVAs of YAKIMA VALLEY, WALLA WALLA VALLEY, Wahluke Slope, Horse Heaven Hills, Rattlesnake Hills, Red Mountain, Columbia Gorge, Snipes Mountain, Puget Sound, Naches Heights and Lake Chelan. Although the heat is not as intense as in California, long summer days with extra hours of sunshine due to the northern latitude seem to increase the intensity of fruit flavours, resulting in red and white wines of great depth. Cabernets Sauvignon and Franc, Merlot, Syrah, Chardonnay, Semillon and Riesling can produce very good wines here.

GEOFF WEAVER *Adelaide Hills, South Australia* Low-yielding vines at Geoff Weaver's Lenswood vineyard produce top-quality fruit, from which he crafts limy Riesling★★, crisply gooseberryish Sauvignon★★ and stylish cool-climate Chardonnay★★. Tasty Pinot Noir.

WEGELER *Bernkastel, Mosel; Oestrich-Winkel, Rheingau, Germany* The Wegeler family's 2 estates are dedicated primarily to Riesling, and dry wines make up the bulk of production. The Wegelers' share of the legendary BERNKASTELer Doctor has been in the family since 1903. Whatever their style, the best wines merit ★★ and will develop well with 5 or more years of aging. Best years: (Mosel) (2011) 10 09 **08 07 06 05 04 02 01**.

WEHLEN *Mosel, Germany* Village whose steep Sonnenuhr vineyard produces some of Germany's most intense Rieslings. Best producers: Kerpen, Dr LOOSEN★★★, MOLITOR★★, J J PRÜM★★★, S A PRUM★, Max Ferd RICHTER★★, SELBACH-OSTER★★, Studert-Prüm, WEGELER★, Dr Weins-Prüm★. Best years: (2011) 10 09 **08** 07 06 05 04 03 01 99.

ROBERT WEIL *Kiedrich, Rheingau, Germany* Huge investment from Japanese drinks giant Suntory, coupled with Wilhelm Weil's devotion to quality, clearly paid off, showing particular flair with majestic sweet Auslese, Beerenauslese and Trockenbeerenauslese Rieslings★★★. Other styles are ★, sometimes ★★, but less remarkable than the sweet wines. Best years: (2011) 10 09 **08** 07 06 05 04 03 02 01.

WEINBACH *Alsace AC, Alsace, France* This Kaysersberg estate is run by the Faller family. The extensive range (which includes cuvées Théo, Ste-Catherine and Laurence) is complicated, with Théo★★ being the lightest; Laurence★ wines are from the Altenbourg locale, but include a Grand Cru Furstentum Gewurztraminer; many of the Ste-Catherine★★ bottlings come from the Grand Cru Schlossberg. The top dry wine is the Ste-Catherine Riesling Grand Cru Schlossberg L'Inédit★★★. Quintessence★★★ is an SGN from Pinot Gris or Gewurztraminer. All the wines are exceptionally balanced and, while delightful on release, can age for many years. Best years: (Grand Cru Riesling) (2011) (10) 09 08 **07** 05 04 02 01 00 99 98 97 96 95 94 93 92 90.

WEISSBURGUNDER See PINOT BLANC.

WELSCHRIESLING Unrelated to the great Riesling of the Rhine, this grape makes some of the best sweet wines in Austria, and, as Graševina, some serious, weighty dry whites in Croatia. It is highly esteemed in Hungary as Olasz Rizling. As Riesling Italico it has virtually disappeared in northern Italy.

WENDOUREE *Clare Valley, South Australia* Small winery making impressive, ageworthy reds★★ from paltry yields off its own very old Shiraz, Cabernet, Malbec and Mataro (Mourvèdre) vines, plus tiny amounts of sweet Muscat★. Some of Australia's best reds, they can, and do, age beautifully for 30 years or more. Best years: (reds) (2010) 08 06 05 04 **03** 02 01 99 98 96 95 94 92 91 90 86 83 82 81 80 78 76 75.

WESTEND *Riverina, New South Wales, Australia* High-quality family winery established in 1945, now expanding with Cool Climate series (whites from CANBERRA, Shiraz and Tempranillo from HILLTOPS and Pinot Noir from Tumbarumba). The 3 Bridges range includes a powerful yet scented Durif★ and the lush, honeyed Golden Mist Botrytis Semillon★. Richland is one of Australia's best budget ranges (especially Pinot Grigio and Sauvignon Blanc).

WESTERN AUSTRALIA Warm-climate vineyards were established near Perth nearly 200 years ago; high-quality, cool-climate viticulture has been established in the state's south-west for just over 40 years, but Western Australia punches well above its weight. With just over 4% of Australia's grape crush it produces about 20% of Australia's premium wines. Thanks to the influence of the Roaring Forties, rainfall is more consistent and poor vintages rarer than in other parts of the country. With more than 260 producers, the focus of attention is on the GREAT SOUTHERN, MARGARET RIVER, Geographe and PEMBERTON.

HERMANN J WIEMER *Finger Lakes AVA, New York State, USA* Wiemer's family has 300 years' experience of winemaking in the MOSEL, so working with local Riesling pioneer Dr Konstantin FRANK was natural before he established his own winery in 1979. Fine sweeter styles (Auslese-style Late Harvest Riesling★★), though in recent years dry wines have shown more pizzazz. Good sparkling wines. Wiemer has now handed the reins over to winemaker Fred Merwarth; the wines continue to excel.

WIEN *Austria* 700ha (1730-acre) wine region within the city limits of Wien (Vienna). The wines are mostly consumed young in the growers' Heurigen (wine inns). The local 'Gemischter Satz' tradition of field-blend vineyards is being revived by many growers. Best producers: Christ, Edlmoser, Mayer★, WIENINGER★★, Zahel. Best years: (2011) 10 **09 08 07 06**.

WIENINGER *Stammersdorf, Wien, Austria* Fritz Wieninger has risen above the parochial standards of many Viennese growers to offer a range of elegant, well-crafted wines from Chardonnay and Pinot Noir. The best range is often the Select★★, the pricier Grand Select★ being sometimes over-oaked. Also brilliant Riesling and 'Gemischter Satz' from the renowned Nussberg★★ vineyard. Best years: (2011) 10 **09 08 07 06**.

WILLAKENZIE ESTATE *Willamette Valley AVA, Oregon, USA* Bernard Lacroute purchased a cattle ranch in 1991 just outside Yamhill, Oregon and named the property after the ancient Willakenzie sedimentary soil. Eleven different clones of Pinot Noir are planted and estate-bottled Pinot Noirs from individual sites are the primary focus: Terres Basses★ and Triple Black Slopes★ are powerful long-aging styles. There is a small amount of rich Pinot Gris★ made from estate fruit and some delightful, rare, Pinot Meunier★ reds. Best years: (Pinot Noir) (2010) 09 **08 07 06**

WILLAMETTE VALLEY AVA *Oregon, USA* Wet winters, generally dry summers, and a good chance of long, cool autumn days provide sound growing conditions for Pinot Noir, Pinot Gris and Chardonnay. The volcanic Dundee Hills is considered the best sub-AVA; others are Yamhill-Carlton, McMinnville, Eola-Amity Hills, Ribbon Ridge and Chehalem Mountains. Best producers: ADELSHEIM★, ARGYLE★, BEAUX FRERES★★, BERGSTROM★★, Cristom★★, DOMAINE DROUHIN★★, DOMAINE SERENE★★, ELK COVE★, Evesham Wood★, Patricia GREEN★, PONZI★, ST INNOCENT★, Shea Wine Cellars, Sineann★, Sokol Blosser, SOTER★★, WILLAKENZIE ESTATE★, Ken WRIGHT★★. Best years: (reds) 2009 **08 06**

WILLIAMS SELYEM *Russian River Valley AVA, California, USA* Exemplary Pinot Noirs (Rochioli Riverblock★★, Westside Road Neighbors★★ – can be ★★★) from various regions, including RUSSIAN RIVER VALLEY, SONOMA COAST and ANDERSON VALLEY. Zins are good too. Best years: (Pinot Noir) 2009 **08 07 06 05 04 03 02 01 00 99 98.**

WINNINGEN *Mosel, Germany* Winningen's steep slopes, particularly the Ühlen and Röttgen sites, can produce excellent Rieslings, especially in a rich dry style. Best producers: Fries, Heddesdorff, HEYMANN-LÖWENSTEIN★★, Knebel★★, Richard Richter★. Best years: (2011) 10 09 **08 07 06 05 04 03.**

WIRRA WIRRA *McLaren Vale, South Australia* Outstanding producer with fine ADELAIDE HILLS whites – well-balanced and tangy Sauvignon Blanc★ and Riesling★ and tight, fine yet creamy Chardonnay★★ – and soft MCLAREN VALE reds led by delicious The Angelus (Dead Ringer outside Australia) Cabernet★★, chocolaty RSW Shiraz★★, rich, balanced Catapult Shiraz-Viognier★ and stylish, concentrated Woodhenge Shiraz★. In 2007 purchased outstanding Rayner vineyard in the McLaren Vale. Best years: (RSW Shiraz) 2010 09 **08 06 05 04 03 02 01 98 96.**

WITHER HILLS *Marlborough, South Island, New Zealand* Large winery now owned by Lion Nathan breweries and struggling to hold on to its cult reputation created by founder Brent Marris (departed in 2007 to run his Marisco Vineyards/'The Ned'). Sauvignon Blanc sadly seems to get sweeter every vintage, but the Chardonnay★ and Pinot Noir★ still do their best to maintain the original Wither Hills style. Best years: (Chardonnay) 2011 **10 09** 07 06.

WITTMANN *Westhofen, Rheinhessen, Germany* Inspiring, family-run biodynamic estate, succeeding equally with bold dry Rieslings★★, Chardonnay★★, Weissburgunder (Pinot Blanc)★★, and voluptuous Trockenbeerenauslese ★★★. Best years: (2011) 10 09 **08 07 06** 05 04.

WÖLFFER ESTATE *Long Island, New York State, USA* One of the few wineries in LONG ISLAND's Hamptons, Wölffer created a sensation in the early 2000s when it released a 'Premier Cru' Merlot priced at a lofty $100. It is good – but overshadowed by the more modestly priced Estate Selection Merlot★, a rich Pinot Gris and a spritely rosé. Winemaker Roman Roth also has his own label, The Grapes of Roth.

WOODWARD CANYON *Walla Walla Valley AVA, Washington State, USA* Big, barrel-fermented Chardonnays★ were the trademark wines for many years, but today the focus is on reds, led by Artist Series★★ Cabernet Sauvignon and Old Vines★★ Cabernet Sauvignon. Merlot★ is rich, velvety and perfumed. Red BORDEAUX-style blend is labelled Charbonneau★, the name of the vineyard where the fruit is grown. Best years: (top Cabernet Sauvignon) (2010) 09 **08** 07 06.

KEN WRIGHT CELLARS *Willamette Valley AVA, Oregon, USA* Ken Wright produces a dozen succulent, single-vineyard Pinot Noirs. Bold and rich with new oak flavour, they range from good to ethereal, led by the Carter★★, Savoya★★, Guadalupe★★, McCrone★★ and Shea★★. Fine Chardonnay★★ and a crisp Freedom Hill Vineyard Pinot Blanc★, made in very small quantities. Best years: (Pinot Noir) (2010) 09 **08 07 06**.

WÜRTTEMBERG *Germany* 11,500ha (28,415-acre) region centred on the river Neckar. 70% of the wine made is red, and the best comes from Lemberger (Blaufränkisch) or Spätburgunder (Pinot Noir) grapes. Massive yields are often responsible for pallid wines, especially from the locally popular Trollinger grape. A few top steep sites are now producing perfumed reds and racy Riesling. Best years: (reds) (2011) (10) 09 **08 07 06** 05.

WÜRZBURG *Franken, Germany* The centre of FRANKEN wines. Some Rieslings can be excellent, but the real star is Silvaner. Best producers: Bürgerspital★, JULIUSSPITAL★★, Staatlicher Hofkeller, Weingut am Stein★. Best years: (2011) 10 09 **08 07 06 05** 04 03.

WYNNS *Coonawarra, South Australia* Part of the giant Treasury Wine Estates, but Wynns' name is still synonymous with COONAWARRA. Investment in vineyard rejuvenation is paying off. Wynns is best known for reds, such as Shiraz★ and Black Label Cabernet Sauvignon★★. Top-end John Riddoch Cabernet Sauvignon★★★ and Michael Shiraz★★★ were deep, ripe, oaky styles, but latest releases show more restraint and elegance and many consider them among the finest reds currently being produced in Australia. Each year Wynns selects a premium single-vineyard red (usually Cabernet) to show Coonawarra's potential: invariably ★★★. Also attractive Chardonnay★ and delightful Riesling★. Best years: (John Riddoch) 2009 08 **06 05 04** 99 98 96 94 91 90 88 86.

XAREL-LO By far the most characterful, structured member of the classic Cava trio, this Catalan grape now dominates blends in top-end Cavas, some of them varietal, and is increasingly vinified as an unfortified white. Best producers: Gramona★★, Recaredo★★.

YAKIMA VALLEY AVA *Washington State, USA* Important valley within the much larger COLUMBIA VALLEY AVA. Yakima is planted mostly to Chardonnay, Merlot and Cabernet Sauvignon and has more than 65 wineries. Best producers: Chinook★, DELILLE CELLARS★★, Hogue Cellars, Wineglass Cellars★.

YALUMBA *Barossa Valley, South Australia* Robert Hill Smith has taken his distinguished family firm to the pinnacle of Australian winemaking. There's an increasingly wide range under the Yalumba label, as well as a labyrinthine group under the banner of Hill Smith Family Vineyards. The latter includes Heggies (minerally Riesling★★, plump Merlot★★, opulent Viognier★★), Hill Smith Estate (Sauvignon Blanc★), Pewsey Vale (Riesling★★★) and TASMANIA's Jansz (vintage★★, non-vintage★). Flagship reds are The Signature Cabernet-Shiraz★★ (sometimes ★★★), Octavius Shiraz★★, Tri-Centenary Grenache★★ and The Menzies Cabernet★★, and all age well. Bush Vine Grenache★★ (sometimes ★★★), Virgilius Viognier★★ and Shiraz-Viognier★ are excellent too. High-quality Y Series varietals★ (sometimes ★★) are among Australia's finest quaffers. Budget-priced Redbank, Mawson's, Oxford Landing (Sauvignon★) and Angas Brut are enjoyable. Museum Reserve fortifieds (Muscat★★) are excellent, but rare. Best years: (The Signature) (2010) (09) 08 **06 05 04 03 02 01 00 99 98 97 96 95 93**.

YARRA VALLEY *Victoria, Australia* Cool-climate Yarra is asking to be judged as Australia's best Pinot Noir region, but superb Chardonnay, fascinating Cabernet-Merlot and small amounts of world-class Shiraz can be even more exciting. Fizz is also very good. Best producers: Arthur's Creek★, COLDSTREAM HILLS★★, CARLEI★★, DE BORTOLI★★, Diamond Valley★★, DOMAINE CHANDON/Green Point★★, Gembrook Hill★, Giant Steps★, Jamsheed★★, Leayton Estate★, Mac Forbes★, Timo Mayer★, Métier★, MOUNT MARY★★, OAKRIDGE★★, TARRAWARRA★★, Toolangi★, The Wanderer★, Wantirna Estate★, Yarrabank★, Yarra Yering★★, Yeringberg★, Yering Station★★.

YATIR *Judean Hills, Israel* Situated in the Negev Desert, with high-altitude vineyards set within Israel's largest forest. Top label Yatir Forest★, a BORDEAUX blend, is deep and supple, with ripe dark fruit backed by Mediterranean herbs; also full-flavoured Cabernet Sauvignon and complex Merlot-Shiraz-Cabernet★. Aromatic Viognier. Best years: (reds) 2008 07 06 **05 04 03 02**.

YEALANDS *Marlborough, South Island, New Zealand* New and ambitious winery with around 1000ha (2470 acres) of vineyards in the AWATERE VALLEY. Delicately grassy Sauvignon Blanc, pretty Gewurztraminer, succulent Pinot Gris, tangy dry Riesling and a light, aromatic Pinot Noir. Range includes some experimental varieties such as Grüner Veltliner and Tempranillo, both showing form. Best years: (Sauvignon Blanc) 2011 **10 09**.

YELLOWTAIL *Riverina, New South Wales, Australia* Yellowtail, Australia's fastest-growing export brand ever, has made the RIVERINA family winery, Casella, a major world player. Artfully crafted but overly sweet wines.

CH. D'YQUEM★★★ *Sauternes AC, 1er Cru Supérieur, Bordeaux, France* Often rated the most sublime sweet wine in the world. Despite a large vineyard (100ha/250 acres), production is tiny. Only fully noble-rotted grapes are picked, often berry by berry, and low yield means each vine produces only a glass of wine! This precious liquid is then fermented in new oak barrels and left to mature for 30 months before bottling. It is one of the world's most expensive wines, in constant demand because of its richness and exotic flavours. A dry white, Ygrec, is made most years. In 1999 LVMH, the luxury goods group, won a takeover battle with the Lur-Saluces family, owners for 406 years. Best years: 2010 09 08 **07 06 05 04 03 02 01 00 99 98 97 96 95 94 90 89 88 86 83 81 79 76 75 71 70 67**.

ZILLIKEN *Saarburg, Mosel, Germany* Estate specializing in steely Rieslings★★ (Auslese, Eiswein often ★★★) from the Saarburger Rausch. Best years: (2011) 10 09 08 **07 06 05 04 03 02**.

ZIND-HUMBRECHT *Alsace AC, Alsace, France* Olivier Humbrecht is a staunch biodynamicist, and one of France's outstanding winemakers, with an approach that emphasizes the individuality of each site and each vintage. Wines from 4 Grand Cru sites – Rangen, Goldert, Hengst and Brand – are superlative (Riesling★★★, Gewurztraminer★★★, Pinot Gris★★★, Muscat★★), as are wines from specific non-Grand Cru vineyards such as Clos Windsbuhl★★ and Clos Jebsal★★. Vendange Tardive and Sélection de Grains Nobles wines are almost invariably of ★★★ quality. Even basic Sylvaners★ and Pinot Blancs★★ are fine. Wines often have some residual sugar, but Olivier says that's just how they naturally turn out. Best years: (Grand Cru Riesling) (2011) 10 09 08 **07 05 04 03 02 01 00 99 98 97 96 95**.

ZINFANDEL CALIFORNIA's versatile red grape can make big, juicy, briary fruit-packed reds – often farmed from very old vines – or insipid, sweetish 'blush' labelled as White Zinfandel, or even late-harvest dessert wine. Some notable Zinfandel is now made in Australia and South Africa. **Best producers: (California)** Bianchi, Brown★★, Cline★★, CHÂTEAU MONTELENA,

Dashe★★, DRY CREEK VINEYARD★★, DUTTON GOLDFIELD★★, Gary FARRELL★★, HARTFORD★★, MARIAH★, Martinelli★★, Michael-David (Earthquake), NALLE★★, Oakville Winery, Peachy Canyon, Preston★, Rafanelli★★, RAVENSWOOD★, RIDGE★★★, Rosenblum★★, Saddleback★★, St Francis★★, SEGHESIO★★, Trinitas★★, TURLEY★★; **(Australia)** CAPE MENTELLE★★, Kangarilla Road, Nepenthe★★, Smidge, Tscharke. See also PRIMITIVO DI MANDURIA.

ZUCCARDI *Mendoza, Argentina* The Zuccardi family have forged a global reputation for the unexpected and delicious. Sebastian Zuccardi, under the brand that bears his name, leads the team behind the finer wines of the estate. The Santa Julia brand delivers top-value varietals and above that, a dizzying array of experimental wines, sparkling and still. The recently revamped Zuccardi 'Q'★ varietals are fine and pure. Top of the range Zeta★ (Malbec-Tempranillo) improves with every vintage. Some of Argentina's best sparklers, as well as an eclectic varietal range under the Innovacíon label, including Bourboulenc, Aglianico and Touriga Nacional, and new Aluvionale label – wines from alluvial soils, doh – are full of intrigue for the adventurous wine lover.

GLOSSARY OF WINE TERMS

AC/AOC/AOP (APPELLATION D'ORIGINE CONTRÔLÉE/PROTÉGÉE)

The top category of French wines, defined by regulations covering vineyard yields, grape varieties, geographical boundaries, alcohol content and production method. Guarantees origin and style of a wine, but not its quality. *See* page 24.

ACID/ACIDITY

Naturally present in grapes and essential to wine, providing balance and stability, a refreshing tang in white wines and appetizing grip in reds.

ADEGA

Portuguese for winery.

AGING

An alternative term for maturation.

ALCOHOLIC CONTENT

The alcoholic strength of wine, expressed as a percentage of the total volume of the wine. Typically in the range of 7–15%.

ALCOHOLIC FERMENTATION

The process whereby yeasts, natural or added, convert the grape sugars into alcohol (ethyl alcohol, or ethanol) and carbon dioxide.

AMONTILLADO

Traditionally dry style of sherry. *See* Jerez y Manzanilla in main A–Z.

ANBAUGEBIET

German for growing region; these names will appear on labels of all QbA and QmP wines. There are 13 Anbaugebiete: Ahr, Baden, Franken, Hessische Bergstrasse, Mittelrhein, Mosel, Nahe, Pfalz, Rheingau, Rheinhessen, Saale-Unstrut, Sachsen and Württemberg.

AUSBRUCH

Austrian Prädikat category used for sweet wines from the town of Rust.

AUSLESE

German and Austrian Prädikat category meaning that the grapes were 'selected' for their higher ripeness.

AVA (AMERICAN VITICULTURAL AREA)

System of appellations of origin for US wines.

AZIENDA AGRICOLA

Italian for estate or farm. It also indicates wine made from grapes grown by the proprietor.

BARREL AGING

Time spent maturing in wood, usually oak, during which wine takes on flavours from the wood.

BARREL FERMENTATION

Oak barrels may be used for fermentation instead of stainless steel to give a rich, oaky flavour to the wine.

BARRIQUE

The *barrique bordelaise* is the traditional Bordeaux oak barrel of 225 litres (50 gallons) capacity.

BAUMÉ

A scale measuring must weight (the amount of sugar in grape juice) to estimate potential alcohol content.

BEERENAUSLESE

German and Austrian Prädikat category applied to wines made from 'individually selected' berries (i.e. grapes) affected by noble rot (*Edelfäule* in German). The wines are rich and sweet. Beerenauslese wines are only produced in the best years in Germany, but in Austria they are a regular occurrence.

BEREICH

German for region or district within a wine region or *Anbaugebiet*. Bereichs tend to be large, and the use of a Bereich name, such as Bereich Bingen, without qualification is seldom an indication of quality – in most cases, quite the reverse.

BIODYNAMIC VITICULTURE

This approach works with the movement of the planets and cosmic forces to achieve health and balance in the soil and in the vine. Vines are treated with infusions of mineral, animal and plant materials, applied in homeopathic quantities. An increasing number of growers are turning to biodynamism, with some astonishing results, but it is labour-intensive and generally confined to smaller estates.

BOTTLE SIZES

CHAMPAGNE

Magnum	1.5 litres	2 bottles
Jeroboam	3 litres	4 bottles
Rehoboam	4.5 litres	6 bottles
Methuselah	6 litres	8 bottles
Salmanazar	9 litres	12 bottles
Balthazar	12 litres	16 bottles
Nebuchadnezzar	15 litres	20 bottles

BORDEAUX

Magnum	1.5 litres	2 bottles
Marie-Jeanne	2.25 litres	3 bottles
Double-magnum	3 litres	4 bottles
Jeroboam	4.5 litres	6 bottles
Imperial	6 litres	8 bottles

BLANC DE BLANCS
White wine made from one or more white grape varieties. Used especially for sparkling wines; in Champagne, denotes wine made entirely from the Chardonnay grape.

BLANC DE NOIRS
White wine made from black grapes only – the juice is separated from the skins to avoid extracting any colour. Most often seen in Champagne, where it describes wine made from Pinot Noir and/or Pinot Meunier grapes.

BLENDING
The art of mixing together wines of different origin, style or age, often to balance out acidity, weight etc. Winemakers often use the term *assemblage*.

BODEGA
Spanish for winery.

BOTRYTIS
See noble rot.

BRUT
French term for dry sparkling wines, especially Champagne.

CARBONIC MACERATION
Winemaking method used to produce fresh fruity reds for drinking young. Whole (uncrushed) bunches of grapes are fermented in closed containers – a process that extracts lots of fruit and colour, but little tannin.

CHAMPAGNE METHOD
Traditional method used for nearly all of the world's finest sparkling wines. A second fermentation takes place in the bottle, producing carbon dioxide which, kept in solution under pressure, gives the wine its fizz.

CHAPTALIZATION
Legal addition of sugar during fermentation to raise a wine's alcoholic strength. More necessary in cool climates where lack of sun produces insufficient natural sugar in the grape.

CHARMAT
See cuve close.

CHÂTEAU
French for castle: widely used in France to describe any wine estate, large or small.

CHIARETTO
Italian for a rosé wine of very light pink colour from around Lake Garda.

CLARET
English for red Bordeaux wines, from the French *clairet*, which was traditionally used to describe a lighter style of red Bordeaux.

CLARIFICATION
Term covering any winemaking process (such as filtering or fining) that involves the removal of solid matter either from the must or the wine.

CLONE
Strain of grape species. The term is usually taken to mean laboratory-produced, virus-free clones, selected to produce higher or lower quantity, or selected for resistance to frost or disease.

CLOS
French for a walled vineyard – as in Burgundy's Clos de Vougeot – also commonly incorporated into the names of estates (e.g. Clos des Papes), whether they are walled or not.

COLD FERMENTATION
Long, slow fermentation at low temperature to extract maximum freshness from the grapes. Crucial for whites in hot climates.

COLHEITA
Aged tawny port from a single vintage. *See* Port in main A–Z.

COMMUNE
A French village and its surrounding area or parish.

CO-OPERATIVE
In a co-operative cellar, growers who are members bring their grapes for vinification and bottling under a collective label. In terms of quantity, the French wine industry is dominated by co-ops. They often use less workaday titles, such as Caves des Vignerons, Producteurs Réunis, Union des Producteurs or Cellier des Vignerons.

CORKED/CORKY
Wine fault derived from a cork which has become contaminated, usually with Trichloroanisole or TCA. The mouldy, stale smell is unmistakable. Nothing to do with pieces of cork in the wine.

COSECHA
Spanish for vintage.

CÔTE
French word for a slope or hillside, which is where many, but not all, of the country's best vineyards are found.

CRÉMANT
French term for traditional-method sparkling wine from Alsace, Bordeaux, Burgundy, Die, Jura, Limoux, Loire and Luxembourg.

CRIANZA
Spanish term for the youngest official category of oak-matured wine. A red Crianza wine must have had at least 2 years' aging (1 in oak, 1 in bottle) before sale, a white or rosé, 1 year.

CRU
French for growth, meaning a specific plot of land or particular estate. In Burgundy, growths are divided into Grands (great) and Premiers (first) Crus, and apply solely to the actual land. In

Champagne the same terms are used for whole villages. In Bordeaux there are various hierarchical levels of Cru referring to estates rather than their vineyards. In Italy the term is used frequently, in an unofficial way, to indicate a single-vineyard or special-selection wine.

CRU BOURGEOIS
Term for a group of châteaux (over 200) in the 8 appellations of Bordeaux's Médoc, ranked below the Crus Classés (Classed Growths) and revised annually after official tastings.

CRU CLASSÉ
The Classed Growths are the aristocracy of Bordeaux, ennobled by the Classifications of 1855 (for the Médoc, Barsac and Sauternes), 1955, 1969, 1986, 1996 and 2006 (for St-Émilion) and 1953 and 1959 (for Graves). Curiously, Pomerol has never been classified. The modern classifications are more reliable than the 1855 version, which was based solely on the price of the wines at the time of the Great Exhibition in Paris, but in terms of prestige the 1855 Classification remains the most important. With the exception of a single alteration in 1973, when Ch. Mouton-Rothschild was elevated to First Growth status, the list has not changed since 1855. It certainly needs revising.

CUVE CLOSE
A bulk process used to produce inexpensive sparkling wines. The second fermentation, which produces the bubbles, takes place in tank rather than in the bottle (as in the superior Traditional Method). Also called Charmat.

CUVÉE
French for the contents of a single vat or tank, but

usually indicates a wine blended from either different grape varieties or the best barrels of wine.

DEGORGEMENT
Stage in the production of Champagne-method wines when the sediment, collected in the neck of the bottle during *remuage*, is removed.

DEMI-SEC
French for medium-dry.

DO/DOP
Spanish quality wine category, regulating origin and production methods. *See* page 38.

DOC
Italian quality wine category, regulating origin, grape varieties, yield and production methods. *See* page 31.

DOC/DOP
Portugal's top regional wine classification. *See* page 39.

DOCA
Spanish quality wine category, intended to be one step up from DO. *See* page 38.

DOCG
The top tier of the Italian classification system. *See* page 31.

DOMAINE
French term for wine estate.

DOSAGE
A sugar and wine mixture added to sparkling wine after *dégorgement* which affects how sweet or dry it will be.

EDELZWICKER
Blended wine from Alsace, usually bland.

EINZELLAGE
German for an individual vineyard site which is generally farmed by several growers. The name is preceded on the label by that of the village: for example, the Wehlener

Sonnenuhr is the Sonnenuhr vineyard in Wehlen. The mention of a particular site should signify a superior wine.

EISWEIN
Rare, chiefly German and Austrian, late-harvested wine made by picking the grapes and pressing them while frozen. This concentrates the sweetness of the grape as most of the liquid is removed as ice. *See also* Icewine.

ERSTE LAGE
In Germany's Mosel, this term is used to indicate outstanding sites.

ERSTES GEWÄCHS
An official classification used in the Rheingau in Germany. Top sites were chosen by a kind of popular vote. Growers tend to use the label only for their best wines. *See also* Grosses Gewächs.

ESCOLHA
Portuguese for selection.

EXTRACTION
Refers to the extraction of colour, tannins and flavour from the grapes during and after fermentation. There are various ways in which extraction can be manipulated by the winemaker, but over-extraction leads to imbalance.

FEINHERB
Disliking the term Halb-trocken, some producers prefer to use Feinherb. No legal definition but usually applies to wines with 9–25g per litre of residual sugar.

FILTERING
Removal of yeasts, solids and any impurities from a wine before bottling.

FINING
Method of clarifying wine by adding a coagulant (e.g. egg whites, isinglass) to remove soluble particles such as proteins and excessive tannins.

FINO
The lightest, freshest style of sherry. *See* Jerez y Manzanilla in main A–Z.

FLOR
A film of yeast which forms on the surface of fino sherries (and some other wines) in the barrel, preventing oxidation and imparting a tangy, dry flavour.

FLYING WINEMAKER
Term coined in the late 1980s to describe enologists, many Australian-trained, brought in to improve the quality of wines in many underperforming wine regions.

FORTIFIED WINE
Wine which has high-alcohol grape spirit added, usually before the initial fermentation is completed, thereby preserving sweetness.

FRIZZANTE
Italian for semi-sparkling wine.

GARAGE WINE
See vin de garage.

GARRAFEIRA
Portuguese term for wine from an outstanding vintage, with 0.5% more alcohol than the minimum required, and 2 years' aging in vat or barrel followed by 1 year in bottle for reds, and 6 months of each for whites. Also used by merchants for their best blended and aged wines. Use of the term is in decline as producers opt for the more readily recognized Reserva as an alternative on the label.

GRAN RESERVA
Top category of Spanish wines from a top vintage, with at least 5 years' aging (2 of them in cask) for reds and 4 for whites.

GRAND CRU
French for great growth. Supposedly the best vineyard sites in Alsace, Burgundy, Champagne and parts of Bordeaux – and should produce the most exciting wines.

GROSSES GEWÄCHS/GG
A vineyard classification in Germany, devised by the VDP growers' association and now widely adopted. Wines must meet both quality and stylistic criteria: essentially for Riesling, dry and very sweet wines.

GROSSLAGE
German term for a grouping of vineyards. Some are not too big, and have the advantage of allowing small amounts of higher QmP wines to be made from the grapes from several vineyards. But sometimes the use of vast Grosslage names (e.g. Niersteiner Gutes Domtal) deceives consumers into believing they are buying something special. Top estates have agreed not to use Gross-lage names on their labels.

HALBTROCKEN
German for medium dry. In Germany and Austria medium-dry wine has 9–18g per litre of residual sugar, though sparkling wine is allowed up to 50g per litre. *See* Feinherb.

ICEWINE
A speciality of Canada, produced from juice squeezed from ripe grapes that have frozen on the vine. *See also* Eiswein.

IGT
Italian classification of regional wines. Both premium and everyday wines may share the same appellation. *See* page 31.

KABINETT
Term used for the lowest level of QmP wines in Germany.

LANDWEIN
German or Austrian 'country' wine. The wine must have a territorial

definition
and may be chaptalized to give it more alcohol.

LATE HARVEST
See Vendange Tardive.

LAYING DOWN
The storing of wine which will improve with age.

LEES
Sediment – dead yeast cells, grape pips (seeds), pulp and tartrates – thrown by wine during fermentation and left behind after racking. Some wines are left on the fine lees for as long as possible to take on extra flavour.

MACERATION
Important winemaking process for red wines whereby colour, flavour and/or tannin are extracted from grape skins before, during or after fermentation. The period lasts from a few days to several weeks.

MALOLACTIC FERMENTATION
Secondary fermentation whereby harsh malic acid is converted into mild lactic acid and carbon dioxide. Normal in red wines but often prevented in whites to preserve a fresh, fruity taste.

MANZANILLA
The tangiest style of sherry, similar to fino. *See* Jerez y Manzanilla in main A–Z.

MATURATION
Term for the beneficial aging of wine.

MERITAGE
American term for red or white wines made from a blend of Bordeaux grape varieties.

MESOCLIMATE
The climate of a specific geographical area, be it a vineyard or simply a hillside or valley.

MIDI
A loose geographical term,

virtually synonymous with Languedoc-Roussillon, covering the vast, sunbaked area of southern France between the Pyrenees and the Rhône Valley.

MOELLEUX
French for soft or mellow, used to describe sweet and medium-sweet wines, particularly in the Loire.

MOUSSEUX
French for sparkling wine.

MUST
The mixture of grape juice, skins, pips and pulp produced after crushing (but prior to completion of fermentation), which will eventually become wine.

MUST WEIGHT
An indicator of the sugar content of juice – and therefore the ripeness of grapes.

NÉGOCIANT
French term for a merchant who buys and sells wine. A *négociant-éléveur* is a merchant who buys, makes, ages and sells wine.

NEW WORLD
When used as a geographical term, New World includes the Americas, South Africa, Australia and New Zealand. By extension, it is also a term used to describe the clean, fruity, upfront style now in evidence all over the world, but pioneered in the USA and Australia.

NOBLE ROT
(*Botrytis cinerea*) Fungus which, when it attacks ripe white grapes, shrivels the fruit and intensifies their sugar while adding a distinctive flavour. A vital factor in creating many of the world's finest sweet wines, such as Sauternes and Trockenbeerenauslese.

OAK
The wood used almost exclusively to make barrels for fermenting and aging fine wines. It adds flavours such as vanilla, and tannins; the newer the wood, the greater the impact.

OECHSLE
German scale measuring must weight (sugar content).

OLOROSO
The darkest, most heavily fortified style of sherry. *See* Jerez y Manzanilla in main A–Z.

OXIDATION
Over-exposure of wine to air, causing loss of fruit and flavour. Slight oxidation, such as occurs through the wood of a barrel or during racking, is part of the aging process and, in wines of sufficient structure, enhances flavour and complexity.

PASSITO
Italian term for wine made from dried grapes. The result is usually a sweet wine with a raisiny intensity of fruit. The drying process is called *appassimento*. *See also* Moscato Passito di Pantelleria, Recioto della Valpolicella, Recioto di Soave and Vin Santo in main A–Z.

PERLWEIN
German for a lightly sparkling wine.

PÉTILLANT
French for a lightly sparkling wine.

PHYLLOXERA
The vine aphid *Phylloxera vastatrix* attacks vine roots. It devastated vineyards around the world in the late 1800s soon after it arrived from America. Since then, the vulnerable *Vitis vinifera* has generally been grafted on to vinously inferior, but phylloxera-resistant, American rootstocks.

PRÄDIKAT
Grades defining quality wines in Germany and Austria. These are (in ascending order) Kabinett (not considered as Prädikat in Austria), Spätlese, Auslese, Beerenauslese, the Austrian-only category Ausbruch, and Trockenbeerenauslese. Strohwein and Eiswein are also Prädikat wines. Some Spätleses and even a few Ausleses are now made as dry wines.

PRÄDIKATSWEIN
The new term for QmP.

PREMIER CRU
First Growth: the top quality classification in parts of Bordeaux, but second to Grand Cru in Burgundy. Used in Champagne to designate vineyards just below Grand Cru.

PRIMEUR
French term for a young wine, often released for sale within a few weeks of the harvest. Beaujolais Nouveau is the best-known example.

QBA (QUALITÄTSWEIN BESTIMMTER ANBAUGEBIETE)
German for quality wine from designated regions. Sugar can be added to increase the alcohol content. Usually pretty ordinary, but from top estates this category offers excellent value. In Austria *Qualitätswein* is equivalent to German QbA.

QMP (QUALITÄTSWEIN MIT PRÄDIKAT)
German for quality wine with distinction. A higher category than QbA, with controlled yields and no sugar addition. QmP covers 6 levels based on the ripeness of the grapes: *see* Prädikat. The term is replaced by Prädikatswein from August 2007.

QUINTA
Portuguese for farm or estate.

RACKING
Gradual clarification of wine: the wine is transferred from one barrel or container to another, leaving the lees behind.

RANCIO
Fortified wine deliberately exposed to the effects of oxidation, found mainly in Languedoc-Roussillon and parts of Spain.

REMUAGE
Process in Champagne-making whereby the bottles, stored on their sides and at a progressively steeper angle in *pupitres*, are twisted, or riddled, each day so that the sediment moves down the sides and collects in the neck of the bottle on the cap, ready for *dégorgement*.

RESERVA
Spanish wines that have fulfilled certain aging requirements: reds must have at least 3 years' aging before sale, of which one must be in oak barrels; whites and rosés must have at least 2 years' age, of which 6 months must be in oak.

RÉSERVE
French for what is, in theory at least, a winemaker's finest wine. The word has no legal definition in France.

RIPASSO
A method used in Valpolicella to make wines with extra depth. Wine is passed over the lees of Recioto or Amarone della Valpolicella, adding extra alcohol and flavour, though also extra tannin and a risk of higher acidity and oxidation.

RISERVA
An Italian term, recognized in many DOCs and DOCGs, for a special selection of wine that has been aged longer before release. It is only a promise of a more pleasurable drink if the wine had enough fruit and structure in the first place.

SAIGNÉE
Rosé wine takes its colour from the skins of red grapes: the juice is bled off (*saignée*) after a short period of contact with the skins.

SEC
French for dry. When applied to Champagne, it means medium-dry.

'SECOND' WINES
A second selection from a designated vineyard, usually lighter and quicker-maturing than the main wine.

SEDIMENT
Usually refers to residue thrown by a wine, particularly red, as it ages in bottle.

SEKT
German for sparkling wine. The best wines are made by the traditional Champagne method, from 100% Riesling or 100% Weissburgunder (Pinot Blanc).

SÉLECTION DE GRAINS NOBLES (SGN)
A superripe category for sweet Alsace wines, now also being used by some producers of Coteaux du Layon in the Loire Valley. *See also* Vendange Tardive.

SMARAGD
The top of the three categories of wine from the Wachau in Austria, the lower two being Federspiel and Steinfeder. Made from very ripe and usually late-harvested grapes, the wines have a minimum of 12.5% alcohol, often 13–14%.

SOLERA
Traditional Spanish system of blending fortified wines, especially sherry and Montilla-Moriles.

SPÄTLESE
German for late-picked (riper) grapes. Often moderately sweet, though there are dry versions.

SPUMANTE
Italian for sparkling. Bottle-fermented wines are often referred to as *metodo classico* or *metodo tradizionale*.

SUPER-TUSCAN
Term coined in the 1980s for top-quality wines that did not conform to local DOC regulations (usually Chianti) and were therefore classed as vini da tavola (table wine). Many are now sold under the regional IGT Toscana.

SUPÉRIEUR
French for a wine with a slightly higher alcohol content than the basic AC.

SUPERIORE
Italian DOC wines with higher alcohol or more aging potential.

SUR LIE
French for on the lees, meaning wine bottled direct from the cask/fermentation vat to gain extra flavour from the lees. Common with quality Muscadet, white Burgundy, similar barrel-aged whites and, increasingly, bulk whites.

TAFELWEIN
German for table wine.

TANNIN
Harsh, bitter, mouth-puckering element in red wine, derived from grape skins and stems, and from oak barrels. Tannins soften with age and are essential for long-term development in red wines.

TERROIR
A French term used to denote the combination of soil, climate and exposure to the sun – that is, the natural physical environment of the vine.

TRADITIONAL METHOD
See Champagne method.

TROCKEN
German for dry. In most parts of Germany and

Austria, Trocken matches the EU definition of dryness – less than 9g per litre residual sugar.

TROCKENBEEREN-AUSLESE (TBA)
German for 'dry berry selected', denoting grapes affected by noble rot (*Edelfäule* in German) – the wines will be lusciously sweet although low in alcohol.

VARIETAL
Wine made from, and named after, a single or dominant grape variety.

VDP
German organization recognizable on the label by a Prussian eagle bearing grapes. The quality of estates included is usually – but not always – high.

VDQS (VIN DÉLIMITÉ DE QUALITÉ SUPÉRIEURE)
For many years, the second-highest classi-fication for French wines, behind AC. Phased out after the 2011 vintage.

VELHO
Portuguese for old. Legally applied only to wines with at least 3 years' aging for reds and 2 years for whites.

VENDANGE TARDIVE
French for late harvest. Grapes are left on the vines beyond the normal harvest time to concentrate flavours and sugars. The term is traditional in Alsace. The Italian term is *vendemmia tardiva*.

VIEILLES VIGNES
French term for a wine made from vines at least 20 years old. Should have greater concentration than wine from younger vines.

VIÑA
Spanish for vineyard.

VIN DE GARAGE
Wines made on so small a scale they could be made in a garage. Such wines may be made from vineyards of a couple of hectares or less, and are often of extreme concentration.

VIN DE PAILLE
Sweet wine found mainly in the Jura region of France. Traditionally, the grapes are left for 2–3 months on straw (*paille*) mats before fermentation to dehydrate, thus concentrating the sugars. The wines are sweet but slightly nutty.

VIN DE PAYS
The term gives a regional identity to wine from the less renowned districts of France. Many are labelled with the grape variety. Gradually being converted to new IGP classification. *See page 24.*

VIN DE TABLE
French for table wine, the lowest quality level; phased out after the 2008 vintage. *See page 24.*

VIN DOUX NATUREL (VDN)
French for a fortified wine, where fermentation has been stopped by the addition of alcohol, leaving the wine 'naturally' sweet, although you could argue that stopping fermentation with a slug of powerful spirit is distinctly unnatural.

VIN JAUNE
A speciality of the Jura region in France, made from the Savagnin grape. In Château-Chalon it is the only permitted style. Made in a similar way to fino sherry but not fortified and aged for 6 years in oak. Unlike fino, *vin jaune* ages well.

VINIFICATION
The process of turning grapes into wine.

VINO DA TAVOLA
The Italian term for table wine, officially Italy's lowest level of production, is a catch-all that until relatively recently applied to more than 80% of the nation's wine, with virtually no regulations controlling quality. Yet this category also provided the arena in the 1970s and 80s for the biggest revolution in quality that Italy has ever seen, with the creation of innovative, DOC-busting 'super-Tuscans'.

VINTAGE
The year's grape harvest, also used to describe wines of a single year. 'Off-vintage' is a year not generally declared as vintage. *See* Port in main A–Z.

VITICULTURE
Vine-growing and vineyard management.

VITIS VINIFERA
Vine species, native to Europe and Central Asia, from which almost all the world's quality wine is made.

VQA (VINTNERS QUALITY ALLIANCE)
Canadian equivalent of France's AC system, defining quality standards and designated viticultural areas.

WEISSHERBST
German rosé wine, a speciality of Baden.

WO (WINE OF ORIGIN)
South African system of appellations which certifies area of origin, grape variety and vintage.

YIELD
The amount of fruit, and ultimately wine, produced from a vineyard. Measured in hectolitres per hectare (hl/ha) in most of Europe, and in the New World as tons per acre or tonnes per hectare. Yield may vary from year to year, and depends on grape variety, age and density of the vines, and viticultural practices.

WHO OWNS WHAT

With Constellation's decision to sell off a great chunk of its wine business, it becomes clear that some of the world's vast drinks conglomerates have become too big to be beneficial to wine. I'm not entirely sure they all know what they're doing and I'm certainly not sure they all have the interest of wine and wine quality – as against business and bottom line – at heart. It's not all bad news: in some cases wineries have benefited from the huge resources that come with corporate ownership, but I can't help feeling nervous knowing that the fate of a winery rests in the hands of distant institutional investors. Below, I list some of the names that crop up again and again in the world of wine.

Other wine companies – which bottle wines under their own names and feature in the main A–Z – are spreading their nets. GALLO has agreements with, among others, Da Vinci winery in Tuscany, MCWILLIAM'S of Australia and Whitehaven of New Zealand. California businessman Donald Hess owns Hess Collection in California, Peter LEHMANN in Australia, GLEN CARLOU in South Africa, and COLOMÉ and Amalaya in Argentina. Besides Ch. MOUTON-ROTHSCHILD, the Rothschild family have other interests in France, co-own OPUS ONE and, in partnership with CONCHA Y TORO, produce ALMAVIVA in Chile.

The never-ending whirl of joint ventures, mergers and takeovers has slowed down a bit this year, but the following can only be a snapshot at the time of going to press.

ACCOLADE WINES

Accolade was created when Constellation Brands (see below) sold 80% of its Australian, South African and European business to Champ, an Australian private equity group, in January 2011. Accolade's wine portfolio includes HARDYS, Banrock Station, Arras, BAY OF FIRES, HOUGHTON, Leasingham, Tintara and Berri Estates in Australia, Kumala and Flagstone in South Africa, Gran Tierra in Chile, Echo Falls and Stowells.

AXA MILLÉSIMES

The French insurance giant AXA's subsidiary owns Bordeaux châteaux PETIT-VILLAGE, PICHON-LONGUEVILLE, Pibran and SUDUIRAUT, plus Dom. de l'Arlot in Burgundy, Mas Belles Eaux in the Languedoc, TOKAJI producer Disznókö and PORT producer Quinta DO NOVAL.

CONSTELLATION BRANDS

US-based Constellation became the world's largest wine company in the first decade of the 21st century through a series of acquisitions in Australia, New Zealand, Canada, South America and South Africa. In 2004 Constellation acquired the prestigious Robert MONDAVI winery and all its entities, including OPUS ONE (a joint venture with the Rothschild family of Ch. MOUTON-ROTHSCHILD), as well as a 40% stake in Italy's RUFFINO (increased to 50% in 2010). Constellation's brands include Blackstone, CLOS DU BOIS, Estancia, FRANCISCAN, Mount Veeder Winery, RAVENSWOOD, Simi and Wild Horse in California, Hogue Cellars in Washington State, Le CLOS JORDANNE, INNISKILLIN, JACKSON-TRIGGS and SUMAC RIDGE in Canada, and Kim Crawford and NOBILO in New Zealand.

FREIXENET

This famous CAVA producer remains a family-owned business, with winery estates and interests around the world. In Spain, alongside FREIXENET Cavas, the portfolio includes Castellblanch, Segura Viudas, Conde de Caralt, René Barbier, Morlanda and Valdubón. Further afield it includes Bordeaux *négociant* and producer Yvon Mau, the Champagne house of Henri Abelé,

Gloria Ferrer in California, Viento Sur in Argentina and Australia's Wingara Wine Group (Deakin Estate, KATNOOK ESTATE).

JACKSON FAMILY WINES

The late Jess Jackson, founder of California's KENDALL-JACKSON, built up a large portfolio of independent wineries in California, including: ARROWOOD, Atalon, Byron, Cambria, Cardinale, Edmeades, Freemark Abbey, HARTFORD, La Crema, La Jota, Lokoya, MATANZAS CREEK, Murphy-Goode, Pepi, Stonestreet and Vérité. Further afield, Jackson also owns Calina (Chile), Yangarra (Australia), Ch. Lassègue (ST-ÉMILION) and Villa Arceno (Tuscany).

LVMH

French luxury goods group Louis Vuitton-Moët Hennessy owns Champagne houses MOËT & CHANDON (including Dom Pérignon), KRUG, Mercier, RUINART and VEUVE CLICQUOT, and has established DOMAINE CHANDON sparkling wine companies in California, Australia and Argentina. It also owns Ch. d'YQUEM, CAPE MENTELLE in Australia, CLOUDY BAY in New Zealand, NEWTON in California, Numanthia in TORO, Spain, and TERRAZAS DE LOS ANDES in Argentina.

PERNOD RICARD

The French spirits giant owns Australia's all-conquering JACOB'S CREEK brand, along with Wyndham Estate and the Orlando, Gramp's, Poet's Corner and Richmond Grove labels. Pernod Ricard's portfolio also encompasses New Zealand's mighty BRANCOTT, CHURCH ROAD and Stoneleigh brands, as well as Champagne producers G H MUMM and PERRIER-JOUËT, Californian fizz MUMM NAPA, Long Mountain in South Africa and a number of Argentinian producers, including Etchart and Graffigna. In Spain, Pernod Ricard controls CAMPO VIEJO, Alcorta, Azpilicueta, Siglo and Ysios, among others, and in Georgia it has a 75% stake in Georgian Wines & Spirits. In China it owns the impressive Helan Mountain winery in Ningxia province.

TREASURY WINE ESTATES

The wine division of Australian brewer Foster's, recently demerged and renamed Treasury Wine Estates, was founded on the twin pillars of Australia's Wolf BLASS and BERINGER in California. In 2005 Foster's won control of Australia's biggest wine conglomerate, Southcorp, and the group currently controls more than 50 wineries and brands. Australian brands include LINDEMANS, PENFOLDS, Rosemount Estate, SEPPELT, WYNNS, COLDSTREAM HILLS, Devil's Lair, Annie's Lane, Baileys of Glenrowan, Leo Buring, Heemskerk, Jamiesons Run, Metala, Mildara, Greg Norman, Rothbury Estate, Rouge Homme, St Huberts, Saltram, Seaview, T'Gallant, Tollana, Yarra Ridge and Yellowglen. In California it owns, among others, CHATEAU ST JEAN, Etude, Meridian, Souverain, St Clement and Stags' Leap Winery. Treasury also owns MATUA VALLEY and Secret Stone in New Zealand, and Castello di Gabbiano in Tuscany.

INDEX OF PRODUCERS

347

348

365

This edition first published in 2012 by Pavilion Books

An imprint of Anova Books Company Ltd
10 Southcombe Street, London W14 0RA

Distributed in the U.S. and Canada by:
Sterling Publishing Co., Inc.
387 Park Avenue South
New York
NY 10016-8810

www.anovabooks.com   www.ozclarke.com

Editor Maggie Ramsay
Editorial assistant Charlotte Selby
Cartographer Andrew Thompson
Photography David Forcina, Michael Wicks
Desktop publishing Jayne Clementson
Proofreader Julie Ross
Indexer Angie Hipkin

21st edition. First published in 1992.
Revised editions published annually.

ISBN 978-1-862-05968-9

Printed by Toppan Leefung Printers Ltd, China
Repro by Mission Productions Ltd, Hong Kong

Photographs: Pages 2–3 Errazuriz Manzanar Vineyard, Aconcagua Costa,
Chile (Viña Errazuriz); page 5 Fromm Vineyard, Marlborough, New Zealand;
page 6 Chilean winery, Elquí Valley (Enoturismo); page 7 Klein Constantia
(Wines of South Africa); page 8 Anova Books (Gary Moyes)

Keep up to date with Oz on his website **www.ozclarke.com**. Here you can
find information about his books, wine recommendations, recipes, wine and
food matching, event details, competitions, special offers and lots more...

Thanks are due to the following people for their invaluable help with the
2013 edition and the generous spirit in which they have shared their
knowledge: Tony Aspler, Nicolas Belfrage MW, Stephen Brook, Bob
Campbell MW, Tina Caputo, Michael Cox, Giles Fallowfield, James
Forbes, Peter Forrestal, Elizabeth Gabay MW, Rosemary George MW,
Richard Hemming, Natasha Hughes, James Lawther MW, John
Livingstone-Learmonth, Angela Lloyd, Wink Lorch, Dan McCarthy, Dave
McIntyre, Charles Metcalfe, Adam Montefiore, Jasper Morris MW, Lisa
Perrotti-Brown MW, Victor de la Serna, Stephen Skelton MW, Paul Strang.

OLDER VINTAGE CHARTS *(top wines only)*

FRANCE										
Alsace (vendanges tardives)	01	00	99	98	97	96	95	90	89	88
	8◆	7◊	6◊	9◆	8◆	8◆	9◆	10◆	9◊	8◊
Champagne (vintage)	00	99	98	97	96	95	90	89	88	85
	6◆	7◊	7◆	6◆	9◆	8◆	9◆	8◆	9◆	8◆
Bordeaux	01	00	99	98	97	96	95	94	90	89
Margaux	9◆	9◊	7◆	7◆	6◆	8◆	8◆	6◊	9◆	8◆
St-Jul., Pauillac, St-Est.	8◆	10◊	7◆	7◆	6◊	9◆	8◆	6◊	9◆	9◆
Graves/Pessac-L. (red)	7◆	9◊	7◆	8◆	6◊	8◆	8◆	6◊	8◆	8◆
St-Émilion, Pomerol	8◆	9◊	7◆	9◆	6◊	7◆	9◆	6◊	9◆	9◆
Bordeaux (cont.)	88	86	85	83	82	81	75	70	66	61
Margaux (cont.)	7◆	8◆	8◆	9◊	8◆	7◊	6◊	8◆	7◊	10◊
St-Jul. etc. (cont.)	8◆	9◆	8◆	7◊	10◆	7◊	8◊	8◆	8◊	10◊
Graves/P-L (red) (cont.)	8◆	6◊	8◆	8◆	9◊	7◊	6◊	8◆	8◊	10◊
St-Émilion etc. (cont.)	8◆	7◊	9◆	7◊	9◊	7◊	8◊	8◆	6◊	10◊
Sauternes	00	99	98	97	96	95	90	89	88	86
	6◆	8◆	7◆	9◆	9◆	7◊	10◆	9◆	9◆	9◆
Sauternes (cont.)	83	80	76	75	71	67	62	59	55	53
	9◆	7◊	8◊	8◊	8◊	9◊	8◊	9◊	8◊	8◊
Burgundy										
Chablis	01	00	99	98	97	96	95	92	90	
	4◊	9◆	7◊	7◊	7◊	8◆	8◆	7◊	9◊	
Côte de Beaune (wh.)	01	00	99	98	97	96	95	93	92	90
	6◆	8◆	8◆	5◊	7◊	6◊	8◊	7◆	8◊	7◊
Côte de Nuits (red)	01	00	99	98	97	96	95	93	90	88
	7◆	7◊	9◊	7◆	7◊	9◊	7◆	8◆	9◆	8◊